Donald E. Knuth, On Bottom-Up.

(excerpted from the preface to "The Art of Computer Programming. Fas http://www-cs-faculty.Stanford.EDU/~knuth/fasel.ps.gz *with his permiss*

Why have a machine language?

Many readers are no doubt thinking, "Why does Knuth replace MIX by another machine instead of just sticking to a high-level programming language? Hardly anybody uses assemblers these days."

Such people are entitled to their opinions, and they need not bother reading the machine-language parts of my books. But the reasons for machine language that I gave in the preface to Volume 1, written in the early 1960s, remains valid today:

> *One of the principal goals of my books is to show how high-level constructions are actually implemented in machines, not simply to show how they are applied. I explain coroutine linkage, tree structures, random number generation, high-precision arithmetic, radix conversion, packing of data, combinatorial searching, recursion, etc., from the ground up.*

> *The programs needed in my books are generally so short that their main points can be grasped easily.*

> *People who are more than casually interested in computers should have at least some idea of what the underlying hardware is like. Otherwise the programs they write will be pretty weird.*

Machine language is necessary in any case, as output of some software that I describe.

> *Expressing basic methods like algorithms for sorting and searching in machine lanuguage makes it possible to carry out meaningful studies of the effects of cache and RAM size and other hardware characteristics (memory speed, pipelining, multiple issue, lookaside buffers, the size of cache backs, etc.) when comparing different schemes.*

> > second edition

introduction to
computing systems

from bits and gates to C and beyond

Yale N. Patt
The University of Texas at Austin

Sanjay J. Patel
University of Illinois at Urbana-Champaign

 **Higher Education**

Boston   Burr Ridge, IL   Dubuque, IA   Madison, WI   New York   San Francisco   St. Louis
Bangkok   Bogotá   Caracas   Kuala Lumpur   Lisbon   London   Madrid   Mexico City
Milan   Montreal   New Delhi   Santiago   Seoul   Singapore   Sydney   Taipei   Toronto

Higher Education

INTRODUCTION TO COMPUTING SYSTEMS: FROM BITS AND GATES TO C AND BEYOND
SECOND EDITION

14 15 QFR/QFR 1 5 4 3

ISBN-13: 978-0-07-246750-5
ISBN-10: 0-07-246750-9

Publisher: *Elizabeth A. Jones*
Developmental editor: *Michelle L. Flomenhoft*
Marketing manager: *Dawn R. Bercier*
Lead project manager: *Jill R. Peter*
Production supervisor: *Kara Kudronowicz*
Senior media project manager: *Jodi K. Banowetz*
Senior media technology producer: *Phillip Meek*
Designer: *Rick D. Noel*
Cover/interior designer: *Kaye Farmer*
Cover images: *©Photodisc, AA048376 Green Abstract, AA003317 Circuit Board Detail*
Senior photo research coordinator: *Lori Hancock*
Compositor: *UG/GGS Information Services, Inc.*
Typeface: *10.5/12 Times Roman*
Printer: *Quad/Graphics, Fairfield, PA*

Library of Congress Cataloging-in-Publication Data

Patt, Yale N.
  Introduction to computing systems: from bits and Gates to C and beyond / Yale N. Patt, Sanjay J. Patel.—2nd ed.
    p.   cm.
  Includes index.
  ISBN 0-07-246750-9—ISBN 0-07-121503-4 (ISE)
  1. Computer science. 2. C (Computer program language). I. Patel, Sanjay J. II. Title.

QA76.P367   2004
004—dc21
                                                                          2003051002
                                                                          CIP

www.mhhe.com

contents

16 Pointers and Arrays 427

17 Recursion 457

18 I/O in C 481

19 Data Structures 497

A The LC-3 ISA 521

It is a pleasure to be writing a preface to the second edition of this book. Three years have passed since the first edition came out. We have received an enormous number of comments from students who have studied the material in the book and from instructors who have taught from it. Almost all have been very positive. It is gratifying to know that a lot of people agree with our approach, and that this agreement is based on real firsthand experience learning from it (in the case of students) or watching students learn from it (in the case of instructors). The excitement displayed in their e-mail continues to be a high for us.

However, as we said in the preface to the first edition, this book will always be a "work in progress." Along with the accolades, we have received some good advice on how to make it better. We thank you for that. We have also each taught the course two more times since the first edition came out, and that, too, has improved our insights into what we think we did right and what needed improvement. The result has been a lot of changes in the second edition, while hopefully maintaining the essence of what we had before. How well we have succeeded we hope to soon learn from you.

Major Changes to the First Edition

The LC-3

One of the more obvious changes in the second edition is the replacement of the LC-2 with the LC-3. We insisted on keeping the basic concept of the LC-2: a rich ISA that can be described in a few pages, and hopefully mastered in a short time. We kept the 16-bit instruction and 4-bit opcode. One of our students pointed out that the subroutine return instruction (RET) was just a special case of LC-2's JMPR instruction, so we eliminated RET as a separate opcode. The LC-3 specifies only 15 opcodes—and leaves one for future use (perhaps, the third edition!).

We received a lot of push-back on the PC-concatenate addressing mode, particularly for branches. The addressing mode had its roots in the old PDP-8 of the mid-1960s. A major problem with it comes up when an instruction on one page wants to dereference the next (or previous) page. This has been a major hassle, particularly for forward branches close to a page boundary. A lot of people have asked us to use the more modern PC+offset, and we agreed. We have replaced all uses of PC'offset with PC+SEXT(offset).

We incorporated other changes in the LC-3. Stacks now grow toward 0, in keeping with current conventional practice. The offset in LDR/STR is now a signed value, so addresses can be computed plus or minus a base address. The opcode 1101 is not specified. The JSR/JMP opcodes have been reorganized slightly. Finally, we expanded the condition codes to a 16-bit processor status register (PSR) that includes a privilege mode and a priority level. As in the first edition, Appendix A specifies the LC-3 completely.

Additional Material

Although no chapter in the book has remained untouched, some chapters have been changed more than others. We added discussions to Chapter 1 on the nature and importance of abstraction and the interplay of hardware and software because it became clear that these points needed to be made explicit. We added a full section to Chapter 3 on finite state control and its implementation as a sequential switching circuit because we believe the concept of state and finite state control are among the most important concepts a computer science or engineering student encounters. We feel it is also useful to the understanding of the von Neumann model of execution discussed in Chapter 4. We added a section to Chapter 4 giving a glimpse of the underlying microarchitecture of the LC-3, which is spelled out in all its detail in the overhauled Appendix C. We were told by more than one reader that Chapter 5 was too terse. We added little new material, but lots of figures and explanations that hopefully make the concepts clearer. We also added major new sections on interrupt-driven I/O to Chapters 8 and 10.

Just as in the first edition, Chapters 11 through 14 introduce the C programming language. Unlike the first edition, these chapters are more focused on the essential aspects of the language useful to a beginning programmer. Specialized features, for example the C switch construct, are relegated to the ends of the chapters (or to Appendix D), out of the main line of the text. All of these chapters include more examples than the first edition. The second edition also places a heavier emphasis on "how to program" via problem-solving examples that demonstrate how newly introduced C constructs can be used in C programming. In Chapter 14, students are exposed to a new LC-3 calling convention that more closely reflects the calling convention used by real systems. Chapter 15 contains a deeper treatment of testing and debugging. Based on our experiences teaching the introductory course, we have decided to swap the order of the chapter on recursion with the chapter on pointers and arrays. Moving recursion later (now Chapter 17) in the order of treatment allows students to gain more experience with basic programming concepts before they start programming recursive functions.

The Simulator

Brian Hartman has updated the simulator that runs on Windows to incorporate the changes to the LC-3. Ashley Wise has written an LC-3 simulator that runs on UNIX. Both have incorporated interrupt-driven I/O into the simulator's functionality. We believe strongly that there is no substitute for hands-on practice testing one's knowledge. With the addition of interrupt-driven I/O to the simulator, the student can now interrupt an executing program by typing a key on the keyboard and invoke an interrupt service routine.

Alternate Uses of the Book

We wrote the book as a textbook for a freshman introduction to computing. We strongly believe, as stated more completely in the preface to our first edition, that our motivated bottom-up approach is the best way for students to learn the fundamentals of computing. We have seen lots of evidence that suggests that in general, students who understand the fundamentals of how the computer works are better able to grasp the stuff that they encounter later, including the high-level programming languages that they must work in, and that they can learn the rules of these programming languages with far less memorizing because everything makes sense. For us, the best use of the book is a one-semester freshman course for particularly motivated students, or a two-semester sequence where the pace is tempered. If you choose to go the route of a one-semester course heavy on high-level language programming, you probably want to leave out the material on sequential machines and interrupt-driven I/O. If you choose to go the one-semester route heavy on the first half of the book, you probably want to leave out much of Chapters 15, 17, 18, and 19.

We have also seen the book used effectively in each of the following environments:

Two Quarters, Freshman Course

In some sense this is the best use of the book. In the first quarter, Chapters 1 through 10 are covered; in the second quarter, Chapters 11 through 19. The pace is brisk, but the entire book can be covered in two academic quarters.

One-Semester Second Course

The book has been used successfully as a second course in computing, after the student has spent the first course with a high-level programming language. The rationale is that after exposure to high-level language programming in the first course, the second course should treat at an introductory level digital logic, basic computer organization, and assembly language programming. Most of the semester is spent on Chapters 1 through 10, with the last few weeks spent on a few topics from Chapters 11 through 19, showing how some of the magic from the students' first course can actually be implemented. Functions, activation records, recursion, pointer variables, and some elementary data structures are typically the topics that get covered.

A Sophomore-Level Computer Organization Course

The book has been used to delve deeply into computer implementation in the sophomore year. The semester is spent in Chapters 1 through 10, sometimes culminating in a thorough study of Appendix C, which provides the complete microarchitecture of a microprogrammed LC-3. We note, however, that some very important ideas in computer architecture are not covered here, most notably cache memory, pipelining, and virtual memory. We agree that these topics are very important to the education of a computer scientist or computer engineer, but we feel these topics are better suited to a senior course in computer architecture and design. This book is not intended for that purpose.

Acknowledgments

Our book continues to benefit greatly from important contributions of many, many people. We particularly want to acknowledge Brian Hartman and Matt Starolis.

Brian Hartman continues to be a very important part of this work, both for the great positive energy he brings to the table and for his technical expertise. He is now out of school more than three years and remains committed to the concept. He took the course the first year it was offered at Michigan (Winter term, 1996), TAed it several times as an undergraduate student, and wrote the first LC-2 simulator for Windows while he was working on his master's degree. He recently upgraded the Windows simulator to incorporate the new LC-3.

Matt Starolis took the freshman course at UT two years ago and TAed it as a junior last fall. He, too, has been very important to us getting out this second edition. He has been both critic of our writing and helpful designer of many of the figures. He also updated the tutorials for the simulators, which was necessary in order to incorporate the new characteristics of the LC-3. When something needed to be done, Matt volunteered to do it. His enthusiasm for the course and the book has been a pleasure.

With more than 100 adopters now, we regularly get enthusiastic e-mail with suggestions from professors from all over the world. Although we realize we have undoubtedly forgotten some, we would at least like to thank Professors Vijay Pai, Rice; Richard Johnson, Western New Mexico; Tore Larsen, Tromso; Greg Byrd, NC State; Walid Najjar, UC Riverside; Sean Joyce, Heidelberg College; James Boettler, South Carolina State; Steven Zeltmann, Arkansas; Mike McGregor, Alberta; David Lilja, Minnesota; Eric Thompson, Colorado, Denver; and Brad Hutchings, Brigham Young.

Between the two of us, we have taught the course four more times since the first edition came out, and that has produced a new enthusiastic group of believers, both TAs and students. Kathy Buckheit, Mustafa Erwa, Joseph Grzywacz, Chandresh Jain, Kevin Major, Onur Mutlu, Moinuddin Qureshi, Kapil Sachdeva, Russell Schreiber, Paroma Sen, Santhosh Srinath, Kameswar Subramaniam, David Thompson, Francis Tseng, Brian Ward, and Kevin Woley have all served as TAs and have demonstrated a commitment to helping students learn that can only be described as wonderful. Linda Bigelow, Matt Starolis, and Lester Guillory all took the course as freshmen, and two years later they were among the most enthusiastic TAs the course has known.

Ashley Wise developed the Linux version of the LC-3 simulator. Ajay Ladsaria ported the LCC compiler to generate LC-3 code. Gregory Muthler and Francesco Spadini enthusiastically provided critical feedback on drafts of the chapters in the second half. Brian Fahs provided solutions to the exercises.

Kathy Buckheit wrote introductory tutorials to help students use the LC-2 simulator because she felt it was necessary.

Several other faculty members at The University of Texas have used the book and shared their insights with us: Tony Ambler, Craig Chase, Mario Gonzalez, and Earl Swartzlander in ECE, and Doug Burger, Chris Edmundson, and Steve Keckler in CS. We thank them.

We continue to celebrate the commitment displayed by our editors, Betsy Jones and Michelle Flomenhoft.

As was the case with the first edition, our book has benefited from extensive reviews provided by faculty members from many universities. We thank Robert Crisp, Arkansas; Allen Tannenbaum, Georgia Tech; Nickolas Jovanovic, Arkansas–Little Rock; Dean Brock, North Carolina–Asheville; Amar Raheja, Cal State–Pomona; Dayton Clark, Brooklyn College; William Yurcik, Illinois State; Jose Delgado-Frias, Washington State; Peter Drexel, Plymouth State; Mahmoud Manzoul, Jackson State; Dan Connors, Colorado; Massoud Ghyam, Southern Cal; John Gray, UMass–Dartmouth; John Hamilton, Auburn; Alan Rosenthal, Toronto; and Ron Taylor, Wright State.

Finally, there are those who have contributed in many different and often unique ways. Without listing their individual contributions, we simply list them and say thank you. Amanda, Bryan, and Carissa Hwu, Mateo Valero, Rich Belgard, Janak Patel, Matthew Frank, Milena Milenkovic, Lila Rhoades, Bruce Shriver, Steve Lumetta, and Brian Evans. Sanjay would like to thank Ann Yeung for all her love and support.

A Final Word

It is worth repeating our final words from the preface to the first edition: We are mindful that the current version of this book will always be a work in progress, and we welcome your comments on any aspect of it. You can reach us by e-mail at patt@ece.utexas.edu and sjp@crhc.uiuc.edu. We hope you will.

Yale N. Patt
Sanjay J. Patel
May, 2003

This textbook has evolved from EECS 100, the first computing course for computer science, computer engineering, and electrical engineering majors at the University of Michigan, that Kevin Compton and the first author introduced for the first time in the fall term, 1995.

EECS 100 happened because Computer Science and Engineering faculty had been dissatisfied for many years with the lack of student comprehension of some very basic concepts. For example, students had a lot of trouble with pointer variables. Recursion seemed to be "magic," beyond understanding.

We decided in 1993 that the conventional wisdom of starting with a high-level programming language, which was the way we (and most universities) were doing it, had its shortcomings. We decided that the reason students were not getting it was that they were forced to memorize technical details when they did not understand the basic underpinnings.

The result is the bottom-up approach taken in this book. We treat (in order) MOS transistors (very briefly, long enough for students to grasp their global switch-level behavior), logic gates, latches, logic structures (MUX, Decoder, Adder, gated latches), finally culminating in an implementation of memory. From there, we move on to the Von Neumann model of execution, then a simple computer (the LC-2), machine language programming of the LC-2, assembly language programming of the LC-2, the high level language C, recursion, pointers, arrays, and finally some elementary data structures.

We do not endorse today's popular information hiding approach when it comes to learning. Information hiding is a useful productivity enhancement technique after one understands what is going on. But until one gets to that point, we insist that information hiding gets in the way of understanding. Thus, we continually build on what has gone before, so that nothing is magic, and everything can be tied to the foundation that has already been laid.

We should point out that we do not disagree with the notion of top-down *design*. On the contrary, we believe strongly that top-down design is correct design. But there is a clear difference between how one approaches a design problem (after one understands the underlying building blocks), and what it takes to get to the point where one does understand the building blocks. In short, we believe in top-down design, but bottom-up learning for understanding.

What Is in the Book

The book breaks down into two major segments, a) the underlying structure of a computer, as manifested in the LC-2; and b) programming in a high level language, in our case C.

The LC-2

We start with the underpinnings that are needed to understand the workings of a real computer. Chapter 2 introduces the bit and arithmetic and logical operations on bits, Then we begin to build the structure needed to understand the LC-2. Chapter 3 takes the student from a MOS transistor, step by step, to a real memory. Our real memory consists of 4 words of 3 bits each, rather than 64 megabytes. The picture fits on a single page (Figure 3.20), making it easy for a student to grasp. By the time the students get there, they have been exposed to all the elements that make memory work. Chapter 4 introduces the Von Neumann execution model, as a lead-in to Chapter 5, the LC-2.

The LC-2 is a 16-bit architecture that includes physical I/O via keyboard and monitor; TRAPs to the operating system for handling service calls; conditional branches on N, Z, and P condition codes; a subroutine call/return mechanism; a minimal set of operate instructions (ADD, AND, and NOT); and various addressing modes for loads and stores (direct, indirect, Base+offset, and an immediate mode for loading effective addresses).

Chapter 6 is devoted to programming methodology (stepwise refinement) and debugging, and Chapter 7 is an introduction to assembly language programming. We have developed a simulator and an assembler for the LC-2. Actually, we have developed two simulators, one that runs on Windows platforms and one that runs on UNIX. The Windows simulator is available on the website and on the CD-ROM. Students who would rather use the UNIX version can download and install the software from the web at no charge.

Students use the simulator to test and debug programs written in LC-2 machine language and in LC-2 assembly language. The simulator allows online debugging (deposit, examine, single-step, set breakpoint, and so on). The simulator can be used for simple LC-2 machine language and assembly language programming assignments, which are essential for students to master the concepts presented throughout the first 10 chapters.

Assembly language is taught, but not to train expert assembly language programmers. Indeed, if the purpose was to train assembly language programmers, the material would be presented in an upper-level course, not in an introductory course for freshmen. Rather, the material is presented in Chapter 7 because it is consistent with the paradigm of the book. In our bottom-up approach, by the time the student reaches Chapter 7, he/she can handle the process of transforming assembly language programs to sequences of 0s and 1s. We go through the process of assembly step-by-step for a very simple LC-2 Assembler. By hand assembling, the student (at a very small additional cost in time) reinforces the important fundamental concept of translation.

It is also the case that assembly language provides a user-friendly notation to describe machine instructions, something that is particularly useful for the second half of the book. Starting in Chapter 11, when we teach the semantics of C statements, it is far easier for the reader to deal with ADD R1, R2, R3 than with 0001001010000011.

Chapter 8 deals with physical input (from a keyboard) and output (to a monitor). Chapter 9 deals with TRAPs to the operating system, and subroutine calls and returns. Students study the operating system routines (written in LC-2 code) for carrying out physical I/O invoked by the TRAP instruction.

The first half of the book concludes with Chapter 10, a treatment of stacks and data conversion at the LC-2 level, and a comprehensive example that makes use of both. The example is the simulation of a calculator, which is implemented by a main program and 11 subroutines.

The Language C

From there, we move on to C. The C programming language occupies the second half of the book. By the time the student gets to C, he/she has an understanding of the layers below.

The C programming language fits very nicely with our bottom-up approach. Its low-level nature allows students to see clearly the connection between software and the underlying hardware. In this book we focus on basic concepts such as control structures, functions, and arrays. Once basic programming concepts are mastered, it is a short step for students to learn more advanced concepts such as objects and abstraction.

Each time a new construct in C is introduced, the student is shown the LC-2 code that a compiler would produce. We cover the basic constructs of C (variables, operators, control, and functions), pointers, recursion, arrays, structures, I/O, complex data structures, and dynamic allocation.

Chapter 11 is a gentle introduction to high-level programming languages. At this point, students have dealt heavily with assembly language and can understand the motivation behind what high-level programming languages provide. Chapter 11 also contains a simple C program, which we use to kick-start the process of learning C.

Chapter 12 deals with values, variables, constants, and operators. Chapter 13 introduces C control structures. We provide many complete program examples to give students a sample of how each of these concepts is used in practice. LC-2 code is used to demonstrate how each C construct affects the machine at the lower levels.

In Chapter 14, students are exposed to techniques for debugging high-level source code. Chapter 15 introduces functions in C. Students are not merely exposed to the syntax of functions. Rather they learn how functions are actually executed using a run-time stack. A number of examples are provided.

Chapter 16 teaches recursion, using the student's newly gained knowledge of functions, activation records, and the run-time stack. Chapter 17 teaches pointers and arrays, relying heavily on the student's understanding of how memory is organized. Chapter 18 introduces the details of I/O functions in C, in particular, streams, variable length argument lists, and how C I/O is affected by the various format specifications. This chapter relies on the student's earlier exposure to physical I/O in Chapter 8. Chapter 19 concludes the coverage of C with structures, dynamic memory allocation, and linked lists.

Along the way, we have tried to emphasize good programming style and coding methodology by means of examples. Novice programmers probably learn at least as much from the programming examples they read as from the rules they are forced to study. Insights that accompany these examples are highlighted by means of lightbulb icons that are included in the margins.

We have found that the concept of pointer variables (Chapter 17) is not at all a problem. By the time students encounter it, they have a good understanding of what memory is all about, since they have analyzed the logic design of a small memory (Chapter 3). They know the difference, for example, between a memory location's address and the data stored there.

Recursion ceases to be magic since, by the time a student gets to that point (Chapter 16), he/she has already encountered all the underpinnings. Students understand how stacks work at the machine level (Chapter 10), and they understand the call/return mechanism from their LC-2 machine language programming experience, and the need for linkages between a called program and the return to the caller (Chapter 9). From this foundation, it is not a large step to explain functions by introducing run-time activation records (Chapter 15), with a lot of the mystery about argument passing, dynamic declarations, and so on, going away. Since a function can call a function, it is one additional small step (certainly no magic involved) for a function to call itself.

How to Use This Book

We have discovered over the past two years that there are many ways the material in this book can be presented in class effectively. We suggest six presentations below:

1. The Michigan model. First course, no formal prerequisites. Very intensive, this course covers the entire book. We have found that with talented, very highly motivated students, this works best.

2. Normal usage. First course, no prerequisites. This course is also intensive, although less so. It covers most of the book, leaving out Sections 10.3 and 10.4 of Chapter 10, Chapters 16 (recursion), 18 (the details of C I/O), and 19 (data structures).

3. Second course. Several schools have successfully used the book in their second course, after the students have been exposed to programming with an object-oriented programming language in a milder first course. In this second course, the entire book is covered, spending the first two-thirds of the semester on the first 10 chapters, and the last one-third of the semester on the second half of the book. The second half of the book can move more quickly, given that it follows both Chapters 1–10 and the

introductory programming course, which the student has already taken. Since students have experience with programming, lengthier programming projects can be assigned. This model allows students who were introduced to programming via an object-oriented language to pick up C, which they will certainly need if they plan to go on to advanced software courses such as operating systems.

4. Two quarters. An excellent use of the book. No prerequisites, the entire book can be covered easily in two quarters, the first quarter for Chapters 1–10, the second quarter for Chapters 11–19.

5. Two semesters. Perhaps the optimal use of the book. A two-semester sequence for freshmen. No formal prerequisites. First semester, Chapters 1–10, with supplemental material from Appendix C, the Microarchitecture of the LC-2. Second semester, Chapters 11–19 with additional substantial programming projects so that the students can solidify the concepts they learn in lectures.

6. A sophomore course in computer hardware. Some universities have found the book useful for a sophomore level breadth-first survey of computer hardware. They wish to introduce students in one semester to number systems, digital logic, computer organization, machine language and assembly language programming, finishing up with the material on stacks, activation records, recursion, and linked lists. The idea is to tie the hardware knowledge the students have acquired in the first part of the course to some of the harder to understand concepts that they struggled with in their freshman programming course. We strongly believe the better paradigm is to study the material in this book before tackling an object-oriented language. Nonetheless, we have seen this approach used successfully, where the sophomore student gets to understand the concepts in this course, after struggling with them during the freshman year.

Some Observations

Understanding, Not Memorizing

Since the course builds from the bottom up, we have found that less memorization of seemingly arbitrary rules is required than in traditional programming courses. Students understand that the rules make sense since by the time a topic is taught, they have an awareness of how that topic is implemented at the levels below it. This approach is good preparation for later courses in design, where understanding of and insights gained from fundamental underpinnings are essential to making the required design tradeoffs.

The Student Debugs the Student's Program

We hear complaints from industry all the time about CS graduates not being able to program. Part of the problem is the helpful teaching assistant, who contributes far too much of the intellectual component of the student's program, so the student never has to really master the art. Our approach is to push the student to do the job without the teaching assistant (TA). Part of this comes from the bottom-up approach where memorizing is minimized and the student builds on what he/she already knows. Part of this is the simulator, which the student uses from day one. The student is taught debugging from the beginning and is required to use the debugging tools of the simulator to get his/her programs to work from the very beginning. The combination of the simulator and the order in which the subject material is taught results in students actually debugging their own programs instead of taking their programs to the TA for help . . . and the common result that the TAs end up writing the programs for the students.

Preparation for the Future: Cutting Through Protective Layers

In today's real world, professionals who use computers in systems but remain ignorant of what is going on underneath are likely to discover the hard way that the effectiveness of their solutions is impacted adversely by things other than the actual programs they write. This is true for the sophisticated computer programmer as well as the sophisticated engineer.

Serious programmers will write more efficient code if they understand what is going on beyond the statements in their high-level language. Engineers, and not just computer engineers, are having to interact with their computer systems today more and more at the device or pin level. In systems where the computer is being used to sample data from some metering device such as a weather meter or feedback control system, the engineer needs to know more than just how to program in FORTRAN. This is true of mechanical, chemical, and aeronautical engineers today, not just electrical engineers. Consequently, the high-level programming language course, where the compiler protects the student from everything "ugly" underneath, does not serve most engineering students well, and certainly does not prepare them for the future.

Rippling Effects Through the Curriculum

The material of this text clearly has a rippling effect on what can be taught in subsequent courses. Subsequent programming courses can not only assume the students know the syntax of C but also understand how it relates to the underlying architecture. Consequently, the focus can be on problem solving and more sophisticated data structures. On the hardware side, a similar effect is seen in courses in digital logic design and in computer organization. Students start the logic design course with an appreciation of what the logic circuits they master are good for. In the computer organization course, the starting point is much further along than when students are seeing the term Program Counter for the first time. Feedback from Michigan faculty members in the follow-on courses have noticed substantial improvement in students' comprehension, compared to what they saw before students took EECS 100.

Acknowledgments

This book has benefited greatly from important contributions of many, many people. At the risk of leaving out some, we would at least like to acknowledge the following.

First, Professor Kevin Compton. Kevin believed in the concept of the book since it was first introduced at a curriculum committee meeting that he chaired at Michigan in 1993. The book grew out of a course (EECS 100) that he and the first author developed together, and co-taught the first three semesters it was offered at Michigan in fall 1995, winter 1996, and fall 1996. Kevin's insights into programming methodology (independent of the syntax of the particular language) provided a sound foundation for the beginning student The course at Michigan and this book would be a lot less were it not for Kevin's influence.

Several other students and faculty at Michigan were involved in the early years of EECS 100 and the early stages of the book. We are particularly grateful for the help of Professor David Kieras, Brian Hartman, David Armstrong, Matt Postiff, Dan Friendly, Rob Chappell, David Cybulski, Sangwook Kim, Don Winsor, and Ann Ford.

We also benefited enormously from TAs who were committed to helping students learn. The focus was always on how to explain the concept so the student gets it. We acknowledge, in particular, Fadi Aloul, David Armstrong, David Baker, Rob Chappell, David Cybulski, Amolika Gurujee, Brian Hartman, Sangwook Kim, Steve Maciejewski, Paul Racunas, David Telehowski, Francis Tseng, Aaron Wagner, and Paul Watkins.

We were delighted with the response from the publishing world to our manuscript. We ultimately decided on McGraw-Hill in large part because of the editor, Betsy Jones. Once she checked us out, she became a strong believer in what we are trying to accomplish. Throughout the process, her commitment and energy level have been greatly appreciated. We also appreciate what Michelle Flomenhoft has brought to the project. It has been a pleasure to work with her.

Our book has benefited from extensive reviews provided by faculty members at many universities. We gratefully acknowledge reviews provided by Carl D. Crane III, Florida, Nat Davis, Virginia Tech, Renee Elio, University of Alberta, Kelly Flangan, BYU, George Friedman, UIUC, Franco Fummi, Universita di Verona, Dale Grit, Colorado State, Thor Guisrud, Stavanger College, Brad Hutchings, BYU, Dave Kaeli, Northeastern, Rasool Kenarangui, UT at Arlington, Joel Kraft, Case Western Reserve, Wei-Ming Lin, UT at San Antonio, Roderick Loss, Montgomery College, Ron Meleshko, Grant MacEwan Community College, Andreas Moshovos, Northwestern, Tom Murphy, The Citadel, Murali Narayanan, Kansas State, Carla Purdy, Cincinnati, T. N. Rajashekhara, Camden County College, Nello Scarabottolo, Universita degli Studi di Milano, Robert Schaefer, Daniel Webster College, Tage Stabell-Kuloe, University of Tromsoe, Jean-Pierre Steger, Burgdorf School of Engineering, Bill Sverdlik, Eastern Michigan, John Trono, St. Michael's College, Murali Varansi, University of South Florida, Montanez Wade, Tennessee State, and Carl Wick, US Naval Academy.

In addition to all these people, there were others who contributed in many different and sometimes unique ways. Space dictates that we simply list them and say thank you. Susan Kornfield, Ed DeFranco, Evan Gsell, Rich Belgard, Tom Conte, Dave Nagle, Bruce Shriver, Bill Sayle, Steve Lumetta, Dharma Agarwal, David Lilja, and Michelle Chapman.

Finally, if you will indulge the first author a bit: This book is about developing a strong foundation in the fundamentals with the fervent belief that once that is accomplished, students can go as far as their talent and energy can take them. This objective was instilled in me by the professor who taught me how to be a professor, Professor William K. Linvill. It has been more than 35 years since I was in his classroom, but I still treasure the example he set.

A Final Word

We hope you will enjoy the approach taken in this book. Nonetheless, we are mindful that the current version will always be a work in progress, and both of us welcome your comments on any aspect of it. You can reach us by email at patt@ece.utexas.edu and sjp@crhc.uiuc.edu. We hope you will.

Yale N. Patt
Sanjay J. Patel
March, 2000

1

Welcome Aboard

1.1 What We Will Try to Do

Welcome to *From Bits and Gates to C and Beyond*. Our intent is to introduce you over the next 632 pages to come, to the world of computing. As we do so, we have one objective above all others: to show you very clearly that there is no magic to computing. The computer is a deterministic system—every time we hit it over the head in the same way and in the same place (provided, of course, it was in the same starting condition), we get the same response. The computer is not an electronic genius; on the contrary, if anything, it is an electronic idiot, doing exactly what we tell it to do. It has no mind of its own.

What appears to be a very complex organism is really just a huge, systematically interconnected collection of very simple parts. Our job throughout this book is to introduce you to those very simple parts, and, step-by-step, build the interconnected structure that you know by the name *computer*. Like a house, we will start at the bottom, construct the foundation first, and then go on to add layers and layers, as we get closer and closer to what most people know as a full-blown computer. Each time we add a layer, we will explain what we are doing, tying the new ideas to the underlying fabric. Our goal is that when we are done, you will be able to write programs in a computer language such as C, using the sophisticated features of that language, and understand what is going on underneath, inside the computer.

1.2 How We Will Get There

We will start (in Chapter 2) by noting that the computer is a piece of electronic equipment and, as such, consists of electronic parts interconnected by wires. Every wire in the computer, at every moment in time, is either at a high voltage or a low voltage. We do not differentiate exactly how high. For example, we do not distinguish voltages of 115 volts from voltages of 118 volts. We only care whether there is or is not a large voltage relative to 0 volts. That absence or presence of a large voltage relative to 0 volts is represented as 0 or 1.

We will encode all information as sequences of 0s and 1s. For example, one encoding of the letter *a* that is commonly used is the sequence 01100001. One encoding of the decimal number *35* is the sequence 00100011. We will see how to perform operations on such encoded information.

Once we are comfortable with information represented as codes made up of 0s and 1s and operations (addition, for example) being performed on these representations, we will begin the process of showing how a computer works. In Chapter 3, we will see how the transistors that make up today's microprocessors work. We will further see how those transistors are combined into larger structures that perform operations, such as addition, and into structures that allow us to save information for later use. In Chapter 4, we will combine these larger structures into the Von Neumann machine, a basic model that describes how a computer works. In Chapter 5, we will begin to study a simple computer, the LC-3. *LC-3* stands for Little Computer 3; we started with LC-1 but needed two more shots at it before we got it right! The LC-3 has all the important characteristics of the microprocessors that you may have already heard of, for example, the Intel 8088, which was used in the first IBM PCs back in 1981. Or the Motorola 68000, which was used in the Macintosh, vintage 1984. Or the Pentium IV, one of the high-performance microprocessors of choice in the PC of the year 2003. That is, the LC-3 has all the important characteristics of these "real" microprocessors, without being so complicated that it gets in the way of your understanding.

Once we understand how the LC-3 works, the next step is to program it, first in its own language (Chapter 6), then in a language called *assembly language* that is a little bit easier for humans to work with (Chapter 7). Chapter 8 deals with the problem of getting information into (input) and out of (output) the LC-3. Chapter 9 covers two sophisticated LC-3 mechanisms, TRAPs and subroutines.

We conclude our introduction to programming the LC-3 in Chapter 10 by first introducing two important concepts (stacks and data conversion), and then by showing a sophisticated example: an LC-3 program that carries out the work of a handheld calculator.

In the second half of the book (Chapters 11–19), we turn our attention to a high-level programming language, C. We include many aspects of C that are usually not dealt with in an introductory textbook. In almost all cases, we try to tie high-level C constructs to the underlying LC-3, so that you will understand what you demand of the computer when you use a particular construct in a C program.

Our treatment of C starts with basic topics such as variables and operators (Chapter 12), control structures (Chapter 13), and functions (Chapter 14). We then move on to the more advanced topics of debugging C programs (Chapter 15), recursion (Chapter 16), and pointers and arrays (Chapter 17).

We conclude our introduction to C by examining two very common high-level constructs, input/output in C (Chapter 18) and the linked list (Chapter 19).

1.3 Two Recurring Themes

Two themes permeate this book that we have previously taken for granted, assuming that everyone recognized their value and regularly emphasized them to students of engineering and computer science. Lately, it has become clear to us that from the git-go, we need to make these points explicit. So, we state them here up front. The two themes are (a) the notion of abstraction and (b) the importance of not separating in your mind the notions of hardware and software. Their value to your development as an effective engineer or computer scientist goes well beyond your understanding of how a computer works and how to program it.

The notion of abstraction is central to all that you will learn and expect to use in practicing your craft, whether it be in mathematics, physics, any aspect of engineering, or business. It is hard to think of any body of knowledge where the notion of abstraction is not central. The misguided hardware/software separation is directly related to your continuing study of computers and your work with them. We will discuss each in turn.

1.3.1 The Notion of Abstraction

The use of abstraction is all around us. When we get in a taxi and tell the driver, "Take me to the airport," we are using abstraction. If we had to, we could probably direct the driver each step of the way: "Go down this street ten blocks, and make a left turn." And, when he got there, "Now take this street five blocks and make a right turn." And on and on. You know the details, but it is a lot quicker to just tell the driver to take you to the airport.

Even the statement "Go down this street ten blocks..." can be broken down further with instructions on using the accelerator, the steering wheel, watching out for other vehicles, pedestrians, etc.

Our ability to abstract is very much a productivity enhancer. It allows us to deal with a situation at a higher level, focusing on the essential aspects, while keeping the component ideas in the background. It allows us to be more efficient in our use of time and brain activity. It allows us to not get bogged down in the detail when everything about the detail is working just fine.

There is an underlying assumption to this, however: "when everything about the detail is just fine." What if everything about the detail is not just fine? Then, to be successful, our ability to abstract must be combined with our ability to un-abstract. Some people use the word *deconstruct*—the ability to go from the abstraction back to its component parts.

Two stories come to mind.

The first involves a trip through Arizona the first author made a long time ago in the hottest part of the summer. At the time I was living in Palo Alto, California, where the temperature tends to be mild almost always. I knew enough to take the car to a mechanic before making the trip, and I told him to check the cooling system. That was the abstraction: cooling system. What I had not mastered was that the capability of a cooling system for Palo Alto, California is not the same as the capability of a cooling system for the summer deserts of Arizona. The result: two days in Deer Lodge, Arizona (population 3), waiting for a head gasket to be shipped in.

The second story (perhaps apocryphal) is supposed to have happened during the infancy of electric power generation. General Electric Co. was having trouble with one of its huge electric power generators and did not know what to do. On the front of the generator were lots of dials containing lots of information, and lots of screws that could be rotated clockwise or counterclockwise as the operator wished. Something on the other side of the wall of dials and screws was malfunctioning and no one knew what to do. So, as the story goes, they called in one of the early giants in the electric power industry. He looked at the dials and listened to the noises for a minute, then took a small pocket screwdriver out of his geek pack and rotated one screw 35 degrees counterclockwise. The problem immediately went away. He submitted a bill for $1,000 (a lot of money in those days) without any elaboration. The controller found the bill for two minutes' work a little unsettling, and asked for further clarification. Back came the new bill:

```
Turning a screw 35 degrees counterclockwise:  $  0.75
Knowing which screw to turn and by how much:     999.25
```

In both stories the message is the same. It is more efficient to think of entities as abstractions. One does not want to get bogged down in details unnecessarily. And as long as nothing untoward happens, we are OK. If I had never tried to make the trip to Arizona, the abstraction "cooling system" would have been sufficient. If the electric power generator never malfunctioned, there would have been no need for the power engineering guru's deeper understanding.

When one designs a logic circuit out of gates, it is much more efficient to not have to think about the internals of each gate. To do so would slow down the process of designing the logic circuit. One wants to think of the gate as a component. But if there is a problem with getting the logic circuit to work, it is often helpful to look at the internal structure of the gate and see if something about its functioning is causing the problem.

When one designs a sophisticated computer application program, whether it be a new spreadsheet program, word processing system, or computer game, one wants to think of each of the components one is using as an abstraction. If one spent time thinking about the details of a component when it is not necessary, the distraction could easily prevent the total job from ever getting finished. But when there is a problem putting the components together, it is often useful to examine carefully the details of each component in order to uncover the problem.

The ability to abstract is a most important skill. In our view, one should try to keep the level of abstraction as high as possible, consistent with getting everything to work effectively. Our approach in this book is to continually raise the level of abstraction. We describe logic gates in terms of transistors. Once we understand the abstraction of gates, we no longer think in terms of transistors. Then we build larger structures out of gates. Once we understand these larger abstractions, we no longer think in terms of gates.

The Bottom Line

Abstractions allow us to be much more efficient in dealing with all kinds of situations. It is also true that one can be effective without understanding what is below the abstraction as long as everything behaves nicely. So, one should not pooh-pooh the notion of abstraction. On the contrary, one should celebrate it since it allows us to be more efficient.

In fact, if we never have to combine a component with anything else into a larger system, and if nothing can go wrong with the component, then it is perfectly fine to understand this component only at the level of its abstraction.

But if we have to combine multiple components into a larger system, we should be careful not to allow their abstractions to be the deepest level of our understanding. If we don't know the components below the level of their abstractions, then we are at the mercy of them working together without our intervention. If they don't work together, and we are unable to go below the level of abstraction, we are stuck. And that is the state we should take care not to find ourselves in.

1.3.2 Hardware versus Software

Many computer scientists and engineers refer to themselves as hardware people or software people. By hardware, they generally mean the physical computer and all the specifications associated with it. By software, they generally mean the programs, whether operating systems like UNIX or Windows, or database systems like Oracle or DB-terrific, or application programs like Excel or Word. The implication is that the person knows a whole lot about one of these two things and precious little about the other. Usually, there is the further implication that it is OK to be an expert at one of these (hardware OR software) and clueless about the other. It is as if there were a big wall between the hardware (the computer and how it actually works) and the software (the programs that direct the computer's bidding), and that one should be content to remain on one side of that wall or the other.

As you approach your study and practice of computing, we urge you to take the opposite approach—that hardware and software are names for components of two parts of a computing system that work best when they are designed by someone who took into account the capabilities and limitations of both.

Microprocessor designers who understand the needs of the programs that will execute on that microprocessor they are designing can design much more effective microprocessors than those who don't. For example, Intel, Motorola, and other major producers of microprocessors recognized a few years ago that a large fraction of future programs would contain video clips as part of e-mail, video games, and full-length movies. They recognized that it would be important for such programs to execute efficiently. The result: most microprocessors today contain special hardware capability to process these video clips. Intel defined additional instructions, collectively called their MMX instruction set, and developed special hardware for it. Motorola, IBM, and Apple did essentially the same thing, resulting in the AltiVec instruction set and special hardware to support it.

A similar story can be told about software designers. The designer of a large computer program who understands the capabilities and limitations of the hardware that will carry out the tasks of that program can design the program more efficiently than the designer who does not understand the nature of the hardware. One important task that almost all large software systems have to carry out is called sorting, where a number of items have to be arranged in some order. The words in a dictionary are arranged in alphabetical order. Students in a class are often arranged in numeric order, according to their scores on the final exam. There are a huge number of fundamentally different programs one can write to arrange a collection of items in order. Donald Knuth devoted 391 pages to the task in *The Art of Computer Programming*, vol. 3. Which sorting program works best is often very dependent on how much the software designer is aware of the characteristics of the hardware.

The Bottom Line

We believe that whether your inclinations are in the direction of a computer hardware career or a computer software career, you will be much more capable if you master both. This book is about getting you started on the path to mastering both hardware and software. Although we sometimes ignore making the point explicitly when we are in the trenches of working through a concept, it really is the case that each sheds light on the other.

When you study data types, a software concept (in C, Chapter 12), you will understand how the finite word length of the computer, a hardware concept, affects our notion of data types.

When you study functions (in C, Chapter 14), you will be able to tie the *rules* of calling a function with the hardware implementation that makes those rules necessary.

When you study recursion (a powerful algorithmic device, in Chapter 16), you will be able to tie it to the hardware. If you take the time to do that, you will better understand when the additional time to execute a procedure recursively is worth it.

When you study pointer variables (in C, in Chapter 17), your knowledge of computer memory will provide a deeper understanding of what pointers provide, when they should be used, and when they should be avoided.

When you study data structures (in C, in Chapter 19), your knowledge of computer memory will help you better understand what must be done to manipulate the actual structures in memory efficiently.

We understand that most of the terms in the preceding five short paragraphs are not familiar to you *yet*. That is OK; you can reread this page at the end of the semester. What is important to know right now is that there are important topics in the software that are very deeply interwoven with topics in the hardware. Our contention is that mastering either is easier if you pay attention to both.

Most importantly, most computing problems yield better solutions when the problem solver has the capability of both at his or her disposal.

1.4 A Computer System

We have used the word *computer* many times in the preceding paragraphs, and although we did not say so explicitly, we used it to mean a mechanism that does two things: It directs the processing of information and it performs the actual processing of information. It does both of these things in response to a computer program. When we say "directing the processing of information," we mean figuring out which task should get carried out next. When we say "performing the actual processing," we mean doing the actual additions, multiplications, and so forth that are necessary to get the job done. A more precise term for this mechanism is a central processing unit (CPU), or simply a processor. This textbook is primarily about the processor and the programs that are executed by the processor.

Twenty years ago, the processor was constructed out of ten or more 18-inch electronic boards, each containing 50 or more electronic parts known as integrated circuit packages (see Figure 1.1). Today, a processor usually consists of a single microprocessor chip, built on a piece of silicon material, measuring less than an inch square, and containing many millions of transistors (see Figure 1.2).

However, when most people use the word *computer*, they usually mean more than the processor. They usually mean the collection of parts that in combination

Figure 1.1   A processor board, vintage 1980s (Courtesy of Emilio Salgueiro, Unisys Corporation.)

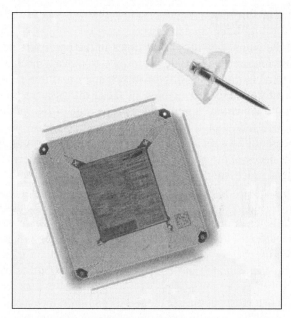

Figure 1.2   A microprocessor, vintage 1998 (Courtesy of Intel Corporation.)

Figure 1.3   A personal computer (Courtesy of Dell Computer.)

form their *computer system* (see Figure 1.3). A computer system usually includes, in addition to the processor, a keyboard for typing commands, a mouse for clicking on menu entries, a monitor for displaying information that the computer system has produced, a printer for obtaining paper copies of that information, memory for temporarily storing information, disks and CD-ROMs of one sort or another for storing information for a very long time, even after the computer has been turned off, and the collection of programs (the software) that the user wishes to execute.

These additional items are useful in helping the computer user do his or her job. Without a printer, for example, the user would have to copy by hand what is displayed on the monitor. Without a mouse, the user would have to type each command, rather than simply clicking on the mouse button.

So, as we begin our journey, which focuses on how we get less than 1 square inch of silicon to do our bidding, we note that the computer systems we use contain a lot of other components to make our life more comfortable.

1.5 Two Very Important Ideas

Before we leave this first chapter, there are two very important ideas that we would like you to understand, ideas that are at the core of what computing is all about.

Idea 1:   All computers (the biggest and the smallest, the fastest and the slowest, the most expensive and the cheapest) are capable of computing exactly the same things if they are given enough time and enough memory. That is, anything a fast computer can do, a slow computer can do also. The slow computer just does it more slowly. A more expensive computer cannot figure out something that a cheaper computer is unable to figure out as long as the cheap computer can access enough memory. (You may have to go to the store to buy disks whenever it runs out of memory in order to keep increasing memory.) **All** computers can do **exactly** the same things. Some computers can do things faster, but none can do **more** than any other.

Idea 2:   We describe our problems in English or some other language spoken by people. Yet the problems are solved by electrons running around inside the computer. It is necessary to transform our problem from the language of humans to the voltages that influence the flow of electrons. This transformation is really a sequence of systematic transformations, developed and improved over the last 50 years, which combine to give the computer the ability to carry out what appears to be some very complicated tasks. In reality, these tasks are simple and straightforward.

The rest of this chapter is devoted to discussing these two ideas.

1.6 Computers as Universal Computational Devices

It may seem strange that an introductory textbook begins by describing how computers work. After all, mechanical engineering students begin by studying physics, not how car engines work. Chemical engineering students begin by studying chemistry, not oil refineries. Why should computing students begin by studying computers?

The answer is that computers are different. To learn the fundamental principles of computing, you must study computers or machines that can do what computers can do. The reason for this has to do with the notion that computers are *universal computational devices*. Let's see what that means.

Before modern computers, there were many kinds of calculating machines. Some were *analog machines*—machines that produced an answer by measuring some physical quantity such as distance or voltage. For example, a slide rule is an analog machine that multiplies numbers by sliding one logarithmically graded ruler next to another. The user can read a logarithmic "distance" on the second ruler. Some early analog adding machines worked by dropping weights on a scale. The difficulty with analog machines is that it is very hard to increase their accuracy.

This is why *digital machines*—machines that perform computations by manipulating a fixed finite set of digits or letters—came to dominate computing. You are familiar with the distinction between analog and digital watches. An analog watch has hour and minute hands, and perhaps a second hand. It gives the time by the positions of its hands, which are really angular measures. Digital watches give the time in digits. You can increase accuracy just by adding more digits. For example, if it is important for you to measure time in hundredths of a second, you can buy a watch that gives a reading like 10:35.16 rather than just 10:35. How would you get an analog watch that would give you an accurate reading to one one-hundredth of a second? You could do it, but it would take a mighty long second hand! When we talk about computers in this book, we will always mean digital machines.

Before modern digital computers, the most common digital machines in the West were adding machines. In other parts of the world another digital machine, the abacus, was common. Digital adding machines were mechanical or electromechanical devices that could perform a specific kind of computation: adding integers. There were also digital machines that could multiply integers. There were digital machines that could put a stack of cards with punched names in alphabetical order. The main limitation of all of these machines is that they could do only one specific kind of computation. If you owned only an adding machine and wanted to multiply two integers, you had some pencil and paper work to do.

This is why computers are different. You can tell a computer how to add numbers. You can tell it how to multiply. You can tell it how to alphabetize a list or perform any computation you like. When you think of a new kind of computation, you do not have to buy or design a new computer. You just give the old computer a new set of instructions (or program) to carry out the computation. This is why we say the computer is a *universal computational device*. Computer scientists believe that *anything that can be computed, can be computed by a computer* provided it has enough time and enough memory. When we study computers, we study the fundamentals of all computing. We learn what computation is and what can be computed.

The idea of a universal computational device is due to Alan Turing. Turing proposed in 1937 that all computations could be carried out by a particular kind of machine, which is now called a Turing machine. He gave a mathematical description of this kind of machine, but did not actually build one. Digital computers were not operating until 1946. Turing was more interested in solving a philosophical problem: defining computation. He began by looking at the kinds of actions that people perform when they compute; these include making marks

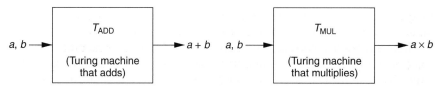

Figure 1.4   Black box models of Turing machines

on paper, writing symbols according to certain rules when other symbols are present, and so on. He abstracted these actions and specified a mechanism that could carry them out. He gave some examples of the kinds of things that these machines could do. One Turing machine could add two integers; another could multiply two integers.

Figure 1.4 provides what we call "black box" models of Turing machines that add and multiply. In each case, the operation to be performed is described in the box. The data on which to operate is shown as input to the box. The result of the operation is shown as output from the box. A black box model provides no information as to exactly how the operation is performed, and indeed, there are many ways to add or multiply two numbers.

Turing proposed that every computation can be performed by some Turing machine. We call this *Turing's thesis*. Although Turing's thesis has never been proved, there does exist a lot of evidence to suggest it is true. We know, for example, that various enhancements one can make to Turing machines do not result in machines that can compute more.

Perhaps the best argument to support Turing's thesis was provided by Turing himself in his original paper. He said that one way to try to construct a machine more powerful than any particular Turing machine was to make a machine U that could simulate *all* Turing machines. You would simply describe to U the particular Turing machine you wanted it to simulate, say a machine to add two integers, give U the input data, and U would compute the appropriate output, in this case the sum of the inputs. Turing then showed that there was, in fact, a Turing machine that could do this, so even this attempt to find something that could not be computed by Turing machines failed.

Figure 1.5 further illustrates the point. Suppose you wanted to compute $g \cdot (e + f)$. You would simply provide to U descriptions of the Turing machines to add and to multiply, and the three inputs, e, f, and g. U would do the rest.

In specifying U, Turing had provided us with a deep insight: He had given us the first description of what computers do. In fact, both a computer (with as much

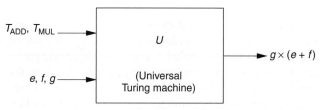

Figure 1.5   Black box model of a universal Turing machine

memory as it wants) and a universal Turing machine can compute exactly the same things. In both cases you give the machine a description of a computation and the data it needs, and the machine computes the appropriate answer. Computers and universal Turing machines can compute anything that can be computed because they are *programmable*.

This is the reason that a big or expensive computer cannot do more than a small, cheap computer. More money may buy you a faster computer, a monitor with higher resolution, or a nice sound system. But if you have a small, cheap computer, you already have a universal computational device.

1.7 How Do We Get the Electrons to Do the Work?

Figure 1.6 shows the process we must go through to get the electrons (which actually do the work) to do our bidding. We call the steps of this process the

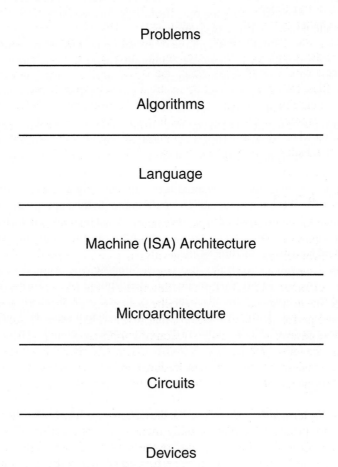

Problems

Algorithms

Language

Machine (ISA) Architecture

Microarchitecture

Circuits

Devices

Figure 1.6   Levels of transformation

"Levels of Transformation." As we will see, at each level we have choices. If we ignore any of the levels, our ability to make the best use of our computing system can be very adversely affected.

1.7.1 The Statement of the Problem

We describe the problems we wish to solve with a computer in a "natural language." Natural languages are languages that people speak, like English, French, Japanese, Italian, and so on. They have evolved over centuries in accordance with their usage. They are fraught with a lot of things unacceptable for providing instructions to a computer. Most important of these unacceptable attributes is ambiguity. Natural language is filled with ambiguity. To infer the meaning of a sentence, a listener is often helped by the tone of voice of the speaker, or at the very least, the context of the sentence.

An example of ambiguity in English is the sentence, "Time flies like an arrow." At least three interpretations are possible, depending on whether (1) one is noticing how fast time passes, (2) one is at a track meet for insects, or (3) one is writing a letter to the Dear Abby of Insectville. In the first case, a simile, one is comparing the speed of time passing to the speed of an arrow that has been released. In the second case, one is telling the timekeeper to do his/her job much like an arrow would. In the third case, one is relating that a particular group of flies (time flies, as opposed to fruit flies) are all in love with the same arrow.

Such ambiguity would be unacceptable in instructions provided to a computer. The computer, electronic idiot that it is, can only do as it is told. To tell it to do something where there are multiple interpretations would cause the computer to not know which interpretation to follow.

1.7.2 The Algorithm

The first step in the sequence of transformations is to transform the natural language description of the problem to an algorithm, and in so doing, get rid of the objectionable characteristics. An algorithm is a step-by-step procedure that is guaranteed to terminate, such that each step is precisely stated and can be carried out by the computer. There are terms to describe each of these properties.

We use the term *definiteness* to describe the notion that each step is precisely stated. A recipe for excellent pancakes that instructs the preparer to "stir until lumpy" lacks definiteness, since the notion of lumpiness is not precise.

We use the term *effective computability* to describe the notion that each step can be carried out by a computer. A procedure that instructs the computer to "take the largest prime number" lacks effective computability, since there is no largest prime number.

We use the term *finiteness* to describe the notion that the procedure terminates.

For every problem there are usually many different algorithms for solving that problem. One algorithm may require the fewest number of steps. Another algorithm may allow some steps to be performed concurrently. A computer that allows more than one thing to be done at a time can often solve the problem in less time, even though it is likely that the total number of steps to be performed has increased.

1.7.3 The Program

The next step is to transform the algorithm into a computer program, in one of the programming languages that are available. Programming languages are "mechanical languages." That is, unlike natural languages, mechanical languages did not evolve through human discourse. Rather, they were invented for use in specifying a sequence of instructions to a computer. Therefore, mechanical languages do not suffer from failings such as ambiguity that would make them unacceptable for specifying a computer program.

There are more than 1,000 programming languages. Some have been designed for use with particular applications, such as Fortran for solving scientific calculations and COBOL for solving business data-processing problems. In the second half of this book, we will use C, a language that was designed for manipulating low-level hardware structures.

Other languages are useful for still other purposes. Prolog is the language of choice for many applications that require the design of an expert system. LISP was for years the language of choice of a substantial number of people working on problems dealing with artificial intelligence. Pascal is a language invented as a vehicle for teaching beginning students how to program.

There are two kinds of programming languages, high-level languages and low-level languages. High-level languages are at a distance (a high level) from the underlying computer. At their best, they are independent of the computer on which the programs will execute. We say the language is "machine independent." All the languages mentioned thus far are high-level languages. Low-level languages are tied to the computer on which the programs will execute. There is generally one such low-level language for each computer. That language is called the *assembly language* for that computer.

1.7.4 The ISA

The next step is to translate the program into the instruction set of the particular computer that will be used to carry out the work of the program. The instruction set architecture (ISA) is the complete specification of the interface between programs that have been written and the underlying computer hardware that must carry out the work of those programs.

The ISA specifies the set of instructions the computer can carry out, that is, what operations the computer can perform and what data is needed by each operation. The term *operand* is used to describe individual data values. The ISA specifies the acceptable representations for operands. They are called *data types*. A *data type* is a legitimate representation for an operand such that the computer can perform operations on that representation. The ISA specifies the mechanisms that the computer can use to figure out where the operands are located. These mechanisms are called *addressing modes*.

The number of operations, data types, and addressing modes specified by an ISA vary among the different ISAs. Some ISAs have as few as a half dozen operations, whereas others have as many as several hundred. Some ISAs have only one data type, while others have more than a dozen. Some ISAs have one or two addressing modes, whereas others have more than 20. The x86, the ISA used in the PC, has more than 100 operations, more than a dozen data types, and more than two dozen addressing modes.

The ISA also specifies the number of unique locations that comprise the computer's memory and the number of individual 0s and 1s that are contained in each location.

Many ISAs are in use today. The most common example is the x86, introduced by Intel Corporation in 1979 and currently also manufactured by AMD and other companies. Other ISAs are the Power PC (IBM and Motorola), PA-RISC (Hewlett Packard), and SPARC (Sun Microsystems).

The translation from a high-level language (such as C) to the ISA of the computer on which the program will execute (such as x86) is usually done by a translating program called a *compiler*. To translate from a program written in C to the x86 ISA, one would need an x86 C compiler. For each high-level language and each desired target computer, one must provide a corresponding compiler.

The translation from the unique assembly language of a computer to its ISA is done by an assembler.

1.7.5 The Microarchitecture

The next step is to transform the ISA into an implementation. The detailed organization of an implementation is called its *microarchitecture*. So, for example, the x86 has been implemented by several different microprocessors over the years, each having its own unique microarchitecture. The original implementation was the 8086 in 1979. More recently, in 2001, Intel introduced the Pentium IV microprocessor. Motorola and IBM have implemented the Power PC ISA with more than a dozen different microprocessors, each having its own microarchitecture. Two of the more recent implementations are the Motorola MPC 7455 and the IBM Power PC 750FX.

Each implementation is an opportunity for computer designers to make different trade-offs between the cost of the microprocessor and the performance that microprocessor will provide. Computer design is always an exercise in trade-offs, as the designer opts for higher (or lower) performance at greater (or lesser) cost.

The automobile provides a good analogy of the relationship between an ISA and a microarchitecture that implements that ISA. The ISA describes what the driver sees as he/she sits inside the automobile. All automobiles provide the same interface (an ISA different from the ISA for boats and the ISA for airplanes). Of the three pedals on the floor, the middle one is always the brake. The one on the right is the accelerator, and when it is depressed, the car will move faster. The ISA is about basic functionality. All cars can get from point A to point B, can move forward and backward, and can turn to the right and to the left.

The implementation of the ISA is about what goes on under the hood. Here all automobile makes and models are different, depending on what cost/performance trade-offs the automobile designer made before the car was manufactured. So, some automobiles come with disc brakes, others (in the past, at least) with drums. Some automobiles have eight cylinders, others run on six cylinders, and still others have four. Some are turbocharged, some are not. In each case, the "microarchitecture" of the specific automobile is a result of the automobile designers' decisions regarding cost and performance.

1.7.6 The Logic Circuit

The next step is to implement each element of the microarchitecture out of simple logic circuits. Here, also, there are choices, as the logic designer decides how to best make the trade-offs between cost and performance. So, for example, even for the simple operation of addition, there are several choices of logic circuits to perform this operation at differing speeds and corresponding costs.

1.7.7 The Devices

Finally, each basic logic circuit is implemented in accordance with the requirements of the particular device technology used. So, CMOS circuits are different from NMOS circuits, which are different, in turn, from gallium arsenide circuits.

1.7.8 Putting It Together

In summary, from the natural language description of a problem to the electrons running around that actually solve the problem, many transformations need to be performed. If we could speak electron, or the electrons could understand English, perhaps we could just walk up to the computer and get the electrons to do our bidding. Since we can't speak electron and they can't speak English, the best we can do is this systematic sequence of transformations. At each level of transformation, there are choices as to how to proceed. Our handling of those choices determines the resulting cost and performance of our computer.

In this book, we describe each of these transformations. We show how transistors combine to form logic circuits, how logic circuits combine to form the microarchitecture, and how the microarchitecture implements a particular ISA, in our case, the LC-3. We complete the process by going from the English-language description of a problem to a C program that solves the problem, and we show how that C program is translated (i.e., compiled) to the ISA of the LC-3.

We hope you enjoy the ride.

1.1   Explain the first of the two important ideas stated in Section 1.5.

1.2   Can a higher-level programming language instruct a computer to compute more than a lower-level programming language?

1.3   What difficulty with analog computers encourages computer designers to use digital designs?

1.4   Name one characteristic of natural languages that prevents them from being used as programming languages.

1.5   Say we had a "black box," which takes two numbers as input and outputs their sum. See Figure 1.7a. Say we had another box capable of multiplying two numbers together. See Figure 1.7b. We can connect these boxes together to calculate $p \times (m + n)$. See Figure 1.7c. Assume we have an unlimited number of these boxes. Show how to connect them together to calculate:

a. $ax + b$
b. The average of the four input numbers w, x, y, and z
c. $a^2 + 2ab + b^2$ (Can you do it with one add box and one multiply box?)

1.6   Write a statement in a natural language and offer two different interpretations of that statement.

1.7   The discussion of abstraction in Section 1.3.1 noted that one does not need to understand the makeup of the components as long as "everything about the detail is just fine." The case was made that when everything is not fine, one must be able to deconstruct the components, or be at the mercy of the abstractions. In the taxi example, suppose you did not understand the component, that is, you had no clue how to get to the airport. Using the notion of abstraction, you simply tell the driver,

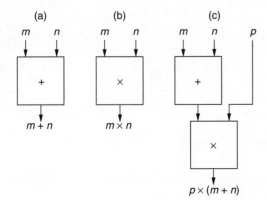

Figure 1.7   "Black boxes" capable of (a) addition, (b) multiplication, and (c) a combination of addition and multiplication

"Take me to the airport." Explain when this is a productivity enhancer, and when it could result in very negative consequences.

1.8 John said, "I saw the man in the park with a telescope." What did he mean? How many reasonable interpretations can you provide for this statement? List them. What property does this sentence demonstrate that makes it unacceptable as a statement in a program.

1.9 Are natural languages capable of expressing algorithms?

1.10 Name three characteristics of algorithms. Briefly explain each of these three characteristics.

1.11 For each characteristic of an algorithm, give an example of a procedure that does not have the characteristic, and is therefore not an algorithm.

1.12 Are items *a* through *e* in the following list algorithms? If not, what qualities required of algorithms do they lack?

a. Add the first row of the following matrix to another row whose first column contains a nonzero entry. (*Reminder*: Columns run vertically; rows run horizontally.)

$$\begin{bmatrix} 1 & 2 & 0 & 4 \\ 0 & 3 & 2 & 4 \\ 2 & 3 & 10 & 22 \\ 12 & 4 & 3 & 4 \end{bmatrix}$$

b. In order to show that there are as many prime numbers as there are natural numbers, match each prime number with a natural number in the following manner. Create pairs of prime and natural numbers by matching the first prime number with 1 (which is the first natural number) and the second prime number with 2, the third with 3, and so forth. If, in the end, it turns out that each prime number can be paired with each natural number, then it is shown that there are as many prime numbers as natural numbers.

c. Suppose you're given two vectors each with 20 elements and asked to perform the following operation. Take the first element of the first vector and multiply it by the first element of the second vector. Do the same to the second elements, and so forth. Add all the individual products together to derive the dot product.

d. Lynne and Calvin are trying to decided who will take the dog for a walk. Lynne suggests that they flip a coin and pulls a quarter out of her pocket. Calvin does not trust Lynne and suspects that the quarter may be weighted (meaning that it might favor a particular outcome when tossed) and suggests the following procedure to fairly determine who will walk the dog.
   1. Flip the quarter twice.
   2. If the outcome is heads on the first flip and tails on the second, then I will walk the dog.
   3. If the outcome is tails on the first flip, and heads on the second, then you will walk the dog.

4. If both outcomes are tails or both outcomes are heads, then we flip twice again.

Is Calvin's technique an algorithm?

e. Given a number, perform the following steps in order:
1. Multiply it by four
2. Add four
3. Divide by two
4. Subtract two
5. Divide by two
6. Subtract one
7. At this point, add one to a counter to keep track of the fact that you performed steps 1 through 6. Then test the result you got when you subtracted one. If 0, write down the number of times you performed steps 1 through 6 and stop. If not 0, starting with the result of subtracting 1, perform the above 7 steps again.

1.13   Two computers, A and B, are identical except for the fact that A has a subtract instruction and B does not. Both have add instructions. Both have instructions that can take a value and produce the negative of that value. Which computer is able to solve more problems, A or B? Prove your result.

1.14   Suppose we wish to put a set of names in alphabetical order. We call the act of doing so *sorting*. One algorithm that can accomplish that is called the bubble sort. We could then program our bubble sort algorithm in C, and compile the C program to execute on an x86 ISA. The x86 ISA can be implemented with an Intel Pentium IV microarchitecture. Let us call the sequence "Bubble Sort, C program, x86 ISA, Pentium IV microarchitecture" one *transformation process*.

Assume we have available four sorting algorithms and can program in C, C++, Pascal, Fortran, and COBOL. We have available compilers that can translate from each of these to either x86 or SPARC, and we have available three different microarchitectures for x86 and three different microarchitectures for SPARC.

a. How many transformation processes are possible?
b. Write three examples of transformation processes.
c. How many transformation processes are possible if instead of three different microarchitectures for x86 and three different microarchitectures for SPARC, there were two for x86 and four for SPARC?

1.15   Identify one advantage of programming in a higher-level language compared to a lower-level language. Identify one disadvantage.

1.16   Name at least three things specified by an ISA.

1.17   Briefly describe the difference between an ISA and a microarchitecture.

1.18   How many ISAs are normally implemented by a single microarchitecture? Conversely, how many microarchitectures could exist for a single ISA?

1.19   List the levels of transformation and name an example for each level.

1.20   The levels of transformation in Figure 1.6 are often referred to as levels of abstraction. Is that a reasonable characterization? If yes, give an example. If no, why not?

1.21   Say you go to the store and buy some word processing software. What form is the software actually in? Is it in a high-level programming language? Is it in assembly language? Is it in the ISA of the computer on which you'll run it? Justify your answer.

1.22   Suppose you were given a task at one of the transformation levels shown in Figure 1.6, and required to tranform it to the level just below. At which level would it be most difficult to perform the transformation to the next lower level? Why?

1.23   Why is an ISA unlikely to change between successive generations of microarchitectures that implement it? For example, why would Intel want to make certain that the ISA implemented by the Pentium III is the same as the one implemented by the Pentium II? *Hint:* When you upgrade your computer (or buy one with a newer CPU), do you need to throw out all your old software?

2

Bits, Data Types, and Operations

2.1 Bits and Data Types

2.1.1 The Bit as the Unit of Information

We noted in Chapter 1 that the computer was organized as a system with several levels of transformation. A problem stated in a natural language such as English is actually solved by the electrons moving around inside the electronics of the computer.

Inside the computer, millions of very tiny, very fast devices control the movement of those electrons. These devices react to the presence or absence of voltages in electronic circuits. They could react to the actual voltages, rather than simply to the presence or absence of voltages. However, this would make the control and detection circuits more complex than they need to be. It is much easier simply to detect whether or not a voltage exists between a pair of points in a circuit than it is to measure exactly what that voltage is.

To understand this, consider any wall outlet in your home. You could measure the exact voltage it is carrying, whether 120 volts or 115 volts, or 118.6 volts, for example. However, the detection circuitry to determine *only* whether there is a voltage (any of the above three will do) or whether there is no voltage is much simpler. Your finger casually inserted into the wall socket, for example, will suffice.

We symbolically represent the presence of a voltage as "1" and the absence of a voltage as "0." We refer to each 0 and each 1 as a "bit," which is a shortened form of binary digit. Recall the digits you have been using since you were a child—0, 1, 2, 3, . . . , 9. There are 10 of them, and they are referred to as decimal digits. In the case of binary digits, there are two of them, 0 and 1.

To be perfectly precise, it is not really the case that the computer differentiates the *absolute* absence of a voltage (that is, 0) from the *absolute* presence of a voltage (that is, 1). Actually, the electronic circuits in the computer differentiate voltages *close to* 0 from voltages *far from* 0. So, for example, if the computer expects a voltage of 2.9 volts or a voltage of 0 volts (2.9 volts signifying 1 and 0 volts signifying 0), then a voltage of 2.6 volts will be taken as a 1 and 0.2 volts will be taken as a 0.

To get useful work done by the computer, it is necessary to be able to identify uniquely a large number of distinct values. The voltage on one wire can represent uniquely one of only two things. One thing can be represented by 0, the other thing can be represented by 1. Thus, to identify uniquely many things, it is necessary to combine multiple bits. For example, if we use eight bits (corresponding to the voltage present on eight wires), we can represent one particular value as 01001110, and another value as 11100111. In fact, if we are limited to eight bits, we can differentiate at most only 256 (that is, 2^8) different values. In general, with k bits, we can distinguish at most 2^k distinct items. Each pattern of these k bits is a code; that is, it corresponds to a particular value.

2.1.2 Data Types

There are many ways to represent the same value. For example, the number five can be written as a 5. This is the standard decimal notation that you are used to. The value five can also be represented by someone holding up one hand, with all fingers and thumb extended. The person is saying, "The number I wish to communicate can be determined by counting the number of fingers I am showing." A written version of that scheme would be the value 11111. This notation has a name also—*unary*. The Romans had yet another notation for five—the character V. We will see momentarily that a fourth notation for five is the binary representation 00000101.

It is not enough simply to represent values; we must be able to operate on those values. We say a particular representation is a *data type* if there are operations in the computer that can operate on information that is encoded in that representation. Each ISA has its own set of data types and its own set of instructions that can operate on those data types. In this book, we will mainly use two data types: *2's complement integers* for representing positive and negative integers that we wish to perform arithmetic on, and *ASCII codes* for representing characters on the keyboard that we wish to input to a computer or display on the computer's monitor. Both data types will be explained shortly.

There are other representations of information that could be used, and indeed that are present in most computers. Recall the "scientific notation" from high school chemistry where you were admonished to represent the decimal number 621 as $6.21 \cdot 10^2$. There are computers that represent numbers in that form, and they provide operations that can operate on numbers so represented. That data type is usually called *floating point*. We will show you its representation in Section 2.6.

2.2 Integer Data Types

2.2.1 Unsigned Integers

The first representation of information, or data type, that we shall look at is the unsigned integer. Unsigned integers have many uses in a computer. If we wish to perform a task some specific number of times, unsigned integers enable us to keep track of this number easily by simply counting how many times we have performed the task "so far." Unsigned integers also provide a means for identifying different memory locations in the computer, in the same way that house numbers differentiate 129 Main Street from 131 Main Street.

We can represent unsigned integers as strings of binary digits. To do this, we use a positional notation much like the decimal system that you have been using since you were three years old.

You are familiar with the decimal number 329, which also uses positional notation. The 3 is worth much more than the 9, even though the absolute value of 3 standing alone is only worth 1/3 the value of 9 standing alone. This is because, as you know, the 3 stands for 300 ($3 \cdot 10^2$) due to its position in the decimal string 329, while the 9 stands for $9 \cdot 10^0$.

The 2's complement representation works the same way, except that the digits used are the binary digits 0 and 1, and the base is 2, rather than 10. So, for example, if we have five bits available to represent our values, the number 6 is represented as 00110, corresponding to

$$0 \cdot 2^4 + 0 \cdot 2^3 + 1 \cdot 2^2 + 1 \cdot 2^1 + 0 \cdot 2^0$$

With k bits, we can represent in this positional notation exactly 2^k integers, ranging from 0 to $2^k - 1$. In our five-bit example, we can represent the integers from 0 to 31.

2.2.2 Signed Integers

However, to do useful arithmetic, it is often (although not always) necessary to be able to deal with negative quantities as well as positive. We could take our 2^k distinct patterns of k bits and separate them in half, half for positive numbers, and half for negative numbers. In this way, with five-bit codes, instead of representing integers from 0 to +31, we could choose to represent positive integers from +1 to +15 and negative integers from −1 to −15. There are 30 such integers. Since 2^5 is 32, we still have two 5-bit codes unassigned. One of them, 00000, we would presumably assign to the value 0, giving us the full range of integer values from −15 to +15. That leaves one more five-bit code to assign, and there are different ways to do this, as we will see momentarily.

We are still left with the problem of determining what codes to assign to what values. That is, we have 32 codes, but which value should go with which code?

Positive integers are represented in the straightforward positional scheme. Since there are k bits, and we wish to use exactly half of the 2^k codes to represent the integers from 0 to $2^{k-1} - 1$, all positive integers will have a leading 0 in their representation. In our example (with $k = 5$), the largest positive integer +15 is represented as 01111.

Representation	Value Represented		
	Signed Magnitude	1's Complement	2's Complement
00000	0	0	0
00001	1	1	1
00010	2	2	2
00011	3	3	3
00100	4	4	4
00101	5	5	5
00110	6	6	6
00111	7	7	7
01000	8	8	8
01001	9	9	9
01010	10	10	10
01011	11	11	11
01100	12	12	12
01101	13	13	13
01110	14	14	14
01111	15	15	15
10000	−0	−15	−16
10001	−1	−14	−15
10010	−2	−13	−14
10011	−3	−12	−13
10100	−4	−11	−12
10101	−5	−10	−11
10110	−6	−9	−10
10111	−7	−8	−9
11000	−8	−7	−8
11001	−9	−6	−7
11010	−10	−5	−6
11011	−11	−4	−5
11100	−12	−3	−4
11101	−13	−2	−3
11110	−14	−1	−2
11111	−15	−0	−1

Figure 2.1   Three representations of signed integers

Note that in all three data types shown in Figure 2.1, the representation for 0 and all the positive integers start with a leading 0. What about the representations for the negative numbers (in our five-bit example, −1 to −15)? The first thought that usually comes to mind is: If a leading 0 signifies a *positive* integer, how about letting a leading 1 signify a *negative* integer? The result is the *signed-magnitude* data type shown in Figure 2.1. A second idea (which was actually used on some early computers such as the Control Data Corporation 6600) was the following: Let a negative number be represented by taking the representation of the positive number having the same magnitude, and "flipping" all the bits. So, for example, since +5 is represented as 00101, we designate −5 as 11010. This data type is referred to in the computer engineering community as *1's complement*, and is also shown in Figure 2.1.

At this point, you might think that a computer designer could assign any bit pattern to represent any integer he or she wants. And you would be right! Unfortunately, that could complicate matters when we try to build a logic circuit to add two integers. In fact, the signed-magnitude and 1's complement data types both require unnecessarily cumbersome hardware to do addition. Because computer designers knew what it would take to design a logic circuit to add two integers, they chose representations that simplified that logic circuit. The result is the *2's complement* data type, also shown in Figure 2.1. It is used on just about every computer manufactured today.

2.3   2's Complement Integers

We see in Figure 2.1 the representations of the integers from −16 to +15 for the 2's complement data type. Why were the representations chosen that way?

The positive integers, we saw, are represented in the straightforward positional scheme. With five bits, we use exactly half of the 2^5 codes to represent 0 and the positive integers from 1 to $2^4 - 1$.

The choice of representations for the negative integers was based, as we said previously, on the wish to keep the logic circuits as simple as possible. Almost all computers use the same basic mechanism to do addition. It is called an *arithmetic and logic unit*, usually known by its acronym ALU. We will get into the actual structure of the ALU in Chapters 3 and 4. What is relevant right now is that an ALU has two inputs and one output. It performs addition by adding the binary bit patterns at its inputs, producing a bit pattern at its output that is the sum of the two input bit patterns.

For example, if the ALU processed five-bit input patterns, and the two inputs were 00110 and 00101, the result (output of the ALU) would be 01011. The addition is as follows:

```
 00110
 00101
 01011
```

The addition of two binary strings is performed in the same way addition of two decimal strings is performed, from right to left, column by column. If the addition in a column generates a carry, the carry is added to the column immediately to its left.

What is particularly relevant is that the binary ALU does not know (and does not care) what the two patterns it is adding represent. It simply adds the two binary patterns. Since the binary ALU only ADDs and does not CARE, it would be a nice benefit of our assignment of codes to the integers if it resulted in the ALU doing the right thing.

For starters, it would be nice if, when the ALU adds the representation for an arbitrary integer to the integer of the same magnitude and opposite sign, the sum is 0. That is, if the inputs to the ALU are the representations of non-zero integers A and $-A$, the output of the ALU should be 00000.

To accomplish that, the 2's complement data type specifies the representation for each negative integer so that when the ALU adds it to the representation of the positive integer of the same magnitude, the result will be the representation for 0. For example, since 00101 is the representation of +5, 11011 is chosen as the representation for -5.

Moreover, and more importantly, as we sequence from representations of -15 to $+15$, the ALU is adding 00001 to each successive representation.

We can express this mathematically as:

$$\text{REPRESENTATION(value} + 1) =$$
$$\text{REPRESENTATION(value)} + \text{REPRESENTATION(1)}.$$

This is sufficient to guarantee (as long as we do not get a result larger than $+15$ or smaller than -16) that the binary ALU will perform addition correctly.

Note in particular the representations for -1 and 0, that is, 11111 and 00000. When we add 00001 to the representation for -1, we do get 00000, but we also generate a carry. That carry does not influence the result. That is, the correct result of adding 00001 to the representation for -1 is 0, not 100000. Therefore, the carry is ignored. In fact, because the carry obtained by adding 00001 to 11111 is ignored, the carry can *always* be ignored when dealing with 2's complement arithmetic.

Note: A shortcut for figuring out the representation for $-A(A \neq 0)$, if we know the representation for A, is as follows: Flip all the bits of A (the term for "flip" is *complement*), and add 1 to the complement of A. The sum of A and the complement of A is 11111. If we then add 00001 to 11111, the final result is 00000. Thus, the representation for $-A$ can be easily obtained by adding 1 to the complement of A.

Example 2.1	What is the 2's complement representation for -13?

1. Let A be $+13$. Then the representation for A is 01101.

2. The complement of A is 10010.

3. Adding 1 to 10010 gives us 10011, the 2's complement representation for -13.

   We can verify our result by adding the representations for A and $-A$,

   ```
    01101
    10011
    00000
   ```

You may have noticed that the addition of 01101 and 10011, in addition to producing 00000, also produces a carry out of the five-bit ALU. That is, the binary addition of 01101 and 10011 is really 100000. However, as we saw previously, this carry out can be ignored in the case of the 2's complement data type.

At this point, we have identified in our five-bit scheme 15 positive integers. We have constructed 15 negative integers. We also have a representation for 0. With $k = 5$, we can uniquely identify 32 distinct quantities, and we have accounted for only 31 ($15 + 15 + 1$). The remaining representation is 10000. What value shall we assign to it?

We note that -1 is 11111, -2 is 11110, -3 is 11101, and so on. If we continue this, we note that -15 is 10001. Note that, as in the case of the positive representations, as we sequence backwards from representations of -1 to -15, the ALU is subtracting 00001 from each successive representation. Thus, it is convenient to assign to 10000 the value -16; that is the value one gets by subtracting 00001 from 10001 (the representation for -15).

In Chapter 5 we will specify a computer that we affectionately have named the LC-3 (for Little Computer 3). The LC-3 operates on 16-bit values. Therefore, the 2's complement integers that can be represented in the LC-3 are the integers from $-32,768$ to $+32,767$.

2.4 Binary-Decimal Conversion

It is often useful to convert integers between the 2's complement data type and the decimal representation that you have used all your life.

2.4.1 Binary to Decimal Conversion

We convert from 2's complement to a decimal representation as follows: For purposes of illustration, we will assume 2's complement representations of eight bits, corresponding to decimal integer values from -128 to $+127$.

Recall that an eight-bit 2's complement number takes the form

$$a_7\ a_6\ a_5\ a_4\ a_3\ a_2\ a_1\ a_0$$

where each of the bits a_i is either 0 or 1.

1. Examine the leading bit a_7. If it is a 0, the integer is positive, and we can begin evaluating its magnitude. If it is a 1, the integer is negative. In that case, we need to first obtain the 2's complement representation of the positive number having the same magnitude.

2. The magnitude is simply

$$a_6 \cdot 2^6 + a_5 \cdot 2^5 + a_4 \cdot 2^4 + a_3 \cdot 2^3 + a_2 \cdot 2^2 + a_1 \cdot 2^1 + a_0 \cdot 2^0$$

which we obtain by simply adding the powers of 2 that have coefficients of 1.

3. Finally, if the original number is negative, we affix a minus sign in front. Done!

| Example 2.2 | Convert the 2's complement integer 11000111 to a decimal integer value. |

1. Since the leading binary digit is a 1, the number is negative. We must first find the 2's complement representation of the positive number of the same magnitude. This is 00111001.

2. The magnitude can be represented as

$$0 \cdot 2^6 + 1 \cdot 2^5 + 1 \cdot 2^4 + 1 \cdot 2^3 + 0 \cdot 2^2 + 0 \cdot 2^1 + 1 \cdot 2^0$$

or,

$$32 + 16 + 8 + 1.$$

3. The decimal integer value corresponding to 11000111 is -57.

2.4.2 Decimal to Binary Conversion

Converting from decimal to 2's complement is a little more complicated. The crux of the method is to note that a positive binary number is *odd* if the rightmost digit is 1 and *even* if the rightmost digit is 0.

Consider again our generic eight-bit representation:

$$a_7 \cdot 2^7 + a_6 \cdot 2^6 + a_5 \cdot 2^5 + a_4 \cdot 2^4 + a_3 \cdot 2^3 + a_2 \cdot 2^2 + a_1 \cdot 2^1 + a_0 \cdot 2^0$$

We can illustrate the conversion best by first working through an example.

Suppose we wish to convert the value $+105$ to a 2's complement binary code. We note that $+105$ is positive. We first find values for a_i, representing the magnitude 105. Since the value is positive, we will then obtain the 2's complement result by simply appending a_7, which we know is 0.

Our first step is to find values for a_i that satisfy the following:

$$105 = a_6 \cdot 2^6 + a_5 \cdot 2^5 + a_4 \cdot 2^4 + a_3 \cdot 2^3 + a_2 \cdot 2^2 + a_1 \cdot 2^1 + a_0 \cdot 2^0$$

Since 105 is odd, we know that a_0 is 1. We subtract 1 from both sides of the equation, yielding

$$104 = a_6 \cdot 2^6 + a_5 \cdot 2^5 + a_4 \cdot 2^4 + a_3 \cdot 2^3 + a_2 \cdot 2^2 + a_1 \cdot 2^1$$

We next divide both sides of the equation by 2, yielding

$$52 = a_6 \cdot 2^5 + a_5 \cdot 2^4 + a_4 \cdot 2^3 + a_3 \cdot 2^2 + a_2 \cdot 2^1 + a_1 \cdot 2^0$$

We note that 52 is even, so a_1, the only coefficient not multiplied by a power of 2, must be equal to 0.

We now iterate the process, each time subtracting the rightmost digit from both sides of the equation, then dividing both sides by 2, and finally noting whether the new decimal number on the left side is odd or even. Starting where we left off, with

$$52 = a_6 \cdot 2^5 + a_5 \cdot 2^4 + a_4 \cdot 2^3 + a_3 \cdot 2^2 + a_2 \cdot 2^1$$

the process produces, in turn:

$$26 = a_6 \cdot 2^4 + a_5 \cdot 2^3 + a_4 \cdot 2^2 + a_3 \cdot 2^1 + a_2 \cdot 2^0$$

Therefore, $a_2 = 0$.

$$13 = a_6 \cdot 2^3 + a_5 \cdot 2^2 + a_4 \cdot 2^1 + a_3 \cdot 2^0$$

Therefore, $a_3 = 1$.

$$6 = a_6 \cdot 2^2 + a_5 \cdot 2^1 + a_4 \cdot 2^0$$

Therefore, $a_4 = 0$.

$$3 = a_6 \cdot 2^1 + a_5 \cdot 2^0$$

Therefore, $a_5 = 1$.

$$1 = a_6 \cdot 2^0$$

Therefore, $a_6 = 1$, and we are done. The binary representation is 01101001.

Let's summarize the process. If we are given a decimal integer value N, we construct the 2's complement representation as follows:

1. We first obtain the binary representation of the magnitude of N by forming the equation

   $$N = a_6 \cdot 2^6 + a_5 \cdot 2^5 + a_4 \cdot 2^4 + a_3 \cdot 2^3 + a_2 \cdot 2^2 + a_1 \cdot 2^1 + a_0 \cdot 2^0$$

   and repeating the following, until the left side of the equation is 0:

   a. If N is odd, the rightmost bit is 1. If N is even, the rightmost bit is 0.

   b. Subtract 1 or 0 (according to whether N is odd or even) from N, remove the least significant term from the right side, and divide both sides of the equation by 2.

   Each iteration produces the value of one coefficient a_i.

2. If the original decimal number is positive, append a leading 0 sign bit, and you are done.

3. If the original decimal number is negative, append a leading 0 and then form the negative of this 2's complement representation, and then you are done.

2.5 Operations on Bits—Part I: Arithmetic

2.5.1 Addition and Subtraction

Arithmetic on 2's complement numbers is very much like the arithmetic on decimal numbers that you have been doing for a long time.

Addition still proceeds from right to left, one digit at a time. At each point, we generate a sum digit and a carry. Instead of generating a carry after 9 (since 9 is the largest decimal digit), we generate a carry after 1 (since 1 is the largest binary digit).

| Example 2.3 | Using our five-bit notation, what is $11 + 3$? |

```
The decimal value 11 is represented as 01011
The decimal value 3 is represented as  00011
The sum, which is the value 14, is      01110
```

Subtraction is simply addition, preceded by determining the negative of the number to be subtracted. That is, $A - B$ is simply $A + (-B)$.

| Example 2.4 | What is $14 - 9$? |

```
The decimal value 14 is represented as    01110
The decimal value 9 is represented as     01001


First we form the negative, that is, -9: 10111


Adding 14 to -9, we get                   01110
                                          10111


which results in the value 5.             00101
```

Note again that the carry out is ignored.

| Example 2.5 | What happens when we add a number to itself (e.g., $x + x$)? |

    Let's assume for this example eight-bit codes, which would allow us to represent integers from -128 to 127. Consider a value for x, the integer 59, represented as 00111011. If we add 59 to itself, we get the code 01110110. Note that the bits have all shifted to the left by one position. Is that a curiosity, or will that happen all the time as long as the sum $x + x$ is not too large to represent with the available number of bits?

    Using our positional notation, the number 59 is

$$0 \cdot 2^6 + 1 \cdot 2^5 + 1 \cdot 2^4 + 1 \cdot 2^3 + 0 \cdot 2^2 + 1 \cdot 2^1 + 1 \cdot 2^0$$

The sum $59 + 59$ is $2 \cdot 59$, which, in our representation, is

$$2 \cdot (0 \cdot 2^6 + 1 \cdot 2^5 + 1 \cdot 2^4 + 1 \cdot 2^3 + 0 \cdot 2^2 + 1 \cdot 2^1 + 1 \cdot 2^0)$$

But that is nothing more than

$$0 \cdot 2^7 + 1 \cdot 2^6 + 1 \cdot 2^5 + 1 \cdot 2^4 + 0 \cdot 2^3 + 1 \cdot 2^2 + 1 \cdot 2^1$$

which shifts each digit one position to the left. Thus, adding a number to itself (provided there are enough bits to represent the result) is equivalent to shifting the representation one bit position to the left.

2.5.2 Sign-Extension

It is often useful to represent a small number with fewer bits. For example, rather than represent the value 5 as 0000000000000101, there are times when it is useful to allocate only six bits to represent the value 5: 000101. There is little confusion, since we are all used to adding leading zeros without affecting the value of a number. A check for $456.78 and a check for $0000456.78 are checks having the same value.

What about negative representations? We obtained the negative representation from its positive counterpart by complementing the positive representation and adding 1. Thus, the representation for −5, given that 5 is represented as 000101, is 111011. If 5 is represented as 0000000000000101, then the representation for −5 is 1111111111111011. In the same way that leading 0s do not affect the value of a positive number, leading 1s do not affect the value of a negative number.

In order to add representations of different lengths, it is first necessary to represent them with the same number of bits. For example, suppose we wish to add the number 13 to −5, where 13 is represented as 0000000000001101 and −5 is represented as 111011. If we do not represent the two values with the same number of bits, we have

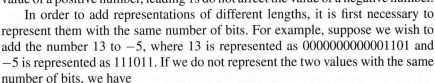

```
0000000000001101
   +    111011
```

When we attempt to perform the addition, what shall we do with the missing bits in the representation for −5? If we take the absence of a bit to be a 0, then we are no longer adding −5 to 13. On the contrary, if we take the absence of bits to be 0s, we have changed the −5 to the number represented as 0000000000111011, that is +59. Not surprisingly, then, our result turns out to be the representation for 72.

However, if we understand that a six-bit −5 and a 16-bit −5 differ only in the number of meaningless leading 1s, then we first extend the value of −5 to 16 bits before we perform the addition. Thus, we have

```
     0000000000001101
  +  1111111111111011
     0000000000001000
```

and the result is +8, as we should expect.

The value of a positive number does not change if we extend the sign bit 0 as many bit positions to the left as desired. Similarly, the value of a negative number does not change by extending the sign bit 1 as many bit positions to the left as desired. Since in both cases, it is the sign bit that is extended, we refer to the operation as *Sign-EXTension*, often abbreviated SEXT. Sign-extension is performed in order to be able to operate on bit patterns of different lengths. It does not affect the values of the numbers being represented.

2.5.3 Overflow

Up to now, we have always insisted that the sum of two integers be small enough to be represented by the available bits. What happens if such is not the case?

You are undoubtedly familiar with the odometer on the front dashboard of your automobile. It keeps track of how many miles your car has been driven—but only up to a point. In the old days, when the odometer registered 99992 and you drove it 100 miles, its new reading became 00092. A brand new car! The problem, as you know, is that the largest value the odometer could store was 99999, so the value 100092 showed up as 00092. The carryout of the ten-thousands digit was lost. (Of course, if you grew up in Boston, the carryout was not lost at all—it was in full display in the rusted chrome all over the car.)

We say the odometer *overflowed*. Representing 100092 as 00092 is unacceptable. As more and more cars lasted more than 100,000 miles, car makers felt the pressure to add a digit to the odometer. Today, practically all cars overflow at 1,000,000 miles, rather than 100,000 miles.

The odometer provides an example of unsigned arithmetic. The miles you add are always positive miles. The odometer reads 000129 and you drive 50 miles. The odometer now reads 000179. Overflow is a carry out of the leading digit.

In the case of signed arithmetic, or more particularly, 2's complement arithmetic, overflow is a little more subtle.

Let's return to our five-bit 2's complement data type, which allowed us to represent integers from -16 to $+15$. Suppose we wish to add $+9$ and $+11$. Our arithmetic takes the following form:

```
  01001
  01011
  10100
```

Note that the sum is larger than $+15$, and therefore too large to represent with our 2's complement scheme. The fact that the number is too large means that the number is larger than 01111, the largest positive number we can represent with a five-bit 2's complement data type. Note that because our positive result was larger than $+15$, it generated a carry into the leading bit position. But this bit position is used to indicate the sign of a value. Thus detecting that the result is too large is an easy matter. Since we are adding two positive numbers, the result must be positive. Since the ALU has produced a negative result, something must be wrong. The thing that is wrong is that the sum of the two positive numbers is too large to be represented with the available bits. We say that the result has *overflowed* the capacity of the representation.

Suppose instead, we had started with negative numbers, for example, -12 and -6. In this case our arithmetic takes the following form:

```
  10100
  11010
  01110
```

Here, too, the result has overflowed the capacity of the machine, since $-12 + -6$ equals -18, which is "more negative" than -16, the negative number with the largest allowable magnitude. The ALU obliges by producing a positive result. Again, this is easy to detect since the sum of two negative numbers cannot be positive.

Note that the sum of a negative number and a positive number never presents a problem. Why is that? See Exercise 2.25.

2.6 Operations on Bits—Part II: Logical Operations

We have seen that it is possible to perform arithmetic (e.g., add, subtract) on values represented as binary patterns. Another class of operations that it is useful to perform on binary patterns is the set of *logical* operations.

Logical operations operate on logical variables. A logical variable can have one of two values, 0 or 1. The name *logical* is a historical one; it comes from the fact that the two values 0 and 1 can represent the two logical values *false* and *true*, but the use of logical operations has traveled far from this original meaning.

There are several basic logic functions, and most ALUs perform all of them.

2.6.1 The AND Function

AND is a binary logical function. This means it requires two pieces of input data. Said another way, AND requires two source operands. Each source is a logical variable, taking the value 0 or 1. The output of AND is 1 only if both sources have the value 1. Otherwise, the output is 0. We can think of the AND operation as the ALL operation; that is, the output is 1 only if ALL two inputs are 1. Otherwise, the output is 0.

A convenient mechanism for representing the behavior of a logical operation is the *truth table*. A truth table consists of $n + 1$ columns and 2^n rows. The first n columns correspond to the n source operands. Since each source operand is a logical variable and can have one of two values, there are 2^n unique values that these source operands can have. Each such set of values (sometimes called an input combination) is represented as one row of the truth table. The final column in the truth table shows the output for each input combination.

In the case of a two-input AND function, the truth table has two columns for source operands, and four (2^2) rows for unique input combinations.

A	B	AND
0	0	0
0	1	0
1	0	0
1	1	1

We can apply the logical operation AND to two bit patterns of m bits each. This involves applying the operation individually to each pair of bits in the two source operands. For example, if a and b in Example 2.6 are 16-bit patterns, then c is the AND of a and b. This operation is often called a *bit-wise AND*.

Example 2.6

If c is the AND of a and b, where $a = 0011101001101001$ and $b = 0101100100100001$, what is c?

We form the AND of a and b by bit-wise ANDing the two values.

That means individually ANDing each pair of bits a_i and b_i to form c_i. For example, since $a_0 = 1$ and $b_0 = 1$, c_0 is the AND of a_0 and b_0, which is 1.

Since $a_6 = 1$ and $b_6 = 0$, c is the AND of a_6 and b_6, which is 0.

The complete solution for c is

```
a:  0011101001101001
b:  0101100100100001
c:  0001100000100001
```

Example 2.7

Suppose we have an eight-bit pattern, let's call it A, in which the rightmost two bits have particular significance. The computer could be asked to do one of four tasks depending on the value stored in the two rightmost bits of A. Can we isolate those two bits?

Yes, we can, using a bit mask. A *bit mask* is a binary pattern that enables the bits of A to be separated into two parts—generally the part you care about and the part you wish to ignore. In this case, the bit mask 00000011 ANDed with A produces 0 in bit positions 7 through 2, and the original values of bits 1 and 0 of A in bit positions 1 and 0. The bit mask is said to *mask out* the values in bit positions 7 through 2.

If A is 01010110, the AND of A and the bit mask 00000011 is 00000010. If A is 11111100, the AND of A and the bit mask 00000011 is 00000000.

That is, the result of ANDing any eight-bit pattern with the mask 00000011 is one of the four patterns 00000000, 00000001, 00000010, or 00000011. The result of ANDing with the mask is to highlight the two bits that are relevant.

2.6.2 The OR Function

OR is also a binary logical function. It requires two source operands, both of which are logical variables. The output of OR is 1 if any source has the value 1. Only if both sources are 0 is the output 0. We can think of the OR operation as the ANY operation; that is, the output is 1 if ANY of the two inputs are 1.

The truth table for a two-input OR function is

A	B	OR
0	0	0
0	1	1
1	0	1
1	1	1

In the same way that we applied the logical operation AND to two m-bit patterns, we can apply the OR operation bit-wise to two m-bit patterns.

If c is the OR of a and b, where $a = 0011101001101001$ and $b = 0101100100100001$, as before, what is c?

Example 2.8

We form the OR of a and b by bit-wise ORing the two values. That means individually ORing each pair of bits ai and bi to form ci. For example, since $a0 = 1$ and $b0 = 1$, $c0$ is the OR of $a0$ and $b0$, which is 1. Since $a6 = 1$ and $b6 = 0$, c is the OR of $a6$ and $b6$, which is also 1.

The complete solution for c is

```
a:  0011101001101001
b:  0101100100100001
c:  0111101101101001
```

Sometimes this OR operation is referred to as the *inclusive-OR* in order to distinguish it from the exclusive-OR function, which we will discuss momentarily.

2.6.3 The NOT Function

NOT is a unary logical function. This means it operates on only one source operand. It is also known as the *complement* operation. The output is formed by complementing the input. We sometimes say the output is formed by *inverting* the input. A 1 input results in a 0 output. A 0 input results in a 1 output.

The truth table for the NOT function is

```
A │ NOT
──┼────
0 │  1
1 │  0
```

In the same way that we applied the logical operation AND and OR to two m-bit patterns, we can apply the NOT operation bit-wise to one m-bit pattern. If a is as before, then c is the NOT of a.

```
a:  0011101001101001
c:  1100010110010110
```

2.6.4 The Exclusive-OR Function

Exclusive-OR, often abbreviated XOR, is a binary logical function. It, too, requires two source operands, both of which are logical variables. The output of XOR is 1 if the two sources are different. The output is 0 if the two sources are the same.

The truth table for the XOR function is

A	B	XOR
0	0	0
0	1	1
1	0	1
1	1	0

In the same way that we applied the logical operation AND to two m-bit patterns, we can apply the XOR operation bit-wise to two m-bit patterns.

Example 2.9   If a and b are 16-bit patterns as before, then c (shown here) is the XOR of a and b.

```
a:  0011101001101001
b:  0101100100100001
c:  0110001101001000
```

Note the distinction between the truth table for XOR shown here and the truth table for OR shown earlier. In the case of exclusive-OR, if both source operands are 1, the output is 0. That is, the output is 1 if the first operand is 1 but the second operand is not 1 or if the second operand is 1 but the first operand is not 1. The term *exclusive* is used because the output is 1 if *only* one of the two sources is 1. The OR function, on the other hand, produces an output 1 if only one of the two sources is 1, or if both sources are 1. Ergo, the name *inclusive-OR*.

Example 2.10   Suppose we wish to know if two patterns are identical. Since the XOR function produces a 0 only if the corresponding pair of bits is identical, two patterns are identical if the output of the XOR is all zeros.

2.7 Other Representations

Four other representations of information that we will find useful in our work are the bit vector, the floating point data type, ASCII codes, and hexadecimal notation.

2.7.1 The Bit Vector

It is often useful to describe a complex system made up of several units, each of which is individually and independently *busy* or *available*. This system could be a manufacturing plant where each unit is a particular machine. Or the system could be a taxicab network where each unit is a particular taxicab. In both cases, it is important to identify which units are busy and which are available, so that work can be assigned as needed.

Say we have n such units. We can keep track of these n units with an n-bit binary pattern we call a *bit vector*, where a bit is 1 if the unit is free and 0 if the unit is busy.

Suppose we have eight machines that we want to monitor with respect to their availability. We can keep track of them with an eight-bit BUSYNESS bit vector, where a bit is 1 if the unit is free and 0 if the unit is busy. The bits are labeled, from right to left, from 0 to 7.

Example 2.11

The BUSYNESS bit vector 11000010 corresponds to the situation where only units 7, 6, and 1 are free, and therefore available for work assignment.

Suppose work is assigned to unit 7. We update our BUSYNESS bit vector by performing the logical AND, where our two sources are the current bit vector 11000010 and the bit mask 01111111. The purpose of the bit mask is to clear bit 7 of the BUSYNESS bit vector. The result is the bit vector 01000010.

Recall that we encountered the concept of bit mask in Example 2.7. Recall that a bit mask enables one to interact some bits of a binary pattern while ignoring the rest. In this case, the bit mask clears bit 7 and leaves unchanged (ignores) bits 6 through 0.

Suppose unit 5 finishes its task and becomes idle. We can update the BUSYNESS bit vector by performing the logical OR of it with the bit mask 00100000. The result is 01100010.

2.7.2 Floating Point Data Type

Most of the arithmetic we will do in this book uses integer values. For example, the LC-3 uses the 16-bit, 2's complement data type, which provides, in addition to one bit to identify positive or negative, 15 bits to represent the magnitude of the value. With 16 bits used in this way, we can express values between $-32,768$ and $+32,767$, that is, between -2^{15} and $+2^{15} - 1$. We say the *precision* of our value is 15 bits, and the *range* is 2^{15}. As you learned in high school chemistry or physics, sometimes we need to express much larger numbers, but we do not require so many digits of precision. In fact, recall the value $6.023 \cdot 10^{23}$, which you may have been required to memorize back then. The range required to express this value is far greater than the 2^{15} available with 16-bit 2's complement integers. On the other hand, the 15 bits of precision available with 16-bit 2's complement integers is overkill. We need only enough bits to express four significant decimal digits (6023).

So we have a problem. We have more bits than we need for precision. But we don't have enough bits to represent the range.

The *floating point* data type is the solution to the problem. Instead of using all the bits (except the sign bit) to represent the precision of a value, the floating point data type allocates some of the bits to the range of values (i.e., how big or small) that can be expressed. The rest of the bits (except for the sign bit) are used for precision.

Most ISAs today specify more than one floating point data type. One of them, usually called *float*, consists of 32 bits, allocated as follows:

```
 1 bit for the sign (positive or negative)
 8 bits for the range (the exponent field)
23 bits for precision (the fraction field)
```

$$N = (-1)^S \times 1.fraction \times 2^{exponent-127}, 1 \le exponent \le 254$$

Figure 2.2   The floating point data type

In most computers manufactured today, these bits represent numbers according to the formula in Figure 2.2. This formula is part of the IEEE Standard for Floating Point Arithmetic.

Recall that we said that the floating point data type was very much like the scientific notation you learned in high school, and we gave the example $6.023 \cdot 10^{23}$. This representation has three parts: the sign, which is positive, the significant digits 6.023, and the exponent 23. We call the significant digits the *fraction*. Note that the fraction is normalized, that is, exactly one nonzero decimal digit appears to the left of the decimal point.

The data type and formula of Figure 2.2 also consist of these three parts. Instead of a fraction (i.e., significant digits) of four decimal digits, we have 23 binary digits. Note that the fraction is normalized, that is, exactly one nonzero binary digit appears to the left of the binary point. Since the nonzero binary digit has to be a 1 (1 is the only nonzero binary digit) there is no need to represent that bit explicitly. Thus, the formula of Figure 2.2 shows 24 bits of precision, the 23 bits from the data type and the leading one bit to the left of the binary point that is unnecessary to represent explicitly.

Instead of an exponent of two decimal digits as in $6.023 \cdot 10^{23}$, we have in Figure 2.2 eight binary digits. Instead of a radix of 10, we have a radix of 2. With eight bits to represent the exponent, we can represent 256 exponents. Note that the formula only gives meaning to 254 of them. If the exponent field contains 00000000 (that is, 0) or 11111111 (that is, 255), the formula does not tell you how to interpret the bits. We will look at those two special cases momentarily.

For the remaining 254 values in the exponent field of the floating point data type, the explanation is as follows: The actual exponent being represented is the unsigned number in the data type minus 127. For example, if the actual exponent is $+8$, the exponent field contains 10000111, which is the unsigned number 135. Note that $135 - 127 = 8$. If the actual exponent is -125, the exponent field contains 00000010, which is the unsigned number 2. Note that $2 - 127 = -125$.

The third part is the sign bit: 0 for positive numbers, 1 for negative numbers. The formula contains the factor -1^s, which evaluates to $+1$ if $s = 0$, and -1 if $s = 1$.

How is the number $-6\frac{5}{8}$ represented in the floating point data type?

First, we express $-6\frac{5}{8}$ as a binary number: -110.101.

$$-(1 \cdot 2^2 + 1 \cdot 2^1 + 0 \cdot 2^0 + 1 \cdot 2^{-1} + 0 \cdot 2^{-2} + 1 \cdot 2^{-3})$$

Then we normalize the value, yielding $-1.10101 \cdot 2^2$.

The sign bit is 1, reflecting the fact that $-6\frac{5}{8}$ is a negative number. The exponent field contains 10000001, the unsigned number 129, reflecting the fact that the real exponent is $+2$ ($129 - 127 = +2$). The fraction is the 23 bits of precision, after removing the leading 1. That is, the fraction is 10101000000000000000000. The result is the number $-6\frac{5}{8}$, expressed as a floating point number:

1 10000001 10101000000000000000000

What does the floating point data type

00111101100000000000000000000000

represent?

The leading bit is a 0. This signifies a positive number. The next eight bits represent the unsigned number 123. If we subtract 127, we get the actual exponent -4. The last 23 bits are all 0. Therefore the number being represented is $+1.00000000000000000000000 \cdot 2^{-4}$, which is $\frac{1}{16}$.

We noted that the interpretation of the 32 bits required that the exponent field contain neither 00000000 nor 11111111. The IEEE Standard for Floating Point Arithmetic also specifies how to interpret the 32 bits if the exponent field contains 00000000 or 11111111.

If the exponent field contains 00000000, the exponent is -126, and the significant digits are obtained by starting with a leading 0, followed by a binary point, followed by the 23 bits of the fraction field, as follows:

$$-1^s \cdot 0.\,fraction \cdot 2^{-126}$$

For example, the floating point data representation

0 00000000 00001000000000000000000

can be evaluated as follows: The leading 0 means the number is positive. The next eight bits, a zero exponent, means the exponent is -126. The last 23 bits form the number 0.00001000000000000000000, which equals 2^{-5}. Thus, the number represented is $2^{-5} \cdot 2^{-126}$, which is 2^{-131}.

This allows very tiny numbers to be represented.

Example 2.12

Example 2.13

Example 2.14

The following four examples provide further illustrations of the interpretation of the 32-bit floating point data type according to the rules of the IEEE standard.

$$0\ \ 10000011\ \ 00101000000000000000000 \text{ is } 1.00101 \cdot 2^4 = 18.5$$

The exponent field contains the unsigned number 131. Since $131 - 127$ is 4, the exponent is +4. Combining a 1 to the left of the binary point with the fraction field to the right of the binary point yields 1.00101. If we move the binary point four positions to the right, we get 10010.1, which is 18.5.

$$110000\ \ 010\ \ 00101000000000000000000 \text{ is } -1 \cdot 1.00101 \cdot 2^3 = -9.25$$

The sign bit is 1, signifying a negative number. The exponent is 130, signifying an exponent of $130 - 127$, or +3. Combining a 1 to the left of the binary point with the fraction field to the right of the binary point yields 1.00101. Moving the binary point three positions to the right, we get 1001.01, which is −9.25.

$$011111\ \ 110\ \ 11111111111111111111111 \text{ is } \sim 2^{128}$$

The sign is +. The exponent is $254 - 127$, or +127. Combining a 1 to the left of the binary point with the fraction field to the right of the binary point yields $1.11111111 \ldots 1$, which is approximately 2. Therefore, the result is approximately 2^{128}.

$$1\ \ 00000000\ \ 00000000000000000000001 \text{ is } -2^{-149}$$

The sign is −. The exponent field contains all 0s, signifying an exponent of −126. Combining a 0 to the left of the binary point with the fraction field to the right of the binary point yields 2^{-23} for the fraction. Therefore, the number represented is $-2^{-23} \cdot 2^{-126}$, which equals -2^{-149}.

A detailed understanding of IEEE Floating Point Arithmetic is well beyond what should be expected in this first course. Indeed, we have not even considered how to interpret the 32 bits if the exponent field contains 11111111. Our purpose in including this section in the textbook is to at least let you know that there is, in addition to 2's complement integers, another very important data type available in almost all ISAs. This data type is called *floating point*; it allows very large and very tiny numbers to be expressed at the expense of reducing the number of binary digits of precision.

2.7.3 ASCII Codes

Another representation of information is the standard code that almost all computer equipment manufacturers have agreed to use for transferring character codes between the main computer processing unit and the input and output devices. That code is an eight-bit code referred to as *ASCII*. ASCII stands for American Standard Code for Information Interchange. It (ASCII) greatly simplifies the interface between a keyboard manufactured by one company, a computer made by another company, and a monitor made by a third company.

Each key on the keyboard is identified by its unique ASCII code. So, for example, the digit 3 expanded to 8 bits with a leading 0 is 00110011, the digit 2 is 00110010, the lowercase *e* is 01100101, and the carriage return is 00001101. The entire set of eight-bit ASCII codes is listed in Figure E.3 of Appendix E. When you type a key on the keyboard, the corresponding eight-bit code is stored and made available to the computer. Where it is stored and how it gets into the computer is discussed in Chapter 8.

Most keys are associated with more than one code. For example, the ASCII code for the letter *E* is 01000101, and the ASCII code for the letter *e* is 01100101. Both are associated with the same key, although in one case the Shift key is also depressed while in the other case, it is not.

In order to display a particular character on the monitor, the computer must transfer the ASCII code for that character to the electronics associated with the monitor. That, too, is discussed in Chapter 8.

2.7.4 Hexadecimal Notation

We have seen that information can be represented as 2's complement integers, as bit vectors, in floating point format, or as an ASCII code. There are other representations also, but we will leave them for another book. However, before we leave this topic, we would like to introduce you to a representation that is used more as a convenience for humans than as a data type to support operations being performed by the computer. This is the *hexadecimal* notation. As we will see, it evolves nicely from the positional binary notation and is useful for dealing with long strings of binary digits without making errors.

It will be particularly useful in dealing with the LC-3 where 16-bit binary strings will be encountered often.

An example of such a binary string is

```
0011110101101110
```

Let's try an experiment. Cover the preceding 16-bit binary string of 0s and 1s with one hand, and try to write it down from memory. How did you do? Hexadecimal notation is about being able to do this without making mistakes. We shall see how.

In general, a 16-bit binary string takes the form

$$a_{15}\ a_{14}\ a_{13}\ a_{12}\ a_{11}\ a_{10}\ a_9\ a_8\ a_7\ a_6\ a_5\ a_4\ a_3\ a_2\ a_1\ a_0$$

where each of the bits a_i is either 0 or 1.

If we think of this binary string as an unsigned integer, its value can be computed as

$$a_{15} \cdot 2^{15} + a_{14} \cdot 2^{14} + a_{13} \cdot 2^{13} + a_{12} \cdot 2^{12} + a_{11} \cdot 2^{11} + a_{10} \cdot 2^{10}$$
$$+ a_9 \cdot 2^9 + a_8 \cdot 2^8 + a_7 \cdot 2^7 + a_6 \cdot 2^6 + a_5 \cdot 2^5 + a_4 \cdot 2^4 + a_3 \cdot 2^3$$
$$+ a_2 \cdot 2^2 + a_1 \cdot 2^1 + a_0 \cdot 2^0$$

We can factor 2^{12} from the first four terms, 2^8 from the second four terms, 2^4 from the third set of four terms, and 2^0 from the last four terms, yielding

$$2^{12}[a_{15} \cdot 2^3 + a_{14} \cdot 2^2 + a_{13} \cdot 2^1 + a_{12} \cdot 2^0]$$
$$+ 2^8[a_{11} \cdot 2^3 + a_{10} \cdot 2^2 + a_9 \cdot 2^1 + a_8 \cdot 2^0]$$
$$+ 2^4[a_7 \cdot 2^3 + a_6 \cdot 2^2 + a_5 \cdot 2^1 + a_4 \cdot 2^0]$$
$$+ 2^0[a_3 \cdot 2^3 + a_2 \cdot 2^2 + a_1 \cdot 2^1 + a_0 \cdot 2^0]$$

Note that the largest value inside a set of square brackets is 15, which would be the case if each of the four bits is 1. If we replace what is inside each square bracket by a symbol representing its value (from 0 to 15), and we replace 2^{12} by its equivalent 16^3, 2^8 by 16^2, 2^4 by 16^1, and 2^0 by 16^0, we have

$$h_3 \cdot 16^3 + h_2 \cdot 16^2 + h_1 \cdot 16^1 + h_0 \cdot 16^0$$

where h_3, for example, is a symbol representing

$$a_{15} \cdot 2^3 + a_{14} \cdot 2^2 + a_{13} \cdot 2^1 + a_{12} \cdot 2^0$$

Since the symbols must represent values from 0 to 15, we assign symbols to these values as follows: 0, 1, 2, 3, 4, 5, 6, 7, 8, 9, A, B, C, D, E, F. That is, we represent 0000 with the symbol 0, 0001 with the symbol 1, ... 1001 with 9, 1010 with A, 1011 with B, ... 1111 with F. The resulting notation is hexadecimal, or base 16.

So, for example, if the hex digits E92F represent a 16-bit 2's complement integer, is the value of that integer positive or negative? How do you know?

Now, then, what is this hexadecimal representation good for, anyway? It seems like just another way to represent a number without adding any benefit. Let's return to the exercise where you tried to write from memory the string

$$0011110101101110$$

If we had first broken the string at four-bit boundaries

$$0011 \quad 1101 \quad 0110 \quad 1110$$

and then converted each four-bit string to its equivalent hex digit

$$3 \quad D \quad 6 \quad E$$

it would have been no problem to jot down (with the string covered) 3D6E.

In summary, hexadecimal notation is mainly used as a convenience for humans. It can be used to represent binary strings that are integers or floating point numbers or sequences of ASCII codes, or bit vectors. It simply reduces the number of digits by a factor of 4, where each digit is in hex (0, 1, 2, ... F) instead of binary (0, 1). The usual result is far fewer copying errors due to too many 0s and 1s.

2.1   Given n bits, how many distinct combinations of the n bits exist?

2.2   There are 26 characters in the alphabet we use for writing English. What is the least number of bits needed to give each character a unique bit pattern? How many bits would we need to distinguish between upper- and lowercase versions of all 26 characters?

2.3   *a.* Assume that there are about 400 students in your class. If every student is to be assigned a unique bit pattern, what is the minimum number of bits required to do this?
        b. How many more students can be admitted to the class without requiring additional bits for each student's unique bit pattern?

2.4   Given n bits, how many unsigned integers can be represented with the n bits? What is the range of these integers?

2.5   Using 5 bits to represent each number, write the representations of 7 and -7 in 1's complement, signed magnitude, and 2's complement integers.

2.6   Write the 6-bit 2's complement representation of -32.

2.7   Create a table showing the decimal values of all 4-bit 2's complement numbers.

2.8   *a.* What is the largest positive number one can represent in an 8-bit 2's complement code? Write your result in binary and decimal.
        b. What is the greatest magnitude negative number one can represent in an 8-bit 2's complement code? Write your result in binary and decimal.
        c. What is the largest positive number one can represent in n-bit 2's complement code?
        d. What is the greatest magnitude negative number one can represent in n-bit 2's complement code?

2.9   How many bits are needed to represent Avogadro's number ($6.02 \cdot 10^{23}$) in 2's complement binary representation?

2.10   Convert the following 2's complement binary numbers to decimal.

        a. `1010`
        b. `01011010`
        c. `11111110`
        d. `0011100111010011`

2.11   Convert these decimal numbers to 8-bit 2's complement binary numbers.

        a. 102
        b. 64
        c. 33
        d. -128
        e. 127

2.12 If the last digit of a 2's complement binary number is 0, then the number is even. If the last two digits of a 2's complement binary number are 00 (e.g., the binary number 01100), what does that tell you about the number?

2.13 Without changing their values, convert the following 2's complement binary numbers into 8-bit 2's complement numbers.

   a. `1010`   *c.* `111111000`
   b. `011001`   *d.* `01`

2.14 Add the following bit patterns. Leave your results in binary form.

   a. `1011 + 0001`
   b. `0000 + 1010`
   c. `1100 + 0011`
   d. `0101 + 0110`
   e. `1111 + 0001`

2.15 It was demonstrated in Example 2.5 that shifting a binary number one bit to the left is equivalent to multiplying the number by 2. What operation is performed when a binary number is shifted one bit to the right?

2.16 Write the results of the following additions as both 8-bit binary and decimal numbers. For each part, use standard binary addition as described in Section 2.5.1.

   a. Add the 1's complement representation of 7 to the 1's complement representation of −7.
   b. Add the signed magnitude representation of 7 to the signed magnitude representation of −7.
   c. Add the 2's complement representation of 7 to the 2's complement representation of −7.

2.17 Add the following 2's complement binary numbers. Also express the answer in decimal.

   a. `01 + 1011`
   b. `11 + 01010101`
   c. `0101 + 110`
   d. `01 + 10`

2.18 Add the following unsigned binary numbers. Also, express the answer in decimal.

   a. `01 + 1011`
   b. `11 + 01010101`
   c. `0101 + 110`
   d. `01 + 10`

2.19 Express the negative value −27 as a 2's complement integer, using eight bits. Repeat, using 16 bits. Repeat, using 32 bits. What does this illustrate with respect to the properties of sign extension as they pertain to 2's complement representation?

2.20 The following binary numbers are 4-bit 2's complement binary numbers. Which of the following operations generate overflow? Justify your answer by translating the operands and results into decimal.

    a. `1100 + 0011`   *d.* `1000 - 0001`
    b. `1100 + 0100`   *e.* `0111 + 1001`
    c. `0111 + 0001`

2.21 Describe what conditions indicate overflow has occurred when two 2's complement numbers are added.

2.22 Create two 16-bit 2's complement integers such that their sum causes an overflow.

2.23 Describe what conditions indicate overflow has occurred when two unsigned numbers are added.

2.24 Create two 16-bit unsigned integers such that their sum causes an overflow.

2.25 Why does the sum of a negative 2's complement number and a positive 2's complement number never generate an overflow?

2.26 You wish to express −64 as a 2's complement number.

    a. How many bits do you need (the minimum number)?
    b. With this number of bits, what is the largest positive number you can represent? (Please give answer in both decimal and binary).
    c. With this number of bits, what is the largest unsigned number you can represent? (Please give answer in both decimal and binary).

2.27 The LC-3, a 16-bit machine adds the two 2's complement numbers 0101010101010101 and 0011100111001111, producing 1000111100100100. Is there a problem here? If yes, what is the problem? If no, why not?

2.28 When is the output of an AND operation equal to 1?

2.29 Fill in the following truth table for a one-bit AND operation.

X	Y	X AND Y
0	0	
0	1	
1	0	
1	1	

2.30 Compute the following. Write your results in binary.

    a. `01010111 AND 11010111`
    b. `101 AND 110`
    c. `11100000 AND 10110100`
    d. `00011111 AND 10110100`
    e. `(0011 AND 0110) AND 1101`
    f. `0011 AND (0110 AND 1101)`

2.31 When is the output of an OR operation equal to 1?

2.32 Fill in the following truth table for a one-bit OR operation.

X	Y	X OR Y
0	0	
0	1	
1	0	
1	1	

2.33 Compute the following:

   a. `01010111 OR 11010111`
   b. `101 OR 110`
   c. `11100000 OR 10110100`
   d. `00011111 OR 10110100`
   e. `(0101 OR 1100) OR 1101`
   f. `0101 OR (1100 OR 1101)`

2.34 Compute the following:

   a. `NOT(1011) OR NOT(1100)`
   b. `NOT(1000 AND (1100 OR 0101))`
   c. `NOT(NOT(1101))`
   d. `(0110 OR 0000) AND 1111`

2.35 In Example 2.11, what are the masks used for?

2.36 Refer to Example 2.11 for the following questions.

   a. What mask value and what operation would one use to indicate that machine 2 is busy?
   b. What mask value and what operation would one use to indicate that machines 2 and 6 are no longer busy? (Note: This can be done with only one operation.)
   c. What mask value and what operation would one use to indicate that all machines are busy?
   d. What mask value and what operation would one use to indicate that all machines are idle?
   e. Develop a procedure to isolate the status bit of machine 2 as the sign bit. For example, if the BUSYNESS pattern is 01011100, then the output of this procedure is 10000000. If the BUSYNESS pattern is 01110011, then the output is 00000000. In general, if the BUSYNESS pattern is:

b7	b6	b5	b4	b3	b2	b1	b0

   the output is:

b2	0	0	0	0	0	0	0

   Hint: What happens when you ADD a bit pattern to itself?

2.37 If n and m are both 4-bit 2's complement numbers, and s is the 4-bit result of adding them together, how can we determine, using only the logical operations described in Section 2.6, if an overflow occurred during the addition? Develop a "procedure" for doing so. The inputs to the procedure are n, m, and s, and the output will be a bit pattern of all zeros (0000) if no overflow occurred and 1000 if an overflow did occur.

2.38 If n and m are both 4-bit unsigned numbers, and s is the 4-bit result of adding them together, how can we determine, using only the logical operations described in Section 2.6, if an overflow occurred during the addition? Develop a "procedure" for doing so. The inputs to the procedure are n, m, and s, and the output will be a bit pattern of all zeros (0000) if no overflow occurred and 1000 if an overflow did occur.

2.39 Write IEEE floating point representation of the following decimal numbers.

   a. 3.75
   b. $-55\frac{23}{64}$
   c. 3.1415927
   d. 64,000

2.40 Write the decimal equivalents for these IEEE floating point numbers.

   a. 0　10000000　00000000000000000000000
   b. 1　10000011　00010000000000000000000
   c. 0　11111111　00000000000000000000000
   d. 1　10000000　10010000000000000000000

2.41 *a.* What is the largest exponent the IEEE standard allows for a 32-bit floating point number?
   b. What is the smallest exponent the IEEE standard allows for a 32-bit floating point number?

2.42 A computer programmer wrote a program that adds two numbers. The programmer ran the program and observed that when 5 is added to 8, the result is the character m. Explain why this program is behaving erroneously.

2.43 Translate the following ASCII codes into strings of characters by interpreting each group of eight bits as an ASCII character.

   a. x48656c6c6f21
   b. x68454c4c4f21
   c. x436f6d70757465727321
   d. x4c432d32

2.44 What operation(s) can be used to convert the binary representation for 3 (i.e., 0000 0011) into the ASCII representation for 3 (i.e., 0011 0011)? What about the binary 4 into the ASCII 4? What about any digit?

2.45 Convert the following unsigned binary numbers to hexadecimal.

a. 1101 0001 1010 1111
b. 001 1111
c. 1
d. 1110 1101 1011 0010

2.46 Convert the following hexadecimal numbers to binary.

a. x10
b. x801
c. xF731
d. x0F1E2D
e. xBCAD

2.47 Convert the following hexadecimal representations of 2's complement binary numbers to decimal numbers.

a. xF0
b. x7FF
c. x16
d. x8000

2.48 Convert the following decimal numbers to hexadecimal representations of 2's complement numbers.

a. 256
b. 111
c. 123,456,789
d. −44

2.49 Perform the following additions. The corresponding 16-bit binary numbers are in 2's complement notation. Provide your answers in hexadecimal.

a. x025B + x26DE
b. x7D96 + xF0A0
c. xA397 + xA35D
d. x7D96 + x7412
e. What else can you say about the answers to parts *c* and *d*?

2.50 Perform the following logical operations. Express your answers in hexadecimal notation.

a. x5478 AND xFDEA
b. xABCD OR x1234
c. NOT((NOT(xDEFA)) AND (NOT(xFFFF)))
d. x00FF XOR x325C

2.51 What is the hexadecimal representation of the following numbers?

    a. 25,675

    b. 675.625 (that is, $675\frac{5}{8}$), in the IEEE 754 floating point standard

    c. The ASCII string: Hello

2.52 Consider two hexadecimal numbers: x434F4D50 and x55544552. What values do they represent for each of the five data types shown?

	x434F4D50	x55544552
Unsigned binary		
1's complement		
2's complement		
IEEE 754 floating point		
ASCII string		

2.53 Fill in the truth table for the equations given. The first line is done as an example.

$$Q_1 = \text{NOT(A AND B)}$$

$$Q_2 = \text{NOT(NOT(A) AND NOT(B))}$$

A	B	Q_1	Q_2
0	0	1	0

    Express Q_2 another way.

2.54 Fill in the truth table for the equations given. The first line is done as an example.

$$Q_1 = \text{NOT(NOT(X) OR (X AND Y AND Z))}$$

$$Q_2 = \text{NOT((Y OR Z) AND (X AND Y AND Z))}$$

X	Y	Z	Q_1	Q_2
0	0	0	0	1

2.55 We have represented numbers in base-2 (binary) and in base-16 (hex). We are now ready for unsigned base-4, which we will call quad numbers. A quad digit can be 0, 1, 2, or 3.

    a. What is the maximum unsigned decimal value that one can represent with 3 quad digits?

    b. What is the maximum unsigned decimal value that one can represent with n quad digits (Hint: your answer should be a function of n)?

    c. Add the two unsigned quad numbers: 023 and 221.

    d. What is the quad representation of the decimal number 42?

    e. What is the binary representation of the unsigned quad number 123.3?

    f. Express the unsigned quad number 123.3 in IEEE floating point format.

    g. Given a black box which takes m quad digits as input and produces one quad digit for output, what is the maximum number of unique functions this black box can implement?

2.56 Define a new 8-bit floating point format with 1 sign bit, 4 bits of exponent, using an excess-7 code (that is, the bias is 7), and 3 bits of fraction. If xE5 is the bit pattern for a number in this 8-bit floating point format, what value does it have? (Express as a decimal number.)

Digital Logic Structures

In Chapter 1, we stated that computers were built from very large numbers of very simple structures. For example, Intel's Pentium IV microprocessor, first offered for sale in 2000, was made up of more than 42 million MOS transistors. The IBM Power PC 750 FX, released in 2002, consists of more than 38 million MOS transistors. In this chapter, we will explain how the MOS transistor works (as a logic element), show how these transistors are connected to form logic gates, and then show how logic gates are interconnected to form larger units that are needed to construct a computer. In Chapter 4, we will connect those larger units into a computer.

But first, the transistor.

3.1 The Transistor

Most computers today, or rather most microprocessors (which form the core of the computer) are constructed out of MOS transistors. MOS stands for *metal-oxide semiconductor*. The electrical properties of metal-oxide semiconductors are well beyond the scope of what we want to understand in this course. They are below our lowest level of abstraction, which means that if somehow transistors start misbehaving, we are at their mercy. It is unlikely that we will have any problems from the transistors.

However, it is useful to know that there are two types of MOS transistors: p-type and n-type. They both operate "logically," very similar to the way wall switches work.

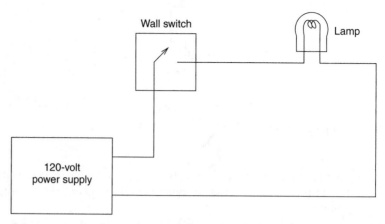

Figure 3.1   A simple electric circuit showing the use of a wall switch

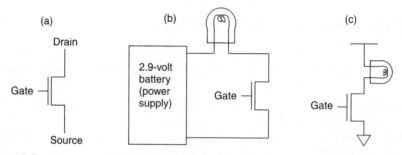

Figure 3.2   The n-type MOS transistor

Figure 3.1 shows the most basic of electrical circuits: a power supply (in this case, the 120 volts that come into your house), a wall switch, and a lamp (plugged into an outlet in the wall). In order for the lamp to glow, electrons must flow; in order for electrons to flow, there must be a closed circuit from the power supply to the lamp and back to the power supply. The lamp can be turned on and off by simply manipulating the wall switch to make or break the closed circuit.

Instead of the wall switch, we could use an n-type or a p-type MOS transistor to make or break the closed circuit. Figure 3.2 shows a schematic rendering of an n-type transistor (a) by itself, and (b) in a circuit. Note (Figure 3.2a) that the transistor has three terminals. They are called the *gate*, the *source*, and the *drain*. The reasons for the names source and drain are not of interest to us in this course. What is of interest is the fact that if the gate of the n-type transistor is supplied with 2.9 volts, the connection from source to drain acts like a piece of wire. We say (in the language of electricity) that we have a *closed circuit* between the source and drain. If the gate of the n-type transistor is supplied with 0 volts, the connection between the source and drain is broken. We say that between the source and drain we have an *open circuit*.

Figure 3.2b shows the n-type transistor in a circuit with a battery and a bulb. When the gate is supplied with 2.9 volts, the transistor acts like a piece of wire,

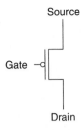

Figure 3.3   A p-type MOS transistor

completing the circuit and causing the bulb to glow. When the gate is supplied with 0 volts, the transistor acts like an open circuit, breaking the circuit, and causing the bulb not to glow.

Figure 3.2c is a shorthand notation for describing the circuit of Figure 3.2b. Rather than always showing the power supply and the complete circuit, electrical engineers usually show only the terminals of the power supply. The fact that the power supply itself provides the completion of the completed circuit is well understood, and so is not usually shown.

The p-type transistor works in exactly the opposite fashion from the n-type transistor. Figure 3.3 shows the schematic representation of a p-type transistor. When the gate is supplied with 0 volts, the p-type transistor acts (more or less) like a piece of wire, closing the circuit. When the gate is supplied with 2.9 volts, the p-type transistor acts like an open circuit. Because the p-type and n-type transistors act in this complementary way, we refer to circuits that contain both p-type and n-type transistors as CMOS circuits, for *complementary metal-oxide semiconductor*.

3.2 Logic Gates

One step up from the transistor is the logic gate. That is, we construct basic logic structures out of individual MOS transistors. In Chapter 2, we studied the behavior of the AND, the OR, and the NOT functions. In this chapter we construct transistor circuits that implement each of these functions. The corresponding circuits are called AND, OR, and NOT gates.

3.2.1 The NOT Gate (Inverter)

Figure 3.4 shows the simplest logic structure that exists in a computer. It is constructed from two MOS transistors, one p-type and one n-type. Figure 3.4a is the schematic representation of that circuit. Figure 3.4b shows the behavior of the circuit if the input is supplied with 0 volts. Note that the p-type transistor conducts and the n-type transistor does not conduct. The output is, therefore, connected to 2.9 volts. On the other hand, if the input is supplied with 2.9 volts, the p-type transistor does not conduct, but the n-type transistor does conduct. The output in this case is connected to ground (i.e., 0 volts). The complete behavior

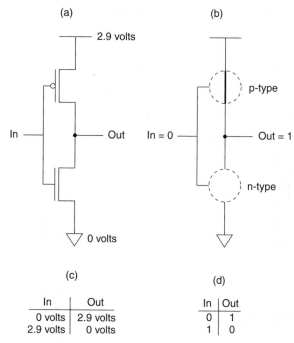

Figure 3.4   A CMOS inverter

of the circuit can be described by means of a table, as shown in Figure 3.4c. If we replace 0 volts by the symbol 0 and 2.9 volts by the symbol 1, we have the truth table (Figure 3.4d) for the complement or NOT function, which we studied in Chapter 2.

In other words, we have just shown how to construct an electronic circuit that implements the NOT logic function discussed in Chapter 2. We call this circuit a *NOT gate*, or an *inverter*.

3.2.2 OR and NOR Gates

Figure 3.5 illustrates a NOR gate. Figure 3.5a is a schematic of a circuit that implements a NOR gate. It contains two p-type and two n-type transistors.

Figure 3.5b shows the behavior of the circuit if A is supplied with 0 volts and B is supplied with 2.9 volts. In this case, the lower of the two p-type transistors produces an open circuit, and the output C is disconnected from the 2.9-volt power supply. However, the leftmost n-type transistor acts like a piece of wire, connecting the output C to 0 volts.

Note that if both A and B are supplied with 0 volts, the two p-type transistors conduct, and the output C is connected to 2.9 volts. Note further that there is no ambiguity here, since both n-type transistors act as open circuits, and so C is disconnected from ground.

If either A or B is supplied with 2.9 volts, the corresponding p-type transistor results in an open circuit. That is sufficient to break the connection from C to

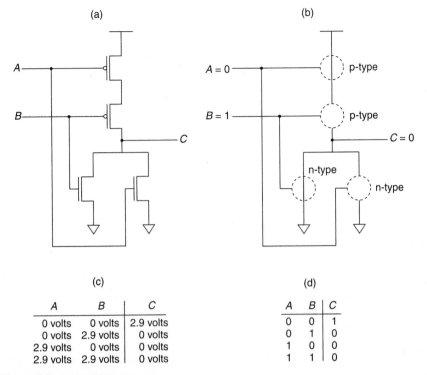

(a)   (b)

(c)

A	B	C
0 volts	0 volts	2.9 volts
0 volts	2.9 volts	0 volts
2.9 volts	0 volts	0 volts
2.9 volts	2.9 volts	0 volts

(d)

A	B	C
0	0	1
0	1	0
1	0	0
1	1	0

Figure 3.5 The NOR gate

the 2.9-volt source. However, 2.9 volts supplied to the gate of one of the n-type transistors is sufficient to cause that transistor to conduct, resulting in C being connected to ground (i.e., 0 volts).

Figure 3.5c summarizes the complete behavior of the circuit of Figure 3.5a. It shows the behavior of the circuit for each of the four pairs of voltages that can be supplied to A and B. That is,

$$A = 0 \text{ volts,} \qquad B = 0 \text{ volts}$$
$$A = 0 \text{ volts,} \qquad B = 2.9 \text{ volts}$$
$$A = 2.9 \text{ volts,} \qquad B = 0 \text{ volts}$$
$$A = 2.9 \text{ volts,} \qquad B = 2.9 \text{ volts}$$

If we replace the voltages with their logical equivalents, we have the truth table of Figure 3.5d. Note that the output C is exactly the opposite of the logical OR function that we studied in Chapter 2. In fact, it is the NOT-OR function, more typically abbreviated as NOR. We refer to the circuit that implements the NOR function as a NOR gate.

If we augment the circuit of Figure 3.5a by adding an inverter at the output, as shown in Figure 3.6a, we have at the output D the logical function OR. Figure 3.6a is the circuit for an OR gate. Figure 3.6b describes the behavior of this circuit if the input variable A is set to 0 and the input variable B is set to 1. Figure 3.6c shows the circuit's truth table.

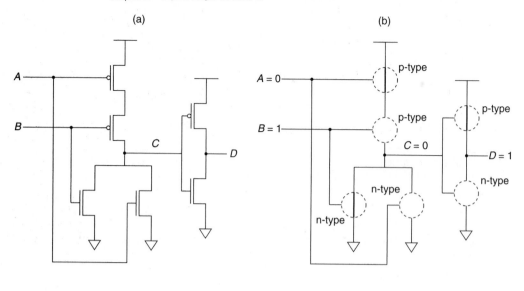

(a)   (b)

(c)

A	B	C	D
0	0	1	0
0	1	0	1
1	0	0	1
1	1	0	1

Figure 3.6   The OR gate

3.2.3 AND and NAND Gates

Figure 3.7 shows an AND gate. Note that if either A or B is supplied with 0 volts, there is a direct connection from C to the 2.9-volt power supply. The fact that C is at 2.9 volts means the n-type transistor whose gate is connected to C provides a path from D to ground. Therefore, if either A or B is supplied with 0 volts, the output D of the circuit of Figure 3.7 is 0 volts.

Again, we note that there is no ambiguity. The fact that at least one of the two inputs A or B is supplied with 0 volts means that at least one of the two n-type transistors whose gates are connected to A or B is open, and that consequently, C is disconnected from ground. Furthermore, the fact that C is at 2.9 volts means the p-type transistor whose gate is connected to C is open-circuited. Therefore, D is not connected to 2.9 volts.

On the other hand, if both A and B are supplied with 2.9 volts, then both of their corresponding p-type transistors are open. However, their corresponding n-type transistors act like pieces of wire, providing a direct connection from C to ground. Because C is at ground, the rightmost p-type transistor acts like a closed circuit, forcing D to 2.9 volts.

(a)

(b)

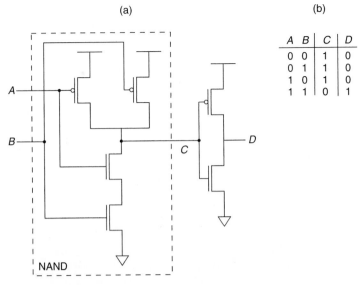

A	B	C	D
0	0	1	0
0	1	1	0
1	0	1	0
1	1	0	1

Figure 3.7   The AND gate

Figure 3.7b summarizes in truth table form the behavior of the circuit of Figure 3.7a. Note that the circuit is an AND gate. The circuit shown within the dashed lines (i.e., having output C) is a NOT-AND gate, which we generally abbreviate as NAND.

The gates just discussed are very common in digital logic circuits and in digital computers. There are millions of inverters (NOT gates) in the Pentium IV microprocessor. As a convenience, we can represent each of these gates by standard symbols, as shown in Figure 3.8. The bubble shown in the inverter, NAND, and NOR gates signifies the complement (i.e., NOT) function.

From now on, we will not draw circuits showing the individual transistors. Instead, we will raise our level of abstraction and use the symbols shown in Figure 3.8.

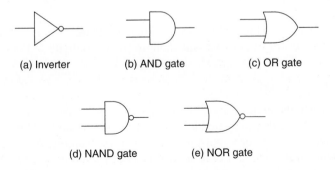

(a) Inverter   (b) AND gate   (c) OR gate

(d) NAND gate   (e) NOR gate

Figure 3.8   Basic logic gates

(a)   (b)

(c)

A	B	$\bar{A}$	$\bar{B}$	AND	C
0	0	1	1	1	0
0	1	1	0	0	1
1	0	0	1	0	1
1	1	0	0	0	1

Figure 3.9   DeMorgan's law

3.2.4 DeMorgan's Law

Note (see Figure 3.9a) that one can complement an input before applying it to a gate. Consider the effect on the two-input AND gate if we apply the complements of A and B as inputs to the gate, and also complement the output of the AND gate. The "bubbles" at the inputs to the AND gate designate that the inputs A and B are complemented before they are used as inputs to the AND gate.

Figure 3.9b shows the behavior of this structure for the input combination $A = 0, B = 1$. For ease of representation, we have moved the bubbles away from the inputs and the output of the AND gate. That way, we can more easily see what happens to each value as it passes through a bubble.

Figure 3.9c summarizes by means of a truth table the behavior of the logic circuit of Figure 3.9a for all four combinations of input values. Note that the NOT of A is represented as $\bar{A}$.

We can describe the behavior of this circuit algebraically:

$$\overline{\bar{A} \text{ AND } \bar{B}} = A \text{ OR } B$$

We can also state this behavior in English:

"It is not the case that both A and B are false" is equivalent to saying "At least one of A and B is true."

This equivalence is known as DeMorgan's law. Is there a similar result if one inverts both inputs to an OR gate, and then inverts the output?

3.2.5 Larger Gates

Before we leave the topic of logic gates, we should note that the notion of AND, OR, NAND, and NOR gates extends to larger numbers of inputs. One could build a three-input AND gate or a four-input OR gate, for example. An n-input AND gate has an output value of 1 only if ALL n input variables have values of 1. If any of the n inputs has a value of 0, the output of the n-input AND gate is 0. An n-input OR gate has an output value of 1 if ANY of the n input variables has a value of 1. That is, an n-input OR gate has an output value of 0 only if ALL n input variables have values of 0.

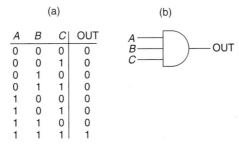

A	B	C	OUT
0	0	0	0
0	0	1	0
0	1	0	0
0	1	1	0
1	0	0	0
1	0	1	0
1	1	0	0
1	1	1	1

Figure 3.10   A three-input AND gate

Figure 3.10 illustrates a three-input AND gate. Figure 3.10a shows its truth table. Figure 3.10b shows the symbol for a three-input AND gate.

Can you draw a transistor-level circuit for a three-input AND gate? How about a four-input AND gate? How about a four-input OR gate?

3.3 Combinational Logic Circuits

Now that we understand the workings of the basic logic gates, the next step is to build some of the logic structures that are important components of the microarchitecture of a computer.

There are fundamentally two kinds of logic structures, those that include the storage of information and those that do not. In Sections 3.4, 3.5, and 3.6, we will deal with structures that store information. In this section, we will deal with those that do not. These structures are sometimes referred to as *decision elements*. Usually, they are referred to as *combinational logic structures*, because their outputs are strictly dependent on the combination of input values that are being applied to the structure *right now*. Their outputs are not at all dependent on any past history of information that is stored internally, since no information can be stored internally in a combinational logic circuit.

We will next examine a decoder, a mux, and a full adder.

3.3.1 Decoder

Figure 3.11 shows a logic gate description of a two-input decoder. A decoder has the property that exactly one of its outputs is 1 and all the rest are 0s. The one output that is logically 1 is the output corresponding to the input pattern that it is expected to detect. In general, decoders have n inputs and 2^n outputs. We say the output line that detects the input pattern is *asserted*. That is, that output line has the value 1, rather than 0 as is the case for all the other output lines. In Figure 3.11, note that for each of the four possible combinations of inputs A and B, exactly one output has the value 1 at any one time. In Figure 3.11b, the input to the decoder is 10, resulting in the third output line being asserted.

The decoder is useful in determining how to interpret a bit pattern. We will see in Chapter 5 that the work to be carried out by each instruction in the LC-3 is

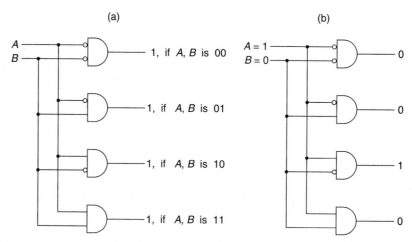

Figure 3.11   A two-input decoder

determined by a four-bit pattern, called an *opcode*, that is part of the instruction. A 4-to-16 decoder is a simple combinational logic structure for identifying what work is to be performed by each instruction.

3.3.2 Mux

Figure 3.12a shows a gate-level description of a two-input multiplexer, more commonly referred to as a *mux*. The function of a mux is to select one of the inputs and connect it to the output. The select signal (S in Figure 3.12) determines which input is connected to the output. The mux of Figure 3.12 works as follows: Suppose $S = 0$, as shown in Figure 3.12b. Since the output of an AND gate is 0 unless all inputs are 1, the output of the rightmost AND gate is 0. Also, the output of the leftmost AND gate is whatever the input A is. That is, if $A = 0$, then the output of the leftmost AND gate is 0, and if $A = 1$, then the output is 1. Since the output of the rightmost AND gate is 0, it has no effect on the OR gate. Consequently, the output at C is exactly the same as the output of the leftmost AND gate. The net result of all this is that if $S = 0$, the output C is identical to the input A.

On the other hand, if $S = 1$, it is B that is ANDed with 1, resulting in the output of the OR gate having the value of B.

In summary, the output C is always connected to either the input A or the input B—which one depends on the value of the select line S. We say S selects the source of the mux (either A or B) to be routed through to the output C. Figure 3.12c shows the standard representation for a mux.

In general, a mux consists of 2^n inputs and n select lines. Figure 3.13a shows a gate-level description of a four-input mux. It requires two select lines. Figure 3.13b shows the standard representation for a four-input mux.

Can you construct the gate-level representation for an eight-input mux? How many select lines must you have?

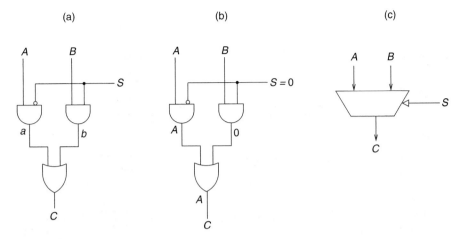

Figure 3.12   A 2-to-1 mux

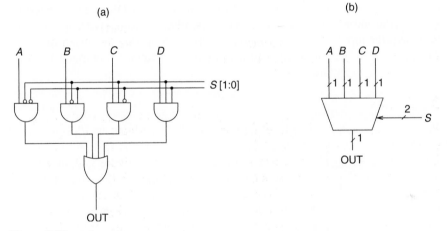

Figure 3.13   A four-input mux

3.3.3 Full Adder

In Chapter 2, we discussed binary addition. Recall that a simple algorithm for binary addition is to proceed as you have always done in the case of decimal addition, from right to left, one column at a time, adding the two digits from the two values plus the carry in, and generating a sum digit and a carry to the next column. The only difference is you get a carry after 1, rather than after 9.

Figure 3.14 is a truth table that describes the result of binary addition on *one column* of bits within two *n*-bit operands. At each column, there are three values that must be added: one bit from each of the two operands and the carry from the previous column. We designate these three bits as a_i, b_i, and $carry_i$. There are two results, the sum bit (s_i) and the carryover to the next column, $carry_{i+1}$. Note that if only one of the three bits equals 1, we get a sum of 1, and no carry (i.e., $carry_{i+1} = 0$). If two of the three bits equal 1, we get a sum of 0, and a carry

a_i	b_i	$carry_i$	$carry_{i+1}$	s_i
0	0	0	0	0
0	0	1	0	1
0	1	0	0	1
0	1	1	1	0
1	0	0	0	1
1	0	1	1	0
1	1	0	1	0
1	1	1	1	1

Figure 3.14   A truth table for a binary adder

of 1. If all three bits equal 1, the sum is 3, which in binary addition corresponds to a sum of 1 and a carry of 1.

Figure 3.15 is the gate-level description of the truth table of Figure 3.14. Note that each AND gate in Figure 3.15 produces an output 1 for exactly one of the eight input combinations of a_i, b_i, and $carry_i$. The output of the OR gate for C_{i+1} must be 1 in exactly those cases where the corresponding input combinations in Figure 3.14 produce an output 1. Therefore the inputs to the OR gate that generates C_{i+1} are the outputs of the AND gates corresponding to those input combinations. Similarly, the inputs to the OR gate that generates S_i are the outputs of the AND gates corresponding to the input combinations that require an output 1 for S_i in the truth table of Figure 3.14.

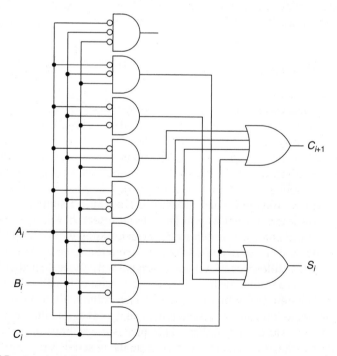

Figure 3.15   Gate-level description of a full adder

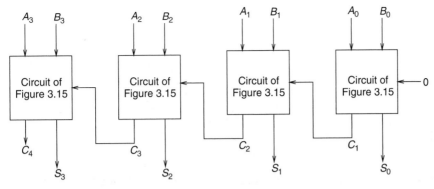

Figure 3.16 A circuit for adding two 4-bit binary numbers

Note that since the input combination 000 does not result in an output 1 for either C_{i+1} or S_i, its corresponding AND gate is not an input to either of the two OR gates.

We call the logic circuit of Figure 3.15 that provides three inputs (a_i, b_i, and $carry_i$) and two outputs (the sum bit s_i and the carryover to the next column $carry_{i+1}$) a *full adder*.

Figure 3.16 illustrates a circuit for adding two 4-bit binary numbers, using four of the full adder circuits of Figure 3.15. Note that the carryout of column i is an input to the addition performed in column $i + 1$.

3.3.4 The Programmable Logic Array (PLA)

Figure 3.17 illustrates a very common building block for implementing any collection of logic functions one wishes to. The building block is called a programmable logic array (PLA). It consists of an array of AND gates (called an AND array) followed by an array of OR gates (called an OR array). The number of AND gates corresponds to the number of input combinations (rows) in the truth table. For n input logic functions, we need a PLA with 2^n n-input AND gates. In Figure 3.17, we have 2^3 3-input AND gates. The number of OR gates corresponds to the number of output columns in the truth table. The implementation algorithm is simply to connect the output of an AND gate to the input of an OR gate if the corresponding row of the truth table produces an output 1 for that output column. Hence the notion of programmable. That is, we say we program the connections from AND gate outputs to OR gate inputs to implement our desired logic functions.

Figure 3.15 showed eight AND gates connected to two OR gates since our requirement was to implement two functions (sum and carry) of three input variables. Figure 3.17 shows a PLA that can implement any four functions of three variables one wishes to, by appropriately connecting AND gate outputs to OR gate inputs.

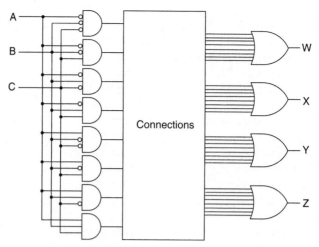

Figure 3.17   A programmable logic array

3.3.5 Logical Completeness

Before we leave the topic of combinational logic circuits, it is worth noting an important property of building blocks for logic circuits: logical completeness. We showed in Section 3.3.4 that any logic function we wished to implement could be accomplished with a PLA. We saw that the PLA consists of only AND gates, OR gates, and inverters. That means that any logic function we wish to implement can be accomplished, provided that enough AND, OR, and NOT gates are available. We say that the set of gates {AND, OR, NOT} is *logically complete* because we can build a circuit to carry out the specification of any truth table we wish without using any other kind of gate. That is, the set of gates {AND, OR, and NOT} is logically complete because a barrel of AND gates, a barrel of OR gates, and a barrel of NOT gates are sufficient to build a logic circuit that carries out the specification of any desired truth table. The barrels may have to be big ones, but the point is, we do not need any other kind of gate to do the job.

3.4 Basic Storage Elements

Recall our statement at the beginning of Section 3.3 that there are two kinds of logic structures, those that involve the storage of information and those that do not. We have discussed three examples of those that do not: the decoder, the mux, and the full adder. Now we are ready to discuss logic structures that do include the storage of information.

3.4.1 The R-S Latch

A simple example of a storage element is the R-S latch. It can store one bit of information. The R-S latch can be implemented in many ways, the simplest being the one shown in Figure 3.18. Two 2-input NAND gates are connected such that the output of each is connected to one of the inputs of the other. The remaining inputs S and R are normally held at a logic level 1.

The R-S latch works as follows: We start with what we call the *quiescent* (or quiet) state, where inputs S and R both have logic value 1. We consider first the case where the output a is 1. Since that means the input A equals 1 (and we know the input R equals 1 since we are in the quiescent state), the output b must be 0. That, in turn, means the input B must be 0, which results in the output a equal to 1. As long as the inputs S and R remain 1, the state of the circuit will not change. We say the R-S latch stores the value 1 (the value of the output a).

If, on the other hand, we assume the output a is 0, then the input A must be 0, and the output b must be 1. This, in turn, results in the input B equal to 1, and combined with the input S equal to 1 (again due to quiescence) results in the output a equal to 0. Again, as long as the inputs S and R remain 1, the state of the circuit will not change. In this case, we say the R-S latch stores the value 0.

The latch can be set to 1 by momentarily setting S to 0, provided we keep the value of R at 1. Similarly, the latch can be set to 0 by momentarily setting R to 0, provided we keep the value of S at 1. We use the term *set* to denote setting a variable to 0 or 1, as in "set to 0" or "set to 1." In addition, we often use the term *clear* to denote the act of setting a variable to 0.

If we clear S, then a equals 1, which in turn causes A to equal 1. Since R is also 1, the output at b must be 0. This causes B to be 0, which in turn makes a equal to 1. If we now return S to 1, it does not affect a, since B is also 0, and only one input to a NAND gate must be 0 in order to guarantee that the output of the NAND gate is 1. Thus, the latch continues to store a 1 long after S returns to 1.

In the same way, we can clear the latch (set the latch to 0) by momentarily setting R to 0.

We should also note that in order for the R-S latch to work properly, one must take care that it is never the case that both S and R are allowed to be set to 0 at the same time. If that does happen, the outputs a and b are both 1, and the final state of the latch depends on the electrical properties of the transistors making up the gates and not on the logic being performed. How the electrical properties of the transistors will determine the final state in this case is a subject we will have to leave for a later semester.

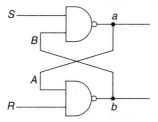

Figure 3.18   An R-S latch

3.4.2 The Gated D Latch

To be useful, it is necessary to control when a latch is set and when it is cleared. A simple way to accomplish this is with the gated latch.

Figure 3.19 shows a logic circuit that implements a gated D latch. It consists of the R-S latch of Figure 3.18, plus two additional gates that allow the latch to be set to the value of D, but *only* when WE is asserted. WE stands for *write enable*. When WE is not asserted (i.e., when WE equals 0), the outputs S and R are both equal to 1. Since S and R are also inputs to the R-S latch, if they are kept at 1, the value stored in the latch remains unchanged, as we explained in Section 3.4.1. When WE is momentarily asserted (i.e., set to 1), exactly one of the outputs S or R is set to 0, depending on the value of D. If D equals 1, then S is set to 0. If D equals 0, then both inputs to the lower NAND gate are 1, resulting in R being set to 0. As we saw earlier, if S is set to 0, the R-S latch is set to 1. If R is set to 0, the R-S latch is set to 0. Thus, the R-S latch is set to 1 or 0 according to whether D is 1 or 0. When WE returns to 0, S and R return to 1, and the value stored in the R-S latch persists.

3.4.3 A Register

We have already seen in Chapter 2 that it is useful to deal with values consisting of more than one bit. In Chapter 5, we will introduce the LC-3 computer, where most values are represented by 16 bits. It is useful to be able to store these larger numbers of bits as self-contained units. The *register* is a structure that stores a number of bits, taken together as a unit. That number can be as large as is useful or as small as 1. In the LC-3, we will need many 16-bit registers, and also a few one-bit registers. We will see in Figure 3.33, which describes the internal structure of the LC-3, that PC, IR, and MAR are all 16-bit registers, and that N, Z, and P are all one-bit registers.

Figure 3.20 shows a four-bit register made up of four gated D latches. The four-bit value stored in the register is Q_3, Q_2, Q_1, Q_0. The value D_3, D_2, D_1, D_0 can be written into the register when WE is asserted.

Note: A common shorthand notation to describe a sequence of bits that are numbered as just described is $Q[3:0]$. That is, each bit is assigned its own bit number. The rightmost bit is bit [0], and the numbering continues from right to

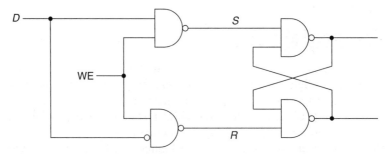

Figure 3.19 A gated D latch

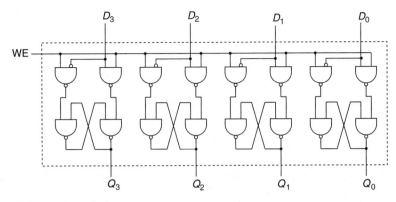

Figure 3.20 A four-bit register

left. If there are *n* bits, the leftmost bit is bit [*n* − 1]. For example, in the following 16-bit pattern,

```
0011101100011110
```

bit [15] is 0, bit [14] is 0, bit [13] is 1, bit [12] is 1, and so on.

We can designate a subunit of this pattern with the notation $Q[l:r]$, where l is the leftmost bit in the subunit and r is the rightmost bit in the subunit. We call such a subunit a *field*.

In this 16-bit pattern, if $A[15:0]$ is the entire 16-bit pattern, then, for example:

```
A[15:12] is 0011
A[13:7] is 1110110
A[2:0] is 110
A[1:1] is 1
```

We should also point out that the numbering scheme from right to left is purely arbitrary. We could just as easily have designated the leftmost bit as bit [0] and numbered them from left to right. Indeed, many people do. So, it is not important whether the numbering scheme is left to right or right to left. But it is important that the bit numbering be consistent in a given setting, that is, that it is always done the same way. In our work, we will always number bits from right to left.

3.5 The Concept of Memory

We now have all the tools we need to describe one of the most important structures in the electronic digital computer, its *memory*. We will see in Chapter 4 how memory fits into the basic scheme of computer processing, and you will see throughout the rest of the book and indeed the rest of your work with computers how important the concept of memory is to computing.

Memory is made up of a (usually large) number of locations, each uniquely identifiable and each having the ability to store a value. We refer to the unique identifier associated with each memory location as its *address*. We refer to the number of bits of information stored in each location as its *addressability*.

For example, an advertisement for a personal computer might say, "This computer comes with 16 megabytes of memory." Actually, most ads generally use the abbreviation 16 MB. This statement means, as we will explain momentarily, that the computer system includes 16 million memory locations, each containing 1 byte of information.

3.5.1 Address Space

We refer to the total number of uniquely identifiable locations as the memory's *address space*. A 16 MB memory, for example, refers to a memory that consists of 16 million uniquely identifiable memory locations.

Actually, the number *16 million* is only an approximation, due to the way we identify memory locations. Since everything else in the computer is represented by sequences of 0s and 1s, it should not be surprising that memory locations are identified by binary addresses as well. With n bits of address, we can uniquely identify 2^n locations. Ten bits provide 1,024 locations, which is approximately 1,000. If we have 20 bits to represent each address, we have 2^{20} uniquely identifiable locations, which is approximately 1 million. Thus 16 mega really corresponds to the number of uniquely identifiable locations that can be specified with 24 address bits. We say the address space is 2^{24}, which is *exactly* 16,777,216 locations, rather than 16,000,000, although we colloquially refer to it as 16 million.

3.5.2 Addressability

The number of bits stored in each memory location is the memory's addressability. A 16 megabyte memory is a memory consisting of 16,777,216 memory locations, each containing 1 byte (i.e., 8 bits) of storage. Most memories are byte-addressable. The reason is historical; most computers got their start processing data, and one character stroke on the keyboard corresponds to one 8-bit ASCII character, as we learned in Chapter 2. If the memory is byte-addressable, then each ASCII code occupies one location in memory. Uniquely identifying each byte of memory allowed individual bytes of stored information to be changed easily.

Many computers that have been designed specifically to perform large scientific calculations are 64-bit addressable. This is due to the fact that numbers used in scientific calculations are often represented as 64-bit floating point quantities. Recall that we discussed the floating point data type in Chapter 2. Since scientific calculations are likely to use numbers that require 64 bits to represent them, it is reasonable to design a memory for such a computer that stores one such number in each uniquely identifiable memory location.

3.5.3 A 2^2-by-3-Bit Memory

Figure 3.21 illustrates a memory of size 2^2 by 3 bits. That is, the memory has an address space of four locations, and an addressability of 3 bits. A memory of size 2^2 requires 2 bits to specify the address. A memory of addressability 3 stores 3 bits

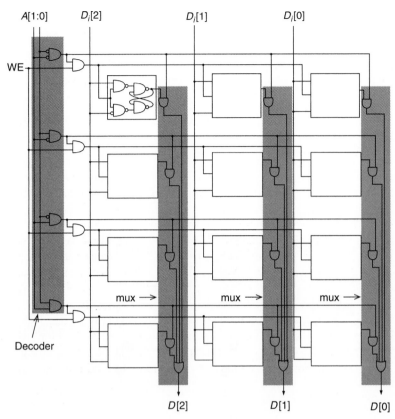

Figure 3.21   A 2^2-by-3-bit memory

of information in each memory location. Accesses of memory require decoding the address bits. Note that the address decoder takes as input $A[1:0]$ and asserts exactly one of its four outputs, corresponding to the *word line* being addressed. In Figure 3.21, each row of the memory corresponds to a unique three-bit word; thus the term *word line*. Memory can be read by applying the address $A[1:0]$, which asserts the word line to be read. Note that each bit of the memory is ANDed with its word line and then ORed with the corresponding bits of the other words. Since only one word line can be asserted at a time, this is effectively a mux with the output of the decoder providing the select function to each bit line. Thus, the appropriate word is read.

   Figure 3.22 shows the process of reading location 3. The code for 3 is 11. The address $A[1:0] = 11$ is decoded, and the bottom word line is asserted. Note that the three other decoder outputs are not asserted. That is, they have the value 0. The value stored in location 3 is 101. These three bits are each ANDed with their word line producing the bits 101, which are supplied to the three output OR gates. Note that all other inputs to the OR gates are 0, since they have been produced by ANDing with unasserted word lines. The result is that $D[2:0] = 101$. That is, the value stored in location 3 is output by the OR gates. Memory can be written in a similar fashion. The address specified by $A[1:0]$ is presented to

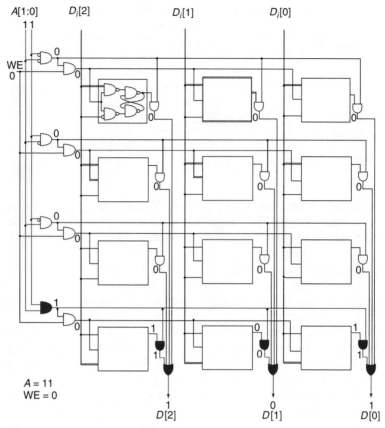

Figure 3.22   Reading location 3 in our 2^2-by-3-bit memory

the address decoder, resulting in the correct word line being asserted. With WE asserted as well, the three bits $D_i[2:0]$ can be written into the three gated latches corresponding to that word line.

3.6 Sequential Logic Circuits

In Section 3.3, we discussed digital logic structures that process information (decision structures, we call them) wherein the outputs depend solely on the values that are present on the inputs **now**. Examples are muxes, decoders, and full adders. We call these structures combinational logic circuits. In these circuits there is no sense of the past. Indeed, there is no capability for storing any information of anything that happened before the present time. In Sections 3.4 and 3.5, we described structures that do store information—in Section 3.4, some basic storage elements, and in Section 3.5, a simple 2^2-by-3-bit memory.

In this section, we discuss digital logic structures that can **both** process information (i.e., make decisions) **and** store information. That is, these structures base their decisions not only on the input values now present, but also (and this is

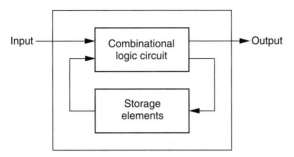

Figure 3.23 Sequential logic circuit block diagram

very important) on what has happened before. These structures are usually called **sequential logic circuits**. They are distinguishable from combinational logic circuits because, unlike combinational logic circuits, they contain storage elements that allow them to keep track of prior history information. Figure 3.23 shows a block diagram of a sequential logic circuit. Note the storage elements. Note, also, that the output can be dependent on both the inputs now and the values stored in the storage elements. The values stored in the storage elements reflect the history of what has happened before.

Sequential logic circuits are used to implement a very important class of mechanisms called finite state machines. We use finite state machines in essentially all branches of engineering. For example, they are used as controllers of electrical systems, mechanical systems, aeronautical systems, and so forth. A traffic light controller that sets the traffic light to red, yellow, or green depends on the light that is currently on (history information) and input information from sensors such as trip wires on the road and optical devices that are monitoring traffic.

We will see in Chapter 4 when we introduce the von Neumann model of a computer that a finite state controller is at the heart of the computer. It controls the processing of information by the computer.

3.6.1 A Simple Example: The Combination Lock

A simple example shows the difference between combinational logic structures and sequential logic structures. Suppose one wishes to secure a bicycle with a lock, but does not want to carry a key. A common solution is the combination lock. The person memorizes a "combination" and uses this to open the lock. Two common types of locks are shown in Figure 3.24.

In Figure 3.24a, the lock consists of a dial, with the numbers from 0 to 30 equally spaced around its circumference. To open the lock, one needs to know the "combination." One such combination could be: R13-L22-R3. If this were the case, one would open the lock by turning the dial two complete turns to the right, and then continuing until the dial points to 13, followed by one complete turn to the left, and then continuing until the dial points to 22, followed by turning the dial again to the right until it points to 3. At that point, the lock opens. What is important here is the *sequence* of the turns. The lock will not open, for example

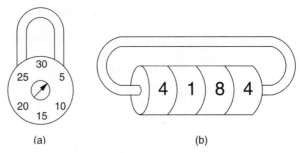

Figure 3.24   Combination locks

if one performed two turns to the right, and then stopped on 20, followed by one complete turn to the left, ending on 22, followed by one turn to the right, ending on 3. That is, even though the final position of the dial is 3, the lock would not open. Why? Because the lock stores the previous rotations and makes its decision (open or don't open) on the basis of the current input value (R3) *and* the history of the past operations. This mechanism is a simple example of a sequential structure.

Another type of lock is shown in Figure 3.24b. The mechanism consists of (usually) four wheels, each containing the digits 0 through 9. When the digits are lined up properly, the lock will open. In this case, the combination is the set of four digits. Whether or not this lock opens is totally independent of the past rotations of the four wheels. The lock does not care at all about past rotations. The only thing important is the current value of each of the four wheels. This is a simple example of a combinational structure.

It is curious that in our everyday speech, both mechanisms are referred to as "combination locks." In fact, only the lock of Figure 3.24b is a combinational lock. The lock of Figure 3.24a would be better called a sequential lock!

3.6.2 The Concept of State

For the mechanism of Figure 3.24a to work properly, it has to keep track of the sequence of rotations leading up to the opening of the lock. In particular, it has to differentiate the correct sequence R13-L22-R3 from all other sequences. For example, R13-L29-R3 must not be allowed to open the lock. Likewise, R10-L22-R3 must also not be allowed to open the lock. The problem is that, at any one time, the only external input to the lock is the current rotation.

For the lock of Figure 3.24a to work, it must identify several relevant situations, as follows:

A. The lock is not open, and NO relevant operations have been performed.

B. The lock is not open, but the user has just completed the R13 operation.

C. The lock is not open, but the user has just completed R13, followed by L22.

D. The lock is open.

We have labeled these four situations A, B, C, and D. We refer to each of these situations as the *state* of the lock.

The notion of **state** is a very important concept in computer engineering, and actually, in just about all branches of engineering. The state of a mechanism—more generally, the state of a system—is a snapshot of that system in which all relevant items are explicitly expressed.

That is: *The state of a system is a snapshot of all the relevant elements of the system at the moment the snapshot is taken.*

In the case of the lock of Figure 3.24a, there are four states A, B, C, and D. Either the lock is open (State D), or if it is not open, we have already performed either zero (State A), one (State B), or two (State C) correct operations. This is the sum total of all possible states that can exist. Exercise: Why is that the case? That is, what would be the snapshot of a fifth state that describes a possible situation for the combination lock?

There are many common examples of systems that can be easily described by means of states.

The state of a game of basketball can be described by the scoreboard in the basketball arena. Figure 3.25 shows the state of the basketball game as Texas 73, Oklahoma 68, 7 minutes and 38 seconds left in the second half, 14 seconds left on the shot clock, Texas with the ball, and Texas and Oklahoma each with four team fouls. This is a snapshot of the basketball game. It describes the state of the basketball game right now. If, 12 seconds later, a Texas player were to score a two-point shot, the new state would be described by the updated scoreboard. That is, the score would then be Texas 75, Oklahoma 68, the time remaining in the game would be 7 minutes and 26 seconds, the shot clock would be back to 25 seconds, and Oklahoma would have the ball.

The game of tic-tac-toe can also be described in accordance with the notion of state. Recall that the game is played by two people (or, in our case, a person

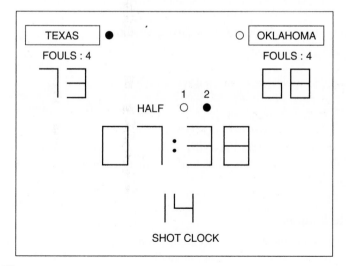

Figure 3.25 An example of a state

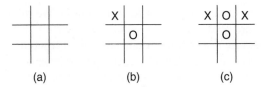

Figure 3.26   Three states in a tic-tac-toe machine

and the computer). The state is a snapshot of the game in progress each time the computer asks the person to make a move. The game is played as follows: There are nine locations on the diagram. The person and then the computer take turns placing an X (the person) and an O (the computer) in an empty location. The person goes first. The winner is the first to place three symbols (three Xs for the person, three Os for the computer) in a straight line, either vertically, horizontally, or diagonally.

The initial state, before either the person or computer has had a turn, is shown in Figure 3.26a. Figure 3.26b shows a possible state of the game when the person is prompted for a second move, if he/she put an X in the upper left corner as the first move. In the state shown, the computer put an O in the middle square as its first move. Figure 3.26c shows a possible state of the game when the person is being prompted for a third move if he/she put an X in the upper right corner on the second move (after putting the first X in the upper left corner). In the state shown, the computer put its second O in the upper middle location.

3.6.3 Finite State Machines

We have seen that a state is a snapshot of all relevant parts of a system at a particular point in time. At other times, that system can be in other states. The behavior of a system can often be best understood by describing it as a *finite state machine*.

A finite state machine consists of five elements:

```
1.  a finite number of states
2.  a finite number of external inputs
3.  a finite number of external outputs
4.  an explicit specification of all state transitions
5.  an explicit specification of what determines each external
    output value.
```

The set of states represents all possible situations (or snapshots) that the system can be in. Each state transition describes what it takes to get from one state to another.

The State Diagram

A finite state machine can be conveniently represented by means of a *state diagram*. Figure 3.27 is an example of a state diagram. A state diagram is drawn as a set of circles, where each circle corresponds to one state, and a set of connections

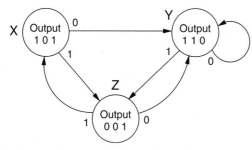

Figure 3.27 A state diagram

between some of the states, where each connection is drawn as an arrow. The more sophisticated term for "connection" is *arc*. Each arc identifies the transition from one state to another. The arrowhead on each arc specifies which state the system is coming from, and which state it is going to. We refer to the state the system is coming from as the *current state*, and the state it is going to as the *next state*. The finite state machine represented by the state diagram of Figure 3.27 consists of three states, with six state transitions. Note that there is no state transition from state Y to state X.

It is often the case that from a current state there are multiple transitions to next states. The state transition that occurs depends on the values of the external inputs. In Figure 3.27, if the current state is state X and the external input has value 0, the next state is state Y. If the current state is state X and the external input has the value 1, the next state is state Z. In short, the next state is determined by the combination of the current state and the current external input.

The output values of a system can be determined just by the current state of the system, or they can be determined by the combination of the current state and the values of the current external inputs. In all the cases we will study, the output values are specified by the current state of the system. In Figure 3.27, the output is 101 when the system is in state X, the output is 110 when the system is in state Y, and 001 when the system is in state Z.

Figure 3.28 is a state diagram of the combination lock of Figure 3.24a, for which the correct combination is R13, L22, R3. Note the four states, labeled A, B, C, D, identifying whether the lock is open, or, in the cases where it is not open, the number of correct rotations performed up to now. The external inputs are the possible rotation operations. The output is the condition "open" or "do not open." The output is explicitly associated with each state. That is, in states A, B, and C, the output is "do not open." In state D, the output is "open." Note further that the "arcs" out of each state comprise all possible operations that one could perform when the mechanism is in that state. For example, when in state B, all possible rotations can be described as (1) L22 and (2) everything except L22. Note that there are two arrows emanating from state B in Figure 3.28, corresponding to these two cases.

We could similarly draw a state diagram for the basketball game we described earlier, where each state would be one possible configuration of the scoreboard. A transition would occur if either the referee blew a whistle or the other team got the

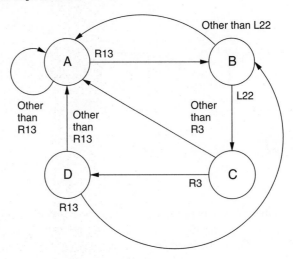

Figure 3.28   State diagram of the combination lock of Figure 3.24

ball. We showed earlier the transition that would be caused by Texas scoring a two-point shot. Clearly, the number of states in the finite state machine describing a basketball game would be huge. Also clearly, the number of legitimate transitions from one state to another is small, compared to the number of arcs one could draw connecting arbitrary pairs of states. The input is the activity that occurred on the basketball court since the last transition. Some input values are: Texas scored two points, Oklahoma scored three points, Texas stole the ball, Oklahoma successfully rebounded a Texas shot, and so forth. The output is the final result of the game. The output has three values: Game still in progress, Texas wins, Oklahoma wins.

Can one have an arc from a state where the score is Texas 30, Oklahoma 28 to a state where the score is tied, Texas 30, Oklahoma 30? See Exercise 3.38.

Is it possible to have two states, one where Texas is ahead 30-28 and the other where the score is tied 30-30, but no arc between the two? See Exercise 3.39.

The Clock

There is still one important property of the behavior of finite state machines that we have not discussed—the mechanism that triggers the transition from one state to the next. In the case of the "sequential" combination lock, the mechanism is the completion of rotating the dial in one direction, and the start of rotating the dial in the opposite direction. In the case of the basketball game, the mechanism is triggered by the referee blowing a whistle, or someone scoring or the other team otherwise getting the ball.

Frequently, the mechanism that triggers the transition from one state to the next is a clock circuit. A clock circuit, or, more commonly, a *clock*, is a signal whose value alternates between 0 volts and some specified fixed voltage. In digital logic terms, a clock is a signal whose value alternates between 0 and 1. Figure 3.29 illustrates the value of the clock signal as a function of time. A *clock cycle* is one interval of the repeated sequence of intervals shown in Figure 3.29.

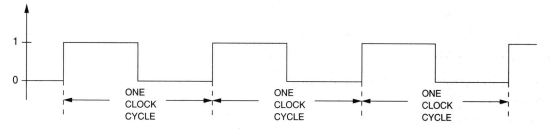

Figure 3.29 A clock signal

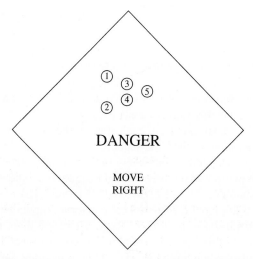

Figure 3.30 A traffic danger sign

In electronic circuit implementations of a finite state machine, the transition from one state to another occurs at the start of each clock cycle.

3.6.4 An Example: The Complete Implementation of a Finite State Machine

We conclude this section with the logic specification of a sequential logic circuit that implements a finite state machine. Our example is a controller for a traffic danger sign, as shown in Figure 3.30. Note the sign says, "Danger, Move Right." The sign also contains five lights (labeled 1 through 5 in the figure).

Like many sequential logic circuits, the purpose of our controller is to direct the behavior of a system. In our case, the system is the set of lights on the traffic danger sign. The controller's job is to have the five lights flash on and off as follows: During one cycle, all lights will be off. The next cycle, lights 1 and 2 will be on. The next cycle, lights 1, 2, 3, and 4 will be on. The next cycle, all five lights will be on. Then the sequence repeats: next cycle, no lights on, followed by 1 and 2 on, followed by 1, 2, 3, and 4 on, and so forth. Each cycle is to last $\frac{1}{2}$ second.

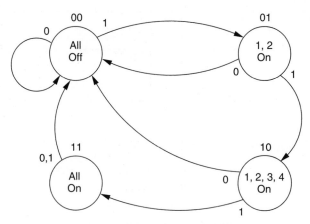

Figure 3.31   State diagram for the traffic danger sign controller

Figure 3.31 is a finite state machine that describes the behavior of the traffic danger sign. Note that there are four states, one for each of the four relevant situations. Note the transitions from each state to the next state. If the switch is on (input = 1), the lights flash in the sequence described. If the switch is turned off, the state always transfers immediately to the "all off" state.

Figure 3.32 shows the implementation of a sequential logic circuit that implements the finite state machine of Figure 3.31. Figure 3.32a is a block diagram, similar to Figure 3.23. Note that there is one external input, a switch that determines whether or not the lights should flash. There are three external outputs, one to control when lights 1 and 2 are on, one to control when lights 3 and 4 are on, and one to control when light 5 is on. Note that there are two internal storage elements that are needed to keep track of which state the controller is in, which is determined by the past behavior of the traffic danger sign. Note finally that there is a clock signal that must have a cycle time of $\frac{1}{2}$ second in order for the state transitions to occur every $\frac{1}{2}$ second.

The only relevant history that must be retained is the state that we are transitioning from. Since there are only four states, we can uniquely identify them with two bits. Therefore, only two storage elements are needed. Figure 3.31 shows the two-bit code used to identify each of the four states.

Combinational Logic

Figure 3.32b shows the combinational logic circuit required to complete the implementation of the controller for the traffic danger sign. Two sets of outputs of the combinational logic circuit are required for the controller to work properly: a set of external outputs for the lights and a set of internal outputs to determine the inputs to the two storage elements that keep track of the state.

First, let us look at the outputs that control the lights. As we have said, there are only three outputs necessary to control the lights. Light 5 is controlled by the output of the AND gate labeled X, since the only time light 5 is on is if the switch is on, and the controller is in state 11. Lights 3 and 4 are controlled by the output of the OR gate labeled Y, since there are two states in which those lights are on,

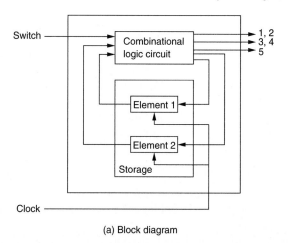

(a) Block diagram

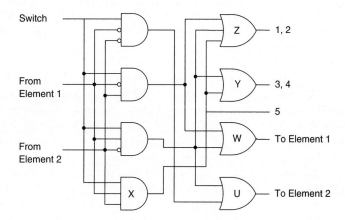

(b) The combinational logic circuit

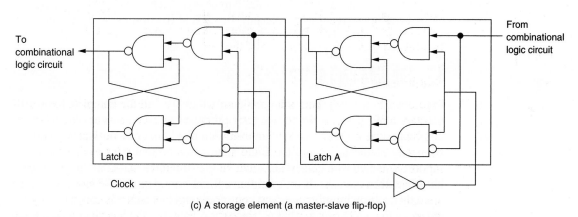

(c) A storage element (a master-slave flip-flop)

Figure 3.32 Sequential logic circuit implementation of Figure 3.30

those labeled 10 and 11. Why are lights 1 and 2 controlled by the output of the OR gate labeled Z? See Exercise 3.42.

Next, let us look at the internal outputs that control the storage elements. Storage element 1 should be set to 1 for the next clock cycle if the next state is to be 10 or 11. This is true only if the switch is on and the current state is either 01 or 10. Therefore the output signal that will make storage element 1 be 1 in the next clock cycle is the output of the OR gate labeled W. Why is the next state of storage element 2 controlled by the output of the OR gate labeled U? See Exercise 3.42.

Storage Elements

The last piece of logic needed for the traffic danger sign controller is the logic circuit for the two storage elements shown in Figure 3.32a. Why can't we use the the gated *D* latch discussed in Section 3.4, one might ask? The reason is as follows: During the current clock cycle the output of the storage element is an internal input to the combinational logic circuit, and the output of the combinational logic circuit is an input to the storage element that must not take effect until the *start* of the next clock cycle. If we used a gated *D* latch, the input would take effect immediately and overwrite the value in the storage element, instead of waiting for the start of the next cycle.

To prevent that from happening, a simple logic circuit for implementing the storage element is the *master-slave flip-flop*. A master-slave flip-flop can be constructed out of two gated *D* latches, as shown in Figure 3.32c. During the first half of the clock cycle, it is not possible to change the value stored in latch A. Thus, whatever is in latch A is passed to latch B, which is an internal input to the combinational logic circuit. During the second half of the clock cycle, it is not possible to change the value stored in latch B, so the value present during the first half of the clock cycle remains in latch B as the input to the combinational logic circuit for the entire cycle. However, during the second half of the clock cycle, it is possible to change the value stored in latch A. Thus the master-slave flip-flop allows the current state to remain intact for the entire cycle, while the next state is produced by the combinational logic to change latch A during the second half of the cycle so as to be ready to change latch B at the start of the next cycle.

3.7 The Data Path of the LC-3

In Chapter 5, we will specify a computer, which we call the LC-3, and you will have the opportunity to write computer programs to execute on it. We close out this chapter with Figure 3.33, which shows a block diagram of what we call the *data path* of the LC-3 and the finite state machine that controls all the LC-3 actions. The data path consists of all the logic structures that combine to process information in the core of the computer. Right now, Figure 3.33 is undoubtedly more than a little intimidating, and you should not be concerned by that. You are not ready to analyze it yet. That will come in Chapter 5. We have included it here, however, only to show you that you are already familiar with many of the basic structures that make up a computer. That is, you already know how most of the

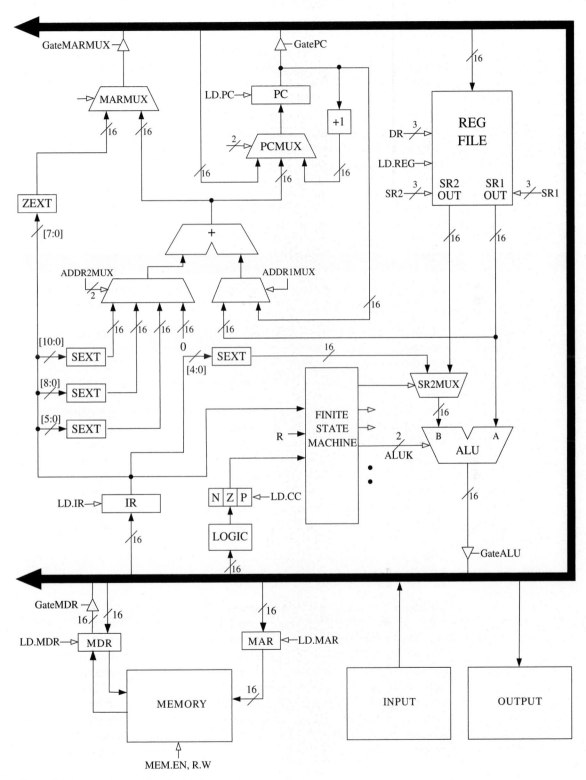

Figure 3.33   The data path of the LC-3 computer

elements in the data path work, and furthermore, you know how those elements are constructed from gates. For example, PC, IR, MAR, and MDR are registers and store 16 bits of information each. Each wire that is labeled with a cross-hatch 16 represents 16 wires, each carrying one bit of information. N, Z, and P are one-bit registers. They could be implemented as master-slave flip-flops. There are five muxes, one supplying a 16-bit value to the PC register, one supplying an address to the MAR, one selecting one of two sources to the B input of the ALU, and two selecting inputs to a 16-bit adder. In Chapter 5, we will see why these elements must be connected as shown in order to execute the programs written for the LC-3 computer. For now, just enjoy the fact that the components look familiar. In Chapters 4 and 5, we will raise the level of abstraction again and put these components together into a working computer.

Exercises

3.1   In the following table, write whether each type of transistor will act as an open circuit or a closed circuit.

	n-type	p-type
Gate = 1		
Gate = 0		

3.2   Replace the missing parts in the circuit below with either a wire or no wire to give the output OUT a logical value of 0 when the input IN is a logical 1.

3.3   A two-input AND and a two-input OR are both examples of two-input logic functions. How many different two-input logic functions are possible?

3.4   Replace the missing parts in the circuit below with either a wire or no
wire to give the output C a logical value of 1. Describe a set of inputs that
give the output C a logical value of 0. Replace the missing parts with
wires or no wires corresponding to that set of inputs.

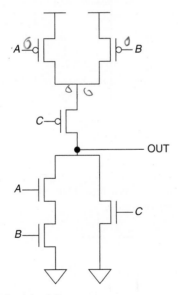

3.5   Complete a truth table for the transistor-level circuit in Figure 3.34.

Figure 3.34   Diagram for Exercise 3.5

3.6   For the transistor-level circuit in Figure 3.35, fill in the truth table. What is Z in terms of A and B?

A	B	C	D	Z
0	0			

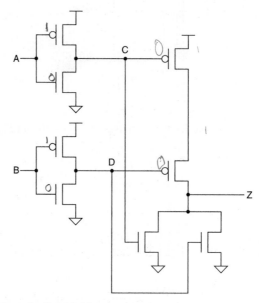

Figure 3.35   Diagram for Exercise 3.6

3.7   The circuit below has a major flaw. Can you identify it? *Hint*: Evaluate the circuit for all sets of inputs.

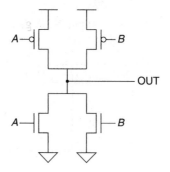

3.8   The transistor-level circuit below implements the logic equation given below. Label the inputs to all the transistors.

Y = NOT (A AND (B OR C))

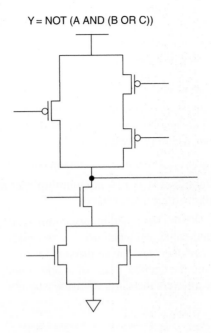

3.9   Fill in the truth table for the logical expression NOT(NOT(A) OR NOT(B)). What single logic gate has the same truth table?

A	B	NOT(NOT(A) OR NOT(B))
0	0	
0	1	
1	0	
1	1	

3.10   Fill in the truth table for a two-input NOR gate.

A	B	A NOR B
0	0	
0	1	
1	0	
1	1	

3.11   *a.* Draw a transistor-level diagram for a three-input AND gate and a three-input OR gate. Do this by extending the designs from Figures 3.6a and 3.7a.

      b. Replace the transistors in your diagrams from part *a* with either a wire or no wire to reflect the circuit's operation when the following inputs are applied.

        (1) $A = 1$, $B = 0$, $C = 0$
        (2) $A = 0$, $B = 0$, $C = 0$
        (3) $A = 1$, $B = 1$, $C = 1$

3.12   Following the example of Figure 3.11a, draw the gate-level schematic of a three-input decoder. For each output of this decoder, write the input conditions under which that output will be 1.

3.13   How many output lines will a five-input decoder have?

3.14   How many output lines will a 16-input multiplexer have? How many select lines will this multiplexer have?

3.15   If A and B are four-bit unsigned binary numbers, 0111 and 1011, complete the table obtained when using a two-bit full adder from Figure 3.15 to calculate each bit of the sum, S, of A and B. Check your answer by adding the decimal value of A and B and comparing the sum with S. Are the answers the same? Why or why not?

C_{in}				0
A	0	1	1	1
B	1	0	1	1
S				
C_{out}				

3.16   Given the following truth table, generate the gate-level logic circuit, using the implementation algorithm referred to in Section 3.3.4.

A	B	C	Z
0	0	0	1
0	0	1	0
0	1	0	0
0	1	1	1
1	0	0	0
1	0	1	1
1	1	0	1
1	1	1	0

3.17 *a.* Given four inputs, A, B, C, and D and one output, Z, create a truth table for a circuit with at least seven input combinations generating 1s at the output. (How many rows will this truth table have?)

b. Now that you have a truth table, generate the gate-level logic circuit that implements this truth table. Use the implementation algorithm referred to in Section 3.3.4.

3.18 Implement the following functions using AND, OR, and NOT logic gates. The inputs are A, B, and the output is F.

a. F has the value 1 only if A has the value 0 and B has the value 1.

b. F has the value 1 only if A has the value 1 and B has the value 0.

c. Use your answers from (a) and (b) to implement a 1-bit adder. The truth table for the 1-bit adder is given below.

A	B	Sum
0	0	0
0	1	1
1	0	1
1	1	0

d. Is it possible to create a 4-bit adder (a circuit that will correctly add two 4-bit quantities) using only four copies of the logic diagram from (c)? If not, what information is missing? *Hint:* When $A = 1$ and $B = 1$, a sum of 0 is produced. What information is not dropped?

3.19 Logic circuit 1 in Figure 3.36 has inputs A, B, C. Logic circuit 2 in Figure 3.37 has inputs A and B. Both logic circuits have an output D. There is a fundamental difference between the behavioral characteristics of these two circuits. What is it? *Hint:* What happens when the voltage at input A goes from 0 to 1 in both circuits?

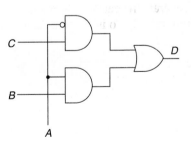

Figure 3.36 Logic circuit 1 for Exercise 3.19

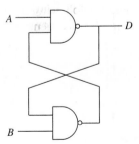

Figure 3.37 Logic circuit 2 for Exercise 3.19

3.20 Generate the gate-level logic that implements the following truth table. From the gate-level structure, generate a transistor diagram that implements the logic structure. Verify that the transistor diagram implements the truth table.

in_0	in_1	$f(in_0, in_1)$
0	0	1
0	1	0
1	0	1
1	1	1

3.21 You know a byte is 8 bits. We call a 4-bit quantity a *nibble*. If a byte-addressable memory has a 14-bit address, how many nibbles of storage are in this memory?

3.22 Implement a 4-to-1 mux using only 2-to-1 muxes making sure to properly connect all of the terminals. Remember that you will have 4 inputs, 2 control signals, and 1 output. Write out the truth table for this circuit.

3.23 Given the logic circuit in Figure 3.38, fill in the truth table for the output value Z.

A	B	C	Z
0	0	0	
0	0	1	
0	1	0	
0	1	1	
1	0	0	
1	0	1	
1	1	0	
1	1	1	

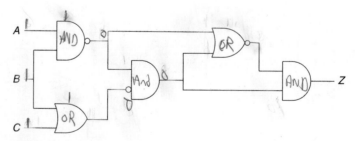

Figure 3.38   Diagram for Exercise 3.23

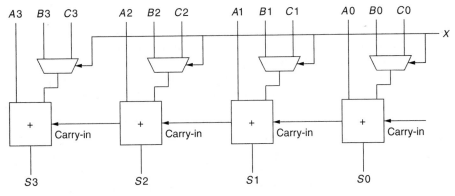

Figure 3.39   Diagram for Exercise 3.24

3.24 *a.* Figure 3.39 shows a logic circuit that appears in many of today's processors. Each of the boxes is a full-adder circuit. What does the value on the wire X do? That is, what is the difference in the output of this circuit if $X = 0$ versus if $X = 1$?

   b. Construct a logic diagram that implements an adder/subtracter. That is, the logic circuit will compute $A + B$ or $A - B$ depending on the value of X. *Hint*: Use the logic diagram of Figure 3.39 as a building block.

3.25 Say the speed of a logic structure depends on the largest number of logic gates through which any of the inputs must propagate to reach an output. Assume that a NOT, an AND, and an OR gate all count as one gate delay. For example, the propagation delay for a two-input decoder shown in Figure 3.11 is 2 because some inputs propagate through two gates.

   a. What is the propagation delay for the two-input mux shown in Figure 3.12?

   b. What is the propagation delay for the 1-bit full adder in Figure 3.15?

   c. What is the propagation delay for the 4-bit adder shown in Figure 3.16?

   d. What if the 4-bit adder were extended to 32 bits?

3.26 Recall that the adder was built with individual "**slices**" that produced a sum bit and carryout bit based on the two operand bits A and B and the carryin bit. We called such an element a full adder. Suppose we have a 3-to-8 decoder and two six-input OR gates, as shown below. Can we connect them so that we have a full adder? If so, please do. (*Hint*: If an input to an OR gate is not needed, we can simply put an input 0 on it and it will have no effect on anything. For example, see the figure below.)

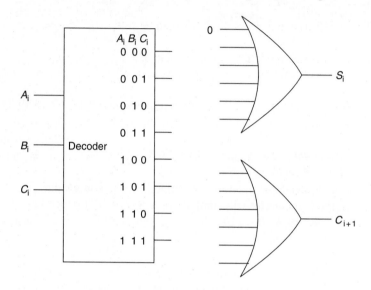

3.27 For this question, refer to the figure below.

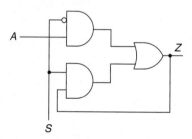

a. Describe the output of this logic circuit when the select line S is a logical 0. That is, what is the output Z for each value of A?

b. If the select line S is switched from a logical 0 to 1, what will the output be?

c. Is this logic circuit a storage element?

3.28 Having designed a binary adder, you are now ready to design a 2-bit by 2-bit unsigned binary multiplier. The multiplier takes two 2-bit inputs A[1:0] and B[1:0] and produces an output Y which is the product of A[1:0] and B[1:0]. The standard notation for this is:

$$Y = A[1:0] \cdot B[1:0]$$

    a. What is the maximum value that can be represented in 2 bits for $A(A[1:0])$?

    b. What is the maximum value that can be represented in 2 bits for $B(B[1:0])$?

    c. What is the maximum possible value of Y?

    d. What is the number of required bits to represent the maximum value of Y?

    e. Write a truth table for the multiplier described above. You will have a four-input truth table with the inputs being A[1], A[0], B[1], and B[0].

    f. Implement the third bit of output, Y[2] from the truth table using only AND, OR, and NOT gates.

3.29 A 16-bit register contains a value. The value x75A2 is written into it. Can the original value be recovered?

3.30   A comparator circuit has two 1-bit inputs A and B and three 1-bit outputs G (greater), E (Equal), and L (less than). Refer to Figures 3.40 and 3.41 for this problem.

G is 1 if $A > B$ E is 1 if $A = B$ L is 1 if $A < B$
0 otherwise   0 otherwise   0 otherwise

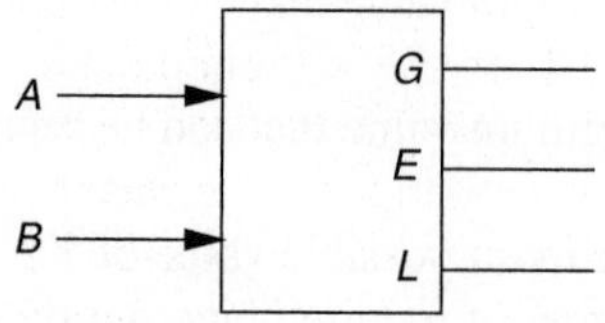

Figure 3.40   Diagram for Exercise 3.30

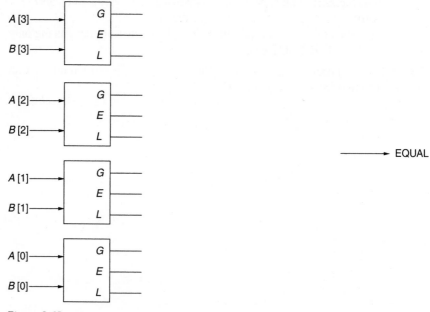

Figure 3.41   Diagram for Exercise 3.30

a. Draw the truth table for a 1-bit comparator.

A	B	G	E	L
0	0			
0	1			
1	0			
1	1			

b. Implement G, E, and L using AND, OR, and NOT gates.
c. Using the 1-bit comparator as a basic building block, construct a four-bit equality checker, such that output EQUAL is 1 if $A[3:0] = B[3:0]$, 0 otherwise.

3.31 If a computer has eight-byte addressability and needs three bits to access a location in memory, what is the total size of memory in bytes?

3.32 Distinguish between a memory address and the memory's addressability.

3.33 Using Figure 3.21, the diagram of the 4-entry, 2^2-by-3-bit memory.

    a. To read from the fourth memory location, what must the values of $A[1:0]$ and WE be?

    b. To change the number of entries in the memory from 4 to 60, how many address lines would be needed? What would the addressability of the memory be after this change was made?

    c. Suppose the minimum width (in bits) of the program counter (the program counter is a special register within a CPU, and we will discuss it in detail in the next chapter) is the minimum number of bits needed to address all 60 locations in our memory from part (b). How many additional memory locations could be added to this memory without having to alter the width of the program counter?

3.34 For the memory shown in Figure 3.42:

    a. What is the address space?

    b. What is the addressability?

    c. What is the data at address 2?

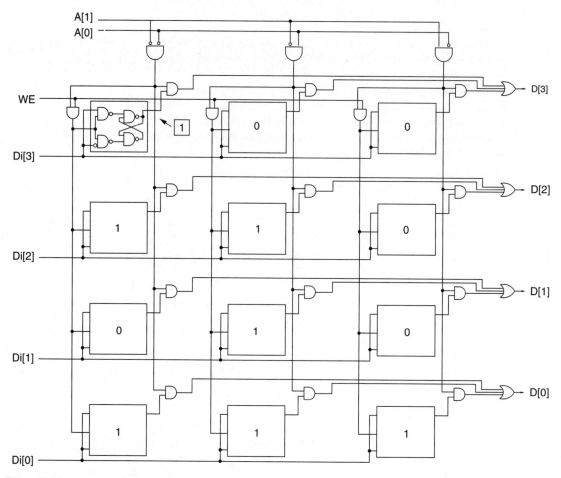

Figure 3.42 Diagram for Exercise 3.34

3.35 Given a memory that is addressed by 22 bits and is 3-bit addressable, how many bits of storage does the memory contain?

3.36 A combinational logic circuit has two inputs. The values of those two inputs during the past ten cycles were 01, 10, 11, 01, 10, 11, 01, 10, 11, and 01. The values of these two inputs during the current cycle are 10. Explain the effect on the current output due to the values of the inputs during the previous ten cycles.

3.37 In the case of the lock of Figure 3.24a, there are four states A, B, C, and D, as described in Section 3.6.2. Either the lock is open (State D), or if it is not open, we have already performed either zero (State A), one (State B), or two (State C) correct operations. This is the sum total of all possible states that can exist. Exercise: Why is that the case? That is, what would be the snapshot of a fifth state that describes a possible situation for the combination lock?

3.38 Recall Section 3.6.2. Can one have an arc from a state where the score is Texas 30, Oklahoma 28 to a state where the score is tied, Texas 30, Oklahoma 30? Draw an example of the scoreboards (like the one in Figure 3.25) for the two states.

3.39 Recall again Section 3.6.2. Is it possible to have two states, one where Texas is ahead 30-28 and the other where the score is tied 30-30, but no arc between the two? Draw an example of two scoreboards, one where the score is 30-28 and the other where the score is 30-30, but there can be no arc between the two. For each of the three output values, game in progress, Texas wins, Oklahoma wins, draw an example of a scoreboard that corresponds to a state that would produce that output.

3.40 Refer to Section 3.6.2. Draw a partial finite state machine for the game of tic-tac-toe.

3.41 The IEEE campus society office sells sodas for 35 cents. Suppose they install a soda controller that only takes the following three inputs: nickel, dime, and quarter. After you put in each coin, you push a pushbutton to register the coin. If at least 35 cents has been put in the controller, it will output a soda and proper change (if applicable). Draw a finite state machine that describes the behavior of the soda controller. Each state will represent how much money has been put in (*Hint*: There will be seven of these states). Once enough money has been put in, the controller will go to a final state where the person will receive a soda and proper change (*Hint*: There are five such final states). From the final state, the next coin that is put in will start the process again.

3.42 Refer to Figure 3.32b. Why are lights 1 and 2 controlled by the output of the OR gate labeled Z? Why is the next state of storage element 2 controlled by the output of the OR gate labeled U?

3.43 Shown in Figure 3.43 is an implementation of a finite state machine with an input X and output Z.

    a. Complete the rest of the following table.
        S1, S0 specifies the present state.
        D1, D0 specifies the next state.

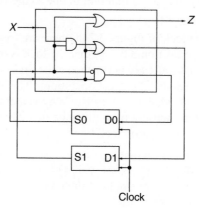

Figure 3.43   Diagram for Exercise 3.43

S1	S0	X	D1	D0	Z
0	0	0			
0	0	1			
0	1	0			
0	1	1	1	0	1
1	0	0			
1	0	1			
1	1	0			
1	1	1			

    b. Draw the state diagram for the truth table from part *a*.

3.44 Prove that the NAND gate, by itself, is logically complete (see Section 3.3.5) by constructing a logic circuit that performs the AND function, a logic circuit that performs the NOT function, and a logic circuit that performs the OR function. Use only NAND gates in these three logic circuits.

4

The von Neumann Model

We are now ready to raise our level of abstraction another notch. We will build on the logic structures that we studied in Chapter 3, both decision elements and storage elements, to construct the basic computer model first proposed by John von Neumann in 1946.

4.1 Basic Components

To get a task done by a computer, we need two things: a computer program that specifies what the computer must to do to complete the task, and the computer itself that is to carry out the task.

A computer program consists of a set of instructions, each specifying a well-defined piece of work for the computer to carry out. The *instruction* is the smallest piece of work specified in a computer program. That is, the computer either carries out the work specified by an instruction or it does not. The computer does not have the luxury of carrying out a piece of an instruction.

John von Neumann proposed a fundamental model of a computer for processing computer programs in 1946. Figure 4.1 shows its basic components. We have taken a little poetic license and added a few of our own minor embellishments to von Neumann's original diagram. The von Neumann model consists of five parts: *memory, a processing unit, input, output*, and *a control unit*. The computer program is contained in the computer's memory. The control of the order in which the instructions are carried out is performed by the control unit.

We will describe each of the five parts of the von Neumann model.

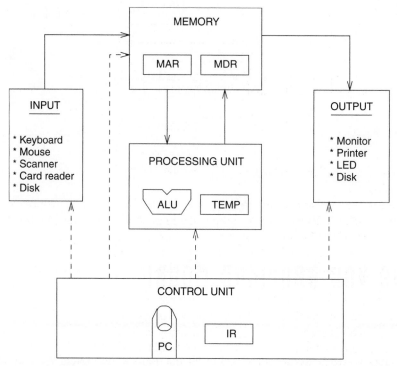

Figure 4.1   The von Neumann model, overall block diagram

4.1.1 Memory

Recall that in Chapter 3 we examined a simple 2^2-by-3-bit memory that was constructed out of gates and latches. A more realistic memory for one of today's computer systems is 2^{28} by 8 bits. That is, a typical memory in today's world of computers consists of 2^{28} distinct memory locations, each of which is capable of storing 8 bits of information. We say that such a memory has an *address space* of 2^{28} uniquely identifiable locations, and an *addressability* of 8 bits. We refer to such a memory as a 256-megabyte memory (abbreviated, 256 MB). The "256 mega" refers to the 2^{28} locations, and the "byte" refers to the 8 bits stored in each location. The term *byte* is, by definition, the word used to describe 8 bits, much the way *gallon* describes four quarts.

We note (as we will note again and again) that with k bits, we can represent uniquely 2^k items. Thus, to uniquely identify 2^{28} memory locations, each location must have its own 28-bit address. In Chapter 5, we will begin the complete definition of the instruction set architecture (ISA) of the LC-3 computer. We will see that the memory address space of the LC-3 is 2^{16}, and the addressability is 16 bits.

Recall from Chapter 3 that we access memory by providing the address from which we wish to read, or to which we wish to write. To read the contents of a memory location, we first place the address of that location in the memory's address register (**MAR**), and then interrogate the computer's memory. The information

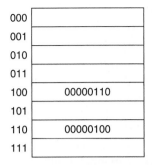

000	
001	
010	
011	
100	00000110
101	
110	00000100
111	

Figure 4.2   Location 6 contains the value 4; location 4 contains the value 6

stored in the location having that address will be placed in the memory's data register (**MDR**). To write (or store) a value in a memory location, we first write the address of the memory location in the MAR, and the value to be stored in the MDR. We then interrogate the computer's memory with the Write Enable signal asserted. The information contained in the MDR will be written into the memory location whose address is in the MAR.

Before we leave the notion of memory for the moment, let us again emphasize the two characteristics of a memory location: its address and what is stored there. Figure 4.2 shows a representation of a memory consisting of eight locations. Its addresses are shown at the left, numbered in binary from 0 to 7. Each location contains 8 bits of information. Note that the value 6 is stored in the memory location whose address is 4, and the value 4 is stored in the memory location whose address is 6. These represent two very different situations.

Finally, an analogy comes to mind: the post office boxes in your local post office. The box number is like the memory location's address. Each box number is unique. The information stored in the memory location is like the letters contained in the post office box. As time goes by, what is contained in the post office box at any particular moment can change. But the box number remains the same. So, too, with each memory location. The value stored in that location can be changed, but the location's memory address remains unchanged.

4.1.2 Processing Unit

The actual processing of information in the computer is carried out by the *processing unit*. The processing unit in a modern computer can consist of many sophisticated complex functional units, each performing one particular operation (divide, square root, etc.). The simplest processing unit, and the one normally thought of when discussing the basic von Neumann model, is the **ALU**. *ALU* is the abbreviation for Arithmetic and Logic Unit, so called because it is usually capable of performing basic arithmetic functions (like ADD and SUBTRACT) and basic logic operations (like bit-wise AND, OR, and NOT that we have already studied in Chapter 2). As we will see in Chapter 5, the LC-3 has an ALU, which can perform ADD, AND, and NOT operations.

The size of the quantities normally processed by the ALU is often referred to as the *word length* of the computer, and each element is referred to as a *word*. In the LC-3, the ALU processes 16-bit quantities. We say the LC-3 has a word length of 16 bits. Each ISA has its own word length, depending on the intended use of the computer. Most microprocessors today that are used in PCs or workstations have a word length of either 32 bits (as is the case with Intel's Pentium IV) or 64 bits (as is the case with Sun's SPARC-V9 processors and Intel's Itanium processor). For some applications, like the microprocessors used in pagers, VCRs, and cellular telephones, 8 bits are usually enough. Such microprocessors, we say, have a word length of 8 bits.

It is almost always the case that a computer provides some small amount of storage very close to the ALU to allow results to be temporarily stored if they will be needed to produce additional results in the near future. For example, if a computer is to calculate $(A + B) \cdot C$, it could store the result of $A + B$ in memory, and then subsequently read it in order to multiply that result by C. However, the time it takes to access memory is long compared to the time it takes to perform the ADD or MULTIPLY. Almost all computers, therefore, have temporary storage for storing the result of $A + B$ in order to avoid the unnecessarily longer access time that would be necessary when it came time to multiply. The most common form of temporary storage is a set of registers, like the register described in Section 3.4.3. Typically, the size of each register is identical to the size of values processed by the ALU, that is, they each contain one word. The LC-3 has eight registers (R0, R1, ... R7), each containing 16 bits. The SPARC-V9 ISA has 32 registers (R0, R1, ... R31), each containing 64 bits.

4.1.3 Input and Output

In order for a computer to process information, the information must get into the computer. In order to use the results of that processing, those results must be displayed in some fashion outside the computer. Many devices exist for the purposes of input and output. They are generically referred to in computer jargon as *peripherals* because they are in some sense accessories to the processing function. Nonetheless, they are no less important.

In the LC-3 we will have the two most basic of input and output devices. For input, we will use the keyboard; for output, we will use the monitor.

There are, of course, many other input and output devices in computer systems today. For input we have among other things the mouse, digital scanners, and floppy disks. For output we have among other things printers, LED displays, and disks. In the old days, much input and output was carried out by punched cards. Fortunately, for those who would have to lug boxes of cards around, the use of punched cards has largely disappeared.

4.1.4 Control Unit

The control unit is like the conductor of an orchestra; it is in charge of making all the other parts play together. As we will see when we describe the step-by-step process of executing a computer program, it is the control unit that keeps track of both where we are within the process of executing the program and where we are in the process of executing each instruction.

To keep track of which instruction is being executed, the control unit has an *instruction register* to contain that instruction. To keep track of which instruction is to be processed next, the control unit has a register that contains the next instruction's address. For historical reasons, that register is called the *program counter* (abbreviated PC), although a better name for it would be the *instruction pointer*, since the contents of this register are, in some sense, "pointing" to the next instruction to be processed. Curiously, Intel does in fact call that register the instruction pointer, but the simple elegance of that name has not caught on.

4.2 The LC-3: An Example von Neumann Machine

In Chapter 5, we will introduce in detail the LC-3, a simple computer that we will study extensively. We have already shown you its data path in Chapter 3 (Figure 3.33) and identified several of its structures in Section 4.1. In this section, we will pull together all the parts of the LC-3 we need to describe it as a von Neumann computer (see Figure 4.3). We constructed Figure 4.3 by starting with the LC-3's full data path (Figure 3.33) and removing all elements that are not essential to pointing out the five basic components of the von Neumann model.

Note that there are two kinds of arrowheads in Figure 4.3: filled-in and not-filled-in. Filled-in arrowheads denote data elements that flow along the corresponding paths. Not-filled-in arrowheads denote control signals that control the processing of the data elements. For example, the box labeled ALU in the processing unit processes two 16-bit values and produces a 16-bit result. The two sources and the result are all data, and are designated by filled-in arrowheads. The operation performed on those two 16-bit data elements (it is labeled ALUK) is part of the control—therefore, a not-filled-in arrowhead.

MEMORY consists of the storage elements, along with the MAR for addressing individual locations and the MDR for holding the contents of a memory location on its way to/from the storage. Note that the MAR contains 16 bits, reflecting the fact that the memory address space of the LC-3 is 2^{16} memory locations. The MDR contains 16 bits, reflecting the fact that each memory location contains 16 bits—that is, that the LC-3 is 16-bit addressable.

INPUT/OUTPUT consists of a keyboard and a monitor. The simplest keyboard requires two registers, a data register (KBDR) for holding the ASCII codes of keys struck, and a status register (KBSR) for maintaining status information about the keys struck. The simplest monitor also requires two registers, one (DDR) for holding the ASCII code of something to be displayed on the screen, and one (DSR) for maintaining associated status information. These input and output registers will be discussed in more detail in Chapter 8.

THE PROCESSING UNIT consists of a functional unit that can perform arithmetic and logic operations (ALU) and eight registers (R0, ... R7) for storing temporary values that will be needed in the near future as operands

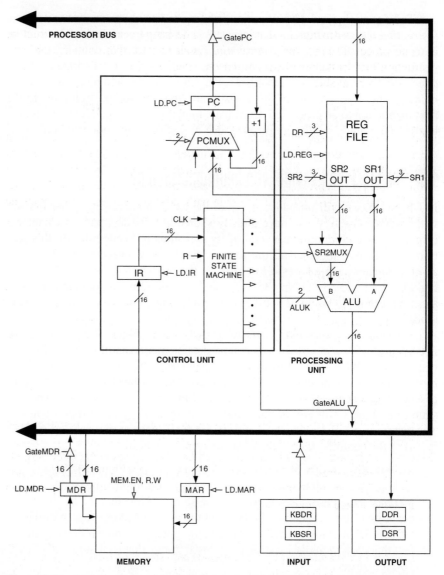

Figure 4.3   The LC-3 as an example of the von Neumann model

for subsequent instructions. The LC-3 ALU can perform one arithmetic operation (addition) and two logical operations (bitwise AND and bitwise complement).

THE CONTROL UNIT consists of all the structures needed to manage the processing that is carried out by the computer. Its most important structure is the finite state machine, which directs all the activity. Recall the finite state machines in Section 3.6. Processing is carried out step by step, or rather, clock cycle by clock cycle. Note the CLK input to the finite state machine in Figure 4.3. It specifies how long each clock cycle lasts. The instruction register (IR) is also an input to the finite state machine since what LC-3 instruction is being processed determines what activities must be carried out. The program counter (PC) is also a part of the control unit; it keeps track of the next instruction to be executed after the current instruction finishes.

Note that all the external outputs of the finite state machine in Figure 4.3 have arrowheads that are not filled in. These outputs control the processing throughout the computer. For example, one of these outputs (two bits) is ALUK, which controls the operation performed in the ALU (add, and, or not) during the current clock cycle. Another output is GateALU, which determines whether or not the output of the ALU is provided to the processor bus during the current clock cycle.

The complete description of the data path, control, and finite state machine for one implementation of the LC-3 is the subject of Appendix C.

4.3 Instruction Processing

The central idea in the von Neumann model of computer processing is that the program and data are both stored as sequences of bits in the computer's memory, and the program is executed one instruction at a time under the direction of the control unit.

4.3.1 The Instruction

The most basic unit of computer processing is the instruction. It is made up of two parts, the *opcode* (what the instruction does) and the *operands* (who it is to do it to). In Chapter 5, we will see that each LC-3 instruction consists of 16 bits (one word), numbered from left to right, bit [15] to bit [0]. Bits [15:12] contain the opcode. This means there are at most 2^4 distinct opcodes. Bits [11:0] are used to figure out where the operands are.

The ADD Instruction   The ADD instruction requires three operands: two source operands (the data that is to be added) and one destination operand (the sum that is to be stored after the addition is performed). We said that the processing unit of the LC-3 contained eight registers for purposes of storing data that may be needed later. In fact, the ADD instruction **requires** that at least one of the two source operands (and often both) is contained in one of these registers, and that the result of the ADD is put into one of these eight registers. Since there are eight registers, three bits are necessary to identify each register. Thus the 16-bit LC-3 ADD instruction has the following form (we say *format*):

Example 4.1

15	14	13	12	11	10	9	8	7	6	5	4	3	2	1	0
0	0	0	1	1	1	0	0	1	0	0	0	0	1	1	0

| | ADD | | | R6 | | | R2 | | | | R6 | |

The 4-bit opcode for ADD, contained in bits [15:12], is 0001. Bits [11:9] identify the location to be used for storing the result, in this case register 6 (R6). Bits [8:6] and bits [2:0] identify the registers to be used to obtain the source operands, in this case R2 and R6. Bits [5:3] have a purpose that it is not necessary to understand in the context of this example. We will save the explanation of bits [5:3] for Section 5.2.

Thus, the instruction we have just encoded is interpreted, "Add the contents of register 2 (R2) to the contents of register 6 (R6) and store the result back into register 6 (R6)."

Example 4.2   **The LDR Instruction**   The LDR instruction requires two operands. *LD* stands for load, which is computerese for "go to a particular memory location, read the value that is contained there, and store it in one of the registers." The two operands that are required are the value to be read from memory and the destination register, which will contain that value after the instruction is processed. The *R* in LDR identifies the mechanism that will be used to calculate the address of the memory location to be read. That mechanism is called the *addressing mode*, and the particular addressing mode identified by the use of the letter *R* is called **Base+offset**. Thus, the 16-bit LC-3 LDR instruction has the following format:

15	14	13	12	11	10	9	8	7	6	5	4	3	2	1	0
0	1	1	0	0	1	0	0	1	1	0	0	0	1	1	0
	LDR				R2			R3					6		

The four-bit opcode for LDR is 0110. Bits [11:9] identify the register that will contain the value read from memory after the instruction is executed. Bits [8:0] are used to calculate the address of the location to be read. In particular, since the addressing mode is BASE+offset, this address is computed by adding the 2's complement integer contained in bits [5:0] of the instruction to the contents of the register specified by bits [8:6]. Thus, the instruction we have just encoded is interpreted: "Add the contents of R3 to the value 6 to form the address of a memory location. Load the contents stored in that memory location into R2."

4.3.2 The Instruction Cycle

Instructions are processed under the direction of the control unit in a very systematic, step-by-step manner. The sequence of steps is called the *instruction cycle*, and each step is referred to as a *phase*. There are fundamentally six phases to the instruction cycle, although many computers have been designed such that not all instructions require all six phases. We will discuss this momentarily.

But first, we will examine the six phases of the instruction cycle:

```
FETCH
DECODE
EVALUATE ADDRESS
FETCH OPERANDS
```

```
EXECUTE
STORE RESULT
```

The process is as follows (again refer to Figure 4.3, our simplified version of the LC-3 data path):

FETCH

The FETCH phase obtains the next instruction from memory and loads it into the instruction register (IR) of the control unit. Recall that a computer program consists of a collection of instructions, that each instruction is represented by a sequence of bits, and that the entire program (in the von Neumann model) is stored in the computer's memory. In order to carry out the work of the next instruction, we must first identify where it is. The program counter (PC) contains the address of the next instruction. Thus, the FETCH phase takes multiple steps:

```
First the MAR is loaded with the contents of the PC.
Next, the memory is interrogated, which results
in the next instruction being placed by the memory
into the MDR.
Finally, the IR is loaded with the contents
of the MDR.
```

We are now ready for the next phase, decoding the instruction. However, when the instruction cycle is complete, and we wish to fetch the next instruction, we would like the PC to contain the address of the next instruction. Therefore, one more step the FETCH phase must perform is to increment the PC. In that way, at the completion of the execution of this instruction, the FETCH phase of the next instruction will load into IR the contents of the next memory location, provided the execution of the current instruction does not involve changing the value in the PC.

The complete description of the FETCH phase is as follows:

```
Step 1:  Load the MAR with the contents of the PC, and
         simultaneously increment the PC.
Step 2:  Interrogate memory, resulting in the instruction
         being placed in the MDR.
Step 3:  Load the IR with the contents of the MDR.
```

Each of these steps is under the direction of the control unit, much like, as we said previously, the instruments in an orchestra are under the control of a conductor's baton. Each stroke of the conductor's baton corresponds to one *machine cycle*. We will see in Section 4.4.1 that the amount of time taken by each machine cycle is one clock cycle. In fact, we often use the two terms interchangeably. Step 1 takes one machine cycle. Step 2 could take one machine cycle, or many machine cycles, depending on how long it takes to access the computer's memory. Step 3 takes one machine cycle. In a modern digital computer, a machine cycle takes a very small fraction of a second. Indeed, a 3.3-GHz Intel Pentium IV completes 3.3. billion machine cycles (or clock cycles) in one second. Said another way, one machine cycle (or clock cycle) takes 0.303 billionths of a second (0.303 nanoseconds). Recall that the light bulb that is helping you read this text is switching on and off at the rate of 60 times a second. Thus, in the time it takes a light bulb to switch on and off once, today's computers can complete 55 million machine cycles!

DECODE

The DECODE phase examines the instruction in order to figure out what the microarchitecture is being asked to do. Recall the decoders we studied in Chapter 3. In the LC-3, a 4-to-16 decoder identifies which of the 16 opcodes is to be processed. Input is the four-bit opcode IR[15:12]. The output line asserted is the one corresponding to the opcode at the input. Depending on which output of the decoder is asserted, the remaining 12 bits identify what else is needed to process that instruction.

EVALUATE ADDRESS

This phase computes the address of the memory location that is needed to process the instruction. Recall the example of the LDR instruction: The LDR instruction causes a value stored in memory to be loaded into a register. In that example, the address was obtained by adding the value 6 to the contents of R3. This calculation was performed during the EVALUATE ADDRESS phase.

FETCH OPERANDS

This phase obtains the source operands needed to process the instruction. In the LDR example, this phase took two steps: loading MAR with the address calculated in the EVALUATE ADDRESS phase, and reading memory, which resulted in the source operand being placed in MDR.

In the ADD example, this phase consisted of obtaining the source operands from R2 and R6. (In most current microprocessors, this phase [for the ADD instruction] can be done at the same time the instruction is being decoded. Exactly how we can speed up the processing of an instruction in this way is a fascinating subject, but one we are forced to leave for later in your education.)

EXECUTE

This phase carries out the execution of the instruction. In the ADD example, this phase consisted of the single step of performing the addition in the ALU.

STORE RESULT

The final phase of an instruction's execution. The result is written to its designated destination.

Once the sixth phase (STORE RESULT) has been completed, the control unit begins anew the instruction cycle, starting from the top with the FETCH phase.

Since the PC was updated during the previous instruction cycle, it contains at this point the address of the instruction stored in the next sequential memory location. Thus the next sequential instruction is fetched next. Processing continues in this way until something breaks this sequential flow.

ADD [eax], edx   This is an example of an Intel x86 instruction that requires all six phases of the instruction cycle. All instructions require the first two phases, FETCH and DECODE. This instruction uses the eax register to calculate the address of a memory location (EVALUATE ADDRESS). The contents of that memory location are then read (FETCH OPERAND), added to the contents of the edx register (EXECUTE), and the result written into the memory location that originally contained the first source operand (STORE RESULT).

The LC-3 ADD and LDR instructions do not require all six phases. In particular, the ADD instruction does not require an EVALUATE ADDRESS phase. The LDR instruction does not require an EXECUTE phase.

4.4 Changing the Sequence of Execution

Everything we have said thus far suggests that a computer program is executed in sequence. That is, the first instruction is executed, then the second instruction is executed, followed by the third instruction, and so on.

We have identified two types of instructions, the ADD, which is an example of an *operate instruction* in that it processes data, and the LDR, which is an example of a *data movement instruction* in that it moves data from one place to another. There are other examples of both operate instructions and data movement instructions, as we will discover in Chapter 5 when we study the LC-3 in detail.

There is a third type of instruction, the *control instruction*, whose purpose is to change the sequence of instruction execution. For example, there are times, as we shall see, when it is desirable to first execute the first instruction, then the second, then the third, then the first again, the second again, then the third again, then the first for the third time, the second for the third time, and so on. As we know, each instruction cycle starts with loading the MAR with the PC. Thus, if we wish to change the sequence of instructions executed, we must change the PC between the time it is incremented (during the FETCH phase of one instruction) and the start of the FETCH phase of the next.

Control instructions perform that function by loading the PC during the EXECUTE phase, which wipes out the incremented PC that was loaded during the FETCH phase. The result is that, at the start of the next instruction cycle, when the computer accesses the PC to obtain the address of an instruction to fetch, it will get the address loaded during the previous EXECUTE phase, rather than the next sequential instruction in the computer's program.

| Example 4.5 | **The JMP Instruction**   Consider the LC-3 instruction JMP, whose format follows. Assume this instruction is stored in memory location x36A2. |

15	14	13	12	11	10	9	8	7	6	5	4	3	2	1	0
1	1	0	0	0	0	0	1	1	0	0	0	0	0	0	0

JMP   R3

The 4-bit opcode for JMP is 1100. Bits [8:6] specify the register which contains the address of the next instruction to be processed. Thus, the instruction encoded here is interpreted, "Load the PC (during the EXECUTE phase) with the contents of R3 so that the next instruction processed will be the one at the address obtained from R3."

Processing will go on as follows. Let's start at the beginning of the instruction cycle, with PC = x36A2. The FETCH phase results in the IR being loaded with the JMP instruction and the PC updated to contain the address x36A3. Suppose the content of R3 at the start of this instruction is x5446. During the EXECUTE phase, the PC is loaded with x5446. Therefore, in the next instruction cycle, the instruction processed will be the one at address x5446, rather than the one at address x36A3.

4.4.1 Control of the Instruction Cycle

We have described the instruction cycle as consisting of six phases, each of which has some number of steps. We also noted that one of the six phases, FETCH, required the three sequential steps of loading the MAR with the contents of the PC, reading memory, and loading the IR with the contents of the MDR. Each step of the FETCH phase, and indeed, each step of every operation in the computer is controlled by the finite state machine in the control unit.

Figure 4.4 shows a very abbreviated part of the state diagram corresponding to the finite state machine that directs all phases of the instruction cycle. As is the case with the finite state machines studied in Section 3.6, each state corresponds to one clock cycle of activity. The processing controlled by each state is described within the node representing that state. The arcs show the next state transitions.

Processing starts with state 1. The FETCH phase takes three clock cycles. In the first clock cycle, the MAR is loaded with the contents of the PC, and the PC is incremented. In order for the contents of the PC to be loaded into the MAR (see Figure 4.3), the finite state machine must assert GatePC and LD.MAR. GatePC connects the PC to the processor bus. LD.MAR, the write enable signal of the MAR register, latches the contents of the bus into the MAR at the end of the current clock cycle. (Latches are loaded at the end of the clock cycle if the corresponding control signal is asserted.)

In order for the PC to be incremented (again, see Figure 4.3), the finite state machine must assert the PCMUX select lines to choose the output of the box labeled +1 and must also assert the LD.PC signal to latch the output of the PCMUX at the end of the current cycle.

The finite state machine then goes to state 2. Here, the MDR is loaded with the instruction, which is read from memory.

In state 3, the data is transferred from MDR to the instruction register (IR). This requires the finite state machine to assert GateMDR and LD.IR, which causes

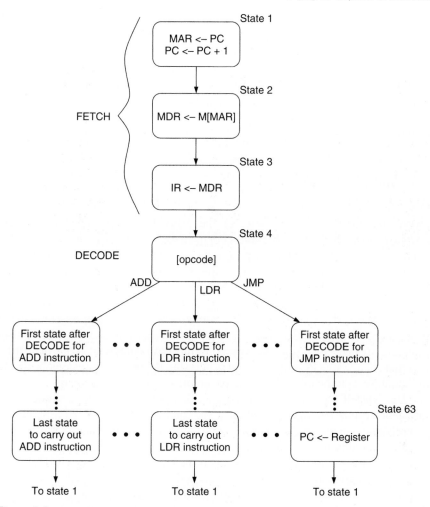

Figure 4.4   An abbreviated state diagram of the LC-3

the IR to be latched at the end of the clock cycle, concluding the FETCH phase of the instruction.

The DECODE phase takes one cycle. In state 4, using the external input IR, and in particular the opcode bits of the instruction, the finite state machine can go to the appropriate next state for processing instructions depending on the particular opcode in IR[15:12]. Processing continues cycle by cycle until the instruction completes execution, and the next state logic returns the finite state machine to state 1.

As we mentioned earlier in this section, it is sometimes necessary not to execute the next sequential instruction but rather to jump to another location to find the next instruction to execute. As we have said, instructions that change the flow of instruction processing in this way are called control instructions. This can be done very easily by loading the PC during the EXECUTE phase of the control instruction, as in state 63 of Figure 4.4, for example.

Appendix C contains a full description of the implementation of the LC-3, including its full state diagram and data path. We will not go into that level of detail in this chapter. Our objective here is to show you that there is nothing magic about the processing of the instruction cycle, and that a properly completed state diagram would be able to control, clock cycle by clock cycle, all the steps required to execute all the phases of every instruction cycle. Since each instruction cycle ends by returning to state 1, the finite state machine can process, cycle by cycle, a complete computer program.

4.5 Stopping the Computer

From everything we have said, it appears that the computer will continue processing instructions, carrying out the instruction cycle again and again, *ad nauseum*. Since the computer does not have the capacity to be bored, must this continue until someone pulls the plug and disconnects power to the computer?

Usually, user programs execute under the control of an operating system. UNIX, DOS, MacOS, and Windows NT are all examples of operating systems. Operating systems are just computer programs themselves. So as far as the computer is concerned, the instruction cycle continues whether a user program is being processed or the operating system is being processed. This is fine as far as user programs are concerned since each user program terminates with a control instruction that changes the PC to again start processing the operating system—often to initiate the execution of another user program.

But what if we actually want to stop this potentially infinite sequence of instruction cycles? Recall our analogy to the conductor's baton, beating at the rate of millions of machine cycles per second. Stopping the instruction sequencing requires stopping the conductor's baton. We have pointed out many times that there is, inside the computer, a component that corresponds very closely to the conductor's baton. It is called the **clock**, and it defines the machine cycle. It enables the finite state machine to continue on to the next machine cycle, whether that machine cycle is the next step of the current phase or the first step of the next phase of the instruction cycle. Stopping the instruction cycle requires stopping the clock.

Figure 4.5a shows a block diagram of the clock circuit, consisting primarily of a clock generator and a RUN latch. The clock generator is a crystal oscillator, a piezoelectric device that you may have studied in your physics or chemistry class. For our purposes, the crystal oscillator is a black box (recall our definition of black

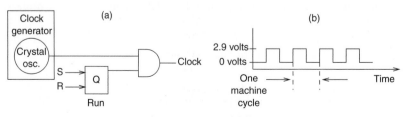

Figure 4.5   The clock circuit and its control

box in Section 1.4) that produces the oscillating voltage shown in Figure 4.5b. Note the resemblance of that voltage to the conductor's baton. Every machine cycle, the voltage rises to 2.9 volts and then drops back to 0 volts.

If the RUN latch is in the 1 state (i.e., $Q = 1$), the output of the clock circuit is the same as the output of the clock generator. If the RUN latch is in the 0 state (i.e., $Q = 0$), the output of the clock circuit is 0.

Thus, stopping the instruction cycle requires only clearing the RUN latch. Every computer has some mechanism for doing that. In some older machines, it is done by executing a HALT instruction. In the LC-3, as in many other machines, it is done under control of the operating system, as we will see in Chapter 9.

Question: If a HALT instruction can clear the RUN latch, thereby stopping the instruction cycle, what instruction is needed to set the RUN latch, thereby reinitiating the instruction cycle?

Exercises

4.1   Name the five components of the von Neumann model. For each component, state its purpose.

4.2   Briefly describe the interface between the memory and the processing unit. That is, describe the method by which the memory and the processing unit communicate.

4.3   What is misleading about the name *program counter*? Why is the name *instruction pointer* more insightful?

4.4   What is the word length of a computer? How does the word length of a computer affect what the computer is able to compute? That is, is it a valid argument, in light of what you learned in Chapter 1, to say that a computer with a larger word size can process more information and therefore is capable of computing more than a computer with a smaller word size?

4.5   The following table represents a small memory. Refer to this table for the following questions.

Address	Data
0000	0001 1110 0100 0011
0001	1111 0000 0010 0101
0010	0110 1111 0000 0001
0011	0000 0000 0000 0000
0100	0000 0000 0110 0101
0101	0000 0000 0000 0110
0110	1111 1110 1101 0011
0111	0000 0110 1101 1001

    a. What binary value does location 3 contain? Location 6?

    b. The binary value within each location can be interpreted in many ways. We have seen that binary values can represent unsigned numbers, 2's complement signed numbers, floating point numbers, and so forth.

      (1) Interpret location 0 and location 1 as 2's complement integers.

      (2) Interpret location 4 as an ASCII value.

      (3) Interpret locations 6 and 7 as an IEEE floating point number. Location 6 contains number [15:0]. Location 7 contains number [31:16].

      (4) Interpret location 0 and location 1 as unsigned integers.

    c. In the von Neumann model, the contents of a memory location can also be an instruction. If the binary pattern in location 0 were interpreted as an instruction, what instruction would it represent?

    d. A binary value can also be interpreted as a memory address. Say the value stored in location 5 is a memory address. To which location does it refer? What binary value does that location contain?

4.6 What are the two components of an instruction? What information do these two components contain?

4.7 Suppose a 32-bit instruction takes the following format:

OPCODE	SR	DR	IMM

If there are 60 opcodes and 32 registers, what is the range of values that can be represented by the immediate (IMM)? Assume IMM is a 2's complement value.

4.8 Suppose a 32-bit instruction takes the following format:

OPCODE	DR	SR1	SR2	UNUSED

If there are 225 opcodes and 120 registers,

    a. What is the minimum number of bits required to represent the OPCODE?

    b. What is the minimum number of bits required to represent the Destination Register (DR)?

    c. What is maximum number of UNUSED bits in the instruction encoding?

4.9 The FETCH phase of the instruction cycle does two important things. One is that it loads the instruction to be processed next into the IR. What is the other important thing?

4.10 Examples 4.1, 4.2, and 4.5 illustrate the processing of the ADD, LDR, and JMP instructions. The PC, IR, MAR, and MDR are written in various phases of the instruction cycle, depending on the opcode of the particular instruction. In each location in the table below, enter the opcodes which write to the corresponding register (row) during the corresponding phase (column) of the instruction cycle.

	Fetch Instruction	Decode	Evaluate Address	Fetch Data	Execute	Store Result
PC						
IR						
MAR						
MDR						

4.11 State the phases of the instruction cycle and briefly describe what operations occur in each phase.

4.12 For the instructions ADD, LDR, and JMP, write the operations that occur in each phase of the instruction cycle.

4.13 Say it takes 100 cycles to read from or write to memory and only one cycle to read from or write to a register. Calculate the number of cycles it takes for each phase of the instruction cycle for both the IA-32 instruction "ADD [eax], edx" (refer to Example 4.3) and the LC-3 instruction "ADD R6, R2, R6." Assume each phase (if required) takes one cycle, unless a memory access is required.

4.14 Describe the execution of the JMP instruction if R3 contains x369C (refer to Example 4.5).

4.15 If a HALT instruction can clear the RUN latch, thereby stopping the instruction cycle, what instruction is needed to set the RUN latch, thereby reinitiating the instruction cycle?

4.16 *a.* If a machine cycle is 2 nanoseconds (i.e., $2 \cdot 10^{-9}$ seconds), how many machine cycles occur each second?

    b. If the computer requires on the average eight cycles to process each instruction, and the computer processes instructions one at a time from beginning to end, how many instructions can the computer process in 1 second?

    c. Preview of future courses: In today's microprocessors, many features are added to increase the number of instructions processed each second. One such feature is the computer's equivalent of an assembly line. Each phase of the instruction cycle is implemented as one or more separate pieces of logic. Each step in the processing of an instruction picks up where the previous step left off in the previous machine cycle. Using this feature, an instruction can be fetched from memory every machine cycle and handed off at the end of the machine cycle to the decoder, which performs the decoding function during the next machine cycle while the next instruction is being fetched. Ergo, the assembly line. Assuming instructions are located at sequential addresses in memory, and nothing breaks the sequential flow, how many instructions can the microprocessor execute each second if the assembly line is present? (The assembly line is called a pipeline, which you will encounter in your advanced courses. There are many reasons why the assembly line cannot operate at its maximum rate, a topic you will consider at length in some of these courses.)

chapter

5

The LC-3

In Chapter 4, we discussed the basic components of a computer—its memory, its processing unit, including the associated temporary storage (usually a set of registers), input and output devices, and the control unit that directs the activity of all the units (including itself!). We also studied the six phases of the instruction cycle—FETCH, DECODE, ADDRESS EVALUATION, OPERAND FETCH, EXECUTE, and STORE RESULT. We are now ready to introduce a "real" computer, the LC-3. To be more nearly exact, we are ready to introduce the instruction set architecture (ISA) of the LC-3. We have already teased you with a few facts about the LC-3 and a few of its instructions. Now we will examine the ISA of the LC-3 in a more comprehensive way.

Recall from Chapter 1 that the ISA is the interface between what the software commands and what the hardware actually carries out. In this chapter and in Chapters 8 and 9, we will point out the important features of the ISA of the LC-3. You will need these features to write programs in the LC-3's own language, that is, in the LC-3's *machine language*.

A complete description of the ISA of the LC-3 is contained in Appendix A.

5.1 The ISA: Overview

The ISA specifies all the information about the computer that the software has to be aware of. In other words, the ISA specifies everything in the computer that is available to a programmer when he/she writes programs in the computer's own machine language. Thus, the ISA also specifies everything in the computer that is available to someone who wishes to translate programs written in a high-level language like C or Pascal or Fortran or COBOL into the machine language of the computer.

The ISA specifies the memory organization, register set, and instruction set, including opcodes, data types, and addressing modes.

5.1.1 Memory Organization

The LC-3 memory has an address space of 2^{16} (i.e., 65,536) locations, and an addressability of 16 bits. Not all 65,536 addresses are actually used for memory locations, but we will leave that discussion for Chapter 8. Since the normal unit of data that is processed in the LC-3 is 16 bits, we refer to 16 bits as one *word*, and we say the LC-3 is *word-addressable*.

5.1.2 Registers

Since it usually takes far more than one machine cycle to obtain data from memory, the LC-3 provides (like almost all computers) additional temporary storage locations that can be accessed in a single machine cycle.

The most common type of temporary storage locations and the one used in the LC-3 is the general purpose register set. Each register in the set is called a *general purpose register* (GPR). Registers have the same property as memory locations in that they are used to store information that can be retrieved later. The number of bits stored in each register is usually one word. In the LC-3, this means 16 bits.

Registers must be uniquely identifiable. The LC-3 specifies eight GPRs, each identified by a 3-bit register number. They are referred to as R0, R1, ... R7. Figure 5.1 shows a snapshot of the LC-3's register set, sometimes called a *register file*, with the eight values 1, 3, 5, 7, −2, −4, −6, and −8 stored in R0, ... R7, respectively.

Register 0	(R0)	0000000000000001
Register 1	(R1)	0000000000000011
Register 2	(R2)	0000000000000101
Register 3	(R3)	0000000000000111
Register 4	(R4)	1111111111111110
Register 5	(R5)	1111111111111100
Register 6	(R6)	1111111111111010
Register 7	(R7)	1111111111111000

Figure 5.1   The register file before the ADD instruction

Register 0	(R0)	0000000000000001
Register 1	(R1)	0000000000000011
Register 2	(R2)	0000000000000100
Register 3	(R3)	0000000000000111
Register 4	(R4)	1111111111111110
Register 5	(R5)	1111111111111100
Register 6	(R6)	1111111111111010
Register 7	(R7)	1111111111111000

Figure 5.2   The register file after the ADD instruction

Recall that the instruction to ADD the contents of R0 to R1 and store the result in R2 is specified as

15	14	13	12	11	10	9	8	7	6	5	4	3	2	1	0
0	0	0	1	0	1	0	0	0	0	0	0	0	0	0	1

$$\underbrace{\quad}_{ADD}\qquad\underbrace{\quad}_{R2}\qquad\underbrace{\quad}_{R0}\qquad\qquad\underbrace{\quad}_{R1}$$

where the two *sources* of the ADD instruction are specified in bits [8:6] and bits [2:0]. The *destination* of the ADD result is specified in bits [11:9]. Figure 5.2 shows the contents of the register file of Figure 5.1 AFTER the instruction ADD R2, R1, R0 is executed.

5.1.3 The Instruction Set

An instruction is made up of two things, its *opcode* (what the instruction is asking the computer to do) and its *operands* (who the computer is expected to do it to). The instruction set of an ISA is defined by its set of opcodes, *data types*, and *addressing modes*. The addressing modes determine where the operands are located.

You have just seen an example of one opcode ADD and one addressing mode *register mode*. The operation the instruction is asking the computer to perform is 2's complement integer addition, and the locations where the computer is expected to find the operands are the general purpose registers.

5.1.4 Opcodes

Some ISAs have a very large set of opcodes, one for each of a large number of tasks that a program may wish to carry out. Other ISAs have a very small set of opcodes. Some ISAs have specific opcodes to help with processing scientific calculations. For example, the Hewlett Packard *Precision Architecture* has an instruction that performs a multiply, followed by an add $(A \cdot B) + C$ on three source operands. Other ISAs have instructions that process video images obtained from the World Wide Web. The Intel x86 ISA added a number of instructions Intel calls *MMX instructions* because they e**X**tend the ISA to assist with **M**ulti**M**edia applications that use the Web. Still other ISAs have specific opcodes to help with handling the tasks of the operating system. For example, the VAX architecture, popular in the 1980s, had an opcode to save all the information associated with one program that was running prior to switching to another program. Almost all computers prefer to use a long sequence of instructions to ask the computer to carry out the task of saving all that information. Although that sounds counterintuitive, there is a rationale for it. Unfortunately, the topic will have to wait for a later semester. The decision as to which instructions to include or leave out of an ISA is usually a hotly debated topic in a company when a new ISA is being specified.

The LC-3 ISA has 15 instructions, each identified by its unique opcode. The opcode is specified by bits [15:12] of the instruction. Since four bits are used to specify the opcode, 16 distinct opcodes are possible. However, the LC-3 ISA specifies only 15 opcodes. The code 1101 has been left unspecified, reserved for some future need that we are not able to anticipate today.

There are three different types of instructions, which means three different types of opcodes: *operates*, *data movement*, and *control*. Operate instructions process information. Data movement instructions move information between memory and the registers and between registers/memory and input/output devices. Control instructions change the sequence of instructions that will be executed. That is, they enable the execution of an instruction other than the one that is stored in the next sequential location in memory.

Figure 5.3 lists all the instructions of the LC-3, the bit encoding [15:12] for each opcode, and the format of each instruction. The use of these formats will be further explained in Sections 5.2, 5.3, and 5.4.

5.1.5 Data Types

A *data type* is a representation of information such that the ISA has opcodes that operate on that representation. There are many ways to represent the same information in a computer. That should not surprise us. In our daily lives, we regularly represent the same information in many different ways. For example, a child, when asked how old he is, might hold up three fingers, signifying he is 3 years old. If the child is particularly precocious, he might write the decimal digit *3* to indicate his age. Or, if he is a CS or CE major at the university, he might write 0000000000000011, the 16-bit binary representation for 3. If he is a chemistry major, he might write $3.0 \cdot 10^0$. All four represent the same entity: 3.

If the ISA has an opcode that operates on information represented by a data type, then we say the ISA **supports** that data type. In Chapter 2, we introduced the only data type supported by the ISA of the LC-3: 2's complement integers.

5.1.6 Addressing Modes

An addressing mode is a mechanism for specifying where the operand is located. An operand can generally be found in one of three places: in memory, in a register, or as a part of the instruction. If the operand is a part of the instruction, we refer to it as a *literal* or as an *immediate* operand. The term *literal* comes from the

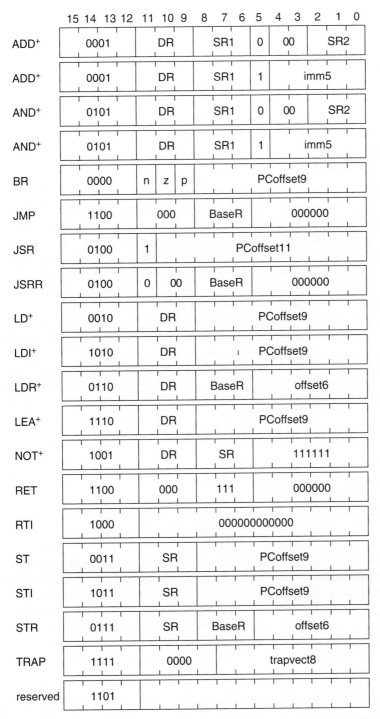

Figure 5.3   Formats of the entire LC-3 instruction set. NOTE: $^+$ indicates instructions that modify condition codes

fact that the bits of the instruction literally form the operand. The term *immediate* comes from the fact that we have the operand immediately, that is, we don't have to look elsewhere for it.

The LC-3 supports five addressing modes: immediate (or literal), register, and three memory addressing modes: *PC-relative*, *indirect*, and *Base+offset*. We will see in Section 5.2 that operate instructions use two addressing modes: register and immediate. We will see in Section 5.3 that data movement instructions use all five modes.

5.1.7 Condition Codes

One final item will complete our overview of the ISA of the LC-3: condition codes. Almost all ISAs allow the instruction sequencing to change on the basis of a previously generated result. The LC-3 has three single-bit registers that are set (set to 1) or cleared (set to 0) each time one of the eight general purpose registers is written. The three single-bit registers are called N, Z, and P, corresponding to their meaning: negative, zero, and positive. Each time a GPR is written, the N, Z, and P registers are individually set to 0 or 1, corresponding to whether the result written to the GPR is negative, zero, or positive. That is, if the result is negative, the N register is set, and Z and P are cleared. If the result is zero, Z is set and N and P are cleared. Finally, if the result is positive, P is set and N and Z are cleared.

Each of the three single-bit registers is referred to as a *condition code* because the condition of that bit can be used by one of the control instructions to change the execution sequence. The x86 and SPARC are two examples of ISAs that use condition codes to do this. We show how the LC-3 does it in Section 5.4.

5.2 Operate Instructions

Operate instructions process data. Arithmetic operations (like ADD, SUB, MUL, and DIV) and logical operations (like AND, OR, NOT, XOR) are common examples. The LC-3 has three operate instructions: ADD, AND, and NOT.

The **NOT** (opcode = 1001) instruction is the only operate instruction that performs a *unary* operation, that is, the operation requires one source operand. The NOT instruction bit-wise complements a 16-bit source operand and stores the result of this operation in a destination. NOT uses the register addressing mode for both its source and destination. Bits [8:6] specify the source register and bits [11:9] specify the destination register. Bits [5:0] must contain all 1s.

If R5 initially contains 0101000011110000, after executing the following instruction:

15	14	13	12	11	10	9	8	7	6	5	4	3	2	1	0
1	0	0	1	0	1	1	1	0	1	1	1	1	1	1	1
NOT				R3			R5								

R3 will contain 1010111100001111.

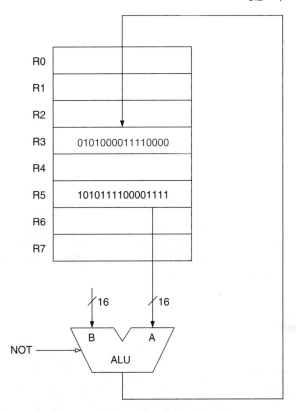

R0	
R1	
R2	
R3	0101000011110000
R4	
R5	1010111100001111
R6	
R7	

Figure 5.4 Data path relevant to the execution of NOT R3, R5

Figure 5.4 shows the key parts of the data path that are used to perform the NOT instruction shown here. Since NOT is a unary operation, only the A input of the ALU is relevant. It is sourced from R5. The control signal to the ALU directs the ALU to perform the bit-wise complement operation. The output of the ALU (the result of the operation) is stored into R3.

The **ADD** (opcode = 0001) and **AND** (opcode = 0101) instructions both perform *binary* operations; they require two 16-bit source operands. The ADD instruction performs a 2's complement addition of its two source operands. The AND instruction performs a bit-wise AND of each pair of bits in its two 16-bit operands. Like the NOT, the ADD and AND use the register addressing mode for one of the source operands and for the destination operand. Bits [8:6] specify the source register and bits [11:9] specify the destination register (where the result will be written).

The second source operand for both ADD and AND instructions can be specified by either register mode or as an immediate operand. Bit [5] determines which is used. If bit [5] is 0, then the second source operand uses a register, and bits [2:0] specify which register. In that case, bits [4:3] are set to 0 to complete the specification of the instruction.

For example, if R4 contains the value 6 and R5 contains the value −18, then after the following instruction is executed

15	14	13	12	11	10	9	8	7	6	5	4	3	2	1	0
0	0	0	1	0	0	1	1	0	0	0	0	0	1	0	1

    ADD   R1   R4   R5

R1 will contain the value −12.

If bit [5] is 1, the second source operand is contained within the instruction. In fact, the second source operand is obtained by sign-extending bits [4:0] to 16 bits before performing the ADD or AND. Figure 5.5 shows the key parts of the data path that are used to perform the instruction ADD R1, R4, #−2.

Since the immediate operand in an ADD or AND instruction must fit in bits [4:0] of the instruction, not all 2's complement integers can be immediate operands. Which integers are OK (i.e., which integers can be used as immediate operands)?

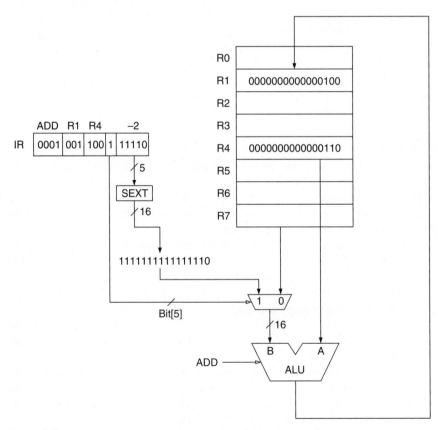

Figure 5.5   Data path relevant to the execution of ADD R1, R4, #-2

What does the following instruction do?   Example 5.1

15	14	13	12	11	10	9	8	7	6	5	4	3	2	1	0
0	1	0	1	0	1	0	0	1	0	1	0	0	0	0	0

ANSWER: Register 2 is cleared (i.e., set to all 0s).

What does the following instruction do?   Example 5.2

15	14	13	12	11	10	9	8	7	6	5	4	3	2	1	0
0	0	0	1	1	1	0	1	1	0	1	0	0	0	0	1

ANSWER: Register 6 is incremented (i.e., R6 ← R6 + 1).
Note that a register can be used as a source and also as a destination in the same instruction. This is true for all the instructions in the LC-3.

Recall that the 2's complement of a number can be obtained by complementing the   Example 5.3
number and adding 1. Therefore, assuming the values A and B are in R0 and R1, what
sequence of three instructions performs "A minus B" and writes the result into R2?

ANSWER:

15	14	13	12	11	10	9	8	7	6	5	4	3	2	1	0
1	0	0	1	0	0	1	0	0	1	1	1	1	1	1	1
	NOT				R1				R1						

R1 ← NOT(B)

15	14	13	12	11	10	9	8	7	6	5	4	3	2	1	0
0	0	0	1	0	1	0	0	0	1	1	0	0	0	0	1
	ADD				R2				R1				1		

R2 ← -B

15	14	13	12	11	10	9	8	7	6	5	4	3	2	1	0
0	0	0	1	0	1	0	0	0	0	0	0	0	0	1	0
	ADD				R2				R0				R2		

R2 ← A + (-B)

Question: What distasteful result is also produced by this sequence? How can it
easily be avoided?

5.3 Data Movement Instructions

Data movement instructions move information between the general purpose registers and memory, and between the registers and the input/output devices. We will
ignore for now the business of moving information from input devices to registers
and from registers to output devices. This will be the major topic of Chapter 8 and
an important part of Chapter 9 as well. In this chapter, we will confine ourselves
to moving information between memory and the general purpose registers.

The process of moving information from memory to a register is called a *load*, and the process of moving information from a register to memory is called a *store*. In both cases, the information in the location containing the source operand remains unchanged. In both cases, the location of the destination operand is overwritten with the source operand, destroying the prior value in the destination location in the process.

The LC-3 contains seven instructions that move information: LD, LDR, LDI, LEA, ST, STR, and STI.

The format of the load and store instructions is as follows:

15	14	13	12	11	10	9	8	7	6	5	4	3	2	1	0
opcode				DR or SR			Addr Gen bits								

Data movement instructions require two operands, a source and a destination. The source is the data to be moved; the destination is the location where it is moved to. One of these locations is a register, the second is a memory location or an input/output device. As we said earlier, in this chapter the second operand will be assumed to be in memory. We will save for Chapter 8 the cases where the second operand specifies an input or output device.

Bits [11:9] specify one of these operands, the register. If the instruction is a load, *DR* refers to the destination register that will contain the value after it is read from memory (at the completion of the instruction cycle). If the instruction is a store, *SR* refers to the register that contains the value that will be written to memory.

Bits [8:0] contain the *address generation bits*. That is, bits [8:0] encode information that is used to compute the 16-bit address of the second operand. In the case of the LC-3's data movement instructions, there are four ways to interpret bits [8:0]. They are collectively called *addressing modes*. The opcode specifies how to interpret bits [8:0]. That is, the LC-3's opcode specifies which addressing mode should be used to obtain the operand from bits [8:0] of the instruction.

5.3.1 PC-Relative Mode

LD (opcode = 0010) and **ST** (opcode = 0011) specify the *PC-relative* addressing mode. This addressing mode is so named because bits [8:0] of the instruction specify an offset relative to the PC. The memory address is computed by sign-extending bits [8:0] to 16 bits, and adding the result to the incremented PC. The incremented PC is the contents of the program counter after the FETCH phase; that is, after the PC has been incremented. If a load, the memory location corresponding to the computed memory address is read, and the result loaded into the register specified by bits [11:9] of the instruction.

If the instruction

15	14	13	12	11	10	9	8	7	6	5	4	3	2	1	0
0	0	1	0	0	1	0	1	1	0	1	0	1	1	1	1
LD				R2			x1AF								

is located at x4018, it will cause the contents of x3FC8 to be loaded into R2.

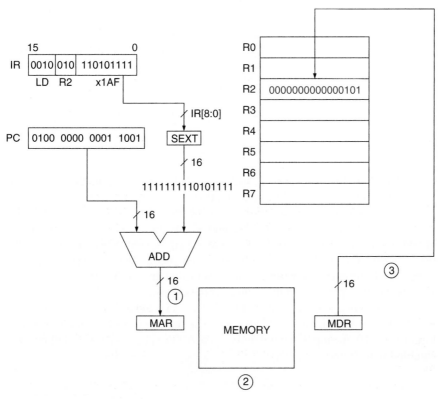

Figure 5.6   Data path relevant to execution of LD R2, x1AF

Figure 5.6 shows the relevant parts of the data path required to execute this instruction. The three steps of the LD instruction are identified. In step 1, the incremented PC (x4019) is added to the sign-extended value contained in IR[8:0] (xFFAF), and the result (x3FC8) is loaded into the MAR. In step 2, memory is read and the contents of x3FC8 are loaded into the MDR. Suppose the value stored in x3FC8 is 5. In step 3, the value 5 is loaded into R2, completing the instruction cycle.

Note that the address of the memory operand is limited to a small range of the total memory. That is, the address can only be within +256 or −255 locations of the LD or ST instruction since the PC is incremented before the offset is added. This is the range provided by the sign-extended value contained in bits [8:0] of the instruction.

5.3.2 Indirect Mode

LDI (opcode = 1010) and **STI** (opcode = 1011) specify the *indirect* addressing mode. An address is first formed exactly the same way as with LD and ST. However, instead of this address **being** the address of the operand to be loaded or stored, it **contains** the address of the operand to be loaded or stored. Hence the name *indirect*. Note that the address of the operand can be anywhere in the computer's memory, not just within the range provided by bits [8:0] of the instruction as is the case for LD and ST. The destination register for the LDI and the source register for STI, like all the other loads and stores, are specified in bits [11:9] of the instruction.

If the instruction

15	14	13	12	11	10	9	8	7	6	5	4	3	2	1	0
1	0	1	0	0	1	1	1	1	1	0	0	1	1	0	0

LDI   R3   x1CC

is in x4A1B, and the contents of x49E8 is x2110, execution of this instruction results in the contents of x2110 being loaded into R3.

Figure 5.7 shows the relevant parts of the data path required to execute this instruction. As is the case with the LD and ST instructions, the first step consists of adding the incremented PC (x4A1C) to the sign-extended value contained in IR[8:0] (xFFCC), and the result (x49E8) loaded into the MAR. In step 2, memory is read and the contents of x49E8 (x2110) is loaded into the MDR. In step 3, since x2110 is not the operand, but the address of the operand, it is loaded into the MAR. In step 4, memory is again read, and the MDR again loaded. This time the MDR is loaded with the contents of x2110. Suppose the value −1 is stored in memory location x2110. In step 5, the contents of the MDR (i.e., −1) are loaded into R3, completing the instruction cycle.

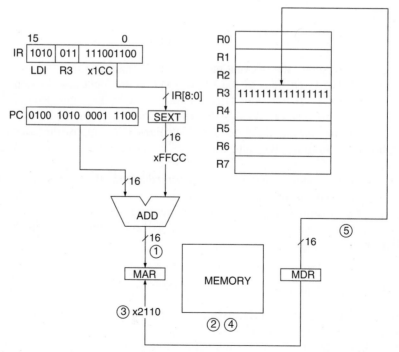

Figure 5.7   Data path relevant to the execution of LDI R3, x1CC

5.3.3 Base+offset Mode

LDR (opcode = 0110) and **STR** (opcode = 0111) specify the *Base+offset* addressing mode. The Base+offset mode is so named because the address of the operand is obtained by adding a sign-extended 6-bit offset to a base register. The 6-bit offset is **literally** taken from the instruction, bits [5:0]. The base register is specified by bits [8:6] of the instruction.

The Base+offset addressing uses the 6-bit value as a 2's complement integer between −32 and +31. Thus it must first be sign-extended to 16 bits before it is added to the base register.

If R2 contains the 16-bit quantity x2345, the instruction

15	14	13	12	11	10	9	8	7	6	5	4	3	2	1	0
0	1	1	0	0	0	1	0	1	0	0	1	1	1	0	1
	LDR				R1			R2				x1D			

loads R1 with the contents of x2362.

Figure 5.8 shows the relevant parts of the data path required to execute this instruction. First the contents of R2 (x2345) are added to the sign-extended value contained in IR[5:0] (x001D), and the result (x2362) is loaded into the MAR. Second, memory is read, and the contents of x2362 are loaded into the MDR. Suppose the value stored in memory location x2362 is x0F0F. Third, and finally, the contents of the MDR (in this case, x0F0F) are loaded into R1.

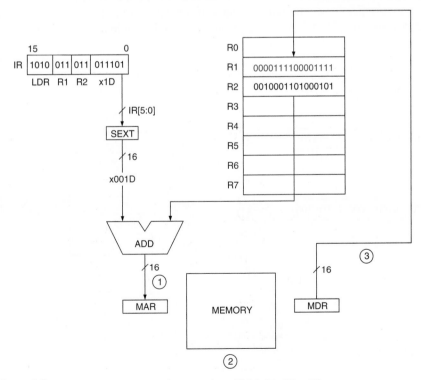

Figure 5.8   Data path relevant to the execution of LDR R1, R2, x1D

Note that the Base+offset addressing mode also allows the address of the operand to be anywhere in the computer's memory.

5.3.4 Immediate Mode

The fourth and last addressing mode used by the data movement instructions is the *immediate* (or, *literal*) addressing mode. It is used only with the load effective address (LEA) instruction. **LEA** (opcode = 1110) loads the register specified by bits [11:9] of the instruction with the value formed by adding the incremented program counter to the sign-extended bits [8:0] of the instruction. The immediate addressing mode is so named because the operand to be loaded into the destination register is obtained immediately, that is, without requiring any access of memory.

The LEA instruction is useful to initialize a register with an address that is very close to the address of the instruction doing the initializing. If memory location x4018 contains the instruction LEA R5, #−3, and the PC contains x4018,

15	14	13	12	11	10	9	8	7	6	5	4	3	2	1	0
1	1	1	0	1	0	1	1	1	1	1	1	1	1	0	1
LEA				R5						−3					

R5 will contain x4016 after the instruction at x4018 is executed.

Figure 5.9 shows the relevant parts of the data path required to execute the LEA instruction. Note that no access to memory is required to obtain the value to be loaded.

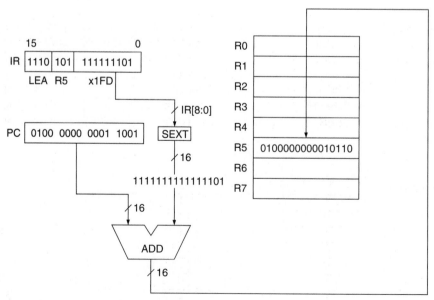

Figure 5.9   Data path relevant to the execution of LEA R5, #−3

Again, LEA is the *only* load instruction that does not access memory to obtain the information it will load into the DR. It loads into the DR the address formed from the incremented PC and the address generation bits of the instruction.

5.3.5 An Example

We conclude our study of addressing modes with a comprehensive example. Assume the contents of memory locations x30F6 through x30FC are as shown in Figure 5.10, and the PC contains x30F6. We will examine the effects of carrying out the instruction cycle seven consecutive times.

The PC points initially to location x30F6. That is, the content of the PC is the address x30F6. Therefore, the first instruction to be executed is the one stored in location x30F6. The opcode of that instruction is 1110, which identifies the load effective address instruction (LEA). LEA loads the register specified by bits [11:9] with the address formed by sign-extending bits [8:0] of the instruction and adding the result to the incremented PC. The 16-bit value obtained by sign-extending bits [8:0] of the instruction is xFFFD. The incremented PC is x30F7. Therefore, at the end of execution of the LEA instruction, R1 contains x30F4, and the PC contains x30F7.

The second instruction to be executed is the one stored in location x30F7. The opcode 0001 identifies the ADD instruction, which stores the result of adding the contents of the register specified in bits [8:6] to the sign-extended immediate in bits [4:0] (since bit [5] is 1) in the register specified by bits [11:9]. Since the previous instruction loaded x30F4 into R1, and the sign-extended immediate value is x000E, the value to be loaded into R2 is x3102. At the end of execution of this instruction, R2 contains x3102, and the PC contains x30F8. R1 still contains x30F4.

The third instruction to be executed is stored in x30F8. The opcode 0011 specifies the ST instruction, which stores the contents of the register specified by bits [11:9] of the instruction into the memory location whose address is computed using the PC-relative addressing mode. That is, the address is computed by adding the incremented PC to the 16-bit value obtained by sign-extending bits [8:0] of the instruction. The 16-bit value obtained by sign-extending bits [8:0] of the instruction is xFFFB. The incremented PC is x30F9. Therefore, at the end of

Address	15	14	13	12	11	10	9	8	7	6	5	4	3	2	1	0	
x30F6	1	1	1	0	0	0	1	1	1	1	1	1	1	1	0	1	R1 <- PC-3
x30F7	0	0	0	1	0	1	0	0	0	1	1	0	1	1	1	0	R2 <- R1+14
x30F8	0	0	1	1	0	1	0	1	1	1	1	1	1	0	1	1	M[x30F4] <- R2
x30F9	0	1	0	1	0	1	0	0	1	0	1	0	0	0	0	0	R2 <- 0
x30FA	0	0	0	1	0	1	0	0	1	0	1	0	0	1	0	1	R2 <- R2+5
x30FB	0	1	1	1	0	1	0	0	0	1	0	0	1	1	1	0	M[R1+14] <- R2
x30FC	1	0	1	0	0	1	1	1	1	1	1	1	0	1	1	1	R3 <- M[M[x3F04]]

Figure 5.10   Addressing mode example

execution of the ST instruction, memory location x30F4 contains x3102, and the PC contains x30F9.

At x30F9, we find the opcode 0101, which represents the AND instruction. After execution, R2 contains the value 0, and the PC contains x30FA.

At x30FA, we find the opcode 0001, signifying the ADD instruction. After execution, R2 contains the value 5, and the PC contains x30FB.

At x30FB, we find the opcode 0111, signifying the STR instruction. The STR instruction (like the LDR instruction) uses the Base+offset addressing mode. The memory address is obtained by adding the contents of the register specified by bits [8:6] (the BASE register) to the sign-extended offset contained in bits [5:0]. In this case, bits [8:6] specify R1. The contents of R1 are still x30F4. The 16-bit sign-extended offset is x000E. Since x30F4 + x000E is x3102, the memory address is x3102. The STR instruction stores into x3102 the contents of the register specified by bits [11:9], that is, R2. Recall that the previous instruction (at x30FA) stored the value 5 into R2. Therefore, at the end of execution of this instruction, location x3102 contains the value 5, and the PC contains x30FC.

At x30FC, we find the opcode 1010, signifying the LDI instruction. The LDI instruction (like the STI instruction) uses the indirect addressing mode. The memory address is obtained by first forming an address as is done in the PC-relative addressing mode. In this case, the 16-bit value obtained by sign-extending bits [8:0] of the instruction is xFFF7. The incremented PC is x30FD. Their sum is x30F4, which is the address of the operand address. Memory location x30F4 contains x3102. Therefore, x3102 is the operand address. The LDI instruction loads the value found at this address (in this case 5) into the register identified by bits [11:9] of the instruction (in this case R3). At the end of execution of this instruction, R3 contains the value 5 and the PC contains x30FD.

5.4 Control Instructions

Control instructions change the sequence of the instructions that are executed. If there were no control instructions, the next instruction fetched after the current instruction finishes would be the instruction located in the next sequential memory location. As you know, this is because the PC is incremented in the FETCH phase of each instruction. We will see momentarily that it is often useful to be able to break that sequence.

The LC-3 has five opcodes that enable this sequential flow to be broken: conditional branch, unconditional jump, subroutine (sometimes called *function*) call, TRAP, and return from interrupt. In this section, we will deal almost exclusively with the most common control instruction, the *conditional branch*. We will also introduce the unconditional jump and the TRAP instruction. The TRAP instruction is particularly useful because, among other things, it allows a programmer to get information into and out of the computer without fully understanding the intricacies of the input and output devices. However, most of the discussion of the TRAP instruction and all of the discussion of the subroutine call and the return from interrupt we will leave for Chapters 9 and 10.

5.4.1 Conditional Branches

The format of the conditional branch instruction (opcode = 0000) is as follows:

15	14	13	12	11	10	9	8 7 6 5 4 3 2 1 0
0	0	0	0	N	Z	P	PCoffset

Bits [11], [10], and [9] correspond to the three condition codes discussed in Section 5.1.7. Recall that in the LC-3, **all** instructions that write values into the general purpose registers set the three condition codes (i.e., the single-bit registers N, Z, P) in accordance with whether the value written is negative, zero, or positive. These instructions are ADD, AND, NOT, LD, LDI, LDR, and LEA.

The condition codes are used by the conditional branch instruction to determine whether to change the instruction flow; that is, whether to depart from the usual sequential execution of instructions that we get as a result of incrementing PC during the FETCH phase of each instruction.

The instruction cycle is as follows: FETCH and DECODE are the same for all instructions. The PC is incremented during FETCH. The EVALUATE ADDRESS phase is the same as that for LD and ST: the address is computed by adding the incremented PC to the 16-bit value formed by sign-extending bits [8:0] of the instruction.

During the EXECUTE phase, the processor examines the condition codes whose corresponding bits in the instruction are 1. That is, if bit [11] is 1, condition code N is examined. If bit [10] is 1, condition code Z is examined. If bit [9] is 1, condition code P is examined. If any of bits [11:9] are 0, the corresponding condition codes are not examined. If any of the condition codes that are examined are in state 1, then the PC is loaded with the address obtained in the EVALUATE ADDRESS phase. If none of the condition codes that are examined are in state 1, the PC is left unchanged. In that case, in the next instruction cycle, the next sequential instruction will be fetched.

For example, if the last value loaded into a general purpose register was 0, then the current instruction (located at x4027) shown here

15	14	13	12	11	10	9	8	7	6	5	4	3	2	1	0
0	0	0	0	0	1	0	0	1	1	0	1	1	0	0	1
BR				n	z	p				x0D9					

would load the PC with x4101, and the next instruction executed would be the one at x4101, rather than the instruction at x4028.

Figure 5.11 shows the data path elements that are required to execute this instruction. Note the logic required to determine whether the sequential instruction flow should be broken. In this case the answer is yes, and the PC is loaded with x4101, replacing x4028, which had been loaded during the FETCH phase of the conditional branch instruction.

If all three bits [11:9] are 1, then all three condition codes are examined. In this case, since the last result stored into a register had to be either negative, zero, or positive (there are no other choices), one of the three condition codes must be in state 1. Since all three are examined, the PC is loaded with the address obtained in the EVALUATE ADDRESS phase. We call this an *un*conditional branch since

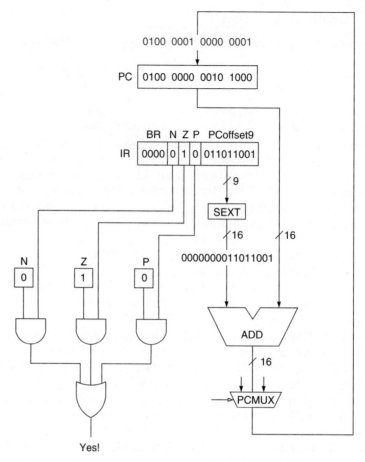

Figure 5.11   Data path relevant to the execution of BRz x0D9

the instruction flow is changed unconditionally, that is, independent of the data that is being processed.

For example, if the following instruction,

15	14	13	12	11	10	9	8	7	6	5	4	3	2	1	0
0	0	0	0	1	1	1	1	1	0	0	0	0	1	0	1
	BR			n	z	p				x185					

located at x507B, is executed, the PC is loaded with x5001.

What happens if all three bits [11:9] in the BR instruction are 0?

5.4.2 An Example

We are ready to show by means of a simple example the value of having control instructions in the instruction set.

Suppose we know that the 12 locations x3100 to x310B contain integers, and we wish to compute the sum of these 12 integers.

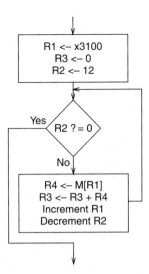

Figure 5.12   An algorithm for adding 12 integers

A flowchart for an algorithm to solve the problem is shown in Figure 5.12.

First, as in all algorithms, we must *initialize our variables*. That is, we must set up the initial values of the variables that the computer will use in executing the program that solves the problem. There are three such variables: the address of the next integer to be added (assigned to R1), the running sum (assigned to R3), and the number of integers left to be added (assigned to R2). The three variables are initialized as follows: The address of the first integer to be added is put in R1. R3, which will keep track of the running sum, is initialized to 0. R2, which will keep track of the number of integers left to be added, is initialized to 12. Then the process of adding begins.

The program repeats the process of loading into R4 one of the 12 integers, and adding it to R3. Each time we perform the ADD, we increment R1 so it will point to (i.e., contain the address of) the next number to be added and decrement R2 so we will know how many numbers still need to be added. When R2 becomes zero, the Z condition code is set, and we can detect that we are done.

The 10-instruction program shown in Figure 5.13 accomplishes the task.

The details of the program execution are as follows: The program starts with PC = x3000. The first instruction (at location x3000) loads R1 with the address x3100. (The incremented PC is x3001; the sign-extended PCoffset is x00FF.)

The instruction at x3001 clears R3. R3 will keep track of the running sum, so it must start off with the value 0. As we said previously, this is called *initializing* the SUM to zero.

The instructions at x3002 and x3003 set the value of R2 to 12, the number of integers to be added. R2 will keep track of how many numbers have already been added. This will be done (by the instruction contained in x3008) by decrementing R2 after each addition takes place.

The instruction at x3004 is a conditional branch instruction. Note that bit [10] is a 1. That means that the Z condition code will be examined. If it is set, we

Address	15	14	13	12	11	10	9	8	7	6	5	4	3	2	1	0	
x3000	1	1	1	0	0	0	1	0	1	1	1	1	1	1	1	1	R1<- 3100
x3001	0	1	0	1	0	1	1	0	1	1	1	0	0	0	0	0	R3 <- 0
x3002	0	1	0	1	0	1	0	0	1	0	1	0	0	0	0	0	R2 <- 0
x3003	0	0	0	1	0	1	0	0	1	0	1	0	1	1	0	0	R2 <- 12
x3004	0	0	0	0	0	1	0	0	0	0	0	0	0	1	0	1	BRz x300A
x3005	0	1	1	0	1	0	0	0	0	1	0	0	0	0	0	0	R4 <- M[R1]
x3006	0	0	0	1	0	1	1	0	1	1	0	0	0	1	0	0	R3 <- R3+R4
x3007	0	0	0	1	0	0	1	0	0	1	1	0	0	0	0	1	R1 <- R1+1
x3008	0	0	0	1	0	1	0	0	1	0	1	1	1	1	1	1	R2 <- R2-1
x3009	0	0	0	0	1	1	1	1	1	1	1	1	1	0	1	0	BRnzp x3004

Figure 5.13   A program that implements the algorithm of Figure 5.12

know R2 must have just been decremented to 0. That means there are no more numbers to be added and we are done. If it is clear, we know we still have work to do and we continue.

The instruction at x3005 loads the contents of x3100 (i.e., the first integer) into R4, and the instruction at x3006 adds it to R3.

The instructions at x3007 and x3008 perform the necessary bookkeeping. The instruction at x3007 increments R1, so R1 will point to the next location in memory containing an integer to be added (in this case, x3101). The instruction at x3008 decrements R2, which is keeping track of the number of integers still to be added, as we have already explained, and sets the N, Z, and P condition codes.

The instruction at x3009 is an unconditional branch, since bits [11:9] are all 1. It loads the PC with x3004. It also does not affect the condition codes, so the next instruction to be executed (the conditional branch at x3004) will be based on the instruction executed at x3008.

This is worth saying again. The conditional branch instruction at x3004 follows the instruction at x3009, which does not affect condition codes, which in turn follows the instruction at x3008. Thus, the conditional branch instruction at x3004 will be based on the condition codes set by the instruction at x3008. The instruction at x3008 sets the condition codes depending on the value produced by decrementing R2. As long as there are still integers to be added, the ADD instruction at x3008 will produce a value greater than zero and therefore clear the Z condition code. The conditional branch instruction at x3004 examines the Z condition code. As long as Z is clear, the PC will not be affected, and the next instruction cycle will start with an instruction fetch from x3005.

The conditional branch instruction causes the execution sequence to follow: x3000, x3001, x3002, x3003, x3004, x3005, x3006, x3007, x3008, x3009, x3004, x3005, x3006, x3007, x3008, x3009, x3004, x3005, and so on until the value in R2 becomes 0. The next time the conditional branch instruction at x3004 is executed, the PC is loaded with x300A, and the program continues at x300A with its next activity.

Finally, it is worth noting that we could have written a program to add these 12 integers **without** any control instructions. We still would have needed the LEA instruction in x3000 to initialize R1. We would not have needed the instruction at x3001 to initialize the running sum, nor the instructions at x3002, and x3003 to initialize the number of integers left to be added. We could have loaded the contents of x3100 directly into R3, and then repeatedly (by incrementing R1, loading the next integer into R4, and adding R4 to the running sum in R3) added the remaining 11 integers. After the addition of the twelfth integer, we would go on to the next task, as does the example of Figure 5.13 with the branch instruction in x3004.

Unfortunately, instead of a 10-instruction program, we would have had a 35-instruction program. Moreover, if we had wished to add 100 integers without any control instructions instead of 12, we would have had a 299-instruction program instead of 10. The control instructions in the example of Figure 5.13 permit the reuse of sequences of code by breaking the sequential instruction execution flow.

5.4.3 Two Methods for Loop Control

We use the term *loop* to describe a sequence of instructions that get executed again and again under some controlling mechanism. The example of adding 12 integers contains a loop. Each time the *body* of the loop executes, one more integer is added to the running total, and the counter is decremented so we can detect whether there are any more integers left to add. Each time the loop body executes is called one *iteration* of the loop.

There are two common methods for controlling the number of iterations of a loop. One method we just examined: the use of a counter. If we know we wish to execute a loop *n* times, we simply set a counter to *n*, then after each execution of the loop, we decrement the counter and check to see if it is zero. If it is not zero, we set the PC to the start of the loop and continue with another iteration.

A second method for controlling the number of executions of a loop is to use a *sentinel*. This method is particularly effective if we do not know ahead of time how many iterations we will want to perform. Each iteration is usually based on processing a value. We append to our sequence of values to be processed a value that we know ahead of time can never occur (i.e., the sentinel). For example, if we are adding a sequence of numbers, a sentinel could be a # or a *, that is, something that is not a number. Our loop test is simply a test for the occurrence of the sentinel. When we find it, we know we are done.

5.4.4 Example: Adding a Column of Numbers Using a Sentinel

Suppose in our example of Section 5.4.2, we know the values stored in locations x3100 to x310B are all positive. Then we could use any negative number as a sentinel. Let's say the sentinel stored at memory address x310C is −1. The resulting flowchart for the program is shown in Figure 5.14 and the resulting program is shown in Figure 5.15.

As before, the instruction at x3000 loads R1 with the address of the first value to be added, and the instruction at x3001 initializes R3 (which keeps track of the sum) to 0.

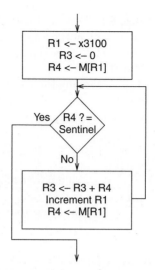

Figure 5.14   An algorithm showing the use of a sentinel for loop control

Address	15	14	13	12	11	10	9	8	7	6	5	4	3	2	1	0	
x3000	1	1	1	0	0	0	1	0	1	1	1	1	1	1	1	1	R1<- x3100
x3001	0	1	0	1	0	1	1	0	1	1	1	0	0	0	0	0	R3 <- 0
x3002	0	1	1	0	1	0	0	0	0	1	0	0	0	0	0	0	R4 <- M[R1]
x3003	0	0	0	0	1	0	0	0	0	0	0	0	0	1	0	0	BRn x3008
x3004	0	0	0	1	0	1	1	0	1	1	0	0	0	1	0	0	R3 <- R3+R4
x3005	0	0	0	1	0	0	1	0	0	1	1	0	0	0	0	1	R1 <- R1+1
x3006	0	1	1	0	1	0	0	0	0	1	0	0	0	0	0	0	R4 <- M[R1]
x3007	0	0	0	0	1	1	1	1	1	1	1	1	1	0	1	1	BRnzp x3003

Figure 5.15   A program that implements the algorithm of Figure 5.14

At x3002, we load the contents of the next memory location into R4. If the sentinel is loaded, the N condition code is set.

The conditional branch at x3003 examines the N condition code, and if it is set, sets PC to x3008 and onto the next task to be done. If the N condition code is clear, R4 must contain a valid number to be added. In this case, the number is added to R3 (x3004), R1 is incremented to point to the next memory location (x3005), R4 is loaded with the contents of the next memory location (x3006), and the PC is loaded with x3003 to begin the next iteration (x3007).

5.4.5 The JMP Instruction

The conditional branch instruction, for all its capability, does have one unfortunate limitation. The next instruction executed must be within the range of addresses that can be computed by adding the incremented PC to the sign-extended offset obtained from bits [8:0] of the instruction. Since bits [8:0] specify a 2's complement integer, the next instruction executed after the conditional branch can be at most +256 or −255 locations from the branch instruction itself. What if we would like to execute next an instruction that is 1,000 locations from the current instruction. We cannot fit the value 1,000 into the 9-bit field; ergo, the conditional branch instruction does not work.

The LC-3 ISA does provide an instruction **JMP** (opcode = 1100) that can do the job. An example follows:

15	14	13	12	11	10	9	8	7	6	5	4	3	2	1	0
1	1	0	0	0	0	0	0	1	0	0	0	0	0	0	0
JMP							R2								

The JMP instruction loads the PC with the contents of the register specified by bits [8:6] of the instruction. If this JMP instruction is located at address x4000, R2 contains the value x6600, and the PC contains x4000, then the instruction at x4000 (the JMP instruction) will be executed, followed by the instruction located at x6600. Since registers contain 16 bits, the full address space of memory, the JMP instruction has no limitation on where the next instruction to be executed must reside.

5.4.6 The TRAP Instruction

Finally, because it will be useful long before Chapter 9 to get data into and out of the computer, we introduce the TRAP instruction now. The **TRAP** (opcode = 1111) instruction changes the PC to a memory address that is part of the operating system so that the operating system will perform some task in behalf of the program that is executing. In the language of operating system jargon, we say the TRAP instruction invokes an operating system SERVICE CALL. Bits [7:0] of the TRAP instruction form the *trapvector*, which identifies the service call that the program wishes the operating system to perform. Table A.2 contains the trapvectors for all the service calls that we will use with the LC-3 in this book.

15	14	13	12	11	10	9	8	7	6	5	4	3	2	1	0
1	1	1	1	0	0	0	0				trapvector				

Once the operating system is finished performing the service call, the program counter is set to the address of the instruction following the TRAP instruction, and the program continues. In this way, a program can, during its execution, request services from the operating system and continue processing after each such service is performed. The services we will require for now are

```
* Input a character from the keyboard (trapvector = x23).
* Output a character to the monitor (trapvector = x21).
* Halt the program (trapvector = x25).
```

Exactly how the LC-3 carries out the interaction between operating system and executing programs is an important topic for Chapter 9.

5.5 Another Example: Counting Occurrences of a Character

We will finish our introduction to the ISA of the LC-3 with another example program. We would like to be able to input a character from the keyboard and then count the number of occurrences of that character in a file. Finally, we would like to display that count on the monitor. We will simplify the problem by assuming that the number of occurrences of any character that we would be interested in is small. That is, there will be at most nine occurrences. This simplification allows us to not have to worry about complex conversion routines between the binary count and the ASCII display on the monitor—a subject we will get into in Chapter 10, but not today.

Figure 5.16 is a flowchart of the algorithm that solves this problem. Note that each step is expressed both in English and also (in parentheses) in terms of an LC-3 implementation.

The first step is (as always) to initialize all the variables. This means providing starting values (called *initial values*) for R0, R1, R2, and R3, the four registers the computer will use to execute the program that will solve the problem. R2 will keep track of the number of occurrences; in Figure 5.16, it is referred to as *count*. It is initialized to zero. R3 will point to the next character in the file that is being examined. We refer to it as *pointer* since it contains the **address** of the location where the next character of the file that we wish to examine resides. The pointer is initialized with the address of the **first** character in the file. R0 will hold the character that is being counted; we will input that character from the keyboard and put it in R0. R1 will hold, in turn, each character that we get from the file being examined.

We should also note that there is no requirement that the file we are examining be close to or far away from the program we are developing. For example, it is perfectly reasonable for the program we are developing to start at x3000, and the file we are examining to start at x9000. If that were the case, in the initialization process, R3 would be initialized to x9000.

The next step is to count the number of occurrences of the input character. This is done by processing, in turn, each character in the file being examined, until the file is exhausted. Processing each character requires one iteration of a loop. Recall from Section 5.4.3 that there are two common methods for keeping track of iterations of a loop. We will use the sentinel method, using the ASCII code for EOT (End of Text) (00000100) as the sentinel. A table of ASCII codes is in Appendix E.

In each iteration of the loop, the contents of R1 are first compared to the ASCII code for EOT. If they are equal, the loop is exited, and the program moves on to the final step, displaying on the screen the number of occurrences. If not, there is work to do. R1 (the current character under examination) is compared to R0 (the character input from the keyboard). If they match, R2 is incremented. In either case, we get the next character, that is, R3 is incremented, the next character is loaded into R1, and the program returns to the test that checks for the sentinel at the end of the file.

When the end of the file is reached, all the characters have been examined, and the count is contained as a binary number in R2. In order to display the count

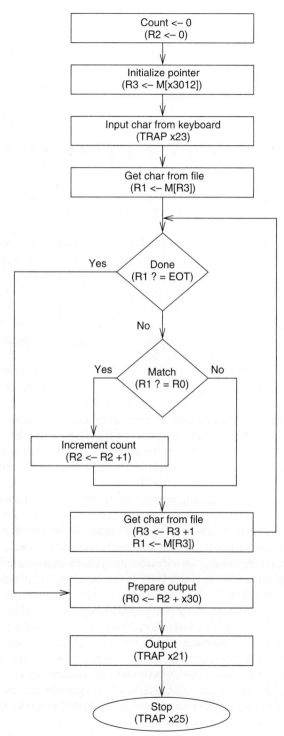

Figure 5.16   An algorithm to count occurrences of a character

Address	15	14	13	12	11	10	9	8	7	6	5	4	3	2	1	0	
x3000	0	1	0	1	0	1	0	0	1	0	1	0	0	0	0	0	R2 <- 0
x3001	0	0	1	0	0	1	1	0	0	0	0	1	0	0	0	0	R3 <- M[x3012]
x3002	1	1	1	1	0	0	0	0	0	0	1	0	0	0	1	1	TRAP x23
x3003	0	1	1	0	0	0	1	0	1	1	0	0	0	0	0	0	R1 <- M[R3]
x3004	0	0	0	1	1	0	0	0	0	1	1	1	1	1	0	0	R4 <- R1-4
x3005	0	0	0	0	0	1	0	0	0	0	0	0	1	0	0	0	BRz x300E
x3006	1	0	0	1	0	0	1	0	0	1	1	1	1	1	1	1	R1 <- NOT R1
x3007	0	0	0	1	0	0	1	0	0	1	1	0	0	0	0	1	R1 <- R1 + 1
x3008	0	0	0	1	0	0	1	0	0	1	0	0	0	0	0	0	R1 <- R1 + R0
x3009	0	0	0	0	1	0	1	0	0	0	0	0	0	0	0	1	BRnp x300B
x300A	0	0	0	1	0	1	0	0	1	0	1	0	0	0	0	1	R2 <- R2 + 1
x300B	0	0	0	1	0	1	1	0	1	1	1	0	0	0	0	1	R3 <- R3 + 1
x300C	0	1	1	0	0	0	1	0	1	1	0	0	0	0	0	0	R1 <- M[R3]
x300D	0	0	0	0	1	1	1	1	1	1	1	1	0	1	1	0	BRnzp x3004
x300E	0	0	1	0	0	0	0	0	0	0	0	0	0	1	0	0	R0 <- M[x3013]
x300F	0	0	0	1	0	0	0	0	0	0	0	0	0	0	1	0	R0 <- R0 + R2
x3010	1	1	1	1	0	0	0	0	0	0	1	0	0	0	0	1	TRAP x21
x3011	1	1	1	1	0	0	0	0	0	0	1	0	0	1	0	1	TRAP x25
x3012	Starting address of file																
x3013	0	0	0	0	0	0	0	0	0	0	1	1	0	0	0	0	ASCII TEMPLATE

Figure 5.17   A machine language program that implements the algorithm of Figure 5.16

on the monitor, it is necessary to first convert it to an ASCII code. Since we have assumed the count is less than 10, we can do this by putting a leading 0011 in front of the 4-bit binary representation of the count. Note in Figure E.2 the relationship between the binary value of each decimal digit between 0 and 9 and its corresponding ASCII code. Finally, the count is output to the monitor, and the program terminates.

Figure 5.17 is a machine language program that implements the flowchart of Figure 5.16.

First the initialization steps. The instruction at x3000 clears R2 by ANDing it with x0000; the instruction at x3001 loads the value stored in x3012 into R3. This is the address of the first character in the file that is to be examined for occurrences of our character. Again, we note that this file can be anywhere in memory. Prior to starting execution at x3000, some sequence of instructions must have stored the first address of this file in x3012. Location x3002 contains the TRAP instruction, which requests the operating system to perform a service call on behalf of this program. The function requested, as identified by the 8-bit trapvector 00100011 (or, x23), is to input a character from the keyboard and load it into R0. Table A.2 lists trapvectors for all operating system service calls that can be performed on behalf of a user program. Note (from Table A.2) that x23 directs the operating system to perform the service call that reads the next character struck and loads it into R0. The instruction at x3003 loads the character pointed to by R3 into R1.

Then the process of examining characters begins. We start (x3004) by sub-tracting 4 (the ASCII code for EOT) from R1, and storing it in R4. If the result is zero, the end of the file has been reached, and it is time to output the count. The instruction at x3005 conditionally branches to x300E, where the process of outputting the count begins.

If R4 is not equal to zero, the character in R1 is legitimate and must be examined. The sequence of instructions at locations x3006, x3007, and x3008 determine if the contents of R1 and R0 are identical. The sequence of instructions perform the following operation:

$$R0 + (NOT (R1) + 1)$$

This produces all zeros only if the bit patterns of R1 and R0 are identical. If the bit patterns are not identical, the conditional branch at x3009 branches to x300B, that is, it skips the instruction x300A, which increments R2, the counter.

The instruction at x300B increments R3, so it will point to the next character in the file being examined, the instruction at x300C loads that character into R1, and the instruction at x300D unconditionally takes us back to x3004 to start processing that character.

When the sentinel (EOT) is finally detected, the process of outputting the count begins (at x300E). The instruction at x300E loads 00110000 into R0, and the instruction at x300F adds the count to R0. This converts the binary representation of the count (in R2) to the ASCII representation of the count (in R0). The instruction at x3010 invokes a TRAP to the operating system to output the contents of R0 on the monitor. When that is done and the program resumes execution, the instruction at x3011 invokes a TRAP instruction to terminate the program.

5.6   The Data Path Revisited

Before we leave Chapter 5, let us revisit the data path diagram that we first encountered in Chapter 3 (Figure 3.33). Now we are ready to examine all the structures that are needed to implement the LC-3 ISA. Many of them we have seen earlier in this chapter in Figures 5.4, 5.5, 5.6, 5.7, 5.8, 5.9, and 5.11. We reproduce this diagram as Figure 5.18. Note at the outset that there are two kinds of arrows in the data path, those with arrowheads filled in, and those with arrowheads not filled in. Filled-in arrowheads designate information that is processed. Unfilled-in arrowheads designate control signals. Control signals emanate from the block labeled "Control." The connections from Control to most control signals have been left off Figure 5.18 to reduce unnecessary clutter in the diagram.

5.6.1 Basic Components of the Data Path

The Global Bus

You undoubtedly first notice the heavy black structure with arrowheads at both ends. This represents the data path's global bus. The LC-3 global bus consists of 16 wires and associated electronics. It allows one structure to transfer up to 16 bits of information to another structure by making the necessary electronic connections on the bus. Exactly one value can be transferred on the bus at one time. Note that each structure that supplies values to the bus has a triangle just

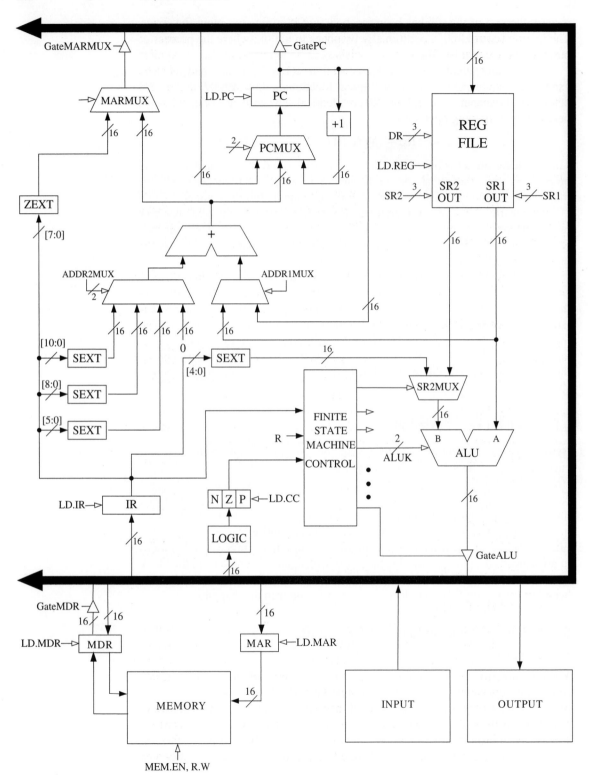

Figure 5.18   The data path of the LC-3

behind its input arrow to the bus. This triangle (called a *tri-state device*) allows the computer's control logic to enable exactly one supplier to provide information to the bus at any one time. The structure wishing to obtain the value being supplied can do so by asserting its LD.x (load enable) signal (recall our discussion of gated latches in Section 3.4.2). Not all computers have a single global bus. The pros and cons of a single global bus is yet another one of those topics that will have to wait for later in your education.

Memory

One of the most important parts of any computer is the memory that contains both instructions and data. Memory is accessed by loading the memory address register (MAR) with the address of the location to be accessed. If a load is being performed, control signals then read the memory, and the result of that read is delivered by the memory to the memory data register (MDR). On the other hand, if a store is being performed, the data to be stored is first loaded into the MDR. Then the control signals specify that WE is asserted in order to store into that memory location.

The ALU and the Register File

The ALU is the processing element. It has two inputs, source 1 from a register and source 2 from either a register or the sign-extended immediate value provided by the instruction. The registers (R0 through R7) can provide two values, source 1, which is controlled by the 3-bit register number SR1, and source 2, which is controlled by the 3-bit register number SR2. SR1 and SR2 are fields in the LC-3 operate instruction. The selection of a second register operand or a sign-extended immediate operand is determined by bit [5] of the LC-3 instruction. Note the mux that provides source 2 to the ALU. The select line of that mux, coming from the control logic, is bit [5] of the LC-3 operate instruction.

The result of an ALU operation is a result that is stored in one of the registers, and the three single-bit condition codes. Note that the ALU can supply 16 bits to the bus, and that value can then be written into the register specified by the 3-bit register number DR. Also, note that the 16 bits supplied to the bus are also input to logic that determines whether that 16-bit quantity is negative, zero, or positive, and sets the three registers N, Z, and P accordingly.

The PC and the PCMUX

The PC supplies via the global bus to the MAR the address of the instruction to be fetched at the start of the instruction cycle. The PC, in turn, is supplied via the three-to-one PCMUX, depending on the instruction being executed. During the FETCH phase of the instruction cycle, the PC is incremented and written into the PC. That is shown as the rightmost input to the PCMUX.

If the current instruction is a control instruction, then the relevant source of the PCMUX depends on which control instruction is currently being processed. If the current instruction is a conditional branch and the branch is taken, then the PC is loaded with the incremented PC + PCoffset (the 16-bit value obtained by sign-extending IR[8:0]). Note that this addition takes place in the special adder and not in the ALU. The output of the adder is the middle input to PCMUX. The third input to PCMUX is obtained from the global bus. Its use will become clear after we discuss the other control instructions in Chapters 9 and 10.

The MARMUX

As you know, memory is accessed by supplying the address to the MAR. The MARMUX controls which of two sources will supply the MAR with the appropriate address during the execution of a load, a store, or a TRAP instruction. The right input to the MARMUX is obtained by adding either the incremented PC or a base register to a literal value or zero supplied by the IR. Whether the PC or a base register and what literal value depends on which opcode is being processed. The control signal ADDR1MUX specifies the PC or base register. The control signal ADDR2MUX specifies which of four values to be added. The left input to MARMUX provides the zero-extended trapvector, which is needed to invoke service calls, as will be discussed in further detail in Chapter 9.

5.6.2 The Instruction Cycle

We complete our tour of the LC-3 data path by following the flow through an instruction cycle. Suppose the content of the PC is x3456 and the content of location x3456 is 0110011010000100. And suppose the LC-3 has just completed processing the instruction at x3455, which happened to be an ADD instruction.

FETCH

As you know, the instruction cycle starts with the FETCH phase. That is, the instruction is obtained by accessing memory with the address contained in the PC. In the first cycle, the contents of the PC are loaded via the global bus into the MAR, and the PC is incremented and loaded into the PC. At the end of this cycle, the PC contains x3457. In the next cycle (if memory can provide information in one cycle), the memory is read, and the instruction 0110011010000100 is loaded into the MDR. In the next cycle, the contents of the MDR are loaded into the instruction register (IR), completing the FETCH phase.

DECODE

In the next cycle, the contents of the IR are decoded, resulting in the control logic providing the correct control signals (unfilled arrowheads) to control the processing of the rest of this instruction. The opcode is 0110, identifying the LDR instruction. This means that the Base+offset addressing mode is to be used to determine the address of data to be loaded into the destination register R3.

EVALUATE ADDRESS

In the next cycle, the contents of R2 (the base register) and the sign-extended bits [5:0] of the IR are added and supplied via the MARMUX to the MAR. The SR1 field specifies 010, the register to be read to obtain the base address. ADDR1MUX selects SR1OUT, and ADDR2MUX selects the second from the right source.

OPERAND FETCH

In the next cycle (or more than one, if memory access takes more than one cycle), the data at that address is loaded into the MDR.

EXECUTE

The LDR instruction does not require an EXECUTE phase, so this phase takes zero cycles.

STORE RESULT

In the last cycle, the contents of the MDR are loaded into R3. The DR control field specifies 011, the register to be loaded.

5.1 Given instructions ADD, JMP, LEA, and NOT, identify whether the instructions are operate instructions, data movement instructions, or control instructions. For each instruction, list the addressing modes that can be used with the instruction.

5.2 A memory's addressibility is 64 bits. What does that tell you about the size of the MAR and MDR?

5.3 There are two common ways to terminate a loop. One way uses a counter to keep track of the number of iterations. The other way uses an element called a ____. What is the distinguishing characteristic of this element?

5.4 Say we have a memory consisting of 256 locations, and each location contains 16 bits.

   a. How many bits are required for the address?

   b. If we use the PC-relative addressing mode, and want to allow control transfer between instructions 20 locations away, how many bits of a branch instruction are needed to specify the PC-relative offset?

   c. If a control instruction is in location 3, what is the PC-relative offset of address 10. Assume that the control transfer instructions work the same way as in the LC-3.

5.5 *a.* What is an addressing mode?

   b. Name three places an instruction's operands might be located.

   c. List the five addressing modes of the LC-3, and for each one state where the operand is located (from part b).

   d. What addressing mode is used by the ADD instruction shown in Section 5.1.2?

146   chapter 5   The LC-3

5.6   Recall the machine busy example from Section 2.7.1. Assuming the BUSYNESS bit vector is stored in R2, we can use the LC-3 instruction 0101 011 010 1 00001 (AND R3, R2, #1) to determine whether machine 0 is busy or not. If the result of this instruction is 0, then machine 0 is busy.

  a. Write an LC-3 instruction that determines whether machine 2 is busy.
  b. Write an LC-3 instruction that determines whether both machines 2 and 3 are busy.
  c. Write an LC-3 instruction that indicates none of the machines are busy.
  d. Can you write an LC-3 instruction that determines whether machine 6 is busy? Is there a problem here?

5.7   What is the largest positive number we can represent literally (i.e., as an immediate value) within an LC-3 ADD instruction?

5.8   We want to increase the number of registers that we can specify in the LC-3 ADD instruction to 32. Do you see any problem with that? Explain.

5.9   We would like to have an instruction that does nothing. Many ISAs actually have an opcode devoted to doing nothing. It is usually called NOP, for NO OPERATION. The instruction is fetched, decoded, and executed. The execution phase is to do nothing! Which of the following three instructions could be used for NOP and have the program still work correctly?

  a. 0001 001 001 1 00000
  b. 0000 111 000000001
  c. 0000 000 000000000

  What does the ADD instruction do that the others do not do?

5.10   What is the difference between the following LC-3 instructions A and B? How are they similar? How are they different?

A: 0000111101010101
B: 0100111101010101

5.11   We wish to execute a single LC-3 instruction that will subtract the decimal number 20 from register 1 and put the result into register 2. Can we do it? If yes, do it. If not, explain why not.

5.12   After executing the following LC-3 instruction: ADD R2, R0, R1, we notice that R0[15] equals R1[15], but is different from R2[15]. We are told that R0 and R1 contain UNSIGNED integers (that is, nonnegative integers between 0 and 65,535). Under what conditions can we trust the result in R2?

5.13   *a.* How might one use a single LC-3 instruction to move the value in R2 into R3?

   b. The LC-3 has no subtract instruction. How could one perform the following operation using only three LC-3 instructions:

$$R1 \leftarrow R2 - R3$$

   c. Using only one LC-3 instruction and without changing the contents of any register, how might one set the condition codes based on the value that resides in R1?

   d. Is there a sequence of LC-3 instructions that will cause the condition codes at the end of the sequence to be N = 1, Z = 1, and P = 0? Explain.

   e. Write an LC-3 instruction that clears the contents of R2.

5.14   The LC-3 does not have an opcode for the logical function OR. That is, there is no instruction in the LC-3 ISA that performs the OR operation. However, we can write a sequence of instructions to implement the OR operation. The four instruction sequence below performs the OR of the contents of register 1 and register 2 and puts the result in register 3. Fill in the two missing instructions so that the four instruction sequence will do the job.

```
(1): 1001 100 001 111111
(2):
(3): 0101 110 100 000 101
(4):
```

5.15   State the contents of R1, R2, R3, and R4 after the program starting at location x3100 halts.

Address	Data
0011 0001 0000 0000	1110 001 000100000
0011 0001 0000 0001	0010 010 000100000
0011 0001 0000 0010	1010 011 000100000
0011 0001 0000 0011	0110 100 010 000001
0011 0001 0000 0100	1111 0000 0010 0101
:	:
:	:
0011 0001 0010 0010	0100 0101 0110 0110
0011 0001 0010 0011	0100 0101 0110 0111
:	:
:	:
0100 0101 0110 0111	1010 1011 1100 1101
0100 0101 0110 1000	1111 1110 1101 0011

5.16 Which LC-3 addressing mode makes the most sense to use under the following conditions. (There may be more than one correct answer to each of these; therefore, justify your answers with some explanation.)

   a. You want to load one value from an address which is less than $\pm 2^8$ locations away.
   b. You want to load one value from an address which is more than 2^8 locations away.
   c. You want to load an array of sequential addresses.

5.17 How many times does the LC-3 make a read or write request to memory during the processing of the LD instruction? How many times during the processing of the LDI instruction? How many times during the processing of the LEA instruction? Processing includes all phases of the instruction cycle.

5.18 The program counter contains the address of an LDR instruction. In order for the LC-3 to process that instruction, how many memory accesses must be made? Repeat this task for STI and TRAP.

5.19 The LC-3 Instruction Register (IR) is made up of 16 bits, of which the least significant nine bits [8:0] represent the PC-relative offset for the LD instruction. If we change the ISA so that bits [6:0] represent the PC-relative offset, what is the new range of addresses we can load data from using the LD instruction?

5.20 If we made the LC-3 ISA such that we allow the LD instruction to load data only ± 32 locations away from the incremented PC value, how many bits would be required for the PC-relative offset in the LD instruction?

5.21 What is the maximum number of TRAP service routines that the LC-3 ISA can support? Explain.

5.22 The PC contains x3010. The following memory locations contain values as shown:

```
x3050:          x70A4
x70A2:          x70A3
x70A3:          xFFFF
x70A4:          x123B
```

The following three LC-3 instructions are then executed, causing a value to be loaded into R6. What is that value?

```
x3010           1110 0110 0011 1111
x3011           0110 1000 1100 0000
x3012           0110 1101 0000 0000
```

We could replace the three-instruction sequence with a single instruction. What is it?

5.23 Suppose the following LC-3 program is loaded into memory starting at location x30FF:

LEA   x30FF   1110 0010 0000 0001   *R1 will contain x30FD*

LDR   x3100   0110 0100 0100 0010   *3 → SEXT 03   R2 = x3100*

TRAP x3101   1111 0000 0010 0101

ADD   x3102   0001 0100 0100 0001

ADD   x3103   0001 0100 1000 0010

If the program is executed, what is the value in R2 at the end of execution?

5.24 An LDR instruction, located at x3200, uses R4 as its base register. The value currently in R4 is x4011. What is the largest address that this instruction can load from? Suppose we redefine the LDR offset to be zero-extended, rather than sign-extended. Then what would be the largest address that this instruction could load from? With the new definition, what would be the smallest address that this instruction could load from?

5.25 Write an LC-3 program that compares two numbers in R2 and R3 and puts the larger number in R1. If the numbers are equal, then R1 is set equal to 0.

5.26 Your task is to consider the successor to the LC-3. We will add 16 additional instructions to the ISA and expand the register set from 8 to 16. We would like our machine to have an addressability of 1 byte and a total memory size of 64K bytes. We will keep the size of an instruction at 16 bits. Also, we will encode all new instructions with the same five fields as the original 16 instructions, although it may be necessary to change the size of some of those fields.

   a. How many bits do we need in the PC to be able to address all of memory?
   b. What is the largest immediate value that can be represented in an arithmetic instruction?
   c. If we want 128 different operating system routines to be able to be accessed with a trap instruction and we form the address of each of these routines by shifting the trap vector to the left by 5 bits, what is the minimum amount of memory required by the trap service routines?
   d. If, in the new version of the LC-3, we reduced the number of registers from eight to four and kept the number of opcodes at 16, what is the largest immediate value we could represent in an ADD instruction on this new machine?

5.27 Before the seven instructions are executed in the example of Section 5.3.5, R2 contains the value xAAAA. How many different values are contained in R2 during the execution of the seven instructions? What are they?

5.28 It is the case that we REALLY don't need to have load indirect (1010) and store indirect (1011) instructions. We can accomplish the same results using other instruction sequences instead of using these instructions. Replace the store indirect (1011) instruction in the code below with whatever instructions are necessary to perform the same function.

```
x3000    0010 0000 0000 0010
x3001    1011 0000 0000 0010
x3002    1111 0000 0010 0101
x3003    0000 0000 0100 1000
x3004    1111 0011 1111 1111
```

5.29 The LC-3 ISA contains the instruction LDR DR, BaseR, offset. After the instruction is decoded, the following operations (called microinstructions) are carried out to complete the processing of the LDR instruction:

```
MAR ← BaseR + SEXT(Offset6) ; set up the memory address
MDR ← Memory[MAR] ; read mem at BaseR + offset
DR  ← MDR ; load DR
```

Suppose that the architect of the LC-3 wanted to include an instruction MOVE DR, SR that would copy the memory location with address given by SR and store it into the memory location whose address is in DR.

a. The MOVE instruction is not really necessary since it can be accomplished with a sequence of existing LC-3 instructions. What sequence of existing LC-3 instructions implements (also called "emulates") MOVE R0,R1?

b. If the MOVE instruction were added to the LC-3 ISA, what sequence of microinstructions, following the decode operation, would emulate MOVE DR,SR?

5.30 The following table shows a part of the LC-3's memory:

Address	Data
0011 0001 0000 0000	1001 001 001 111111
0011 0001 0000 0001	0001 010 000 000 001
0011 0001 0000 0010	1001 010 010 111111
0011 0001 0000 0011	0000 010 111111100

State what is known about R1 and R0 if the conditional branch redirects control to location x3100.

5.31 The figure at the top of the next page shows a snapshot of the 8 registers of the LC-3 before and after the instruction at location x1000 is executed. Fill in the bits of the instruction at location x1000.

BEFORE   AFTER

R0	x0000
R1	x1111
R2	x2222
R3	x3333
R4	x4444
R5	x5555
R6	x6666
R7	x7777

R0	x0000
R1	x1111
R2	x2222
R3	x3333
R4	x4444
R5	xFFF8
R6	x6666
R7	x7777

0x1000 : [0 | 0 | 0 | 1 | | | | | | | | | | | |]

5.32 If the condition codes have values $N = 0, Z = 0, P = 1$ at the beginning of the execution of the following sequence of LC-3 instructions?

x3050	0000 0010 0000 0010
x3051	0101 0000 0010 0000
x3052	0000 1110 0000 0010
x3053	0101 0000 0010 0000
x3054	0001 0000 0011 1111

5.33 If the value stored in R0 is 5 at the end of the execution of the following instructions, what can be inferred about R5?

x3000	0101 1111 1110 0000
x3001	0001 1101 1110 0001
x3002	0101 1001 0100 0110
x3003	0000 0100 0000 0001
x3004	0001 0000 0010 0001
x3005	0001 1101 1000 0110
x3006	0001 1111 1110 0001
x3007	0001 0011 1111 1000
x3008	0000 1001 1111 1001
x3009	0101 1111 1110 0000

5.34 Using the overall data path in Figure 5.18, identify the elements that implement the NOT instruction of Figure 5.4.

5.35 Using the overall data path in Figure 5.18, identify the elements that implement the ADD instruction of Figure 5.5.

5.36 Using the overall data path in Figure 5.18, identify the elements that implement the LD instruction of Figure 5.6.

5.37 Using the overall data path in Figure 5.18, identify the elements that implement the LDI instruction of Figure 5.7.

5.38 Using the overall data path in Figure 5.18, identify the elements that implement the LDR instruction of Figure 5.8.

5.39 Using the overall data path in Figure 5.18, identify the elements that implement the LEA instruction of Figure 5.9.

5.40 The logic diagram below shows part of the control structure of the LC-3 machine. What is the purpose of the signal labeled A?

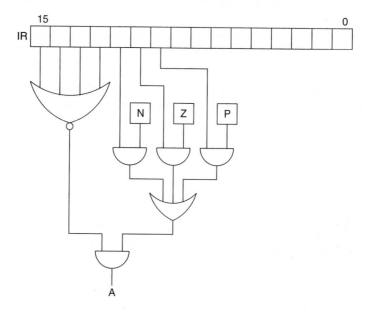

5.41 A part of the implementation of the LC-3 architecture is shown on the top of the next page.

a. What information does Y provide?

b. The signal X is the control signal that gates the gated D latch. Is there an error in the logic that produces X?

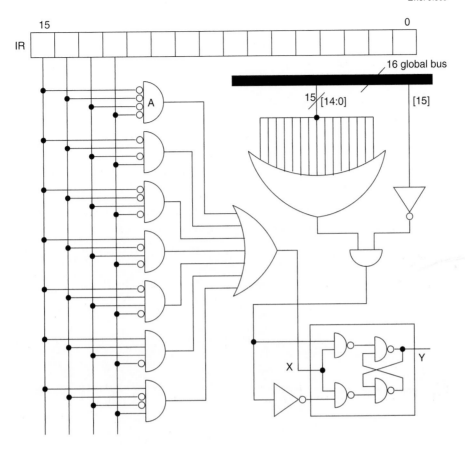

5.42 The LC-3 macho-company had decided to use opcode 1101 to implement a new instruction. They need you help to pick the most useful one from the following:

a. MOVE Ri, Rj; The contents of Rj are copied into Ri.

b. NAND Ri, Rj, Rk; Ri is the bit-wise NAND of Rj, Rk

c. SHFL Ri, Rj, #2; The contents of Rj are shifted left 2 bits and stored into Ri.

d. MUL Ri, Rj, Rk; Ri is the product of 2's complement integers in Rj, Rk.

Justify your answer.

6

Programming

We are now ready to start developing programs to solve problems with the computer. In this chapter we attempt to do two things: first, we develop a methodology for constructing programs; and second, we develop a methodology for fixing those programs under the likely condition that we did not get it right the first time. There is a long tradition that the errors present in programs are referred to as *bugs*, and the process of removing those errors *debugging*. The opportunities for introducing bugs into a complicated program are so great that it usually takes much more time to get the program to work (debugging) than it does to create it in the first place.

6.1 Problem Solving

6.1.1 Systematic Decomposition

Recall from Chapter 1 that in order for electrons to solve a problem, we need to go through several levels of transformation to get from a natural language description of the problem (in our case English, although some of you might prefer Italian, Mandarin, Hindi, or something else) to something electrons can deal with. Once we have a natural language description of the problem, the next step is to transform the problem statement into an algorithm. That is, the next step is to transform the problem statement into a step-by-step procedure that has the properties of finiteness (it terminates), definiteness (each step is precisely stated), and effective computability (each step can be carried out by a computer).

In the late 1960s, the concept of *structured programming* emerged as a way to improve the ability of average programmers to take a complex description of a problem and systematically decompose it into sufficiently smaller, manageable units that they could ultimately write as a program that executed correctly. The mechanism has also been called *systematic decomposition* because the larger tasks are systematically broken down into smaller ones.

We will find the systematic decomposition model a useful technique for designing computer programs to carry out complex tasks.

6.1.2 The Three Constructs: Sequential, Conditional, Iterative

Systematic decomposition is the process of taking a task, that is, a unit of work (see Figure 6.1a), and breaking it down into smaller units of work such that the collection of smaller units carries out the same task as the one larger unit. The idea is that if one starts with a large, complex task and applies this process again and again, one will end up with very small units of work, and consequently, be able to easily write a program to carry out each of these small units of work. The process is also referred to as *stepwise refinement,* because the process is applied one step at a time, and each step refines one of the tasks that is still too complex into a collection of simpler subtasks.

The idea is to replace each larger unit of work with a construct that correctly decomposes it. There are basically three constructs for doing this: *sequential, conditional,* and *iterative.*

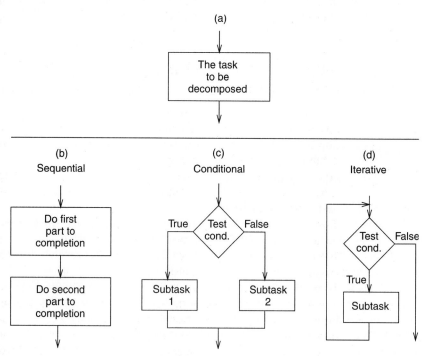

Figure 6.1   The basic constructs of structured programming

The **sequential** construct (Figure 6.1b) is the one to use if the designated task can be broken down into two subtasks, one following the other. That is, the computer is to carry out the first subtask completely, *then* go on and carry out the second subtask completely—never going back to the first subtask after starting the second subtask.

The **conditional** construct (Figure 6.1c) is the one to use if the task consists of doing one of two subtasks but not both, depending on some condition. If the condition is true, the computer is to carry out one subtask. If the condition is not true, the computer is to carry out a different subtask. Either subtask may be vacuous, that is, it may "do nothing." Regardless, after the correct subtask is completed, the program moves onward. The program never goes back and retests the condition.

The **iterative** construct (Figure 6.1d) is the one to use if the task consists of doing a subtask a number of times, but only as long as some condition is true. If the condition is true, do the subtask. After the subtask is finished, go back and test the condition again. As long as the result of the condition tested is true, the program continues to carry out the same subtask. The first time the test is not true, the program proceeds onward.

Note in Figure 6.1 that whatever the task of Figure 6.1a, work starts with the arrow into the top of the "box" representing the task and finishes with the arrow out of the bottom of the box. There is no mention of what goes on *inside* the box. In each of the three possible decompositions of Figure 6.1a (i.e., Figures 6.1b, 1c, and 1d), there is exactly *one entrance into the construct* and *one exit out of the construct*. Thus, it is easy to replace any task of the form of Figure 6.1a with whichever of its three decompositions apply. We will see how in the following example.

6.1.3 LC-3 Control Instructions to Implement the Three Constructs

Before we move on to an example, we illustrate in Figure 6.2 the use of LC-3 control instructions to direct the program counter to carry out each of the three decomposition constructs. That is, Figures 6.2b, 6.2c, and 6.2d correspond respectively to the three constructs shown in Figures 6.1b, 6.1c, and 6.1d.

We use the letters A, B, C, and D to represent addresses in memory containing LC-3 instructions. A, for example, is used in all three cases to represent the address of the first LC-3 instruction to be executed.

Figure 6.2b illustrates the control flow of the sequential decomposition. Note that no control instructions are needed since the PC is incremented from Address B_1 to Address B_1+1. The program continues to execute instructions through address D_1. It does not return to the first subtask.

Figure 6.2c illustrates the control flow of the conditional decomposition. First, a condition is generated, resulting in the setting of one of the condition codes. This condition is tested by the conditional branch instruction at Address B_2. If the condition is true, the PC is set to Address C_2+1, and subtask 1 is executed. (Note: x corresponds to the number of instructions in subtask 2.) If the condition is false, the PC (which had been incremented during the FETCH

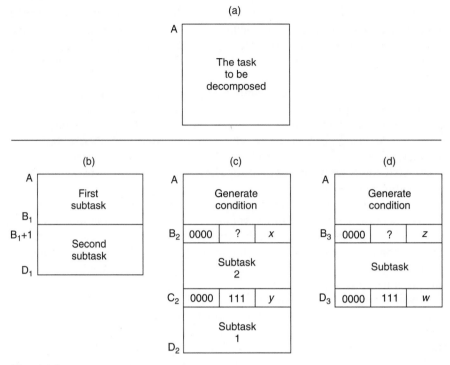

Figure 6.2   Use of LC-3 control instructions to implement structured programming

phase of the branch instruction) fetches the instruction at Address B_2+1, and subtask 2 is executed. Subtask 2 terminates in a branch instruction that at Address C_2 unconditionally branches to D_2+1. (Note: y corresponds to the number of instructions in subtask 1.)

Figure 6.2d illustrates the control flow of the iterative decomposition. As in the case of the conditional construct, first a condition is generated, a condition code is set, and a conditional branch is executed. In this case, the condition bits of the instruction at address B_3 are set to cause a conditional branch if the condition generated is false. If the condition is false, the PC is set to address D_3+1. (Note: z corresponds to the number of instructions in the subtask in Figure 6.2d.) On the other hand, as long as the condition is true, the PC will be incremented to B_3+1, and the subtask will be executed. The subtask terminates in an unconditional branch instruction at address D_3, which sets the PC to A to again generate and test the condition. (Note: w corresponds to the total number of instructions in the decomposition shown as Figure 6.2d.)

Now, we are ready to move on to an example.

6.1.4 The Character Count Example from Chapter 5, Revisited

Recall the example of Section 5.5. The statement of the problem is as follows: "We wish to count the number of occurrences of a character in a file. The character

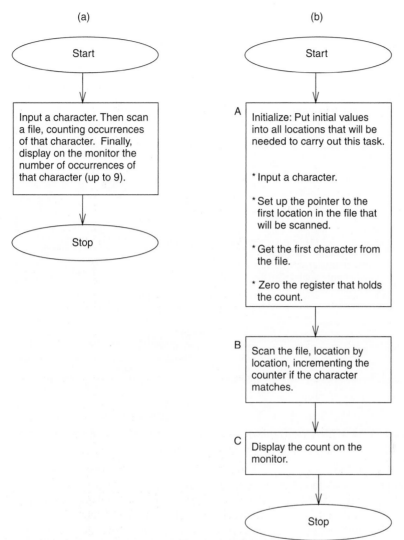

(a)   (b)

Figure 6.3   Stepwise refinement of the character count program

in question is to be input from the keyboard; the result is to be displayed on the monitor."

The systematic decomposition of this English language statement of the problem to the final LC-3 implementation is shown in Figure 6.3. Figure 6.3a is a brief statement of the problem.

In order to solve the problem, it is always a good idea first to examine exactly what is being asked for, and what is available to help solve the problem. In this case, the statement of the problem says that we will get the character of interest from the keyboard, and that we must examine all the characters in a file and determine how many are identical to the character obtained from the keyboard. Finally, we must output the result.

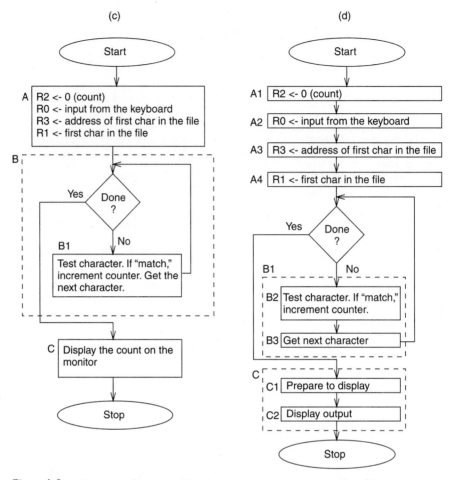

Figure 6.3   Stepwise refinement of the character count program (**continued**)

To do this, we will need a mechanism for scanning all the characters in a file, and we will need a counter so that when we find a match, we can increment that counter.

We will need places to hold all these pieces of information:

1. The character input from the keyboard.
2. Where we are (a pointer) in our scan of the file.
3. The character in the file that is currently being examined.
4. The count of the number of occurrences.

We will also need some mechanism for knowing when the file terminates.

The problem decomposes naturally (using the sequential construct) into three parts as shown in Figure 6.3b: (A) initialization, which includes keyboard input of the character to be "counted," (B) the actual process of determining how many

(e)

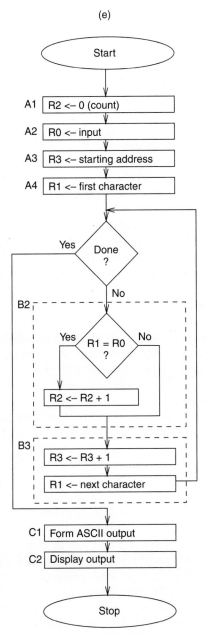

Figure 6.3   Stepwise refinement of the character count program (**continued**)

occurrences of the character are present in the file, and (C) displaying the count on the monitor.

We have seen the importance of proper initialization in several examples already. Before a computer program can get to the crux of the problem, it must have the correct initial values. These initial values do not just show up in the GPRs by magic. They get there as a result of the first set of steps in every algorithm: the initialization of its variables.

In this particular algorithm, initialization (as we said in Chapter 5) consists of starting the counter at 0, setting the pointer to the address of the first character in the file to be examined, getting an input character from the keyboard, and getting the first character from the file. Collectively, these four steps comprise the initialization of the algorithm shown in Figure 6.3b as A.

Figure 6.3c decomposes B into an iteration construct, such that as long as there are characters in the file to examine, the loop iterates. B1 shows what gets accomplished in each iteration. The character is tested and the count incremented if there is a match. Then the next character is prepared for examination. Recall from Chapter 5 that there are two basic techniques for controlling the number of iterations of a loop: the sentinel method and the use of a counter. This program uses the sentinel method by terminating the file we are examining with an EOT (end of text) character. The test to see if there are more legitimate characters in the file is a test for the ASCII code for EOT.

Figure 6.3c also shows the initialization step in greater detail. Four LC-3 registers (R0, R1, R2, and R3) have been specified to handle the four requirements of the algorithm: the input character from the keyboard, the current character being tested, the counter, and the pointer to the next character to be tested.

Figure 6.3d decomposes both B1 and C using the sequential construct. In the case of B1, first the current character is tested (B2), and the counter incremented if we have a match, and then the next character is fetched (B3). In the case of C, first the count is prepared for display by converting it from a 2's complement integer to ASCII (C1), and then the actual character output is performed (C2).

Finally, Figure 6.3e completes the decomposition, replacing B2 with the elements of the condition construct and B3 with the sequential construct (first the pointer is incremented, and then the next character to be scanned is loaded).

The last step (and the easy part, actually) is to write the LC-3 code corresponding to each box in Figure 6.3e. Note that Figure 6.3e is essentially identical to Figure 5.7 of Chapter 5 (except now you know where it all came from!).

Before leaving this topic, it is worth pointing out that it is not always possible to understand everything at the outset. When you find that to be the case, it is not a signal simply to throw up your hands and quit. In such cases (which realistically are most cases), you should see if you can make sense of a piece of the problem, and expand from there. Problems are like puzzles; initially they can be opaque, but the more you work at it, the more they yield under your attack. Once you do understand what is given, what is being asked for, and how to proceed, you are ready to return to square one (Figure 6.3a) and restart the process of systematically decomposing the problem.

6.2 Debugging

Debugging a program is pretty much applied common sense. A simple example comes to mind: You are driving to a place you have never visited, and somewhere along the way you made a wrong turn. What do you do now? One common "driving debugging" technique is to wander aimlessly, hoping to find your way back. When that does not work, and you are finally willing to listen to the person sitting next to you, you turn around and return to some "known" position on the route. Then, using a map (very difficult for some people), you follow the directions provided, periodically comparing where you are (from landmarks you see out the window) with where the map says you should be, until you reach your desired destination.

Debugging is somewhat like that. A logical error in a program can make you take a wrong turn. The simplest way to keep track of where you are as compared to where you want to be is to *trace* the program. This consists of keeping track of the **sequence** of instructions that have been executed and the **results** produced by each instruction executed. When you examine the sequence of instructions executed, you can detect errors in the control flow of the program. When you compare what each instruction has done to what it is supposed to do, you can detect logical errors in the program. In short, when the behavior of the program as it is executing is different from what it should be doing, you know there is a bug.

A useful technique is to partition the program into parts, often referred to as *modules*, and examine the results that have been computed at the end of execution of each module. In fact, the structured programming approach discussed in Section 6.1 can help you determine where in the program's execution you should examine results. This allows you to systematically get to the point where you are focusing your attention on the instruction or instructions that are causing the problem.

6.2.1 Debugging Operations

Many sophisticated debugging tools are offered in the marketplace, and undoubtedly you will use many of them in the years ahead. In Chapter 15, we will examine some debugging techniques available through **dbx**, the source-level debugger for the programming language C. Right now, however, we wish to stay at the level of the machine architecture, and so we will see what we can accomplish with a few very elementary interactive debugging operations. When debugging interactively, the user sits in front of the keyboard and monitor and issues commands to the computer. In our case, this means operating an LC-3 simulator, using the menu available with the simulator.

It is important to be able to

1. Deposit values in memory and in registers.
2. Execute instruction sequences in a program.
3. Stop execution when desired.
4. Examine what is in memory and registers at any point in the program.

These few simple operations will go a long way toward debugging programs.

Set Values

It is useful to deposit values in memory and in registers in order to test the execution of a part of a program in isolation, without having to worry about parts of the program that come before it. For example, suppose one module in your program supplies input from a keyboard, and a subsequent module operates on that input. Suppose you want to test the second module before you have finished debugging the first module. If you know that the keyboard input module ends up with an ASCII code in R0, you can test the module that operates on that input by first placing an ASCII code in R0.

Execute Sequences

It is important to be able to execute a sequence of instructions and then stop execution in order to examine the values that the program has computed. Three simple mechanisms are usually available for doing this: run, step, and set breakpoints.

The **Run** command causes the program to execute until something makes it stop. This can be either a HALT instruction or a breakpoint.

The **Step** command causes the program to execute a fixed number of instructions and then stop. The interactive user enters the number of instructions he/she wishes the simulator to execute before it stops. When that number is 1, the computer executes one instruction, then stops. Executing one instruction and then stopping is called *single-stepping*. It allows the person debugging the program to examine the individual results of every instruction executed.

The **Set Breakpoint** command causes the program to stop execution at a specific instruction in a program. Executing the debugging command Set Breakpoint consists of adding an address to a list maintained by the simulator. During the FETCH phase of each instruction, the simulator compares the PC with the addresses in that list. If there is a match, execution stops. Thus, the effect of setting a breakpoint is to allow execution to proceed until the PC contains the address of the breakpoint. This is useful if one wishes to know what has been computed up to a particular point in the program. One sets a breakpoint at that address in the program and executes the Run command. The program executes until that point, thereby allowing the user to examine what has been computed up to that point. (When one no longer wishes to have the program stop execution at that point, one can remove the breakpoint by executing the Clear Breakpoint command.)

Display Values

Finally, it is useful to examine the results of execution when the simulator has stopped execution. The Display command allows the user to examine the contents of any memory location or any register.

6.2.2 Examples: Use of the Interactive Debugger

We conclude this chapter with four examples, showing how the use of the interactive debugging operations can help us find errors in a program. We have chosen the following four errors: (1) incorrectly setting the loop control so that the loop executes an incorrect number of times, (2) confusing the load instruction 0010, which loads a register with the contents of a memory location, with the load effective address instruction 1110, which loads a register with the address of a memory location, (3) forgetting which instructions set the condition codes, resulting in a branch instruction testing the wrong condition, and (4) not covering all possible cases of input values.

Example 1: Multiplying Without a Multiply Instruction

Consider the program of Figure 6.4a. The goal of the program is to multiply the two positive numbers contained in R4 and R5. A program is necessary since the LC-3 does not have a multiply instruction.

If we go through the program instruction by instruction, we note that the program first clears R2 (that is, initializes R2 to 0) and then attempts to perform the multiplication by adding R4 to itself a number of times equal to the initial value in R5. Each time an add is performed, R5 is decremented. When R5 = 0, the program terminates.

It sounds like the program should work! Upon execution, however, we find that if R4 is initially 10 and R5 is initially 3, the program produces the value 40. What went wrong?

Our first thought is to trace the program. Before we do that, we note that the program assumes positive integers in R4 and R5. Using the Set Values command, we put the value 10 in R4 and the value 3 in R5.

It is also useful to annotate each instruction with some algorithmic description of **exactly** what each instruction is doing. While this can be very tedious and not

(a)

Address	15	14	13	12	11	10	9	8	7	6	5	4	3	2	1	0	
x3200	0	1	0	1	0	1	0	0	1	0	1	0	0	0	0	0	R2 <- 0
x3201	0	0	0	1	0	1	0	0	1	0	0	0	0	1	0	0	R2 <- R2 + R4
x3202	0	0	0	1	1	0	1	1	0	1	1	1	1	1	1	1	R5 <- R5 - 1
x3203	0	0	0	0	0	1	1	1	1	1	1	1	1	1	0	1	BRzp x3201
x3204	1	1	1	1	0	0	0	0	0	0	1	0	0	1	0	1	HALT

(b)

PC	R2	R4	R5
x3201	0	10	3
x3202	10	10	3
x3203	10	10	2
x3201	10	10	2
x3202	20	10	2
x3203	20	10	1
x3201	20	10	1
x3202	30	10	1
x3203	30	10	0
x3201	30	10	0
x3202	40	10	0
x3203	40	10	-1
x3204	40	10	-1
	40	10	-1

(c)

PC	R2	R4	R5
x3203	10	10	2
x3203	20	10	1
x3203	30	10	0
x3203	40	10	-1

Figure 6.4   The use of interactive debugging to find the error in Example 1. (a) An LC-3 program to multiply (without a Multiply instruction). (b) A trace of the Multiply program. (c) Tracing with breakpoints.

very helpful in a 10,000 instruction program, it often can be very helpful after one
has isolated a bug to within a few instructions. There is a big difference between
quickly eyeballing a sequence of instructions and stating precisely what each
instruction is doing. We have included in Figure 6.4a, next to each instruction,
such an annotation.

Figure 6.4b shows a trace of the program, which we can obtain by single-
stepping. The column labeled *PC* shows the contents of the PC at the start of each
instruction. R2, R4, and R5 show the values in those three registers at the start
of each instruction. If we examine the contents of the registers, we see that the
branch condition codes were set wrong; that is, the conditional branch should be
taken as long as R5 is positive, not as long as R5 is nonnegative, as is the case in
x3203. That causes an extra iteration of the loop, resulting in 10 being added to
itself four times, rather than three.

The program can be corrected by simply replacing the instruction at x3203
with

15	14	13	12	11	10	9	8	7	6	5	4	3	2	1	0
0	0	0	0	0	0	1	1	1	1	1	1	1	1	0	1

BR   n   z   p   −3

We should also note that we could have saved some of the work of tracing the
program by using a breakpoint. That is, instead of examining the results of **each
instruction,** setting a breakpoint at x3203 allows us to examine the results of
each iteration of the loop. Figure 6.4c shows the results of tracing the program,
where each step is one iteration of the loop. We see that the loop executed four
times rather than three, as it should have.

One last comment before we leave this example. Before we started tracing
the program, we initialized R4 and R5 with values 10 and 3. When testing a
program, it is important to judiciously choose the initial values for the test. Here,
the program stated that the program had to work only for positive integers. So, 10
and 3 are probably OK. What if a (different) multiply program had been written
to work for all integers? Then, we could have tried initial values of −6 and 3, 4
and −12, and perhaps −5 and −7. The problem with this set of tests is that we
have left out one of the most important initial values of all: 0. For the program
to work for "all" integers, it has to work for 0 as well. The point is that, for a
program to work, it must work for all values, and a good test of such a program
is to initialize its variables to the unusual values, the ones the programmer may
have failed to consider. These values are often referred to colloquially as *corner
cases*.

Example 2: Adding a Column of Numbers

The program of Figure 6.5 is supposed to add the numbers stored in the 10
locations starting with x3100, and leave the result in R1. The contents of the 20
memory locations starting at location x3100 are shown in Figure 6.6.

The program should work as follows. The instructions in x3000 to x3003
initialize the variables. In x3000, the sum (R1) is initialized to 0. In x3001 and
x3002, the loop control (R4), which counts the number of values added to R1, is

(a)

Address	15	14	13	12	11	10	9	8	7	6	5	4	3	2	1	0	
x3000	0	1	0	1	0	0	1	0	0	1	1	0	0	0	0	0	R1 <- 0
x3001	0	1	0	1	1	0	0	1	0	0	1	0	0	0	0	0	R4 <- 0
x3002	0	0	0	1	1	0	0	1	0	0	1	0	1	0	1	0	R4 <- R4 + 10
x3003	0	0	1	0	0	1	0	0	1	1	1	1	1	1	0	0	R2 <- M[x3100]
x3004	0	1	1	0	0	1	1	0	1	0	0	0	0	0	0	0	R3 <- M[R2]
x3005	0	0	0	1	0	1	0	0	1	0	1	0	0	0	0	1	R2 <- R2 + 1
x3006	0	0	0	1	0	0	1	0	0	1	0	0	0	0	1	1	R1 <- R1 + R3
x3007	0	0	0	1	1	0	0	1	0	0	1	1	1	1	1	1	R4 <- R4 - 1
x3008	0	0	0	0	0	0	1	1	1	1	1	1	1	0	1	1	BRp x3004
x3009	1	1	1	1	0	0	0	0	0	0	1	0	0	1	0	1	HALT

(b)

PC	R1	R2	R4
x3001	0	x	x
x3002	0	x	0
x3003	0	x	#10
x3004	0	x3107	#10

Figure 6.5   The use of interactive debugging to find the error in Example 2. (a) An LC-3 program to add 10 integers. (b) A trace of the first four instructions of the Add program

Address	Contents
x3100	x3107
x3101	x2819
x3102	x0110
x3103	x0310
x3104	x0110
x3105	x1110
x3106	x11B1
x3107	x0019
x3108	x0007
x3109	x0004
x310A	x0000
x310B	x0000
x310C	x0000
x310D	x0000
x310E	x0000
x310F	x0000
x3110	x0000
x3111	x0000
x3112	x0000
x3113	x0000

Figure 6.6   Contents of memory locations x3100 to x3113 for Example 2

initialized to #10. The program subtracts 1 each time through the loop and repeats until R4 contains 0. In x3003, the base register (R2) is initialized to the starting location of the values to be added: x3100.

From there, each time through the loop, one value is loaded into R3 (in x3004), the base register is incremented to get ready for the next iteration (x3005), the value in R3 is added to R1, which contains the running sum (x3006), the counter is decremented (x3007), the P bit is tested, and if true, the PC is set to x3004 to begin the loop again (x3008). After 10 times through the loop, R4 contains 0, the P bit is 0, the branch is not taken, and the program terminates (x3009).

It looks like the program should work. However, when we execute the program and then check the value in R1, we find the number x0024, which is not x8135, the sum of the numbers stored in locations x3100 to x3109. What went wrong?

We turn to the debugger and trace the program. Figure 6.5b shows a trace of the first four instructions executed. Note that after the instruction at x3003 has executed, R2 contains x3107, not x3100, as we had expected. The problem is that the opcode 0010 loaded the **contents** of x3100 into R2, not the **address** x3100. Our mistake: We should have used the opcode 1110, which would have loaded the address of x3100 into R2. We correct the bug by replacing the opcode 0010 with 1110, and the program runs correctly.

Example 3: Determining Whether a Sequence of Memory Locations Contains a 5

The program of Figure 6.7 has been written to examine the contents of the 10 memory locations starting at address x3100 and to store a 1 in R0 if any of them contains a 5 and a 0 in R0 if none of them contains a 5.

The program is supposed to work as follows: The first six instructions (at x3000 to x3005) initialize R0 to 1, R1 to −5, and R3 to 10. In each case, the register is first cleared by ANDing it with 0, and then ADDing the corresponding immediate value. For example, in x3003, −5 is added to R1, and the result is stored in R1.

The instruction at x3006 initializes R4 to the starting address (x3100) of the values to be tested, and x3007 loads the contents of x3100 into R2.

x3008 and x3009 determine if R2 contains the value 5 by adding −5 to it and branching to x300F if the result is 0. Since R0 is initialized to 1, the program terminates with R0 reporting the presence of a 5 among the locations tested.

x300A increments R4, preparing to load the next value. x300B decrements R3, indicating the number of values remaining to be tested. x300C loads the next value into R2. x300D branches back to x3008 to repeat the process if R3 still indicates more values to be tested. If R3 = 0, we have exhausted our tests, so R0 is set to 0 (x300E), and the program terminates (x300F).

When we run the program for some sample data that contains a 5 in location x3108, the program terminates with R0 = 0, indicating there were no 5s in locations x3100 to x310A.

What went wrong? We examine a trace of the program, with a breakpoint set at x300D. The results are shown in Figure 6.7b.

(a)

Address	15	14	13	12	11	10	9	8	7	6	5	4	3	2	1	0	
x3000	0	1	0	1	0	0	0	0	0	0	1	0	0	0	0	0	R0 <- 0
x3001	0	0	0	1	0	0	0	0	0	0	1	0	0	0	0	1	R0 <- R0 + 1
x3002	0	1	0	1	0	0	1	0	0	1	1	0	0	0	0	0	R1 <- 0
x3003	0	0	0	1	0	0	1	0	0	1	1	1	1	0	1	1	R1 <- R1 - 5
x3004	0	1	0	1	0	1	1	0	1	1	1	0	0	0	0	0	R3 <- 0
x3005	0	0	0	1	0	1	1	0	1	1	1	0	1	0	1	0	R3 <- R3 + 10
x3006	0	0	1	0	1	0	0	0	0	0	0	0	1	0	0	1	R4 <- M[x3010]
x3007	0	1	1	0	0	1	0	1	0	0	0	0	0	0	0	0	R2 <- M[R4]
x3008	0	0	0	1	0	1	0	0	1	0	0	0	0	0	0	1	R2 <- R2 + R1
x3009	0	0	0	0	0	1	0	0	0	0	0	0	0	1	0	1	BRz x300F
x300A	0	0	0	1	1	0	0	1	0	0	1	0	0	0	0	1	R4 <- R4 + 1
x300B	0	0	0	1	0	1	1	0	1	1	1	1	1	1	1	1	R3 <- R3 - 1
x300C	0	1	1	0	0	1	0	1	0	0	0	0	0	0	0	0	R2 <- M[R4]
x300D	0	0	0	0	0	0	1	1	1	1	1	1	1	0	1	0	BRp x3008
x300E	0	1	0	1	0	0	0	0	0	0	1	0	0	0	0	0	R0 <- 0
x300F	1	1	1	1	0	0	0	0	0	0	1	0	0	1	0	1	HALT
x3010	0	0	1	1	0	0	0	1	0	0	0	0	0	0	0	0	x3100

(b)

PC	R1	R2	R3	R4
x300D	−5	7	9	3101
x300D	−5	32	8	3102
x300D	−5	0	7	3013

Figure 6.7   The use of interactive debugging to find the error in Example 3. (a) An LC-3 program to detect the presence of a 5. (b) Tracing Example 3 with a breakpoint at x300D.

The first time the PC is at x300D, we have already tested the value stored in x3100, we have loaded 7 (the contents of x3101) into R2, and R3 indicates there are still nine values to be tested. R4 contains the address from which we most recently loaded R2.

The second time the PC is at x300D, we have loaded 32 (the contents of x3102) into R2, and R3 indicates there are eight values still to be tested. The third time the PC is at x300D, we have loaded 0 (the contents of x3103) into R2, and R3 indicates seven values still to be tested.

However, the value 0 stored in x3103 causes the load instruction at x300C to clear the P condition code. This, in turn, causes the branch at x300D not to be taken, R0 is set to 0 (x300E), and the program terminates (x300F).

The error in the program was putting a load instruction at x300C between x300B, which kept track of how many values still needed to be tested, and x300D, the branch instruction that returned to x3008 to perform the next test. The load instruction sets condition codes. Therefore, the branch at x300D was based on the value loaded into R2, rather than on the count of how many values remained to be tested. If we remove the instruction at x300C and change the target of the branch in x300D to x3007, the program executes correctly.

Example 4: Finding the First 1 in a Word

Our last example contains an error that is usually one of the hardest to find, as we will see presently. The program of Figure 6.8 has been written to examine the contents of a memory location, find the first bit (reading left to right) that is set, and store the bit position of that bit into R1. If no bit is set, the program is to store -1 in R1. For example, if the location examined contained 0010000000000000, the program would terminate with R1 $= 13$. If the location contained 0000000000000100, the program would terminate with R1 $= 2$.

(a)

Address	15	14	13	12	11	10	9	8	7	6	5	4	3	2	1	0	
x3000	0	1	0	1	0	0	1	0	0	1	1	0	0	0	0	0	R1 <- 0
x3001	0	0	0	1	0	0	1	0	0	1	1	0	1	1	1	1	R1 <- R1 + 15
x3002	1	0	1	0	0	1	0	0	0	0	0	0	0	1	1	0	R2 <- M[M[x3009]]
x3003	0	0	0	0	1	0	0	0	0	0	0	0	0	1	0	0	BRn x3008
x3004	0	0	0	1	0	0	1	0	0	1	1	1	1	1	1	1	R1 <- R1 - 1
x3005	0	0	0	1	0	1	0	0	1	0	0	0	0	0	1	0	R2 <- R2 + R2
x3006	0	0	0	0	1	0	0	0	0	0	0	0	0	0	0	1	BRn x3008
x3007	0	0	0	0	1	1	1	1	1	1	1	1	1	1	0	0	BRnzp x3004
x3008	1	1	1	1	0	0	0	0	0	0	1	0	0	1	0	1	HALT
x3009	0	0	1	1	0	0	0	1	0	0	0	0	0	0	0	0	x3100

(b)

PC	R1
x3007	14
x3007	13
x3007	12
x3007	11
x3007	10
x3007	9
x3007	8
x3007	7
x3007	6
x3007	5
x3007	4
x3007	3
x3007	2
x3007	1
x3007	0
x3007	-1
x3007	-2
x3007	-3
x3007	-4

Figure 6.8   The use of interactive debugging to find the error in Example 4. (a) An LC-3 program to find the first 1 in a word. (b) Tracing Example 4 with a breakpoint at x3007.

The program is supposed to work as follows (and it usually does): x3000 and x3001 initialize R1 in the same way as we have done in the previous examples. In this case, R1 is initialized to 15.

x3002 loads R2 with the contents of x3100, the value to be examined. It does this by the load indirect instruction, which finds the location of the value to be loaded in x3009.

x3003 tests the high bit of that value, and if it is a 1, it branches to x3008, where the program terminates with R1 = 15. If the high bit is a 0, the branch is not taken and R1 is decremented (x3004), indicating the next bit to be tested is bit [14].

In x3005, the value in R2 is added to itself, and the result is stored back in R2. That is, the value in R2 is multiplied by 2. This is the same as shifting the contents of R2 one bit to the left. This causes the value in bit [14] to move into the bit [15] position, where it can be tested by a branch on negative instruction. x3006 performs the test of bit [14] (now in the bit [15] position), and if the bit is 1, the branch is taken, and the program terminates with R1 = 14.

If the bit is 0, x3007 takes an unconditional branch to x3004, where the process repeats. That is, R1 is decremented (x3004), indicating the next lower bit number, R2, is shifted one bit to the left (x3005), and the new occupant of bit [15] is tested (x3006).

The process continues until the first 1 is found. The program works almost all the time. However, when we ran the program on our data, the program failed to terminate. What went wrong?

A trace of the program, with a breakpoint set at x3007, is illuminating. Each time the PC contained the address x3007, R1 contained a value smaller by 1 than the previous time. The reason is as follows: After R1 was decremented and the value in R2 shifted left, the bit tested was a 0, and so the program did not terminate. This continued for values in R1 equal to 14, 13, 12, 11, 10, 9, 8, 7, 6, 5, 4, 3, 2, 1, 0, −1, −2, −3, −4, and so forth.

The problem was that the initial value in x3100 was x0000; that is, there were no 1s present. The program worked fine as long as there was at least one 1 present. For the case where x3100 contained all zeros, the conditional branch at x3006 was never taken, and so the program continued with execution of x3007, then x3004, x3005, x3006, x3007, and then back again to x3004. There was no way to break out of the sequence x3004, x3005, x3006, x3007, and back again to x3004. We call the sequence x3004 to x3007 a loop. Because there is no way for the program execution to break out of this loop, we call it an *infinite loop*. Thus, the program never terminates, and so we can never get the correct answer.

Again, we emphasize that this is often the hardest error to detect. It is also often the most important one. That is, it is not enough for a program to execute correctly most of the time; it must execute correctly all the time, independent of the data that the program is asked to process. We will see more examples of this kind of error later in the book.

6.1   Can a procedure that is *not* an algorithm be constructed from the three basic constructs of structured programming? If so, demonstrate through an example.

6.2   The LC-3 has no Subtract instruction. If a programmer needed to subtract two numbers he/she would have to write a routine to handle it. Show the systematic decomposition of the process of subtracting two integers.

6.3   Recall the machine busy example from previous chapters. Suppose memory location x4000 contains an integer between 0 and 15 identifying a particular machine that has just become busy. Suppose further that the value in memory location x4001 tells which machines are busy and which machines are idle. Write an LC-3 machine language program that sets the appropriate bit in x4001 indicating that the machine in x4000 is busy.

   For example, if x4000 contains x0005 and x4001 contains x3101 at the start of execution, x4001 should contain x3121 after your program terminates.

6.4   Write a short LC-3 program that compares the two numbers in R1 and R2 and puts the value 0 in R0 if R1 = R2, 1 if R1 > R2 and −1 if R1 < R2.

6.5   Which of the two algorithms for multiplying two numbers is preferable and why? $88 \cdot 3 = 88 + 88 + 88$ OR $3 + 3 + 3 + 3 + \ldots + 3$?

6.6   Use your answers from Exercises 6.3 and 6.4 to develop a program that efficiently multiplies two integers and places the result in R3. Show the complete systematic decomposition, from the problem statement to the final program.

6.7 What does the following LC-3 program do?

```
x3001    1110  0000  0000  1100
x3002    1110  0010  0001  0000
x3003    0101  0100  1010  0000
x3004    0010  0100  0001  0011
x3005    0110  0110  0000  0000
x3006    0110  1000  0100  0000
x3007    0001  0110  1100  0100
x3008    0111  0110  0000  0000
x3009    0001  0000  0010  0001
x300A    0001  0010  0110  0001
x300B    0001  0100  1011  1111
x300C    0000  0011  1111  1000
x300D    1111  0000  0010  0101
x300E    0000  0000  0000  0101
x300F    0000  0000  0000  0100
x3010    0000  0000  0000  0011
x3011    0000  0000  0000  0110
x3012    0000  0000  0000  0010
x3013    0000  0000  0000  0100
x3014    0000  0000  0000  0111
x3015    0000  0000  0000  0110
x3016    0000  0000  0000  1000
x3017    0000  0000  0000  0111
x3018    0000  0000  0000  0101
```

6.8 Why is it necessary to initialize R2 in the character counting example in Section 6.1.4? In other words, in what manner might the program behave incorrectly if the R2 ← 0 step were removed from the routine?

6.9 Using the iteration construct, write an LC-3 machine language routine that displays exactly 100 Zs on the screen.

6.10 Using the conditional construct, write an LC-3 machine language routine that determines if a number stored in R2 is odd.

6.11 Write an LC-3 machine language routine to increment each of the numbers stored in memory location A through memory location B. Assume these locations have already been initialized with meaningful numbers. The addresses A and B can be found in memory locations x3100 and x3101.

6.12 *a.* Write an LC-3 machine language routine that echoes the last character typed at the keyboard. If the user types an *R*, the program then immediately outputs an *R* on the screen.

b. Expand the routine from part *a* such that it echoes a line at a time. For example, if the user types:

The quick brown fox jumps over the lazy dog.

then the program waits for the user to press the Enter key (the ASCII code for which is x0A) and then outputs the same line.

6.13 Notice that we can shift a number to the left by one bit position by adding it to itself. For example, when the binary number 0011 is added to itself, the result is 0110. Shifting a number one bit pattern to the right is not as easy. Devise a routine in LC-3 machine code to shift the contents of memory location x3100 to the right by one bit.

6.14 Consider the following machine language program:

```
                      DR    SR1    SR2
        x3000   0101  0100   1010   0000
        x3001   0001  0010   0111   1111
        x3002   0001  0010   0111   1111
        x3003   0001  0010   0111   1111
        x3004   0000  1000   0000   0010
        x3005   0001  0100   1010   0001
        x3006   0000  1111   1111   1010
        x3007   1111  0000   0010   0101
```

What are the possible initial values of R1 that cause the final value in R2 to be 3?

6.15 Shown below are the contents of memory and registers **before** and **after** the LC-3 instruction at location x3010 is executed. Your job: Identify the instruction stored in x3010. Note: There is enough information below to uniquely specify the instruction at x3010.

	Before	After
R0:	x3208	x3208
R1:	x2d7c	x2d7c
R2:	xe373	xe373
R3:	x2053	x2053
R4:	x33ff	x33ff
R5:	x3f1f	x3f1f
R6:	xf4a2	xf4a2
R7:	x5220	x5220
...		
x3400:	x3001	x3001
x3401:	x7a00	x7a00
x3402:	x7a2b	x7a2b
x3403:	xa700	xa700
x3404:	xf011	xf011
x3405:	x2003	x2003
x3406:	x31ba	xe373
x3407:	xc100	xc100
x3408:	xefef	xefef
...		

6.16 An LC-3 program is located in memory locations x3000 to x3006. It starts executing at x3000. If we keep track of all values loaded into the MAR as the program executes, we will get a sequence that starts as follows. Such a sequence of values is referred to as a trace.

MAR Trace

x3000
x3005
x3001
x3002
x3006
x4001
x3003
x0021

We have shown below some of the bits stored in locations x3000 to x3006. Your job is to fill in each blank space with a 0 or a 1, as appropriate.

x3000	0	0	1	0	0	0	0									
x3001	0	0	0	1	0	0	0	0	0	0	1	0	0	0	0	1
x3002	1	0	1	1	0	0	0									
x3003																
x3004	1	1	1	1	0	0	0	0	0	0	1	0	0	1	0	1
x3005	0	0	0	0	0	0	0	0	0	0	1	1	0	0	0	0
x3006																

6.17 Shown below are the contents of registers before and after the LC-3 instruction at location x3210 is executed. Your job: Identify the instruction stored in x3210. Note: There is enough information below to uniquely specify the instruction at x3210.

	Before	After
R0:	xFF1D	xFF1D
R1:	x301C	x301C
R2:	x2F11	x2F11
R3:	x5321	x5321
R4:	x331F	x331F
R5:	x1F22	x1F22
R6:	x01FF	x01FF
R7:	x341F	x3211
PC:	x3210	x3220
N:	0	0
Z:	1	1
P:	0	0

6.18 The LC-3 has no Divide instruction. A programmer needing to divide two numbers would have to write a routine to handle it. Show the systematic decomposition of the process of dividing two positive integers. Write an LC-3 machine language program starting at location x3000 which divides the number in memory location x4000 by the number in memory location x4001 and stores the quotient at x5000 and the remainder at x5001.

6.19 It is often necessary to encrypt messages to keep them away from prying eyes. A message can be represented as a string of ASCII characters, one per memory location, in consecutive memory locations. Bits [15:8] of each location contains 0, and the location immediately following the string contains x0000.

A student who has not taken this course has written the following LC-3 machine language program to encrypt the message starting at location x4000 by adding 4 to each character and storing the resulting message at x5000. For example, if the message at x4000 is "Matt," then the encrypted message at x5000 is "Qeyy." However, there are four bugs in his code. Find and correct these errors so that the program works correctly.

```
x3000    1110  0000  0000  1010
x3001    0010  0010  0000  1010
x3002    0110  0100  0000  0000
x3003    0000  0100  0000  0101
x3004    0001  0100  1010  0101
x3005    0111  0100  0100  0000
x3006    0001  0000  0010  0001
x3007    0001  0010  0110  0001
x3008    0000  1001  1111  1001
x3009    0110  0100  0100  0000
x300A    1111  0000  0010  0101
x300B    0100  0000  0000  0000
x300C    0101  0000  0000  0000
```

6.20 Redo Exercise 6.18 for all integers, not just positive integers.

7

Assembly Language

By now, you are probably a little tired of 1s and 0s and keeping track of 0001 meaning ADD and 1001 meaning NOT. Also, wouldn't it be nice if we could refer to a memory location by some meaningful symbolic name instead of memorizing its 16-bit address? And wouldn't it be nice if we could represent each instruction in some more easily comprehensible way, instead of having to keep track of which bit of the instruction conveys which individual piece of information about the instruction. It turns out that help is on the way.

In this chapter, we introduce assembly language, a mechanism that does all that, and more.

7.1 Assembly Language Programming—Moving Up a Level

Recall the levels of transformation identified in Figure 1.6 of Chapter 1. Algorithms are transformed into programs described in some mechanical language. This mechanical language can be, as it is in Chapter 5, the machine language of a particular computer. Recall that a program is in a computer's machine language if every instruction in the program is from the ISA of that computer.

On the other hand, the mechanical language can be more user-friendly. We generally partition mechanical languages into two classes, high-level and low-level. Of the two, high-level languages are much more user-friendly. Examples are C, C++, Java, Fortran, COBOL, Pascal, plus more than a thousand others. Instructions in a high-level language almost (but not quite) resemble statements in a natural language such as English. High-level languages tend to be ISA independent. That is, once you learn how to program in C (or Fortran or Pascal) for one ISA, it is a small step to write programs in C (or Fortran or Pascal) for another ISA.

Before a program written in a high-level language can be executed, it must be translated into a program in the ISA of the computer on which it is expected to execute. It is usually the case that each statement in the high-level language specifies several instructions in the ISA of the computer. In Chapter 11, we will introduce the high-level language C, and in Chapters 12 through 19, we will show the relationship between various statements in C and their corresponding translations in LC-3 code. In this chapter, however, we will only move up a small notch from the ISA we dealt with in Chapter 5.

A small step up from the ISA of a machine is that ISA's assembly language. Assembly language is a low-level language. There is no confusing an instruction in a low-level language with a statement in English. Each assembly language instruction usually specifies a single instruction in the ISA. Unlike high-level languages, which are usually ISA independent, low-level languages are very much ISA dependent. In fact, it is usually the case that each ISA has only one assembly language.

The purpose of assembly language is to make the programming process more user-friendly than programming in machine language (i.e., the ISA of the computer with which we are dealing), while still providing the programmer with detailed control over the instructions that the computer can execute. So, for example, while still retaining control over the detailed instructions the computer is to carry out, we are freed from having to remember what opcode is 0001 and what opcode is 1001, or what is being stored in memory location 0011111100001010 and what is being stored in location 0011111100000101. Assembly languages let us use mnemonic devices for opcodes, such as ADD and NOT, and they let us give meaningful symbolic names to memory locations, such as SUM or PRODUCT, rather than use their 16-bit addresses. This makes it easier to differentiate which memory location is keeping track of a SUM and which memory location is keeping track of a PRODUCT. We call these names *symbolic addresses*.

We will see, starting in Chapter 11, that when we take the larger step of moving up to a higher-level language (such as C), programming will be even more user-friendly, but we will relinquish control of exactly which detailed instructions are to be carried out in behalf of a high-level language statement.

7.2 An Assembly Language Program

We will begin our study of the LC-3 assembly language by means of an example. The program in Figure 7.1 multiplies the integer intially stored in NUMBER by 6 by adding the integer to itself six times. For example, if the integer is 123, the program computes the product by adding $123 + 123 + 123 + 123 + 123 + 123$.

The program consists of 21 lines of code. We have added a *line number* to each line of the program in order to be able to refer to individual lines easily. This is a common practice. These line numbers are not part of the program. Ten lines start with a semicolon, designating that they are strictly for the benefit of the human reader. More on this momentarily. Seven lines (06, 07, 08, 0C, 0D,

```
01  ;
02  ; Program to multiply an integer by the constant 6.
03  ; Before execution, an integer must be stored in NUMBER.
04  ;
05          .ORIG   x3050
06          LD      R1,SIX
07          LD      R2,NUMBER
08          AND     R3,R3,#0      ; Clear R3. It will
09                                ; contain the product.
0A  ; The inner loop
0B  ;
0C  AGAIN   ADD     R3,R3,R2
0D          ADD     R1,R1,#-1     ; R1 keeps track of
0E          BRp     AGAIN         ; the iterations
0F  ;
10          HALT
11  ;
12  NUMBER  .BLKW   1
13  SIX     .FILL   x0006
14  ;
15          .END
```

Figure 7.1   An assembly language program

0E, and 10) specify assembly language instructions to be translated into machine language instructions of the LC-3, which will actually be carried out when the program runs. The remaining four lines (05, 12, 13, and 15) contain pseudo-ops, which are messages from the programmer to the translation program to help in the translation process. The translation program is called an *assembler* (in this case the LC-3 assembler), and the translation process is called *assembly*.

7.2.1 Instructions

Instead of an instruction being 16 0s and 1s, as is the case in the LC-3 ISA, an instruction in assembly language consists of four parts, as follows:

LABEL   OPCODE   OPERANDS   ; COMMENTS

Two of the parts (LABEL and COMMENTS) are optional. More on that momentarily.

Opcodes and Operands

Two of the parts (OPCODE and OPERANDS) are **mandatory**. An instruction must have an OPCODE (the thing the instruction is to do), and the appropriate number of OPERANDS (the things it is supposed to do it to). Not surprisingly, this was exactly what we encountered in Chapter 5 when we studied the LC-3 ISA.

The OPCODE is a symbolic name for the opcode of the corresponding LC-3 instruction. The idea is that it is easier to remember an operation by the symbolic name ADD, AND, or LDR than by the 4-bit quantity 0001, 0101, or 0110. Figure 5.3 (also Figure A.2) lists the OPCODES of the 15 LC-3 instructions. Pages 526 through 541 show the assembly language representations for the 15 LC-3 instructions.

The number of operands depends on the operation being performed. For example, the ADD instruction (line 0C) requires three operands (two sources to obtain the numbers to be added, and one destination to designate where the result is to be placed). All three operands must be explicitly identified in the instruction.

```
AGAIN      ADD     R3,R3,R2
```

The operands to be added are obtained from register 2 and from register 3. The result is to be placed in register 3. We represent each of the registers 0 through 7 as R0, R1, R2, ..., R7.

The LD instruction (line 07) requires two operands (the memory location from which the value is to be read and the destination register that is to contain the value after the instruction completes its execution). We will see momentarily that memory locations will be given symbolic addresses called *labels*. In this case, the location from which the value is to be read is given the label *NUMBER*. The destination into which the value is to be loaded is register 2.

```
LD   R2, NUMBER
```

As we discussed in Section 5.1.6, operands can be obtained from registers, from memory, or they may be literal (i.e., immediate) values in the instruction. In the case of register operands, the registers are explicitly represented (such as R2 and R3 in line 0C). In the case of memory operands, the symbolic name of the memory location is explicitly represented (such as NUMBER in line 07 and SIX in line 06). In the case of immediate operands, the actual value is explicitly represented (such as the value 0 in line 08).

```
AND  R3, R3, #0 ; Clear R3. It will contain the product.
```

A literal value must contain a symbol identifying the representation base of the number. We use # for decimal, x for hexadecimal, and b for binary. Sometimes there is no ambiguity, such as in the case 3F0A, which is a hex number. Nonetheless, we write it as x3F0A. Sometimes there is ambiguity, such as in the case 1000. x1000 represents the decimal number 4096, b1000 represents the decimal number 8, and #1000 represents the decimal number 1000.

Labels

Labels are symbolic names that are used to identify memory locations that are referred to explicitly in the program. In LC-3 assembly language, a label consists of from one to 20 alphanumeric characters (i.e., a capital or lowercase letter of the alphabet, or a decimal digit), starting with a letter of the alphabet. NOW, Under21, R2D2, and C3PO are all examples of possible LC-3 assembly language labels.

There are two reasons for explicitly referring to a memory location.

1. The location contains the target of a branch instruction (for example, AGAIN in line 0C).

2. The location contains a value that is loaded or stored (for example, NUMBER, line 12, and SIX, line 13).

The location AGAIN is specifically referenced by the branch instruction in line 0E.

```
BRp    AGAIN
```

If the result of ADD R1,R1,#–1 is positive (as evidenced by the P condition code being set), then the program branches to the location explicitly referenced as AGAIN to perform another iteration.

The location NUMBER is specifically referenced by the load instruction in line 07. The value stored in the memory location explicitly referenced as NUMBER is loaded into R2.

If a location in the program is not explicitly referenced, then there is no need to give it a label.

Comments

Comments are messages intended only for human consumption. They have no effect on the translation process and indeed are not acted on by the LC-3 assembler. They are identified in the program by semicolons. A semicolon signifies that the rest of the line is a comment and is to be ignored by the assembler. If the semicolon is the first nonblank character on the line, the entire line is ignored. If the semicolon follows the operands of an instruction, then only the comment is ignored by the assembler.

The purpose of comments is to make the program more comprehensible to the human reader. They help explain a nonintuitive aspect of an instruction or a set of instructions. In lines 08 and 09, the comment "Clear R3; it will contain the product" lets the reader know that the instruction on line 08 is initializing R3 prior to accumulating the product of the two numbers. While the purpose of line 08 may be obvious to the programmer today, it may not be the case two years from now, after the programmer has written an additional 30,000 lines of code and cannot remember why he/she wrote AND R3,R3,#0. It may also be the case that two years from now, the programmer no longer works for the company and the company needs to modify the program in response to a product update. If the task is assigned to someone who has never seen the code before, comments go a long way toward improving comprehension.

It is important to make comments that provide additional insight and not just restate the obvious. There are two reasons for this. First, comments that restate the obvious are a waste of everyone's time. Second, they tend to obscure the comments that say something important because they add clutter to the program. For example, in line 0D, the comment "Decrement R1" would be a bad idea. It would provide no additional insight to the instruction, and it would add clutter to the page.

Another purpose of comments, and also the judicious use of extra blank spaces to a line, is to make the visual presentation of a program easier to understand. So, for example, comments are used to separate pieces of the program from each other to make the program more readable. That is, lines of code that work together to compute a single result are placed on successive lines, while pieces of a program that produce separate results are separated from each other. For example, note that lines 0C through 0E are separated from the rest of the code by lines 0B and 0F. There is nothing on lines 0B and 0F other than the semicolons.

Extra spaces that are ignored by the assembler provide an opportunity to align elements of a program for easier readability. For example, all the opcodes start in the same column on the page.

7.2.2 Pseudo-ops (Assembler Directives)

The LC-3 assembler is a program that takes as input a string of characters representing a computer program written in LC-3 assembly language and translates it into a program in the ISA of the LC-3. Pseudo-ops are helpful to the assembler in performing that task.

Actually, a more formal name for a pseudo-op is *assembler directive*. They are called pseudo-ops because they do not refer to operations that will be performed by the program during execution. Rather, the pseudo-op is strictly a message to the assembler to help the assembler in the assembly process. Once the assembler handles the message, the pseudo-op is discarded. The LC-3 assembler contains five pseudo-ops: .ORIG, .FILL, .BLKW, .STRINGZ, and .END. All are easily recognizable by the dot as their first character.

.ORIG

.ORIG tells the assembler where in memory to place the LC-3 program. In line 05, .ORIG x3050 says, start with location x3050. As a result, the LD R1,SIX instruction will be put in location x3050.

.FILL

.FILL tells the assembler to set aside the next location in the program and initialize it with the value of the operand. In line 13, the ninth location in the resultant LC-3 program is initialized to the value x0006.

.BLKW

.BLKW tells the assembler to set aside some number of sequential memory locations (i.e., a **BL**oc**K** of **W**ords) in the program. The actual number is the operand of the .BLKW pseudo-op. In line 12, the pseudo-op instructs the assembler to set aside one location in memory (and also to label it NUMBER, incidentally).

The pseudo-op .BLKW is particularly useful when the actual value of the operand is not yet known. For example, one might want to set aside a location in memory for storing a character input from a keyboard. It will not be until the program is run that we will know the identity of that keystroke.

.STRINGZ

.STRINGZ tells the assembler to initialize a sequence of $n + 1$ memory locations. The argument is a sequence of n characters, inside double quotation marks. The first *n* words of memory are initialized with the zero-extended ASCII codes of the corresponding characters in the string. The final word of memory is initialized to 0. The last character, x0000, provides a convenient sentinel for processing the string of ASCII codes.

For example, the code fragment

```
        .ORIG     x3010
HELLO   .STRINGZ  "Hello, World!"
```

would result in the assembler initializing locations x3010 through x301D to the following values:

```
x3010:  x0048
x3011:  x0065
x3012:  x006C
x3013:  x006C
x3014:  x006F
x3015:  x002C
x3016:  x0020
x3017:  x0057
x3018:  x006F
x3019:  x0072
x301A:  x006C
x301B:  x0064
x301C:  x0021
x301D:  x0000
```

.END

.END tells the assembler where the program ends. Any characters that come after .END will not be used by the assembler. *Note:* .END does not stop the program during execution. In fact, .END does not even exist at the time of execution. It is simply a delimiter—it marks the end of the source program.

7.2.3 Example: The Character Count Example of Section 5.5, Revisited

Now we are ready for a complete example. Let's consider again the problem of Section 5.5. We wish to write a program that will take a character that is input from the keyboard and a file and count the number of occurrences of that character in that file. As before, we first develop the algorithm by constructing the flowchart. Recall that in Section 6.1, we showed how to decompose the problem systematically so as to generate the flowchart of Figure 5.16. In fact, the final step of that process in Chapter 6 is the flowchart of Figure 6.3e, which is essentially identical to Figure 5.16. Next, we use the flowchart to write the actual program. This time, however, we enjoy the luxury of not worrying about 0s and 1s and instead write the program in LC-3 assembly language. The program is shown in Figure 7.2.

```
01    ;
02    ; Program to count occurrences of a character in a file.
03    ; Character to be input from the keyboard.
04    ; Result to be displayed on the monitor.
05    ; Program works only if no more than 9 occurrences are found.
06    ;
07    ;
08    ; Initialization
09    ;
0A            .ORIG    x3000
0B            AND      R2,R2,#0     ; R2 is counter, initialize to 0
0C            LD       R3,PTR       ; R3 is pointer to characters
0D            TRAP     x23          ; R0 gets character input
0E            LDR      R1,R3,#0     ; R1 gets the next character
0F    ;
10    ; Test character for end of file
11    ;
13    TEST    ADD      R4,R1,#-4    ; Test for EOT
14            BRz      OUTPUT       ; If done, prepare the output
15    ;
16    ; Test character for match.  If a match, increment count.
17    ;
18            NOT      R1,R1
19            ADD      R1,R1,R0     ; If match, R1 = xFFFF
1A            NOT      R1,R1        ; If match, R1 = x0000
1B            BRnp     GETCHAR      ; If no match, do not increment
1C            ADD      R2,R2,#1
1D    ;
1E    ; Get next character from the file
1F    ;
20    GETCHAR ADD      R3,R3,#1     ; Increment the pointer
21            LDR      R1,R3,#0     ; R1 gets the next character to test
22            BRnzp    TEST
23    ;
24    ; Output the count.
25    ;
26    OUTPUT  LD       R0,ASCII     ; Load the ASCII template
27            ADD      R0,R0,R2     ; Convert binary to ASCII
28            TRAP     x21          ; ASCII code in R0 is displayed
29            TRAP     x25          ; Halt machine
2A    ;
2B    ; Storage for pointer and ASCII template
2C    ;
2D    ASCII   .FILL    x0030
2E    PTR     .FILL    x4000
2F            .END
```

Figure 7.2   The assembly language program to count occurrences of a character

A few notes regarding this program:

Three times during this program, assistance in the form of a service call is required of the operating system. In each case, a TRAP instruction is used. TRAP x23 causes a character to be input from the keyboard and placed in R0 (line 0D). TRAP x21 causes the ASCII code in R0 to be displayed on the monitor (line 28). TRAP x25 causes the machine to be halted (line 29). As we said before, we will leave the details of how the TRAP instruction is carried out until Chapter 9.

The ASCII codes for the decimal digits 0 to 9 (0000 to 1001) are x30 to x39. The conversion from binary to ASCII is done simply by adding x30 to the binary value of the decimal digit. Line 2D shows the label ASCII used to identify the memory location containing x0030.

The file that is to be examined starts at address x4000 (see line 2E). Usually, this starting address would not be known to the programmer who is writing this program since we would want the program to work on files that will become available in the future. That situation will be discussed in Section 7.4.

7.3 The Assembly Process

7.3.1 Introduction

Before an LC-3 assembly language program can be executed, it must first be translated into a machine language program, that is, one in which each instruction is in the LC-3 ISA. It is the job of the LC-3 assembler to perform that translation.

If you have available an LC-3 assembler, you can cause it to translate your assembly language program into a machine language program by executing an appropriate command. In the LC-3 assembler that is generally available via the Web, that command is *assemble* and requires as an argument the filename of your assembly language program. For example, if the filename is solution1.asm, then

```
assemble solution1.asm outfile
```

produces the file outfile, which is in the ISA of the LC-3. It is necessary to check with your instructor for the correct command line to cause the LC-3 assembler to produce a file of 0s and 1s in the ISA of the LC-3.

7.3.2 A Two-Pass Process

In this section, we will see how the assembler goes through the process of translating an assembly language program into a machine language program. We will use as our input to the process the assembly language program of Figure 7.2.

You remember that there is in general a one-to-one correspondence between instructions in an assembly language program and instructions in the final machine language program. We could try to perform this translation in one pass through the assembly language program. Starting from the top of Figure 7.2, the assembler discards lines 01 to 09, since they contain only comments. Comments are strictly for human consumption; they have no bearing on the translation process. The assembler then moves on to line 0A. Line 0A is a pseudo-op; it tells the assembler that the machine language program is to start at location x3000. The assembler then moves on to line 0B, which it can easily translate into LC-3 machine code. At this point, we have

```
x3000:   0101010010100000
```

The LC-3 assembler moves on to translate the next instruction (line 0C). Unfortunately, it is unable to do so since it does not know the meaning of the symbolic address PTR. At this point the assembler is stuck, and the assembly process fails.

To prevent this from occurring, the assembly process is done in two complete passes (from beginning to .END) through the entire assembly language program. The objective of the first pass is to identify the actual binary addresses corresponding to the symbolic names (or labels). This set of correspondences is known as the *symbol table*. In pass 1, we construct the symbol table. In pass 2, we translate the individual assembly language instructions into their corresponding machine language instructions.

Thus, when the assembler examines line 0C for the purpose of translating

```
LD R3,PTR
```

during the second pass, it already knows the correspondence between PTR and x3013 (from the first pass). Thus it can easily translate line 0C to

```
x3001:   0010011000010001
```

The problem of not knowing the 16-bit address corresponding to PTR no longer exists.

7.3.3 The First Pass: Creating the Symbol Table

For our purposes, the symbol table is simply a correspondence of symbolic names with their 16-bit memory addresses. We obtain these correspondences by passing through the assembly language program once, noting which instruction is assigned to which address, and identifying each label with the address of its assigned entry.

Recall that we provide labels in those cases where we have to refer to a location, either because it is the target of a branch instruction or because it contains data that must be loaded or stored. Consequently, if we have not made any programming mistakes, and if we identify all the labels, we will have identified all the symbolic addresses used in the program.

The preceding paragraph assumes that our entire program exists between our .ORIG and .END pseudo-ops. This is true for the assembly language program of Figure 7.2. In Section 7.4, we will consider programs that consist of multiple parts, each with its own .ORIG and .END, wherein each part is assembled separately.

The first pass starts, after discarding the comments on lines 01 to 09, by noting (line 0A) that the first instruction will be assigned to address x3000. We keep track of the location assigned to each instruction by means of a location counter (LC). The LC is initialized to the address specified in .ORIG, that is, x3000.

The assembler examines each instruction in sequence and increments the LC once for each assembly language instruction. If the instruction examined contains a label, a symbol table entry is made for that label, specifying the current contents of LC as its address. The first pass terminates when the .END instruction is encountered.

The first instruction that has a label is at line 13. Since it is the fifth instruction in the program and since the LC at that point contains x3004, a symbol table entry is constructed thus:

Symbol	Address
TEST	x3004

The second instruction that has a label is at line 20. At this point, the LC has been incremented to x300B. Thus a symbol table entry is constructed, as follows:

Symbol	Address
GETCHAR	x300B

At the conclusion of the first pass, the symbol table has the following entries:

Symbol	Address
TEST	x3004
GETCHAR	x300B
OUTPUT	x300E
ASCII	x3012
PTR	x3013

7.3.4 The Second Pass: Generating the Machine Language Program

The second pass consists of going through the assembly language program a second time, line by line, this time with the help of the symbol table. At each line, the assembly language instruction is translated into an LC-3 machine language instruction.

Starting again at the top, the assembler again discards lines 01 through 09 because they contain only comments. Line 0A is the .ORIG pseudo-op, which the assembler uses to initialize LC to x3000. The assembler moves on to line 0B and produces the machine language instruction 0101010010100000. Then the assembler moves on to line 0C.

This time, when the assembler gets to line 0C, it can completely assemble the instruction since it knows that PTR corresponds to x3013. The instruction is LD, which has an opcode encoding of 0010. The destination register (DR) is R3, that is, 011.

PCoffset is computed as follows: We know that PTR is the label for address x3013, and that the incremented PC is LC+1, in this case x3002. Since PTR (x3013) must be the sum of the incremented PC (x3002) and the sign-extended PCoffset, PCoffset must be x0011. Putting this all together, x3001 is set to 0010011000010001, and the LC is incremented to x3002.

Note: In order to use the LD instruction, it is necessary that the source of the load, in this case the address whose label is PTR, is not more than +256 or −255 memory locations from the LD instruction itself. If the address of PTR had been greater than LC+1 +255 or less than LC+1 −256, then the offset would not fit in bits [8:0] of the instruction. In such a case, an assembly error would have occurred, preventing the assembly process from finishing successfully. Fortunately, PTR is close enough to the LD instruction, so the instruction assembled correctly.

The second pass continues. At each step, the LC is incremented and the location specified by LC is assigned the translated LC-3 instruction or, in the case of .FILL, the value specified. When the second pass encounters the .END instruction, assembly terminates.

The resulting translated program is shown in Figure 7.3.

Address	Binary
	0011000000000000
x3000	0101010010100000
x3001	0010011000010001
x3002	1111000000100011
x3003	0110001011000000
x3004	0001100001111100
x3005	0000010000001000
x3006	1001001001111111
x3007	0001001001000000
x3008	1001001001111111
x3009	0000101000000001
x300A	0001010010100001
x300B	0001011011100001
x300C	0110001011000000
x300D	0000111111110110
x300E	0010000000000011
x300F	0001000000000010
x3010	1111000000100001
x3011	1111000000100101
x3012	0000000000110000
x3013	0100000000000000

Figure 7.3   The machine language program for the assembly language program of Figure 7.2

That process was, on a good day, merely tedious. Fortunately, you do not have to do it for a living—the LC-3 assembler does that. And, since you now know LC-3 assembly language, there is no need to program in machine language. Now we can write our programs symbolically in LC-3 assembly language and invoke the LC-3 assembler to create the machine language versions that can execute on an LC-3 computer.

7.4 Beyond the Assembly of a Single Assembly Language Program

Our purpose in this chapter has been to take you up one more notch from the ISA of the computer and introduce assembly language. Although it is still quite a large step from C or C++, assembly language does, in fact, save us a good deal of pain. We have also shown how a rudimentary two-pass assembler actually works to translate an assembly language program into the machine language of the LC-3 ISA.

There are many more aspects to sophisticated assembly language programming that go well beyond an introductory course. However, our reason for teaching assembly language is not to deal with its sophistication, but rather to show its innate simplicity. Before we leave this chapter, however, there are a few additional highlights we should explore.

7.4.1 The Executable Image

When a computer begins execution of a program, the entity being executed is called an *executable image*. The executable image is created from modules often created independently by several different programmers. Each module is translated separately into an object file. We have just gone through the process of performing that translation ourselves by mimicking the LC-3 assembler. Other modules, some written in C perhaps, are translated by the C compiler. Some modules are written by users, and some modules are supplied as library routines by the operating system. Each object file consists of instructions in the ISA of the computer being used, along with its associated data. The final step is to *link* all the object modules together into one executable image. During execution of the program, the FETCH, DECODE, ... instruction cycle is applied to instructions in the executable image.

7.4.2 More than One Object File

It is very common to form an executable image from more than one object file. In fact, in the real world, where most programs invoke libraries provided by the operating system as well as modules generated by other programmers, it is much more common to have multiple object files than a single one.

A case in point is our example character count program. The program counts the number of occurrences of a character in a file. A typical application could easily have the program as one module and the input data file as another. If this were the case, then the starting address of the file, shown as x4000 in line 2E of Figure 7.2, would not be known when the program was written. If we replace line 2E with

```
PTR    .FILL    STARTofFILE
```

then the program of Figure 7.2 will not assemble because there will be no symbol table entry for STARTofFILE. What can we do?

If the LC-3 assembly language, on the other hand, contained the pseudo-op .EXTERNAL, we could identify STARTofFILE as the symbolic name of an address that is not known at the time the program of Figure 7.2 is assembled. This would be done by the following line

```
.EXTERNAL    STARTofFILE,
```

which would send a message to the LC-3 assembler that the absence of label STARTofFILE is not an error in the program. Rather, STARTofFILE is a label in some other module that will be translated independently. In fact, in our case, it will be the label of the location of the first character in the file to be examined by our character count program.

If the LC-3 assembly language had the pseudo-op .EXTERNAL, and if we had designated STARTofFILE as .EXTERNAL, the LC-3 would be able to create a symbol table entry for STARTofFILE, and instead of assigning it an address, it would mark the symbol as belonging to another module. At *link time,* when all the modules are combined, the linker (the program that manages the "combining" process) would use the symbol table entry for STARTofFILE in another module to complete the translation of our revised line 2E.

In this way, the .EXTERNAL pseudo-op allows references by one module to symbolic locations in another module without a problem. The proper translations are resolved by the linker.

Exercises

7.1   An assembly language program contains the following two instructions. The assembler puts the translated version of the LDI instruction that follows into location x3025 of the object module. After assembly is complete, what is in location x3025?

```
PLACE    .FILL    x45A7
         LDI      R3, PLACE
```

7.2   An LC-3 assembly language program contains the instruction:

```
ASCII    LD  R1, ASCII
```

The symbol table entry for ASCII is x4F08. If this instruction is executed during the running of the program, what will be contained in R1 immediately after the instruction is executed?

7.3   What is the problem with using the string AND as a label?

7.4   Create the symbol table entries generated by the assembler when translating the following routine into machine code:

```
              .ORIG    x301C
              ST       R3, SAVE3
              ST       R2, SAVE2
              AND      R2, R2, #0
TEST          IN
              BRz      TEST
              ADD      R1, R0, #-10
              BRn      FINISH
              ADD      R1, R0, #-15
              NOT      R1, R1
              BRn      FINISH
              HALT
FINISH        ADD      R2, R2, #1
              HALT
SAVE3         .FILL    X0000
SAVE2         .FILL    X0000
              .END
```

7.5   *a.* What does the following program do?

```
            .ORIG    x3000
            LD       R2, ZERO
            LD       R0, M0
            LD       R1, M1
LOOP        BRz      DONE
            ADD      R2, R2, R0
            ADD      R1, R1, -1
            BR       LOOP
DONE        ST       R2, RESULT
            HALT
RESULT      .FILL    x0000
ZERO        .FILL    x0000
M0          .FILL    x0004
M1          .FILL    x0803
            .END
```

   b. What value will be contained in RESULT after the program runs to completion?

7.6   Our assembler has crashed and we need your help! Create a symbol table and assemble the instructions at labels D, E, and F for the program below. You may assume another module deposits a positive value into A before this module executes.

```
            .ORIG    x3000
            AND      R0, R0, #0
D           LD       R1, A
            AND      R2, R1, #1
            BRp      B
E           ADD      R1, R1, #-1
B           ADD      R0, R0, R1
            ADD      R1, R1, #-2
F           BRp      B
            ST       R0, C
            TRAP     x25
A           .BLKW    1
C           .BLKW    1
            .END
```

   In no more than 15 words, what does the above program do?

7.7   Write an LC-3 assembly language program that counts the number of 1s in the value stored in R0 and stores the result into R1. For example, if R0 contains 0001001101110000, then after the program executes, the result stored in R1 would be 0000 0000 0000 0110.

7.8   An engineer is in the process of debugging a program she has written.
She is looking at the following segment of the program, and decides to
place a breakpoint in memory at location 0xA404. Starting with the
PC = 0xA400, she initializes all the registers to zero and runs the
program until the breakpoint is encountered.

```
Code Segment:
. . .
0xA400   THIS1   LEA     R0,  THIS1
0xA401   THIS2   LD      R1,  THIS2
0xA402   THIS3   LDI     R2,  THIS5
0xA403   THIS4   LDR     R3,  R0,  #2
0xA404   THIS5   .FILL   xA400
. . .
```

Show the contents of the register file (in hexadecimal) when the
breakpoint is encountered.

7.9   What is the purpose of the .END pseudo-op? How does it differ from the
HALT instruction?

7.10 The following program fragment has an error in it. Identify the error and
explain how to fix it.

```
          ADD     R3,  R3,  #30
          ST      R3,  A
          HALT
A         .FILL   #0
```

Will this error be detected when this code is assembled or when this code
is run on the LC-3?

7.11 The LC-3 assembler must be able to convert constants represented in
ASCII into their appropriate binary values. For instance, x2A translates
into 00101010 and #12 translates into 00001100. Write an LC-3
assembly language program that reads a decimal or hexadecimal constant
from the keyboard (i.e., it is preceded by a # character signifying it is a
decimal, or x signifying it is hex) and prints out the binary representation.
Assume the constants can be expressed with no more than two decimal or
hex digits.

7.12   What does the following LC-3 program do?

```
                .ORIG   x3000
                AND     R5, R5, #0
                AND     R3, R3, #0
                ADD     R3, R3, #8
                LDI     R1, A
                ADD     R2, R1, #0
        AG      ADD     R2, R2, R2
                ADD     R3, R3, #-1
                BRnp    AG
                LD      R4, B
                AND     R1, R1, R4
                NOT     R1, R1
                ADD     R1, R1, #1
                ADD     R2, R2, R1
                BRnp    NO
                ADD     R5, R5, #1
        NO      HALT
        B       .FILL   xFF00
        A       .FILL   x4000
                .END
```

7.13   The following program adds the values stored in memory locations A, B, and C, and stores the result into memory. There are two errors in the code. For each, describe the error and indicate whether it will be detected at assembly time or at run time.

```
Line No.
1                       .ORIG  x3000
2           ONE         LD  R0, A
3                       ADD R1, R1, R0
4           TWO         LD  R0, B
5                       ADD R1, R1, R0
6           THREE       LD  R0, C
7                       ADD R1, R1, R0
8                       ST  R1, SUM
9                       TRAP  x25
10          A           .FILL x0001
11          B           .FILL x0002
12          C           .FILL x0003
13          D           .FILL x0004
14                      .END
```

7.14   *a.*   Assemble the following program:

```
        .ORIG   x3000
        STI     R0, LABEL
        OUT
        HALT
LABEL   .STRINGZ "%"
        .END
```

      b.   The programmer intended the program to output a **%** to the monitor, and then halt. Unfortunately, the programmer got confused about the semantics of each of the opcodes (that is, exactly what function is carried out by the LC-3 in response to each opcode). Replace exactly **one** opcode in this program with the correct opcode to make the program work as intended.

      c.   The original program from part *a* was executed. However, execution exhibited some very strange behavior. The strange behavior was in part due to the programming error, and in part due to the fact that the value in R0 when the program started executing was x3000. Explain what the strange behavior was and why the program behaved that way.

7.15   The following is an LC-3 program that performs a function. Assume a sequence of integers is stored in consecutive memory locations, one integer per memory location, starting at the location x4000. The sequence terminates with the value x0000. What does the following program do?

```
        .ORIG   x3000
        LD      R0, NUMBERS
        LD      R2, MASK
LOOP    LDR     R1, R0, #0
        BRz     DONE
        AND     R5, R1, R2
        BRz     L1
        BRnzp   NEXT
L1      ADD     R1, R1, R1
        STR     R1, R0, #0
NEXT    ADD     R0, R0, #1
        BRnzp   LOOP
DONE    HALT
NUMBERS .FILL   x4000
MASK    .FILL   x8000
        .END
```

7.16 Assume a sequence of nonnegative integers is stored in consecutive memory locations, one integer per memory location, starting at location x4000. Each integer has a value between 0 and 30,000 (decimal). The sequence terminates with the value −1 (i.e., xFFFF).

What does the following program do?

```
            .ORIG    x3000
            AND      R4, R4, #0
            AND      R3, R3, #0
            LD       R0, NUMBERS
LOOP        LDR      R1, R0, #0
            NOT      R2, R1
            BRz      DONE
            AND      R2, R1, #1
            BRz      L1
            ADD      R4, R4, #1
            BRnzp    NEXT
L1          ADD      R3, R3, #1
NEXT        ADD      R0, R0, #1
            BRnzp    LOOP
DONE        TRAP     x25
NUMBERS     .FILL    x4000
            .END
```

7.17 Suppose you write two separate assembly language modules that you expect to be combined by the linker. Each module uses the label AGAIN, and neither module contains the pseudo-op .EXTERNAL AGAIN. Is there a problem using the label AGAIN in both modules? Why or why not?

7.18 The following LC-3 program compares two character strings of the same length. The source strings are in the .STRINGZ form. The first string starts at memory location x4000, and the second string starts at memory location x4100. If the strings are the same, the program terminates with the value 0 in R5. Insert instructions at (a), (b), and (c) that will complete the program.

```
            .ORIG  x3000
            LD     R1, FIRST
            LD     R2, SECOND
            AND    R0, R0, #0
LOOP        -------------- (a)
            LDR    R4, R2, #0
            BRz    NEXT
            ADD    R1, R1, #1
            ADD    R2, R2, #1
            -------------- (b)
            -------------- (c)
            ADD    R3, R3, R4
            BRz    LOOP
            AND    R5, R5, #0
            BRnzp  DONE
NEXT        AND    R5, R5, #0
            ADD    R5, R5, #1
DONE        TRAP   x25
FIRST       .FILL  x4000
SECOND      .FILL  x4100
            .END
```

7.19 When the following LC-3 program is executed, how many times will the instruction at the memory address labeled LOOP execute?

```
            .ORIG    x3005
            LEA      R2, DATA
            LDR      R4, R2, #0
LOOP        ADD      R4, R4, #-3
            BRzp     LOOPk                    TRAP      x25
DATA        .FILL    x000B
            .END
```

7.20 LC-3 assembly language modules (a) and (b) have been written by different programmers to store x0015 into memory location x4000. What is fundamentally different about their approaches?

a.
```
            .ORIG    x5000
            AND      R0, R0, #0
            ADD      R0, R0, #15
            ADD      R0, R0, #6
            STI      R0, PTR
            HALT
PTR         .FILL    x4000
            .END
```

b.
```
            .ORIG    x4000
            .FILL    x0015
            .END
```

7.21 Assemble the following LC-3 assembly language program.

```
            .ORIG    x3000
            AND      R0, R0, #0
            ADD      R2, R0, #10
            LD       R1, MASK
            LD       R3, PTR1
LOOP        LDR      R4, R3, #0
            AND      R4, R4, R1
            BRz      NEXT
            ADD      R0, R0, #1
NEXT        ADD      R3, R3, #1
            ADD      R2, R2, #-1
            BRp      LOOP
            STI      R0, PTR2
HALT
MASK        .FILL    x8000
PTR1        .FILL    x4000
PTR2        .FILL    x5000
            .END
```

What does the program do (in no more than 20 words)?

7.22 The LC-3 assembler must be able to map an instruction's mnemonic opcode into its binary opcode. For instance, given an ADD, it must generate the binary pattern 0001. Write an LC-3 assembly language program that prompts the user to type in an LC-3 assembly language opcode and then displays its binary opcode. If the assembly language opcode is invalid, it displays an error message.

7.23 The following LC-3 program determines whether a character string is a palindrome or not. A palindrome is a string that reads the same backwards as forwards. For example, the string "racecar" is a palindrome. Suppose a string starts at memory location x4000, and is in the .STRINGZ format. If the string is a palindrome, the program terminates with the value 1 in R5. If not, the program terminates with the value 0 in R5. Insert instructions at (a)–(e) that will complete the program.

```
        .ORIG   x3000
        LD      R0, PTR
        ADD     R1, R0, #0
AGAIN   LDR     R2, R1, #0
        BRz     CONT
        ADD     R1, R1, #1
        BRnzp   AGAIN
CONT    -------------- (a)
LOOP    LDR     R3, R0, #0
        -------------- (b)
        NOT     R4, R4
        ADD     R4, R4, #1
        ADD     R3, R3, R4
        BRnp    NO
        -------------- (c)
        -------------- (d)
        NOT     R2, R0
        ADD     R2, R2, #1
        ADD     R2, R1, R2
        BRnz    YES
        -------------- (e)
YES     AND     R5, R5, #0
        ADD     R5, R5, #1
        BRnzp   DONE
NO      AND     R5, R5, #0
DONE    HALT
PTR     .FILL   x4000
        .END
```

7.24 We want the following program fragment to shift R3 to the left by four bits, but it has an error in it. Identify the error and explain how to fix it.

```
        .ORIG   x3000
        AND     R2, R2, #0
        ADD     R2, R2, #4
LOOP    BRz     DONE
        ADD     R2, R2, #-1
        ADD     R3, R3, R3
        BR      LOOP
DONE    HALT
        .END
```

7.25 What does the pseudo-op .FILL xFF004 do? Why?

8

I / O

Up to now, we have paid little attention to input/output (I/O). We did note (in Chapter 4) that input/output is an important component of the von Neumann model. There must be a way to get information into the computer in order to process it, and there must be a way to get the result of that processing out of the computer so humans can use it. Figure 4.1 depicts a number of different input and output devices.

We suggested (in Chapter 5) that input and output can be accomplished by executing the TRAP instruction, which asks the operating system to do it for us. Figure 5.17 illustrates this for input (at address x3002) and for output (at address x3010).

In this chapter, we are ready to do I/O by ourselves. We have chosen to study the keyboard as our input device and the monitor display as our output device. Not only are they the simplest I/O devices and the ones most familiar to us, but they have characteristics that allow us to study important concepts about I/O without getting bogged down in unnecessary detail.

8.1 I/O Basics

8.1.1 Device Registers

Although we often think of an I/O device as a single entity, interaction with a single I/O device usually means interacting with more than one *device register*. The simplest I/O devices usually have at least two device registers: one to hold the data being transferred between the device and the computer, and one to indicate status information about the device. An example of status information is whether the device is available or is still busy processing the most recent I/O task.

8.1.2 Memory-Mapped I/O versus Special Input/Output Instructions

An instruction that interacts with an input or output device register must identify the particular input or output device register with which it is interacting. Two schemes have been used in the past. Some computers use special input and output instructions. Most computers prefer to use the same data movement instructions that are used to move data in and out of memory.

The very old PDP-8 (from Digital Equipment Corporation, light years ago— 1965) is an example of a computer that used special input and output instructions. The 12-bit PDP-8 instruction contained a 3-bit opcode. If the opcode was 110, an I/O instruction was indicated. The remaining nine bits of the PDP-8 instruction identified which I/O device register and what operation was to be performed.

Most computer designers prefer not to specify an additional set of instructions for dealing with input and output. They use the same data movement instructions that are used for loading and storing data between memory and the general purpose registers. For example, a load instruction, in which the source address is that of an input device register, is an input instruction. Similarly, a store instruction in which the destination address is that of an output device register is an output instruction.

Since programmers use the same data movement instructions that are used for memory, every input device register and every output device register must be uniquely identified in the same way that memory locations are uniquely identified. Therefore, each device register is assigned an address from the memory address space of the ISA. That is, the I/O device registers are *mapped* to a set of addresses that are allocated to I/O device registers rather than to memory locations. Hence the name *memory-mapped I/O*.

The original PDP-11 ISA had a 16-bit address space. All addresses wherein bits $[15:13] = 111$ were allocated to I/O device registers. That is, of the 2^{16} addresses, only 57,344 corresponded to memory locations. The remaining 2^{13} were memory-mapped I/O addresses.

The LC-3 uses memory-mapped I/O. Addresses x0000 to xFDFF are allocated to memory locations. Addresses xFE00 to xFFFF are reserved for input/output device registers. Table A.3 lists the memory-mapped addresses of the LC-3 device registers that have been assigned so far. Future uses and sales of LC-3 microprocessors may require the expansion of device register address assignments as new and exciting applications emerge!

8.1.3 Asynchronous versus Synchronous

Most I/O is carried out at speeds very much slower than the speed of the processor. A typist, typing on a keyboard, loads an input device register with one ASCII code every time he/she types a character. A computer can read the contents of that device register every time it executes a load instruction, where the operand address is the memory-mapped address of that input device register.

Many of today's microprocessors execute instructions under the control of a clock that operates well in excess of 300 MHz. Even for a microprocessor operating at only 300 MHz, a clock cycle lasts only 3.3 nanoseconds. Suppose a processor executed one instruction at a time, and it took the processor 10 clock cycles to execute the instruction that reads the input device register and stores its contents. At that rate, the processor could read the contents of the input device register once every 33 nanoseconds. Unfortunately, people do not type fast enough to keep this processor busy full-time reading characters. *Question:* How fast would a person have to type to supply input characters to the processor at the maximum rate the processor can receive them? Assume the average word length is six characters. See Exercise 8.3.

We could mitigate this speed disparity by designing hardware that would accept typed characters at some slower fixed rate. For example, we could design a piece of hardware that accepts one character every 30 million cycles. This would require a typing speed of 100 words/minute, which is certainly doable. Unfortunately, it would also require that the typist work in lockstep with the computer's clock. That is not acceptable since the typing speed (even of the same typist) varies from moment to moment.

What's the point? The point is that I/O devices usually operate at speeds very different from that of a microprocessor, and not in lockstep. This latter characteristic we call *asynchronous*. Most interaction between a processor and I/O is asynchronous. To control processing in an asynchronous world requires some protocol or *handshaking* mechanism. So it is with our keyboard and monitor display. In the case of the keyboard, we will need a 1-bit status register, called a *flag,* to indicate if someone has or has not typed a character. In the case of the monitor, we will need a 1-bit status register to indicate whether or not the most recent character sent to the monitor has been displayed.

These flags are the simplest form of *synchronization*. A single flag, called the *Ready bit,* is enough to synchronize the output of the typist who can type characters at the rate of 100 words/minute with the input to a processor that can accept these characters at the rate of 300 million characters/second. Each time the typist types a character, the Ready bit is set. Each time the computer reads a character, it clears the Ready bit. By examining the Ready bit before reading a character, the computer can tell whether it has already read the last character typed. If the Ready bit is clear, no characters have been typed since the last time the computer read a character, and so no additional read would take place. When the computer detects that the Ready bit is set, it could only have been caused by a **new** character being typed, so the computer would know to again read a character.

The single Ready bit provides enough handshaking to ensure that the asynchronous transfer of information between the typist and the microprocessor can be carried out accurately.

If the typist could type at a constant speed, and we did have a piece of hardware that would accept typed characters at precise intervals (for example, one character every 30 million cycles), then we would not need the Ready bit. The computer would simply know, after 30 million cycles of doing other stuff, that the typist had typed exactly one more character, and the computer would read that character. In this hypothetical situation, the typist would be typing in lockstep with the processor, and no additional synchronization would be needed. We would say the computer and typist were operating *synchronously,* or the input activity was synchronous.

8.1.4 Interrupt-Driven versus Polling

The processor, which is computing, and the typist, who is typing, are two separate entities. Each is doing its own thing. Still, they need to interact, that is, the data that is typed has to get into the computer. The issue of *interrupt-driven* versus *polling* is the issue of who controls the interaction. Does the processor do its own thing until being interrupted by an announcement from the keyboard, "Hey, a key has been struck. The ASCII code is in the input device register. You need to read it." This is called *interrupt-driven I/O,* where the keyboard controls the interaction. Or, does the processor control the interaction, specifically by interrogating (usually, again and again) the Ready bit until it (the processor) detects that the Ready bit is set. At that point, the processor knows it is time to read the device register. This second type of interaction is called *polling,* since the Ready bit is polled by the processor, asking if any key has been struck.

Section 8.2.2 describes how the polling method works. Section 8.5 explains interrupt-driven I/O.

8.2 Input from the Keyboard

8.2.1 Basic Input Registers (the KBDR and the KBSR)

We have already noted that in order to handle character input from the keyboard, we need two things: a data register that contains the character to be input, and a synchronization mechanism to let the processor know that input has occurred. The synchronization mechanism is contained in the status register associated with the keyboard.

These two registers are called the *keyboard data register* (KBDR) and the *keyboard status register* (KBSR). They are assigned addresses from the memory address space. As shown in Table A.3, KBDR is assigned to xFE02; KBSR is assigned to xFE00.

Even though a character needs only eight bits and the synchronization mechanism needs only one bit, it is easier to assign 16 bits (like all memory addresses in the LC-3) to each. In the case of KBDR, bits [7:0] are used for the data, and bits [15:8] contain x00. In the case of KBSR, bit [15] contains the synchronization mechanism, that is, the Ready bit. Figure 8.1 shows the two device registers needed by the keyboard.

8.2.2 The Basic Input Service Routine

KBSR[15] controls the synchronization of the slow keyboard and the fast processor. When a key on the keyboard is struck, the ASCII code for that key is loaded into KBDR[7:0] and the electronic circuits associated with the keyboard

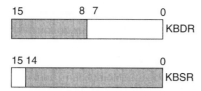

Figure 8.1   Keyboard device registers

automatically set KBSR[15] to 1. When the LC-3 reads KBDR, the electronic circuits associated with the keyboard automatically clear KBSR[15], allowing another key to be struck. If KBSR[15] = 1, the ASCII code corresponding to the last key struck has not yet been read, and so the keyboard is disabled.

If input/output is controlled by the processor (i.e., via polling), then a program can repeatedly test KBSR[15] until it notes that the bit is set. At that point, the processor can load the ASCII code contained in KBDR into one of the LC-3 registers. Since the processor only loads the ASCII code if KBSR[15] is 1, there is no danger of reading a single typed character multiple times. Furthermore, since the keyboard is disabled until the previous code is read, there is no danger of the processor missing characters that were typed. In this way, KBSR[15] provides the mechanism to guarantee that each key typed will be loaded exactly once.

The following input routine loads R0 with the ASCII code that has been entered through the keyboard and then moves on to the NEXT_TASK in the program.

```
01      START   LDI     R1, A           ; Test for
02              BRzp    START           ; character input
03              LDI     R0, B
04              BRnzp   NEXT_TASK       ; Go to the next task
05      A       .FILL   xFE00           ; Address of KBSR
06      B       .FILL   xFE02           ; Address of KBDR
```

As long as KBSR[15] is 0, no key has been struck since the last time the processor read the data register. Lines 01 and 02 comprise a loop that tests bit [15] of KBSR. Note the use of the LDI instruction, which loads R1 with the contents of xFE00, the memory-mapped address of KBSR. If the Ready bit, bit [15], is clear, BRzp will branch to START and another iteration of the loop. When someone strikes a key, KBDR will be loaded with the ASCII code of that key and the Ready bit of KBSR will be set. This will cause the branch to fall through and the instruction at line 03 to be executed. Again, note the use of the LDI instruction, which this time loads R0 with the contents of xFE02, the memory-mapped address of KBDR. The input routine is now done, so the program branches unconditionally to its NEXT_TASK.

8.2.3 Implementation of Memory-Mapped Input

Figure 8.2 shows the additional data path required to implement memory-mapped input. You are already familiar, from Chapter 5, with the data path required to

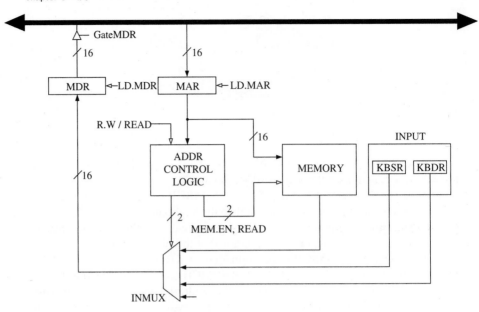

Figure 8.2   Memory-mapped input

carry out the EXECUTE phase of the load instructions. Essentially three steps are required:

1. The MAR is loaded with the address of the memory location to be read.
2. Memory is read, resulting in MDR being loaded with the contents at the specified memory location.
3. The destination register (DR) is loaded with the contents of MDR.

In the case of memory-mapped input, the same set of steps are carried out, **except** instead of MAR being loaded with the address of a memory location, MAR is loaded with the address of a device register. Instead of the address control logic enabling memory to read, the address control logic selects the corresponding device register to provide input to the MDR.

8.3 Output to the Monitor

8.3.1 Basic Output Registers (the DDR and the DSR)

Output works in a way very similar to input, with DDR and DSR replacing the roles of KBDR and KBSR, respectively. DDR stands for Display Data Register, which drives the monitor display. DSR stands for Display Status Register. In the LC-3, DDR is assigned address xFE06. DSR is assigned address xFE04.

As is the case with input, even though an output character needs only eight bits and the synchronization mechanism needs only one bit, it is easier to assign 16 bits (like all memory addresses in the LC-3) to each output device register. In the case of DDR, bits [7:0] are used for data, and bits [15:8] contain x00. In the

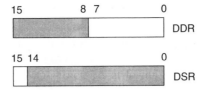

Figure 8.3   Monitor device registers

case of DSR, bit [15] contains the synchronization mechanism, that is, the Ready bit. Figure 8.3 shows the two device registers needed by the monitor.

8.3.2 The Basic Output Service Routine

DSR[15] controls the synchronization of the fast processor and the slow monitor display. When the LC-3 transfers an ASCII code to DDR[7:0] for outputting, the electronics of the monitor automatically clear DSR[15] as the processing of the contents of DDR[7:0] begins. When the monitor finishes processing the character on the screen, it (the monitor) automatically sets DSR[15]. This is a signal to the processor that it (the processor) can transfer another ASCII code to DDR for outputting. As long as DSR[15] is clear, the monitor is still processing the previous character, so the monitor is disabled as far as additional output from the processor is concerned.

　　If input/output is controlled by the processor (i.e., via polling), then a program can repeatedly test DSR[15] until it notes that the bit is set, indicating that it is OK to write a character to the screen. At that point, the processor can store the ASCII code for the character it wishes to write into DDR[7:0], setting up the transfer of that character to the monitor's display.

　　The following routine causes the ASCII code contained in R0 to be displayed on the monitor:

```
01      START   LDI     R1, A           ; Test to see if
02              BRzp    START           ; output register is ready
03              STI     R0, B
04              BRnzp   NEXT_TASK
05      A       .FILL   xFE04           ; Address of DSR
06      B       .FILL   xFE06           ; Address of DDR
```

Like the routine for KBDR and KBSR in Section 8.2.2, lines 01 and 02 repeatedly poll DSR[15] to see if the monitor electronics is finished yet with the last character shipped by the processor. Note the use of LDI and the indirect access to xFE04, the memory-mapped address of DSR. As long as DSR[15] is clear, the monitor electronics is still processing this character, and BRzp branches to START for another iteration of the loop. When the monitor electronics finishes with the last character shipped by the processor, it automatically sets DSR[15] to 1, which causes the branch to fall through and the instruction at line 03 to be executed. Note the use of the STI instruction, which stores R0 into xFE06, the memory-mapped address of DDR. The write to DDR also clears DSR[15], disabling for the moment DDR from further output. The monitor electronics takes over and writes the character to the screen. Since the output routine is now done, the program unconditionally branches (line 04) to its NEXT_TASK.

8.3.3 Implementation of Memory-Mapped Output

Figure 8.4 shows the additional data path required to implement memory-mapped output. As we discussed previously with respect to memory-mapped input, the mechanisms for handling the device registers provide very little additional complexity to what already exists for handling memory accesses.

In Chapter 5, you became familiar with the process of carrying out the EXECUTE phase of the store instructions.

1. The MAR is loaded with the address of the memory location to be written.

2. The MDR is loaded with the data to be written to memory.

3. Memory is written, resulting in the contents of MDR being stored in the specified memory location.

In the case of memory-mapped output, the same steps are carried out, **except** instead of MAR being loaded with the address of a memory location, MAR is loaded with the address of a device register. Instead of the address control logic enabling memory to write, the address control logic asserts the load enable signal of DDR.

Memory-mapped output also requires the ability to **read** output device registers. You saw in Section 8.3.2 that before the DDR could be loaded, the Ready

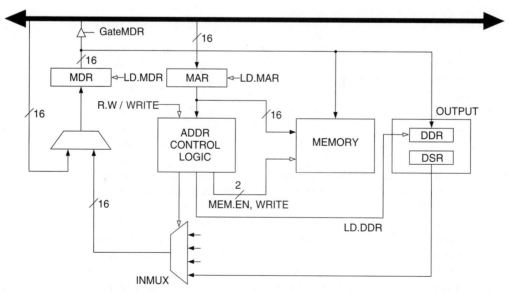

Figure 8.4   Memory-mapped output

bit had to be in state 1, indicating that the previous character had already been written to the screen. The LDI and BRzp instructions on lines 01 and 02 perform that test. To do this the LDI reads the output device register DSR, and BRzp tests bit [15]. If the MAR is loaded with xFE04 (the memory-mapped address of the DSR), the address control logic selects DSR as the input to the MDR, where it is subsequently loaded into R1 and the condition codes are set.

8.3.4 Example: Keyboard Echo

When we type at the keyboard, it is helpful to know exactly what characters we have typed. We can get this echo capability easily (without any sophisticated electronics) by simply combining the two routines we have discussed. The key typed at the keyboard is displayed on the monitor.

```
01      START   LDI     R1, KBSR      ; Test for character input
02              BRzp    START
03              LDI     R0, KBDR
04      ECHO    LDI     R1, DSR       ; Test output register ready
05              BRzp    ECHO
06              STI     R0, DDR
07              BRnzp   NEXT_TASK
08      KBSR    .FILL   xFE00         ; Address of KBSR
09      KBDR    .FILL   xFE02         ; Address of KBDR
0A      DSR     .FILL   xFE04         ; Address of DSR
0B      DDR     .FILL   xFE06         ; Address of DDR
```

8.4 A More Sophisticated Input Routine

In the example of Section 8.2.2, the input routine would be a part of a program being executed by the computer. Presumably, the program requires character input from the keyboard. But how does the person sitting at the keyboard know when to type a character? Sitting there, the person may wonder whether or not the program is actually running, or if perhaps the computer is busy doing something else.

To let the person sitting at the keyboard know that the program is waiting for input from the keyboard, the computer typically prints a message on the monitor. Such a message is often referred to as a *prompt*. The symbol that is displayed by your operating system (for example, % or **C:**) or by your editor (for example, **:**) are examples of prompts.

The program fragment shown in Figure 8.5 obtains keyboard input via polling as we have shown in Section 8.2.2 already. It also includes a prompt to let the person sitting at the keyboard know when it is time to type a key. Let's examine this program fragment in parts.

You are already familiar with lines 13 through 19 and lines 25 through 28, which correspond to the code in Section 8.3.4 for inputting a character via the

```
01   START    ST      R1,SaveR1    ; Save registers needed
02            ST      R2,SaveR2    ; by this routine
03            ST      R3,SaveR3
04   ;
05            LD      R2,Newline
06   L1       LDI     R3,DSR
07            BRzp    L1           ; Loop until monitor is ready
08            STI     R2,DDR       ; Move cursor to new clean line
09   ;
0A            LEA     R1,Prompt    ; Starting address of prompt string
0B   Loop     LDR     R0,R1,#0     ; Write the input prompt
0C            BRz     Input        ; End of prompt string
0D   L2       LDI     R3,DSR
0E            BRzp    L2           ; Loop until monitor is ready
0F            STI     R0,DDR       ; Write next prompt character
10            ADD     R1,R1,#1     ; Increment prompt pointer
11            BRnzp   Loop         ; Get next prompt character
12   ;
13   Input    LDI     R3,KBSR
14            BRzp    Input        ; Poll until a character is typed
15            LDI     R0,KBDR      ; Load input character into R0
16   L3       LDI     R3,DSR
17            BRzp    L3           ; Loop until monitor is ready
18            STI     R0,DDR       ; Echo input character
19   ;
1A   L4       LDI     R3,DSR
1B            BRzp    L4           ; Loop until monitor is ready
1C            STI     R2,DDR       ; Move cursor to new clean line
1D            LD      R1,SaveR1    ; Restore registers
1E            LD      R2,SaveR2    ; to original values
1F            LD      R3,SaveR3
20            BRnzp   NEXT_TASK    ; Do the program's next task
21   ;
22   SaveR1   .BKLW   1            ; Memory for registers saved
23   SaveR2   .BKLW   1
24   SaveR3   .BKLW   1
25   DSR      .FILL   xFE04
26   DDR      .FILL   xFE06
27   KBSR     .FILL   xFE00
28   KBDR     .FILL   xFE02
29   Newline .FILL    x000A        ; ASCII code for newline
2A   Prompt   .STRINGZ ''Input a character>''
```

Figure 8.5   The input routine for the LC-3 keyboard

keyboard and echoing it on the monitor. Lines 01 through 03, lines 1D through 1F, and lines 22 through 24 recognize that this input routine needs to use general purpose registers R1, R2, and R3. Unfortunately, they most likely contain values that will still be needed after this routine has finished. To prevent the loss of those values, the ST instructions in lines 01 through 03 save them in memory locations SaveR1, SaveR2, and SaveR3, before the input routine starts its business. These three memory locations have been allocated by the .BLKW pseudo-ops in lines 22 through 24. After the input routine is finished and before the program branches unconditionally to its NEXT_TASK (line 20), the LD instructions in lines 1D through 1F restore the original values saved to their rightful locations in R1, R2, and R3.

This leaves lines 05 through 08, 0A through 11, 1A through 1C, 29 and 2A. These lines serve to alert the person sitting at the keyboard that it is time to type a character.

Lines 05 through 08 write the ASCII code x0A to the monitor. This is the ASCII code for a *new line*. Most ASCII codes correspond to characters that are visible on the screen. A few, like x0A, are control characters. They cause an action to occur. Specifically, the ASCII code x0A causes the cursor to move to the far left of the next line on the screen. Thus the name *Newline*. Before attempting to write x0A, however, as is always the case, DSR[15] is tested (line 6) to see if DDR can accept a character. If DSR[15] is clear, the monitor is busy, and the loop (lines 06 and 07) is repeated. When DSR[15] is 1, the conditional branch (line 7) is not taken, and x0A is written to DDR for outputting (line 8).

Lines 0A through 11 cause the prompt `Input a character>` to be written to the screen. The prompt is specified by the .STRINGZ pseudo-op on line 2A and is stored in 19 memory locations—18 ASCII codes, one per memory location, corresponding to the 18 characters in the prompt, and the terminating sentinel x0000.

Line 0C iteratively tests to see if the end of the string has been reached (by detecting x0000), and if not, once DDR is free, line 0F writes the next character in the input prompt into DDR. When x0000 is detected, the program knows that the entire input prompt has been written to the screen and branches to the code that handles the actual keyboard input (starting at line 13).

After the person at the keyboard has typed a character and it has been echoed (lines 13 to 19), the program writes one more new line (lines 1A through 1C) before branching to its NEXT_TASK.

8.5   Interrupt-Driven I/O

In Section 8.1.4, we noted that interaction between the processor and an I/O device can be controlled by the processor (i.e., polling) or it can be controlled by the I/O device (i.e., interrupt driven). In Sections 8.2, 8.3, and 8.4, we have studied several examples of polling. In each case, the processor tested the Ready bit of the status register, again and again, and when it was finally 1, the processor branched to the instruction that did the input or output operation.

We are now ready to study the case where the interaction is controlled by the I/O device.

8.5.1   What Is Interrupt-Driven I/O?

The essence of interrupt-driven I/O is the notion that an I/O device that may or may not have anything to do with the program that is running can (1) force that

```
              .
              .
              .
     Program A is executing instruction n
     Program A is executing instruction n+1
     Program A is executing instruction n+2
  1: Interrupt signal is detected
  1: Program A is put into suspended animation
  2: The needs of the I/O device start being carried out
  2: The needs of the I/O device are being carried out
  2: The needs of the I/O device are being carried out
  2: The needs of the I/O device are being carried out
  2: The needs of the I/O device have been carried out
  3: Program A is brought back to life
     Program A is executing instruction n+3
     Program A is executing instruction n+4
              .
              .
              .
```

Figure 8.6   Instruction execution flow for interrupt-driven I/O

program to stop, (2) have the processor carry out the needs of the I/O device, and then (3) have the stopped program resume execution as if nothing had happened. These three stages of the instruction execution flow are shown in Figure 8.6.

As far as Program A is concerned, the work carried out and the results computed are no different from what would have been the case if the interrupt had never happened; that is, as if the instruction execution flow had been the following:

```
              .
              .
     Program A is executing instruction n
     Program A is executing instruction n+1
     Program A is executing instruction n+2
     Program A is executing instruction n+3
     Program A is executing instruction n+4
              .
              .
```

8.5.2 Why Have Interrupt-Driven I/O?

As is undoubtedly clear, polling requires the processor to waste a lot of time spinning its wheels, re-executing again and again the LDI and BR instructions until the Ready bit is set. With interrupt-driven I/O, none of that testing and branching has to go on. Interrupt-driven I/O allows the processor to spend its time doing what is hopefully useful work, executing some other program perhaps, until it is notified that some I/O device needs attention.

Example 8.1

Suppose we are asked to write a program that takes a sequence of 100 characters typed on a keyboard and processes the information contained in those 100 characters. Assume the characters are typed at the rate of 80 words/minute, which corresponds to one character every 0.125 seconds. Assume the processing of the 100-character sequence takes 12.49999 seconds, and that our program is to perform this process on 1,000 consecutive sequences. How long will it take our program to complete the task? (Why did we pick 12.49999? To make the numbers come out nice!)

We could obtain each character input by polling, as in Section 8.2. If we did, we would waste a lot of time waiting for the "next" character to be typed. It would take $100 \cdot 0.125$ or 12.5 seconds to get a 100-character sequence.

On the other hand, if we use interrupt-driven I/O, the processor does not waste any time re-executing the LDI and BR instructions while waiting for a character to be typed. Rather, the processor can be busy working on the previous 100-character sequence that was typed, **except** for those very small fractions of time when it is interrupted by the I/O device to read the next character typed. Let's say that to read the next character typed requires executing a 10-instruction program that takes on the average 0.00000001 seconds to execute each instruction. That means 0.0000001 seconds for each character typed, or 0.00001 seconds for the entire 100-character sequence. That is, with interrupt-driven I/O, since the processor is only needed when characters are actually being read, the time required for each 100-character sequence is 0.00001 seconds, instead of 12.50000 seconds. The remaining 12.49999 of every 12.50000 seconds, the processor is available to do useful work. For example, it can process the previous 100-character sequence.

The bottom line: With polling, the time to complete the entire task for each sequence is 24.9999 seconds, 12.5 seconds to obtain the 100 characters + 12.49999 seconds to process them. With interrupt-driven I/O, the time to complete the entire task for each sequence after the first is 12.5 seconds, 0.00001 seconds to obtain the characters + 12.49999 seconds to process them. For 1,000 sequences that is the difference between 7 hours and $3\frac{1}{2}$ hours.

8.5.3 Generation of the Interrupt Signal

There are two parts to interrupt-driven I/O, (1) the enabling mechanism that allows an I/O device to interrupt the processor when it has input to deliver or is ready to accept output, and (2) the mechanism that manages the transfer of the I/O data. The two parts can be briefly described as:

1. generating the interrupt signal, which stops the currently executing process, and

2. handling the request demanded by this signal.

The first part we will study momentarily. We will examine the various things that must come together to force the processor to stop what it is doing and pay attention to the interrupt request.

The second part, unfortunately, we will have to put off until Section 10.2. To handle interrupt requests, the LC-3 uses a stack, and we will not get to stacks until Chapter 10.

Now, then, part 1. Several things must be true for an I/O device to actually interrupt the processor:

1. The I/O device must want service.

2. The device must have the right to request the service.

3. The device request must be more urgent than what the processor is currently doing.

If all three elements are present, the processor stops executing the program and takes care of the interrupt.

The Interrupt Signal from the Device

For an I/O device to generate an interrupt request, the first two elements in the previous list must be true: The device must want service, and it must have the right to request that service.

The first element we have discussed at length in the study of polling. It is the Ready bit of the KBSR or the DSR. That is, if the I/O device is the keyboard, it wants service if someone has typed a character. If the I/O device is the monitor, it wants service (i.e., the next character to output) if the associated electronic circuits have successfully completed the display of the last character. In both cases, the I/O device wants service when the corresponding Ready bit is set.

The second element is an interrupt enable bit, which can be set or cleared by the processor, depending on whether or not the processor wants to give the I/O device the right to request service. In most I/O devices, this interrupt enable (IE) bit is part of the device status register. In the KBSR and DSR shown in Figure 8.7, the IE bit is bit [14]. The **interrupt request from the I/O device** is the logical AND of the IE bit and the Ready bit, as is also shown in Figure 8.7.

If the interrupt enable bit (bit [14]) is clear, it does not matter whether the Ready bit is set; the I/O device will not be able to interrupt the processor. In that case, the program will have to poll the I/O device to determine if it is ready.

If bit [14] is set, then interrupt-driven I/O is enabled. In that case, as soon as someone types a key (or as soon as the monitor has finished processing the

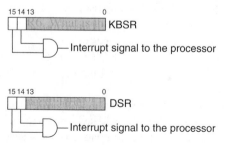

Figure 8.7   Interrupt enable bits and their use

last character), bit [15] is set. This, in turn, asserts the output of the AND gate, causing an interrupt request to be generated from the I/O device.

The Importance of Priority

The third element in the list of things that must be true for an I/O device to actually interrupt the processor is whether the request is sufficiently urgent. Every instruction that the processor executes, it does with a stated level of urgency. The term we give for the urgency of execution is *priority*.

We say that a program is being executed at a specified priority level. Almost all computers have a set of priority levels that programs can run at. The LC-3 has eight priority levels, PL0, .. PL7. The higher the number, the more urgent the program. The PL of a program is usually the same as the PL (i.e., urgency) of the request to run that program. If a program is running at one PL, and a higher-level PL request seeks access to the computer, the lower-priority program suspends processing until the higher-PL program executes and satisfies that more urgent request. For example, a computer's payroll program may run overnight, and at PL0. It has all night to finish—not terribly urgent. A program that corrects for a nuclear plant current surge may run at PL6. We are perfectly happy to let the payroll wait while the nuclear power correction keeps us from being blown to bits.

For our I/O device to successfully stop the processor and start an interrupt-driven I/O request, the priority of the request must be higher than the priority of the program it wishes to interrupt. For example, we would not normally want to allow a keyboard interrupt from a professor checking e-mail to interrupt the nuclear power correction program.

We will see momentarily that the processor will stop executing its current program and service an interrupt request if the INT signal is asserted. Figure 8.8 shows what is required to assert the INT signal and where the notion of priority level comes into play. Figure 8.8 shows the status registers of several devices operating at various priority levels. Any device that has bits [14] and [15] both set asserts its interrupt request signal. The interrupt request signals are input to a priority encoder, a combinational logic structure that selects the highest priority request from all those asserted. If the PL of that request is higher than the PL of the currently executing program, the INT signal is asserted and the executing program is stopped.

The Test for INT

The final step in the first part of interrupt-driven I/O is the test to see if the processor should stop and handle an interrupt. Recall from Chapter 4 that the instruction cycle sequences through the six phases of FETCH, DECODE, EVALUATE ADDRESS, FETCH OPERAND, EXECUTE, and STORE RESULT. Recall further that after the sixth phase, the control unit returns to the first phase, that is, the FETCH of the next instruction.

The additional logic to test for the interrupt signal is to replace that last sequential step of **always** going from STORE RESULT back to FETCH, as follows: The STORE RESULT phase is instead accompanied by a test for the interrupt signal INT. If INT is not asserted, then it is business as usual, with the control unit

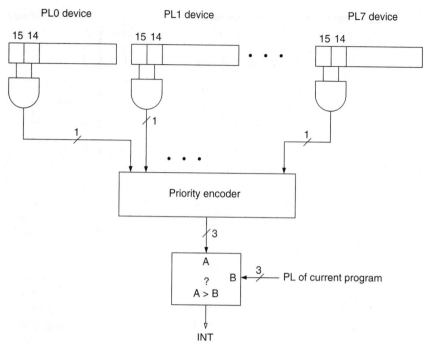

Figure 8.8   Generation of the INT signal

returning to the FETCH phase to start processing the next instruction. If INT is asserted, then the control unit does two things before returning to the FETCH phase. First it saves enough state information to be able to return to the interrupted program where it left off. Second it loads the PC with the starting address of the program that is to carry out the requirements of the I/O device. How it does that is the topic of Section 10.2, which we will study after we learn how stacks work.

8.6 Implementation of Memory-Mapped I/O, Revisited

We showed in Figures 8.2 and 8.4 partial implementations of the data path to handle (separately) memory-mapped input and memory-mapped output. We have also learned that in order to support interrupt-driven I/O, the two status registers must be writeable as well as readable.

Figure 8.9 (reproduced from Figure C.3 of Appendix C) shows the data path necessary to support the full range of features we have discussed for the I/O device registers. The Address Control Logic block controls the input or output operation. Note that there are three inputs to this block. MIO.EN indicates whether a data movement from/to memory or I/O is to take place this clock cycle. MAR contains the address of the memory location or the memory-mapped address of an I/O device register. R.W indicates whether a load or a store is to take place. Depending on the values of these three inputs, the Address Control Logic does nothing (MIO.EN = 0), or provides the control signals to direct the transfer of data between the MDR and the memory or I/O registers.

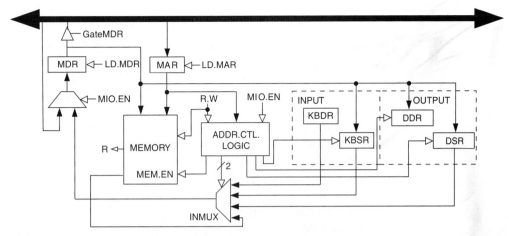

Figure 8.9   Partial data path implementation of memory-mapped I/O

If R.W indicates a load, the transfer is from memory or I/O device to the MDR. The Address Control Logic block provides the select lines to INMUX to source the appropriate I/O device register or memory (depending on MAR) and also enables the memory if MAR contains the address of a memory location.

If R.W indicates a store, the contents of the MDR are written either to memory or to one of the device registers. The Address Control Logic either enables a write to memory or it asserts the load enable line of the device register specified by the contents of the MAR.

Exercises

8.1 *a.* What is a device register?
b. What is a device data register?
c. What is a device status register?

8.2 Why is a Ready bit not needed if synchronous I/O is used?

8.3 In Section 8.1.3, the statement is made that a typist would have trouble supplying keyboard input to a 300-MHz processor at the maximum rate (one character every 33 nanoseconds) that the processor can accept it. Assume an average word (including spaces between words) consists of six characters. How many words/minute would the typist have to type in order to exceed the processor's ability to handle the input?

8.4 Are the following interactions usually synchronous or asynchronous?

a. Between a remote control and a television set
b. Between the mailcarrier and you, via a mailbox
c. Between a mouse and your PC

Under what conditions would each of them be synchronous? Under what conditions would each of them be asynchronous?

8.5   What is the purpose of bit [15] in the KBSR?

8.6   What problem could occur if a program does not check the Ready bit of the KBSR before reading the KBDR?

8.7   Which of the following combinations describe the system described in Section 8.2.2?

  a. Memory mapped and interrupt driven
  b. Memory mapped and polling
  c. Special opcode for I/O and interrupt driven
  d. Special opcode for I/O and polling

8.8   Write a program that checks the initial value in memory location x4000 to see if it is a valid ASCII code and if it is a valid ASCII code, prints the character. If the value in x4000 is not a valid ASCII code, the program prints nothing.

8.9   What problem is likely to occur if the keyboard hardware does not check the KBSR before writing to the KBDR?

8.10   What problem could occur if the display hardware does not check the DSR before writing to the DDR?

8.11   Which is more efficient, interrupt-driven I/O or polling? Explain.

8.12   Adam H. decided to design a variant of the LC-3 that did not need a keyboard status register. Instead, he created a readable/writable keyboard data and status register (KBDSR), which contains the same data as the KBDR. With the KBDSR, a program requiring keyboard input would wait until a nonzero value appeared in the KBDSR. The nonzero value would be the ASCII value of the last key press. Then the program would write a zero into the KBDSR indicating that it had read the key press. Modify the basic input service of Section 8.2.2 to implement Adam's scheme.

8.13   Some computer engineering students decided to revise the LC-3 for their senior project. In designing the LC-4, they decided to conserve on device registers by combining the KBSR and the DSR into one status register: the IOSR (the input/output status register). IOSR[15] is the keyboard device Ready bit and IOSR[14] is the display device Ready bit. What are the implications for programs wishing to do I/O? Is this a poor design decision?

8.14   An LC-3 Load instruction specifies the address xFE02. How do we know whether to load from the KBDR or from memory location xFE02?

8.15 Interrupt-driven I/O:

a. What does the following LC-3 program do?

```
              .ORIG    x3000
              LD       R3, A
              STI      R3, KBSR
      AGAIN   LD       R0, B
              TRAP     x21
              BRnzp    AGAIN
      A       .FILL    x4000
      B       .FILL    x0032
      KBSR    .FILL    xFE00
              .END
```

b. If someone strikes a key, the program will be interrupted and the keyboard interrupt service routine will be executed as shown below. What does the keyboard interrupt service routine do?

```
              .ORIG    x1000
              LDI      R0,  KBDR
              TRAP     x21
              TRAP     x21
              RTI
      KBDR    .FILL    xFE02
              .END
```

NOTE: RTI will be studied in chapter 10.

c. Finally, suppose the program of part *a* started executing, and someone sitting at the keyboard struck a key. What would you see on the screen?

8.16 What does the following LC-3 program do?

```
              .ORIG    x3000
              LD       R0,ASCII
              LD       R1,NEG
      AGAIN   LDI      R2,DSR
              BRzp     AGAIN
              STI      R0,DDR
              ADD      R0,R0,#1
              ADD      R2,R0,R1
              BRnp     AGAIN
              HALT
      ASCII   .FILL    x0041
      NEG     .FILL    xFFB6    ; -x004A
      DSR     .FILL    xFE04
      DDR     .FILL    xFE06
              .END
```

c h a p t e r

9

TRAP Routines and Subroutines

9.1 LC-3 TRAP Routines

9.1.1 Introduction

Recall Figure 8.5 of the previous chapter. In order to have the program successfully obtain input from the keyboard, it was necessary for the programmer (in Chapter 8) to know several things:

1. The hardware data registers for both the keyboard and the monitor: the monitor so a prompt could be displayed, and the keyboard so the program would know where to look for the input character.

2. The hardware status registers for both the keyboard and the monitor: the monitor so the program would know when it was OK to display the next character in the input prompt, and the keyboard so the program would know when someone had struck a key.

3. The asynchronous nature of keyboard input relative to the executing program.

This is beyond the knowledge of most application programmers. In fact, in the real world, if application programmers (or user programmers, as they are sometimes called) had to understand I/O at this level, there would be much less I/O and far fewer programmers in the business.

There is another problem with allowing user programs to perform I/O activity by directly accessing KBDR and KBSR. I/O activity involves the use of device registers that are shared by many programs. This means that if a user programmer

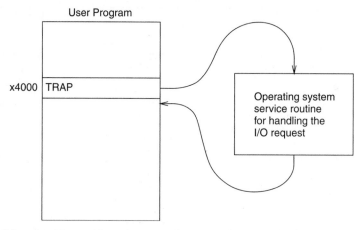

Figure 9.1   Invoking an OS service routine by means of the TRAP instruction

were allowed to access the hardware registers, and he/she messed up, it could create havoc for other user programs. Thus, it is ill-advised to give user programmers access to these registers. We say the hardware registers are **privileged** and accessible only to programs that have the proper degree of *privilege*.

The notion of privilege introduces a pretty big can of worms. Unfortunately, we cannot do much more than mention it here and leave serious treatment for later. For now, we simply note that there are resources that are not accessible to the user program, and access to those resources is controlled by endowing some programs with sufficient privilege and other programs without. Having said that, we move on to our problem at hand, a "better" solution for user programs that require input and/or output.

The simpler solution as well as the safer solution to the problem of user programs requiring I/O involves the TRAP instruction and the operating system. The operating system does have the proper degree of privilege.

We were introduced to the TRAP instruction in Chapter 5. We saw that for certain tasks, a user program could get the operating system to do the job for it by invoking the TRAP instruction. That way, the user programmer does not have to know the gory details previously mentioned, and other user programs are protected from the consequences of inept user programmers.

Figure 9.1 shows a user program that, upon reaching location x4000, needs an I/O task performed. The user program requests the operating system to perform the task on behalf of the user program. The operating system takes control of the computer, handles the request specified by the TRAP instruction, and then returns control to the user program, at location x4001. We often refer to the request made by the user program as a *service call* or a *system call*.

9.1.2 The TRAP Mechanism

The TRAP mechanism involves several elements, as follows:

1. **A set of service routines** executed on behalf of user programs by the operating system. These are part of the operating system and start at

⋮	⋮
x0020	x0400
x0021	x0430
x0022	x0450
x0023	x04A0
x0024	x04E0
x0025	xFD70
⋮	⋮

Figure 9.2   The Trap Vector Table

arbitrary addresses in memory. The LC-3 was designed so that up to 256 service routines can be specified. Table A.2 in Appendix A contains the LC-3's current complete list of operating system service routines.

2. **A table of the starting addresses** of these 256 service routines. This table is stored in memory locations x0000 to x00FF. The table is referred to by various names by various companies. One company calls this table the System Control Block. Another company calls it the Trap Vector Table. Figure 9.2 provides a snapshot of the Trap Vector Table of the LC-3, with specific starting addresses highlighted. Among the starting addresses are the one for the character output service routine (location x0430), which is contained in location x0021, the one for the keyboard input service routine (location x04A0), contained in location x0023, and the one for the machine halt service routine (location xFD70), contained in location x0025.

3. **The TRAP instruction.** When a user program wishes to have the operating system execute a specific service routine on behalf of the user program, and then return control to the user program, the user program uses the TRAP instruction.

4. **A linkage** back to the user program. The service routine must have a mechanism for returning control to the user program.

9.1.3 The TRAP Instruction

The TRAP instruction causes the service routine to execute by doing two things:

- It changes the PC to the starting address of the relevant service routine on the basis of its trap vector.

- It provides a way to get back to the program that initiated the TRAP instruction. The "way back" is referred to as a *linkage*.

The TRAP instruction is specified as follows. The **TRAP** instruction is made up of two parts: the TRAP opcode 1111 and the trap vector (bits [7:0]). Bits [11:8] must be zero. The trap vector identifies the service routine the user program wants the operating system to perform. In the following example, the trap vector is x23.

15	14	13	12	11	10	9	8	7	6	5	4	3	2	1	0
1	1	1	1	0	0	0	0	0	0	1	0	0	0	1	1

TRAP   trap vector

The EXECUTE phase of the TRAP instruction's instruction cycle does four things:

1. The 8-bit trap vector is zero-extended to 16 bits to form an address, which is loaded into the MAR. For the trap vector x23, that address is x0023, which is the address of an entry in the Trap Vector Table.

2. The Trap Vector Table is in memory locations x0000 to x00FF. The entry at x0023 is read and its contents, in this case x04A0 (see Figure 9.2), are loaded into the MDR.

3. The general purpose register R7 is loaded with the current contents of the PC. This will provide a way back to the user program, as will become clear momentarily.

4. The contents of the MDR are loaded into the PC, completing the instruction cycle.

Since the PC now contains x04A0, processing continues at memory address x04A0.

Location x04A0 is the starting address of the operating system service routine to input a character from the keyboard. We say the trap vector "points" to the starting address of the TRAP routine. Thus, TRAP x23 causes the operating system to start executing the keyboard input service routine.

In order to return to the instruction following the TRAP instruction in the user program (after the service routine has ended), there must be some mechanism for saving the address of the user program's next instruction. Step 3 of the EXECUTE phase listed above provides this linkage. By storing the PC in R7 before loading the PC with the starting address of the service routine, the TRAP instruction provides the service routine with all the information it needs to return control to the user program at the proper location. You know that the PC was already updated (in the FETCH phase of the TRAP instruction) to point to the next instruction. Thus, at the start of execution of the trap service routine, R7 contains the address of the instruction in the user program that follows the TRAP instruction.

9.1.4 The Complete Mechanism

We have shown in detail how the TRAP instruction invokes the service routine to do the user program's bidding. We have also shown how the TRAP instruction provides the information that the service routine needs to return control to the correct place in the user program. The only thing left is to show the actual instruction in the service routine that returns control to the correct place in the user program. Recall the JMP instruction from Chapter 5. Assume that during the execution of the trap service routine, the contents of R7 was not changed. If

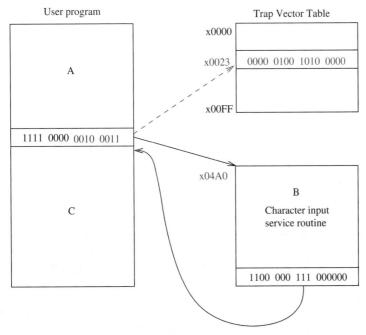

User program

Trap Vector Table

x0000

x0023   0000 0100 1010 0000

A

x00FF

1111 0000 0010 0011

x04A0

B

Character input
service routine

C

1100 000 111 000000

Figure 9.3   Flow of control from a user program to an OS service routine and back

that is the case, control can return to the correct location in the user program by executing JMP R7 as the last instruction in the trap service routine.

Figure 9.3 shows the LC-3 using the TRAP instruction and the JMP instruction to implement the example of Figure 9.1. The flow of control goes from (A) within a user program that needs a character input from the keyboard, to (B) the operating system service routine that performs that task on behalf of the user program, back to the user program (C) that presumably uses the information contained in the input character.

Recall that the computer continually executes its instruction cycle (FETCH, DECODE, etc.). As you know, the way to change the flow of control is to change the contents of the PC during the EXECUTE phase of the current instruction. In that way, the next FETCH will be at a redirected address.

Thus, to request the character input service routine, we use the TRAP instruction with trap vector x23 in our user program. Execution of that instruction causes the contents of memory location x0023 (which, in this case, contains x04A0) to be loaded into the PC and the address of the instruction following the TRAP instruction to be loaded into R7. The dashed lines on Figure 9.3 show the use of the trap vector to obtain the starting address of the trap service routine from the Trap Vector Table.

The next instruction cycle starts with the FETCH of the contents of x04A0, which is the first instruction of the operating system service routine that requests (and accepts) keyboard input. That service routine, as we will see momentarily, is patterned after the keyboard input routine we studied in Section 8.4. Recall that upon completion of that input routine (see Figure 8.5), R0 contains the ASCII code of the key that was typed.

The trap service routine executes to completion, ending with the JMP R7 instruction. Execution of JMP R7 loads the PC with the contents of R7. If R7 was not changed during execution of the service routine, it still contains the address of the instruction following the TRAP instruction in the initiating user program. Thus, the user program resumes execution, with R0 containing the ASCII code of the keyboard character that was typed.

The JMP R7 instruction is so convenient for providing a return to the user program that the LC-3 assembly language provides the mnemonic RET for this instruction, as follows:

15	14	13	12	11	10	9	8	7	6	5	4	3	2	1	0
1	1	0	0	0	0	0	1	1	1	0	0	0	0	0	0

RET

The following program is provided to illustrate the use of the TRAP instruction. It can also be used to amuse the average four-year-old!

Example 9.1

Write a game program to do the following: A person is sitting at a keyboard. Each time the person types a capital letter, the program outputs the lowercase version of that letter. If the person types a 7, the program terminates.

The following LC-3 assembly language program will do the job.

```
01                  .ORIG x3000
02            LD    R2,TERM   ; Load -7
03            LD    R3,ASCII  ; Load ASCII difference
04   AGAIN    TRAP  x23       ; Request keyboard input
05            ADD   R1,R2,R0  ; Test for terminating
06            BRz   EXIT      ; character
07            ADD   R0,R0,R3  ; Change to lowercase
08            TRAP  x21       ; Output to the monitor
09            BRnzp AGAIN     ; ... and do it again!
0A   TERM     .FILL xFFC9     ; FFC9 is negative of ASCII 7
0B   ASCII    .FILL x0020
0C   EXIT     TRAP  x25       ; Halt
0D            .END
```

The program executes as follows: The program first loads constants xFFC9 and x0020 into R2 and R3. The constant xFFC9, which is the negative of the ASCII code for 7, is used to test the character typed at the keyboard to see if the four-year-old wants to continue playing. The constant x0020 is the zero-extended difference between the ASCII code for a capital letter and the ASCII code for that same letter's lowercase representation. For example, the ASCII code for **A** is x41; the ASCII code for **a** is x61. The ASCII codes for **Z** and **z** are x5A and x7A, respectively.

Then TRAP x23 is executed, which invokes the keyboard input service routine. When the service routine is finished, control returns to the application program (at line 05), and R0 contains the ASCII code of the character typed. The ADD and BRz instructions test for the terminating character 7. If the character typed is not a 7, the ASCII uppercase/lowercase difference (x0020) is added to the input ASCII code, storing the result in R0. Then a TRAP to the monitor output service routine is called. This causes the lowercase representation of the same letter to be displayed on the monitor. When control returns to the application program (this time at line 09), an unconditional BR to AGAIN is executed, and another request for keyboard input appears.

The correct operation of the program in this example assumes that the person sitting at the keyboard only types capital letters and the value 7. What if the person types a $? A better solution to Example 9.1 would be a program that tests the character typed to be sure it really is a capital letter from among the 26 capital letters in the alphabet, and if it is not, takes corrective action.

Question: Augment this program to add the test for bad data. That is, write a program that will type the lowercase representation of any capital letter typed and will terminate if anything other than a capital letter is typed. See Exercise 9.6.

9.1.5 TRAP Routines for Handling I/O

With the constructs just provided, the input routine described in Figure 8.5 can be slightly modified to be the input service routine shown in Figure 9.4. Two changes are needed: (1) We add the appropriate .ORIG and .END pseudo-ops. .ORIG specifies the starting address of the input service routine—the address found at location x0023 in the Trap Vector Table. And (2) we terminate the input service routine with the JMP R7 instruction (mnemonically, RET) rather than the BR NEXT_TASK, as is done on line 20 in Figure 8.5. We use JMP R7 because the service routine is invoked by TRAP x23. It is not part of the user program, as was the case in Figure 8.5.

The output routine of Section 8.3.2 can be modified in a similar way, as shown in Figure 9.5. The results are input (Figure 9.4) and output (Figure 9.5) service routines that can be invoked simply and safely by the TRAP instruction with the appropriate trap vector. In the case of input, upon completion of TRAP x23, R0 contains the ASCII code of the keyboard character typed. In the case of output, the initiating program must load R0 with the ASCII code of the character it wishes displayed on the monitor and then invoke TRAP x21.

9.1.6 TRAP Routine for Halting the Computer

Recall from Section 4.5 that the RUN latch is ANDed with the crystal oscillator to produce the clock that controls the operation of the computer. We noted that if that 1-bit latch was cleared, the output of the AND gate would be 0, stopping the clock.

Years ago, most ISAs had a HALT instruction for stopping the clock. Given how infrequently that instruction is executed, it seems wasteful to devote an opcode to it. In many modern computers, the RUN latch is cleared by a TRAP

```
01        ;   Service Routine for Keyboard Input
02        ;
03                .ORIG    x04A0
04        START   ST       R1,SaveR1        ; Save the values in the registers
05                ST       R2,SaveR2        ; that are used so that they
06                ST       R3,SaveR3        ; can be restored before RET
07        ;
08                LD       R2,Newline
09        L1      LDI      R3,DSR           ; Check DDR --  is it free?
0A                BRzp     L1
0B                STI      R2,DDR           ; Move cursor to new clean line
0C        ;
0D                LEA      R1,Prompt        ; Prompt is starting address
0E                                         ; of prompt string
1F        Loop    LDR      R0,R1,#0         ; Get next prompt character
10                BRz      Input            ; Check for end of prompt string
11        L2      LDI      R3,DSR
12                BRzp     L2
13                STI      R0,DDR           ; Write next character of
14                                          ; prompt string
15                ADD      R1,R1,#1         ; Increment prompt pointer
16                BRnzp    Loop
17        ;
18        Input   LDI      R3,KBSR          ; Has a character been typed?
19                BRzp     Input
1A                LDI      R0,KBDR          ; Load it into R0
1B        L3      LDI      R3,DSR
1C                BRzp     L3
1D                STI      R0,DDR           ; Echo input character
1E                                          ; to the monitor
1F        ;
20        L4      LDI      R3,DSR
21                BRzp     L4
22                STI      R2,DDR           ; Move cursor to new clean line
23                LD       R1,SaveR1        ; Service routine done, restore
24                LD       R2,SaveR2        ; original values in registers.
25                LD       R3,SaveR3
26                RET                       ; Return from trap (i.e., JMP R7)
27        ;
28        SaveR1  .BLKW    1
29        SaveR2  .BLKW    1
2A        SaveR3  .BLKW    1
2B        DSR     .FILL    xFE04
2C        DDR     .FILL    xFE06
2D        KBSR    .FILL    xFE00
2E        KBDR    .FILL    xFE02
2F        Newline .FILL    x000A            ; ASCII code for newline
30        Prompt  .STRINGZ "Input a character>"
31                .END
```

Figure 9.4   Character input service routine

```
01                    .ORIG    x0430         ; System call starting address
02              ST      R1, SaveR1          ; R1 will be used to poll the DSR
03                                          ; hardware
04      ; Write the character
05      TryWrite LDI    R1, DSR             ; Get status
06               BRzp   TryWrite            ; Bit 15 on says display is ready
07      WriteIt  STI    R0, DDR             ; Write character
08
09      ; return from trap
0A      Return   LD     R1, SaveR1          ; Restore registers
0B               RET                        ; Return from trap (JMP R7, actually)
0C      DSR      .FILL  xFE04               ; Address of display status register
0D      DDR      .FILL  xFE06               ; Address of display data register
0E      SaveR1   .BLKW  1
0F               .END
```

Figure 9.5   Character output service routine

routine. In the LC-3, the RUN latch is bit [15] of the Machine Control Register, which is memory-mapped to location xFFFE. Figure 9.6 shows the trap service routine for halting the processor, that is, for stopping the clock.

First (lines 02, 03, and 04), registers R7, R1, and R0 are saved. R1 and R0 are saved because they are needed by the service routine. R7 is saved because its contents will be overwritten after TRAP x21 executes (line 09). Then (lines 08 through 0D), the banner *Halting the machine* is displayed on the monitor. Finally (lines 11 through 14), the RUN latch (MCR[15]) is cleared by ANDing the MCR with 0111111111111111. That is, MCR[14:0] remains unchanged, but MCR[15] is cleared. *Question*: What instruction (or trap service routine) can be used to start the clock?

```
01                     .ORIG    xFD70     ; Where this routine resides
02               ST      R7, SaveR7
03               ST      R1, SaveR1 ; R1: a temp for MC register
04               ST      R0, SaveR0 ; R0 is used as working space
05
06  ; print message that machine is halting
07
08               LD      R0, ASCIINewLine
09               TRAP    x21
0A               LEA     R0, Message
0B               TRAP    x22
0C               LD      R0, ASCIINewLine
0D               TRAP    x21
0E  ;
0F  ; clear bit 15 at xFFFE to stop the machine
10  ;
11               LDI     R1, MCR       ; Load MC register into R1
12               LD      R0, MASK      ; R0 = x7FFF
13               AND     R0, R1, R0 ; Mask to clear the top bit
14               STI     R0, MCR       ; Store R0 into MC register
15  ;
```

Figure 9.6   HALT service routine for the LC-3

```
16   ; return from HALT routine.
17   ; (how can this routine return if the machine is halted above?)
18   ;
19                    LD      R1, SaveR1 ; Restore registers
1A                    LD      R0, SaveR0
1B                    LD      R7, SaveR7
1C                    RET                ; JMP R7, actually
1D   ;
1E   ; Some constants
1F   ;
20   ASCIINewLine     .FILL    x000A
21   SaveR0           .BLKW    1
22   SaveR1           .BLKW    1
23   SaveR7           .BLKW    1
24   Message          .STRINGZ "Halting the machine."
25   MCR              .FILL    xFFFE     ; Address of MCR
26   MASK             .FILL    x7FFF     ; Mask to clear the top bit
27                    .END
```

Figure 9.6   HALT service routine for the LC-3 (continued)

9.1.7 Saving and Restoring Registers

One item we have mentioned in passing that we should emphasize more explicitly is the need to save the value in a register

- if the value will be destroyed by some subsequent action, and

- if we will need to use it after that subsequent action.

Suppose we want to input from the keyboard 10 decimal digits, convert their ASCII codes into their binary representations, and store the binary values in 10 successive memory locations, starting at the address Binary. The following program fragment does the job.

```
01               LEA     R3,Binary    ; Initialize to first location
02               LD      R6,ASCII     ; Template for line 05
03               LD      R7,COUNT     ; Initialize to 10
04    AGAIN      TRAP    x23          ; Get keyboard input
05               ADD     R0,R0,R6     ; Strip ASCII template
06               STR     R0,R3,#0     ; Store binary digit
07               ADD     R3,R3,#1     ; Increment pointer
08               ADD     R7,R7,#-1    ; Decrement COUNT.
09               BRp     AGAIN        ; More characters?
0A               BRnzp   NEXT_TASK    ;
0B    ASCII      .FILL   xFFD0        ; Negative of x0030.
0C    COUNT      .FILL   #10
0D    Binary     .BLKW   #10
```

The first step in the program fragment is initialization. We load R3 with the starting address of the memory space set aside to store the 10 decimal digits. We load R6 with the negative of the ASCII template. This is used to subtract x0030 from each ASCII code. We load R7 with 10, the initial value of the count. Then we execute the loop 10 times, each time getting a character from the keyboard, stripping away the ASCII template, storing the binary result, and testing to see if we are done. But the program does not work! Why? *Answer:* The TRAP instruction in line 04 replaces the value 10 that was loaded into R7 in line 03 with the address of the ADD R0,R0,R6 instruction. Therefore, the instructions in lines 08 and 09 do not perform the loop control function they were programmed to do.

The message is this: If a value in a register will be needed after something else is stored in that register, we must *save* it before the something else happens and *restore* it before we can subsequently use it. We save a register value by storing it in memory; we restore it by loading it back into the register. In Figure 9.6, line 03 contains the ST instruction that saves R1, line 11 contains the LDI instruction that loads R1 with a value to do the work of the trap service routine, line 19 contains the LD instruction that restores R1 to its original value before the service routine was called, and line 22 sets aside a location in memory for storing R1.

The save/restore problem can be handled either by the initiating program before the TRAP occurs or by the called program (for example, the service routine) after the TRAP instruction executes. We will see in Section 9.2 that the same problem exists for another class of calling/called programs, the subroutine mechanism.

We use the term *caller-save* if the calling program handles the problem. We use the term *callee-save* if the called program handles the problem. The appropriate one to handle the problem is the one that knows which registers will be destroyed by subsequent actions.

The callee knows which registers it needs to do the job of the called program. Therefore, before it starts, it saves those registers with a sequence of stores. After it finishes, it restores those registers with a sequence of loads. And it sets aside memory locations to save those register values. In Figure 9.6, the HALT routine needs R0 and R1. So it saves their values with ST instructions in lines 03 and 04, restores their values with LD instructions in lines 19 and 1A, and sets aside memory locations for these values in lines 21 and 22.

The caller knows what damage will be done by instructions under its control. Again, in Figure 9.6, the caller knows that each instance of the TRAP instruction will destroy what is in R7. So, before the first TRAP instruction in the HALT service routine is executed, R7 is saved. After the last TRAP instruction in the HALT service routine is executed, R7 is restored.

9.2 Subroutines

We have just seen how programmers' productivity can be enhanced if they do not have to learn details of the I/O hardware, but can rely instead on the operating system to supply the program fragments needed to perform those tasks. We also mentioned in passing that it is kind of nice to have the operating system access these device registers so we do not have to be at the mercy of some other user programmer.

We have seen that a request for a service routine is invoked in the user program by the TRAP instruction and handled by the operating system. Return to the initiating program is obtained via the JMP R7 instruction.

In a similar vein, it is often useful to be able to invoke a program fragment multiple times within the same program without having to specify its details all over again in the source program each time it is needed. In addition, it is sometimes the case that one person writes a program that requires such fragments and another person writes the fragments.

Also, one might require a fragment that has been supplied by the manufacturer or by some independent software supplier. It is almost always the case that collections of such fragments are available to user programmers to free them from having to write their own. These collections are referred to as *libraries*. An example is the Math Library, which consists of fragments that execute such functions as **square root, sine,** and **arctangent.**

For all of these reasons, it is good to have a way to use program fragments efficiently. Such program fragments are called *subroutines,* or alternatively, *procedures*, or in C terminology, *functions*. The mechanism for using them is referred to as a *Call/Return mechanism.*

9.2.1 The Call/Return Mechanism

Figure 9.4 provides a simple illustration of a fragment that must be executed multiple times within the same program. Note the three instructions starting at symbolic address L1. Note also the three instructions starting at addresses L2, L3, and L4. Each of these four 3-instruction sequences do the following:

```
LABEL    LDI    R3,DSR
         BRzp   LABEL
         STI    Reg,DDR
```

Two of the four program fragments store the contents of R0 and the other two store the contents of R2, but that is easy to take care of, as we will see. The main point is that, aside from the small nuisance of which register is being used for the source for the STI instruction, the four program fragments do exactly the same thing. The Call/Return mechanism allows us to execute this one 3-instruction sequence multiple times while requiring us to include it as a subroutine in our program only once.

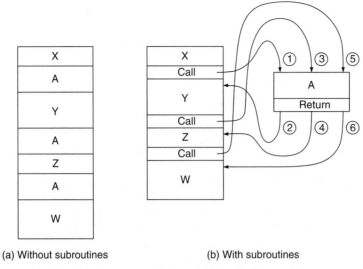

(a) Without subroutines   (b) With subroutines

Figure 9.7   Instruction execution flow with/without subroutines

The call mechanism computes the starting address of the subroutine, loads it into the PC, and saves the return address for getting back to the next instruction in the calling program. The return mechanism loads the PC with the return address. Figure 9.7 shows the instruction execution flow for a program with and without subroutines.

The Call/Return mechanism acts very much like the TRAP instruction in that it redirects control to a program fragment while saving the linkage back to the calling program. In both cases, the PC is loaded with the starting address of the program fragment, while R7 is loaded with the address that is needed to get back to the calling program. The last instruction in the program fragment, whether the fragment is a trap service routine or a subroutine, is the JMP R7 instruction, which loads the PC with the contents of R7, thereby returning control to the instruction following the calling instruction.

There is an important difference between subroutines and the service routines that are called by the TRAP instruction. Although it is somewhat beyond the scope of this course, we will mention it briefly. It has to do with the nature of the work that the program fragment is being asked to do. In the case of the TRAP instruction (as we saw), the service routines involve operating system resources, and they generally require privileged access to the underlying hardware of the computer. They are written by systems programmers charged with managing the resources of the computer. In the case of subroutines, they are either written by the same programmer who wrote the program containing the calling instruction, or they are written by a colleague, or they are provided as part of a library. In all cases, they involve resources that cannot mess up other people's programs, and so we are not concerned that they are part of a user program.

9.2.2 The JSR(R) Instruction

The LC-3 specifies one opcode for calling subroutines, **0100.** The instruction uses one of two addressing modes for computing the starting address of the subroutine, PC-relative addressing or Base addressing. The LC-3 assembly language provides two different mnemonic names for the opcode, JSR and JSRR, depending on which addressing mode is used.

The instruction does two things. It saves the return address in R7 and it computes the starting address of the subroutine and loads it into the PC. The return address is the incremented PC, which points to the instruction following the JSR or JSRR instruction in the calling program.

The JSR(R) instruction consists of three parts.

15	14	13	12	11	10	9	8	7	6	5	4	3	2	1	0
Opcode				A				Address evaluation bits							

Bits [15:12] contain the opcode, 0100. Bit [11] specifies the addressing mode, the value 1 if the addressing mode is PC-relative, and the value 0 if the addressing mode is Base addressing. Bits [10:0] contain information that is used to evaluate the starting address of the subroutine. The only difference between JSR and JSRR is the addressing mode that is used for evaluating the starting address of the subroutine.

JSR

The **JSR** instruction computes the target address of the subroutine by sign-extending the 11-bit offset (bits [10:0]) of the instruction to 16 bits and adding that to the incremented PC. This addressing mode is almost identical to the addressing mode of the LD and ST instructions, except 11 bits of PCoffset are used, rather than nine bits as is the case for LD and ST.

If the following JSR instruction is stored in location x4200, its execution will cause the PC to be loaded with x3E05 and R7 to be loaded with x4201.

15	14	13	12	11	10	9	8	7	6	5	4	3	2	1	0
0	1	0	0	1	1	0	0	0	0	0	0	0	1	0	0
JSR				A				PCoffset11							

JSRR

The JSRR instruction is exactly like the JSR instruction except for the addressing mode. **JSRR** obtains the starting address of the subroutine in exactly the same way the JMP instruction does, that is, it uses the contents of the register specified by bits [8:6] of the instruction.

If the following JSRR instruction is stored in location x420A, and if R5 contains x3002, the execution of the JSRR will cause R7 to be loaded with x420B, and the PC to be loaded with x3002.

Question: What important feature does the JSRR instruction provide that the JSR instruction does not provide?

15	14	13	12	11	10	9	8	7	6	5	4	3	2	1	0
0	1	0	0	0	0	0	1	0	1	0	0	0	0	0	0

JSRR   A   BaseR

9.2.3 The TRAP Routine for Character Input, Revisited

Let's look again at the keyboard input service routine of Figure 9.4. In particular, let's look at the three-line sequence that occurs at symbolic addresses L1, L2, L3, and L4:

```
LABEL    LDI    R3,DSR
         BRzp   LABEL
         STI    Reg,DDR
```

Can the JSR/RET mechanism enable us to replace these four occurrences of the same sequence with a single subroutine? *Answer:* Yes, **almost.**

Figure 9.8, our "improved" keyboard input service routine, contains

```
         JSR    WriteChar
```

at lines 05, 0B, 11, and 14, and the four-instruction subroutine

```
WriteChar    LDI    R3,DSR
             BRzp   WriteChar
             STI    R2,DDR
             RET
```

at lines 1D through 20. Note the RET instruction (actually, JMP R7) that is needed to terminate the subroutine.

Note the hedging: *almost.* In the original sequences starting at L2 and L3, the STI instruction forwards the contents of R0 (not R2) to the DDR. We can fix that easily enough, as follows: In line 09 of Figure 9.8, we use

```
         LDR    R2,R1,#0
```

instead of

```
         LDR    R0,R1,#0
```

This causes each character in the prompt to be loaded into R2. The subroutine Writechar forwards each character from R2 to the DDR.

In line 10 of Figure 9.8, we insert the instruction

```
         ADD    R2,R0,#0
```

in order to move the keyboard input (which is in R0) into R2. The subroutine Writechar forwards it from R2 to the DDR. Note that R0 still contains the keyboard input. Furthermore, since no subsequent instruction in the service routine loads R0, R0 still contains the keyboard input after control returns to the user program.

In line 13 of Figure 9.8, we insert the instruction

```
         LD     R2,Newline
```

in order to move the "newline" character into R2. The subroutine Writechar forwards it from R2 to the DDR.

Finally, we note that unlike Figure 9.4, this trap service routine contains several instances of the JSR instruction. Thus any linkage back to the calling

```
01                    .ORIG    x04A0
02      START         ST       R7,SaveR7
03                    JSR      SaveReg
04                    LD       R2,Newline
05                    JSR      WriteChar
06                    LEA      R1,PROMPT
07      ;
08      ;
09      Loop          LDR      R2,R1,#0     ; Get next prompt char
0A                    BRz      Input
0B                    JSR      WriteChar
0C                    ADD      R1,R1,#1
0D                    BRnzp    Loop
0E      ;
0F      Input         JSR      ReadChar
10                    ADD      R2,R0,#0     ; Move char to R2 for writing
11                    JSR      WriteChar    ; Echo to monitor
12      ;
13                    LD       R2, Newline
14                    JSR      WriteChar
15                    JSR      RestoreReg
16                    LD       R7,SaveR7
17                    RET                   ; JMP R7 terminates
18      ;                                     the TRAP routine
19      SaveR7        .FILL    x0000
1A      Newline       .FILL    x000A
1B      Prompt        .STRINGZ "Input a character>"
1C      ;
1D      WriteChar     LDI      R3,DSR
1E                    BRzp     WriteChar
1F                    STI      R2,DDR
20                    RET                   ; JMP R7 terminates subroutine
21      DSR           .FILL    xFE04
22      DDR           .FILL    xFE06
23      ;
24      ReadChar      LDI      R3,KBSR
25                    BRzp     ReadChar
26                    LDI      R0,KBDR
27                    RET
28      KBSR          .FILL    xFE00
29      KBDR          .FILL    xFE02
2A      ;
2B      SaveReg       ST       R1,SaveR1
2C                    ST       R2,SaveR2
2D                    ST       R3,SaveR3
2E                    ST       R4,SaveR4
2F                    ST       R5,SaveR5
30                    ST       R6,SaveR6
31                    RET
32      ;
33      RestoreReg    LD       R1,SaveR1
34                    LD       R2,SaveR2
35                    LD       R3,SaveR3
36                    LD       R4,SaveR4
37                    LD       R5,SaveR5
38                    LD       R6,SaveR6
39                    RET
3A      SaveR1        .FILL    x0000
3B      SaveR2        .FILL    x0000
3C      SaveR3        .FILL    x0000
3D      SaveR4        .FILL    x0000
3E      SaveR5        .FILL    x0000
3F      SaveR6        .FILL    x0000
40                    .END
```

Figure 9.8   The LC-3 trap service routine for character input

program that was contained in R7 when the service routine started execution was long ago overwritten (by the first JSR instruction, actually, in line 03). Therefore, we save R7 in line 02 before we execute our first JSR instruction, and we restore R7 in line 16 after we execute our last JSR instruction.

Figure 9.8 is the actual LC-3 trap service routine provided for keyboard input.

9.2.4 PUTS: Writing a Character String to the Monitor

Before we leave the example of Figure 9.8, note the code on lines 09 through 0D. This fragment of the service routine is used to write the sequence of characters *Input a character* to the monitor. A sequence of characters is often referred to as a *string of characters* or a *character string*. This fragment is also present in Figure 9.6, with the result that *Halting the machine* is written to the monitor. In fact, it is so often the case that a user program needs to write a string of characters to the monitor that this function is given its own trap vector in the LC-3 operating system. Thus, if a user program requires a character string to be written to the monitor, it need only provide (in R0) the starting address of the character string, and then invoke TRAP x22. In LC-3 assembly language this TRAP is called *PUTS*.

Thus, PUTS (or TRAP x22) causes control to be passed to the operating system, and the procedure shown in Figure 9.9 is executed. Note that PUTS is the code of lines 09 through 0D of Figure 9.8, with a few minor adjustments.

9.2.5 Library Routines

We noted early in this section that there are many uses for the Call/Return mechanism, among them the ability of a user program to call library subroutines that are usually delivered as part of the computer system. Libraries are provided as a convenience to the user programmer. They are legitimately advertised as "productivity enhancers" since they allow the user programmer to use them without having to know or learn much of their inner details. For example, a user programmer knows what a square root is (we abbreviate **SQRT**), and may need to use sqrt(x) for some value x but does not have a clue as to how to write a program to do it, and probably would rather not have to learn how.

A simple example illustrates the point. We have lost our key and need to get into our apartment. We can lean a ladder up against the wall so that the ladder touches the bottom of our open window, 24 feet above the ground. There is a 10-foot flower bed on the ground along the edge of the wall, so we need to keep the base of the ladder outside the flower bed. How big a ladder do we need so that we can lean it against the wall and climb through the window? Or, stated less colorfully: If the sides of a right triangle are 24 feet and 10 feet, how big is the hypotenuse (see Figure 9.10)?

We remember from high school that Pythagoras answered that one for us:

$$c^2 = a^2 + b^2$$

```
01      ; This service routine writes a NULL-terminated string to the console.
02      ; It services the PUTS service call (TRAP x22).
03      ; Inputs: R0 is a pointer to the string to print.
04      ;
05                      .ORIG   x0450           ; Where this ISR resides
06                      ST      R7, SaveR7      ; Save R7 for later return
07                      ST      R0, SaveR0      ; Save other registers that
08                      ST      R1, SaveR1      ; are needed by this routine
09                      ST      R3, SaveR3      ;
0A      ;
0B      ; Loop through each character in the array
0C      ;
0D      Loop            LDR     R1, R0, #0      ; Retrieve the character(s)
0E                      BRz     Return          ; If it is 0, done
0F      L2              LDI     R3,DSR
10                      BRzp    L2
11                      STI     R1, DDR         ; Write the character
12                      ADD     R0, R0, #1      ; Increment pointer
13                      BRnzp   Loop            ; Do it all over again
14      ;
15      ; Return from the request for service call
16      Return          LD      R3, SaveR3
17                      LD      R1, SaveR1
18                      LD      R0, SaveR0
19                      LD      R7, SaveR7
1A                      RET
1B      ;
1C      ; Register locations
1D      DSR             .FILL   xFE04
1E      DDR             .FILL   xFE06
1F      SaveR0          .FILL   x0000
20      SaveR1          .FILL   x0000
21      SaveR3          .FILL   x0000
22      SaveR7          .FILL   x0000
23                      .END
```

Figure 9.9 The LC-3 PUTS service routine

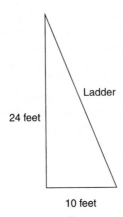

Figure 9.10 Solving for the length of the hypotenuse

Knowing *a* and *b*, we can easily solve for *c* by taking the square root of the sum of a^2 and b^2. Taking the sum is not hard—the LC-3 ADD instruction will do the job. The square is also not hard; we can multiply two numbers by a sequence of additions. But how does one get the square root? The structure of our solution is shown in Figure 9.11.

The subroutine SQRT has yet to be written. If it were not for the Math Library, the programmer would have to pick up a math book (or get someone to do it for him/her), check out the Newton-Raphson method, and produce the missing subroutine.

However, with the Math Library, the problem pretty much goes away. Since the Math Library supplies a number of subroutines (including SQRT), the user programmer can continue to be ignorant of the likes of Newton-Raphson. The user still needs to know the label of the target address of the library routine that performs the square root function, where to put the argument x, and where to expect the result SQRT(x). But these are easy conventions that can be obtained from the documentation associated with the Math Library.

```
01                  . . .
02                  . . .
03            LD    R0,SIDE1
04            BRz   S1
05            JSR   SQUARE
06    S1      ADD   R1,R0,#0
07            LD    R0,SIDE2
08            BRz   S2
09            JSR   SQUARE
0A    S2      ADD   R0,R0,R1
0B            JSR   SQRT
0C            ST    R0,HYPOT
0D            BRnzp NEXT_TASK
0E    SQUARE  ADD   R2,R0,#0
0F            ADD   R3,R0,#0
10    AGAIN   ADD   R2,R2,#-1
11            BRz   DONE
12            ADD   R0,R0,R3
13            BRnzp AGAIN
14    DONE    RET
15    SQRT    . . .          ; R0 <-- SQRT(R0)
16            . . .          ;
17            . . .          ; How do we write this subroutine?
18            . . .          ;
19            . . .          ;
1A            RET
1B    SIDE1   .BLKW 1
1C    SIDE2   .BLKW 1
1D    HYPOT   .BLKW 1
1E            . . .
1F            . . .
```

Figure 9.11 A program fragment to compute the hypotenuse of a right triangle

If the library routine starts at address SQRT, and the argument is provided to the library routine at R0, and the result is obtained from the library routine at R0, Figure 9.11 reduces to Figure 9.12.

Two things are worth noting:

- *Thing 1*—The programmer no longer has to worry about how to compute the square root function. The library routine does that for us.

- *Thing 2*—The pseudo-op .EXTERNAL. We already saw in Section 7.4.2 that this pseudo-op tells the assembler that the label (SQRT), which is needed to assemble the .FILL pseudo-op in line 19, will be supplied by some other program fragment (i.e., module) and will be combined with this program fragment (i.e., module) when the *executable image* is produced. The executable image is the binary module that actually executes. The executable image is produced at *link* time.

This notion of combining multiple modules at link time to produce an executable image is the normal case. Figure 9.13 illustrates the process. You will see concrete examples of this when we work with the programming language C in the second half of this course.

```
01                  . . .
02                  . . .
03                  .EXTERNAL SQRT
04                  . . .
05                  . . .
06             LD      R0,SIDE1
07             BRz     1$
08             JSR     SQUARE
09     1$      ADD     R1,R0,#0
0A             LD      R0,SIDE2
0B             BRz     2$
0C             JSR     SQUARE
0D     2$      ADD     R0,R0,R1   ; R0 contains argument x
0E             LD      R4,BASE
0F             JSRR    R4
10             ST      R0,HYPOT
11             BRnzp   NEXT_TASK
12     SQUARE  ADD     R2,R0,#0
13             ADD     R3,R0,#0
14     AGAIN   ADD     R2,R2,#-1
15             BRz     DONE
16             ADD     R0,R0,R3
17             BRnzp   AGAIN
18     DONE    RET
19     BASE    .FILL   SQRT
1A     SIDE1   .BLKW   1
1B     SIDE2   .BLKW   1
1C     HYPOT   .BLKW   1
1D                  . . .
1E                  . . .
```

Figure 9.12   The program fragment of Figure 9.10, using a library routine

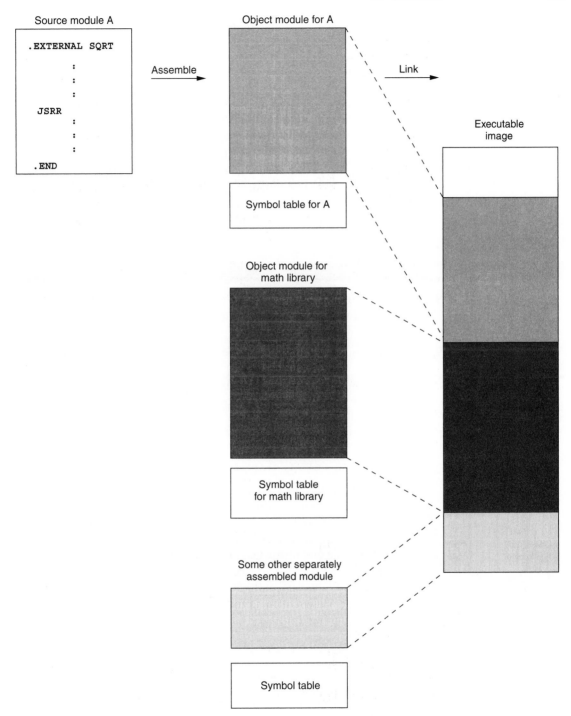

Figure 9.13 An executable image constructed from multiple files

Most application software requires library routines from various libraries. It would be very inefficient for the typical programmer to produce all of them—assuming the typical programmer could produce such routines in the first place. We have mentioned routines from the Math Library. There are also a number of preprocessing routines for producing "pretty" graphic images. There are other routines for a number of other tasks where it would make no sense at all to have the programmer write them from scratch. It is much easier to require only (1) appropriate documentation so that the interface between the library routine and the program that calls that routine is clear, and (2) the use of the proper pseudo-ops such as .EXTERNAL in the source program. The linker can then produce an executable image at link time from the separately assembled modules.

Exercises

9.1   Name some of the advantages of doing I/O through a TRAP routine instead of writing the routine yourself each time you would like your program to perform I/O.

9.2   *a.* How many trap service routines can be implemented in the LC-3? Why?

         b. Why must a RET instruction be used to return from a TRAP routine? Why won't a BR (Unconditional Branch) instruction work instead?

         c. How many accesses to memory are made during the processing of a TRAP instruction? Assume the TRAP is already in the IR.

9.3   Refer to Figure 9.6, the HALT service routine.

         a. What starts the clock after the machine is HALTed? Hint: How can the HALT service routine return after bit [15] of the machine control register is cleared?

         b. Which instruction actually halts the machine?

         c. What is the first instruction executed when the machine is started again?

         d. Where will the RET of the HALT routine return to?

9.4   Consider the following LC-3 assembly language program:

```
            .ORIG    x3000
L1          LEA      R1, L1
            AND      R2, R2, x0
            ADD      R2, R2, x2
            LD       R3, P1
L2          LDR      R0, R1, xC
            OUT
            ADD      R3, R3, #-1
            BRz      GLUE
            ADD      R1, R1, R2
            BR       L2
GLUE        HALT
P1          .FILL    xB
            .STRINGZ "HBoeoakteSmtHaotren!s"
            .END
```

   a. After this program is assembled and loaded, what binary pattern is
      stored in memory location x3005?
   b. Which instruction (provide a memory address) is executed after
      instruction x3005 is executed?
   c. Which instruction (provide a memory address) is executed prior to
      instruction x3006?
   d. What is the output of this program?

9.5   The following LC-3 program is assembled and then executed. There are
      no assemble time or run-time errors. What is the output of this program?
      Assume all registers are initialized to 0 before the program executes.

```
            .ORIG    x3000
            ST       R0, x3007
            LEA      R0, LABEL
            TRAP     x22
            TRAP     x25
LABEL       .STRINGZ "FUNKY"
LABEL2      .STRINGZ "HELLO WORLD"
            .END
```

9.6   The correct operation of the program in Example 9.1 assumes that the
      person sitting at the keyboard only types capital letters and the value 7.
      What if the person types a $? A better program would be one that tests
      the character typed to be sure it really is a capital letter from among the
      26 capital letters in the alphabet, and if it is not, takes corrective action.
      Your job: Augment the program of Example 9.1 to add a test for bad
      data. That is, write a program that will type the lowercase representation
      of any capital letter typed and will terminate if anything other than a
      capital letter is typed.

9.7   Two students wrote interrupt service routines for an assignment. Both
      service routines did exactly the same work, but the first student
      accidentally used RET at the end of his routine, while the second student
      correctly used RTI. There are three errors that arose in the first student's
      program due to his mistake. Describe any two of them.

9.8   Assume that an integer greater than 2 and less than 32,768 is deposited in memory location A by another module before the program below is executed.

```
              .ORIG  x3000
              AND    R4, R4, #0
              LD     R0, A
              NOT    R5, R0
              ADD    R5, R5, #2
              ADD    R1, R4, #2
              ;
REMOD         JSR    MOD
              BRz    STORE0
              ;
              ADD    R7, R1, R5
              BRz    STORE1
              ADD    R1, R1, #1
              BR     REMOD
              ;
STORE1        ADD    R4, R4, #1
STORE0        ST     R4, RESULT
              TRAP   x25
              ;
MOD           ADD    R2, R0, #0
              NOT    R3, R1
              ADD    R3, R3, #1
DEC           ADD    R2, R2, R3
              BRp    DEC
              RET
              ;
A             .BLKW  1
RESULT        .BLKW  1
              .END
```

In 20 words or fewer, what does the above program do?

9.9   Recall the machine busy example. Suppose the bit pattern indicating which machines are busy and which are free is stored in memory location x4001. Write subroutines that do the following.

   a. Check if no machines are busy, and return 1 if none are busy.
   b. Check if all machines are busy, and return 1 if all are busy.
   c. Check how many machines are busy, and return the number of busy machines.
   d. Check how many machines are free, and return the number of free machines.
   e. Check if a certain machine number, passed as an argument in R5, is busy, and return 1 if that machine is busy.
   f. Return the number of a machine that is not busy.

9.10 The starting address of the trap routine is stored at the address specified in the TRAP instruction. Why isn't the first instruction of the trap routine stored at that address instead? Assume each trap service routine requires at most 16 instructions. Modify the semantics of the LC-3 TRAP instruction so that the trap vector provides the starting address of the service routine.

9.11 Following is part of a program that was fed to the LC-3 assembler. The program is supposed to read a series of input lines from the console into a buffer, search for a particular character, and output the number of times that character occurs in the text. The input text is terminated by an EOT and is guaranteed to be no more than 1,000 characters in length. After the text has been input, the program reads the character to count.

The subroutine labeled COUNT that actually does the counting was written by another person and is located at address x3500. When called, the subroutine expects the address of the buffer to be in R5 and the address of the character to count to be in R6. The buffer should have a NULL to mark the end of the text. It returns the count in R6.

The OUTPUT subroutine that converts the binary count to ASCII digits and displays them was also written by another person and is at address x3600. It expects the number to print to be in R6.

Here is the code that reads the input and calls COUNT:

```
            .ORIG   x3000
            LEA     R1, BUFFER
G_TEXT      TRAP    x20              ; Get input text
            ADD     R2, R0, x-4
            BRz     G_CHAR
            STR     R0, R1, #0
            ADD     R1, R1, #1
            BRz     G_TEXT
G_CHAR      STR     R2, R1, #0       ; x0000 terminates buffer
            TRAP    x20              ; Get character to count
            ST      R0, S_CHAR
            LEA     R5, BUFFER
            LEA     R6, S_CHAR
            LD      R4, CADDR
            JSRR    R4               ; Count character
            LD      R4. OADDR
            JSRR    R4               ; Convert R6 and display
            TRAP    x25
CADDR       .FILL   x3500            ; Address of COUNT
OADDR       .FILL   x3600            ; Address of OUTPUT
BUFFER      .BLKW   1001
S_CHAR      .FILL   x0000
            .END
```

There is a problem with this code. What is it, and how might it be fixed? (The problem is *not* that the code for COUNT and OUTPUT is missing.)

9.12 Consider the following LC-3 assembly language program:

```
                .ORIG    x3000
                LEA      R0,DATA
                AND      R1,R1,#0
                ADD      R1,R1,#9
        LOOP1   ADD      R2,R0,#0
                ADD      R3,R1,#0
        LOOP2   JSR      SUB1
                ADD      R4,R4,#0
                BRzp     LABEL
                JSR      SUB2
        LABEL   ADD      R2,R2,#1
                ADD      R3,R3,#-1
                BRP      LOOP2
                ADD      R1,R1,#-1
                BRp      LOOP1
                HALT
        DATA    .BLKW    10 x0000
        SUB1    LDR      R5,R2,#0
                NOT      R5,R5
                ADD      R5,R5,#1
                LDR      R6,R2,#1
                ADD      R4,R5,R6
                RET
        SUB2    LDR      R4,R2,#0
                LDR      R5,R2,#1
                STR      R4,R2,#1
                STR      R5,R2,#0
                RET
                .END
```

Assuming that the memory locations at DATA get filled in before the program executes, what is the relationship between the final values at DATA and the initial values at DATA?

9.13 The following program is supposed to print the number 5 on the screen. It does not work. Why? Answer in no more than ten words, please.

```
                .ORIG    x3000
                JSR      A
                OUT
                BRnzp    DONE
        A       AND      R0,R0,#0
                ADD      R0,R0,#5
                JSR      B
                RET
        DONE    HALT
        ASCII   .FILL    x0030
        B       LD       R1,ASCII
                ADD      R0,R0,R1
                RET
                .END
```

9.14 Figure 9.6 shows a service routine to stop the computer by clearing the RUN latch, bit [15] of the Machine Control Register. The latch is cleared by the instruction in line 14, and the computer stops. What purpose is served by the instructions on lines 19 through 1C?

9.15 Suppose we define a new service routine starting at memory location x4000. This routine reads in a character and echoes it to the screen. Suppose memory location x0072 contains the value x4000. The service routine is shown below.

```
        .ORIG x4000
        ST R7, SaveR7
        GETC
        OUT
        LD R7, SaveR7
        RET
SaveR7  .FILL x0000
```

a. Identify the instruction that will invoke this routine.
b. Will this service routine work? Explain.

9.16 The two code sequences *a* and *b* are assembled separately. There is one error that will be caught at assemble time or at link time. Identify and describe why the bug will cause an error, and whether it will be detected at assemble time or link time.

a.
```
            .ORIG x3200
SQRT    ADD     R0, R0, #0
        ; code to perform square
        ; root function and
        ; return the result in R0
        RET
        .END
```

b.
```
                .EXTERNAL SQRT
                .ORIG   x3000
                LD      R0,VALUE
                JSR     SQRT
                ST      R0,DEST
                HALT
VALUE       .FILL   x30000
DEST        .FILL   x0025
            .END
```

9.17 Shown below is a partially constructed program. The program asks the user his/her name and stores the sentence "Hello, name" as a string starting from the memory location indicated by the symbol HELLO. The program then outputs that sentence to the screen. The program assumes that the user has finished entering his/her name when he/she presses the Enter key, whose ASCII code is x0A. The name is restricted to be not more than 25 characters.

Assuming that the user enters Onur followed by a carriage return when prompted to enter his/her name, the output of the program looks exactly like:

```
Please enter your name: Onur
Hello, Onur
```

Insert instructions at (a)–(d) that will complete the program.

```
          .ORIG x3000
          LEA    R1,HELLO
AGAIN     LDR    R2,R1,#0
          BRz    NEXT
          ADD    R1,R1,#1
          BR     AGAIN
NEXT      LEA    R0,PROMPT
          TRAP   x22            ; PUTS
          ----------- (a)
AGAIN2    TRAP   x20            ; GETC
          TRAP   x21            ; OUT
          ADD    R2,R0,R3
          BRz    CONT
          ----------- (b)
          ----------- (c)
          BR     AGAIN2
CONT      AND    R2,R2,#0
          ----------- (d)
          LEA    R0, HELLO
          TRAP   x22            ; PUTS
          TRAP   x25            ; HALT
NEGENTER  .FILL xFFF6           ; -x0A
PROMPT    .STRINGZ "Please enter your name: "
HELLO     .STRINGZ "Hello, "
          .BLKW #25
          .END
```

9.18 The program below, when complete, should print the following to the monitor:

ABCFGH

Insert instructions at (a)–(d) that will complete the program.

```
                .ORIG x3000
                LEA   R1, TESTOUT
BACK_1          LDR   R0, R1, #0
                BRz   NEXT_1
                TRAP  x21
                ------------ (a)
                BRnzp BACK_1
                ;
NEXT_1          LEA   R1, TESTOUT
BACK_2          LDR   R0, R1, #0
                BRz   NEXT_2
                JSR   SUB_1
                ADD   R1, R1, #1
                BRnzp BACK_2
                ;
NEXT_2          ------------ (b)
                ;
SUB_1           ------------ (c)

K               LDI   R2, DSR
                ------------ (d)

                STI   R0, DDR
                RET
DSR             .FILL xFE04
DDR             .FILL xFE06
TESTOUT         .STRINGZ "ABC"
                .END
```

9.19 A local company has decided to build a real LC-3 computer. In order
to make the computer work in a network, four interrupt-driven I/O
devices are connected. To request service, a device asserts its interrupt
request signal (IRQ). This causes a bit to get set in a special LC-3
memory-mapped interrupt control register called INTCTL which is
mapped to address xFF00. The INTCTL register is shown below. When a
device requests service, the INT signal in the LC-3 data path is asserted.
The LC-3 interrupt service routine determines which device has
requested service and calls the appropriate subroutine for that device. If
more than one device asserts its IRQ signal at the same time, only the
subroutine for the highest priority device is executed. During execution
of the subroutine, the corresponding bit in INTCTL is cleared.

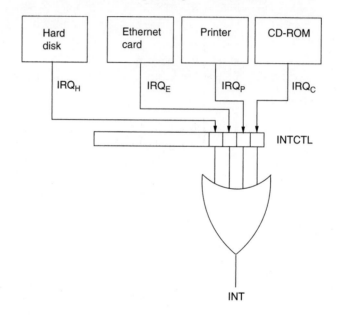

The following labels are used to identify the first instruction of each
device subroutine:

HARDDISK ETHERNET PRINTER CDROM

For example, if the highest priority device requesting service is the
printer, the interrupt service routine will call the printer subroutine with
the following instruction:

JSR PRINTER

Finish the code in the LC-3 interrupt service routine for the following priority scheme by filling in the spaces labeled (a)–(k). The lower the number, the higher the priority of the device.

1. Hard disk
2. Ethernet card
3. Printer
4. CD-ROM

```
                LDI    R1,  INTCTL
        DEV0    LD     R2,  ------  (a)
                AND    R2,  R2, R1
                BRnz   DEV1
                JSR    ----------  (b)
                ----------------  (c)

                ;
        DEV1    LD     R2,  ------  (d)
                AND    R2,  R2,  R1
                BRnz   DEV2
                JSR    ----------  (e)
                ----------------  (f)

                ;
        DEV2    LD     R2,  ------  (g)
                AND    R2,  R2, R1
                BRnz   DEV3
                JSR    ----------  (h)
                ----------------  (i)

                ;
        DEV3    JSR    ----------  (j)
                ;
        END     ----------------  (k)

        INTCTL  .FILL    xFF00
        MASK8   .FILL    x0008
        MASK4   .FILL    x0004
        MASK2   .FILL    x0002
        MASK1   .FILL    x0001
```

10

And, Finally ... The Stack

We have finished our treatment of the LC-3 ISA. Before moving up another level of abstraction in Chapter 11 to programming in C, there is a particularly important fundamental topic that we should spend some time on: the *stack*. First we will explain in detail its basic structure. Then, we will describe three uses of the stack: (1) interrupt-driven I/O—the rest of the mechanism that we promised in Section 8.5, (2) a mechanism for performing arithmetic where the temporary storage for intermediate results is a stack instead of general purpose registers, and (3) algorithms for converting integers between 2's complement binary and ASCII character strings. These three examples are just the tip of the iceberg. You will find that the stack has enormous use in much of what you do in computer science and engineering. We suspect you will be discovering new uses for stacks long after this book is just a pleasant memory.

We will close our introduction to the ISA level with the design of a calculator, a comprehensive application that makes use of many of the topics studied in this chapter.

10.1 The Stack: Its Basic Structure

10.1.1 The Stack—An Abstract Data Type

Throughout your future usage (or design) of computers, you will encounter the storage mechanism known as a *stack*. Stacks can be implemented in many different ways, and we will get to that momentarily. But first, it is important to know that the concept of a stack has nothing to do with how it is implemented. The concept of a stack is the specification of how it is to be *accessed*. That is, the defining

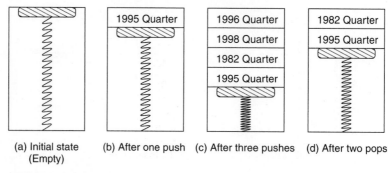

(a) Initial state   (b) After one push   (c) After three pushes   (d) After two pops
(Empty)

Figure 10.1   A coin holder in an auto armrest—example of a stack

ingredient of a stack is that the **last** thing you stored in it is the **first** thing you remove from it. That is what makes a stack different from everything else in the world. Simply put: Last In, First Out, or LIFO.

In the terminology of computer programming languages, we say the stack is an example of an *abstract data type*. That is, an abstract data type is a storage mechanism that is defined by the operations performed on it and not at all by the specific manner in which it is implemented. In Chapter 19, we will write programs in C that use linked lists, another example of an abstract data type.

10.1.2 Two Example Implementations

A coin holder in the armrest of an automobile is an example of a stack. The first quarter you take to pay the highway toll is the last quarter you added to the stack of quarters. As you add quarters, you push the earlier quarters down into the coin holder.

Figure 10.1 shows the behavior of a coin holder. Initially, as shown in Figure 10.1a, the coin holder is empty. The first highway toll is 75 cents, and you give the toll collector a dollar. She gives you 25 cents change, a 1995 quarter, which you insert into the coin holder. The coin holder appears as shown in Figure 10.1b.

There are special terms for the insertion and removal of elements from a stack. We say we *push* an element onto the stack when we insert it. We say we *pop* an element from the stack when we remove it.

The second highway toll is $4.25, and you give the toll collector $5.00. She gives you 75 cents change, which you insert into the coin holder: first a 1982 quarter, then a 1998 quarter, and finally, a 1996 quarter. Now the coin holder is as shown in Figure 10.1c. The third toll is 50 cents, and you remove (pop) the top two quarters from the coin holder: the 1996 quarter first and then the 1998 quarter. The coin holder is then as shown in Figure 10.1d.

The coin holder is an example of a stack, **precisely** because it obeys the LIFO requirement. Each time you insert a quarter, you do so at the top. Each time you remove a quarter, you do so from the top. The last coin you inserted is the first coin you remove; therefore, it is a stack.

Another implementation of a stack, sometimes referred to as a hardware stack, is shown in Figure 10.2. Its behavior resembles that of the coin holder we

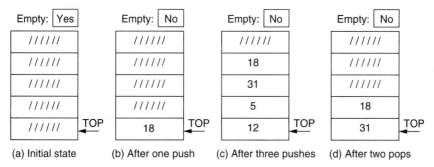

(a) Initial state   (b) After one push   (c) After three pushes   (d) After two pops

Figure 10.2 A stack, implemented in hardware—data entries move

just described. It consists of some number of registers, each of which can store an element. The example of Figure 10.2 contains five registers. As each element is added to the stack or removed from the stack, the elements **already** on the stack **move.**

In Figure 10.2a, the stack is initially shown as empty. Access is always via the first element, which is labeled TOP. If the value 18 is pushed on to the stack, we have Figure 10.2b. If the three values, 31, 5, and 12, are pushed (in that order), the result is Figure 10.2c. Finally, if two elements are popped from the stack, we have Figure 10.2d. The distinguishing feature of the stack of Figure 10.2 is that, like the quarters in the coin holder, as each value is added or removed, all the values already on the stack move.

10.1.3 Implementation in Memory

By far the most common implementation of a stack in a computer is as shown in Figure 10.3. The stack consists of a sequence of memory locations along with a mechanism, called the *stack pointer,* that keeps track of the top of the stack, that is, the location containing the most recent element pushed. Each value pushed is stored in one of the memory locations. In this case, the data already stored on the stack **does not physically move.**

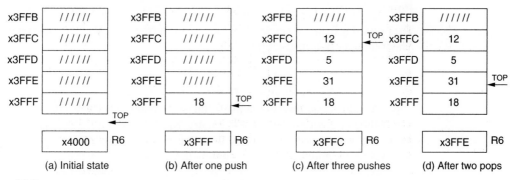

(a) Initial state   (b) After one push   (c) After three pushes   (d) After two pops

Figure 10.3 A stack, implemented in memory—data entries do not move

In the example shown in Figure 10.3, the stack consists of five locations, x3FFF through x3FFB. R6 is the stack pointer.

Figure 10.3a shows an initially empty stack. Figure 10.3b shows the stack after pushing the value 18. Figure 10.3c shows the stack after pushing the values 31, 5, and 12, in that order. Figure 10.3d shows the stack after popping the top two elements off the stack. Note that those top two elements (the values 5 and 12) are still present in memory locations x3FFD and x3FFC. However, as we will see momentarily, those values 5 and 12 cannot be accessed from memory, as long as the access to memory is controlled by the stack mechanism.

Push

In Figure 10.3a, R6 contains x4000, the address just ahead of the first (BASE) location in the stack. This indicates that the stack is initially empty. The BASE address of the stack of Figure 10.3 is x3FFF.

We first push the value 18 onto the stack, resulting in Figure 10.3b. The stack pointer provides the address of the last value pushed, in this case, x3FFF, where 18 is stored. Note that the contents of locations x3FFE, x3FFD, x3FFC, and x3FFB are not shown. As will be seen momentarily, the contents of these locations are irrelevant since they can never be accessed provided that locations x3FFF through x3FFB are accessed *only* as a stack.

When we push a value onto the stack, the stack pointer is decremented and the value stored. The two-instruction sequence

```
        PUSH        ADD     R6,R6,#-1
                    STR     R0,R6,#0
```

pushes the value contained in R0 onto the stack. Thus, for the stack to be as shown in Figure 10.3b, R0 must have contained the value 18 before the two-instruction sequence was executed.

The three values 31, 5, and 12 are pushed onto the stack by loading each in turn into R0, and then executing the two-instruction sequence. In Figure 10.3c, R6 (the stack pointer) contains x3FFC, indicating that 12 was the last element pushed.

Pop

To pop a value from the stack, the value is read and the stack pointer is incremented. The following two-instruction sequence

```
        POP         LDR     R0,R6,#0
                    ADD     R6,R6,#1
```

pops the value contained in the top of the stack and loads it into R0.

If the stack were as shown in Figure 10.3c and we executed the sequence twice, we would pop two values from the stack. In this case, we would first remove the 12, and then the 5. Assuming the purpose of popping two values is to use those two values, we would, of course, have to move the 12 from R0 to some other location before calling POP a second time.

Figure 10.3d shows the stack after that sequence of operations. R6 contains x3FFE, indicating that 31 is now at the top of the stack. Note that the values 12 and 5 are still stored in memory locations x3FFD and x3FFC, respectively. However, since the stack requires that we push by executing the PUSH sequence and pop by executing the POP sequence, we cannot access these two values if we obey the rules. The fancy name for "the rules" is the *stack protocol*.

Underflow

What happens if we now attempt to pop three values from the stack? Since only two values remain on the stack, we would have a problem. Attempting to pop items that have not been previously pushed results in an *underflow* situation. In our example, we can test for underflow by comparing the stack pointer with x4000, which would be the contents of R6 if there were nothing left on the stack to pop. If UNDERFLOW is the label of a routine that handles the underflow condition, our resulting POP sequence would be

```
POP       LD      R1,EMPTY
          ADD     R2,R6,R1     ; Compare stack
          BRz     UNDERFLOW    ; pointer with x4000.
          LDR     R0,R6,#0
          ADD     R6,R6,#1
          RET
EMPTY     .FILL   xC000        ; EMPTY <-- -x4000
```

Rather than have the POP routine immediately jump to the UNDERFLOW routine if the POP is unsuccessful, it is often useful to have the POP routine return to the calling program, with the underflow information contained in a register.

A common convention for doing this is to use a register to provide success/ failure information. Figure 10.4 is a flowchart showing how the POP routine could be augmented, using R5 to report this success/failure information.

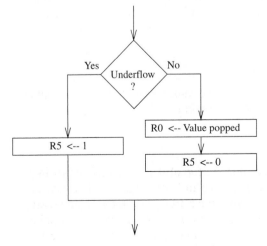

Figure 10.4   POP routine, including test for underflow

Upon return from the POP routine, the calling program would examine R5 to determine whether the POP completed successfully (R5 = 0), or not (R5 = 1).

Note that since the POP routine reports success or failure in R5, whatever was stored in R5 **before** the POP routine was called is lost. Thus, it is the job of the calling program to save the contents of R5 before the JSR instruction is executed. Recall from Section 9.1.7 that this is an example of a caller-save situation.

The resulting POP routine is shown in the following instruction sequence. Note that since the instruction immediately preceding the RET instruction sets/clears the condition codes, the calling program can simply test Z to determine whether the POP was completed successfully.

```
POP         LD      R1,EMPTY
            ADD     R2,R6,R1
            BRz     Failure
            LDR     R0,R6,#0
            ADD     R6,R6,#1
            AND     R5,R5,#0
            RET
Failure     AND     R5,R5,#0
            ADD     R5,R5,#1
            RET
EMPTY       .FILL   xC000           ; EMPTY <-- -x4000
```

Overflow

What happens when we run out of available space and we try to push a value onto the stack? Since we cannot store values where there is no room, we have an *overflow* situation. We can test for overflow by comparing the stack pointer with (in the example of Figure 10.3) x3FFB. If they are equal, we have no room to push another value onto the stack. If OVERFLOW is the label of a routine that handles the overflow condition, our resulting PUSH sequence would be

```
PUSH        LD      R1,MAX
            ADD     R2,R6,R1
            BRz     OVERFLOW
            ADD     R6,R6,#-1
            STR     R0,R6,#0
            RET
MAX         .FILL   xC005           ; MAX <-- -x3FFB
```

In the same way that it is useful to have the POP routine return to the calling program with success/failure information, rather than immediately jumping to the UNDERFLOW routine, it is useful to have the PUSH routine act similarly.

We augment the PUSH routine with instructions to store 0 (success) or 1 (failure) in R5, depending on whether or not the push completed successfully. Upon return from the PUSH routine, the calling program would examine R5 to determine whether the PUSH completed successfully (R5 = 0) or not (R5 = 1).

Note again that since the PUSH routine reports success or failure in R5, we have another example of a caller-save situation. That is, since whatever was stored in R5 before the PUSH routine was called is lost, it is the job of the calling program to save the contents of R5 before the JSR instruction is executed.

Also, note again that since the instruction immediately preceding the RET instruction sets/clears the condition codes, the calling program can simply test Z or P to determine whether the POP completed successfully (see the following PUSH routine).

```
        PUSH       LD      R1,MAX
                   ADD     R2,R6,R1
                   BRz     Failure
                   ADD     R6,R6,#-1
                   STR     R0,R6,#0
                   AND     R5,R5,#0
                   RET
        Failure    AND     R5,R5,#0
                   ADD     R5,R5,#1
                   RET
        MAX        .FILL   xC005         ; MAX <-- -x3FFB
```

10.1.4 The Complete Picture

The POP and PUSH routines allow us to use memory locations x3FFF through x3FFB as a five-entry stack. If we wish to push a value onto the stack, we simply load that value into R0 and execute JSR PUSH. To pop a value from the stack into R0, we simply execute JSR POP. If we wish to change the location or the size of the stack, we adjust BASE and MAX accordingly.

Before leaving this topic, we should be careful to clean up one detail. The subroutines PUSH and POP make use of R1, R2, and R5. If we wish to use the values stored in those registers after returning from the PUSH or POP routine, we had best save them before using them. In the case of R1 and R2, it is easiest to save them in the PUSH and POP routines before using them and then to restore them before returning to the calling program. That way, the calling program does not even have to know that these registers are used in the PUSH and POP routines. This is an example of the callee-save situation described in Section 9.1.7. In the case of R5, the situation is different since the calling program does have to know the success or failure that is reported in R5. Thus, it is the job of the calling program to save the contents of R5 before the JSR instruction is executed if the calling program wishes to use the value stored there again. This is an example of the caller-save situation.

The final code for our PUSH and POP operations is shown in Figure 10.5.

```
01   ;
02   ; Subroutines for carrying out the PUSH and POP functions.  This
03   ; program works with a stack consisting of memory locations x3FFF
04   ; (BASE) through x3FFB (MAX).  R6 is the stack pointer.
05   ;
06   POP           ST     R2,Save2        ; are needed by POP.
07                 ST     R1,Save1
08                 LD     R1,BASE         ; BASE contains -x3FFF.
09                 ADD    R1,R1,#-1       ; R1 contains -x4000.
0A                 ADD    R2,R6,R1        ; Compare stack pointer to x4000.
0B                 BRz    fail_exit       ; Branch if stack is empty.
0C                 LDR    R0,R6,#0        ; The actual "pop"
0D                 ADD    R6,R6,#1        ; Adjust stack pointer.
0E                 BRnzp  success_exit
0F   PUSH          ST     R2,Save2        ; Save registers that
10                 ST     R1,Save1        ; are needed by PUSH.
11                 LD     R1,MAX          ; MAX contains -x3FFB.
12                 ADD    R2,R6,R1        ; Compare stack pointer to -x3FFB.
13                 BRz    fail_exit       ; Branch if stack is full.
14                 ADD    R6,R6,#-1       ; Adjust stack pointer.
15                 STR    R0,R6,#0        ; The actual "push"
16   success_exit  LD     R1,Save1        ; Restore original
17                 LD     R2,Save2        ; register values.
18                 AND    R5,R5,#0        ; R5 <-- success.
19                 RET
1A   fail_exit     LD     R1,Save1        ; Restore original
1B                 LD     R2,Save2        ; register values.
1C                 AND    R5,R5,#0
1D                 ADD    R5,R5,#1        ; R5 <-- failure.
1E                 RET
1F   BASE          .FILL  xC001           ; BASE contains -x3FFF.
20   MAX           .FILL  xC005
21   Save1         .FILL  x0000
22   Save2         .FILL  x0000
```

Figure 10.5   The stack protocol

10.2 Interrupt-Driven I/O (Part 2)

Recall our discussion in Section 8.1.4 about interrupt-driven I/O as an alternative to polling. As you know, in polling, the processor wastes its time spinning its wheels, re-executing again and again the LDI and BR instructions until the Ready bit is set. With interrupt-driven I/O, none of that testing and branching has to go on. Instead, the processor spends its time doing what is hopefully useful work, executing some program, until it is notified that some I/O device needs attention.

You remember that there are two parts to interrupt-driven I/O:

1. the enabling mechanism that allows an I/O device to interrupt the processor when it has input to deliver or is ready to accept output, and

2. the process that manages the transfer of the I/O data.

In Section 8.5, we showed the enabling mechanism for interrupting the processor, that is, asserting the INT signal. We showed how the Ready bit, combined with the Interrupt Enable bit, provided an interrupt request signal. We showed that if the interrupt request signal is at a higher priority level (PL) than the PL of the currently executing process, the INT signal is asserted. We saw (Figure 8.8) that with this mechanism, the processor did not have to waste a lot of time polling. In Section 8.5, we could not study the process that manages the transfer of the I/O data because it involves the use of a stack, and you were not yet familiar with the stack. Now you know about stacks, so we can finish the explanation.

The actual management of the I/O data transfer goes through three stages, as shown in Figure 8.6:

1. Initiate the interrupt.
2. Service the interrupt.
3. Return from the interrupt.

We will discuss these in turn.

10.2.1 Initiate and Service the Interrupt

Recall from Section 8.5 (and Figure 8.8) that an interrupt is initiated because an I/O device with higher priority than the currently running program has caused the INT signal to be asserted. The processor, for its part, tests for the presence of INT each time it completes an instruction cycle. If the test is negative, business continues as usual and the next instruction of the currently running program is fetched. If the test is positive, that next instruction is not fetched.

Instead, preparation is made to interrupt the program that is running and execute the interrupt service routine that deals with the needs of the I/O device that has requested this higher priority service. Two steps must be carried out: (1) Enough of the state of the program that is running must be saved so we can later continue where we left off, and (2) enough of the state of the interrupt service routine must be loaded so we can begin to service the interrupt request.

The State of a Program

The state of a program is a snapshot of the contents of all the resources that the program affects. It includes the contents of the memory locations that are part of the program and the contents of all the general purpose registers. It also includes two very important registers, the PC and the PSR. The PC you are very familiar with; it contains the address of the next instruction to be executed. The PSR, shown here, is the Processor Status Register. It contains several important pieces of information about the status of the running program.

15	14	13	12	11	10	9	8	7	6	5	4	3	2	1	0	
Pr					PL								N	Z	P	**PSR**
Priv					Priority								cond codes			

PSR[15] indicates whether the program is running in privileged (supervisor) or unprivileged (user) mode. In privileged mode, the program has access to important resources not available to user programs. We will see momentarily why that is important in dealing with interrupts. PSR[10:8] specifies the priority level (PL) or sense of urgency of the execution of the program. As has been mentioned previously, there are eight priority levels, PL0 (lowest) to PL7 (highest). Finally, PSR[2:0] is used to store the condition codes. PSR[2] is the N bit, PSR[1] is the Z bit, and PSR[0] is the P bit.

Saving the State of the Interrupted Program

The first step in initiating the interrupt is to save enough of the state of the program that is running so it can continue where it left off after the I/O device request has been satisfied. That means, in the case of the LC-3, saving the PC and the PSR. The PC must be saved since it knows which instruction should be executed next when the interrupted program resumes execution. The condition codes (the N, Z, and P flags) must be saved since they may be needed by a subsequent conditional branch instruction after the program resumes execution. The priority level of the interrupted program must be saved because it specifies the urgency of the interrupted program with respect to all other programs. When the interrupted program resumes execution, it is important to know what priority level programs can interrupt it again and which ones can not. Finally, the privilege level of the program must be saved since it contains information about what processor resources the interrupted program can and can not access.

It is not necessary to save the contents of the general purpose registers since we assume that the service routine will save the contents of any general purpose register it needs before using it, and will restore it before returning to the interrupted program.

The LC-3 saves this state information on a special stack, called the Supervisor Stack, that is used only by programs that execute in privileged mode. A section of memory is dedicated for this purpose. This stack is separate from the User Stack, which is accessed by user programs. Programs access both stacks using R6 as the stack pointer. When accessing the Supervisor Stack, R6 is the Supervisor Stack Pointer. When accessing the User Stack, R6 is the User Stack Pointer. Two internal registers, Saved.SSP and Saved.USP, are used to save the stack pointer not in use. When the privilege mode changes from user to supervisor, the contents of R6 are saved in Saved.USP, and R6 is loaded with the contents of Saved.SSP before processing begins.

That is, before the interrupt service routine starts, R6 is loaded with the contents of the Supervisor Stack Pointer. Then PC and PSR of the interrupted program are pushed onto the Supervisor Stack, where they remain unmolested while the service routine executes.

Loading the State of the Interrupt Service Routine

Once the state of the interrupted program has been safely saved on the Supervisor Stack, the second step is to load the PC and PSR of the interrupt service routine. Interrupt service routines are similar to the trap service routines discussed in Chapter 9. They are program fragments stored in some prearranged set of locations in memory. They service interrupt requests.

Most processors use the mechanism of *vectored interrupts*. You are familiar with this notion from your study of the trap vector contained in the TRAP instruction. In the case of interrupts, the 8-bit vector is provided by the device that is requesting the processor be interrupted. That is, the I/O device transmits to the processor an 8-bit interrupt vector along with its interrupt request signal and its priority level. The interrupt vector corresponding to the highest priority interrupt request is the one supplied to the processor. It is designated INTV. If the interrupt is taken, the processor expands the 8-bit interrupt vector (INTV) to form a 16-bit address, which is an entry into the Interrupt Vector Table. Recall from Chapter 9 that the Trap Vector Table consists of memory locations x0000 to x00FF, each containing the starting address of a trap service routine. The Interrupt Vector Table consists of memory locations x0100 to x01FF, each containing the starting address of an interrupt service routine. The processor loads the PC with the contents of the address formed by expanding the interrupt vector INTV.

The PSR is loaded as follows: Since no instructions in the service routine have yet executed, PSR[2:0] is initially loaded with zeros. Since the interrupt service routine runs in privileged mode, PSR[15] is set to 0. PSR[10:8] is set to the priority level associated with the interrupt request.

This completes the initiation phase and the interrupt service routine is ready to go.

Service the Interrupt

Since the PC contains the starting address of the interrupt service routine, the service routine will execute, and the requirements of the I/O device will be serviced.

For example, the LC-3 keyboard could interrupt the processor every time a key is pressed by someone sitting at the keyboard. The keyboard interrupt vector would indicate the handler to invoke. The handler would then copy the contents of the data register into some preestablished location in memory.

10.2.2 Return from the Interrupt

The last instruction in every interrupt service routine is RTI, return from interrupt. When the processor finally accesses the RTI instruction, all the requirements of the I/O device have been taken care of.

Execution of the **RTI** instruction (opcode = 1000) consists simply of popping the PSR and the PC from the Supervisor Stack (where they have been resting peacefully) and restoring them to their rightful places in the processor. The condition codes are now restored to what they were when the program was interrupted, in case they are needed by a subsequent BR instruction in the program. PSR[15] and PSR[10:8] now reflect the privilege level and priority level of the about-to-be-resumed program. Similarly, the PC is restored to the address of the instruction that would have been executed next if the program had not been interrupted.

With all these things as they were before the interrupt occurred, the program can resume as if nothing had happened.

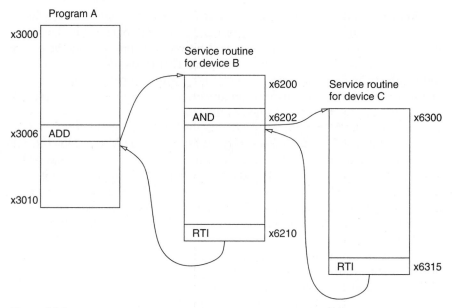

Figure 10.6   Execution flow for interrupt-driven I/O

10.2.3 An Example

We complete the discussion of interrupt-driven I/O with an example.

Suppose program A is executing when I/O device B, having a PL higher than that of A, requests service. During the execution of the service routine for I/O device B, a still more urgent device C requests service.

Figure 10.6 shows the execution flow that must take place.

Program A consists of instructions in locations x3000 to x3010 and was in the middle of executing the ADD instruction at x3006, when device B sent its interrupt request signal and accompanying interrupt vector xF1, causing INT to be asserted.

Note that the interrupt service routine for device B is stored in locations x6200 to x6210; x6210 contains the RTI instruction. Note that the service routine for B was in the middle of executing the AND instruction at x6202, when device C sent its interrupt request signal and accompanying interrupt vector xF2. Since the request associated with device C is of a higher priority than that of device B, INT is again asserted.

Note that the interrupt service routine for device C is stored in locations x6300 to x6315; x6315 contains the RTI instruction.

Let us examine the order of execution by the processor. Figure 10.7 shows several snapshots of the contents of the Supervisor Stack and the PC during the execution of this example.

The processor executes as follows: Figure 10.7a shows the Supervisor Stack and the PC before program A fetches the instruction at x3006. Note that the stack pointer is shown as Saved.SSP, not R6. Since the interrupt has not yet occurred, R6 is pointing to the current contents of the User Stack. The INT signal (caused by an interrupt from device B) is detected at the end of execution of the instruction

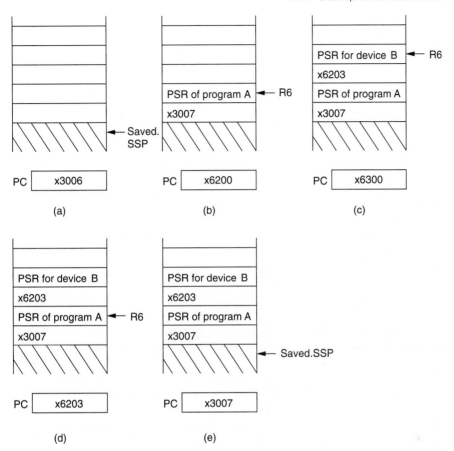

Figure 10.7   Snapshots of the contents of the Supervisor Stack and the PC during interrupt-driven I/O

in x3006. Since the state of program A must be saved on the Supervisor Stack, the first step is to start using the Supervisor Stack. This is done by saving R6 in the Saved.USP register, and loading R6 with the contents of the Saved.SSP register. The address x3007, the PC for the next instruction to be executed in program A, is pushed onto the stack. The PSR of program A, which includes the condition codes produced by the ADD instruction, is pushed onto the stack. The interrupt vector associated with device B is expanded to 16 bits x01F1, and the contents of x01F1 (x6200) are loaded into the PC. Figure 10.7b shows the stack and PC at this point.

The service routine for device B executes until a higher priority interrupt is detected at the end of execution of the instruction at x6202. The address x6203 is pushed onto the stack, along with the PSR of the service routine for B, which includes the condition codes produced by the AND instruction. The interrupt vector associated with device C is expanded to 16 bits (x01F2), and the contents of x01F2 (x6300) are loaded into the PC. Figure 10.7c shows the Supervisor Stack and PC at this point.

The interrupt service routine for device C executes to completion, finishing with the RTI instruction in x6315. The Supervisor Stack is popped twice, restoring the PSR of the service routine for device B, including the condition codes produced by the AND instruction in x6202, and restoring the PC to x6203. Figure 10.7d shows the stack and PC at this point.

The interrupt service routine for device B resumes execution at x6203 and runs to completion, finishing with the RTI instruction in x6210. The Supervisor Stack is popped twice, restoring the PSR of program A, including the condition codes produced by the ADD instruction in x3006, and restoring the PC to x3007. Finally, since program A is in User Mode, the contents of R6 are stored in Saved.SSP and R6 is loaded with the contents of Saved.USP. Figure 10.7e shows the Supervisor Stack and PC at this point.

Program A resumes execution with the instruction at x3007.

10.3 Arithmetic Using a Stack

10.3.1 The Stack as Temporary Storage

There are computers that use a stack instead of general purpose registers to store temporary values during a computation. Recall that our ADD instruction

```
ADD        R0,R1,R2
```

takes source operands from R1 and R2 and writes the result of the addition into R0. We call the LC-3 a *three-address machine* because all three locations (the two sources and the destination) are explicitly identified. Some computers use a stack for source and destination operands and explicitly identify **none** of them. The instruction would simply be

```
ADD
```

We call such a computer a stack machine, or a *zero-address machine*. The hardware would know that the source operands are the top two elements on the stack, which would be popped and then supplied to the ALU, and that the result of the addition would be pushed onto the stack.

To perform an ADD on a stack machine, the hardware would execute two pops, an add, and a push. The two pops would remove the two source operands from the stack, the add would compute their sum, and the push would place the result back on the stack. Note that the pop, push, and add are not part of the ISA of that computer, and therefore not available to the programmer. They are control signals that the hardware uses to make the actual pop, push, and add occur. The control signals are part of the microarchitecture, similar to the load enable signals and mux select signals we discussed in Chapters 4 and 5. As is the case with LC-3 instructions LD and ST, and control signals PCMUX and LD.MDR, the programmer simply instructs the computer to ADD, and the microarchitecture does the rest.

Sometimes (as we will see in our final example of this chapter), it is useful to process arithmetic using a stack. Intermediate values are maintained on the

Source module A

```
.EXTERNAL SQRT
        :
        :
        :
JSRR    :
        :
        :
.END
```

Assemble →

Object module for A

Symbol table for A

Object module for
math library

Symbol table
for math library

Some other separately
assembled module

Symbol table

Link →

Executable
image

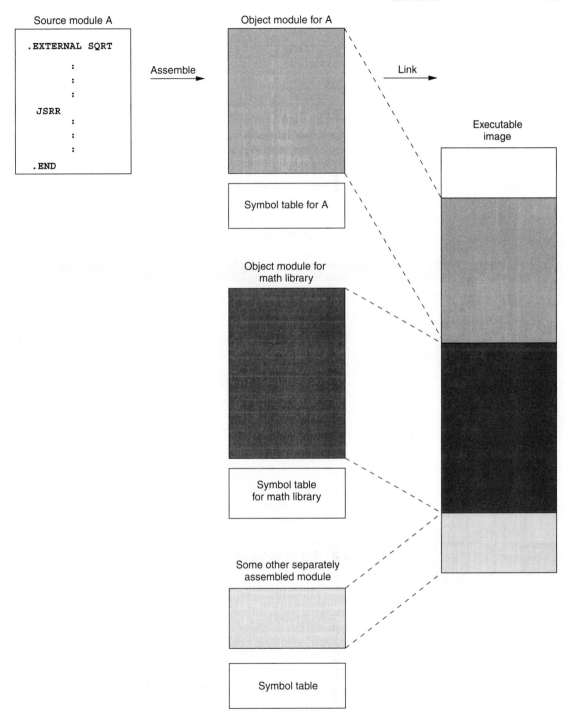

Figure 9.13 An executable image constructed from multiple files

the developers of the system software (the operating system and compiler, for example). If a program uses a library routine, then the linker will find the object code corresponding to the routine and link it within the final executable image. This process of linking in library objects should not be new to you; we described the process in Section 9.2.5 in the context of the LC-3. Usually, library objects are stored in a particular place depending on the computer system. In UNIX, for example, many common library objects can be found in the directory `/usr/lib`.

11.5 A Simple Example

We are now ready to start discussing programming concepts in the C programming language. Many of the new C concepts we present will be coupled with LC-3 code generated by a "hypothetical" LC-3 C compiler. In some cases, we will describe what actually happens when this code is executed. Keep in mind that you are not likely to be using an LC-3–based computer but rather one based on a real ISA such as the x86. For example, if you are using a Windows-based PC, then it is likely that your compiler will generate x86 code, not LC-3 code.

Many of the examples we provide are complete programs that you can compile and execute. For the sake of clearer illustration, some of the examples we provide are not quite complete programs and need to be completed before they can be compiled. In order to keep things straight, we'll refer to these partial code examples as *code segments*.

Let's begin by diving headfirst into a simple C example. Figure 11.3 shows its *source code*. We will use this example to jump-start the process of learning C by pointing out some important aspects of a typical C program. The example is a simple one: It prompts the user to type in a number and then counts down from that number to 0.

You are encouraged to compile and execute this program. At this point, it is not important to completely understand the purpose of each line. There are however several aspects of this example that will help you with writing your own C code and with comprehending the subsequent examples in the text. We'll focus on four such aspects: the function `main`, the code's comments and programming style, preprocessor directives, and the I/O function calls.

11.5.1 The Function `main`

The function `main` begins at the line containing `int main()` (line 17) and ends at the closing brace on the last line of the code. These lines of the source code constitute a *function definition* for the function named `main`. What were called subroutines in LC-3 assembly language programming (discussed in Chapter 9) are referred to as *functions* in C. Functions are a very important part of C, and we will devote all of Chapter 14 to them. In C, the function `main` serves a special purpose: It is where execution of the program begins. Every C program, therefore, requires a function `main`. Note that in ANSI C, `main` must be declared to return

```
1    /*
2     *
3     *    Program Name : countdown, our first C program
4     *
5     *    Description  : This program prompts the user to type in
6     *    a positive number and counts down from that number to 0,
7     *    displaying each number along the way.
8     *
9     */
10
11   /* The next two lines are preprocessor directives */
12   #include <stdio.h>
13   #define STOP 0
14
15   /* Function    : main                                      */
16   /* Description : prompt for input, then display countdown */
17   int main()
18   {
19     /* Variable declarations */
20     int counter;          /* Holds intermediate count values */
21     int startPoint;       /* Starting point for count down    */
22
23     /* Prompt the user for input */
24     printf("===== Countdown Program =====\n");
25     printf("Enter a positive integer: ");
26     scanf("%d", &startPoint);
27
28     /* Count down from the input number to 0 */
29     for (counter = startPoint; counter >= STOP; counter--)
30       printf("%d\n", counter);
31   }
```

Figure 11.3   A program prompts the user for a decimal integer and counts down from that number to 0

an integer value. That is, main must be of type int, thus line 17 of the code is int main().

In this example, the code for function main (i.e., the code in between the curly braces) can be broken down into two components. The first component contains the variable *declarations* for the function. Two variables, one called counter and the other startPoint, are created for use within the function main. Variables are a very useful feature provided by high-level programming languages. They give us a way to symbolically name the values within a program.

The second component contains the *statements* of the function. These statements express the actions that will be performed when the function is executed. For all C programs, execution starts in main and progresses, statement by statement, until the last statement in main is completed.

In this example, the first grouping of statements (lines 24–26) displays a message and prompts the user to input an integer number. Once the user enters a number, the program enters the last statement, which is a for loop (a type of iteration construct that we will discuss in Chapter 13). The loop counts downward from the number typed by the user to 0. For example, if the user entered the number 5, the program's output would look as follows:

```
===== Countdown Program =====
Enter a positive integer: 5
5
4
3
2
1
0
```

Notice in this example that many lines of the source code are terminated by semicolons, ;. In C, semicolons are used to terminate declarations and statements; they are necessary for the compiler to break the program down unambiguously into its constituents.

11.5.2 Formatting, Comments, and Style

C is a free-format language. That is, the amount of spacing between words and between lines within a program does not change the meaning of the program. The programmer is free to structure the program in whatever manner he/she sees fit while obeying the syntactic rules of C. Programmers use this freedom to format the code in a manner that makes it easier to read. In the example program, notice that the `for` loop is indented in such a manner that the statement being iterated is easier to identify. Also in the example, notice the use of blank lines to separate different regions of code in the function `main`. These blank lines are not necessary but are used to provide visual separation of the code. Often, statements that together accomplish a larger task are grouped together into a visually identifiable unit. The C code examples throughout this book use a conventional indentation style typical for C. Styles vary. Programmers sometimes use style as a means of expression. Feel free to define your own style, keeping in mind that the objective is to help convey the meaning of the program through its formatting.

Comments in C are different than in LC-3 assembly language. Comments in C begin with /* and end with */. They can span multiple lines. Notice that this example program contains several lines of comments, some on a single line, some spanning multiple lines. Comments are expressed differently from one programming language to another. For example, comments in C++ can also begin with the sequence // and extend to the end of the line. Regardless of how comments are expressed, the purpose is always the same: They provide a way for programmers to describe in human terms what their code does.

Proper commenting of code is an important part of the programming process. Good comments enhance code readability, allowing someone not familiar with the code to understand it more quickly. Since programming tasks often involve working in teams, code very often gets shared or borrowed between programmers. In order to work effectively on a programming team, or to write code that is worth sharing, you must adopt a good commenting style early on.

One aspect of good commenting style is to provide information at the beginning of each source file that describes the code contained within it, the date it was last modified, and by whom. Furthermore, each function (see function `main` in the example) should have a brief description of what the function accomplishes, along with a description of its inputs and outputs. Also, comments are usually interspersed within the code to explain the intent of the various sections of the code. But overcommenting can be detrimental as it can clutter up your code, making it harder to read. In particular, watch out for comments that provide no additional information beyond what is obvious from the code.

11.5.3 The C Preprocessor

We briefly mentioned the C preprocessor in Section 11.4.1. Recall that it transforms the original C program before it is handed off to the compiler. Our simple example contains two commonly used preprocessor directives: `#define` and `#include`. The C examples in this book rely only on these two directives.

The `#define` directive is a simple yet powerful directive that instructs the C preprocessor to replace occurrences of any text that matches X with text Y. That is, the *macro* X gets *substituted* with Y. In the example, the `#define` causes the text STOP to be substituted with the text 0. So the following source line

```
for (counter = startPoint; counter >= STOP; counter--)
```

is transformed (internally, only between the preprocessor and compiler) into

```
for (counter = startPoint; counter >= 0; counter--)
```

Why is this helpful? Often, the `#define` directive is used to create fixed values within a program. Following are several examples.

```
#define NUMBER_OF_STUDENTS    25
#define MAX_LENGTH            80
#define LENGTH_OF_GAME        300
#define PRICE_OF_FUEL         1.49
#define COLOR_OF_EYES         brown
```

So for example, we can symbolically refer to the price of fuel as PRICE_OF_FUEL. If the price of fuel were to change, we would simply modify the definition of the macro PRICE_OF_FUEL and the preprocessor would handle the actual substitution for us. This can be very convenient—if the cost of fuel was used heavily within a program, we would only need to modify one line in the source code to change the price throughout the code. Notice that the last example is slightly different from the others. In this example, one string of characters COLOR_OF_EYES is being substituted for another, brown. The common programming style is to use uppercase for the macro name.

The `#include` directive instructs the preprocessor literally to insert another file into the source file. Essentially, the `#include` directive itself is replaced by the contents of another file. At this point, the usefulness of this command may not be completely apparent to you, but as we progress deeper into the C language, you will understand how *C header files* can be used to hold `#defines` and declarations that are useful among multiple source files.

For instance, all programs that use the C I/O functions must include the I/O library's header file `stdio.h`. This file defines some relevant information about the I/O functions in the C library. The preprocessor directive, `#include <stdio.h>` is used to insert the header file before compilation begins.

There are two variations of the `#include` directive:

```
#include <stdio.h>
#include "program.h"
```

The first variation uses angle brackets (`< >`) around the filename. This tells the preprocessor that the header file can be found in a predefined directory. This is usually determined by the configuration of the system and contains many system-related and library-related header files, such as `stdio.h`. Often we want to include headers files we have created ourselves for the particular program we are writing. The second variation, using double quotes (`" "`) around the filename, instructs the preprocessor that the header file can be found in the same directory as the C source file.

Notice that none of the preprocessor macros ends with a semicolon. Since `#define` and `#include` are preprocessor directives and not C statements, they are not required to be terminated by semicolons.

11.5.4 Input and Output

We close this chapter by pointing out how to perform input and output from within a C program. We describe these functions at a high level now and save the details for Chapter 18, when we have introduced enough background material to understand C I/O down to a low level. Since all useful programs perform some form of I/O, learning the I/O capabilities of C is an important first step. In C, I/O is performed by library functions, similar to the IN and OUT trap routines provided by the LC-3 system software.

Three lines of the example program perform output using the C library function `printf` or *print formatted* (refer to lines 24, 25, and 30). The function `printf` performs output to the standard output device, which is typically the monitor. It requires a *format string* in which we provide two things: (1) text to print out and (2) specifications on how to print out values within that text. For example, the statement

```
printf("43 is a prime number.");
```

prints out the following text to the output device.

```
43 is a prime number.
```

In addition to text, it is often useful to print out values generated within a program. Specifications within the format string indicate how we want these values to be printed out. Let's examine a few examples.

```
printf("%d is a prime number.", 43);
```

This first example contains the format specification `%d` in its format string. It causes the value listed after the format string to be embedded in the output as a decimal number in place of the `%d`. The resulting output would be

```
43 is a prime number.
```

The following examples show other variants of `printf`.

```
printf("43 plus 59 in decimal is %d.", 43 + 59);
printf("43 plus 59 in hexadecimal is %x.", 43 + 59);
printf("43 plus 59 as a character is %c.", 43 + 59);
```

In the first `printf`, the format specification causes the value 102 to be embedded in the text because the result of "43 + 59" is printed as a decimal number. In the next example, the format specification `%x` causes 66 (because 102 equals x66) to be embedded in the text. Similarly, in the third example, the format specification of `%c` displays the value interpreted as an ASCII character which, in this case, would be lowercase `f`. The output of this statement would be

```
43 plus 59 as a character is f.
```

What is important to notice is that the binary pattern being supplied to `printf` after the format string is the same for all three statements. Here, `printf` interprets the binary pattern 0110 0110 (decimal 102) first as a decimal number, then as a hexadecimal number, and finally as an ASCII character. The C output function `printf` converts the bit pattern into the proper sequence of ASCII characters based on the format sepecifications we provide it. Table D.6 contains a list of all the format specifications that can be used with `printf`. All format specifications begin with the percent sign, `%`.

The final example demonstrates a very common and powerful use of `printf`.

```
printf("The wind speed is %d km/hr.", windSpeed);
```

Here, a value generated during the execution of the program, in this case the variable `windSpeed`, is output as a decimal number. The value displayed depends on the value of `windSpeed` when this line of code is executed. So if `windSpeed` equals 2 when the statement containing `printf` is executed, the following output would result:

```
The wind speed is 2 km/hr.
```

If you were to execute a program containing the five preceding `printf` statements in these examples, you would notice that they would all be displayed on one single line without any line breaks. If we want line breaks to appear, we must put them explicitly within the format string in the places we want them to occur. New lines, tabs, and other special characters require the use of a special backslash (\) sequence. For example, to print a new line character (and thus cause a line break), we use the special sequence \n. We can rewrite the preceding printf statements as such:

```
printf("%d is a prime number.\n", 43);
printf("43 plus 59 in decimal is %d.\n", 43 + 59);
printf("43 plus 59 in hexadecimal is %x.\n", 43 + 59);
printf("43 plus 59 as a character is %c.\n", 43 + 59);
printf("The wind speed is %d km/hr.\n", windSpeed);
```

Notice that each format string ends by printing the new line character \n, so therefore each subsequent printf will begin on a new line. Table D.1 contains a list of other special characters that are useful when generating output. The output generated by these five statements would look as follows:

```
43 is a prime number.
43 plus 59 in decimal is 102.
43 plus 59 in hexadecimal is 66.
43 plus 59 as a character is f.
The wind speed is 2 km/hr.
```

In our sample program in Figure 11.3, printf appears three times in the source. The first two versions display only text and no values (thus, they have no format specifications). The third version prints out the value of variable counter. Generally speaking, we can display as many values as we like within a single printf. The number of format specifications (for example, %d) must equal the number of values that follow the format string.

Question: What happens if we replace the third printf in the example program with the following? The expression "startPoint - counter" calculates the value of startPoint minus the value of counter.

```
printf("%d %d\n", counter, startPoint - counter);
```

Having dealt with output, we now turn to the corresponding input function scanf. The function scanf performs input from the standard input device, which is typically the keyboard. It requires a format string (similar to the one required by printf) and a list of variables into which the values retrieved from the keyboard should be stored. The function scanf reads input from the keyboard and, according to the conversion characters in the format string, converts the input and assigns the converted values to the variables listed. Let's look at an example.

In the example program in Figure 11.3, we use scanf to read in a single decimal number using the format specification %d. Recall from our discussion on LC-3 keyboard input, the value received via the keyboard is in ASCII. The format specification %d informs scanf to expect a sequence of *numeric* ASCII keystrokes (i.e., the digits 0 to 9). This sequence is interpreted as a decimal number and converted into an integer. The resulting binary pattern will be stored in the variable called `startPoint`. The function `scanf` automatically performs type conversions (in this case, from ASCII to integer) for us! The format specification `%d` is one of several that can be used with `scanf`. Table D.5 lists them all. There are specifications to read in a single character, a floating point value, an integer expressed as a hexadecimal value, and so forth.

A very important thing to remember about `scanf` is that variables that are being modified by the `scanf` function (for example, `startPoint`) must be preceded by an `&` character. This may seem a bit mysterious, but we will discuss the reason for this strange notation in Chapter 16.

Following are several more examples of `scanf`.

```
/* Reads in a character and stores it in nextChar */
scanf("%c", &nextChar);

/* Reads in a floating point number into radius */
scanf("%f", &radius);

/* Reads two decimal numbers into length and width */
scanf("%d %d", &length, &width);
```

11.6 Summary

In this chapter, we have introduced some key characteristics of high-level programming languages and provided an initial exposure to the C programming language. We conclude this chapter with a listing of the major topics we've covered.

- **High-Level Programming Languages.** High-level languages aim to make the programming process easier by connecting real-world objects with the low-level concepts, such as bits and operations on bits, that a computer natively deals with. Because computers can only execute machine code, programs in high-level languages must be translated using the process of compilation or interpretation into machine code.

- **The C Programming Language.** The C programming language is an ideal language for a bottom-up exposure to computing because of its low-level nature and because of its root influence on current popular programming languages. The C compilation process involves a preprocessor, a compiler, and a linker.

- **Our First C Program.** We provided a very simple program to illustrate several basic features of C programs. Comments, indentation, and style can help convey the meaning of a program to someone trying to understand the code. Many C programs use the preprocessor macros `#define` and `#include`. The execution of a C program begins at the function `main`, which itself consists of variable declarations and statements. Finally, I/O in C can be accomplished using the library functions `printf` and `scanf`.

11.1   Describe some problems or inconveniences you found when programming in lower-level languages.

11.2   How do higher-level languages help reduce the tedium of programming in lower-level languages?

11.3   What are some disadvantages to programming in a higher-level language?

11.4   Compare and contrast the execution process of an interpreter versus the execution process of a compiled binary. What implication does interpretation have on performance?

11.5   A language is portable if its code can run on different computer systems, say with different ISAs. What makes interpreted languages more portable than compiled languages?

11.6   The UNIX command line shell is an interpreter. Why can't it be a compiler?

11.7   Is the LC-3 simulator a compiler or an interpreter?

11.8   Another advantage of compilation over interpretation is that a compiler can optimize code more thoroughly. Since a compiler can examine the entire program when generating machine code, it can reduce the amount of computation by analyzing what the program is trying to do.

     The following algorithm performs some very straightforward arithmetic based on values typed at the keyboard. It outputs a single result.

1. Get W from the keyboard
2. $X \leftarrow W + W$
3. $Y \leftarrow X + X$
4. $Z \leftarrow Y + Y$
5. Print Z to the screen

a. An interpreter would execute the program statement by statement. In total, five statements would execute. At least how many arithmetic operations would the interpreter perform on behalf of this program? State what the operations would be.

b. A compiler would analyze the entire program before generating machine code, and possibly optimize the code. If the underlying ISA were capable of all arithmetic operations (i.e., addition, subtraction, multiplication, division), at least how many operations would be needed to carry out this program? State what the operations would be.

11.9   For this question refer to Figure 11.2.

a. Describe the input to the C preprocessor.
b. Describe the input to the C compiler.
c. Describe the input to the linker.

11.10   What happens if we changed the second-to-last line of the program in Figure 11.3 from `printf("%d\n", counter);` to:

    a. `printf("%c\n", counter + 'A');`
    b. `printf("%d\n%d\n", counter, startPoint + counter);`
    c. `printf("%x\n", counter);`

11.11   The function `scanf` reads in a character from the keyboard and the function `printf` prints it out. What do the following two statements accomplish?

```
scanf("%c", &nextChar);
printf("%d\n", nextChar);
```

11.12   The following lines of C code appear in a program. What will be the output of each `printf` statement?

```
#define LETTER  '1'
#define ZERO      0
#define NUMBER  123

printf("%c", 'a');

printf("x%x", 12288);

printf("$%d.%c%d\n", NUMBER, LETTER, ZERO);
```

11.13   Describe a program (at this point we do not expect you to be able to write working C code) that reads a decimal number from the keyboard and prints out its hexadecimal equivalent.

12

Variables and Operators

12.1 Introduction

In this chapter, we cover two basic concepts of high-level language programming, variables and operators. *Variables* hold the values upon which a program acts, and *operators* are the language mechanisms for manipulating these values. Variables and operators together allow the programmer to more easily express the work that a program is to carry out.

The following line of C code is a statement that involves both variables and operators. In this statement, the addition operator + is used to add 3 to the original value of the variable score. This new value is then assigned using the assignment operator = back to score. If score was equal to 7 before this statement was executed, it would equal 10 afterwards.

```
score = score + 3;
```

In the first part of this chapter, we'll take a closer look at variables in the C programming language. Variables in C are straightforward: the three most basic flavors are integers, characters, and floating point numbers. After variables, we'll cover C's rich set of operators, providing plenty of examples to help illustrate their operations. One unique feature of our approach is that we can connect both of these high-level concepts back to solid low-level material, and in the third part of the chapter we'll do just that by discussing the compiler's point of view when it tries to deal with variables and operators in generating machine code. We close this chapter with some problem solving and some miscellaneous concepts involving variables and operators in C.

12.2 Variables

A value is any data item upon which a program performs an operation. Examples of values include the iteration counter for a loop, an input value entered by a user, or the partial sum of a series of numbers that are being added together. Programmers spend a lot of effort keeping track of these values.

Because values are such an important programming concept, high-level languages try to make the process of managing them easier on the programmer. High-level languages allow the programmer to refer to values *symbolically*, by a name rather than a memory location. And whenever we want to operate on the value, the language will automatically generate the proper sequence of data movement operations. The programmer can then focus on writing the program and need not worry about where in memory to store a value or about juggling the value between memory and the registers. In high-level languages, these symbolically named values are called *variables*.

In order to properly track the variables in a program, the high-level language translator (the C compiler, for instance) needs to know several characteristics about each variable. It needs to know, obviously, the symbolic name of the variable. It needs to know what type of information the variable will contain. It needs to know where in the program the variable will be accessible. In most languages, C included, this information is provided by the variable's *declaration*.

Let's look at an example. The following declares a variable called echo that will contain an integer value.

```
int echo;
```

Based on this declaration, the compiler reserves an integer's worth of memory for echo (sometimes, the compiler can optimize the program such that echo is stored in a register and therefore does not require a memory location, but that is a subject for a later course). Whenever echo is referred to in the subsequent C code, the compiler generates the appropriate machine code to access it.

12.2.1 Three Basic Data Types: `int, char, double`

By now, you should be very familiar with the following concept: the meaning of a particular bit pattern depends on the data type imposed on the pattern. For example, the binary pattern 0110 0110 might represent the lowercase f or it might represent the decimal number 102, depending on whether we treat the pattern as an ASCII data type or as a 2's complement integer data type. A variable's declaration informs the compiler about the variable's type. The compiler uses a variable's type information to allocate a proper amount of storage for the variable. Also, type indicates how operations on the variable are to be performed at the machine level. For instance, performing an addition on two integer variables can be done on the LC-3 with one ADD instruction. If the two variables were of floating point type, the LC-3 compiler would generate a sequence of instructions to perform the addition because no single LC-3 instruction performs a floating point addition.

C supports three basic data types: integers, characters, and floating point numbers. Variables of these types can be created with the type specifiers `int`, `char`, and `double` (which is short for *double*-precision floating point).

int

The `int` type specifier declares a signed integer variable. The internal representation and range of values of an `int` depends on the ISA of the computer and the specifics of the compiler being used. In the LC-3, for example, an `int` is a 16-bit 2's complement integer that can represent numbers between $-32,768$ and $+32,767$. On an x86-based computer, an `int` is likely to be a 32-bit 2's complement number that can represent numbers between $-2,147,483,648$ and $+2,147,483,647$. In most cases, an `int` is a 2's complement integer in the word length of the underlying ISA.

The following line of code declares an integer variable called `numberOfSeconds`. When the compiler sees this declaration, the compiler sets aside enough storage for this variable (in the case of the LC-3, one memory location).

```
int numberOfSeconds;
```

It should be no surprise that variables of integer type are frequently used in programs. They often conveniently represent the real-world data we want our programs to process. If we wanted to represent time, say for example in seconds, an integer variable would be perfect. In an application that tracks whale migration, we can use an integer to represent the sizes of pods of gray whales seen off the California coast. Integers are also useful for program control. An integer can be useful as the iteration counter for a counter-controlled loop.

char

The `char` type specifier declares a variable whose data value represents a character. Following are two examples. The first declaration creates a variable named `lock`. The second one declares `key`. The second declaration is slightly different; it also contains an *initializer*. In C, any variables can be set to an initial value directly in its declaration. In this example, the variable `key` will have the initial value of the ASCII code for uppercase Q. Also notice that the uppercase Q is surrounded by single quotes, ` ' ' `. In C, characters that are to be interpreted as ASCII *literals* are surrounded by single quotes. What about `lock`? What initial value will it have? We'll address this issue shortly.

```
char lock;
char key = 'Q';
```

Although eight bits are sufficient to hold an ASCII character, for purposes of making the examples in this textbook less cluttered, all `char` variables will occupy 16 bits. That is, `char`s, like `int`s, will each occupy one memory location.

double

The type specifier `double` allows us to declare variables of the floating point type that we examined in Section 2.7.2. Floating point numbers allow us to conveniently deal with numbers that have fractional components or numbers that are very large or very small. Recall from our previous discussion in Section 2.7.2 that at the lowest level, a floating point number is a bit pattern that has three parts: a sign, a fraction, and an exponent.

Here are three examples of variables of type `double`:

```
double costPerLiter;
double electronsPerSecond;
double averageTemp;
```

As with `int`s and `char`s, we can also optionally initialize a floating point number along with its declaration. Before we can completely describe how to initialize floating point variables, we must first discuss how to represent floating point *literals* in C. Floating point literals are represented containing either a decimal point or an exponent, or both, as demonstrated in the example code that follows. The exponent is signified by the character *e* or *E* and can be positive or negative. It represents the power of 10 by which the fractional part (the part that precedes the *e* or *E*) is multiplied. Note that the exponent must be an integer value. For more information on floating point literals, see Appendix D.2.4.

```
double twoPointOne = 2.1;        /* This is 2.1    */
double twoHundredTen = 2.1E2;    /* This is 210.0 */
double twoHundred = 2E2;         /* This is 200.0 */
double twoTenths = 2E-1;         /* This is 0.2    */
double minusTwoTenths = -2E-1;   /* This is -0.2   */
```

Another floating point type specifier in C is called `float`. It declares a single-precision floating point variable; `double` creates one that is double-precision. Recall from our previous discussion on floating point numbers in Chapter 2 that the precision of a floating point number depends on the number of bits of the representation allocated to the fraction. In C, depending on the compiler and the ISA, a `double` may have more bits allocated for the fraction than a `float`, but never fewer. The size of the `double` is dependent upon the ISA and the compiler. Usually, a `double` is 64 bits long and a `float` is 32 bits in compliance with the IEEE 754 floating point standard.

12.2.2 Choosing Identifiers

Most high-level languages have flexible rules for the variable names (more generally known as *identifiers*) that can be chosen within a program. C allows you to create identifiers composed of letters of the alphabet, digits, and the underscore character, _. Only letters and the underscore character, however, can be used to begin an identifier. An identifier can be of any length, but only the first 31 characters are used by the C compiler to differentiate variables— only the first 31 characters matter to the compiler. Also, the use of upper- and lowercase has significance: C will treat `Capital` and `capital` as different indentifiers.

Here are several tips on standard C naming conventions: Variables beginning with an underscore (e.g., `_index_`) conventionally are used only in special library code. Variables are almost never declared in all uppercase letters. The convention of all uppercase is used solely for symbolic values created using the preprocessor directive `#define`. See Section 11.5.3 for examples of symbolic constants. Programmers like to visually partition variables that consist of multiple words. In this book, we use uppercase (e.g., `wordsPerSecond`). Other programmers prefer underscores (e.g., `words_per_second`).

Giving variables meaningful names is important for writing good code. Variable names should be chosen to reflect a characteristic of the value they represent, allowing the programmer to more easily recall what the value is used for. For example, a value used to count the number of words the person at the keyboard types per second might be named `wordsPerSecond`.

There are certain *keywords* in C that have special meaning and are therefore restricted from being used as identifiers. A list of C keywords can be found in Appendix D.2.6. One keyword we have encountered already is `int`, and therefore we cannot use `int` as a variable name. Having a variable named `int` would not only be confusing to someone trying to read through the code but might also confuse the compiler trying to translate it. The compiler may not be able to determine whether a particular `int` refers to the variable or to the type specifier.

12.2.3 Scope: Local versus Global

As we mentioned, a variable's declaration assists the compiler in managing the storage of that variable. In C, a variable's declaration conveys three pieces of information to the compiler: the variable's *identifier*, its *type*, and its *scope*. The first two of these, identifier and type, the C compiler gets explicitly from the variable's declaration. The third piece, scope, the compiler infers from the position of the declaration within the code. The scope of a variable is the region of the program in which the variable is "alive" and accessible.

The good news is that in C, there are only two basic types of scope for a variable. Either the variable is *global* to the entire program,[1] or it is *local*, or private, to a particular block of code.

Local Variables

In C, all variables must be declared before they can be used. In fact, some variables must be declared at the beginning of the *block* in which they appear—these are called local variables. In C, a *block* is any subsection of a program beginning with the open brace character, { and ending with the closing brace character, }. All local variables must be declared immediately following the block's open brace.

The following code is a simple C program that gets a number from the keyboard and redisplays it on the screen. The integer variable `echo` is declared within

---

[1] This is a slight simplification because C allows globals to be optionally declared to be global only to a particular source file and not the entire program, but this caveat is not relevant for our discussion here.

the block that contains the code for function `main`. It is only visible to the function `main`. If the program contained any other functions besides `main`, the variable would not be accessible from those other functions. Typically, most local variables are declared at the beginning of the function in which they are used, as for example `echo` in the code.

```c
#include <stdio.h>

int main()
{
    int echo;

    scanf("%d", &echo);
    printf("%d\n", echo);
}
```

It is possible, and sometimes useful, to declare two different variables with the same name within different blocks of the same function. For instance, it might be convenient to use the name `count` for the counter variable for several different loops within the same program. C allows this, as long as the different variables sharing the same name are declared in seperate blocks. Figure 12.1, which we discuss in the next section, provides an example of this.

Global Variables

In contrast to local variables, which can only be accessed within the block in which they are declared, global variables can be accessed throughout the program. They retain their storage and values throughout the duration of the program.

```c
#include <stdio.h>

int globalVar = 2;              /* This variable is global */

int main()
{
    int localVar = 3;    /* This variable is local to main */

    printf("Global %d Local %d\n", globalVar, localVar);

    {
        int localVar = 4;            /* Local to this sub-block */

        printf("Global %d Local %d\n", globalVar, localVar);
    }

    printf("Global %d Local %d\n", globalVar, localVar);
}
```

Figure 12.1   A C program that demonstrates nested scope

The following code contains both a global variable and a variable local to the function `main`:

```
#include <stdio.h>

int globalVar = 2;              /* This variable is global */

int main()
{
  int localVar = 3;    /* This variable is local to main */

  printf("Global %d Local %d\n", globalVar, localVar);
}
```

Globals can be extremely helpful in certain programming situations, but novice programmers are often instructed to adopt a programming style that uses locals over globals. Because global variables are public and can be modified from anywhere within the code, the heavy use of globals can make your code more vulnerable to bugs and more difficult to reuse and modify. In almost all C code examples in this textbook, we use only local variables.

Let's look at a slightly more complex example. The C program in Figure 12.1 is similar to the previous program except we have added a sub-block within `main`. Within this sub-block, we have declared a new variable `localVar`. It has the same name as the local variable declared at the beginning of `main`. Execute this program and you will notice that when the sub-block is executing the prior version of `localVar` is not visible; that is, the new declaration of a variable of the same name supersedes the previous one. Once the sub-block is done executing, the previous version of `localVar` becomes visible again. This is an example of what is called *nested scope*.

Initialization of Variables

Now that we have discussed global and local variables, let's answer the question we asked earlier: What initial value will a variable have if it has no initializer? In C, by default, local variables start with an unknown value. That is, the storage location a local variable is assigned is not cleared and thus contains whatever last value was stored there. More generally, in C, local variables are uninitialized (in particular, all variables of the *automatic storage class*). Global variables (and all other static *storage class variables*) are, in contrast, initialized to 0 when the program starts execution.

12.2.4 More Examples

Let's examine a couple more examples of variable declarations in C. The following examples demonstrate declarations of the three basic types discussed in this chapter. Some declarations have no initializers; some do. Notice how floating point and character literals are expressed in C.

```
double width;
double pType = 9.44;
double mass = 6.34E2;
double verySmallAmount = 9.1094E-31;
double veryLargeAmount = 7.334553E102;
int average = 12;
int windChillIndex = -21;
int unknownValue;
int mysteryAmount;
char car    = 'A';
char number = '4';
```

In C, it is also possible to have literals that are hexadecimal values. A literal that has the prefix `0x` will be treated as a hexadecimal number. In the following examples, all three integer variables are initialized using hexadecimal literals.

```
int programCounter = 0x3000;
int sevenBits = 0xA1234;
int valueD = 0xD;
```

Questions: What happens if we perform a `printf("%d\n", valueD);` after the declarations? What bit pattern would you expect to find in the memory location associated with `valueD`?

12.3 Operators

Having covered the basics of variables in C, we are now ready to investigate operators. C, like many other high-level languages, supports a rich set of operators that allow the programmer to manipulate variables. Some operators perform arithmetic, some perform logic functions, and others perform comparisons between values. These operators allow the programmer to express a computation in a more natural, convenient, and compact way than by expressing it as a sequence of assembly language instructions.

Given some C code, the compiler's job is to take the code and convert it into machine code that the underlying hardware can execute. In the case of a C program being compiled for the LC-3, the compiler must translate whatever operations the program might contain into the instructions of the LC-3 instruction set—clearly not an easy task given that the LC-3 has very few operate instructions.

To help illustrate this point, we examine the code generated by a simple C statement in which two integers are multiplied together. In the following code segment, x, y, and z are integer variables where x and y are multiplied and the result *assigned* to z.

```
z = x * y;
```

Since there is no single LC-3 instruction to multiply two values, our LC-3 compiler must generate a sequence of code that accomplishes the multiplication of

```
        AND   R0, R0, #0    ;   R0 <= 0

        LDR   R1, R5, #0    ;   load value of x
        LDR   R2, R5, #-1   ;   load value of y
        BRz   DONE          ;   if y is zero, we're done
        BRp   LOOP          ;   if y is positive, start mult


                           ;   y is negative
        NOT   R1, R1        ;
        ADD   R1, R1, #1    ;   R1 <= -x

        NOT   R2, R2
        ADD   R2, R2, #1    ;   R2 <= -y (-y is positive)

LOOP    ADD   R0, R0, R1    ;   Multiply loop
        ADD   R2, R2, #-1   ;   The result is in R2
        BRp   LOOP

DONE:   STR   R0, R5, #-2   ;   z = x * y;
```
Figure 12.2   The LC-3 code for C multiplication

two (possibly negative) integers. One possible manner in which this can be accomplished is by repeatedly adding the value of x to itself a total of y times. This code is similar to the code in the calculator example in Chapter 10. Figure 12.2 lists the resulting LC-3 code generated by the LC-3 compiler. Assume that register 5 (R5) contains the memory address where variable x is allocated. Immediately prior to that location is where variable y is allocated (i.e., R5 − 1), and immediately prior to that is where variable z resides. While this method of allocating variables in memory might seem a little strange at first, we will explain this later in Section 12.5.2.

12.3.1 Expressions and Statements

Before proceeding with our coverage of operators, we'll diverge a little into C syntax to help clarify some syntactic notations used within C programs. We can combine variables and literal values with operators, such as the multiply operator from the previous example, to form a C *expression*. In the previous example, x * y is an expression.

Expressions can be grouped together to form a *statement*. For example, z = x * y; is a statement. Statements in C are like complete sentences in English. Just as a sentence captures a complete thought or action, a C statement expresses a complete unit of work to be carried out by the computer. All statements in C end with a semicolon character, ; (or as we'll see in the next paragraph, a closing brace, }). The semicolon terminates the end of a statement in much the same way a punctuation mark terminates a sentence in English. An interesting (or perhaps odd) feature of C is that it is possible to create statements that do not express any computation but are syntactically considered statements. The null statement is simply a semicolon and it accomplishes nothing.

One or more simple statements can be grouped together to form a compound statement, or *block*, by enclosing the simple statements within braces, { }. Syntactically, compound statements are equivalent to simple statements. We will see many real uses of compound statements in the next chapter.

The following examples show some simple, compound, and null statements.

```
z = x * y;    /* This statement accomplishes some work */

{             /* This is a compound statement            */
  a = b + c;
  i = p * r * t;
}

k = k + 1;    /* This is another simple statement        */
;             /* Null statement -- no work done here     */
```

12.3.2 The Assignment Operator

We've already seen examples of C's assignment operator. Its symbol is the equal sign, =. The operator works by first evaluating the right-hand side of the assignment, and then assigning the value of the right-hand side to the *object* on the left-hand side. For example, in the C statement

```
a = b + c;
```

the value of variable a will be set equal to the value of the expression b + c.

Notice that even though the arithmetic symbol for equality is the same as the C symbol for assignment, they have different meanings. In mathematics, by using the equal sign, =, one is making the assertion that the right-hand and left-hand expressions are equivalent. In C, using the = operator causes the compiler to generate code that will make the left-hand side change its value to equal the value of the right-hand side. In other words, the left-hand side is *assigned* the value of the right-hand side.

Let's examine what happens when the LC-3 C compiler generates code for a statement containing the assignment operator. The C following statement represents the increment by 4 of the integer variable x.

```
x = x + 4;
```

The LC-3 code for this statement is straightforward. Here, R5 contains the address of variable x.

```
        LDR  R0, R5, #0   ;   Get the value of x
        ADD  R0, R0, #4   ;   calculate x + 4
        STR  R0, R5, #0   ;   x = x + 4;
```

In C, all expressions evaluate to a value of a particular type. From the previous example, the expression x + 4 evaluates to an integral value because we are adding an integer 4 to another integer (the variable x). This integer result is then assigned to an integer variable. But what would happen if we constructed an expression of mixed type, for example x + 4.3? The general rule in C is that the mixed expressions like the one shown will be *converted* from integer to floating point. If an expression contains both integer and character types, it will be promoted to integer type. In general, in C shorter types are converted to longer types. What if we tried to assign an expression of one type to a variable of another, for example x = x + 4.3? In C, the type of a variable remains immutable (meaning it cannot be changed), so the expression is converted to the type of the variable. In this case, the floating point expression x + 4.3 is converted to integer. In C, floating point values are rounded into integers by dropping the fractional part. For example, 4.3 will be rounded to 4 when converting from a floating point into an integer; 5.9 will be rounded to 5.

12.3.3 Arithmetic Operators

The arithmetic operators are easy to understand. Many of the operations and corresponding symbols are ones to which we are accustomed, having used them since learning arithmetic in grade school. For instance, + performs addition, - subtraction, * performs multiplication (which is different from the symbol we are accustomed to for multiplication in order to avoid confusion with the letter x), and / performs division. Just as when doing arithmetic by hand, there is an order in which expressions are evaluated. Multiplication and division are evaluated first, followed by addition and subtraction. The order in which operators are evaluated is called *precedence*, and we discuss it in more detail in the next section. Following are several C statements formed using the arithmetic operators:

```
distance = rate * time;
netIncome = income - taxesPaid;
fuelEconomy = milesTraveled / fuelConsumed;
area = 3.14159 * radius * radius;
y = a*x*x + b*x + c;
```

C has another arithmetic operator that might not be as familiar to you as +, -, *, and /. It is the *modulus* operator, % (also known as the integer remainder operator). To illustrate its operation, consider what happens when we divide two integer values. When performing an integer divide in C, the fractional part is dropped and the integral part is the result. The expression 11 / 4 evaluates to 2. The modulus operator % can be used to calculate the integer remainder. For example, 11 % 4 evaluates to 3. Said another way, (11 / 4) * 4 + (11 % 4) is equal to 11. In the following example, all variables are integers.

```
quotient  = x / y;   /* if x = 7 and y = 2, quotient = 3  */
remainder = x % y;   /* if x = 7 and y = 2, remainder = 1 */
```

Table 12.1 lists all the arithmetic operations and their symbols. Multiplication, division, and modulus have higher precedence than addition and subtraction.

Table 12.1	Arithmetic Operators in C	
Operator symbol	Operation	Example usage
*	multiplication	x * y
/	division	x / y
%	modulus	x % y
+	addition	x + y
-	subtraction	x - y

12.3.4 Order of Evaluation

Before proceeding onwards to the next set of C operators, we diverge momentarily to answer an important question: What value is stored in x as a result of the following statement?

```
x = 2 + 3 * 4;
```

Precedence

Just as when doing arithmetic by hand, there is an order to which expressions are evaluated. And this order is called operator *precedence*. For instance, when doing arithmetic, multiplication and division have higher precedence than addition and subtraction. For the arithmetic operators, the C precedence rules are the same as we were taught in grade-school arithmetic. In the preceding statement, x is assigned the value 14 because the multiplication operator has higher precedence than addition. That is, the expression evaluates as if it were $2 + (3 * 4)$.

Associativity

But what about operators of equal precedence? What does the following statement evaluate to?

```
x = 2 + 3 - 4 + 5;
```

Depending on which operator we evaluate first, the value of the expression $2 + 3 - 4 + 5$ could equal 6 or it could equal -4. Since the precedence of both operators is the same (that is, addition has the same precedence as subtraction in C), we clearly need a rule on how such expressions should be evaluated in C. For operations of equal precedence, their *associativity* determines the order in which they are evaluated. In the case of addition and subtraction, both associate from left to right. Therefore $2 + 3 - 4 + 5$ evaluates as if it were $((2 + 3) - 4) + 5$.

The complete set of precedence and associativity rules for all operators in C is provided in Table 12.5 at the end of this chapter and also in Table D.4. We suggest that you do not try to memorize this table (unless you enjoy quoting C trivia to your friends). Instead, it is important to realize that the precedence rules exist and to roughly comprehend the logic behind them. You can always refer to the table whenever you need to know the relationship between particular operators. There is a safeguard, however: parentheses.

Parentheses

Parentheses override the evaluation rules by specifying explicitly which operations are to be performed ahead of others. As in arithmetic, evaluation always begins at the innermost set of parentheses. We can surround a subexpression with parentheses if we want that subexpression to be evaluated first. So in the following example, say the variables a, b, c, and d are all equal to 4. The statement

```
x = a * b + c * d / 2;
```

could be written equivalently as

```
x = (a * b) + ((c * d) / 4);
```

For both statements, x is set to the value of 20. Here the program will always evaluate the innermost subexpression first and move outward before falling back on the precedence rules.

What value would the following expression evaluate to if a, b, c, and d equal 4?

```
x = a * (b + c) * d / 4;
```

Parentheses can help make code more readable, too. Most people reading your code are unlikely to have memorized C's precedence rules. For this reason, for long or complex expressions, it is often stylistically preferable to use parentheses, even if the code works fine without them.

12.3.5 Bitwise Operators

We now return to our discussion of C operators. C has a set of operators called *bitwise* operators that manipulate bits of a value. That is, they perform a logical operation such as AND, OR, NOT, XOR across the individual bits of a value. For example, the C bitwise operator & performs an operation similar to the LC-3 AND instruction. That is, the & operator performs an AND operation bit by bit across the two input operands. The C operator | performs a bitwise OR. The operator ~ performs a bitwise NOT and takes only one operand (i.e., it is a unary operator). The operator ^ performs a bitwise XOR. Examples of expressions using these operators on 16-bit values follow.

```
0x1234 | 0x5678   /* equals 0x567C */
0x1234 & 0x5678   /* equals 0x1230 */
0x1234 ^ 0x5678   /* equals 0x444C */
~0x1234           /* equals 0xEDCB */
1234 & 5678       /* equals 1026  */
```

C's set of bitwise operators includes two shift operators: <<, which performs a left shift, and >>, which performs a right shift. Both are binary operators, meaning they require two operands. The first operand is the value to be shifted and the second operand indicates the number of bit positions to shift by. On a left shift, the vacated bit positions of the value are filled with zeros; on a right shift, the value is sign-extended. The result is the value of the expression; neither of the

Table 12.2	Bitwise Operators in C	
Operator symbol	Operation	Example usage
~	bitwise NOT	~x
«	left shift	x « y
»	right shift	x » y
&	bitwise AND	x & y
^	bitwise XOR	x ^ y
|	bitwise OR	x | y

two original operand values are modified. The following expressions provide examples of these two operators operating on 16-bit integers.

```
0x1234 << 3     /* equals 0x91A0  */
0x1234 >> 2     /* equals 0x048D  */
1234 << 3       /* equals 9872    */
1234 >> 2       /* equals 308     */
0x1234 << 5     /* equals 0x4680  (result is 16 bits)   */
0xFEDC >> 3     /* equals 0xFFDB  (from sign-extension) */
```

Here we show several C statements formed using the bitwise operators. For all of C's bitwise operators, neither operand can be a floating point value. For these statements, f, g, and h are integers.

```
h = f & g;      /* if f = 7, g = 8, h will equal 0     */
h = f | g;      /* if f = 7, g = 8, h will equal 15    */
h = f << 1;     /* if f = 7, g = 8, h will equal 14    */
h = g << f;     /* if f = 7, g = 8, h will equal 1024  */
h = ~f | ~g;    /* if f = 7, g = 8, h will equal -1    */
                /* because h is a signed integer       */
```

Question: Say that on a particular machine, the integer x occupies 16 bits and has the value 1. What happens after the statement x = x << 16; is executed? Conceptually, we are shifting x by its data width, replacing all bits with 0. You might expect the value of x to be 0. To remain generic, C formally defines the result of shifting a value by its width (or more than its data width) as implementation-dependent. This means that the result might be 0 or it might not, depending on the system on which the code is executed.

Table 12.2 lists all the bitwise operations and their symbols. The operators are listed in order of precedence, the NOT operator having highest precedence, and the left and right shift operators having equal precedence, followed by AND, then XOR, then OR. They all associate from left to right. See Table 12.5 for a complete listing of operator precedence.

12.3.6 Relational Operators

C has several operators to test the relationship between two values. As we will see in the next chapter, these operators are often used in C to generate conditional

Table 12.3	Relational Operators in C	
Operator symbol	Operation	Example usage
>	greater than	x > y
>=	greater than or equal	x >= y
<	less than	x < y
<=	less than or equal	x <= y
==	equal	x == y
!=	not equal	x != y

constructs (similar to the conditional constructs we discussed in Section 6.1.2 when we discussed systematic decomposition).

The equality operator, ==, is one of C's relational operators. This operator tests if two values are equal. If they are equal, the expression evaluates to a 1, and if they are not, the expression evaluates to 0. The following shows two examples:

```
q = (312 == 83);    /* q will equal 0 */
z = (x == y);       /* z will equal 1 if x equals y */
```

In the second example, the right-hand side of the assignment operator = is the expression x == y, which evaluates to a 1 or a 0, depending on whether x and y are equal. (Note: The parentheses are not required because the == operator has higher precedence than the = operator. We added them to help make the example clearer).

Opposite the equality operator, the inequality operator, !=, evaluates to a 1 if the operands are not equal. Other relational operators test for greater than, less than, and so on, as described in the following examples. For these examples, the variables f, g, and h are integers. The variable f has the value 7, and g is 8.

```
h = f == g;    /* Equal To operator.      h will equal 0  */
h = f > g;     /* Greater Than operator. h will equal 0  */
h = f != g;    /* Not Equal To operator. h will equal 1  */
h = f <= g;    /* Less Than Or Equal To. h will equal 1  */
```

The next example is a preview of coming attractions. The C relational operators are very useful for performing tests on variables in order to change the flow of the program. In the next chapter, we describe the C if statement in more detail. However, the concept of an if construct is not a new one—we have been dealing with this particular decision construct ever since learning how to program the LC-3 in Chapter 6. Here, a message is printed only if the variable tankLevel is equal to zero.

```
if (tankLevel == 0)
    printf("Warning: Tank Empty!!\n");
```

Table 12.3 lists all the relational operators and provides a simple example of each. The first four operators have higher precedence than the last two. Both sets associate from left to right.

12.3.7 Logical Operators

C's logical operators appear at first glance to be exactly like some of the bitwise operators, and many novice programmers sometimes confuse the two. Before we explain their operation, we need to mention C's concept of logically true and logically false values. C adopts the notion that a nonzero value (i.e., a value other than zero) is logically true. A value of zero is logically false. It is an important concept to remember, and we will see it surface many times as we go through the various components of the C language.

C supports three logical operators: &&, ||, and !. The && operator performs a logical AND of its two operands; it evaluates to an integer value of 1 (which is logically true) if both of its operands are logically true, or nonzero. It evaluates to 0 otherwise. For example, 3 && 4 evaluates to a 1, whereas 3 && 0 evaluates to 0. The || operator is C's logical OR operator. The expression x || y evaluates to a 1 if either x OR y are nonzero. For example, 3 || 4 evaluates to a 1. Also, 3 || 0 evaluates to 1. The negation operator ! evalutes to the other logical state of its operand. So !x is 1 only if x equals 0. It is 0 otherwise.

What are the logical operators useful for? One use is for constructing logical conditions within a program. For example, we can determine if a variable is within a particular range of values using a combination of relational and logical operators. To check if x is between 10 and 20, inclusive, we can use the following expression:

```
(10 <= x) && (x <= 20)
```

Or to test if a character c is a letter of the alphabet:

```
(('a' <= c) && (c <= 'z')) || (('A' <= c) && (c <= 'Z'))
```

Here are some examples of the logical operators, with several previous examples of bitwise operators included to highlight the difference. As in the previous examples, the variables f, g, and h are integers. The variable f has the value 7, and g is 8.

```
h = f & g;      /* bitwise operator: h will equal 0  */
h = f && g;     /* logical operator: h will equal 1  */
h = f | g;      /* bitwise operator: h will equal 15 */
h = f || g;     /* logical operator: h will equal 1  */
h = ~f | ~g;    /* bitwise operator: h will equal -1 */
h = !f && !g;   /* logical operator: h will equal 0  */
h = 29 || -52;  /* logical operator: h will equal 1  */
```

Table 12.4 lists logical operators in C and their symbols. The logical NOT operator has highest precedence, then logical AND, then logical OR. See Table 12.5 for a complete listing of operator precedence.

12.3.8 Increment/Decrement Operators

Because incrementing and decrementing variables is such a commonly performed operation, the designers of the C programming language decided to include special

Table 12.4	Logical Operators in C	
Operator symbol	Operation	Example usage
!	logical NOT	!x
&&	logical AND	x && y
||	logical OR	x || y

Table 12.5   Operator Precedence, from Highest to Lowest. Descriptions of Some Operators are Provided in Parentheses

Precedence	Associativity	Operators
1 (highest)	l to r	() (function call) [ ] (array index) . ->
2	r to l	++ -- (postfix versions)
3	r to l	++ -- (prefix versions)
4	r to l	* (indirection) & (address of) + (unary) - (unary) ~ ! sizeof
5	r to l	(type) (type cast)
6	l to r	* (multiplication) / %
7	l to r	+ (addition) - (subtraction)
8	l to r	« »
9	l to r	< > <= >=
10	l to r	== !=
11	l to r	&
12	l to r	^
13	l to r	|
14	l to r	&&
15	l to r	||
16	l to r	?: (conditional expression)
17 (lowest)	r to l	= += -= *= etc.

operators to perform them. The ++ operator *increments* a variable to the next higher value. The -- operator *decrements* it. For example, the expression x++ increments the value of integer variable x by 1. The expression x-- decrements the value of x by 1. Keep in mind that these operators modify the value of the variable itself. That is, x++ is similar to the operation x = x + 1.

The ++ and -- operators can be used on either side of a variable. The expression ++x operates in a slightly different order than x++. If x++ is part of a larger expression, then the value of x++ is the value of x prior to the increment, whereas the value of ++x is the incremented value of x. If the operator ++ appears before the variable, then it is used in *prefix* form. If it appears after the variable, it is in *postfix* form. The prefix forms are often referred to as *preincrement* and *predecrement*, whereas the postfix are *postincrement* and *postdecrement*.

Let's examine a couple of examples:

```
x = 4;
y = x++;
```

Here, the integer variable x is incremented. However, the original value of x is assigned to the variable y (i.e., the value of x++ evaluates to the original value of x). After this code executes, the variable y will have the value 4, and x will be 5.

Similarly, the following code increments x.

```
x = 4;
y = ++x;
```

However with this code, the expression ++x evaluates to the value after the increment. In this case, the value of both y and x will be 5.

This subtle distinction between the postfix and prefix forms is not too important to understand for now. For the few examples in this book that use these operators, the prefix and postfix forms of these operators can be used interchangeably. You can find a precise description of this difference in Appendix D.5.6.

12.3.9 Expressions with Multiple Operators

Thus far we've only seen examples of expressions with one or two operators. Real and useful expressions sometimes have more. We can combine various operators and operands to form complex expressions. The following example demonstrates a peculiar blend of operators forming a complex expression.

```
y = x & z + 3 || 9 - w % 6;
```

In order to figure out what this statement evaluates to, we need to examine the order of evaluation of operators. Table 12.5 lists all the C operators (including some that we have not yet covered but will cover later in this textbook) and their order of evaluation. According to precedence rules, this statement is equivalent to the following:

```
y = (x & (z + 3)) || (9 - (w % 6));
```

Another more useful expression that consists of multiple operators is given in the example that follows. In this example, if the value of the variable age is between 18 and 25, the expression evaluates to 1. Otherwise it is 0. Notice that even though the parentheses are not required to make the expression evaluate as we described, they do help make the code easier to read.

```
(18 <= age) && (age <= 25)
```

12.4 Problem Solving Using Operators

At this point, we have covered enough C operators to attempt a simple problem-solving exercise. For this problem, we will create a program that performs a simple network calculation: It calculates the amount of time required to transfer some number of bytes across a network with a particular transfer rate (provided in bytes per second). The twist to this problem is that transfer time is to be displayed as hours, minutes, and seconds.

We approach this problem by applying the decomposition techniques described in Chapter 6. That is, we will start with a very rough description of our program and continually refine it using the sequential, decision, and iteration constructs (see Chapter 6 if you need a refresher) until we arrive at something from which we can easily write C code. This technique is called *top-down decomposition* because we start with a rough description of the algorithm and refine it by breaking larger steps into smaller ones, eventually arriving at something that resembles a program. Many experienced programmers rely on their understanding of the lower levels of the system to help make good decisions on how to decompose a problem. That is, in order to reduce a problem into a program, good programmers rely on their understanding of the basic primitives of systems they are programming on. In our case (at this point), these basic primitives are variables of the three C types and the operations we can perform on them.

In the subsequent chapters, we will go through several problem-solving examples to illustrate this top-down process. In doing so, we hope to provide you with a sense of the mental process a programmer might use to solve such problems.

The very first step (step 0) we need to consider for all problems from now on is how we represent the data items that the program will need to manipulate. At this point, we get to select from the three basic C types: integer, character, and floating point. For this problem, we can represent our internal calculations with either floating point values or integers. Since we are ultimately interested in displaying the result as hours, minutes, and seconds, any fractional components of

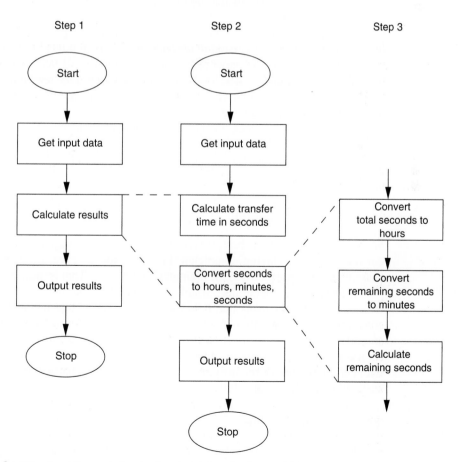

Figure 12.3   Stepwise refinement of a simple network transfer time problem

time are unnecessary. For example, displaying the total transfer time as 10.1 hours, 12.7 minutes, 9.3 seconds does not make sense. Rather, 10 hours, 18 minutes, 51 seconds is the preferred output. Because of this, the better choice of data type for the time calculation is integer (yes, there are rounding issues, but say we can ignore them for this calculation).

Having chosen our data representations, we can now apply stepwise refinement to decompose the problem. Figure 12.3 shows our decomposition of this particular programming problem. Step 1 in the figure shows the initial formulation of the problem. It involves three phases: get input, calculate results, output results. In the first phase, we will query the user about the amount of data to be transfered (in bytes) and the transfer rate of the network (in bytes per second). In the second phase, we will perform all necessary calculations, which we will then output in the third phase.

Step 1 is not detailed enough to translate directly into C code, and therefore we perform another refinement of it in step 2. Here we realize that the calculation phase can be further refined into a subphase that first calculates total time in seconds—which is an easy calculation given the input data—and a subphase to convert total time in seconds into hours, minutes, and seconds.

Step 2 is still not complete enough for mapping into C; we perform another refinement of it in step 3. Most phases of step 2 are fairly simple enough to convert into C, except for the conversion of seconds into hours, minutes, and seconds. In step 3, we refine this phase into three subphases. First we will calculate total hours based on the total number of seconds. Second, we will use the remaining seconds to calculate minutes. Finally, we determine the remaining number of seconds after the minutes have been calculated.

Based on the total breakdown of the problem after three steps of refinement presented in Figure 12.3, it should be fairly straightforward to map out the C code. The complete C program for this problem is presented in Figure 12.4.

12.5   Tying It All Together

We've now covered all the basic C types and operators that we plan to use throughout this textbook. Having completed this first exposure, we are now ready to examine these concepts from the compiler's viewpoint. That is, how does a compiler translate code containing variables and operators into machine code. There are two basic mechanisms that help the compiler do its job of translation. The compiler makes heavy use of a *symbol table* to keep track of variables during compilation. The compiler also follows a systematic partitioning of memory—it carefully allocates memory to these variables based on certain characteristics, with certain regions of memory reserved for objects of a particular class. In this section, we'll take a closer look at these two processes.

12.5.1   Symbol Table

In Chapter 7, we examined how the assembler systematically keeps track of labels within an assembly program by using a symbol table. Like the assembler, the C

```c
#include <stdio.h>

int main()
{
    int amount;     /* The number of bytes to be transferred  */
    int rate;       /* The average network transfer rate       */
    int time;       /* The time, in seconds, for the transfer */

    int hours;      /* The number of hours for the transfer    */
    int minutes;    /* The number of mins for the transfer     */
    int seconds;    /* The number of secs for the transfer     */

    /* Get input: number of bytes and network transfer rate */
    printf("How many bytes of data to be transferred?  ");
    scanf("%d", &amount);

    printf("What is the transfer rate (in bytes/sec)?  ");
    scanf("%d", &rate);

    /* Calculate total time in seconds                        */
    time = amount / rate;

    /* Convert time into hours, minutes, seconds              */
    hours = time / 3600;          /* 3600 seconds in an hour */
    minutes = (time % 3600) / 60; /* 60 seconds in a minute */
    seconds = ((time % 3600) % 60); /* remainder is seconds */

    /* Output results */
    printf("Time : %dh %dm %ds\n", hours, minutes, seconds);
}
```

Figure 12.4   A C program that performs a simple network rate calculation

compiler keeps track of variables in a program with a symbol table. Whenever the compiler reads a variable declaration, it creates a new entry in its symbol table corresponding to the variable being declared. The entry contains enough information for the compiler to manage the storage allocation for the variable and generation of the proper sequence of machine code whenever the variable is used in the program. Each symbol table entry for a variable contains (1) its name, (2) its type, (3) the place in memory the variable has been allocated storage, and (4) an identifier to indicate the block in which the variable is declared (i.e., the scope of the variable).

Figure 12.5 shows the symbol table entries corresponding to the variables declared in the network rate calculation program in Figure 12.4. Since this program contains six variables declarations, the compiler ends up with six entries in its symbol table for them. Notice that the compiler records a variable's location in memory as an offset, with most offsets being negative. This offset indicates the relative position of the variable within the region of memory it is allocated.

Identifier	Type	Location (as an offset)	Scope	Other info...
amount	int	0	main	...
hours	int	−3	main	...
minutes	int	−4	main	...
rate	int	−1	main	...
seconds	int	−5	main	...
time	int	−2	main	...

Figure 12.5   The compiler's symbol table when it compiles the program from Chapter 11

12.5.2 Allocating Space for Variables

There are two regions of memory in which C variables are allocated storage: the *global data section* and the *run-time stack*.[2] The global data section is where all global variables are stored. More generally, it is where variables of the static storage class are allocated (we say more about this in Section 12.6). The run-time stack is where local variables (of the default automatic storage class) are allocated storage.

The offset field in the symbol table provides the precise information about where in memory variables are actually stored. The offset field simply indicates how many locations from the base of the section a variable is allocated storage.

For instance, if a global variable earth has an offset of 4 and the global data section starts at memory location 0x5000, then earth is stored in location 0x5004. All our examples of compiler-generated machine code use R4 to contain the address of the beginning of the global data section—R4 is referred to as the *global pointer*. Loading the variable earth into R3, for example, can be accomplished with the following LC-3 instruction:

```
LDR  R3, R4, #4
```

If earth is instead a local variable, say for example in the function main, the story is slightly more complicated. All local variables for a function are allocated in a "memory template" called an *activation record* or *stack frame*. For now, we'll examine the format of an activation record and leave the motivation for why we need it for Chapter 14 when we discuss functions. An activation record is a region of contiguous memory locations that contains all the local variables for a given function. Every function has an activation record (or more precisely, every invocation of a function has an activation record—more on this later).

---

[2] For examples in this textbook, all variables will be assigned a memory location. However, real compilers perform code optimizations that attempt to allocate variables in registers. Since registers take less time to access than memory, the program will run faster if frequently accessed values are put into registers.

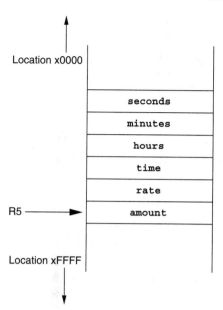

Figure 12.6 An example of an activation record in the LC-3's memory. This function has five local variables. R5 is the frame pointer and points to the first local variable

Whenever we are executing a particular function, the highest memory address of the activation record will be stored in R5—R5 is called the *frame pointer*. For example, the activation record for the function `main` from the code in Figure 12.4 is shown in Figure 12.6. Notice that the variables are allocated in the record in the reverse order in which they are declared. Since the variable `amount` is declared first, it appears nearest to the frame pointer R5.

If we make a reference to a particular local variable, the compiler will use the variable's symbol table entry to generate the proper code to access it. In particular, the offset in the variable's symbol table entry indicates where in the activation record the variable has been allocated storage. To access the variable `seconds`, the compiler would generate the instruction:

```
LDR  R0, R5, #-5
```

A preview of things to come: Whenever we call a function in C (in C, subroutines are called functions), the activation record for the function is pushed on to the run-time stack. That is, the function's activation record is allocated on top of the stack. R5 is appropriately adjusted to point to the base of the record—therefore any code within the function that accesses local variables will now work correctly. Whenever the function completes and control is about to return to the caller, the activation record is popped off the stack. R5 is adjusted to point to the caller's activation record. Throughout all of this, R6 always contains the address of the top of the run-time stack—it is called the *stack pointer*. We will revisit this in more detail in Chapter 14.

Figure 12.7 shows the organization of the LC-3's memory when a program is running. Many UNIX-based systems arrange their memory space similarly.

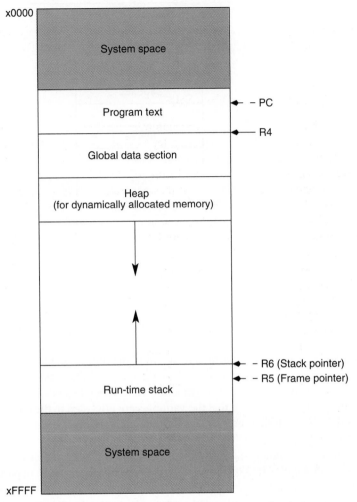

Figure 12.7   The LC-3 memory map showing various sections active during program execution

The program itself occupies a region of memory (labelled Program text in the diagram); so does the run-time stack and the global data section. There is another region reserved for dynamically allocated data called the *heap* (we will discuss this region in Chapter 19). Both the run-time stack and the heap can change size as the program executes. For example, whenever one function calls another, the run-time stack grows because we push another activation record onto the stack—in fact, it grows toward memory address x0000. In contrast, the heap grows toward 0xFFFF. Since the stack grows toward x0000, the organization of an activation record appears to be "upside-down": that is, the first local variable appears at the memory location pointed to by R5, the next one at R5 − 1, the subsequent one at R5 − 2, and so forth (as opposed to R5, R5 + 1, R5 + 2, etc).

During execution, the PC points to a location in the program text, R4 points to the beginning of the global data section, R5 points within the run-time stack, and R6 points to the very top of the run-time stack. There are certain regions of memory, marked System space in Figure 12.7, that are reserved for the operating system, for things such as TRAP routines, vector tables, I/O registers, and boot code.

12.5.3 A Comprehensive Example

Now that we have examined the LC-3 compiler's techniques for tracking and allocating space for variables in memory, let's take a look at a comprehensive C example and its translation into LC-3 code.

Figure 12.8 is a C program that performs some simple operations on integer variables and then outputs the results of these operations. The program contains one global variable, inGlobal, and three local variables, inLocal, outLocalA, and outLocalB, which are local to the function main.

The program starts off by assigning initial values to inLocal and inGlobal. After the initialization step, the variables outLocalA and outLocalB are updated based on two calculations performed using inLocal and inGlobal. After the calculation step, the values of outLocalA and outLocalB are output using the printf library function. Notice because we are using printf, we must include the standard I/O library header file, stdio.h.

When analyzing this code, the LC-3 C compiler will assign the global variable inGlobal the first available spot in the global data section, which is at offset 0. When analyzing the function main, it will assign inLocalA to offset 0, outLocalA to offset −1, and outLocalB to offset −2 within main's activation

```
/* Include the standard I/O header file */
#include <stdio.h>

int inGlobal;      /* inGlobal is a global variable because */
                   /* it is declared outside of all blocks  */

int main()
{
   int inLocal;    /* inLocal, outLocalA, outLocalB are all */
   int outLocalA;  /* local to main                         */
   int outLocalB;

   /* Initialize */
   inLocal  = 5;
   inGlobal = 3;

   /* Perform calculations */
   outLocalA = inLocal & ~inGlobal;
   outLocalB = (inLocal + inGlobal) - (inLocal - inGlobal);

   /* Print out results */
   printf("outLocalA = %d, outLocalB=%d\n", outLocalA, outLocalB);
}
```

Figure 12.8 A C program that performs simple operations

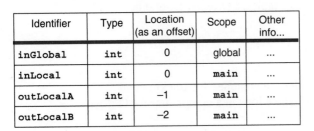

Identifier	Type	Location (as an offset)	Scope	Other info...
inGlobal	int	0	global	...
inLocal	int	0	main	...
outLocalA	int	−1	main	...
outLocalB	int	−2	main	...

(a) Symbol table

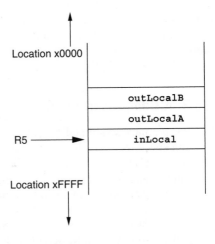

(b) Activation record for main

Figure 12.9   The LC-3 C compiler's symbol table when compiling the program in Figure 12.8 and the activation record format for its function main

record. A snapshot of the compiler's symbol table corresponding to this program along with the activation record of main are shown in Figure 12.9.

The resulting assembly code generated by the LC-3 C compiler is listed in Figure 12.10. Execution starts at the instruction labeled main.

12.6 Additional Topics

The last major section of this chapter involves a set of additional topics involving variables and operators. Some of the topics are advanced issues involving concepts we covered earlier in the chapter; some of the topics are miscellaneous features of C. We provide this section in order to complete our coverage of C, but this material is not essential to your understanding of the material in later chapters. For those of you interested in a more complete coverage of variables and operators in C, read on!

12.6.1 Variations of the Three Basic Types

C gives the programmer the ability to specify larger or smaller sizes for the three basic types int, char, and double. The modifiers long and short can be attached to int with the intent of extending or shortening the default size. For example, a long int can declare an integer that has twice the number of bits as a regular int, thereby allowing us to represent a larger range of integers in a C program. Similarly, the specifier long can be attached to the double type to create a larger floating point type (if supported by the particular system) with greater range and precision.

```
1    main:
2       :
3       :
4       <startup code>
5       :
6       :
7       AND  R0, R0, #0
8       ADD  R0, R0, #5   ;  inLocal is at offset 0
9       STR  R0, R5, #0   ;  inLocal = 5;
10
11      AND  R0, R0, #0
12      ADD  R0, R0, #3   ;  inGlobal is at offset 0, in globals
13      STR  R0, R4, #0   ;  inGlobal = 3;
14
15      LDR  R0, R5, #0   ;  get value of inLocal
16      LDR  R1, R4, #0   ;  get value of inGlobal
17      NOT  R1, R1       ;  ~inGlobal
18      AND  R2, R0, R1   ;  calculate inLocal & ~inGlobal
19      STR  R2, R5, #-1  ;  outLocalA = inLocal & ~inGlobal;
20                        ;  outLocalA is at offset -1
21
22      LDR  R0, R5, #0   ;  get value of inLocal
23      LDR  R1, R4, #0   ;  get value of inGlobal
24      ADD  R0, R0, R1   ;  calculate inLocal + inGlobal
25
26      LDR  R2, R5, #0   ;  get value of inLocal
27      LDR  R3, R4, #0   ;  get value of inGlobal
28      NOT  R3
29      ADD  R3, R3, #1   ;  calculate -inGlobal
30
31      ADD  R2, R2, R3   ;  calculate inLocal - inGlobal
32      NOT  R2
33      ADD  R2, R2, #1   ;  calculate -(inLocal - inGlobal)
34
35      ADD  R0, R0, R2   ;  (inLocal + inGlobal) - (inLocal - inGlobal)
36      STR  R0, R5, #-2  ;  outLocalB = ...
37                        ;  outLocalB is at offset -2
38      :
39      :
40      <code for calling the function printf>
41      :
42      :
```

Figure 12.10 The LC-3 code for the C program in Figure 12.8

The modifier short can be used to create variables that are smaller than the default size, which can be useful when trying to conserve on memory space when handling data that does not require the full range of the default data type. The following example demonstates how the variations are declared:

```
long double particlesInUniverse;
long int worldPopulation;
short int ageOfStudent;
```

Because the size of the three basic C types is closely tied to the types supported by the underlying ISA, many compilers only support these modifiers `long` and `short` if the computer's ISA supports these size variations. Even though a variable can be declared as a `long int`, it may be equivalent to a regular `int` if the underlying ISA has no support for longer versions of the integer data type. See Appendix D.3.2 for more examples and additional information on `long` and `short`.

Another useful variation of the basic `int` data type is the unsigned integer. We can declare an unsigned integer using the `unsigned` type modifier. With unsigned integers, all bits are used to represent nonnegative integers (i.e., positive numbers and zero). In the LC-3 for instance, which has 16-bit integers, an unsigned integer has a value between 0 and 65,535. When dealing with real-world objects that by nature do not take on negative values, unsigned integers might be the data type of choice. The following are examples of unsigned integers:

```
unsigned int numberOfDays;
unsigned int populationSize;
```

Following are some sample variations of the three basic types:

```
long int ounces;
short int gallons;
long double veryVeryLargeNumber = 4.12936E361;
unsigned int sizeOfClass = 900;
float oType = 9.24;
float tonsOfGrain = 2.998E8;
```

12.6.2 Literals, Constants, and Symbolic Values

In C, variables can also be declared as *constants* by adding the `const` qualifier before the type specifier. These constants are really variables whose values do not change during the execution of a program. For example, in writing a program that calculates the area and circumference of a circle of a given radius, it might be useful to create a floating point constant called `pi` initialized to the value 3.14159. Figure 12.11 contains an example of such a program.

This example is useful for making a distinction between three types of constant values that often appear in C code. *Literal* constants are unnamed values that appear *literally* in the source code. In the circle example, the values 2 and 3.14159 are examples of *literal* constants. In C, we can represent literal constants in hexadecimal by prepending a `0x` in front of them, for example `0x1DB`. ASCII literals require single quotes around them, as for example `'R'`, which is the ASCII value of the character R. Floating point literals can be the exponential notation described in Section 12.2.1. An example of the second type of constant value is `pi`, which is declared as a constant value using a variable declaration with the `const` qualifier. The third type of constant value is created using the preprocessor directive `#define`, an example of which is the symbolic value `RADIUS`. All three types create values that do not change during the execution of a program.

```
1    #include <stdio.h>
2
3    #define RADIUS  15.0      /* This value is in centimeters */
4
5    int main()
6    {
7      const double pi = 3.14159;
8      double area;
9      double circumference;
10
11     /* Calculations */
12     area = pi * RADIUS * RADIUS;            /* area = pi*r^2 */
13
14     circumference = 2 * pi * RADIUS;     /* circumference = */
15                                         /*          2*pi*r */
16
17     printf("Area of a circle with radius %f cm is %f cm^2\n",
18            RADIUS, area);
19
20     printf("Circumference of the circle is %f cm\n",
21            circumference);
22   }
```

Figure 12.11 A C program that computes the area and circumference of a circle with a radius of 15 cm

The distinction between constants declared using `const` and symbolic values defined using `#define` might seem a little subtle to you. Using one versus another is really a matter of programming style rather than function. Declared constants are used for things we traditionally think of as constant values, which are values that never change. The constant `pi` is an example. Physical constants such as the speed of light, or the number of days in a week, are conventionally represented by declared constants.

Values that stay constant during a single execution of the program but which might be different from user to user, or possibly from invocation to invocation, are represented by symbolic values using `#define`. Such values can be thought of as parameters for the program. For example, `RADIUS` in Figure 12.11 can be changed and the program recompiled, then re-executed.

In general, naming a constant using `const` or `#define` is preferred over leaving the constant as a literal in your code. Names convey more meaning about your code than unnamed literal values.

12.6.3 Storage Class

Earlier in the chapter, we mentioned three basic properties of a C variable: its identifier, its type, and its scope. There is another: *storage class*. The storage class of a variable indicates how the C compiler allocates its storage, and in particular indicates whether or not the variable loses its value when the block that contains it has completed execution. There are two storage classes in C: *static* and *automatic*.

Static variables retain their values between invocations. Automatic variables lose their values when their block terminates. In C, global variables are of static storage class, that is, they retain their value until the program ends. Local variables are by default of automatic storage class. Local variables can be declared as static class variables by using the `static` modifier on the declaration. For example, the variable declared by `static int localVar;` will retain its value even when its function completes execution. If the function is executed again (during the same program execution), `localVar` will retain its previous value. In particular, the use of the `static` keyword on a local variable causes the compiler to allocate storage for the variable in the global data section, while keeping it private to its block. See Appendix D.3.3 for additional examples on storage class.

12.6.4 Additional C Operators

The C programming language has a collection of unusual operators, which have become a trademark of C programming. Most of these operators are combinations of operators we have already seen. The combinations are such that they make expressing commonly used computations even simpler. However, to someone who is not accustomed to the shorthand notation of these operators, reading and trying to understand C code that contains them can be difficult.

Assignment Operators

C also allows certain arithmetic and bitwise operators to be combined with the assignment operator. For instance, if we wanted to add 29 to variable x, we could use the shorthand operator `+=` as follows:

```
x   += 29;
```

This code is equivalent to

```
x   = x + 29;
```

Table 12.6 lists some of the special operators provided by C. The postfix operators have highest precedence, followed by prefix. The assignment operators have lowest precedence. Each group associates from right to left.

Table 12.6	Assignment Operators in C	
Operator symbol	Operation	Example usage
+=	add and assign	x += y
-=	subtract and assign	x -= y
*=	multiply and assign	x *= y
/=	divide and assign	x /= y
%=	modulus and assign	x %= y
&=	and and assign	x &= y
|=	or and assign	x |= y
^=	xor and assign	x ^= y
«=	left-shift and assign	x «= y
»=	right-shift and assign	x »= y

More examples are as follows:

```
h += g;           /* Equivalent to h = h + g;    */
h %= f;           /* Equivalent to h = h % f;    */
h <<= 3;          /* Equivalent to h = h << 3;    */
```

Conditional Expressions

Conditional expressions are a unique feature of C that allow for simple decisions to be made with a simple expression. The symbols for the conditional expression are the question mark and colon, ? and :. The following is an example:

```
x = a ? b : c;
```

Here variable x will get either the value of b **or** the value of c based on the logical value of a. If a is nonzero, x will get the value of b. Otherwise, it will get the value of c.

Figure 12.12 is a complete program that uses a conditional expression to calculate the maximum of two integers. The maximum of these two input values is determined by a conditional expression and is assigned to the variable maxValue. The value of maxValue is output using printf.

```
1   #include <stdio.h>
2
3   int main()
4   {
5       int maxValue;
6       int input1;
7       int input2;
8
9       printf("Input an integer: ");
10      scanf("%d", &input1);
11      printf("Input another integer: ");
12      scanf("%d", &input2);
13
14      maxValue = (input1 > input2) ? input1 : input2;
15      printf("The larger number is %d\n", maxValue);
16  }
```

Figure 12.12 A C program that uses a conditional expression

12.7 Summary

We conclude this chapter by summarizing the three key concepts we covered.

• **Variables in C.** The C programming language supports variables of three basic types: integers (int), characters (char), and floating point numbers (double). C, like all other high-level languages, provides the programmer the ability to provide symbolic names to these variables. Variables in C can be locally declared within a block of code (such as a function) or globally visible by all blocks.

• **Operators in C.** C's operators can be categorized by the function they perform: assignment, arithmetic, bitwise manipulations, logical and relational tests. We can form expressions using variables and operators such that the expressions get evaluated according to precedence and associativity rules. Expressions are grouped into statements, which express the work the program is to perform.

• **Translating C Variables and Operators into LC-3 Code.** Using a symbol table to keep track of variable declarations, a compiler will allocate local variables for a function within an activation record for the function. The activation record for the function is pushed onto the run-time stack whenever the function is executed. Global variables in a program are allocated in the global data section.

Exercises

12.1   Generate the compiler's symbol table for the following code. Assume all variables occupy one location in memory.

```
{
    double ff;
    char cc;
    int ii;
    char dd;
}
```

12.2   The following variable declaration appears in a program:

```
int r;
```

   a. If r is a local variable, to what value will it be initialized?
   b. If r if a global variable, to what value will it be initialized?

12.3   What are the ranges for the following two variables if they are stored as 32-bit quantities?

```
int plusOrMinus;
unsigned int positive;
```

12.4   Evaluate the following floating point literals. Write their values in standard decimal notation.

   a.   111 E −11
   b.   −0.00021 E 4
   c.   101.101 E 0

12.5 Write the LC-3 code that would result if the following local variable declarations were compiled using the LC-3 C compiler:

```
char  c = 'a';
int   x = 3;
int   y;
int   z = 10;
```

12.6 For the following code, state the values that are printed out by each `printf` statement. The statements are executed in the order A, B, C, D.

```
int t;   /* This variable is global */

{
    int t = 2;

    printf("%d\n", t);        /*  A  */
    {
        printf("%d\n", t);    /*  B  */
        t = 3;
    }
    printf("%d\n", t);        /*  C  */
}

{
    printf("%d\n", t);        /*  D  */
}
```

12.7 Given that a and b are both integers where a and b have been assigned the values 6 and 9, respectively, what is the value of each of the following expressions? Also, if the value of a or b changes, give their new value.

a. a | b
b. a || b
c. a & b
d. a && b
e. !(a + b)
f. a % b
g. b / a
h. a = b
i. a = b = 5
j. ++a + b--
k. a = (++b < 3) ? a : b
l. a <<= b

12.8 For the following questions, write a C expression to perform the following relational test on the character variable `letter`.

a. Test if `letter` is any alphabetic character or a number.
b. Test if `letter` is any character except an alphabetic character or a number.

12.9   *a.* What does the following statement accomplish? The variable
letter is a character variable.

```
letter = ((letter >= 'a' && letter <= 'z') ? '!' : letter);
```

b. Modify the statement in (a) so that it converts lowercase to
uppercase.

12.10   Write a program that reads an integer from the keyboard and displays a
1 if it is divisible by 3 or a 0 otherwise.

12.11   Explain the differences between the following C statements:

a. j = i++;
b. j = ++i;
c. j = i + 1;
d. i += 1;
e. j = i += 1;
f. Which statements modify the value of i? Which ones modify the
value of j? If i = 1 and j = 0 initially, what will the values of
i and j be after each statement is run separately?

12.12   Say variables a and b are both declared locally as long int.

a. Translate the expression a + b into LC-3 code, assuming a
long int occupies two bytes. Assume a is allocated at offset 0 and
b is at offset −1 in the activation record for their function.

b. Translate the same expression, assuming a long int occupies four
bytes, a is allocated offset 0, and b is at offset −2.

12.13   If initially, a = 1, b = 1, c = 3, and result = 999, what are the
values of the variables after the following C statement is executed?

```
result = b + 1 | c + a;
```

12.14   Recall the machine busy example from Chapter 2. Say the integer
variable machineBusy tracks the busyness of all 16 machines. Recall
that a 0 in a particular bit position indicates the machine is busy and
a 1 in that position indicates the machine is idle.

a. Write a C statement to make machine 5 busy.
b. Write a C statement to make machine 10 idle.
c. Write a C statement to make machine n busy. That is, the machine
that has become busy is an integer variable n.
d. Write a C expression to check if machine 3 is idle. If it is idle, the
expression returns a 1. If it is busy, the expression returns a 0.
e. Write a C expression that evaluates to the number of idle machines.
For example, if the binary pattern in machineBusy were
1011 0010 1110 1001, then the expression will evaluate to 9.

12.15 What purpose does the semicolon serve in C?

12.16 Say we are designing a new computer programming language that includes the operators @, #, $ and U. How would the expression
w @ x # y $ z U a get evaluated under the following constraints?

    a. The precedence of @ is higher than # is higher than $ is higher than U. Use parentheses to indicate the order.

    b. The precedence of # is higher than U is higher than @ is higher than $.

    c. Their precedence is all the same, but they associate left to right.

    d. Their precedence is all the same, but they associate right to left.

12.17 Notice that the C assignment operators have the lowest precedence. Say we have developed a new programming language called *Q* that works exactly like C, except that the assignment operator had the highest precedence.

    a. What is the result of the following Q statement? In other words, what would the value of x be after it executed?

```
x = x + 1;
```

    b. How would we change this Q statement so that it works the same way as it would in C?

12.18 Modify the example program in Chapter 11 (Figure 11.3) so that it prompts the user to type a character and then prints every character from that character down to the character ! in the order they appear in the ASCII table.

12.19 Write a C program to calculate the sales tax on a sales transaction. Prompt the user to enter the amount of the purchase and the tax rate. Output the amount of sales tax and the total amount (including tax) on the whole purchase.

12.20 Suppose a program contains the two integer variables x and y, which have values 3 and 4, respectively. Write C statements that will exchange the values in x and y so that after the statements are executed, x is equal to 4 and y is equal to 3.

    a. First, write this routine using a temporary variable for storage.

    b. Now rewrite this routine without using a temporary variable.

13

```
101001 000110 0011
110111 101010 0011
```

```
int Add(int x, int y
{
    return x + y;
}
```

```
x + y
```

```
LDR   R0, R6, 3
LDR   R1, R6, 4
ADD   R2, R0, R1
STR   R2, R6, 0
RET
```

Control Structures

13.1 Introduction

In Chapter 6, we introduced our top-down problem-solving methodology where a problem is systematically refined into smaller, more detailed subtasks using three programming constructs: the sequential construct, the conditional construct, and the iteration construct.

We applied this methodology in the previous chapter to derive a simple C program that calculates network transfer time. The problem's refinement into a program only required the use of the sequential construct. For transforming more complex problems into C programs, we will need a way to invoke the conditional and iteration constructs in our programs. In this chapter, we cover C's version of these two constructs.

We begin this chapter by describing C's conditional constructs. The `if` and `if-else` statements allow us to conditionally execute a statement. After conditional constructs, we move on to C's iteration constructs: the `for`, the `while`, and the `do-while` statements, all of which allow us to express loops. With many of these constructs, we will present the corresponding LC-3 code generated by our hypothetical LC-3 C compiler to better illustrate how these constructs behave at the lower levels. C also provides additional control constructs, such as the `switch`, `break`, and `continue` statements, all of which provide a convenient way to represent some particular control tasks. We discuss these in Section 13.5. In the final part of the chapter, we'll use the top-down problem-solving methodology to solve some complex problems involving control structures.

13.2 Conditional Constructs

Conditional constructs allow a programmer to select an action based on some condition. This is a very common programming construct and is supported by every useful programming language. C provides two types of basic conditional constructs: if and if-else.

13.2.1 The if Statement

The if statement is quite simple. It performs an action if a condition is true. The action is a C statement, and it is executed only if the condition, which is a C expression, evaluates to a nonzero (logically true) value. Let's take a look at an example.

```
if (x <= 10)
    y = x * x + 5;
```

The statement `y = x * x + 5;` is only executed if the expression `x <= 10` is nonzero. Recall from our discussion of the `<=` operator (the less than or equal to operator) that it evaluates to 1 if the relationship is true, 0 otherwise.

    The statement following the condition can also be a *compound statement*, or *block*, which is a sequence of statements beginning with an open brace and ending with a closing brace. Compound statements are used to group one or more simple statements into a single entity. This entity is itself equivalent to a simple statement. Using compound statements with an if statement, we can conditionally execute several statements on a single condition. For example, in the following code, both y and z will be modified if x is less than or equal to 10.

```
if (x <= 10) {
    y = x * x + 5;
    z = (2 * y) / 3;
}
```

As with all statements in C, the format of the if statement is flexible. The line breaks and indentation used in the preceding example are features of a popular style for formatting an if statement. It allows someone reading the code to quickly identify the portion that executes if the condition is true. Keep in mind that the format does not affect the behavior of the program. Even though the following code is indented like the previous code, it behaves differently. The second statement `z = (2 * y) / 3;` is not associated with the if and will execute regardless of the condition.

```
if (x <= 10)
    y = x * x + 5;
    z = (2 * y) / 3;
```

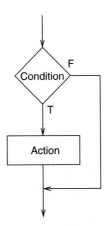

Figure 13.1   The C `if` statement, pictorially represented

Figure 13.1 shows the control flow of an `if` statement. The diagram corresponds to the following code:

```
if (condition)
   action;
```

Syntactically, the condition must be surrounded by parentheses in order to enable the compiler to unambiguously separate the condition from the rest of the `if` statement. The action must be a simple or compound statement.

Here are more examples of `if` statements demonstrating programming situations where this decision construct might be useful.

```
if (temperature <= 0)
   printf("At or below freezing point.\n");

if ('a' <= key && key <= 'z')
   numLowerCase++;

if (current > currentLimit)
   blownFuse = 1;

if (loadMAR & clock)
   registerMAR = bus;

if (month == 4 || month == 6 || month == 9 || month == 11)
   printf("The month has 30 days\n");

if (x = 2)    /* This condition is always true.   */
   y = 5;     /* The variable y will always be 5   */
```

The last example in the preceding code illustrates a very common mistake made when programming in C. (Sometimes even expert C programmers make this mistake. Good C compilers will warn you if they detect such code.) The condition uses the assignment operator = rather than the equality operator, which causes the value of x to change to 2. This condition is always true: expressions containing the assignment operator evaluate to the value being assigned (in this case, 2). Since the condition is always nonzero, y will always get assigned the value 5 and x will always be assigned 2.

Even though they look similar at first glance, the following code is a "repaired" version of the previous code.

```
if (x == 2)
   y = 5;
```

Let's look at the LC-3 code that is generated for this code, assuming that x and y are integers that are locally declared. This means that R5 will point to the variable x and R5 - 1 will point to y.

```
            LDR   R0, R5, #0    ; load x into R0
            ADD   R0, R0, #-2   ; subtract 2 from x
            BRnp  NOT_TRUE      ; If condition is not true,
                                ; then skip the assignment

            AND   R0, R0, #0    ; R0 <- 0
            ADD   R0, R0, #5    ; R0 <- 5
            STR   R0, R5, #-1   ; y = 5;

NOT_TRUE  :                     ; the rest of the program
          :
```

Notice that it is most straightforward for the LC-3 C compiler to generate code that tests for the opposite of the original condition (x not equal to 2) and to branch based on its outcome.

The if statement is itself a statement. Therefore, it is legal to *nest* an if statement as demonstrated in the following C code. Since the statement following the first if is a simple statement (i.e., composed of only one statement), no braces are required.

```
if (x == 3)
   if (y != 6) {
      z = z + 1;
      w = w + 2;
   }
```

The inner `if` statement only executes if x is equal to 3. There is an easier way to express this code. Can you do it with only one `if` statement? The following code demonstrates how.

```
if ((x == 3) && (y != 6)) {
    z = z + 1;
    w = w + 2;
}
```

13.2.2 The `if-else` Statement

If we wanted to perform one set of actions if a condition were true and another set if the same condition were false, we could use the following sequence of `if` statements:

```
if (temperature <= 0)
    printf("At or below freezing point.\n");

if (temperature > 0)
    printf("Above freezing.\n");
```

Here, a single message is printed depending on whether the variable `temperature` is below or equal to zero or if it is above zero. It turns out that this type of conditional execution is a very useful construct in programming. Since expressing code in the preceding way can be a bit cumbersome, C provides a more convenient construct: the `if-else` statement.

The following code is equivalent to the previous code segment.

```
if (temperature <= 0)
    printf("At or below freezing point.\n");
else
    printf("Above freezing.\n");
```

Here, the statement appearing immediately after the `else` keyword executes only if the condition is false.

The flow diagram for the `if-else` is shown in Figure 13.2. The figure corresponds to the following code:

```
if (condition)
    action_if;
else
    action_else;
```

The lines `action_if` and `action_else` can correspond to compound statements and thus consist of multiple statements, as in the following example.

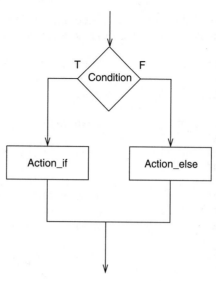

Figure 13.2   The C if-else statement, pictorially represented

```
if (x) {
    y++;
    z--;
}
else {
    y--;
    z++;
}
```

If the variable x is nonzero, the if's condition is true, y is incremented, and z decremented. Otherwise, y is decremented and z incremented. The LC-3 code generated by the LC-3 C compiler is listed in Figure 13.3. The three variables x, y, and z are locally declared integers.

We can connect conditional constructs together to form a longer sequence of conditional tests. The example in Figure 13.4 shows a complex decision structure created using the if and if-else statements. No other control structures are used. This program gets a number of a month from the user and displays the number of days in that month.

At this point, we need to mention a C syntax rule for associating ifs with elses: An else is associated with the closest unassociated if. The following example points out why this is important.

```
if (x != 10)
    if (y > 3)
        z = z / 2;
    else
        z = z * 2;
```

```
1          LDR   R0, R5, #0    ;   load the value of x
2          BRz   ELSE          ;   if x equals 0, perform else part
3
4          LDR   R0, R5, #-1   ;   load y into R0
5          ADD   R0, R0, #1
6          STR   R0, R5, #-1   ;   y++;
7
8          LDR   R0, R5, #-2   ;   load z into R0
9          ADD   R0, R0, #-1
10         STR   R0, R5, #-2   ;   z--;
11         BR DONE
12
13  ELSE: LDR   R0, R5, #-1   ;   load y into R0
14         ADD   R0, R0, #-1
15         STR   R0, R5, #-1   ;   y--;
16
17         LDR   R0, R5, #-2   ;   load z into R0
18         ADD   R0, R0, #1
19         STR   R0, R5, #-2   ;   z++;
20  DONE: :
21        :
```

Figure 13.3   The LC-3 code generated for an if-else statement

```
1   #include <stdio.h>
2
3   int main()
4   {
5     int month;
6
7     printf("Enter the number of the month: ");
8     scanf("%d", &month);
9
10    if (month == 4 || month == 6 || month == 9 || month == 11)
11      printf("The month has 30 days\n");
12    else if (month == 1 || month == 3 || month == 5 ||
13            month == 7 || month == 8 || month == 10 || month == 12)
14      printf("The month has 31 days\n");
15    else if (month == 2)
16      printf("The month has either 28 days or 29 days\n");
17    else
18      printf("Don't know that month\n");
19  }
```

Figure 13.4   A program that determines the number of days in a month

Without this rule, it would not be clear whether the `else` should be paired with the *outer* `if` or the *inner* `if`. For this situation, the rule states that the `else` is coupled with the inner `if` because it is closer than the outer `if` and the inner `if` statement has not already been coupled to another `else` (i.e., it is unassociated). The code is equivalent to the following:

```
if (x != 10) {
    if (y > 3)
        z = z / 2;
    else
        z = z * 2;
}
```

Just as parentheses can be used to modify the order of evaluation of expressions, braces can be used to associate statements. If we wanted to associate the `else` with the outer `if`, we could write the code as

```
if (x != 10) {
    if (y > 3)
        z = z / 2;
}
else
  z = z * 2;
```

Before we leave the `if-else` statement for bigger things, we present a very common use for the `if-else` construct. The `if-else` statement is very handy for checking for bad situations during program execution. We can use it for error checking, as shown in Figure 13.5. This example performs a simple division based on two numbers scanned from the keyboard. Because division by 0 is undefined, if the user enters a 0 divisor, a message is displayed indicating the result cannot be generated. The `if-else` statement serves nicely for this purpose.

Notice that the nonerror case appears in the `if-else` statement first and the error case second. Although we could have coded this either way, having the common, nonerror case first provides a visual cue to someone reading the code that the error case is the uncommon one.

13.3   Iteration Constructs

Being able to iterate, or repeat, a computation is part of the power of computing. Almost all useful programs perform some form of iteration. In C, there are three iteration constructs, each a slight variant of the others: the `while` statement, the `for` statement, and the `do-while` statement.

13.3.1 The `while` Statement

We begin by describing C's simplest iteration statement: the `while`. A `while` loop executes a statement repeatedly *while* a condition is true. Before each iteration

```
1   #include <stdio.h>
2
3   int main()
4   {
5     int dividend;
6     int divisor;
7     int result;
8
9     printf("Enter the dividend: ");
10    scanf("%d", &dividend);
11
12    printf("Enter the divisor: ");
13    scanf("%d", &divisor);
14
15    if (divisor != 0) {
16       result = dividend / divisor;
17       printf("The result of the division is %d\n", result);
18    }
19    else
20       printf("A divisor of zero is not allowed\n");
21  }
```

Figure 13.5 A program that has error-checking code

of the statement, the condition is checked. If the condition evaluates to a logical true (nonzero) value, the statement is executed again.

In the following example program, the loop keeps iterating while the value of variable x is less than 10. It produces the following output:

```
0 1 2 3 4 5 6 7 8 9

#include <stdio.h>

int main()
{
   int x = 0;

   while (x < 10) {
      printf("%d ", x);
      x = x + 1;
   }
}
```

The while statement can be broken down into two components. The test condition is an expression used to determine whether or not to continue executing the loop.

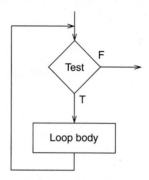

Figure 13.6   The C while statement, pictorially represented

```
while (test)
    loop_body;
```

It is tested before each execution of the loop_body. The loop_body is a statement that expresses the work to be done within the loop. Like all statements, it can be a compound statement.

Figure 13.6 shows the control flow using the notation of systematic decomposition. Two branches are required: one conditional branch to exit the loop and one unconditional branch to loop back to the test to determine whether or not to execute another iteration.

The LC-3 code generated by the compiler for the while example that counts from 0 to 9 is listed in Figure 13.7.

The while statement is useful for coding loops where the iteration process involves testing for a *sentinel* condition. That is, we don't know the number of iterations beforehand but we wish to keep looping until some event (i.e., the

```
1                    AND  R0, R0, #0    ;    clear out R0
2                    STR  R0, R5, #0    ;    x = 0;
3
4                    ; while (x < 10)
5      LOOP:         LDR  R0, R5, #0    ;    perform the test
6                    ADD  R0, R0, #-10
7                    BRpz DONE          ;    x is not less than 10
8
9                    ; loop body
10                   :
11                   <code for calling the function printf>
12                   :
13                   LDR  R0, R5, #0    ;    R0 <- x
14                   ADD  R0, R0, #1    ;    x + 1
15                   STR  R0, R5, #0    ;    x = x + 1;
16                   BR   LOOP          ;    another iteration
17     DONE:         :
18                   :
```

Figure 13.7   The LC-3 code generated for a while loop that counts to 9

```
1    #include <stdio.h>
2
3    int main()
4    {
5      char echo = 'A';    /* Initialize char variable echo */
6
7      while (echo != '\n') {
8        scanf("%c", &echo);
9        printf("%c", echo);
10     }
11   }
```

Figure 13.8   Another program with a simple while loop

sentinel) occurs. For example, when we wrote the character counting program in Chapters 5 and 7, we created a loop that terminated when the sentinel EOT character (a character with ASCII code 4) was detected. If we were coding that program in C rather than LC-3 assembly language, we would use a while loop. The program in Figure 13.8 uses the while statement to test for a sentinel condition. Can you determine what this program does without executing it?[1]

We end our discussion of the while statement by pointing out a common mistake when using while loops. The following program will never terminate because the loop body does not change the looping condition. In this case, the condition always remains true and the loop never terminates. Such loops are called *infinite loops*, and most of the time they occur because of programming errors.

```
#include <stdio.h>

int main()
{
   int x = 0;

   while (x < 10)
      printf("%d ", x);
}
```

13.3.2 The for Statement

Just as the while loop is a perfect match for a sentinel-controlled loop, the C for loop is a perfect match for a counter-controlled loop. In fact, the for loop is a special case of the while loop that happens to work well when the number of iterations is known ahead of time.

---

[1] This program behaves a bit differently than you might expect. You might expect it to print out each input character as the user types it in. Because of the way C deals with keyboard I/O, the program does not get any input until the user hits the Enter key. We explain why this is so when dealing with the low-level issues surrounding I/O in Chapter 18.

In its most straightforward form, the `for` statement allows us to repeat a statement a specified number of times. For example,

```c
#include <stdio.h>

int main()
{
    int x;

    for (x = 0; x < 10; x++)
        printf("%d ", x);
}
```

will produce the following output. It loops exactly 10 times.

```
0 1 2 3 4 5 6 7 8 9
```

The syntax for the C `for` statement may look a little perplexing at first. The `for` statement is composed of four components, broken down as follows:

```c
for (init; test; reinit)
    loop_body;
```

The three components within the parentheses, `init`, `test`, and `reinit`, control the behavior of the loop and must be separated by semicolons. The final component, `loop_body`, specifies the actual computation to be executed in each iteration.

Let's take a look at each component of the `for` loop in detail. The `init` component is an expression that is evaluated before the **first** iteration. It is typically used to initialize variables in preparation for executing the loop.

The `test` is an expression that gets evaluated before *every* iteration to determine if another iteration should be executed. If the `test` expression evaluates to zero, the `for` terminates and the control flow passes to the statement immediately following the `for`. If the expression is nonzero, another iteration of the `loop_body` is performed. Therefore, in the previous code example, the test expression `x < 10` causes the loop to keep repeating as long as `x` is less than 10.

The `reinit` component is an expression that is evaluated at the end of *every* iteration. It is used to prepare (or reinitialize) for the next iteration. In the previous code example, the variable `x` is incremented before each repetition of the loop body.

The `loop_body` is a statement that defines the work to be performed in each iteration. It can be a compound statement.

Figure 13.9 shows the flow diagram of the `for` statement. There are four blocks, one for each of the four components of the `for` statement. There is a conditional branch that determines whether to exit the loop based on the outcome of the `test` expression or to proceed with another iteration. An unconditional

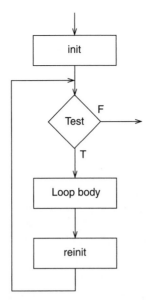

Figure 13.9   The C `for` statement

branch loops back to the `test` at the end of each iteration, after the `reinit` expression is evaluated.

Even though the syntax of a `for` statement allows it to be very flexible, most of the `for` loops you will encounter (or will write) will be of the counter-controlled variety, that is, loops that iterate for a certain number of iterations. Following are some examples of code that demonstrate the counter-controlled nature of `for` loops.

```
/* --- What does the loop output?  --- */
for (x = 0; x <= 10; x++)
    printf("%d ", x);

/* --- What does this one output?  --- */
letter = 'a';

for (c = 0; c < 26; c++)
    printf("%c ", letter + c);

/* --- What does this loop do?    --- */
numberOfOnes = 0;

for (bitNum = 0; bitNum < 16; bitNum++) {
    if (inputValue & (1 << bitNum))
        numberOfOnes++;
}
```

```
 1                   AND   R0, R0, #0    ;    clear out R0
 2                   STR   R0, R5, #-1   ;    sum = 0;
 3
 4                   ; init
 5                   AND   R0, R0, #0    ;    clear out R0
 6                   STR   R0, R5, #0    ;    init (x = 0)
 7
 8                   ; test
 9     LOOP:         LDR   R0, R5, #0    ;    perform the test
10                   ADD   R0, R0, #-10
11                   BRpz DONE           ;    x is not less than 10
12
13                   ; loop body
14                   LDR   R0, R5, #0    ;    get x
15                   LDR   R1, R5, #-1   ;    get sum
16                   ADD   R1, R1, R0    ;    sum + x
17                   STR   R0, R5, #-1   ;    sum = sum + x;
18
19                   ; reinit
20                   LDR   R0, R5, #0    ;    get x
21                   ADD   R0, R0, #1
22                   STR   R0, R5, #0    ;    x++
23                   BR    LOOP
24
25    DONE:         :
26                  :
```

Figure 13.10 The LC-3 code generated for a `for` statement

Let's take a look at the LC-3 translation of a simple `for` loop. The program is a simple one: it calculates the sum of all integers between 0 and 9.

```
#include <stdio.h>

int main()
{
    int x;
    int sum = 0;

    for (x = 0; x < 10; x++)
        sum = sum + x;
}
```

The LC-3 code generated by the compiler is shown in Figure 13.10.

The following code contains a mistake commonly made when using `for` loops.

```
sum = 0;
for (x = 0; x < 10; x++);
   sum = sum + x;

printf("sum = %d\n", sum);
printf("x = %d\n", x);
```

What is output by the first `printf`? The answer is `sum = 10`. Why? The second `printf` outputs `x = 10`. Why? If you look carefully, you might be able to notice a misplaced semicolon.

A `for` loop can be constructed using a `while` loop (actually, vice versa as well). In programming, they can be used interchangeably, to a degree. Which construct to use in which situation may seem puzzling at first, but keep in mind the general rule that `while` is best suited for loops that involve sentinel conditions, whereas `for` fits situations where the number of iterations is known beforehand.

Nested Loops

Figure 13.11 contains an example of a `for` where the loop body is composed of another `for` loop. This construct is referred to as a *nested loop* because the inner loop is nested within the outer. In this example, the program prints out a multiplication table for the numbers 0 through 9. Each iteration of the inner loop prints out a single product in the table. That is, the inner loop iterates 10 times for each iteration of the outer loop. An entire row is printed for each iteration of the outer loop. Notice that the `printf` function call contains a special character sequence in its format string. The `\t` sequence causes a tab character to be printed out. The tab helps align the columns of the multiplication table so the output looks neater.

```
1   #include <stdio.h>
2
3   int main()
4   {
5      int multiplicand;    /* First operand of each multiply  */
6      int multiplier;      /* Second operand of each multiply */
7
8      /* Outer Loop */
9      for (multiplicand = 0; multiplicand < 10; multiplicand++) {
10        /* Inner Loop */
11        for (multiplier = 0; multiplier < 10; multiplier++) {
12           printf("%d\t", multiplier * multiplicand);
13        }
14        printf("\n");
15     }
16  }
```

Figure 13.11 A program that prints out a multiplication table

```
1    #include <stdio.h>
2
3    int main()
4    {
5      int sum = 0;            /* Initial the result variable */
6      int input;              /* Holds user input           */
7      int inner;              /* Iteration variables        */
8      int outer;
9
10     /* Get input */
11     printf("Input an integer: ");
12     scanf("%d", &input);
13
14     /* Perform calculation */
15     for (outer = 1; outer <= input; outer++)
16       for (inner = 0; inner < outer; inner++) {
17         sum += inner;
18       }
19
20     /* Output result */
21     printf("The result is %d\n", sum);
22   }
```

Figure 13.12 A program with a nested `for` loop

Figure 13.12 contains a slightly more complex example. The number of iterations of the inner loop depends on the value of `outer` as determined by the outer loop. The inner loop will first execute 0 time, then 1 time, then 2 times, etc. For a challenging exercise based on this example, see Exercise 13.6 at the end of this chapter.

13.3.3 The `do-while` Statement

With a `while` loop, the condition is always evaluated *before* an iteration is performed. Therefore, it is possible for the `while` loop to execute zero iterations (i.e., when the condition is false from the start). There is a slight variant of the `while` statement in C called `do-while`, which always performs at least one iteration. In a `do-while` loop, the condition is evaluated *after* the first iteration is performed. The operation of the `do-while` is demonstrated in the following example:

```
x = 0;
do {
   printf("%d \n", x);
   x = x + 1;
} while (x < 10);
```

Here, the conditional test, `x < 10`, is evaluated at the end of each iteration. Thus, the loop body will execute at least once. The next iteration is performed

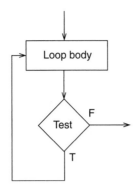

Figure 13.13 The C `do-while` statement

only if the test evaluates to a nonzero value. This code produces the following output:

```
0 1 2 3 4 5 6 7 8 9
```

Syntactically, a `do-while` is composed of two components, exactly like the `while`.

```
do
  loop_body;
while (test);
```

The `loop_body` component is a statement (simple or compound) that describes the computation to be performed by the loop. The `test` is an expression that determines whether another iteration is to be performed.

Figure 13.13 shows the control flow of the `do-while` loop. Notice the slight change from the flow of a `while` loop. The loop body and the test are interchanged. A conditional branch loops back to the top of the loop body, initiating another iteration.

At this point, the differences between the three types of C iteration constructs may seem very subtle, but once you become comfortable with them and build up experience using these constructs, you will more easily be able to pick the right construct to fit the situation. To a large degree, these constructs can be used interchangeably. Stylistically, there are times when one construct makes more sense to use than another—often the type of loop you choose will convey information about the intent of the loop to someone reading your code.

13.4 Problem Solving Using Control Structures

Armed with a new arsenal of control structures, we can attempt to solve more complex programming problems. In this section, we will apply our top-down problem-solving methodology to four problems requiring the use of C control structures.

Being effective at solving programming problems requires that you understand the basic primitives of the system on which you are programming. You will need to invoke them at the appropriate times to solve various programming puzzles. At this point, our list of C primitives includes variables of the three basic types, operators, two decision structures, and three control structures.

13.4.1 Problem 1: Approximating the Value of π

For the first programming problem, we will calculate the value of π using the following series expansion:

$$\pi = 4 - \frac{4}{3} + \frac{4}{5} - \frac{4}{7} + \cdots + (-1)^{n-1} \frac{4}{2n+1} + \cdots$$

The problem is to evaluate this series for the number of terms indicated by the user. If the user enters 3, the program will evaluate $4 - \frac{4}{3} + \frac{4}{5}$. The series is an infinite series, and the more terms we evaluate, the more accurate our approximation of π.

As we did for the problem-solving example in Chapter 12, we first invoke step 0: we select a representation for the data involved in the computation. Since the series deals with fractional numbers, we use the double floating point type for any variables directly involved in the series calculation. Given the nature of the computation, this seems clearly to be the best choice.

Now we invoke stepwise refinement to decompose a roughly stated algorithm into a C program. Roughly, we want the program to initialize all data that requires initialization. Then ask the user to input the number of terms of the series to evaluate. Then evaluate the series for the given number of terms. Finally, print out the result. We have defined the problem as a set of sequential constructs. Figure 13.14 shows the decomposition thus far.

Most of the sequential constructs in Figure 13.14 are very straightforward. Converting them into C code should be quite simple. One of the constructs in the figure, however, requires some additional refinement. We need to put a little thought into the subtask labeled *Evaluate series*. For this subtask, we essentially want to *iterate* through the series, term by term, until we evaluate exactly the number of terms indicated by the user. We want to use a counter-controlled iteration construct. Figure 13.15 shows the decomposition. We maintain a counter for the current loop iteration. If the counter is less than the limit indicated by the user, then we evaluate another term. Notice that the refined version of the subtask looks like the flow diagram for a `for` loop.

We are almost done. The only nontrivial subtask remaining is *Evaluate another term*. Notice that all even terms in the series are subtracted, and all odd terms are added. Within this subtask, we need to determine if the particular term we are evaluating is an odd or an even term, and then accordingly factor it into the current value of the approximation. This involves using a decision construct as shown in Figure 13.16. The complete code resulting from this stepwise refinement is shown in Figure 13.17.

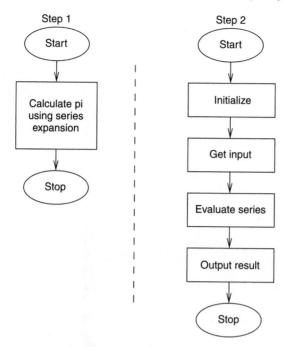

Figure 13.14 The initial decomposition of a program that evaluates the series expansion for π for a given number of terms

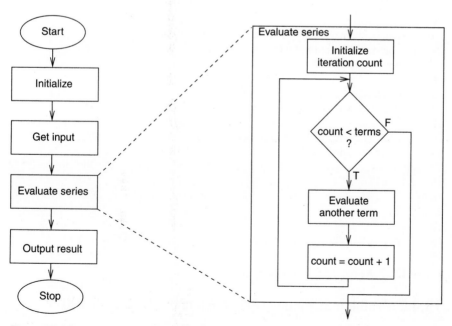

Figure 13.15 The refinement of the subtask Evaluate series into an iteration construct that iterates a given number of times. Within this loop, we evaluate terms for a series expansion for π

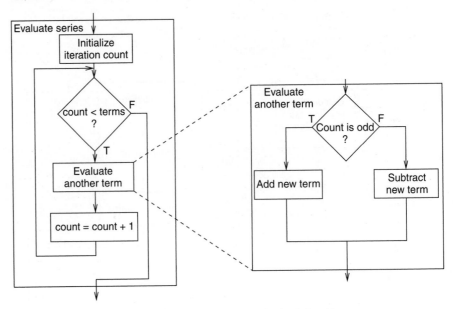

Figure 13.16 Incorporate the current term based on whether it is odd or even

```
1    #include <stdio.h>
2
3    int main()
4    {
5      int count;       /* Iteration variable              */
6      int numOfTerms;  /* Number of terms to evaluate     */
7      double pi = 0;   /* approximation of pi             */
8
9      printf("Number of terms (must be 1 or larger) : ");
10     scanf("%d", &numOfTerms);
11
12     for (count = 1; count <= numOfTerms; count++) {
13       if (count % 2)
14         pi = pi + (4.0 / (2.0 * count - 1)); /* Odd term   */
15       else
16         pi = pi - (4.0 / (2.0 * count - 1)); /* Even term */
17     }
18
19     printf("The approximate value of pi is %f\n", pi);
20   }
```

Figure 13.17 A program to calculate π

13.4.2 Problem 2: Finding Prime Numbers Less than 100

Our next problem-solving example involves finding all the prime numbers that are less than 100. Recall that a number is prime only if the only numbers that evenly divide it are 1 and itself.

Step 1   Step 2   Step 3

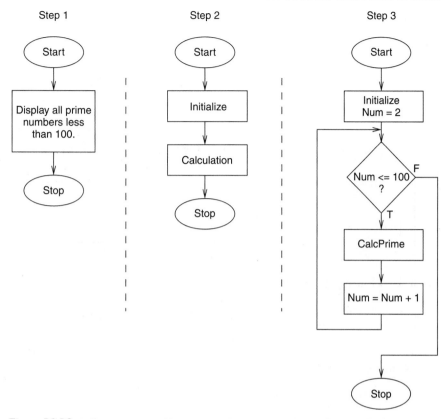

Figure 13.18 Decomposing a problem to compute prime numbers less than 100. The first
three steps involve creating a loop that iterates between the 2 and 100

Step 0, as with our previous examples, is to select an appropriate data representation for the various data associated with the problem. Since the property of prime numbers only applies to integers, using the integer data type for the main computation seems a good choice.

Next we apply stepwise refinement to the problem to reduce it into a C program. We can approach this problem by first stating it as a single task (step 1). We then refine this single task into two separate sequential subtasks: Initialize and then perform the calculation (step 2).

Performing the *Calculation* subtask is the brunt of the programming effort. Essentially, the *Calculation* subtask can be stated as follows: We want to check every integer between 2 and 100 to determine if it is prime. If it is prime, we want to print it out. A counter-controlled loop should work just fine for this purpose. We can further refine the *Calculation* subtask into smaller subtasks, as shown in Figure 13.18. Notice that the flow diagram has the shape of a `for` loop.

Already, the problem is starting to resolve into C code. We still need to refine the *CalcPrime* subtask. In this subtask, we need to determine if the current number is prime or not. Here, we rely on the fact that any number between 2 and 100 that is *not* prime will have at least one divisor between 2 and 10 that is not itself. We

Step 3

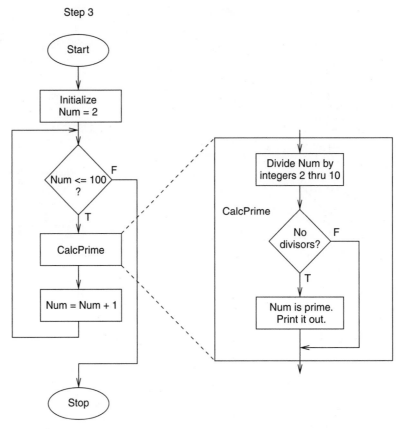

Figure 13.19 Decomposing the CalcPrime subtask

can refine this subtask as shown in Figure 13.19. Basically, we will determine if each number is divisible by an integer between 2 and 10 (being careful to exclude the number itself). If it has no divisors between 2 and 10, except perhaps itself, then the number is prime.

Finally, we need to refine the *Divide number by integers 2 through 10* subtask. It involves dividing the current number by all integers between 2 and 10 and determining if any of them evenly divide it. A simple way to do this is to use another counter-controlled loop to cycle through all the integers between 2 and 10. Figure 13.20 shows the decomposition using the iteration construct.

Now, coding this problem into a C program is a small step forward. The program is listed in Figure 13.21. There are two `for` loops within the program, one of which is nested within the other. The outer loop sequences through all the integers between 2 and 100; it corresponds to the loop created when we decomposed the *Calculation* subtask. An inner loop determines if the number generated by the outer loop has any divisors; it corresponds to the loop created when we decomposed the *Divide number by integers 2 through 10* subtask.

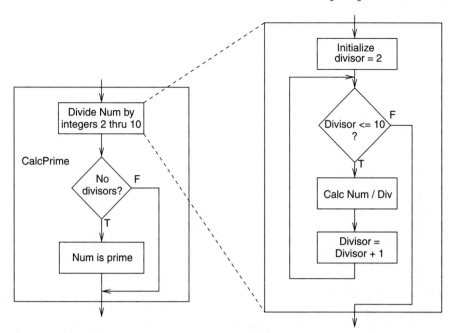

Figure 13.20 Decomposing the Divide numbers by integers 2 through 10 subtask

```
1    #include <stdio.h>
2    #define FALSE 0
3    #define TRUE  1
4
5    int main()
6    {
7      int num;
8      int divisor;
9      int prime;
10
11     /* Start at 2 and go until 100  */
12     for (num = 2; num <= 100; num++) {
13       prime = TRUE;   /* Assume the number is prime */
14
15       /* Test if the candidate number is a prime */
16       for (divisor = 2; divisor <= 10; divisor++)
17         if (((num % divisor) == 0) && num != divisor)
18           prime = FALSE;
19
20       if (prime)
21         printf("The number %d is prime\n", num);
22     }
23   }
```

Figure 13.21 A program that finds all prime numbers between 2 and 100

One item of note: If a divisor between 2 and 10 is found, then a flag variable called prime is set to *false*. It is set to *true* before the inner loop begins. If it remains *true*, then the number generated by the outer loop has no divisors and is therefore prime. To do this, we are utilizing the C preprocessor's macro substitution facility. We have defined, using #define, two symbolic names, FALSE, which maps to the value 0 and TRUE, which maps to 1. The preprocessor will simply replace each occurrence of the word TRUE in the source file with 1 and each occurrence of FALSE with 0.

13.4.3 Problem 3: Analyzing an E-mail Address

Our final problem in this section involves analyzing an e-mail address typed in at the keyboard to determine if it is of valid format. For this problem, we'll use a simple definition of validity: an e-mail address is a sequence of characters that must contain an at sign, "@", and a period, ".", with the at sign preceding the period.

As before, we start by choosing an appropriate data representation for the underlying data of the problem. Here, we are processing text data entered by the user. The type best suited for text is the ASCII character type, char. Actually, the best representation for input text is an array of characters, or *character string*, but as we have not yet introduced arrays into our lexicon of primitive elements (and we will in Chapter 16), we instead target our solution to use a single variable of the char type.

Next, we apply stepwise refinement. The entire process is diagrammed in Figure 13.22. We start with a rough flow of the program where we have two

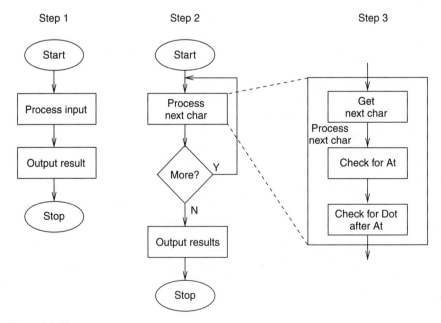

Figure 13.22 A stepwise refinement of the analyze e-mail address program

tasks (step 1): *Process input* and *Output results*. Here, the *Output results* task is straightforward. We will output either that the input text is a valid e-mail address or that it is invalid. The *Process input* task requires more refinement.

In decomposing the *Process input* task (step 2), we need to keep in mind that our choice of data representation (variable of the `char` type) implies that we will need to read and process the user's input one character at a time. We will keep processing, character by character, until we have reached the end of the e-mail address, implying that we select some form of sentinel-controlled loop. Step 2 of the decomposition divides the *Process input* task into a sentinel-controlled iteration construct that terminates when the end of an e-mail address is encountered, which we'll say is either a space or a newline character, \n.

The next step (step 3) of the decomposition involves detailing what processing occurs within the loop. Here, we need to check each character within the e-mail address and remember if we have seen an at sign or a period in the proper order. To do this, we will use two variables to record this status. When the loop terminates

```c
1    #include <stdio.h>
2    #define FALSE 0
3    #define TRUE  1
4
5    int main()
6    {
7      char nextChar;    /* Next character in e-mail address */
8      int gotAt  = FALSE; /* Indicates if At @ was found */
9      int gotDot = FALSE; /* Indicates if Dot . was found */
10
11     printf("Enter your e-mail address: ");
12
13     do {
14       scanf("%c", &nextChar);
15
16       if (nextChar == '@')
17         gotAt = TRUE;
18
19       if (nextChar == '.' && gotAt == TRUE)
20         gotDot = TRUE;
21     }
22     while (nextChar != ' ' && nextChar != '\n');
23
24     if (gotAt == TRUE && gotDot == TRUE)
25       printf("Your e-mail address appears to be valid.\n");
26     else
27       printf("Your e-mail address is not valid!\n");
28   }
```

Figure 13.23 A C program to determine if an e-mail address is valid

and we are ready to display the result, we can examine these variables to display the appropriate output message.

At this point, we are not far from C code. Notice that the loop structure is very similar to the flow diagram of the `do-while` statement. The C code for this problem is provided in Figure 13.23.

13.5 Additional C Control Structures

We complete our coverage of the C control structures by examining the `switch`, `break`, and `continue` statements. These three statements provide specialized program control that programmers occasionally find useful for very particular programming situations. We provide them here primarily for completeness; none of the examples in the remainder of the textbook use any of these three constructs.

13.5.1 The `switch` Statement

Occasionally, we run into programming situations where we want to perform a series of tests on a single value. For example, in the following code, we test the character variable `keyPress` to see if it equals a series of particular characters.

```
char keyPress;

if (keyPress == 'a')
   /* statement A */

else if (keyPress == 'b')
   /* statement B */

else if (keyPress == 'x')
   /* statement C */

else if (keyPress == 'y')
   /* statement D */
```

In this code, one (or none) of the statements labeled A, B, C, or D will execute, depending on the value of the variable `keyPress`. If `keyPress` is equal to the character *a*, then statement A is performed, if it is equal to the character *b*, then statement B is performed, and so forth. If `keyPress` does not equal *a* or *b* or *x* or *y*, then none of the statements are executed.

If there are many of these conditions to check, then many tests will be required in order to find the "matching" one. In order to give the compiler an opportunity to better optimize this code by bypassing some of this testing, C provides the `switch` statement. The following code segment behaves the same as the code in the previous example. It uses a `switch` statement instead of cascaded `if-else` statements.

```
char keyPress;

switch (keyPress) {
case 'a':
  /* statement A */
  break;

case 'b':
  /* statement B */
  break;

case 'x':
  /* statement C */
  break;

case 'y':
  /* statement D */
  break;
}
```

Notice that the `switch` statement contains several lines beginning with the keyword `case`, followed by a label. The program evaluates `keyPress` first. Then it determines which of the following `case` labels matches the value of `keyPress`. If any label matches, then the statements following it are executed.

Let's go through the `switch` construct piece by piece. The `switch` keyword precedes the expression on which to base the decision. This expression must be of integral type (for example, an `int` or a `char`). If one of the `case` labels matches the value of the expression, then program control passes to the statement or block associated with (usually, immediately below) that `case` label. Each `case` consists of a sequence of zero or more statements similar to a compound statement, but no delimiting braces are required. The place within this compound statement to start executing is determined by which `case` matches the value of the `switch` expression. Each `case` label within a `switch` statement must be unique; identical labels are not allowed.

Furthermore, each `case` label must be a constant expression. It cannot be based on a value that changes as the program is executing. The following is not a legal `case` label (assuming `i` is a variable):

```
case i:
```

In the preceding `switch` example, each `case` ends with a `break` statement. The `break` exits the `switch` construct and changes the flow of control directly to the statement after the closing brace of the `switch`. The `break` statements are optional. If they are not used, then control will go from the current `case` to the next. For example, if the break after statement C were omitted, then a match on case 'x' would cause statement C *and* statement D to be executed. However, in practice, cases almost always end with a break.

We can also include a default case. This case is selected if the switch expression matches none of the case constants. If no default case is given, and the expression matches none of the constants, none of the cases are executed.

A stylistic note: The last case of a switch does not need to end with a break since execution of the switch ends there, anyway. However, including a break for the final case is good programming practice. If another case is ever added to the end of the switch, then you will not have to remember to also add the break to the previous case. It is good, defensive programming.

13.5.2 The break and continue Statements

In the previous section, we saw an example of how the C break statement is used with switch. The break statement, and also the continue statement, are occasionally used with iteration constructs.

The break statement causes the compiler to generate code that will prematurely exit a loop or a switch statement. When used within a loop body, break causes the loop to terminate by causing control to jump out of the innermost loop that contains it. The continue statement, on the other hand, causes the compiler to generate code that will end the current iteration and start the next. These statements can occur within a loop body and apply to the iteration construct immediately enclosing them. Essentially, the break and continue statements cause the compiler to generate an unconditional branch instruction that leaves the loop from somewhere in the loop body. Following are two example code segments that use break and continue.

```
/* This code segment produces the output: 0 1 2 3 4 */
for (i = 0; i < 10; i++) {
   if (i == 5)
      break;
   printf("%d ", i);
}
/* This code produces the output: 0 1 2 3 4 6 7 8 9 */
for (i = 0; i < 10; i++) {
   if (i == 5)
      continue;
   printf("%d ", i);
}
```

13.5.3 An Example: Simple Calculator

The program in Figure 13.24 performs a function similar to the calculator example from Chapter 10. The user is prompted for three items: an integer operand,

```
1    #include <stdio.h>
2
3    int main()
4    {
5      int operand1, operand2;     /* Input values            */
6      int result = 0;             /* Result of the operation */
7      char operation;             /* operation to perform    */
8
9      /* Get the input values */
10     printf("Enter first operand: ");
11     scanf("%d", &operand1);
12     printf("Enter operation to perform (+, -, *, /): ");
13     scanf("\n%c", &operation);
14     printf("Enter second operand: ");
15     scanf("%d", &operand2);
16
17     /* Perform the calculation */
18     switch(operation) {
19     case '+':
20       result = operand1 + operand2;
21       break;
22
23     case '-':
24       result = operand1 - operand2;
25       break;
26
27     case '*':
28       result = operand1 * operand2;
29       break;
30
31     case '/':
32       if (operand2 != 0)                /* Error-checking code. */
33         result = operand1 / operand2;
34       else
35         printf("Divide by 0 error!\n");
36       break;
37
38     default:
39       printf("Invalid operation!\n");
40       break;
41     }
42
43     printf("The answer is %d\n", result);
44   }
```

Figure 13.24 Calculator program in C

an operation to perform, and another integer operand. The program performs the operation on the two input values and displays the result. The program makes use of a switch to base its computation on the operator the user has selected.

13.6 Summary

We conclude this chapter by summarizing the key concepts we've covered. The basic objective of this chapter was to enlarge our set of problem-solving primitives by exploring the various control structures supported by the C programming language.

- **Decision Construct in C.** We covered two basic C decision statements: if and if-else. Both of these statements *conditionally* execute a statement depending on whether a specified expression is true or false.

- **Iteration Constructs in C.** C provides three iteration statements: while, for, and do-while. All of these statements execute a statement possibly multiple times until a specified expression becomes false. The while and do-while statements are particularly well-suited for expressing sentinel-controlled loops. The for statement works well for expressing counter-controlled loops.

- **Problem Solving Using Control Structures.** To our arsenal of primitives for problem solving (which already includes the three basic C types, variables, operators, and I/O using printf and scanf), we added control constructs. We practiced some problem-solving examples that required application of these control constructs.

Exercises

13.1   Recreate the LC-3 compiler's symbol table when it compiles the calculator program listed in Figure 13.24.

13.2   *a.* What does the following code look like after it is processed by the preprocessor?

```
#define VERO -2

if (VERO)
    printf("True!");
else
    printf("False!");
```

   b. What is the output produced when this code is run?
   c. If we modified the code to the following, does the code behave differently? If so, how?

```
#define VERO -2

if (VERO)
    printf("True!");
else if (!VERO)
    printf("False!");
```

13.3 An `if-else` statement can be used in place of the C conditional operator (see Section 12.6.3). Rewrite the following statement using an `if-else` rather than the conditional operator.

```
x = a ? b : c;
```

13.4 Describe the behavior of the following statements for the case when x equals 0 and when x equals 1.

a.
```
if (x = 0)
    printf("x equals 0\n");
else
    printf("x does not equal 0\n");
```

b.
```
if (x == 0)
    printf("x equals 0\n");
else
    printf("x does not equal 0\n");
```

c.
```
if (x == 0)
    printf("A\n");
else if (x != 1)
    printf("B\n");
else if (x < 1)
    printf("C\n");
else if (x)
    printf("D\n");
```

d.
```
int x;
int y;

switch (x) {
case 0:
    y = 3;

case 1:
    y = 4;
    break;

default:
    y = 5;
    break;
}
```

e. What happens if x is not equal to 0 or 1 for part 4?

13.5 Provide the LC-3 code generated by our LC-3 C compiler when it compiles the `switch` statement in part 4 of Exercise 13.4.

13.6 Figure 13.12 contains a C program with a nested `for` loop.

a. Mathematically state the series that this program calculates.
b. Write a program to calculate the following function:

$$f(n) = f(n-1) + f(n-2)$$

with the following initial conditions,

$$f(0) = 1, \quad f(1) = 1$$

13.7   Can the following `if-else` statement be converted into a `switch`? If yes, convert it. If no, why not?

```
if (x == 0)
    y = 3;
else if (x == 1)
    y = 4;
else if (x == 2)
    y = 5;
else if (x == y)
    y = 6;
else
    y = 7;
```

13.8   At least how many times will the statement called `loopBody` execute the following constructs?

a.
```
while (condition)
    loopBody;
```

b.
```
do
    loopBody;
while (condition);
```

c.
```
for (init; condition; reinit)
    loopBody;
```

d.
```
while (condition1)
    for (init; condition2; reinit)
        loopBody;
```

e.
```
do
    do
        loopBody;
    while (condition1);
while (condition2);
```

13.9   What is the output of each of the following code segments?

a.
```
a = 2;
while (a > 0) {
    a--;
}
printf("%d", a);
```

b.
```
a = 2;
do {
    a--;
} while (a > 0)
printf("%d", a);
```

c.
```
b = 0;
for (a = 3; a < 10; a += 2)
    b = b + 1;
printf("%d %d", a, b);
```

13.10 Convert the program in Figure 13.4 into one that uses a `switch` statement instead of `if-else`.

13.11 Modify the e-mail address validation program in Figure 13.23 so that it requires that at least one alphabetic character appears prior to the at sign, one appears between the at sign and the period, and one appears after the period in order for an e-mail address to be valid.

13.12 For the following questions, x is an integer with the value 4.

   a. What output is generated by the following code segment?

```
if (7 > x > 2)
    printf("True.");
else
    printf("False.");
```

   b. Does the following code cause an infinite loop?
```
while (x > 0)
    x++;
```

   c. What is the value of x after the following code has executed?
```
for (x = 4; x < 4; x--) {
    if (x < 2)
        break;
    else if (x == 2)
        continue;
    x = -1;
}
```

13.13 Change this program so that it uses a `do-while` loop instead of a `for` loop.

```
int main()
{
    int i;
    int sum;

    for (i = 0; i <= 100; i++) {
        if (i % 4 == 0)
            sum = sum + 2;
        else if (i % 4 == 1)
            sum = sum - 6;
        else if (i % 4 == 2)
            sum = sum * 3;
        else if (i % 4 == 3)
            sum = sum / 2;
    }
    printf("%d\n", sum);
}
```

13.14   Write a C program that accepts as input a single integer k, then writes a pattern consisting of a single 1 on the first line, two 2s on the second line, three 3s on the third line, and so forth, until it writes k occurrences of k on the last line.

For example, if the input is 5, the output should be the following:

```
1
2   2
3   3   3
4   4   4   4
5   5   5   5   5
```

13.15   *a.* Convert the following while loop into a for loop.

```
while (condition)
    loopBody;
```

b. Convert the following for loop into a while loop.

```
for (init; condition; reinit)
    loopBody;
```

13.16   What is the output of the following code?

```
int r = 0;
int s = 0;
int w = 12;
int sum = 0;

for (r = 1; r <= w; r++)
    for (s = r; s <= w; s++)
        sum = sum + s;

printf("sum =%d\n", sum);
```

13.17   The following code performs something quite specific. Describe its output.

```
int i;

scanf("%d", &i);
for (j = 0; j < 16; j++) {
    if (i & (1 << j)) {
        count++;
    }
}

printf("%d\n", count);
```

13.18 Provide the output of each of the following code segments.

a.
```
int x = 20;
int y = 10;

while ((x > 10) && (y & 15)) {
    y = y + 1;
    x = x - 1;
    printf("*");
}
```

b.
```
int x;

for (x = 10; x ; x = x - 1)
    printf("*");
```

c.
```
int x;

for (x = 0; x < 10; x = x + 1) {
    if (x % 2)
        printf("*");
}
```

d.
```
int x = 0;
int i;

while (x < 10) {
    for (i = 0; i < x; i = x + 1)
        printf("*");
    x = x + 1;
}
```

14

Functions

14.1 Introduction

Functions are subprograms, and subprograms are the soul of modern programming languages. Functions provide the programmer with a way to enlarge the set of elementary building blocks with which to write programs. That is, they enable the programmer to extend the set of operations and constructs natively supported by the language to include new primitives. Functions are such an important concept that they have been part of languages since the very early days, and support for them is provided directly in all instruction set architectures, including the LC-3.

Why are they so important? Functions (or procedures, or subroutines, or methods—all of which are variations of the same theme) enable *abstraction*. That is, they increase our ability to separate the "function" of a component from the details of how it accomplishes that "function." Once the component is created and we understand its construction, we can use the component as a building block without giving much thought to its detailed implementation. Without abstraction, our ability to create complex systems such as computers, and the software that runs on them, would be seriously impaired.

Functions are not new to us. We have have been using variants of functions ever since we programmed subroutines in LC-3 assembly language; while there are syntactic differences between subroutines in LC-3 assembly and functions in C, the concepts behind them are largely the same.

The C programming language is heavily oriented around functions. A C program is essentially a collection of functions. Every statement belongs to one (and only one) function. All C programs start and finish execution in the function `main`.

The function main might call other functions along the way, and they might, in turn, call more functions. Control eventually returns to the function main, and when main ends, the program ends (provided something did not cause the program to terminate prematurely).

In this chapter, we provide an introduction to functions in C. We begin by examining several short programs in order to get a sense of the C syntax involving functions. Next, we examine how functions are implemented, examining the low-level operations necessary for functions to work in high-level languages. In the last part of the chapter, we apply our problem-solving methodology to some programming problems that benefit from the use of functions.

14.2 Functions in C

Let's start off with a simple example of a C program involving functions. Figure 14.1 is a program that prints a message using a function named PrintBanner. This program begins execution at the function main, which then calls the function PrintBanner. This function prints a line of text consisting of the = character to the output device.

PrintBanner is the simplest form of a function: it requires no input from its caller to do its job, and it provides its caller with no output data (not counting the banner printed to the screen). In other words, no arguments are passed from main to PrintBanner and no value is returned from PrintBanner to main. We refer to the function main as the *caller* and to PrintBanner as the *callee*.

14.2.1 A Function with a Parameter

The fact that PrintBanner and main require no exchange of information simplifies their interface. In general, however, we'd like to be able to pass some information between the caller and the callee. The next example demonstrates

```
 1   #include <stdio.h>
 2
 3   void PrintBanner();      /* Function declaration */
 4
 5   int main()
 6   {
 7      PrintBanner();        /* Function call        */
 8      printf("A simple C program.\n");
 9      PrintBanner();
10   }
11
12   void PrintBanner()       /* Function definition  */
13   {
14      printf("=============================\n");
15   }
```

Figure 14.1 A C program that uses a function to print a banner message

```
1    #include <stdio.h>
2
3    int Factorial(int n);               /*! Function Declaration !*/
4
5    int main()                          /*  Definition for main   */
6    {
7      int number;                       /*  Number from user      */
8      int answer;                       /*  Answer of factorial   */
9
10     printf("Input a number: ");       /*  Call to printf        */
11
12     scanf("%d", &number);             /*  Call to scanf         */
13
14     answer = Factorial(number);       /*! Call to factorial     !*/
15
16     printf("The factorial of %d is %d\n", number, answer);
17   }
18
19   int Factorial(int n)                /*! Function Definition   !*/
20   {
21     int i;                            /*  Iteration count       */
22     int result = 1;                   /*  Initialized result    */
23
24     for (i = 1; i <= n; i++)          /*  Calculate factorial   */
25       result = result * i;
26
27     return result;                    /*! Return to caller      !*/
28   }
```

Figure 14.2 A C program to calculate factorial

how this is done in C. The code in Figure 14.2 contains a function Factorial that performs an operation based on an input parameter.

Factorial performs a multiplication of all integers between 1 and n, where n is the value provided by the caller function (in this case main). The calculation performed by this function can be algebraically stated as:

$$\text{factorial}(n) = n! = 1 \times 2 \times 3 \times \ldots \times n$$

The value calculated by this function is named result in the C code in Figure 14.2. Its value is returned (using the return statement) to the caller. We say that the function Factorial requires a single integer *argument* from its caller, and it *returns* an integer value back to its caller. In this particular example, the variable answer in the caller is assigned the return value from Factorial (line 14).

Let's take a closer look at the syntax involved with functions in C. In the code in Figure 14.2, there are four lines that are of particular interest to us. The *declaration* for Factorial is at line 3. Its *definition* starts at line 19. The call to Factorial is at line 14; this statement invokes the function. The return from Factorial back to its caller is at line 27.

The Declaration

In the preceding example, the function declaration for Factorial appears at line 3. What is the purpose of a function's declaration? It informs the compiler about some relevant properties of the function in the same way a variable's declaration informs the compiler about a variable. Sometimes called a *function prototype*, a function declaration contains the name of the function, the type of value it returns, and a list of input values it expects. The function declaration ends with a semicolon.

The first item appearing in a function's declaration is the type of the value the function returns. The type can be any C data type (e.g., int, char, double). This type describes the type of the single output value that the function produces. Not all functions return values. For example, the function PrintBanner from the previous example did not return a value. If a function does not return a value, then its return type must be declared as void, indicating to the compiler that the function returns nothing.

The next item on the declaration is the function's name. A function's name can be any legal C identifier. Often, programmers choose function names somewhat carefully to reflect the actions performed by the function. Factorial, for example, is a good choice for the function in our example because the mathematical term for the operation it performs is *factorial*. Also, it is good style to use a naming convention where the names of functions and the names of variables are easily distinguishable. In the examples in this book, we do this by capitalizing the first character of all function names, such as Factorial.

Finally, a function's declaration also describes the type and order of the input *parameters* required by the function. These are the types of values that the function expects to receive from its callers and the order in which it expects to receive them. We can optionally specify (and often do) the name of each parameter in the declaration. For example, the function Factorial takes one integer value as an input parameter, and it refers to this value internally as n. Some functions may not require any input. The function PrintBanner requires no input parameters; therefore its parameter list is empty.

The Call

Line 14 in our example is the function call that invokes Factorial. In this statement, the function main calls Factorial. Before Factorial can start, however, main must transmit a single integer value to Factorial. Such values within the caller that are transmitted to the callee are called *arguments*. Arguments can be any legal expression, but they should match the type expected by the callee. These arguments are enclosed in parentheses immediately after the callee's name. In this example, the function main passes the value of the variable number as the argument. The value returned by Factorial is then assigned to the integer variable answer.

The Definition

The code beginning at line 19 is the function definition for Factorial. Notice that the first line of the definition matches the function declaration (however, minus the semicolon). Within the parentheses after the name of the function is the function's *formal parameter list*. The formal parameter list is a list of variable declarations, where each variable will be initialized with the corresponding argument provided by the caller. In this example, when `Factorial` is called on line 14, the parameter `n` will be initialized to the value of `number` from `main`. From every place in the program where a function is called, the actual arguments appearing in each call should match the type and ordering of the formal parameter list.

The function's body appears in the braces following the parameter list. A function's body consists of declarations and statements that define the computation the function performs. Any variable declared within these braces is local to the function.

A very important concept to realize about functions in C is that none of the local variables of the caller are explicitly visible by the callee function. And in particular, `Factorial` cannot modify the variable `number`. In C, the arguments of the caller are *passed as values* to the callee.

The Return Value

In line 27, control passes back from `Factorial` to the caller `main`. Since `Factorial` is returning a value, an expression must follow the `return` keyword, and the type of this expression should match the return type declared for the function. In the case of `Factorial`, the statement `return result;` transmits the calculated value stored in `result` back to the caller. In general, functions that return a value must include at least one `return` statement in their body. Functions that do not return a value—functions declared as type `void`—do not require a `return` statement; the `return` is optional. For these functions, control passes back to the caller after the last statement has executed.

What about the function `main`? Its type is `int` (as required by the ANSI standard), yet it does not contain a return. Strictly speaking, we should include a `return 0` at the end of `main` in the examples we've seen thus far. In C, if a non-`void` function does not explicitly return a value, the value of the last statement is returned to the caller. Since `main`'s return value will be ignored by most callers (who are the callers of `main`?), we've omitted them in the text to make our examples more compact.

Let's summarize these various syntactic components: A function declaration (or prototype) informs the compiler about the function, indicating its name, the number and types of parameters the function expects from a caller, and the type of value the function returns. A function definition is the actual source code for the function. The definition includes a formal parameter list, which indicates the names of the function's parameters and the order in which they will be expected from the caller. A function is invoked via a function call. Input values, or arguments, for the function are listed within the parentheses of the function call. Literally, the value of each argument listed in the function call is assigned to the corresponding parameter in the parameter list, the first argument assigned to the first parameter, the second argument to the second parameter, and so forth. The return value is the output of the function, and it is passed back to the caller function.

14.2.2 Example: Area of a Ring

We further demonstrate C function syntax with a short example in Figure 14.3. This C program calculates the area of a circle that has a smaller circle removed from it. In other words, it calculates the area of a ring with a specified outer and inner radius. In this program, a function is used to calculate the area of a circle with a given radius. The function AreaOfCircle takes a single parameter of type double and returns a double value back to the caller.

The following point is important for us to reiterate: when function AreaOfCircle is active, it can "see" and modify its local variable pi and its parameter radius. It cannot, however, modify any of the variables within the function main, except via the value it returns.

The function AreaOfCircle in this example has a slightly different usage than the functions that we've seen in the previous examples in this chapter. Notice that there are multiple calls to AreaOfCircle from the function main. In this case, AreaOfCircle performs a useful, primitive computation such that encapsulating it into a function is beneficial. On a larger scale, real programs will include functions that are called from hundreds or thousands of different places. By forming

```c
1    #include <stdio.h>
2
3    /* Function declarations */
4    double AreaOfCircle(double radius);
5
6    int main()
7    {
8      double outer;                           /* Outer radius */
9      double inner;                           /* Inner radius */
10     double areaOfRing;                      /* Area of ring */
11
12     printf("Enter inner radius: ");
13     scanf("%lf", &outer);
14
15     printf("Enter outer radius: ");
16     scanf("%lf", &inner);
17
18     areaOfRing = AreaOfCircle(outer) - AreaOfCircle(inner);
19     printf("The area of the ring is %f\n", areaOfRing);
20   }
21
22   /* Calculate area of circle given a radius */
23   double AreaOfCircle(double radius)
24   {
25     double pi = 3.14159265;
26
27     return pi * radius * radius;
28   }
```

Figure 14.3   A C program calculates the area of a ring

`AreaOfCircle` and similar primitive operations into functions, we potentially save on the amount of code in the program, which is beneficial for code maintenance. The program also takes on a better structure. With `AreaOfCircle`, the intent of the code is more visibly apparent than if the formula were directly embedded in-line.

Some of you might remember our discussion on constant values from Section 12.6.2, where we argue that the variable `pi` should be declared as a constant using the `const` qualifier on line 25 of the code. We omit it here to make the example accessible to those who that might have skipped over the Additional Topics section of Chapter 12.

14.3   Implementing Functions in C

Let's now take a closer look at how functions in C are implemented at the machine level. Functions are the C equivalent of subroutines in LC-3 assembly language (which we discussed in Chapter 9), and the core of their operation is the same. In C, making a function call involves three basic steps: (1) the parameters from the caller are passed to the callee and control is transfered to the callee, (2) the callee does its task, (3) a return value is passed back to the caller, and control returns to the caller. An important constraint that we will put on the calling mechanism is that a function should be *caller-independent*. That is, a function should be callable from any function. In this section we will examine how this is accomplished using the LC-3 to demonstrate.

14.3.1   Run-Time Stack

Before we proceed, we first need to discuss a very important component of functions in C and other modern programming languages. We require a way to "activate" a function when it is called. That is, when a function starts executing, its local variables must be given locations in memory. Let us explain:

Each function has a memory template in which its local variables are stored. Recall from our discussion in Section 12.5.2 that an activation record for a function is a template of the relative positions of its local variables in memory. Each local variable declared in a function will have a position in the activation record. Recall that the frame pointer (R5) indicates the start of the activation record. *Question:* Where in memory does the activation record of a function reside? Let's consider some options.

Option 1: The compiler could systematically assign spots in memory for each function to place its activation record. Function A might be assigned memory location X to place its activation record, function B might be assigned location Y, and so forth, provided, of course, that the activation records do not overlap. While this seems like the most straightforward way to manage the allocation, a serious limitation arises with this option. What happens if function A calls itself? We call this *recursion*, and it is a very important programming concept that we will discuss in Chapter 17. If function A calls itself, then the callee version of function A will overwrite the local values of the caller version of function A, and

the program will not behave as we expect it to. For the C programming language, which allows recursive functions, option 1 will not work.

Option 2: Every time a function is called, an activation record is allocated for it in memory. And when the function returns to the caller, its activation record is reclaimed to be assigned later to another function. While this option appears to be conceptually more difficult than option 1, it permits functions to be recursive. Each *invocation* of a function gets its own space in memory for its locals. For example, if function A calls function A, the callee version will be allocated its own activation record for storing local values, and this record will be different than the caller's. There is a factor that reduces the complexity of making option 2 work: The calling pattern of functions (i.e., function A calls B which calls C, etc.) can be easily tracked with a stack data structure (Chapter 10). Let us demonstrate with an example.

The code in Figure 14.4 contains three functions, main, Watt, and Volta. What each function does is not important for this example, so we've omitted some of their details but provided enough so that the calling pattern between them is

```
1   int main()
2   {
3      int a;
4      int b;
5
6      :
7      b = Watt(a);           /* main calls both    */
8      b = Volta(a, b);
9   }
10
11  int Watt(int a)
12  {
13     int w;
14
15     :
16     w = Volta(w, 10);      /* Watt calls Volta   */
17
18     return w;
19  }
20
21  int Volta(int q, int r)
22  {
23     int k;
24     int m;
25
26     :                      /* Volta calls no one */
27     return k;
28  }
```

Figure 14.4   Code example that demonstrates the stack-like nature of function calls

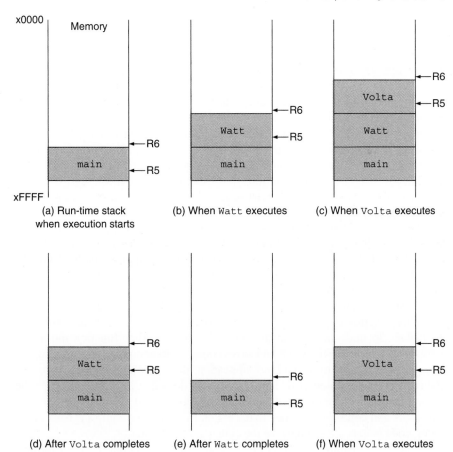

Figure 14.5   Several snapshots of the run-time stack while the program outlined in
Figure 14.4 executes

apparent. The function `main` calls `Watt` and `Watt` calls `Volta`. Eventually, control
returns back to `main` which then calls `Volta`.

Each function has an activation record that consists of its local variables,
some bookkeeping information, and the incoming parameters from the caller
(we'll mention more about the parameters and bookkeeping information in the
subsequent paragraphs). Whenever a function is called, its activation record will
be allocated somewhere in memory, and as we indicated in the previous paragraph,
in a stack-like fashion. This is illustrated in the diagrams of Figure 14.5.

Each of the shaded regions represents the activation record of a particular
function call. The sequence of figures shows how the run-time stack grows and
shrinks as the various functions are called and return to their caller. Keep in mind
that, as we push items onto the stack, the top of the stack moves, or "grows,"
toward lower-numbered memory locations.

Figure 14.5(a) is a picture of the run-time stack when the program starts
execution. Since the execution of a C program starts in `main`, the activation record

for `main` is the first to be allocated on the stack. Figure 14.5(b) shows the run-time stack immediately after `Watt` is called by `main`. Notice that the activation records are allocated in a stack-like fashion. That is, whenever a function is called, its activation record is *pushed* onto the stack. Whenever the function returns, its activation is *popped* off the stack. Figure 14.5 parts (c) through (f) show the state of the run-time stack at various points during the execution of this code. Notice that R5 points to some internal location within the activation record (it points to the base of the local variables). Also notice how R6 always points to the very top of the stack—it is called the stack pointer. Both of these registers have a key role to play in the implementation of the run-time stack and of functions in C in general.

14.3.2 Getting It All to Work

It is clear that there is a lot of work going on at the machine level when a function is called. Parameters must be passed, activation records pushed and popped, control moved from one function to another. Some of this work is accomplished by the caller, some by the callee.

To accomplish all of this, the following steps are required: First, code in the caller function copies its arguments into a region of memory accessible by the callee. Second, the code at the beginning of the callee function pushes its activation record onto the stack and saves some bookkeeping information so that when control returns to the caller, it appears to the caller as if its local variables and registers were untouched. Third, the callee does its thing. Fourth, when the callee function has completed its job, its activation record is popped off the run-time stack and control is returned to the caller. Finally, once control is back in the caller, code is executed to retrieve the callee's return value.

Now we'll examine the actual LC-3 code for carrying out these operations. We do so by examining the LC-3 code associated with the following function call: `w = Volta(w, 10);` from line 18 of the code in Figure 14.4.

The Call

In the statement `w = Volta(w, 10);`, the function `Volta` is called with two arguments. The value returned by `Volta` is then assigned to the local integer variable `w`. In translating this function call, the compiler generates LC-3 code that does the following:

1. Transmits the value of the two arguments to the function `Volta` by pushing them directly onto the top of the run-time stack. Recall that R6 points to the top of the run-time stack. That is, it contains the address of the data item currently at the top of the run-time stack. To push an item onto the stack, we first decrement R6 and then store the data value using R6 as a base address. In the LC-3, the arguments of a C function call are pushed onto the stack from **right-to-left** in order they appear in the function call. In the case of `Watt`, we will first push the value 10 (rightmost argument) and then the value of `w`.

2. Transfers control to `Volta` via the `JSR` instruction.

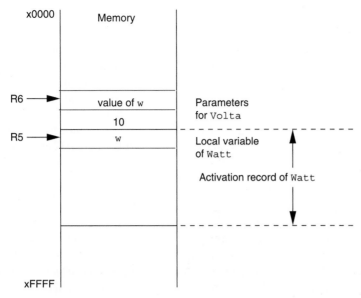

Figure 14.6   The run-time stack Watt pushes the values it wants to pass to Volta

The LC-3 code to perform this function call looks like this:

```
AND   R0, R0, #0   ; R0 <-  0
ADD   R0, R0, #10  ; R0 <- 10
ADD   R6, R6, #-1  ;
STR   R0, R6, #0   ; Push 10

LDR   R0, R5, #0   ; Load w
ADD   R6, R6, #-1  ;
STR   R0, R6, #0   ; Push w

JSR   Volta
```

Figure 14.6 illustrates the modifications made to the run-time stack by these instructions. Notice that the argument values are pushed immediately on top of the activation record of the caller (Watt). The activation record for the callee (Volta) will be constructed on the stack directly on top of the record of the caller.

Starting the Callee Function

The instruction executed immediately after the JSR in the function Watt is the first instruction in the callee function Volta.

The code at the beginning of the callee handles some important bookkeeping associated with the call. The very first thing is the allocation of memory for the return value. The callee will push a memory location onto the stack by decrementing the stack pointer. And this location will be written with the return value prior to the return to the caller.

Next, the callee function saves enough information about the caller so that eventually when the called has finished, the caller can correctly regain program control. In particular, we will need to save the caller's return address, which is in R7 (Why is it in R7? Recall how the JSR instruction works.) and the caller's frame pointer, which is in R5. It is important to make a copy of the caller's frame pointer, which we call the *dynamic link*, so that when control returns to the caller it will be able once again to access its local variables. If either the return address or the dynamic link is destroyed, then we will have trouble restarting the caller correctly when the callee finishes. Therefore it is important that we make copies of both in memory.

Finally, when all of this is done, the callee will allocate enough space on the stack for its local variables by adjusting R6, and it will set R5 to point to the base of its locals.

To recap, here is the list of actions that need to happen at the beginning of a function:

1. The callee saves space on the stack for the return value. The return value is located immediately on top of the parameters for the callee.
2. The callee pushes a copy of the return address in R7 onto the stack.
3. The callee pushes a copy of the dynamic link (caller's frame pointer) in R5 onto the stack.
4. The callee allocates enough space on the stack for its local variables and adjusts R5 to point to the base of the local variables and R6 to point to the top of the stack.

The code to accomplish this for `Volta` is:

```
Volta:
  ADD R6, R6, #-1  ; Allocate spot for the return value

  ADD R6, R6, #-1  ;
  STR R7, R6, #0   ; Push R7 (Return address)

  ADD R6, R6, #-1  ; Push R5 (Caller's frame pointer)
  STR R5, R6, #0   ; We call this the dynamic link

  ADD R5, R6, #-1  ; Set new frame pointer
  ADD R6, R6, #-2  ; Allocate memory for Volta's locals
```

Figure 14.7 summarizes the changes to memory accomplished by the code we have encountered so far. The layout in memory of these two activation records—one for `Watt` and one for `Volta`—is apparent. Notice that some entries of the activation record of `Volta` are written by `Watt`. In particular, these are the parameter fields of `Volta`'s activation record. `Watt` writes the value of its local variable w as the first parameter and the value 10 for the second parameter. Keep in mind that these values are pushed from right to left according to their position in the function call. Therefore, the value of w appears on top of the value 10. Once

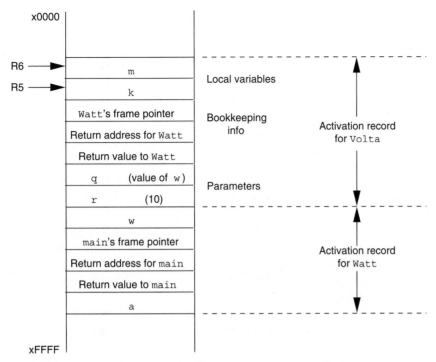

Figure 14.7   The run-time stack after the activation record for `Volta` is pushed onto the stack

invoked, `Volta` will refer to these values with the names `q` and `r`. Question: What are the initial values of `Volta`'s local variable? Recall from Chapter 11 that local variables such as these are uninitialized. See Exercise 14.10 for an exercise on the initial values of local variables.

Notice that each activation record on the stack has the same structure. Each activation record contains locations for the function's local variables, for the bookkeeping information (consisting of the caller's return address and dynamic link), the return value, and the function's parameters.

Ending the Callee Function

Once the callee function has completed its work, it must perform several tasks prior to returning control to the caller function. Firstly, a function that returns a value needs a mechanism for the return value to be transmitted properly to the caller function. Secondly, the callee must pop the current activation record. To enumerate,

1. If there is a return value, it is written into the return value entry of the activation record.
2. The local variables are popped off the stack.
3. The dynamic link is restored.
4. The return address is restored.
5. The RET instruction returns control to the caller function.

The LC-3 instructions corresponding to this for `Volta` are

```
LDR   R0, R5, #0   ; Load local variable k
STR   R0, R5, #3   ; Write it in return value slot

ADD   R6, R5, #1   ; Pop local variables

LDR   R5, R6, #0   ; Pop the dynamic link
ADD   R6, R6, #1   ;

LDR   R7, R6, #0   ; Pop the return address
ADD   R6, R6, #1   ;

RET
```

The first two instructions write the return value, which in this case is the local variable k, into the return value entry of `Volta`'s activation record. Next, the local variables are popped by moving the stack pointer to the location immediately below the frame pointer. The dynamic link is restored, then the return address is restored, and finally we return to the caller.

You should keep in mind that even though the activation record for `Volta` is popped off the stack, the values remain in memory.

Returning to the Caller Function

After the callee function executes the RET instruction, control is passed back to the caller function. In some cases, there is no return value (if the callee is declared of type `void`) and, in some cases, the caller function ignores the return value. Again, from our previous example, the return value is assigned to the variable w in `Watt`.

In particular, there are two actions that must be performed:

1. The return value (if there is one) is popped off the stack.
2. The arguments are popped off the stack.

The code after the JSR looks like the following:

```
JSR   Volta

LDR   R0, R6, #0   ; Load the return value
                   ; at the top of stack
STR   R0, R5, #0   ; w = Volta(w, 10);
ADD   R6, R6, #1   ; Pop return value

ADD   R6, R6, #2   ; Pop arguments
```

Once this code is done, the call is now complete and the caller function can resume its normal operation. Notice that prior to the return to the caller, the callee restores the environment of the caller. To the caller, it appears as if nothing has changed except that a new value (the return value) has been pushed onto the stack.

Caller Save/Callee Save

Before we complete our discussion of the implementation of functions, we need to cover a topic that we've so far swept under the rug. During the execution of a function, R0 through R3 can contain temporary values that are part of an ongoing computation. Registers R4 through R7 are reserved for other purposes: R4 is the pointer to the global data section, R5 is the frame pointer, R6 is the stack pointer, and R7 is used to hold return addresses. If we make a function call, based on the calling convention we've described R4 through R7 do not change or change in predetermined ways. But what happens to registers R0, R1, R2, and R3? In the general case, we'd like to make sure that the callee function does not overwrite them. To address this, calling conventions typically adopt one of two strategies: (1) The caller will save these registers by pushing them onto its activation record. This is called the *caller-save* convention. (We also discussed this in Chapter 9.) When control is returned to the caller, the caller will restore these registers by popping them off the stack. (2) Alternatively, the callee can save these registers by adding four fields in the bookkeeping area of its record. This is called the *callee-save* convention. When the callee is initiated, it will save R0 through R3 and R5 and R7 into the bookkeeping region and restore these registers prior to the return to the caller.

14.3.3 Tying It All Together

The code for the function call in Watt and the beginning and end of Volta is listed in Figure 14.8. The LC-3 code segments presented in the previous sections are all combined, showing the overall structure of the code. This code is more optimized than the previous individual code segments. We've combined the manipulation of the stack pointer R6 associated with pushing and popping the return value into single instructions.

To summarize, our LC-3 C calling convention involves a series of steps that are performed when a function calls another function. The caller function pushes the value of each parameter onto the stack and performs a Jump To Subroutine (JSR) to the callee. The callee allocates a space for the return value, saves some bookkeeping information about the caller, and then allocates space on the stack for its local variables. The callee then proceeds to carry out its task. When the task is complete, the callee writes the return value into the space reserved for it, pops and restores the bookkeeping information, and returns to the caller. The caller then pops the return value and the parameters it placed on the stack and resumes its execution.

You might be wondering why we would go through all these steps just to make a function call. That is, is all this code really required and couldn't the calling convention be made simpler? One of the characteristics of real calling conventions is that in the general case, any function should be able to call any other function. To enable this, the calling convention should be organized so that a caller does not need to know anything about a callee except its interface (that is, the type of value the callee returns and the types of values it expects as parameters). Likewise, a callee is written to be independent of the functions that call it. Because of this generality, the calling convention for C functions require the steps we have outlined here.

```
1    Watt:
2        ...
3        AND   R0, R0, #0   ; R0 <- 0
4        ADD   R0, R0, #10  ; R0 <- 10
5        ADD   R6, R6, #-1  ;
6        STR   R0, R6, #0   ; Push 10
7        LDR   R0, R5, #0   ; Load w
8        ADD   R6, R6, #-1  ;
9        STR   R0, R6, #0   ; Push w
10
11       JSR   Volta
12
13       LDR   R0, R6, #0   ; Load the return value at top of stack
14       STR   R0, R5, #0   ; w = Volta(w, 10);
15       ADD   R6, R6, #3   ; Pop return value, arguments
16       ...
17
18   Volta:
19       ADD R6, R6, #-2  ; Push return value
20       STR R7, R6, #0   ; Push return address
21       ADD R6, R6, #-1  ; Push R5 (Caller's frame pointer)
22       STR R5, R6, #0   ; We call this the dynamic link
23       ADD R5, R6, #-1  ; Set new base pointer
24       ADD R6, R6, #-2  ; Allocate memory for Volta's locals
25
26       ...             ; Volta performs its work
27
28       LDR   R0, R5, #0   ; Load local variable k
29       STR   R0, R5, #3   ; Write it in return value slot
30       ADD   R6, R5, #1   ; Pop local variables
31       LDR   R5, R6, #0   ; Pop the dynamic link
32       ADD   R6, R6, #1   ;
33       LDR   R7, R6, #0   ; Pop the return address
34       ADD   R6, R6, #1   ;
35       RET
```

Figure 14.8   The LC-3 code corresponding to a C function call and return

14.4 Problem Solving Using Functions

For functions to be useful to us, we must somehow integrate them into our programming problem-solving methodology. In this section we will demonstrate the use of functions through two example problems, with each example demonstrating a slightly different application of functions.

Conceptually, functions are a good point of division during the top-down design of an algorithm from a problem. As we decompose a problem, natural "components" will appear in the tasks that are to be performed by the algorithm. And these components are natural candidates for functions. Our first example involves converting text from lowercase into uppercase, and it presents an example of a component function that is naturally apparent during the top-down design process.

Functions are also useful for encapsulating primitive operations that the program requires at various spots in the code. By creating such a function, we are in a sense extending the set of operations of the programming language, tailoring them to the specific problem at hand. In the case of the second problem, which determines Pythagorean Triples, we will develop a primitive function to calculate x^2 to assist with the calculation.

14.4.1 Problem 1: Case Conversion

In this section, we go through the development of a program that reads input from the keyboard and echos it back to the screen. We have already seen an example of a program that does just this in Chapter 13 (see Figure 13.8). However, this time, we throw in a slight twist: We want the program to convert lowercase characters into uppercase before echoing them onto the screen.

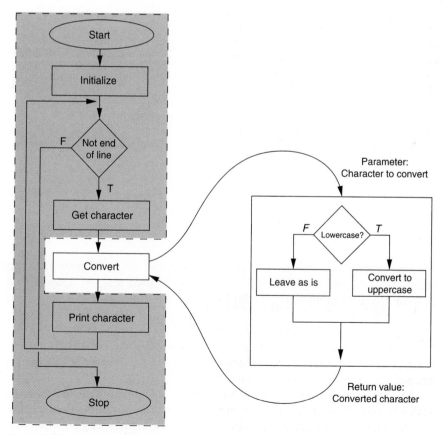

Figure 14.9   The decomposition into smaller subtasks of a program that converts input characters into uppercase

```
1    #include <stdio.h>
2
3    /* Function declaration */ char ToUpper(char inchar);
4
5    /* Function main:                                        */
6    /* Prompt for a line of text, Read one character,        */
7    /* convert to uppercase, print it out, then get another  */
8    int main()
9    {
10     char echo = 'A';          /* Initialize input character */
11     char upcase;                  /* Converted character     */
12
13     while (echo != '\n') {
14        scanf("%c", &echo);
15        upcase = ToUpper(echo);
16        printf("%c", upcase);
17     }
18   }
19
20   /* Function ToUpper:                                      */
21   /* If the parameter is lower case return                 */
22   /* its uppercase ASCII value                             */
23   char ToUpper(char inchar)
24   {
25     char outchar;
26
27     if ('a' <= inchar && inchar <= 'z')
28        outchar = inchar - ('a' - 'A');
29     else
30        outchar = inchar;
31
32     return outchar;
33   }
```

Figure 14.10 A program with a function to convert lowercase letters to uppercase

Our approach to solving this problem is to use the echo program from Figure 13.8 as a starting point. The previous code used a while loop to read an input character from the keyboard and then print it to the output device. To this basic structure, we want to add a component that checks if a character is lowercase and converts it to uppercase if it is. There is a single input and a single output. We could add code to perform this directly into the while loop, but given the self-contained nature of this component, we will create a function to do this job.

The conversion function is called after each character is scanned from the keyboard and before it is displayed to the screen. The function requires a single character as a parameter and returns either the same character (for cases in which the character is already uppercase or is not a character of the alphabet) or it will return an uppercase version of the character. Figure 14.9 shows the flow of this program. The flowchart of the original echo program is shaded. To this original flowchart, we are adding a component function to perform the conversion.

Figure 14.10 shows the complete C program. It takes input from the keyboard, converts each input character into uppercase, and prints out the result. When the input character is the new line character, the program terminates. The conversion process from lowercase to uppercase is done by the function `ToUpper`. Notice the use of ASCII literals in the function body to perform the actual conversion. Keep in mind that a character in single quotes (e.g., `'A'`) is evaluated as the ASCII value of that character. The expression `'a'` - `'A'` is therefore the ASCII value of the character `a` minus the ASCII of `A`.

14.4.2 Problem 2: Pythagorean Triples

Now we'll attempt a programming problem involving calculating all Pythagorean Triples less than a particular input value. A Pythagorean Triple is a set of three **integer** values a, b, and c that satisfy the property $c^2 = a^2 + b^2$. In other words, a and b are the lengths of the sides of a right triangle where c is the hypotenuse. For example, 3, 4, and 5 is a Pythagorean Triple. The problem here is to calculate all Triples a, b, and c where all are less than a limit provided by the user.

For this problem, we will attempt to find all Triples by brute force. That is, if the limit indicated by the user is `max`, we will check all combinations of three integers less than `max` to see if they satisfy the Triple property. In order to check all combinations, we will want to vary each `sideA`, `sideB`, and `sideC` from 1 to `max`. This implies the use of counter-controlled loops. More exactly, we will want to use a `for` loop to vary `sideC`, another to vary `sideB`, and another to vary `sideA`, each *nested* within the other. At the core of these loops, we will check to see if the property holds for the three values, and if so, we'll print them out.

Now, in performing the Triple check, we will need to evaluate the following expression.

```
(sideC * sideC == (sideA * sideA + sideB * sideB))
```

Because the square operation is a primitive operation for this problem—meaning it is required in several spots—we will encapsulate it into a function `Squared` that returns the square of its integer parameter. The preceding expression will be rewritten as follows. Notice that this code gives a clearer indication of what is being calculated.

```
(Squared(sideC) == Squared(sideA) + Squared(sideB))
```

The C program for this is provided in Figure 14.11. There are better ways to calculate Triples than with a brute-force technique of checking all combinations (Can you modify the code to run more efficiently?); the brute-force technique suits our purposes of demonstrating the use of functions.

```
1    #include <stdio.h>
2
3    int Squared(int x);
4
5    int main()
6    {
7       int sideA;
8       int sideB;
9       int sideC;
10      int maxC;
11
12      printf("Enter the maximum length of hypotenuse: ");
13      scanf("%d", &maxC);
14
15      for (sideC = 1; sideC <= maxC; sideC++) {
16        for (sideB = 1; sideB <= maxC; sideB++) {
17          for (sideA = 1; sideA <= maxC; sideA++) {
18            if (Squared(sideC) == Squared(sideA) + Squared(sideB))
19              printf("%d %d %d\n", sideA, sideB, sideC);
20          }
21        }
22      }
23   }
24
25   /* Calculate the square of a number */
26   int Squared(int x)
27   {
28      return x * x;
29   }
```

Figure 14.11 A C program that calculates Pythagorean Triples

14.5 Summary

In this chapter, we introduced the concept of functions in C. The general notion of subprograms such as functions have been part of programming languages since the earliest languages. Functions are useful because they allow us to create new primitive building blocks that might be useful for a particular programming task (or for a variety of tasks). In a sense, they allow us to extend the native operations and constructs supported by the language.

The key notions that you should take away from this chapter are:

- **Syntax of functions in C.** To use a function in C, we must declare the function using a function declaration (which we typically do at the beginning of our code) that indicates the function's name, the type of value the function returns, and the types and order of values the function expects as inputs. A function's definition contains the actual code for the function. A function is invoked when a call to it is executed. A function call contains arguments—values that are to be passed to the function as parameters.

• **Implementation of C functions at the lower level.** Part of the complexity associated with implementing functions is that in C, a function can be called from any other function in the source file (and even from functions in other object files). To assist in dealing with this, we adopt a general calling convention for calling one function from another. To assist with the fact that some functions might even call themselves, we base this calling convention on the run-time stack. The calling convention involves the caller passing the value of its arguments by pushing them onto the stack, then calling the callee. The arguments written by the caller become the parameters of the callee's activation record. The callee does its task and then pops its activation record off the stack, leaving behind its return value for the caller.

• **Using functions when programming.** It is conceivable to write all your programs without ever using functions, the result would be that your code would be hard to read, maintain, and extend and would probably be buggier than if your code used functions. Functions enable abstraction: we can write a function to perform a particular task, debug it, test it, and then use it within the program whereever it is needed.

Exercises

14.1   What is the significance of the function `main`? Why must all programs contain this function?

14.2   Refer to the structure of an activation record for these questions.

   a. What is the purpose of the dynamic link?
   b. What is the purpose of the return address?
   c. What is the purpose of the return value?

14.3   Refer to the C syntax of functions for these questions.

   a. What is a function declaration? What is its purpose?
   b. What is a function prototype?
   c. What is a function definition?
   d. What are arguments?
   e. What are parameters?

14.4   For each of the following items, identify whether the caller function or the callee function performs the action.

   a. Writing the parameters into the activation record.
   b. Writing the return value.
   c. Writing the dynamic link.
   d. Modifying the value in R5 to point within the callee function's activation record.

14.5   What is the output of the following program? Explain.

```
void MyFunc(int z);

int main()
{
  int z = 2;

  MyFunc(z);
  MyFunc(z);
}

void MyFunc(int z)
{
  printf("%d ", z);
  z++;
}
```

14.6   What is the output of the following program?

```
#include <stdio.h>

int Multiply(int d, int b);

int d = 3;

int main()
{
  int a, b, c;
  int e = 4;

  a = 1;
  b = 2;

  c = Multiply(a, b);
  printf("%d %d %d %d %d\n", a, b, c, d, e);
}

int Multiply(int d, int b)
{
  int a;
  a = 2;
  b = 3;

  return (a * b);
}
```

14.7   Following is the code for a C function named `Bump`.

```c
int Bump(int x)
{
    int a;

    a = x + 1;

    return a;
}
```

  a. Draw the activation record for `Bump`.
  b. Write one of the following in each entry of the activation record to indicate what is stored there.
  (1) Local variable
  (2) Argument
  (3) Address of an instruction
  (4) Address of data
  (5) Other
  c. Some of the entries in the activation record for `Bump` are written by the function that calls `Bump`; some are written by `Bump` itself. Identify the entries written by `Bump`.

14.8   What is the output of the following code? Explain why the function `Swap` behaves the way it does.

```c
int main()
{
    int x = 1;
    int y = 2;

    Swap(x, y);
    printf("x = %d    y = %d\n", x, y);
}

void Swap(int y, int x)
{
    int temp

    temp = x;
    x = y;
    y = temp;
}
```

14.9   Are the parameters to a function placed on the stack before or after the JSR to that function? Why?

14.10 A C program containing the function `food` has been compiled into LC-3 assembly language. The partial translation of the function into LC-3 is:

```
food:
    ADD  R6, R6, #-2   ;
    STR  R7, R6, #0    ;
    ADD  R6, R6, #-1   ;
    STR  R5, R6, #0    ;
    ADD  R5, R6, #-1   ;
    ADD  R6, R6, #-4   ;
    . . .
```

  a. How many local variables does this function have?
  b. Say this function takes two integer parameters x and y. Generate the code to evaluate the expression $x + y$.

14.11 Following is the code for a C function named `Unit`.

```
int main()
{
  int a = 1;
  int b = 2;

  a = Init(a);
  b = Unit(b);

  printf("a = %d   b = %d\n", a, b);
}

int Init(int x)
{
    int y = 2;

    return y + x;
}

int Unit(int x)
{
    int z;

    return z + x;
}
```

  a. What is the output of this program?
  b. What determines the value of local variable z when function `Unit` starts execution?

14.12 Modify the example in Figure 14.10 to also convert each character to lowercase. The new program should print out both the lower- and uppercase versions of each input character.

14.13 Write a function to print out an integer value in base 4 (using only the digits 0, 1, 2, 3). Use this function to write a program that reads two integers from the keyboard and displays both numbers and their sum in base 4 on the screen.

14.14 Write a function that returns a 1 if the first integer input parameter is evenly divisible by the second. Using this function, write a program to find the smallest number that is evenly divisible by all integers less than 10.

14.15 The following C program is compiled into LC-3 machine language and loaded into address x3000 before execution. Not counting the JSRs to library routines for I/O, the object code contains three JSRs (one to function f, one to g, and one to h). Suppose the addresses of the three JSR instructions are x3102, x3301, and x3304. And suppose the user provides 4 5 6 as input values. Draw a picture of the run-time stack, providing the contents of locations, if possible, when the program is about to return from function f. Assume the base of the run-time stack is location xEFFF.

```
#include <stdio.h>

int f(int x, int y, int z);
int g(int arg);
int h(int arg1, int arg2);

int main()
{
    int a, b, c;

    printf("Type three numbers: ");
    scanf("%d %d %d", &a, &b, &c);
    printf("%d", f(a, b, c));
}

int f(int x, int y, int z)
{
    int x1;

    x1 = g(x);
    return h(y, z) * x1;
}

int g(int arg)
{
    return arg * arg;
}

int h(int arg1, int arg2)
{
    return arg1 / arg2;
}
```

14.16 Referring once again to the machine-busy example from previous chapters, remember that we represent the busyness of a set of 16 machines with a bit pattern. Recall that a 0 in a particular bit position indicates the corresponding machine is busy and a 1 in that position indicates that machine is idle.

a. Write a function to count the number of busy machines for a given busyness pattern. The input to this function will be a bit pattern (which can be represented by an integer variable), and the output will be an integer corresponding to the number of busy machines.

b. Write a function to take two busyness patterns and determine which machines have changed state, that is, gone from busy to idle, or idle to busy. The output of this function is simply another bit pattern with a 1 in each position corresponding to a machine that has changed its state.

c. Write a program that reads a sequence of 10 busyness patterns from the keyboard and determines the average number of busy machines and the average number of machines that change state from one pattern to the next. The user signals the end of busyness patterns by entering a pattern of all 1s (all machines idle). Use the functions you developed for parts 1 and 2 to write your program.

14.17 *a.* Write a C function that mimics the behavior of a 4-to-1 multiplexor. See Figure 3.13 for a description of a 4-to-1 MUX.

b. Write a C function that mimics the behavior of the LC-3 ALU.

14.18 Notice that on a telephone keypad, the keys labeled 2, 3, 4, ..., 9 also have letters associated with them. For example, the key labeled 2 corresponds to the letters *A*, *B*, and *C*. Write a program that will map a seven-digit telephone number into all possible character sequences that the phone number can represent. For this program, use a function that performs the mapping between digits and characters. The digits 1 and 0 map to nothing.

14.19 The following C program uses a combination of global variables and local variables with different scope. What is the output?

```c
#include <stdio.h>
int t = 1;                  /* Global variable */
int sub1(int fluff);
int main ()
{
    int t = 2;
    int z;
    z = t;
    z = z + 1;
    printf("A: The variable z equals %d\n", z);

    {
        z = t;
        t = 3;

        {
            int t = 4;
            z = t;
            z = z + 1;
            printf("B: The variable z equals %d\n", z);
        }

        z = sub1(z);
        z = z + 1;
        printf("C: The variable z equals %d\n", z);
    }
    z = t;
    z = z + 1;
    printf("D: The variable z equals %d\n", z);
}

int sub1(int fluff)
{
    int i;
    i = t;
    return (fluff + i);
}
```

15

Testing and Debugging

15.1 Introduction

In December 1999, NASA mission controllers lost contact with the Mars Polar Lander as it approached the Martian surface. The Mars Polar Lander was on a mission to study the southern polar region of the Red Planet. Contact was never reestablished, and NASA announced that the spacecraft most probably crashed onto the planet's surface during the landing process. After evaluating the situation, investigators concluded that the likely cause was faulty control software that prematurely caused the on-board engines to shut down when the probe was 40 meters above the surface rather than when the probe had actually landed. The physical complexities of sending probes into space is astounding, and the software systems that control these spacecraft are no less complex. Software is as integral to a system as any mechanical or electrical subsystem, and all the more difficult to make correct because it is "invisible." It cannot be visually observed as easily as, say, a propulsion system or landing system.

Software is everywhere today. It is in your cell phone, in your automobile—even the text of this book was processed by numerous lines of software before appearing in front of you on good old-fashioned printed pages. Because software plays a vital and critical part in our world, it is important that this software behave correctly according to specification. Designing working programs is not automatic. Programs are not correct by construction. That is, just because a program is written does not mean that it functions correctly. We must test and debug it as thoroughly as possible before we can deem it to be complete.

Programmers often spend more time debugging their programs than they spend writing them. A general observation made by experts is that an experienced programmer spends as much time debugging code as he/she does writing it. Because of this inseparable relation between writing code and testing and debugging it, we introduce you to some basic concepts in testing and debugging in this chapter.

Testing is the process of exposing bugs, and debugging is the process of fixing them. Testing a piece of code involves subjecting it to as many input conditions as possible, in order to stress the software into revealing its bugs. For example, in testing the function ToUpper from the previous chapter (recall that this function returns the uppercase version of an alphabetic character passed as a parameter), we might want to pass every possible ASCII value as an input parameter and observe the function's output in order to determine if the function behaves according to specification. If the function produces incorrect output for a particular input, then we've discovered a bug. It is better to find the bug while the code is still in development than to have an unsuspecting user stumble on the bug inadvertently. It would have been better for the NASA software engineers to find the bug in the Mars Polar Lander on the surface of the earth rather than encounter it 40 meters above the surface of Mars.

Using information about a program and its execution, a programmer can apply common sense to deduce where things are going awry. Debugging a program is a bit like solving a puzzle. Like a detective at a crime scene, a programmer must examine the available clues in order to track down the source of the problem. Debugging code is significantly easier if you know how to gather information about the bug—such as the value of key variables during the execution of the program—in a systematic way.

In this chapter, we describe several techniques you can use to find and fix bugs within a program. We first describe some broad categories of errors that can creep into programs. We then describe testing methods for quickly finding these errors. We finally describe some debugging techniques for isolating and repairing these errors, and we provide some defensive programming techniques to minimize the bugs in the code you write.

15.2   Types of Errors

To better understand how to find and fix errors in programs, it is useful to get a sense of the types of errors that can creep into the programs we write. There are three broad categories of errors that you are likely to encounter in your code. *Syntactic errors* are the easiest to deal with because they are caught by the compiler. The compiler notifies us of such errors when it attempts to translate the source code into machine code, often pointing out exactly in which line the error occurred. *Semantic errors*, on the other hand, are problems that can often be very difficult to repair. They occur when the program is syntactically correct but does not behave exactly as we expected. Both syntactic and semantic errors are generally typographic errors: these occur when we type something we did not mean to type. *Algorithmic errors* are errors in which our approach to solving a

```
1    #include <stdio.h>
2
3    int main()
4    {
5        int i
6        int j;
7
8        for (i = 0; i <= 10; i++) {
9            j = i * 7;
10           printf("%d x 7 = %d\n", i, j);
11       }
12   }
```

Figure 15.1   This program contains a syntactic error

problem is wrong. They are often hard to detect and, once detected, can be very hard to fix.

15.2.1 Syntactic Errors

In C, syntactic errors (or *syntax errors* or *parse errors*) are always caught by the compiler. These occur when we ask the compiler to translate code that does not conform to the C specification. For instance, the code listed in Figure 15.1 contains a syntax error, which the compiler will flag when the code is compiled.

The declaration for the variable i is missing a semicolon. As a novice C programmer, missing semicolons and variable declarations will account for a good number of the syntax errors you will encounter. The good news is that these types of errors are easy to find, because the compiler detects them, and are easy to fix, because the compiler indicates where they occur. The real problems start once the syntax errors have been fixed and the harder semantic and algorithmic errors remain.

15.2.2 Semantic Errors

Semantic errors are similar to syntactic errors. They occur for the same reason: Our minds and our fingers are not completely coordinated when typing in a program. Semantic errors do not involve incorrect syntax; therefore, the program gets translated and we are able to execute it. It is not until we analyze the output that we discover that the program is not performing as expected. Figure 15.2 lists an example of the same program as Figure 15.1 with a simple semantic error (the syntax error is fixed). The program should print out a multiplication table for the number 7.

Here, a single execution of the program reveals the problem. Only one entry of the multiplication table is printed. You should be able to deduce, given your knowledge of the C programming language, why this program behaves incorrectly. Why is 11 x 7 = 70 printed out? This program demonstrates something called a *control flow* error. Here, the program's control flow, or the order in which statements are executed, is different than we intended.

The code listed in Figure 15.3 contains a common, but tricky semantic error involving local variables. This example is similar to the factorial program we discussed in Section 14.2.

```
1    #include <stdio.h>
2
3    int main()
4    {
5       int i;
6       int j;
7
8       for (i = 0; i <= 10; i++)
9          j = i * 7;
10         printf("%d x 7 = %d\n", i, j);
11   }
```

Figure 15.2   A program with a semantic error

This program calculates the sum of all integers less than or equal to the number input from the keyboard (i.e., it calculates $1 + 2 + 3 + \ldots + n$). Try executing this program and you will notice that the output is not what you would expect. Why doesn't it work properly? Hint: Draw out the run-time stack for an execution of this program.

Semantic errors are particularly troubling because they often go undetected by both the compiler *and* the programmer until a particular set of inputs triggers

```
1    #include <stdio.h>
2
3    int AllSum(int n);
4
5    int main()
6    {
7       int in;                      /* Input value           */
8       int sum;                     /* Value of 1+2+3+..+n    */
9
10      printf("Input a number: ");
11      scanf("%d", &in);
12
13      sum = AllSum(in);
14      printf("The AllSum of %d is %d\n", in, sum);
15   }
16
17
18   int AllSum(int n)
19   {
20      int result;                  /* Result to be returned */
21      int i;                       /* Iteration count       */
22
23      for (i = 1; i <= n; i++)     /* This calculates sum   */
24         result = result + i;
25
26      return result;               /* Return to caller      */
27   }
```

Figure 15.3   A program with a bug involving local variables

the error. Refer to the `AllSum` program in Figure 15.3, but repair the previous semantic error and notice that if the value passed to `AllSum` is less than or equal to 0 or too large, then `AllSum` may return an erroneous result because it has exceeded the range of the integer variable `result`. Fix the previous bug, compile the program, and input a number smaller than 1 and you will notice another bug.

Some errors are caught during execution because an illegal action is performed by the program. Almost all computer systems have safeguards that prevent a program from performing actions that might affect other unrelated programs. For instance, it is undesirable for a user's program to modify the memory that stores the operating system or to write a control register that might affect other programs, such as a control register that causes the computer to shut down. When such an illegal action is performed by a program, the operating system terminates its execution and prints out a *run-time error* message. Modify the `scanf` statement from the `AllSum` example to the following:

```
scanf("%d", in);
```

In this case, the ampersand character, `&`, as we shall see in Chapter 16, is a special operator in the C language. Omitting it here causes a run-time error because the program has attempted to modify a memory location to which it does not have access. We will look at this example and the reasons for the error in more detail in later chapters.

15.2.3 Algorithmic Errors

Algorithmic errors are the result of an incorrect program design. That is, the program itself behaves exactly as we designed, but the design itself was flawed. These types of errors can be hidden; they may not appear until many trials of the program have been run. Even when they are detected and isolated, they can be very hard to repair. The good news is that these types of errors can often be reduced and even eliminated by proper planning during the design phase, before any code is written.

An example of a program with a simple algorithmic flaw is provided in Figure 15.4. This code takes as input the number of a calendar year and determines if that year is a leap year or not.

At first glance, this code appears to be correct. Leap years do occur every four years. However they are skipped at the turn of every century, **except** every fourth century (i.e., the year 2000 was a leap year, but 2100, 2200, and 2300 will not be). The code works for almost all years, except those falling into these exceptional cases. We categorize this as an algorithmic error, or design flaw.

Another example of an algorithmic error also involving dates is the infamous Year 2000 computer bug, or Y2K bug. Many computer programs minimize the amount of memory required to store dates. They use enough bits to store only the last two digits of the year, and no more. Thus, the year 2000 is indistinguishable from the year 1900 (or 1800 or 2100 for that matter). This presented a problem during the recent century crossover on December 31, 1999. Say, for example, you had checked out a book from the university library in late 1999 and it was due back sometime in early 2000. If the library's computer system suffered from the

```
1   #include <stdio.h>
2
3   int main()
4   {
5     int year;
6
7     printf("Input a year (i.e., 1996): ");
8     scanf("%d", &year);
9
10    if (year % 4 == 0)
11        printf("This year is a leap year"\n);
12    else
13        printf("This year is not a leap year"\n);
14  }
```

Figure 15.4   This program to determine leap years has an algorithmic bug

Y2K bug, you would have gotten an overdue notice in the mail with some hefty fines listed on it. As a consequence, a lot of money and effort were devoted to tracking down Y2K-related bugs before January 1, 2000 rolled around.

15.3 Testing

There is an adage among seasoned programmers that any line of code that is untested is probably buggy. Good testing techniques are crucial to writing good software. What is testing? With testing, we basically put the software through trials where input patterns are applied (in order to mimic what the software might see during real operation) and the output of the program is checked for correctness. Real-world software might undergo millions of trials before it is released.

In an ideal world, we could test a program by examining its operation under every possible input condition. But for a program that is anything more than trivial, testing for every input combination is impossible. For example, if we wanted to test a program that finds prime numbers between integers A and B, where A and B are 32-bit input values, there are $(2^{32})^2$ possible input combinations. Even if we could run 1 million trials in 1 second, it would still take half a million years to completely test the program. Clearly, testing each input combination is not an option. So which input combinations do we test with? We could randomly pick inputs in hopes that some of those random patterns will expose the program's bugs. Software engineers typically rely on more systematic ways of testing their code. In particular, black-box testing is used to check if a program meets its specifications, and white-box testing targets various facets of the program's implementation in order to provide some assurance that every line of code is tested.

15.3.1 Black-Box Testing

With black-box testing, we examine if the program meets its input and output specifications, disregarding the internals of the program. That is, with black-box testing, we are concerned with what the program does and not how it does it. For example, a black-box test of the program AllSum in Figure 15.3 might involve running the program, typing an input number, and comparing the resulting output to what you calculated by hand. If the two do not match, then either the program contains a bug or your arithmetic skills are shoddy. We might continue attempting trials until we are reasonably confident that the program is functional.

For testing larger programs, the testing process is *automated* in order to run more tests per unit time. That is, we construct another program to automatically run the original program, provide some random inputs, check that the output meets specifications, and repeat. With such a process, we can clearly run many more trials than we could if a person performed each trial.

In order to automate the black-box process, however, we need a way to automatically test whether the program's output was correct or incorrect. Here, we might need to construct a checker program that is different than the original program but performs a similar computation. If the original and checker programs had the same bug, it would go undetected by the black-box testing process. For this reason, black-box testers who write checker programs are often not permitted to see the code within the black box they are testing so that we get a truly independent version of the checker.

15.3.2 White-Box Testing

For larger software systems, black-box testing is not enough. With black-box testing, it is not possible to know which lines of code have been tested and which have not, and therefore, according to the adage stated previously, all are presumed to be buggy. Black-box testing is sometimes difficult when the input or output specification of a program is not concrete. For example, black-box testing of an audio player (such as an MP3 player) might be difficult because of the inexact nature of the output. Also, black-box testing can only start once the software is complete—the software must compile and must meet some part of the specification in order to be tested.

Software engineers supplement black-box testing with white-box tests. White-box tests isolate various internal components of the software, and test whether the components conform to their intended design. For example, testing to see that each function performs correctly according to the design is a white-box test. How we divide a program into functions is part of its implementation and not its specification. We can apply the same type of testing to loops and other constructs within a function.

How might a white-box test be constructed? For many tests, we might need to modify the code itself. For example, in order to see whether a function is working correctly, we might add extra code to call the function a few extra times with different inputs and check the outputs. We might add extra printf statements to the code with which we can observe values of internal variables to see if things are working as expected. Once the code is complete and ready for release, these printf statements can be removed.

A common white-box testing technique is the use of error-detecting code strategically placed within a program. This code might check for conditions that indicate that the program is not working correctly. When an incorrect situation is detected, the code prints out a warning message, displays some relevant informa-tion about the situation, or causes the program to prematurely terminate. Since this error-detecting code *asserts* that certain conditions hold during program execution, we generally call these checks *assertions*.

For example, assertions can be used to check whether a function returns a value within an expected range. If the return value is out of this range, an error message is displayed. In the following example, we are checking whether the calculation performed by the function `IncomeTax` is within reasonable bounds. As you can deduce from this code fragment, this function calculates the income tax based on a particular income provided as a parameter to it. We do not pay more tax than we collect in income (fortunately!), and we never pay a negative tax. Here if the calculation within `IncomeTax` is incorrect, a warning message will be displayed by the assertion code.

```
tax = IncomeTax(income);

if (tax < 0 || tax > income)
    printf("Error in function IncomeTax!\n");
```

A thorough testing methodology requires the use of both black-box and white-box tests. It is important to realize that white-box tests alone do not cover the complete functionality of the software—even if all white-box tests pass, there might be a portion of the specification that is missing. Similarly, black-box tests alone do not guarantee that every line of code is tested.

15.4 Debugging

Once a bug is found, we start the process of repairing it, which can often be more tricky than finding it. Debugging an error requires full use of our reasoning skills: We observe a symptom of the error, such as bad output, and we might even have some other information, such as the place in the code where the error occurred, and from this limited information, we will need to use deduction to isolate the source of the error. The key to effective debugging is being able to quickly gather relevant information that will lead to identifying the bug, similar to the way a detective might gather evidence at a crime scene or the way a physician might perform a series of tests in order to diagnose a sick patient's illness.

There are a number of ways you can gather more information in order to diagnose a bug, ranging from ad hoc techniques that are quick and dirty to more systematic techniques that involve the use of software debugging tools.

15.4.1 Ad Hoc Techniques

The simplest thing to do once you realize that there is a problem with your program is to visually inspect the source code. Sometimes the nature of the failure tips you off to the region of the code where the bug is likely to exist. This technique is fine if the region of source code is small and you are very familiar with the code.

Another simple technique is to insert statements within the code to print out information during execution. You might print out, using `printf` statements, the values of important variables that you think will be useful in finding the bug. You can also add `printf` statements at various points within your code to see if the control flow of the program is working correctly. For example, if you wanted to quickly determine if a counter-controlled loop is iterating for the correct number of iterations, you could place a `printf` statement within the loop body. For simple programs, such ad hoc techniques are easy and reasonable to use. Large programs with intricate bugs require the use of more heavy-duty techniques.

15.4.2 Source-Level Debuggers

Often ad hoc techniques cannot provide enough information to uncover the source of a bug. In these cases, programmers often turn to a *source-level debugger* to isolate a bug. A source-level debugger is a tool that allows a program to be executed in a controlled environment, where all aspects of the execution of the program can be controlled and examined by the programmer. For example, a debugger can allow us to execute the program one statement at a time and examine the values of variables (and memory locations and registers, if we so choose) along the way. Source-level debuggers are similar to the LC-3 debugger that we described in Chapter 6, except that a source-level debugger operates in relation to high-level source code rather than LC-3 machine instructions.

For a source-level debugger to be used on a program, the program must be compiled such that the compiler augments the executable image with enough additional information for the debugger to function properly. Among other things, the debugger will need information from the compilation process in order to map every machine language instruction to its corresponding statement in the high-level source program. The debugger also needs information about variable names and their locations in memory (i.e., the symbol table). This is required so that a programmer can examine the value of any variable within the program using its name in the source code.

There are many source-level debuggers available, each of which has its own user interface. Different debuggers are available for UNIX and Windows, each with its own flavor of operation. For example, `gdb` is a free source-level debugger available on most UNIX-based platforms. All debuggers support a core set of necessary operations required to probe a program's execution, many of which are similar to the debugging features of the LC-3 debugger. So rather than describe the user interface for any one particular debugger, in this section we will describe the core set of operations that are universal to any debugger.

The core debugger commands fall into two categories: those that let you control the execution of the program and those that let you examine the value of variables and memory, etc. during the execution.

Breakpoints

Breakpoints allow us to specify points during the execution of a program when the program should be temporarily stopped so that we can examine or modify the state of the program. This is useful because it helps us examine the program's execution in the region of the code where the bug occurs.

For example, we can add a breakpoint at a particular line in the source code or at a particular function. When execution reaches that line, program execution is frozen in time, and we can examine everything about that program at that particular instance. How a breakpoint is added is specific to the user interface of the debugger. Some allow breakpoints to be added by clicking on a line of code. Others require that the breakpoint be added by specifying the line number through a command prompt.

Sometimes it is useful to stop at a line only if a certain condition is true. Such conditional breakpoints are useful for isolating specific situations in which we suspect buggy behavior. For example, if we suspect that the function `PerformCalculation` works incorrectly when its input parameter is 16, then we might want to add a breakpoint that stops execution only when x is equal to 16 in the following code:

```
for (x = 0; x < 100; x++)
    PerformCalculation(x);
```

Alternatively, we can set a *watchpoint* to stop the program at any point where a particular condition is true. For example, we can use a watchpoint to stop execution whenever the variable `LastItem` is equal to 4. This will cause the debugger to stop execution at any statement that causes `LastItem` to equal 4. Unlike breakpoints, watchpoints are not associated with any single line of the code but apply to every line.

Single-Stepping

Once the debugger reaches a breakpoint (or watchpoint), it temporarily suspends program execution and awaits our next command. At this point we can examine program state, such as values of variables, or we can continue with execution.

It is often useful to proceed from a breakpoint one statement at time—a process referred to as *single-stepping*. The LC-3 debugger has a command that executes a single LC-3 instruction and similarly a source-level debugger that allows execution to proceed one statement at a time. The single-step command executes the current source line and then suspends the program again. Most debuggers will also display the source code in a separate window so we can monitor where the program has currently been suspended. Single-stepping through a program is very useful, particularly when executing the region of a program where the bug is suspected to exist. We can set a breakpoint near the suspected region and then check the values of variables as we single-step through the code.

A common use of single-stepping is to verify that the control flow of the program does what we expect. We can single-step through a loop to verify that it performs the correct number of iterations or we can single-step through an `if-else` to verify that we have programmed the condition correctly.

Variations of single-stepping exist that allow us to skip over functions, or to skip to the last iteration of a loop. These variations are useful for skipping over code that we do not suspect to contain errors but are in the execution path between a breakpoint and the error itself.

Displaying Values

The art of debugging is about gathering the information required to logically deduce the source of the error. The debugger is the tool of choice for gathering information when debugging large programs. While execution is suspended at a breakpoint, we can gather information about the bug by examining the values of variables related to the suspected bug. Generally speaking, we can examine all execution states of the program at the breakpoint. We can examine the values of variables, memory, the stack, and even the registers. How this is done is debugger specific. Some debuggers allow you to use the mouse to point to a variable in the source code window, causing a pop-up window to display the variable's current value. Some debuggers require you to type in a command indicating the name of the variable you want to examine.

We encourage you to familiarize yourself with a source-level debugger. At the end of this chapter, we provide several problems that you can use to gain some experience with this useful debugging tool.

15.5 Programming for Correctness

Knowing how to test and debug your code is a prerequisite for being a good programmer. Great programmers know how to avoid many error-causing situations in the first place. Poor programming practices cause bugs. Being aware of some defensive programming techniques can help reduce the amount of time required to get a piece of code up and running. The battle against bugs starts before any line of code is written. Here, we provide three general methods for catching errors even before they become errors.

15.5.1 Nailing Down the Specification

Many bugs arise from poor or incomplete program specifications. Specifications sometimes do not cover all possible operating scenarios, and thus they leave some conditions open for interpretation by the programmer. For example, recall the factorial example from Chapter 14: Figure 14.2 is a program that calculates the factorial of a number typed at the keyboard. You can imagine that the specification for the program might have been "Write a program to take an integer value from the keyboard and calculate its factorial." As such, the specification is incomplete. What if the user enters a negative number? Or zero? What if the user enters a number that is too large and results in an overflow? In these cases, the code as written will not perform correctly, and it is therefore buggy. To fix this, we need to modify the specification of the program to allow the program to indicate an error if the input is less than or equal to zero, or if the input is such that $n! > 2^{31}$, implying n must be less than or equal to 31. In the code that follows we have added an input range check to the `Factorial` function from Chapter 14. Now the function prints a warning message and returns a −1 if its input parameter is out of the correct operating range.

```
1   int Factorial(int n)
2   {
3     int i;                    /* Iteration count          */
4     int result = 1;           /* Initialized result       */
5
6     /* Check for legal parameter values */
7     if (n < 1 || n > 31) {
8       printf("Bad input. Input must be >= 1 and <= 31.\n");
9       return -1;
10    }
11
12    for (i = 1; i <= n; i++)   /* Calculates factorial   */
13      result = result * i;
14
15    return result;            /* Return to caller         */
16  }
```

15.5.2 Modular Design

Functions are useful for extending the functionality of the programming language. With functions we can add new operations and constructs that are helpful for a particular programming task. In this manner, functions enable us to write programs in a modular fashion.

Once a function is complete, we can test it independently in isolation (i.e., as a white-box test) and determine that it is working as we expect. Since a typical function performs a smaller task than the complete program, it is easier to test than the entire program. Once we have tested and debugged each function in isolation, we will have an easier chance getting the program to work when everything is integrated.

This modular design concept of building a program out of simple, pretested, working components is a fundamental concept in systems design. In subsequent chapters we will introduce the concept of a *library*. A library is a collection of pretested components that all programmers can use in writing their code. Modern programming practices are heavily oriented around the use of libraries because of the benefits inherent to modular design. We design not only software, but circuits, hardware, and various other layers of the computing system using a similar modular design philosophy.

15.5.3 Defensive Programming

All seasoned programmers have techniques to prevent bugs from creeping into their code. They construct their code in a such a way that those errors that they suspect might affect the program are eliminated by design. That is, they program *defensively*. We provide a short list of general defensive programming techniques that you should adopt to avoid problems with the programs you write.

- Comment your code. Writing comments makes you think about the code you've written. Code documentation is not only a way to inform others about how your code works, but also is a process that makes you reflect on and reconsider your code. During this process you might discover that you forgot a special case or operating condition that will ultimately break your code.

- Adopt a consistent coding style. For instance, aligning opening and closing braces will let you identify simple semantic errors associated with missing braces. Along these lines, also be consistent in variable naming. The name of a variable should convey some meaningful information about the value the variable contains.

- Avoid assumptions. It is tempting to make simple, innocent assumptions when writing code, but these can ultimately lead to broken code. For example, in writing a function, we might assume that the input parameter will always be within a certain range. If this assumption is not grounded in the program's specification, then the possibility for an error has been introduced. Write code that is free of such assumptions—or at least use assertions and spot checks to indicate when the assumptions do not hold.

- Avoid global variables. While some experienced programmers rely heavily on global variables, many software engineers advocate avoiding them whenever possible. Global variables can make some programming tasks easier. However, they often make code more difficult to understand, and extend, and when a bug is detected, harder to analyze.

- Rely on the compiler. Most good compilers have an option to carefully check your program for suspicious code (for example, an uninitialized variable) or commonly misapplied code constructs (for example, using the assignment operator = instead of the equality operator ==). While these checks are not thorough, they do help identify some commonly made programming mistakes. If you are use the `gcc` compiler, use `gcc -Wall` to enable all warning messages from the compiler.

The defensive techniques mentioned here are particular to the programming concepts we've already discussed. In subsequent chapters, after we introduce new programming concepts, we also discuss how to use defensive techniques when writing programs that use them.

15.6 Summary

In this chapter, we presented methodologies for finding and fixing bugs within your code. Modern systems are increasingly reliant on software, and modern software is often very complex. In order to prevent software bugs from often rendering our cell phones unusable or from occasionally causing airplanes to crash, it is important that software tightly conform to its specifications. The key concepts that we covered in this chapter are:

- **Testing.** Finding bugs in code is not easy, particularly when the program is large. Software engineers use systematic testing to find errors in software. Black-box testing is done to validate that the behavior of a program conforms to specification. White-box testing targets the structure of a program and provides some assurance that every line of code has undergone some level of testing.

- **Debugging.** Debugging an error requires the ability to take the available information and deduce the source of the error. While ad hoc techniques can provide us with a little additional information about the bug, the source-level debugger is the software engineering tool of choice for most debugging tasks. Source-level debuggers allow a programmer to execute a program in a controlled environment and examine various values and states within the program during execution.

- **Programming for correctness.** Experienced programmers try to avoid bugs even before the first line of code is written. Often, the specification of the program is the source of bugs, and nailing down loose ends will help eliminate bugs after the code has been written. Modular design involves writing a larger program out of simple pretested functions and helps reduce the difficulty in testing a large program. Following a defensive programming style helps reduce situations that lead to buggy code.

15.1   The following programs each have a single error that prevents them from operating as specified. With as few changes as possible, correct the programs. They all should output the sum of the integers from 1 to 10, inclusive.

a.
```c
#include <stdio.h>
int main()
{
   int i = 1;
   int sum = 0;

   while (i < 11) {
      sum = sum + i;
      ++i;
      printf("%d\n", sum);
   }
}
```

b.
```c
#include <stdio.h>
int main()
{
   int i;
   int sum = 0;

   for (i = 0; i >= 10; ++i)
      sum = sum + i;
   printf("%d\n", sum);
}
```

c.
```c
#include <stdio.h>
int main()
{
   int i = 0;
   int sum = 0;

   while (i <= 11)
      sum = sum + i++;
   printf("%d\n", sum);
}
```

d.
```c
#include <stdio.h>
int main()
{
   int i = 0;
   int sum = 0;

   for (i = 0; i <= 10;)
      sum = sum + ++i;
   printf("%d\n", sum);
}
```

15.2   The following program fragments have syntax errors and therefore will not compile. Assume that all variables have been properly declared. Fix the errors so that the fragments will not cause compiler errors.

a.
```
i = 0;
j = 0;
while (i < 5)
{
    j = j + 1;
    i = j >> 1
}
```

b.
```
if (cont == 0)
    a = 2;
    b = 3;
else
    a = -2;
    b = -3;
```

c.
```
#define LIMIT 5;

if (LIMIT)
    printf("True");
else
    printf("False");
```

15.3   The following C code was written to find the minimum of a set of positive integers that a user enters from the keyboard. The user signifies the end of the set by entering the value −1. Once all the numbers have been entered and processed, the program outputs the minimum. However, the code contains an error. Identify and suggest ways to fix the error. Use a source-level debugger, if needed, to find it.

```c
#include <stdio.h>
int main()
{
    int smallestNumber = 0;
    int nextInput;

    /* Get the first input number */
    scanf("%d", &nextInput);

    /* Keep reading inputs until user enters -1 */
    while (nextInput != -1) {
        if (nextInput < smallestNumber)
            smallestNumber = nextInput;
        scanf("%d", &nextInput);
    }
    printf("The smallest number is %d\n", smallestNumber);
}
```

15.4   The following program reads in a line of characters from the keyboard and echoes only the alphabetic, numeric, and space characters. For example, if the input were "Let's meet at 6:00pm.", the output should be: "Lets meet at 600pm". The program does not work as specified. Fix it.

```c
#include <stdio.h>
int main()
{
  char echo = '0';

  while (echo != '\n') {
    scanf("%c", &echo);
    if ((echo > 'a' || echo < 'z') &&
        (echo > 'A' || echo < 'Z'))
      printf("%c", echo);
  }
}
```

15.5   Use a source-level debugger to monitor the execution of the following code:

```c
#include <stdio.h>

int IsDivisibleBy(int dividend, int divisor);

int main()
{
    int i;   /* Iteration variable            */
    int j;   /* Iteration variable            */
    int f;   /* The number of factors of a number */


    for (i = 2; i < 1000; i++) {

        f = 0;
        for (j = 2; j < i; j++) {
            if (IsDivisibleBy(i, j))
                f++;
        }
        printf("The number %d has %d factors\n", i, f);
    }
}


int IsDivisibleBy(int dividend, int divisor)

{
    if (dividend % divisor == 0)
        return 1;
    else
        return 0;
}
```

a. Set a breakpoint at the beginning of function `IsDivisibleBy` and examine the parameter values for the first 10 calls. What are they?

b. What is the value of `f` after the inner `for` loop ends and the value of `i` equals 660?

c. Can this program be written more efficiently? Hint: Monitor the value of the arguments when the return value of `IsDivisibleBy` is 1.

15.6   Using a source-level debugger, determine for what values of parameters
the function `Mystery` returns a zero.

```c
#include <stdio.h>

int Mystery(int a, int b, int c);

int main()
{
    int i;             /* Iteration variable      */
    int j;             /* Iteration variable      */
    int k;             /* Iteration variable      */
    int sum = 0;       /* running sum of Mystery  */

    for (i = 100; i > 0; i--) {
      for (j = 1; j < i; j++) {
        for (k = j; k < 100; k++)
          sum = sum + Mystery(i, j, k);
      }
    }
}

int Mystery(int a, int b, int c)
{
    int out;

    out = 3*a*a + 7*a - 5*b*b + 4*b + 5*c ;

    return out;
}
```

15.7   The following program manages flight reservations for a small airline that has only one plane that has SEATS number of seats for passengers. This program processes ticket requests from the airline's website. The command *R* requests a reservation. If there is a seat available, the reservation is approved. If there are no seats, the reservation is denied. Subsequently, a passenger with a reservation can purchase a ticket using the *P* command. This means that for every *P* command, there must be a preceding *R* command; however, not every *R* will materialize into a purchased ticket. The program ends when the *X* command is entered. Following is the program, but it contains serious design errors. Identify the errors. Propose and implement a correct solution.

```c
#include <stdio.h>

#define SEATS 10

int main()
{
  int seatsAvailable = SEATS;
  char request = '0';

  while (request != 'X') {
    scanf("%c", &request);

    if (request == 'R') {
      if (seatsAvailable)
        printf("Reservation Approved!\n");
      else
        printf("Sorry, flight fully booked.\n");
    }

    if (request == 'P') {
      seatsAvailable--;
      printf("Ticket purchased!\n");
    }
  }

  printf("Done! %d seats not sold\n", seatsAvailable);
}
```

16

Pointers and Arrays

16.1 Introduction

In this chapter, we introduce (actually, reintroduce) two simple but powerful programming constructs: pointers and arrays. We used pointers and arrays when writing LC-3 assembly code. Now, we examine them in the context of C.

A pointer is simply the address of a memory object, such as a variable. With pointers, we can *indirectly* access these objects, which provides some very useful capabilities. For example, with pointers, we can create functions that modify the arguments passed by the caller. With pointers, we can create sophisticated data organizations that grow and shrink (like the run-time stack) during a program's execution.

An array is a list of data arranged sequentially in memory. For example, in a few of the LC-3 examples from the first half of the book, we represented a file of characters as a sequence of characters arranged sequentially in memory. This sequential arrangement of characters is known as an *array* of characters. To access a particular item in an array, we need to specify which element we want. As we'll see, an expression like a[4] will access the fifth element in the array named a—it is the fifth element because we start numbering the array at element 0. Arrays are useful because they allow us to conveniently process groups of data such as vectors, matrices, lists, and character strings, which are naturally representative of certain objects in the real world.

16.2 Pointers

We begin our discussion of pointers with a classic example of their utility. In the C
program in Figure 16.1, the function Swap is designed to switch the value of its two
arguments. The function Swap is called from main with the arguments valueA,
which in this case equals 3, and valueB, which equals 4. Once Swap returns
control to main, we expect valueA and valueB to have their values swapped.
However, compile and execute the code and you will notice that the arguments
passed to Swap remain the same.

Let's examine the run-time stack during the execution of Swap to analyze
why. Figure 16.2 shows the state of the run-time stack just prior to the completion
of the function, just after the statement on line 25 has executed but before control
returns to function main. Notice that the function Swap has modified the local
copies of the parameters firstVal and secondVal within its own activation
record. When Swap finishes and control returns to main, these modified values are
lost when the activation record for Swap is popped off the stack. The values from
main's perspective have not been swapped. We have a buggy program.

In C, arguments are always passed from the caller function to the callee *by
value*. C evaluates each argument that appears in a function call as an expression
and pushes the value of the expression onto the run-time stack in order to pass
them to the function being called. For Swap to modify the arguments that the caller

```
1    #include <stdio.h>
2
3    void Swap(int firstVal, int secondVal);
4
5    int main()
6    {
7       int valueA = 3;
8       int valueB = 4;
9
10      printf("Before Swap ");
11      printf("valueA = %d and valueB = %d\n", valueA, valueB);
12
13      Swap(valueA, valueB);
14
15      printf("After Swap ");
16      printf("valueA = %d and valueB = %d\n", valueA, valueB);
17   }
18
19   void Swap(int firstVal, int secondVal)
20   {
21      int tempVal;              /* Holds firstVal when swapping */
22
23      tempVal = firstVal;
24      firstVal = secondVal;
25      secondVal = tempVal;
26   }
```

Figure 16.1   The function Swap attempts to swap the values of its two parameters

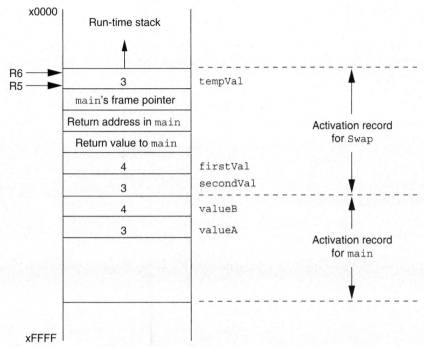

Figure 16.2   A snapshot of the run-time stack when the function Swap is about to return control to main

passes to it, it must have access to the caller function's activation record—it must access the locations at which the arguments are stored in order to modify their values. The function Swap needs the *addresses* of valueA and valueB in main in order to change their values. As we shall see in the next few sections, pointers and their associated operators enable this to happen.

16.2.1 Declaring Pointer Variables

A pointer variable contains the address of a memory object, such as a variable. A pointer is said to *point* to the variable whose address it contains. Associated with a pointer variable is the *type* of object to which it points. So, for instance, an integer pointer variable points to an integer variable. To declare a pointer variable in C, we use the following syntax:

```
int *ptr;
```

Here we have declared a variable named ptr that points to an integer. The asterisk (*) indicates that the identifier that follows is a pointer variable. C programmers will often say that ptr is of type int *star*. Similarly, we can declare

```
char *cp;
double *dp;
```

The variable cp points to a character and dp points to a double-precision floating point number. Pointer variables are initialized in a manner similar to all other variables. If a pointer variable is declared as a local variable, it will not be initialized automatically.

The syntax of declaring a pointer variable using * may seem a bit odd at first, but once we have gone through the pointer operators, the rationale behind the syntax will be more clear.

16.2.2 Pointer Operators

C has two operators for pointer-related manipulations, the address operator & and the indirection operator *.

The Address Operator &

The address operator, whose symbol is an ampersand, &, generates the memory address of its operand, which must be a memory object such as a variable. In the following code sequence, the pointer variable ptr will point to the integer variable object. The expression on the right-hand side of the second assignment statement generates the memory address of object.

```
int object;
int *ptr;

object = 4;
ptr = &object;
```

Let's examine the LC-3 code for this sequence. Both declared variables are locals and are allocated on the stack. Recall that R5, the base pointer, points to the first declared local variable, or object in this case.

```
AND  R0, R0, #0    ;    Clear R0
ADD  R0, R0, #4    ;    R0 = 4
STR  R0, R5, #0    ;    Object = 4;

ADD  R0, R5, #0    ;    Generate memory address of object
STR  R0, R5, #-1   ;    Ptr = &object;
```

Figure 16.3 shows the activation record of the function containing this code after the statement ptr = &object; has executed. In order to make things more concrete, each memory location is labeled with an address, which we've arbitrarily selected to be in the xEFF0 range. The base pointer R5 currently points to xEFF2. Notice that object contains the integer value 4 and ptr contains the memory address of object.

The Indirection Operator *

The second pointer operator is called the *indirection*, or *dereference*, operator, and its symbol is the asterisk, * (pronounced *star* in this context). This operator allows us to indirectly manipulate the value of a memory object. For example, the

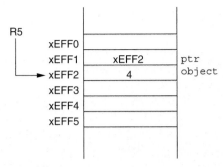

Figure 16.3   The run-time stack frame containing `object` and `ptr` after the statement
`ptr = &object` has executed

expression `*ptr` refers to the value pointed to by the pointer variable `ptr`. Recall
the previous example: `*ptr` refers to the value stored in variable `object`. Here,
`*ptr` and `object` can be used interchangeably. Adding to the previous C code
example,

```
int object;
int *ptr;

object = 4;
ptr = &object;
*ptr = *ptr + 1;
```

Essentially, `*ptr = *ptr + 1;` is another way of saying `object = object + 1;`. Just as with other types of variables we have seen, the `*ptr` means different things depending on which side of the assignment operator it appears on. On the right-hand side of the assignment operator, it refers to the value that appears at that location (in this case the value 4). On the left-hand side, it specifies the location that gets modified (in this case, the address of `object`). Let's examine the LC-3 code for the last statement in the preceding code.

```
LDR   R0, R5, #-1   ;   R0 contains the value of ptr
LDR   R1, R0, #0    ;   R1 <- *ptr
ADD   R1, R1, #1    ;   *ptr + 1
STR   R1, R0, #0    ;   *ptr = *ptr + 1;
```

Notice that this code is different from what would get generated if the final C statement had been `object = object + 1;`. With the pointer dereference, the compiler generates two `LDR` instructions for the indirection operator on the right-hand side, one to load the memory address contained in `ptr` and another to get the value stored at that address. With the dereference on the left-hand side, the compiler generates a `STR R1, R0, #0`. Had the statement been `object = *ptr + 1;`, the compiler would have generated `STR R1, R5, #0`.

16.2.3 Passing a Reference Using Pointers

Using the address and indirection operator, we can repair the Swap function from Figure 16.1 that did not quite accomplish the swap of its two input parameters. Figure 16.4 lists the same program with a revised version of Swap called NewSwap.

The first modification we've made is that the parameters of NewSwap are no longer integers but are now pointers to integers (int *). These two parameters are the memory addresses of the two variables that are to be swapped. Within the function body of NewSwap, we use the indirection operator * to obtain the values that these pointers point to.

Now when we call NewSwap from main, we need to supply the *memory addresses* for the two variables we want swapped, rather than the *values* of the variables as we did in the previous version of the code. For this, the & operator does the trick. Figure 16.5 shows the run-time stack when various statements of the function NewSwap are executed. The three subfigures (A–C) correspond to the run-time stack after lines 23, 24, and 25 execute.

By design, C passes information from the caller function to the callee by value: that is, each argument expression in the call statement is evaluated, and the resulting value is passed to the callee via the run-time stack. However, in NewSwap we created a *call by reference* for the two arguments by using the address

```
1    #include <stdio.h>
2
3    void NewSwap(int *firstVal, int *secondVal);
4
5    int main()
6    {
7      int valueA = 3;
8      int valueB = 4;
9
10     printf("Before Swap ");
11     printf("valueA = %d and valueB = %d\n", valueA, valueB);
12
13     NewSwap(&valueA, &valueB);
14
15     printf("After Swap ");
16     printf("valueA = %d and valueB = %d\n", valueA, valueB);
17   }
18
19   void NewSwap(int *firstVal, int *secondVal)
20   {
21     int tempVal;            /* Holds firstVal when swapping */
22
23     tempVal = *firstVal;
24     *firstVal = *secondVal;
25     *secondVal = tempVal;
26   }
```

Figure 16.4   The function NewSwap swaps the values of its two parameters

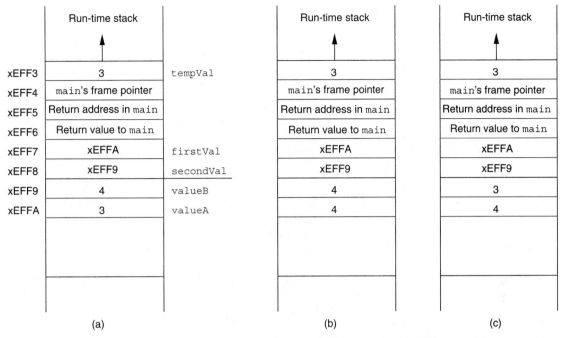

Figure 16.5   Snapshots of the run-time stack when the function `NewSwap` executes the statements in (a) line 23, (b) line 24, (c) line 25.

operator `&`. When an argument is passed as a reference, its **address** is passed to the callee function—for this to be valid, the argument must be a variable or other memory object (i.e., it must have an address). The callee function then can use the indirection operator `*` to access (and modify) the original value of the object.

16.2.4 Null Pointers

Sometimes it is convenient for us to say that a pointer points to nothing. Why such a concept is useful will be eminently clear to you when we discuss dynamic data structures such as linked lists in Chapter 19. For now, let us say that a pointer that points to nothing is a *null* pointer. In C, we make this designation with the following assignment:

```
int *ptr;

ptr = NULL;
```

Here, we are assigning the value of NULL to the pointer variable `ptr`. In C, NULL is a specially defined preprocessor macro that contains a value that no pointer should ever hold unless it is null. For example, NULL might equal 0 on a particular system because no valid memory object can exist at location 0.

16.2.5 Demystifying the Syntax

It is now time to revisit some notation that we introduced in Chapter 11. Now that we know how to pass a reference, let's reexamine the I/O library function `scanf`:

```
scanf("%d", &input);
```

Since function `scanf` needs to update the variable `input` with the decimal value read from the keyboard, `scanf` needs the address of `input` and not its value. Thus, the address operator `&` is required. If we omit the address operator, the program terminates with an error. Can you come up with a plausible reason why this happens? Why is it not possible for `scanf` to work correctly without the use of a reference?

Before we complete our introduction to pointers, let's attempt to make sense of the pointer declaration syntax. To declare a pointer variable, we use a declaration of the following form:

```
type *ptr;
```

where `type` can be any of the predefined (or programmer-defined) types such as `int`, `char`, `double`, and so forth. The name `ptr` is simply any legal variable identifier. With this declaration, we are declaring a variable that, when the `*` (dereference) operator is applied to it, generates a variable of type `type`. That is, `*ptr` is of type `type`.

We can also declare functions to return a pointer type (why we would want to do so will be more apparent in later chapters). For example, we can declare a function using a declaration of the form `int *MaxSwap()`.

As with all other operators, the address and indirection operator are evaluated according to the C precedence and associativity rules. The precedence and associativity of these and all other operators is listed in Table 12.5. Notice that both of the pointer operators have very high precedence.

16.2.6 An Example Problem Involving Pointers

Let's examine an example problem involving pointers. Say we want to develop a program that calculates the quotient and remainder given an integer dividend and integer divisor. That is, the program will calculate *dividend / divisor* and *dividend % divisor* where both values are integers. The structure of this program is very simple and requires only sequential constructs—that is, iteration is not required. The twist, however, is that we want the calculation of quotient and remainder to be performed by a single C function.

We can easily construct a function to generate a single output value (say, quotient) that we can pass back to the caller using the return value mechanism. A function that calculates only the quotient, for example, could consist of the single statement `return dividend / divisor;`. To provide the caller with multiple values, however, we will make use of the call by reference mechanism using pointer variables.

The code in Figure 16.6 contains a function that does just so. The function `IntDivide` takes four parameters, two of which are integers and two of which

```
1    #include <stdio.h>
2
3    int IntDivide(int x, int y, int *quoPtr, int *remPtr);
4
5    int main()
6    {
7      int dividend;        /* The number to be divided       */
8      int divisor;         /* The number to divide by        */
9      int quotient;        /* Integer result of division     */
10     int remainder;       /* Integer remainder of division  */
11     int error;           /* Did something go wrong?        */
12
13     printf("Input dividend: ");
14     scanf("%d", &dividend);
15     printf("Input divisor: ");
16     scanf("%d", &divisor);
17
18     error = IntDivide(dividend,divisor,&quotient,&remainder);
19
20     if (!error)          /* !error indicates no error      */
21       printf("Answer: %d remainder %d\n", quotient, remainder);
22     else
23       printf("IntDivide failed.\n");
24   }
25
26   int IntDivide(int x, int y, int *quoPtr, int *remPtr)
27   {
28     if (y != 0) {
29       *quoPtr = x / y;                /* Modify *quoPtr */
30       *remPtr = x % y;                /* Modify *remPtr */
31       return 0;
32     }
33     else
34       return -1;
35   }
```

Figure 16.6 The function `IntDivide` calculates the integer portion and remainder of an integer divide; it returns a −1 if the divisor is 0

are pointers to integers. The function divides the first parameter x by the second parameter y. The integer portion of the result is assigned to the memory location pointed to by `quoPtr`, and the integer remainder is assigned to the memory location pointed to by `remPtr`.

Notice that the function `IntDivide` also returns a value to indicate its status: It returns a −1 if the `divisor` is zero, indicating to the caller that an error has occurred. It returns a zero otherwise, indicating to the caller that the computation proceeded without a hitch. The function `main`, upon return, checks the return value to determine if the values in quotient and remainder are correct. Using the return value to signal a problem during a function call between caller and callee is an excellent defensive programming practice for conveying error conditions across a call.

16.3 Arrays

Consider a program that keeps track of the final exam scores for each of the 50 students in a computer engineering course. The most convenient way to store this data would be to declare a single object, say examScore, in which we can store 50 different integer values. We can access a particular exam score within this object using an *index* that is an offset from the beginning of the object. For example, examScore[32] provides the exam score for the 33rd student (the very first student's score stored in examScore[0]). The object examScore in this example is an *array* of integers. An array is a collection of similar data items that are stored sequentially in memory. Specifically, all the elements in the array are of the same type (e.g., int, char, etc.).

Arrays are most useful when the data upon which the program operates is naturally expressed as a contiguous sequence of values. Because a lot of real-world data falls into this category (such as exam scores for students in a course), arrays are incredibly useful data structures. For instance, if we wanted to write a program to take a sequence of 100 numbers entered from the keyboard and *sort* them into ascending order, then an array would be the natural choice for storing these numbers in memory. The program would be almost impossible to write using the simple variables we have been using thus far.

16.3.1 Declaring and Using Arrays

First, let's examine how to declare an array in a C program. Like all other variables, arrays must have a type associated with them. The type indicates the properties of the values stored in the array. Following is a declaration for an array of 10 integers:

```
int grid[10];
```

The keyword int indicates that we are declaring something of type integer. The name of the array is grid. The brackets indicate we are declaring an array and the 10 indicates that the array is to contain 10 integers, all of which will be sequentially located in memory. Figure 16.7 shows a pictorial representation of how grid is allocated. The first element, grid[0], is allocated in the lowest memory address and the last element, grid[9], in the highest address. If the array grid were a local variable, then its memory space would be allocated on the run-time stack.

Let's examine how to access different values in this array. Notice in Figure 16.7 that the array's first element is actually numbered 0, which means the last element is numbered 9. To access a particular element, we provide an *index* within brackets. For example,

```
grid[6] = grid[3] + 1;
```

The statement reads the value stored in the fourth (remember, we start numbering with 0) element of grid, adds 1 to it, and stores the result into the seventh element of grid. Let's look at the LC-3 code for this example. Let's say that grid is the only local variable allocated on the run-time stack. This means that the base pointer R5 will point to grid[9].

Memory

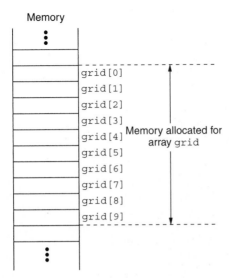

Figure 16.7 The array `grid` allocated in memory

```
ADD  R0, R5, #-9  ;  Put the base address of grid into R0
LDR  R1, R0, #3   ;  R1 <-- grid[3]
ADD  R1, R1, #1   ;  R1 <-- grid[3] + 1
STR  R1, R0, #6   ;  grid[6] = grid[3] + 1;
```

Notice that the first instruction calculates the base address of the array, which is the address of `grid[0]`, and puts it into R0. The base address of an array in general is the address of the first element of the array. We can access any element in the array by adding the index of the desired element to the base address.

The power of arrays comes from the fact that an array's index can be any legal C expression of integer type. The following example demonstrates:

```
grid[x+1] = grid[x] + 2;
```

Let's look at the LC-3 code for this statement. Assume `x` is another local variable allocated on the run-time stack directly on top of the array `grid`.

```
LDR  R0, R5, #-10 ;  Load the value of x
ADD  R1, R5, #-9  ;  Put the base address of grid into R1
ADD  R1, R0, R1   ;  Calculate address of grid[x]
LDR  R2, R1, #0   ;  R2 <-- grid[x]
ADD  R2, R2, #2   ;  R2 <-- grid[x] + 2

LDR  R0, R5, #-10 ;  Load the value of x
ADD  R0, R0, #1   ;  R0 <-- x + 1
ADD  R1, R5, #-9  ;  Put the base address of grid into R1
ADD  R1, R0, R1   ;  Calculate address of grid[x+1]
STR  R2, R1, #0   ;  grid[x+1] = grid[x] + 2;
```

16.3.2 Examples Using Arrays

We start off with a simple C program that adds two arrays together by adding the corresponding elements from each array to form the sum. Each array represents a list of exam scores for students in a course. Each array contains an element for each student's score. To generate the cumulative points for each student, we effectively want to perform `Total[i] = Exam1[i] + Exam2[i]`. Figure 16.8 contains the C code to read in two 10-element integer arrays, add them together into another 10-element array, and print out the sum.

A style note: Notice the use of the preprocessor macro NUM_STUDENTS to represent a constant value of the size of the input set. This is a common use for preprocessor macros, which are usually found at the beginning of the source file (or within C header files). Now, if we want to increase the size of the array, for example if the student enrollment changes, we simply change the definition of

```
1    #include <stdio.h>
2    #define NUM_STUDENTS 10
3
4    int main()
5    {
6      int i;
7      int Exam1[NUM_STUDENTS];
8      int Exam2[NUM_STUDENTS];
9      int Total[NUM_STUDENTS];
10
11     /* Input Exam 1 scores */
12     for (i = 0; i < NUM_STUDENTS; i++) {
13       printf("Input Exam 1 score for student %d : ", i);
14       scanf("%d", &Exam1[i]);
15     }
16     printf("\n");
17
18     /* Input Exam 2 scores */
19     for (i = 0; i < NUM_STUDENTS; i++) {
20       printf("Input Exam 2 score for student %d : ", i);
21       scanf("%d", &Exam2[i]);
22     }
23     printf("\n");
24
25     /* Calculate Total Points */
26     for (i = 0; i < NUM_STUDENTS; i++) {
27       Total[i] = Exam1[i] + Exam2[i];
28     }
29
30     /* Output the Total Points */
31     for (i = 0; i < NUM_STUDENTS; i++) {
32       printf("Total for Student %d = %d\n", i, Total[i]);
33     }
34   }
```

Figure 16.8   A C program that calculates the sum of two 10-element arrays

the macro (one change) and recompile the program. If we did not use the macro, changing the array size would require changes to the code in multiple places. The changes could be potentially difficult to track down, and forgetting to do one would likely result in a program that did not work correctly. Using preprocessor macros for the size of an array is good programming practice.

Now onto a slightly more complex example involving arrays. Figure 16.9 lists a C program that reads in a sequence of decimal numbers (in total MAX_NUMS of them) from the keyboard and determines the number of times each input number is repeated within the sequence. The program then prints out each number, along with the number of times it repeats.

In this program, we use two arrays, numbers and repeats. Both are declared to contain MAX_NUMS integer values. The array numbers stores the input sequence. The array repeats is calculated by the program to contain the number of times the corresponding element in numbers is repeated in the input sequence. For example, if numbers[3] equals 115, and there are a total of four 115s in the input

```
1    #include <stdio.h>
2    #define MAX_NUMS 10
3
4    int main()
5    {
6      int index;              /* Loop iteration variable    */
7      int repIndex;           /* Loop variable for rep loop */
8      int numbers[MAX_NUMS];  /* Original input numbers     */
9      int repeats[MAX_NUMS];  /* Number of repeats          */
10
11     /* Get input */
12     printf("Enter %d numbers.\n", MAX_NUMS);
13     for (index = 0; index < MAX_NUMS; index++) {
14       printf("Input number %d : ", index);
15       scanf("%d", &numbers[index]);
16     }
17
18     /* Scan through entire array, counting number of     */
19     /* repeats per element within the original array      */
20     for (index = 0; index < MAX_NUMS; index++) {
21       repeats[index] = 0;
22       for (repIndex = 0; repIndex < MAX_NUMS; repIndex++) {
23         if (numbers[repIndex] == numbers[index])
24            repeats[index]++;
25       }
26     }
27
28     /* Print the results */
29     for (index = 0; index < MAX_NUMS; index++)
30       printf("Original number %d. Number of repeats %d\n",
31              numbers[index], repeats[index]);
32   }
```

Figure 16.9   A C program that determines the number of repeated values in an array

sequence (i.e., there are four 115s in the array `numbers`), then `repeats[3]` will equal 4.

This program consists of three outer loops, of which the middle loop is actually a *nested loop* (see Section 13.3.2) consisting of two loops. The first and last `for` loops are simple loops that get keyboard input and produce program output.

The middle `for` loop contains the nested loop. This body of code determines how many copies of each element exist within the entire array. The outer loop iterates the variable `index` from 0 through `MAX_NUMS`; we use `index` to scan through the array from the first element `numbers[0]` through the last element `numbers[MAX_NUMS]`. The inner loop also iterates from 0 through `MAX_NUMS`; we use this loop to scan through the array again, this time determining how many of the elements match the element selected by the outer loop (i.e., `numbers[index]`). Each time a copy is detected (i.e., `numbers[repIndex] == numbers[index]`), the corresponding element in the `repeats` array is incremented (i.e., `repeats[index]++`).

16.3.3 Arrays as Parameters

Passing arrays between functions is a useful thing because it allows us to create functions that operate on arrays. Say we want to create a set of functions that calculates the mean and median on an array of integers. We would need either (1) to pass the entire array of values from one function to another or (2) to pass a reference to the array. If the array contains a large number of elements, copying each element from one activation record onto another could be very costly in execution time. Fortunately, C naturally passes arrays by reference. Figure 16.10 is a C program that contains a function `Average` whose single parameter is an array of integers.

When calling the function `Average` from `main`, we pass to it the value associated with the array identifier `numbers`. Notice that here we are not using the standard notation involving brackets `[ ]` that we normally use for arrays. In C, an array's name refers to the address of the base element of the array. The name `numbers` is equivalent to `&numbers[0]`. The type `numbers` is similar to `int *`. It is an address of memory location containing an integer.

In using `numbers` as the argument to the function `Average`, we are causing the address of the array `numbers` to be pushed onto the stack and passed to the function `Average`. Within the function `Average`, the parameter `inputValues` is assigned the address of the array. Within `Average` we can access the elements of the original array using standard array notation. Figure 16.11 shows the run-time stack just prior to the execution of the `return` from `Average` (line 34 of the program).

Notice how the input parameter `inputValues` is specified in the declaration of the function `Average`. The brackets `[ ]` indicate to the compiler that the corresponding parameter will be the base address to an array of the specified type, in this case an array of integers.

Since arrays are passed by reference in C, any modifications to the array values made by the called function will be visible to the caller once control returns to it. How would we go about passing only a single element of an array by value? How about by reference?

```
1    #include <stdio.h>
2    #define MAX_NUMS 10
3
4    int Average(int input_values[]);
5
6    int main()
7    {
8      int index;                 /* Loop iteration variable */
9      int mean;                  /* Average of numbers      */
10     int numbers[MAX_NUMS];     /* Original input numbers   */
11
12
13     /* Get input */
14     printf("Enter %d numbers.\n", MAX_NUMS);
15     for (index = 0; index < MAX_NUMS; index++) {
16       printf("Input number %d : ", index);
17       scanf("%d", &numbers[index]);
18     }
19
20     mean = Average(numbers);
21
22     printf("The average of these numbers is %d\n", mean);
23   }
24
25   int Average(int inputValues[])
26   {
27     int index;
28     int sum = 0;
29
30     for (index = 0; index < MAX_NUMS; index++) {
31       sum = sum + inputValues[index];
32     }
33
34     return (sum / MAX_NUMS);
35   }
```

Figure 16.10 An example of an array as a parameter to a function

16.3.4 Strings in C

A very common use for arrays in C is for *strings*. Strings are sequences of characters that represent text. Strings are simply character arrays, with each subsequent element containing the next character of the string. For example,

```
char word[10];
```

declares an array that can store a string of up to 10 characters. Longer strings require a larger array. What if the string is shorter than 10 characters? In C and many other modern programming languages, the end of a string is denoted by the null character whose ASCII value is 0. It is a sentinel that identifies the end of the string. Such strings are also called *null-terminated strings*. `'\0'` is the special

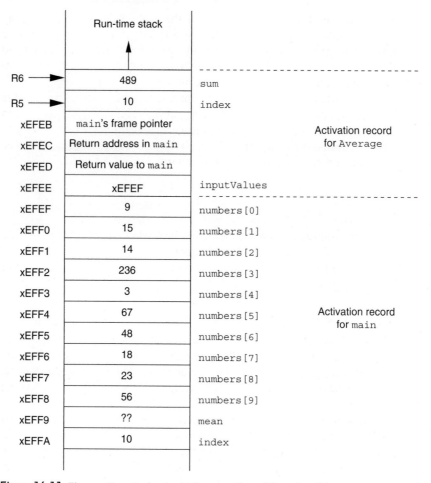

Figure 16.11 The run-time stack prior to the execution of the return from Average

sequence that corresponds to the null character. Continuing with our previous declaration,

```
char word[10];

word[0] = 'H';
word[1] = 'e';
word[2] = 'l';
word[3] = 'l';
word[4] = 'o';
word[5] = '\0';

printf("%s", word);
```

Here, we are assigning each element of the array individually. The array will contain the string "Hello." Notice that the end-of-string character itself is a character that occupies an element of the array. Even though the array is declared for 10 elements, we must reserve one element for the null character, and therefore strings that are longer than nine characters cannot be stored in this array.

We have also used a new `printf` format specification `%s` in this example. This specification prints out a string of characters, starting with the character pointed to by the corresponding parameter and ending at the end-of-string character `'\0'`.

ANSI C compilers also allow strings to be initialized within their declarations. For instance, the preceding example can be rewritten to the following.

```
char word[10] = "Hello";

printf("%s", word);
```

Make note of two things here: First, character strings are distinguished from single characters with double quotes, `" "`. Single quotes are used for single characters, such as `'A'`. Second, notice that the compiler automatically adds the null character to the end of the string.

Examples of Strings

Figure 16.12 contains a program that performs a very simple and useful primitive operation on strings: it calculates the length of a string. Since the size of the array that contains the string does not indicate the actual length of the string (it does, however, tell us the maximum length of the string), we need to examine the string itself to calculate its length.

The algorithm for determining string length is easy. Starting with the first element, we count the number of characters before we encounter the null character. The function `StringLength` in the code in Figure 16.12 performs this calculation.

Notice that we are using the format specification `%s` in the `scanf` statement. This specification causes `scanf` to read in a string of characters from the keyboard until the first *white space* character. In C, any space, tab, new line, carriage return, vertical tab, or form-feed character is considered white space. So if the user types (from *The New Colossus*, by Emma Lazarus)

```
Not like the brazen giant of Greek fame,
With conquering limbs astride from land to land;
```

only the word *Not* is stored in the array `input`. The remainder of the text line is reserved for subsequent `scanf` calls to read. So if we performed another `scanf("%s", input)`, the word *like* will be stored in the array `input`. Notice that the white space is automatically discarded by this `%s` specification. We examine this I/O behavior more closely in Chapter 18 when we take a deeper look into I/O in C.

Notice that the maximum word size is 20 characters. What happens if the first word is longer? The `scanf` function has no information on the size of the array `input` and will keep storing characters to the array address it was provided until white space is encountered. So what then happens if the first word is longer

```
1    #include <stdio.h>
2    #define MAX_STRING 20
3
4    int StringLength(char string[]);
5
6    int main()
7    {
8      char input[MAX_STRING];      /* Input string */
9      int  length = 0;
10
11     printf("Input a word (less than 20 characters): ");
12     scanf("%s", input);
13
14     length = StringLength(input);
15     printf("The word contains %d characters\n", length);
16   }
17
18   int StringLength(char string[])
19   {
20     int index = 0;
21
22     while (string[index] != '\0')
23       index = index + 1;
24
25     return index;
26   }
```

Figure 16.12 A program that calculates the length of a string

than 20 characters? Any local variables that are allocated after the array `input` in the function `main` will be overwritten. Draw out the activation record before and after the call to `scanf` to see why. In the exercises at the end of this chapter, we provide a problem where you need to modify this program in order to catch the scenario where the user enters a word longer than what fits into the `input` array.

Let's examine a slightly more complex example that uses the `StringLength` function from the previous code example. In this example, listed in Figure 16.13, we read an input string from the keyboard using `scanf`, then call a function to reverse the string. The reversed string is then displayed on the output device.

The function `Reverse` performs two tasks in order to reverse the string properly. First it determines the length of the string to reverse using the `StringLength` function from the previous code example. Then it performs the reversal by swapping the first character with the last, the second character with the second to last, the third character with the third to last, and so on.

To perform the swap, it uses a modified version of the `NewSwap` function from Figure 16.4. The reversal loop calls the function `CharSwap` on pairs of characters within the string. First, `CharSwap` is called on the first and last character, then on the second and second to last character, and so forth.

The C standard library provides many prewritten functions for strings. For example, functions to copy strings, merge strings together, compare them, or

```
1    #include <stdio.h>
2    #define MAX_STRING 20
3
4    int StringLength(char string[]);
5    void CharSwap(char *firstVal, char *secondVal);
6    void Reverse(char string[]);
7
8    int main()
9    {
10     char input[MAX_STRING];              /* Input string */
11
12     printf("Input a word (less than 20 characters): ");
13     scanf("%s", input);
14
15     Reverse(input);
16     printf("The word reversed is %s.\n", input);
17   }
18
19   int StringLength(char string[])
20   {
21     int index = 0;
22
23     while (string[index] != '\0')
24       index = index + 1;
25
26     return index;
27   }
28
29   void CharSwap(char *firstVal, char *secondVal)
30   {
31     char tempVal;    /* Temporary location for swapping */
32
33     tempVal = *firstVal;
34     *firstVal = *secondVal;
35     *secondVal = tempVal;
36   }
37
38   void Reverse(char string[])
39   {
40     int index;
41     int length;
42
43     length = StringLength(string);
44
45     for (index = 0; index < (length / 2); index++)
46       CharSwap(&string[index], &string[length - (index + 1)]);
47   }
```

Figure 16.13 A program that reverses a string

Table 16.1	The Relationship Between Pointers and Arrays	
`cptr`	`word`	`&word[0]`
`(cptr + n)`	`word + n`	`&word[n]`
`*cptr`	`*word`	`word[0]`
`*(cptr + n)`	`*(word + n)`	`word[n]`

calculate their length can be found in the C standard library, and the declarations for these functions can be included via the `<string.h>` header file. More information on some of these string functions can be found in Appendix D.9.2.

16.3.5 The Relationship Between Arrays and Pointers in C

You might have noticed that there is a similarity between an array's name and a pointer variable to an element of the same type as the array. For instance,

```
char word[10];
char *cptr;

cptr = word;
```

is a legal, and sometimes useful, sequence of code. Here, we have assigned the pointer variable `cptr` to point to the base address of the array `word`. Because they are both pointers to characters, `cptr` and `word` can be used interchangeably. For example, we can access the fourth character within the string either by using `word[3]` or `*(cptr + 3)`.

One difference between the two, though, is that `cptr` is a variable and can be reassigned. The array identifier `word`, on the other hand, cannot be. For example, the following statement is illegal: `word = newArray`. The identifier always points to a fixed spot in memory where the compiler has placed the array. Once it has been allocated, it cannot be moved.

Table 16.1 shows the equivalence of several expressions involving pointer and array notation. Rows in the table are expressions with the same meaning.

16.3.6 Problem Solving: Insertion Sort

With this initial exposure to arrays under our belt, we can now attempt an interesting and sizeable (and useful!) problem: we will write C code to *sort* an array of integers into ascending order. That is, the code arranges the array `a[]` such that `a[0] ≤ a[1] ≤ a[2] ....`

To accomplish this, we will use an algorithm for sorting called Insertion Sort. Sorting is an important primitive operation, and people in computing have devoted considerable time to understanding, analyzing, and refining the sorting process. As a result, there are many algorithms for sorting, and you will gain exposure to some basic techniques in subsequent computing courses. We use insertion sort here because it parallels how we might sort items in the real world. It is quite straightforward.

Insertion sort is best described by an example. Say you want to sort your compact disc collection into alphabetical order by artist. If you were sorting your compact discs using insertion sort, you would split the CDs into two groups, the sorted group and the unsorted group. Initially, the sorted group would be empty as all your CDs would be yet unsorted. The sorting process proceeds by taking a CD from the unsorted group and *inserting* it into the proper position among the sorted CDs. For example, if the sorted group contained three CDs, one by John Coltrane, one by Charles Mingus, and one by Thelonious Monk, then inserting the Miles Davis CD would mean inserting it between the Coltrane CD and the Mingus CD. You keep doing this until all CDs in the unsorted group have been inserted into the sorted group. This is insertion sort.

How would we go about applying this same technique to sort an array of integers? Applying systematic decomposition to the preceding algorithm, we see that the core of the program involves iterating through the elements of the array, inserting each element into the proper spot in a new array where all items are in ascending order. This process continues until all elements of the original array have been inserted into the new array. Once done, the new array will contain the same elements as the first array, except in sorted order.

For this technique we basically need to represent two groups of items, the original unsorted elements and the sorted elements. And for this we could use two separate arrays. It turns out, however, that we can represent both groups of elements within the original array. Doing so results in code that requires less memory and is more compact, though slightly more complex upon first glance. The initial part of the array contains the sorted elements and the remainder of the array contains the unsorted elements. We pick the next unsorted item and insert it into the sorted part at the correct point. We keep doing this until we have gone through the entire array.

The actual `InsertionSort` routine (shown in Figure 16.14) contains a nested loop. The outer loop scans through all the unsorted items (analogous to going through the unsorted CDs, one by one). The inner loop scans through the already sorted items, scanning for the place at which to insert the new item. Once we detect an already sorted element that is larger than the one we are inserting, we insert the new element between the larger and the one before it.

Let's take a closer look by examining what happens during a pass of the insertion sort. Say we examine the insertion sort process (lines 33–43) when the variable `unsorted` is equal to 4. The array `list` contains the following 10 elements:

```
2 16 69 92 15 37 92 38 82 19
```

During this pass, the code inserts `list[4]`, or 15, into the already sorted portion of the array, elements `list[0]` through `list[3]`.

The inner loop iterates the variable `sorted` through the list of already sorted elements. It does this from the highest numbered element down to 0 (i.e., starting at 3 down to 0). Notice that the condition on the `for` loop terminates the loop once a list item *less* than the current item, 15, is found.

```
1    #include <stdio.h>
2    #define MAX_NUMS 10
3
4    void InsertionSort(int list[]);
5
6    int main()
7    {
8      int index;                /* Iteration variable        */
9      int numbers[MAX_NUMS];    /* List of numbers to be sorted */
10
11     /* Get input */
12     printf("Enter %d numbers.\n", MAX_NUMS);
13     for (index = 0; index < MAX_NUMS; index++) {
14       printf("Input number %d : ", index);
15       scanf("%d", &numbers[index]);
16     }
17
18     InsertionSort(numbers);   /* Call sorting routine       */
19
20     /* Print sorted list */
21     printf("\nThe input set, in ascending order:\n");
22     for (index = 0; index < MAX_NUMS; index++)
23       printf("%d\n", numbers[index]);
24   }
25
26   void InsertionSort(int list[])
27   {
28     int unsorted;           /* Index for unsorted list items */
29     int sorted;             /* Index for sorted items        */
30     int unsortedItem;       /* Current item to be sorted     */
31
32     /* This loop iterates from 1 thru MAX_NUMS  */
33     for (unsorted = 1; unsorted < MAX_NUMS; unsorted++) {
34       unsortedItem = list[unsorted];
35
36       /* This loop iterates from unsorted thru 0, unless
37          we hit an element smaller than current item */
38       for (sorted = unsorted - 1;
39            (sorted >= 0) && (list[sorted] > unsortedItem);
40            sorted--)
41         list[sorted + 1] = list[sorted];
42
43       list[sorted + 1] = unsortedItem; /* Insert item       */
44     }
45   }
```

Figure 16.14 Insertion sort program

In each iteration of this inner loop (lines 38–41), an element in the sorted part of the array is copied to the next position in the array. In the first iteration, `list[3]` is copied to `list[4]`. So after the first iteration of the inner loop, the array `list` contains

```
2 16 69 92 92 37 92 38 82 19
```

Notice that we have overwritten 15 (`list[4]`). This is OK because we have a copy of its value in the variable `unsortedItem` (from line 34). The second iteration performs the same operation on `list[2]`. After the second iteration, `list` contains

```
2 16 69 69 92 37 92 38 82 19
```

After the third iteration, `list` contains:

```
2 16 16 69 92 37 92 38 82 19
```

Now the `for` loop terminates because the evaluation condition is no longer true. More specifically, `list[sorted] > unsortedItem` is not true. The current sorted list item `list[0]`, which is 2, is not larger than the current unsorted item `unsortedItem`, which is 15. Now the inner loop terminates, and the statement following it, `list[sorted + 1] = unsortedItem;` executes. Now `list` contains, and the sorted part of the array contains, one more element.

```
2 15 16 69 92 37 92 38 82 19
```

This process continues until all items have been sorted, meaning the outer loop has iterated through all elements of the array `list`.

16.3.7 Common Pitfalls with Arrays in C

Unlike some other modern programming languages, C does not provide protection against exceeding the size (or bounds) of an array. It is a common error made with arrays in C programming. C provides no support for ensuring that an array index is actually within an array. The compiler blindly generates code for the expression `a[i]`, even if the index `i` accesses a memory location beyond the end of the array. To demonstrate, the code in Figure 16.15 lists an example of how exceeding the array bounds can lead to a serious debugging effort. Enter a number larger than the array size and this program exhibits some peculiar behavior.[1]

Analyze this program by drawing out the run-time stack and you will see more clearly why this bug causes the behavior it does.

C does not perform bounds checking on array accesses. C code tends to be faster because array accesses incur less overhead. This is yet another manner in

---

[1] Depending on the compiler you are using, you might need to enter a number larger than 16, or you might need to declare `index` after `array` in order to observe the problem.

```
1   #include <stdio.h>
2   #define MAX_SIZE 10
3
4   int main()
5   {
6     int index;
7     int array[MAX_SIZE];
8     int limit;
9
10    printf("Enter limit (integer): ");
11    scanf("%d", &limit);
12
13    for(index = 0; index < limit; index++) {
14      array[index] = 0;
15      printf("array[%d] is set to 0\n", index);
16    }
17  }
```

Figure 16.15 This C program has peculiar behavior if the user enters a number that is too large

which C provides more control to the programmer than other languages. If you are not careful in your coding, this bare-bones philosophy can, however, lead to undue debugging effort. To counter this, experienced C programmers often use some specific defensive programming techniques when it comes to arrays.

Another common pitfall with arrays in C revolves around the fact that arrays (in particular, statically declared arrays such as the ones we've seen) must be of a fixed size. We must know the size of the array when we compile the program. C does not support array declarations with variable expressions. The following code in C is illegal. The size of array temp must be known when the compiler analyzes the source code.

```
void SomeFunction(int num_elements)
{
  int temp[num_elements];   /* Generates a syntax error */

  :
}
```

To deal with this limitation, experienced C programmers carefully analyze the situations in which their code will be used and then allocate arrays with ample space. To supplement this built-in assumption in their code, bounds checks are added to warn if the size of the array is not sufficient. Another option is to use dynamic memory allocation to allocate the array at run-time. More on this in Chapter 19.

16.4 Summary

In this chapter we covered two important high-level programming constructs: pointers and arrays. Both constructs enable us to access memory *indirectly*. The key notions we covered in this chapter are:

• **Pointers.** Pointers are variables that contain addresses of other memory objects (such as other variables). With pointers we can indirectly access and manipulate these other objects. A very simple application of pointers is to use them to pass parameters by reference. Pointers have more substantial applications, and we will see them in subsequent chapters.

• **Arrays.** An array is a collection of elements of the same type arranged sequentially in memory. We can access a particular element within an array by providing an index to the element that is its offset from the beginning of the array. Many real-world objects are best represented within a computer program as an array of items, thus making the array a significant structure for organizing data. With arrays, we can represent character strings that hold text data, for example. We examine several important array operations, including the sorting operation via insertion sort.

Exercises

16.1   Write a C function that takes as a parameter a character string of unknown length, containing a single word. Your function should translate this string from English into Pig Latin. This translation is performed by removing the first letter of the string, appending it onto the end, and concatenating the letters *ay*. You can assume that the array contains enough space for you to add the extra characters.

   For example, if your function is passed the string "Hello," after your function returns, the string should have the value "elloHay." The first character of the string should be "e."

16.2   Write a C program that accepts a list of numbers from the user until a number is repeated (i.e., is the same as the number preceding it). The program then prints out the number of numbers entered (excluding the last) and their sum. When the program is run, the prompts and responses will look like the following:

```
Number: 5
Number: -6
Number: 0
Number: 45
Number: 45
4 numbers were entered and their sum is 44
```

16.3   What is the output when the following code is compiled and run?

```
int x;

int main()
{
    int *px = &x;
    int x = 7;

    *px = 4;
    printf("x = %d\n", x);
}
```

16.4   Create a string function that takes two input strings, stringA and stringB, and returns a 0 if both strings are the same, a 1 if stringA appears before stringB in the sorted order of a dictionary, or a 2 if stringB appears before stringA.

16.5   Using the function developed for Exercise 16.4, modify the Insertion Sort program so that it operates upon strings instead of integers.

16.6   Translate the following C function into LC-3 assembly language.

```
int main()
{
    int a[5], i;

    i = 4;
    while (i >= 0) {
        a[i] = i;
        i--;
    }
}
```

16.7 For this question, examine the following program. Notice that the variable `ind` is a pointer variable that points to another pointer variable. Such a construction is legal in C.

```c
#include <stdio.h>

int main()
{
    int apple;
    int *ptr;
    int **ind;
    ind = &ptr;
    *ind = &apple;
    **ind = 123;

    ind++;
    *ptr++;
    apple++;

    printf("%x %x %d\n", ind, ptr, apple);
}
```

Analyze what this program performs by drawing out the run-time stack at the point just after the statement `apple++;` executes.

16.8 The following code contains a call to the function `triple`. What is the minimum size of the activation record of `triple`?

```c
int main()
{
    int array[3];

    array[0] = 1;
    array[1] = 2;
    array[2] = 3;

    triple(array);
}
```

16.9 Write a program to remove any duplicates from a sequence of numbers. For example, if the list consisted of the numbers 5, 4, 5, 5, and 3, the program would output 5, 4, 3.

16.10 Write a program to find the median of a set of numbers. Recall that the median is a number within the set in which half the numbers are larger and half are smaller. *Hint:* To perform this, you may need to sort the list first.

16.11   For this question, refer to the following C program:

```c
int FindLen(char *);

int main()
{
    char str[10];

    printf("Enter a string : ");
    scanf("%s", str);
    printf("%s has %d characters\n", str, FindLen(str));
}

int FindLen(char * s)
{
    int len=0;

    while (*s != '\0') {
        len++;
        s++;
    }

    return len;
}
```

a. For the preceding C program, what is the size of the activation record for the functions `main` and `FindLen`?

b. Show the contents of the stack just before the function `FindLen` returns if the input string is `apple`.

c. What would the activation record look like if the program were run and the user typed a string of length greater than 10 characters? What would happen to the program?

16.12 The following code reads a string from the keyboard and prints out a version with any uppercase characters converted to lowercase. However, it has a flaw. Identify it.

```c
#include <stdio.h>
#define MAX_LEN   10
char *LowerCase(char *s);

int main()
{
    char str[MAX_LEN];

    printf("Enter a string : ");
    scanf("%s", str);

    printf("Lowercase: %s \n", LowerCase(str));
}

char *LowerCase(char *s) {
  char newStr[MAX_LEN];
  int index;

  for (index = 0; index < MAX_LEN; index++) {
     if ('A' <= s[index] && s[index] <= 'Z')
       newStr[index] = s[index] + ('a' - 'A');
     else
       newStr[index] = s[index];
  }

  return newStr;
}
```

16.13 Consider the following declarations.

```c
#define STACK_SIZE 100

int   stack[STACK_SIZE];
int   topOfStack;

int   Push(int item);
```

a. Write a funtion `Push` (the declaration is provided) that will push the value of `item` onto the top of the stack. If the stack is full and the item cannot be added, the function should return a 1. If the item is successfully pushed, the function should return a 0.

b. Write a function `Pop` that will pop an item from the top of the stack. Like `Push`, this function will return a 1 if the operation is unsuccessful. That is, a `Pop` was attempted on an empty stack. It should return a 0 if successful. Consider carefully how the popped value can be returned to the caller.

17

Recursion

17.1 Introduction

We start this chapter by describing a recursive procedure that you might already be familiar with. Suppose we want to find a particular student's exam in a set of exams that are already in alphabetical order. We might randomly examine the name on an exam about halfway through the set. If that randomly chosen exam is not the one we are looking for, we search the appropriate half using the very same technique. That is, we repeat the search on the first half or the second half, depending on whether the name we are looking for is less than or greater than the name on the exam at the halfway point. For example, say we are looking for Babe Ruth's exam and, at the halfway point, we find Mickey Mantle's exam. We then repeat the search on the second half of the original stack. Fairly quickly, we will locate Babe Ruth's exam, if it exists in the set. This technique of searching through a set of elements already in sorted order is *recursive*. We are applying the same searching algorithm to continually smaller and smaller subsets of exams.

The idea behind recursion is simple: A recursive function solves a task by calling itself on a smaller subtask. As we shall see, recursion is another way of expressing iterative program constructs. The power of recursion lies in its ability to elegantly capture the flow of control for certain tasks. There are some programming problems for which the recursive solution is far simpler than the corresponding solution using conventional iteration. In this chapter, we introduce you to the concept of recursion via five different examples. We examine how recursive functions are implemented on the LC-3. The elegance of the run-time stack mechanism is that recursive functions require no special handling—they execute in the same manner as any other function. The main purpose of this chapter is to provide you with an initial but deep exposure to recursion so that you can analyze and reason about recursive programs. Being able to understand recursive code is a necessary ingredient for writing recursive code, and ultimately for recursion to become part of your problem-solving toolkit for attacking programming problems.

17.2 What Is Recursion?

A function that calls itself is a recursive function, as in the function RunningSum in Figure 17.1.

This function calculates the sum of all the integers between the input parameter n and 1. For example, RunningSum(4) calculates $4 + 3 + 2 + 1$. However, it does the calculation recursively. Notice that the running sum of 4 is really 4 plus the running sum of 3. Likewise, the running sum of 3 is 3 plus the running sum of 2. This *recursive* definition is the basis for a recursive algorithm. In other words,

$$\text{RunningSum}(n) = n + \text{RunningSum}(n - 1)$$

In mathematics, we use *recurrence equations* to express such functions. The preceding equation is a recurrence equation for RunningSum. In order to complete the evaluation of this equation, we must also supply an initial case. So in addition to the preceding formula, we need to state

$$\text{RunningSum}(1) = 1$$

before we can completely evaluate the recurrence, which we do as follows:

$$\text{RunningSum}(4) = 4 + \text{RunningSum}(3)$$
$$= 4 + 3 + \text{RunningSum}(2)$$
$$= 4 + 3 + 2 + \text{RunningSum}(1)$$
$$= 4 + 3 + 2 + 1$$

The C version of RunningSum works in the same manner as the recurrence equation. During execution of the function call RunningSum(4), RunningSum makes a function call to itself, with an argument of 3 (i.e., RunningSum(3)). However, before RunningSum(3) ends, it makes a call to RunningSum(2). And before RunningSum(2) ends, it makes a call to RunningSum(1). RunningSum(1), however, makes no additional recursive calls and returns the value 1 to

```
1   int RunningSum(int n)
2   {
3      if (n == 1)
4          return 1;
5      else
6          return (n + RunningSum(n-1));
7   }
```

Figure 17.1 A recursive function

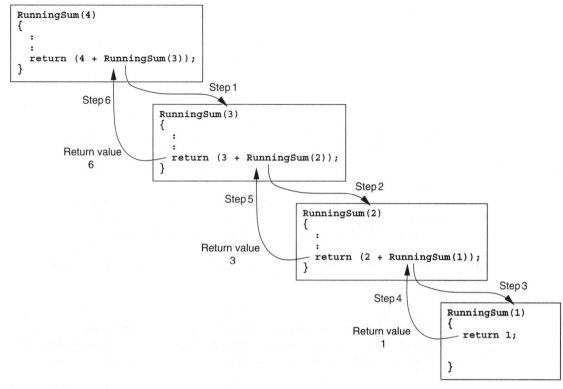

Figure 17.2   The flow of control when RunningSum(4) is called

RunningSum(2), which enables RunningSum(2) to end, and return the value $2 + 1$ back to RunningSum(3). This enables RunningSum(3) to end and pass a value of $3 + 2 + 1$ to RunningSum(4). Figure 17.2 pictorially shows how the execution of RunningSum(4) proceeds.

17.3 Recursion versus Iteration

Clearly, we could have written RunningSum using a for loop, and the code would have been more straightforward than its recursive counterpart. We provided a recursive version here in order to demonstrate a recursive call in the context of an easy-to-understand example.

There is a parallel between using recursion and using conventional iteration (such as for and while loops) in programming. All recursive functions can be written using iteration. For certain programming problems, however, the recursive version is simpler and more elegant than the iterative version. Solutions to certain problems are naturally expressed in a recursive manner, such as problems that are expressed with recurrence equations. It is because of such problems that recursion is an indispensable programming technique. Knowing which problems require recursion and which are better solved with iteration is part of the art of computer programming; you will become better at when to use which with experience.

Recursion, as useful as it is, comes at a cost. As an experiment, write an iterative version of `RunningSum` and compare the running time for large n with the recursive version. To do this you can use library functions to get the time of day (for example, `gettimeofday`) before the function starts and when it ends. Plot the running time for a variety of values of n and you will notice that the recursive version is relatively slow (provided the compiler did not optimize away the recursion). As we shall see in Section 17.5, recursive functions incur function call overhead that iterative solutions do not.

17.4   Towers of Hanoi

One problem for which the recursive solution is the simpler solution is the classic puzzle Towers of Hanoi. The puzzle involves a platform with three posts. On one of the posts sit a number of wooden disks, each smaller than the one below it. The objective is to move all the disks from their current post to one of the other posts. However, there are two rules for moving disks: only one disk can be moved at a time, and a larger disk can never be placed upon a smaller disk. For example, Figure 17.3 shows a puzzle where five disks are on post 1. To solve this puzzle, these five disks must be moved to one of the other posts obeying the two rules.

As the legend associated with the puzzle goes, when the world was created, the priests at the Temple of Brahma were given the task of moving 64 disks from one post to another. When they completed their task, the world would end.

Now how would we go about writing a computer program to solve this puzzle? If we view the problem from the end first, we can make the following observation: the final sequence of moves **must** involve moving the largest disk from post 1 to the target post, say post 3, and then moving the other disks back on top of it. Conceptually, we need to move all $n - 1$ disks off the largest disk and onto the intermediate post, then move the largest disk from its post onto the target post. Finally, we move all $n - 1$ disks from the intermediate post onto the target post. And we are done! Actually, we are not quite done because moving $n - 1$ disks in one move is not legal. However, we have stated the problem in such a manner that we can solve it if we can solve the

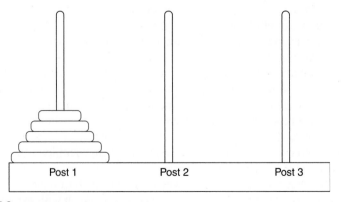

Figure 17.3   The Towers of Hanoi puzzle

```
/*
** Inputs
**    diskNumber is the disk to be moved (disk1 is smallest)
**    startPost is the post the disk is currently on
**    endPost is the post we want the disk to end on
**    midPost is the intermediate post
*/
MoveDisk(diskNumber, startPost, endPost, midPost)
{
    if (diskNumber > 1) {
        /* Move n-1 disks off the current disk on          */
        /* startPost and put them on the midPost            */
        MoveDisk(diskNumber-1, startPost, midPost, endPost);

        /* Move the largest disk.                           */
        printf("Move disk %d from post %d to post %d.\n",
                diskNumber, startPost, endPost);

        /* Move all n-1 disks from midPost onto endPost    */
        MoveDisk(diskNumber-1, midPost, endPost, startPost);
    }
    else
        printf("Move disk 1 from post %d to post %d.\n",
                startPost, endPost);
}
```

Figure 17.4 A recursive function to solve the Towers of Hanoi puzzle

two smaller subproblems of it. Once the largest disk is on the target post, we do not need to deal with it any further. Now the $n - 1^{th}$ disk becomes the largest disk, and the subobjective becomes to move it to the target pole. We can therefore apply the same technique but on a smaller subproblem.

We now have a recursive definition of the problem: In order to move n disks to the target post, which we symbolically represent as Move(n, target), we first move $n - 1$ disks to the intermediate post—Move(n-1, intermediate)—then move the nth disk to the target, and finally move $n - 1$ disks from the intermediate to the target, or Move(n-1, target). So in order to Move(n, target), two recursive calls are made to solve two smaller subproblems involving $n - 1$ disks.

As with recurrence equations in mathematics, all recursive definitions require a *base case*, which ends the recursion. In the way we have formulated the problem, the base case involves moving the smallest disk (disk 1). Moving disk 1 requires no other disks to be moved since it is always on top and can be moved directly from one post to any another without moving any other disks. Without a base case, a recursive function would have an infinite recursion, similar to an infinite loop in conventional iteration.

Taking our recursive definition to C code is fairly straightforward. Figure 17.4 is a recursive C function of this algorithm.

Let's see what happens when we play a game with three disks. Following is an initial function call to MoveDisk. We start off by saying that we want to move

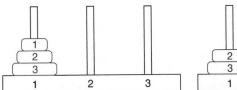

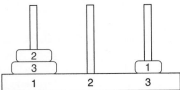

Figure 17.5   The Towers of Hanoi puzzle, initial configuration

Figure 17.6   The Towers of Hanoi puzzle, after first move

disk 3 (the largest disk) from post 1 to post 3, using post 2 as the intermediate storage post. That is, we want to solve a three-disk Towers of Hanoi puzzle. See Figure 17.5.

```
/* diskNumber 3; startPost 1; endPost 3; midPost 2 */
MoveDisk(3, 1, 3, 2)
```

This call invokes another call to `MoveDisk` to move disks 1 and 2 off disk 3 and onto post 2 using post 3 as intermediate storage. The call is performed at line 15 in the source code.

```
/* diskNumber 2; startPost 1; endPost 2; midPost 3 */
MoveDisk(2, 1, 2, 3)
```

To move disk 2 from post 1 to post 2, we must first move disk 1 off disk 2 and onto post 3 (the intermediate post). So this triggers another call to `MoveDisk` again from the call on line 15.

```
/* diskNumber 1; startPost 1; endPost 3; midPost 2 */
MoveDisk(1, 1, 3, 2)
```

Since disk 1 can be directly moved, the second `printf` statement is executed. See Figure 17.6.

```
Move disk number 1 from post 1 to post 3.
```

Now, this invocation of `MoveDisk` returns to its caller, which was the call `MoveDisk(2, 1, 2, 3)`. Recall that we were waiting for all disks on top of disk 2 to be moved to post 3. Since that is now complete, we can now move disk 2 from post 1 to post 2. The `printf` is the next statement to execute, signaling another disk to be moved. See Figure 17.7.

```
Move disk number 2 from post 1 to post 2.
```

Next, a call is made to move all disks that were on disk 2 back onto disk 2. This happens at the call on line 22 of the source code for `MoveDisk`.

```
/* diskNumber 1; startPost 3; endPost 2; midPost 1 */
MoveDisk(1, 3, 2, 1)
```

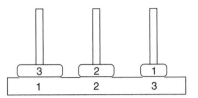

Figure 17.7   The Towers of Hanoi
              puzzle, after second
              move

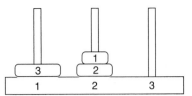

Figure 17.8   The Towers of Hanoi
              puzzle, after third move

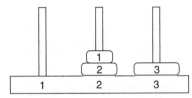

Figure 17.9   The Towers of Hanoi
              puzzle, after fourth
              move

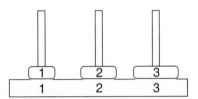

Figure 17.10 The Towers of Hanoi
              puzzle, after fifth move

Again, since disk 1 has no disks on top of it, we see the move printed. See Figure 17.8.

```
Move disk number 1 from post 3 to post 2.
```

Now control passes back to the call `MoveDisk(2, 1, 2, 3)` which, having completed its task of moving disk 2 (and all disks on top of it) from post 1 to post 2, returns to its caller. Its caller is `MoveDisk(3, 1, 3, 2)`. Now, all disks have been moved off disk 3 and onto post 2. Disk 3 can be moved from post 1 onto post 3. The `printf` is the next statement executed. See Figure 17.9.

```
Move disk number 3 from post 1 to post 3.
```

The next subtask remaining is to move disk 2 (and all disks on top of it) from post 2 onto post 3. We can use post 1 for intermediate storage. The following call occurs on line 22 of the source code.

```
/* diskNumber 2; startPost 2; endPost 3; midPost 1 */
MoveDisk(2, 2, 3, 1)
```

In order to do so, we must first move disk 1 from post 2 onto post 1. This call is made from line 15 in the source code.

```
/* diskNumber 1; startPost 2; endPost 1; midPost 3 */
MoveDisk(1, 2, 1, 3)
```

The move requires no submoves. See Figure 17.10.

```
Move disk number 1 from post 2 to post 1.
```

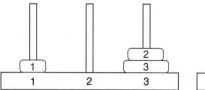

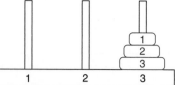

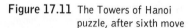

Figure 17.11 The Towers of Hanoi
puzzle, after sixth move

Figure 17.12 The Towers of Hanoi
puzzle, completed

Return passes back to the caller `MoveDisk(2, 2, 3, 1)`, and disk 2 is moved onto post 3. See Figure 17.11.

```
Move disk number 2 from post 2 to post 3.
```

The only thing remaining is to move all disks that were on disk 2 back on top.

```
/* diskNumber 1; startPost 1; endPost 3; midPost 2 */
MoveDisk(1, 1, 3, 2)
```

The move is done immediately. See Figure 17.12.

```
Move disk number 1 from post 1 to post 3.
```

and the puzzle is completed!

Let's summarize the action of the recursion by examining the sequence of function calls that were made in solving the three-disk puzzle:

```
MoveDisk(3, 1, 3, 2)   /* Initial Call */
MoveDisk(2, 1, 2, 3)
MoveDisk(1, 1, 3, 2)
MoveDisk(1, 2, 3, 1)
MoveDisk(2, 2, 3, 1)
MoveDisk(1, 2, 1, 3)
MoveDisk(1, 1, 3, 2)
```

Consider how you would write an iterative version of a program to solve this puzzle and you will appreciate the simplicity of the recursive version. Returning to the legend of the Towers of Hanoi: the world will end when the monks finish solving a 64-disk version of the puzzle. If each move takes one second, how long will it take the monks to solve the puzzle?

17.5 Fibonacci Numbers

The following recurrence equations generate a well-known sequence of numbers called the *Fibonacci numbers*, which has some interesting mathematical, geometrical, and natural properties.

$$f(n) = f(n-1) + f(n-2)$$
$$f(1) = 1$$
$$f(0) = 1$$

In other words, the nth Fibonacci number is the sum of the previous two. The series is $1, 1, 2, 3, 5, 8, 13, \ldots$ This series was first formulated by the Italian mathematician Leonardo of Pisa around the year 1200. His father's name was Bonacci, thus he often called himself Fibonacci as a shortening of *filius Bonacci*, or son of Bonacci. Fibonacci formulated this series as a way of estimating breeding rabbit populations, and we have since discovered some facinating ways in which the series models some other natural phenomena such as the structure of a spiral shell or the pattern of petals on a flower.

We can formulate a recursive function to calculate the nth Fibonacci number directly from the recurrence equations. Fibonacci (n) is recursively calculated by Fibonacci (n-1) + Fibonacci (n-2). The base case of the recursion is simply the fact that Fibonacci (1) and Fibonacci (0) both equal 1. Figure 17.13 lists the recursive code to calculate the nth Fibonacci number.

```
1    #include <stdio.h>
2
3    int Fibonacci(int n);
4
5    int main()
6    {
7      int in;
8      int number;
9
10     printf("Which Fibonacci number? ");
11     scanf("%d", &in);
12
13     number = Fibonacci(in);
14     printf("That Fibonacci number is %d\n", number);
15   }
16
17   int Fibonacci(int n)
18   {
19     int sum;
20
21     if (n == 0 || n == 1)
22        return 1;
23     else {
24        sum = (Fibonacci(n-1) + Fibonacci(n-2));
25        return sum;
26     }
27   }
```

Figure 17.13 Fibonacci is a recursive C function to calculate the nth Fibonacci number

We will use this example to examine how recursion works from the perspective of the lower levels of the computing system. In particular, we will examine the run-time stack mechanism and how it deals with recursive calls. Whenever the function is called, whether from itself or another function, a new copy of its activation record is pushed onto the run-time stack. That is, each invocation of the function gets a new, private copy of parameters and local variables, where each copy is different than any other copy. This must be the case in order for recursion to work, and the run-time stack enables this. If the variables of this function were statically allocated in memory, each recursive call to Fibonacci would overwrite the values of the previous call.

Let's see what happens when we call the function Fibonacci with the parameter 3, Fibonacci(3). We start off with the activation record for Fibonacci(3) on top of the run-time stack. Figure 17.14 shows the progression of the stack as the original function call is evaluated.

The function call Fibonacci(3) will calculate first Fibonacci(3-1), as the expression Fibonacci(n-1) + Fibonacci(n-2) is evaluated left to right. Therefore, a call is first made to Fibonacci(2), and an activation record for Fibonacci(2) is pushed onto the run-time stack (see Figure 17.14, step 2).

For Fibonacci(2), the parameter n equals 2 and does not meet the terminal condition, therefore a call is made to Fibonacci(1) (see Figure 17.14, step 3). This call is made in the course of evaluating Fibonacci(2-1) + Fibonacci(2-2).

The call Fibonacci(1) results in no more recursive calls because the parameter n meets the terminal condition. The value 1 is returned to Fibonacci(2), which now can complete the evaluation of Fibonacci(1) + Fibonacci(0) by calling Fibonacci(0) (see Figure 17.14, step 4). The call Fibonacci(0) immediately returns a 1.

Now, the call Fibonacci(2) can complete and return its subcalculation (its result is 2) to its caller, Fibonacci(3). Having completed the left-hand component of the expression Fibonacci(2) + Fibonacci(1), Fibonacci(3) calls Fibonacci(1) (see Figure 17.14, step 5), which immediately returns the value 1. Now Fibonacci(3) is done—its result is 3 (Figure 17.14, step 6).

We could state the recursion of Fibonacci(3) algebraically, as follows:

```
Fibonacci(3) = Fibonacci(2) + Fibonacci(1)
             = (Fibonacci(1) + Fibonacci(0)) + Fibonacci(1)
             = 1 + 1 + 1 = 3
```

The sequence of function calls made during the evaluations of Fibonacci(3) is as follows:

```
Fibonacci(3)
Fibonacci(2)
Fibonacci(1)
Fibonacci(0)
Fibonacci(1)
```

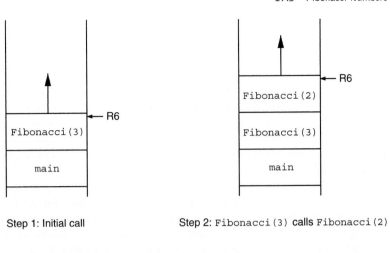

Step 1: Initial call   Step 2: Fibonacci(3) calls Fibonacci(2)

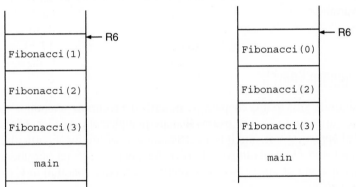

Step 3: Fibonacci(2) calls Fibonacci(1)   Step 4: Fibonacci(2) calls Fibonacci(0)

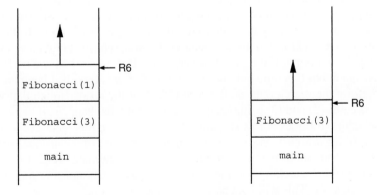

Step 5: Fibonacci(3) calls Fibonacci(1)   Step 6: Back to the starting point

Figure 17.14 Snapshots of the run-time stack for the function call Fibonacci(3)

Walk through the execution of `Fibonacci(4)` and you will notice that the sequence of calls made by `Fibonacci(3)` is a subset of the calls made by `Fibonacci(4)`. No surprise, since `Fibonacci(4)` = `Fibonacci(3)` + `Fibonacci(2)`. Likewise, the sequence of calls made by `Fibonacci(4)` is a subset of the calls made by `Fibonacci(5)`. There is an exercise at the end of this chapter involving calculating the number of function calls made during the evaluation of `Fibonacci(n)`.

The LC-3 C compiler generates the following code for this program, listed in Figure 17.15. Notice that no special treatment was required because this function is recursive. Because of the run-time stack mechanism for activating functions, a recursive function gets treated like every other function. If you examine this code closely, you will notice that the compiler generated a temporary variable in order to translate line 24 of `Fibonacci` properly. Most compilers will generate such temporaries when compiling complex expressions. Such temporary values are allocated storage in the activation on top of the space for the programmer-declared local variables.

17.6 Binary Search

In the introduction to this chapter, we described a recursive technique for finding a particular exam in a set of exams that are in alphabetical order. The technique is called *binary search*, and it is a very rapid way of finding a particular element within a list of elements in sorted order. At this point, given our understanding of recursion and of arrays, we can specify a recursive function in C to perform binary search.

Say we want to find a particular integer value in an array of integers that is in ascending order. The function should return the index of the integer, or a −1 if the integer does not exist. To accomplish this, we will use the binary search technique as such: given an array and an integer to search for, we will examine the midpoint of the array and determine if the integer is (1) equal to the value at the midpoint, (2) less than the value at the midpoint, or (3) greater than the value at the midpoint. If it is equal, we are done. If it is less than, we perform the search again, but this time only on the first half of the array. If it is greater than, we perform the search only on the second half of the array. Notice that we can express cases (2) and (3) using recursive calls. But what happens if the value we are searching for does not exist within the array? Given this recursive technique of performing searches on smaller and smaller subarrays of the original array, we eventually perform a search on an array that has no elements (e.g., of size 0) if the item we are searching for does not exist. If we encounter this situation, we will return a −1. This will be a base case in the recursion.

Figure 17.16 contains the recursive implementation of the binary search algorithm in C. Notice that in order to determine the size of the array at each step, we pass the starting point and ending point of the subarray along with each call to `BinarySearch`. Each call refines the variables `start` and `end` to search smaller and smaller subarrays of the original array `list`.

```
1    Fibonacci:
2       ADD  R6, R6, #-2 ; push return value/address
3       STR  R7, R6, #0  ; store return address
4       ADD  R6, R6, #-1 ; push caller's frame pointer
5       STR  R5, R6, #0  ;
6       ADD  R5, R6, #-1 ; set new frame pointer
7       ADD  R6, R6, #-2 ; allocate space for locals and temps
8
9       LDR  R0, R5, #4  ; load the parameter n
10      BRZ  FIB_BASE    ; n==0
11      ADD  R0, R0, #-1 ;
12      BRZ  FIB_BASE    ; n==1
13
14      LDR  R0, R5, #4  ; load the parameter n
15      ADD  R0, R0, #-1 ; calculate n-1
16      ADD  R6, R6, #-1 ; push n-1
17      STR  R0, R6, #0  ;
18      JSR  Fibonacci   ; call to Fibonacci(n-1)
19
20      LDR  R0, R6, #0  ; read the return value at top of stack
21      ADD  R6, R6, #-1 ; pop return value
22      STR  R0, R5, #-1 ; store it into temporary value
23      LDR  R0, R5, #4  ; load the parameter n
24      ADD  R0, R0, #-2 ; calculate n-2
25      ADD  R6, R6, #-1 ; push n-2
26      STR  R0, R6, #0  ;
27      JSR  Fibonacci   ; call to Fibonacci(n-2)
28
29      LDR  R0, R6, #0  ; read the return value at top of stack
30      ADD  R6, R6, #-1 ; pop return value
31      LDR  R1, R5, #-1 ; read temporary value: Fibonacci(n-1)
32      ADD  R0, R0, R1  ; Fibonacci(n-1) + Fibonacci(n-2)
33      BR   FIB_END     ; branch to end of code
34
35   FIB_BASE:
36      AND  R0, R0, #0  ; clear R0
37      ADD  R0, R0, #1  ; R0 = 1
38
39   FIB_END:
40      STR  R0, R5, #3  ; write the return value
41      ADD  R6, R5, #1  ; pop local variables
42      LDR  R5, R6, #0  ; restore caller's frame pointer
43      ADD  R6, R6, #1  ;
44      LDR  R7, R6, #0  ; pop return address
45      ADD  R6, R6, #1  ;
46      RET
```

Figure 17.15 Fibonacci in LC-3 assembly code

```
1    /*
2    ** This function returns the position of 'item' if it exists
3    ** between list[start] and list[end], or -1 if it does not.
4    */
5    int BinarySearch(int item, int list[], int start, int end)
6    {
7      int middle = (end + start) / 2;
8
9      /* Did we not find what we are looking for? */
10     if (end < start)
11       return -1;
12
13     /* Did we find the item? */
14     else if (list[middle] == item)
15       return middle;
16
17     /* Should we search the first half of the array? */
18     else if (item < list[middle])
19         return BinarySearch(item, list, start, middle - 1);
20
21     /* Or should we search the second half of the array? */
22     else
23         return BinarySearch(item, list, middle + 1, end);
24   }
```

Figure 17.16 A recursive C function to perform binary search

Figure 17.17 provides a pictorial representation of this code during execution. The array list contains 11 elements as shown. The initial call to BinarySearch passes the value we are looking for (item) and the array to be searched (recall from Chapter 16 that this is the address of the very first element, or base address, of the array). Along with the array, we provide the *extent* of the array. That is, we provide the starting point and ending point of the portion of the array to be searched. In every subsequent recursive call to BinarySearch, this extent is made smaller, eventually reaching a point where the subset of the array we are searching has either only one element or no elements at all. These two situations are the base cases of the recursion.

Instead of resorting to a technique like binary search, we could have attempted a more straightforward sequential search through the array. That is, we could examine list[0], then list[1], then list[2], etc., and eventually either find the item or determine that it does not exist. Binary search, however, will require fewer comparisons and can potentially execute faster if the array is large enough. In subsequent computing courses you will analyze binary search and derive that its running time is proportional to $\log_2 n$, where n is the size of the array. Sequential search, on the other hand, is proportional to n.

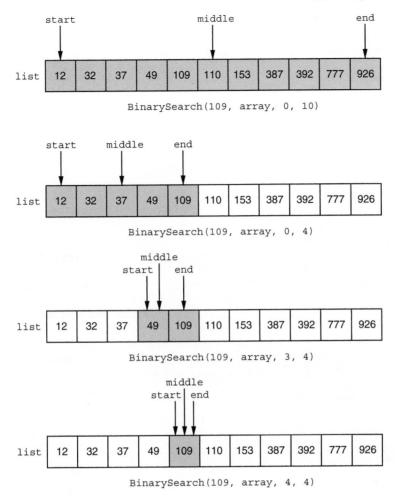

BinarySearch(109, array, 0, 10)

BinarySearch(109, array, 0, 4)

BinarySearch(109, array, 3, 4)

BinarySearch(109, array, 4, 4)

Figure 17.17 BinarySearch performed on an array of 11 elements. We are searching for the element 109

17.7 Integer to ASCII

Our final example of a recursive function is a function that converts an arbitrary integer value into a string of ASCII characters. Recall from Chapter 10 that in order to display an integer value on the screen, each digit of the value must be individually extracted, converted into ASCII, and then displayed on the output device. In Chapter 10, we wrote an LC-3 routine to do this using a straightforward iterative technique.

We can do this recursively with the following recursive formulation: if the number to be displayed is a single digit, we convert it to ASCII and display it and we are done (base case). If the number is multiple digits, we make a recursive

```
1    #include <stdio.h>
2
3    void IntToAscii(int i);
4
5    int main()
6    {
7      int in;
8
9      printf("Input number: ");
10     scanf("%d", &in);
11
12     IntToAscii(in);
13     printf("\n");
14   }
15
16   void IntToAscii(int num)
17   {
18     int prefix;
19     int currDigit;
20
21     if (num < 10)                    /* The terminal case     */
22        printf("%c", num + '0');
23     else {
24        prefix = num / 10;            /* Convert the number    */
25        IntToAscii(prefix);          /* without last digit    */
26
27        currDigit = num % 10;        /* Then print last digit */
28        printf("%c", currDigit + '0');
29     }
30   }
```

Figure 17.18 IntToAscii is a recursive function that converts a positive integer to ASCII

call on the number without the least significant (rightmost) digit, and when the recursive call returns we display the rightmost digit.

Figure 17.18 lists the recursive C function. It takes a positive integer value and converts each digit of the value into ASCII and displays the resulting characters.

The recursive function IntToAscii works as follows: to print out a number, say 21,669, for example (i.e., we are making the call IntToAscii(21669)), the function will subdivide the problem into two parts. First 2166 must be printed out via a recursive call to IntToAscii, and once the call is done, the 9 will be printed.

The function removes the least significant digit of the parameter num by shifting it to the right one digit by dividing by 10. With this new (and smaller) value, we make a recursive call. If the input value num is only a single digit, it is converted to ASCII and displayed to the screen—no recursive calls necessary for this case.

Once control returns to each call, the digit that was removed is converted to ASCII and displayed. To clarify, we present the series of calls for the original call of IntToAscii(12345):

```
IntToAscii(12345)
IntToAscii(1234)
IntToAscii(123)
IntToAscii(12)
IntToAscii(1)
printf('1')
printf('2')
printf('3')
printf('4')
printf('5')
```

17.8 Summary

In this chapter, we introduced the concept of recursion. We can solve a problem recursively by using a function that calls itself on smaller subproblems. With recursion, we state the function, say $f(n)$, in terms of the same function on smaller values of n, say for example, $f(n-1)$. The Fibonacci series, for example, is recursively stated as

```
Fibonacci(n) = Fibonacci(n-1) + Fibonacci(n-2);
```

For the recursion to eventually terminate, recursive calls require a base case.

Recursion is a powerful programming tool that, when applied to the right problem, can make the task of programming considerably easier. For example, the Towers of Hanoi puzzle can be solved in a simple manner with recursion. It is much harder to formulate using iteration. In future courses, you will examine ways of organizing data involving pointers (e.g., trees and graphs) where the simplest techniques to manipulate the data structure involve recursive functions. At the lower levels, recursive functions are handled in exactly the same manner as any other function call. The run-time stack mechanism enables this by allowing us to allocate in memory an activation record for each function invocation so that it does not conflict with any other invocation's activation record.

Exercises

17.1   For these questions, refer to the examples that appear in the chapter.

    a. How many calls to `RunningSum` (see Section 17.2) are made for the call `RunningSum(10)`?

    b. How about for the call `RunningSum(n)`? Give your answer in terms of n.

    c. How many calls to `MoveDisk` are made in the Towers of Hanoi problem if the initial call is `MoveDisk(4, 1, 3, 2)`? This call plays out a four-disk game.

    d. How many calls are made for an n-disk game?

    e. How many calls to `Fibonacci` (see Figure 17.13) are made for the initial call `Fibonacci(10)`?

    f. How many calls are required for the nth Fibonacci number?

17.2   Is the return address for a recursive function always the same at each function call? Why or why not?

17.3   What would happen if we swapped the `printf` call with the recursive call in the code for `IntToAscii` in Figure 17.18?

17.4   What does the following function produce for `count(20)`?

```c
int count(int arg)
{
    if (arg < 1)
        return 0;

    else if (arg % 2)
        return(1 + count(arg - 2));
    else
        return(1 + count(arg - 1));
}
```

17.5   Consider the following C program:

```c
#include <stdio.h>

int Power(int a, int b);

int main(void)
{
    int x, y, z;

    printf("Input two numbers: ");
    scanf("%d %d", &x, &y);

    if (x > 0 && y > 0)
      z = Power(x,y);
    else
      z = 0;

    printf("The result is %d.\n", z);
}

int Power(int a, int b)
{
    if (a < b)
        return 0;
    else
        return 1 + Power(a/b, b);
}
```

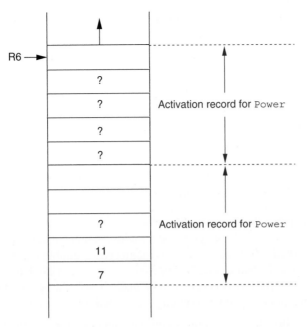

Figure 17.19 Run-time stack after function `Power` is called

    a. State the complete output if the input is

        (1) `4 9`

        (2) `27 5`

        (3) `−1 3`

    b. What does the function `Power` compute?

    c. Figure 17.19 is a snapshot of the stack after a call to the function `Power`. Two activation records are shown, with some of the entries filled in. Assume the snapshot was taken just before execution of one of the `return` statements in `Power`. What are the values in the entries marked with a question mark? If an entry contains an address, use an arrow to indicate the location the address refers to.

17.6   Consider the following C function:

```
int Sigma( int k )
{
    int l;

    l = k -1;

    if (k==0)
        return 0;
    else
        return (k + Sigma(l));
}
```

    a. Convert the recursive function into a nonrecursive function. Assume `Sigma()` will always be called with a nonnegative argument.

    b. Exactly 1 KB of contiguous memory is available for the run-time stack, and addresses and integers are 16 bits wide. How many recursive function calls can be made before the program runs out of memory? Assume no storage is needed for temporary values.

17.7   The following C program is compiled and executed on the LC-3. When the program is executed, the run-time stack starts at memory location xFEFF and grows toward xC000 (the stack can occupy up to 16 KBytes of memory).

```
SevenUp(int x)
{
    if (x == 1)
        return 7;
    else
        return (7 + sevenUp(x - 1));
}

int main()
{
    int a;

    printf("Input a number \n");
    scanf("%d", &a);

    a = SevenUp(a);

    printf("%d is 7 times the number\n", a);
}
```

    a. What is the largest input value for which this program will run correctly? Explain your answer.

    b. If the run-time stack can occupy only 4 KBytes of memory, what is the largest input value for which this program will run correctly? Explain your answer.

17.8 Write an iterative version of a function to find the nth Fibonacci number. Plot the running time of this iterative version to the running time of the recursive version on a variety of values for n. Why is the recursive version significantly slower when n is sufficiently large?

17.9 The binary search routine shown in Figure 17.16 searches through an array that is in ascending order. Rewrite the code so that it works for arrays in descending order.

17.10 Following is a very famous algorithm whose recursive version is significantly easier to express than the iterative one. For the following subproblems, provide the final value returned by the function.

```
int ea(int x, int y)
{
    int a;

    if (y == 0)
        return x;
    else {
        a = x % y;
        return (ea(y, a));
    }
}
```

a. ea(12, 15)
b. ea(6, 10)
c. ea(110, 24)
d. What does this function calculate? Consider how you might construct an iterative version to calculate the same thing.

17.11 Write a program without recursive functions equivalent to the following C program.

```
int main()
{
    printf("%d", M());
}

void M()
{
    int num, x;
    printf("Type a number: ");
    scanf("%d", &num);
    if (num <= 0)
        return 0;
    else {
        x = M();
        if (num > x)
            return num;
        else
            return x;
    }
}
```

17.12   Consider the following recursive function:

```
int func (int arg)
{
   if (arg % 2 != 0)
      return func(arg - 1);
   if (arg <= 0)
      return 1;

   return func(arg/2) + 1;
}
```

a. Is there a value of `arg` that causes an infinite recursion? If so, what is it?

b. Suppose that the function `func` is part of a program whose `main` function follows. How many function calls are made to `func` when the program is executed?

```
int main()
{
   printf("The value is %d\n", func(10));
}
```

c. What value is output by the program?

17.13   The following function is a recursive function that takes a string of characters of unknown length and determines if it contains balanced parentheses. The function `Balanced` is designed to match parentheses. It returns a 0 if the parentheses in the character array string are balanced and a nonzero value if the parentheses are not balanced. The initial call to `Balanced` would be: `Balanced(string, 0, 0);`

The function `Balanced` that follows, however, is missing a few key pieces of code. Fill in the three underlined missing portions in the code.

```
int Balanced(char string[], int position, int count)
{
   if (_____)
      return count;

   else if (string[position] == _____)
      return Balanced( string, ++position, ++count);

   else if (string[position] == _____)
      return Balanced( string, ++position, --count);

   else
      return Balanced( string, ++position, count);
}
```

17.14 What is the output of the following C program?

```c
#include <stdio.h>

void Magic(int in);
int Even(int n);

int main()
{
   Magic(10);
}

void Magic(int in)
{
   if (in == 0)
      return;
   if (Even(in))
      printf("%i\n", in);
   Magic(in - 1);
   if (!Even(in))
      printf("%i\n", in);
   return;
}

int Even(int n)
{
   /* even, return 1; odd, return 0 */
   return (n % 2) == 0 ? 1 : 0;
}
```

18

I/O in C

18.1 Introduction

Whether it be to the screen, to a file, or to another computer across a network, all useful programs perform output of some sort or another. Most programs also require some form of input. As is the case with many other modern programming languages, input and output are not directly supported by C. Instead input/output (I/O) is handled by a set of standard library functions that extend the base language. The behavior of these standard library functions is precisely defined by the ANSI C standard.

In this chapter, we will discuss several functions in the C standard library that support simple I/O. The functions `putchar` and `printf` write to the output device and `getchar` and `scanf` read from the input device. The more general functions `fprintf` and `fscanf` perform file I/O, such as to a file on disk. We have used `printf` and `scanf` extensively throughout the second half of this book. In this chapter, we examine the details of how these functions work. Along the way, we will introduce the notion of variable argument lists and demonstrate how parameter-passing on the LC-3 run-time stack handles function calls with a variable number of arguments.

18.2 The C Standard Library

The C standard library is a major extension of the C programming language. It provides support for input/ouput, character string manipulations, mathematical functions, file access functions, and various system utilities that are not specifically required for a single program but are generally useful in many programs. The standard library is intended to be a repository of useful, primitive functions that serve as *components* for building complex software. This component-based library approach is a characteristic of many programming languages: C++ and Java also have similar standard libraries of primitive functions. We provide a short description of some useful C library functions in Appendix D.9. The library's functions are typically written by designers of the compiler and operating system, and on many occasions they are optimized for the system on which they are installed.

To use a function defined within the C standard library, we must include the appropriate header file (`.h` file). The functions within the standard library are grouped according to their functionality. Each of these groups has a header file associated with it. For example, mathematical functions such as `sin` and `tan` use the common header file `math.h`. The standard I/O functions use the header file `stdio.h`. These header files contain, among other things, function declarations for the I/O functions and preprocessor macros relating to I/O. A library header file does *not* contain the source code for library functions.

If the header files do not contain source code, how does the machine code for, say, `printf` get added to our programs? Each library function called within a program is linked in when the executable image is formed. The object files containing the library functions are stored somewhere on the system and are accessed by the linker, which links together the various function binaries into a single executable program.

As an aside, programs can be linked *dynamically*. With certain types of libraries (dynamically linked libraries [DLLs] or *shared* libraries), the machine code for a library routine does not appear within the executable image but is "linked" on demand, while the program executes.

18.3 I/O, One Character at a Time

We'll start by examining two of the simplest I/O functions provided by the C library. The functions `getchar` and `putchar` perform input and output on a single character at a time. Input is read in as ASCII and output is written out as ASCII, in a manner similar to the IN and OUT TRAP routines of the LC-3.

18.3.1 I/O Streams

Conceptually, all character-based input and output is performed on *streams*. The sequence of ASCII characters typed by the user at the keyboard is an example of an input stream. As each character is typed, it is added to the end of the stream. Whenever a program reads keyboard input, it reads from the beginning of the stream. The sequence of ASCII characters printed by a program, similarly, is added to the end of the output stream. In other words, this stream abstraction allows us to further decouple the producer from the consumer, which is helpful because the two are usually operating at different rates (see Chapter 8). For example, if a program wants to perform some output, it adds characters to the end of the output stream without being required to wait for the output device to finish displaying the previous character. Many other popular languages such as C++ provide a similar stream-based abstraction for I/O.

In C the standard input stream is referred to as `stdin` and is mapped to the keyboard by default. The standard output stream is referred to as `stdout` and is mapped by default to the display. The functions `getchar` and `putchar` operate on these two streams.

18.3.2 `putchar`

The function `putchar` is the high-level language equivalent of the LC-3 OUT TRAP routine. The function `putchar` displays on the `stdout` output stream the ASCII value of the parameter passed to it. It performs no type conversions—the value passed to it is assumed to be ASCII and is added directly to the output stream. All the calls to `putchar` in the following code segment cause the same character (lowercase h) to be displayed. A `putchar` function call is treated like any other function call, except here the function resides within the standard library. The function declaration for `putchar` appears in the `stdio.h` header file. Its code will be linked into the executable during the compiler's link phase.

```
char c = 'h';

:
putchar(c);
putchar('h');
putchar(104);
```

18.3.3 `getchar`

The function `getchar` is the high-level language equivalent of the LC-3 IN TRAP function. It returns the ASCII value of the next input character appearing in the `stdin` input stream. By default, the `stdin` input stream is simply the stream of characters typed at the keyboard. In the following code segment, `getchar` returns the ASCII value of the next character typed at the keyboard. This return value is assigned to the variable `c`.

```
char c;

c = getchar();
```

18.3.4 Buffered I/O

Run the C code in Figure 18.1 and you will notice something peculiar. The program prompts the user for the first input character and waits for that input to be typed in. Type in a single character (say z, for example) and nothing happens. The second prompt does not appear, as if the call to `getchar` has missed the

```
1   #include <stdio.h>
2
3   int main()
4   {
5     char inChar1;
6     char inChar2;
7
8     printf("Input character 1:\n");
9     inChar1 = getchar();
10
11    printf("Input character 2:\n");
12    inChar2 = getchar();
13
14    printf("Character 1 is %c\n", inChar1);
15    printf("Character 2 is %c\n", inChar2);
16  }
```

Figure 18.1   An example of buffered input

keystroke. In fact, the program seems to make no progress at all until the Enter key is pressed. Such behavior seems unexpected considering that getchar is specified to read only a single character from the keyboard input stream.

This unexpected behavior is due to *buffering* of the keyboard input stream. On most computer systems, I/O streams are buffered. Every key typed on the keyboard is captured by the low-level operating system software and kept in a *buffer*, which is a small array, until it is released into the input stream. In the case of the input stream, the buffer is released when the user presses Enter. The Enter key itself appears as a newline character in the input stream. So in the example in Figure 18.1, if the user types the character A and presses Enter, the variable inChar1 will equal the ASCII value of A (which is 65) and the variable inChar2 will equal the ASCII value of newline (which is 10).

There is a good reason for buffering, particularly for keyboard input: Pressing the Enter key allows the user to *confirm* the input. Say you mistyped some input and wanted to correct it before the program detects it. You can edit what you type using the backspace and delete keys, and then confirm your input by pressing Enter.

The output stream is similarly buffered. Observe by running the program in Figure 18.2.

This program uses a new library function called sleep that suspends the execution of the program for approximately the number of seconds provided as the integer argument, which in this case is 5. This library function requires that we include the unistd.h header file. Run this code and you will notice that the output of the character a does not happen quite as you might expect. Instead of appearing prior to the five-second delay, the character a appears *afterwards*, only after the newline character releases the output buffer to the output stream. We say that the putchar('\n') causes output to be *flushed*. Add a putchar('\n') statement immediately after line 6 and the program will behave differently.

Despite the slightly complex behavior of buffered I/O streams, the underlying mechanism used to make this happen are the IN and OUT TRAP routines described

```
1    #include <stdio.h>
2    #include <unistd.h>
3
4    int main()
5    {
6       putchar('a');
7
8       sleep(5);
9
10      putchar('b');
11      putchar('\n');
12   }
```

Figure 18.2 An example of buffered output

in Chapter 8. The buffering of streams is accomplished by extra layers of software surrounding the IN and OUT service routines.

18.4 Formatted I/O

The functions putchar and getchar suffice for simple I/O tasks but are cumbersome for performing non-ASCII I/O. The functions printf and scanf perform more sophisticated *formatted* I/O, and they are designed to more conveniently handle I/O of integer and floating point values.

18.4.1 printf

The function printf writes formatted text to the output stream. Using printf, we can print out ASCII text embedded with values generated by the running program. The printf function takes care of all the type conversions necessary for this to occur. For example, the following code prints out the value of integer variable x. In doing so, the printf must convert the integer value of x into a sequence of ASCII characters that can be embedded in the output stream.

```
int x;

printf("The value is %d\n", x);
```

Generally speaking, printf writes its first parameter to the output stream. The first parameter is the *format string*. It is a character string (i.e., of type char*) containing text to be displayed on the output device. Embedded within the format string are zero or more *conversion specifications*.

The conversion specifications indicate how to print out any of the parameters that follow the format string in the function call. Conversion specifications all begin with a % character. As their name implies, they indicate how the values of the parameters that follow the format string should be treated when converted to ASCII. In many of the examples we have encountered so far, integers have been printed out as decimal numbers using the %d specification. We could also use the %x specification to print integers as hexadecimal numbers, or %b to print them as binary numbers (represented as ASCII text, of course). Other conversions include: %c causes a value to be interpreted as straight ASCII, the %s specification is used for strings and causes characters stored consecutively in memory to be output (for this the corresponding parameter is expected to be of type char*). The specification %f interprets the corresponding parameter as a floating point number and displays it in a floating point format. What if we wanted to print out the % character itself? We use the sequence %%. See Appendix D for a full listing of conversion specifiers.

As mentioned in Chapter 11, special characters such as newline can also be embedded in the format string. The \n prints a new line and a \t character prints a tab; both are examples of these special characters. All special characters begin with a \ and they can appear anywhere within a format string. In order to print out a backslash character, we use a \\. See Table D.1 in the appendix for a list of special characters.

Here are some examples of various format specifications:

```
int   a = 102;
int   b = 65;
char c = 'z';
char banner[10]  = "Hola!";
double pi = 3.14159;

printf("The variable 'a' decimal : %d\n", a);
printf("The variable 'a' hex : %x\n", a);
printf("The variable 'a' binary : %b\n", a);
printf("'a' plus 'b' as character : %c\n", a + b);
printf("Char %c.\t String %s\n Float %f\n", c, banner, pi);
```

The function printf begins by examining the format string a single character at a time. If the current character is not a % or \, then the character is directly written to the output stream. (Recall that the output stream is buffered so the output might not appear on the display until a new line is written.) If the character is a \, then the next character indicates the particular special character to print out. For instance, the escape sequence \n indicates a newline character. If the current character is a %, indicating a conversion specification, then the next character indicates how the next pending parameter should be interpreted. For instance, if the conversion specification is a %d and the next pending parameter is the bit pattern 0000000001101000, then the number 104 is written to the output stream. If the conversion character is a %c, then the character h is written. A different value is printed if %f is the conversion specification. The conversion specifier indicates to printf how the next parameter should be interpreted. It is important to realize that, within the printf routine, there is no relationship between a conversion specification and the type of a parameter. The programmer is free to choose how things are to be interpreted as they are displayed to the screen. *Question:* What happens with the following function call?

```
printf("The value of nothing is %d\n");
```

There is no argument corresponding to the `%d` specification. When the `printf` routine is called, it assumes the correct number of values were written onto the stack, so it blindly reads a value off the stack for the `%d` spec, assuming it was intentionally placed there by the caller. Here, a garbage value is displayed to the screen. However, it is displayed in decimal.

18.4.2 `scanf`

The function `scanf` is used to read formatted ASCII data from the input stream. A call to `scanf` is similar to a call to `printf`. Both calls require a format string as the first argument followed by a variable number of other arguments. Both functions are controlled by characters within the format string. The function `scanf` differs in that all arguments following the format string *must* be pointers. As we discussed in Chapter 16, `scanf` must be able to access the original locations of the objects in memory in order to assign new values to them.

The format string for `scanf` contains ASCII text and conversion specifications, just like the format string for `printf`. The conversion characters are similar to those used for `printf`. A table of these specifications can be found in Appendix D. Essentially, the format string represents the format of the input stream. For example, the format string `"%d"` indicates to `scanf` that the next sequence of non–white space characters (white space is defined as spaces, tabs, new lines, carriage returns, vertical tabs, and form feeds) is a sequence of digits in ASCII representing an integer in decimal notation. After this decimal number is read from the input stream, it is converted into an integer and stored in the corresponding argument. Since `scanf` modifies the values of the variables passed to it, arguments are passed *by reference* using the `&` operator. In addition to conversion specifications, the format string also can contain plain text, which `scanf` tries to match with the input stream. We use the following code to demonstrate.

```
char name[100];
int month, day, year;
double gpa;

printf("Enter : lastname birthdate grade_point_average\n");
scanf("%s %d/%d/%d %lf", name, &month, &day, &year, &gpa);

printf("\n");
printf("Name : %s\n", name);
printf("Birthday : %d/%d/%d\n", month, day, year);
printf("GPA : %f\n", gpa);
```

In this `scanf` statement, the first specification is a `%s` that scans a string of characters from the input stream. In this context, all characters starting from the first non–white space character and ending with the next white space character (conceptually, the next *word* in the input stream) are stored in memory starting at the address of `name`. An `\0` character is automatically added to signify the end of the string. Since the argument `name` is an array, it is automatically passed by reference, that is, the address of the first element of the array is passed to `scanf`.

The next specification is for a decimal number, `%d`. Now, `scanf` expects to find a sequence of digits (at least one digit) as the next set of non–white space characters in the standard input stream. Characters from standard input are analyzed white space characters are discarded, and the decimal number (i.e., a sequence of digits terminated by a nondigit) is read in. The number is converted from a sequence of ASCII characters into a binary integer and stored in the memory location indicated by the argument `&month`.

The next input field is the ASCII character `/`. Now, `scanf` expects to find this character, possibly surrounded by white space, in the input stream. Since this input field is not a conversion specification, it is not assigned to any variable. Once it is read in from the input stream, it is discarded, and `scanf` moves onto the next field of the format string. Similarly, the next three input fields `%d/%d` read in two decimal numbers separated by a `/`. These values are converted into integers and are assigned to the locations indicated by the pointers appearing as the next two arguments (which correspond to the addresses of the variables `day` and `year`).

The last field in the format string specifies that the input stream contains a *long* floating point number, which is the specification used to read in a value of type `double`. For this specifier, `scanf` expects to see a sequence of decimal numbers, and possibly a decimal point, possibly an `E` or `e` signifying exponential notation, in the input stream (see Appendix D.2.4). This field is terminated once a nondigit (excluding the first `E`, or the decimal point or a plus or minus sign for the fraction or exponent) or white space is detected. The `scanf` routine takes this sequence of ASCII characters and converts them into a properly expressed, double-precision floating point number and stores it into `gpa`.

Once it is done processing the format string, `scanf` returns to the caller. It also returns an integer value. The number of format specifications that were successfully scanned in the input stream is passed back to the caller. In this case, if everything went correctly, `scanf` would return the value 5. In the preceding code example, we chose to ignore the return value.

So, for example, the following line of input yields the following output:

```
Enter : lastname birthdate grade_point_average
Mudd 02/16/69 3.02

Name : Mudd
Birthday : 2/16/69
GPA : 3.02
```

Since `scanf` ignores white space for this format string, the following input stream yields the same results. Remember, newline characters are considered white space.

```
Enter : lastname birthdate grade_point_average
Mudd     02
/
16 / 69      3.02

Name : Mudd
Birthday : 2/16/69
GPA : 3.02
```

What if the format of the input stream does not match the format string? For instance, what happens with the following stream?

```
Enter : lastname birthdate grade_point_average
Mudd 02 16 69 3.02
```

Here, the input stream does not contain the / characters encoded in the format string. In this case, `scanf` returns the value 2, since the variables `name` and `month` are correctly assigned before the mismatch between the format string and the input stream is detected. The remaining variables go unmodified. Since the input stream is buffered, unused input is not discarded, and subsequent reads of the input stream begin where the last call left off.

If the next two reads of the input stream are

```
a = getchar();
b = getchar();
```

what do `a` and `b` contain? The answer ' ' (the space character) and 1 should be no surprise.

18.4.3 Variable Argument Lists

By now, you might have noticed something different about the functions `printf` and `scanf` from all other functions we have described thus far. The two functions have a *variable* number of arguments passed to them. The number of arguments passed to `printf` and `scanf` depends on the number of items being printed or scanned. We say such functions have variable argument lists.

There is a one-to-one correspondence between each conversion specification in the format string and each argument that appears after the format string in such function calls. The following `printf` statement is from a previous example:

```
printf("Char %c.\t String %s\n Float %f\n", c, banner, pi);
```

The format string contains three format specifications; therefore, three arguments follow it in the function call. The `%c` spec in the string is associated with the first argument that follows (the variable `c`). The `%s` is associated with `banner`, and

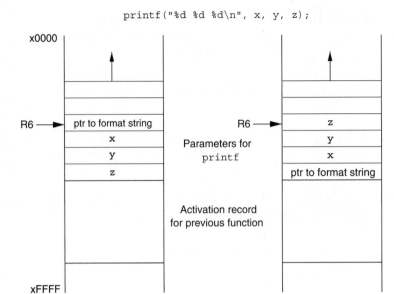

Figure 18.3   Subfigure (a) shows the stack if the arguments to the `printf` call are pushed from right to left. Subfigure (b) shows the stack if the arguments are pushed left to right.

`%f` with `pi`. There are three values to be printed; therefore, this call contains four arguments altogether. If we want to print five values, the function call contains six arguments.

Recall from Chapter 14 that our LC-3 calling convention pushed items onto the run-time stack from *right to left* of the order in which they appear on the function call. This places the pointer to the format string immediately at the top of the stack when `printf` or `scanf` takes over. Since it is the leftmost argument, it will always be the last item pushed onto the stack before the function call occurs. Once `printf` or `scanf` takes over, they can access the first parameter directly off the top of the stack. Once this parameter (which is the format string) is analyzed, the functions can determine the other parameters on the stack. If the arguments on a function call were pushed from left to right, it would be much more difficult for `printf` and `scanf` to discern the location of the format string parameter. Figure 18.3 shows two diagrams of the run-time stack. In diagram (a), the arguments to the call for `printf` are passed from right to left and in (b) from left to right. Consider for which case the resulting LC-3 code for `printf` will be simpler. In version (a), the offset of the format string from the stack pointer will always be zero, regardless of the number of other parameters on the stack. In version (b), the offset of the format string from the stack pointer depends on the number of parameters on the stack.

The format string, like all other strings embedded within a program's source code, is stored in a special region of memory reserved for constants, or *literal values*.

18.5 I/O from Files

Say we wanted to process a large set of data, such as the daily closing price of IBM stock for the last 20 years. To ask the user to type this via keyboard would render it very "user-unfriendly." Instead, we would want the program to read the data off a file on disk, and possibly write its output to disk. I/O in C is based on streams, as we described earlier, and these streams are conceptually all bound to files.

That is, the functions `printf` and `scanf` are in actuality special cases of more general-purpose C I/O functions. These two functions operate specifically on two special files called `stdin` and `stdout`. In C, `stdin` and `stdout` are mapped by default to the keyboard and the display.

The general-purpose version of `printf` is called `fprintf`, and the general-purpose version of `scanf` is called `fscanf`. The functions `fprintf` and `fscanf` work like their counterparts, with the main difference being that they allow us to specify the stream on which they act. For example, we can inform `fprintf` to write its output to a specific file on disk. Let's examine how this can be accomplished.

Before we can perform file I/O, we need to declare a *file pointer* for each file we want to manipulate. Typically, files are stored on the file system of the computer system. In C, we can declare a file pointer called `infile` as follows:

```
FILE *infile;
```

Here we are declaring a pointer to something of type `FILE`. The type `FILE` is defined within the header file `stdio.h`. Its details are not important for our discussion.

Once the file pointer is declared, we need to map it to a file on the computer's file system. The C library call `fopen` performs this mapping. Each `fopen` call requires two arguments: the name of the file to open and the description of what type of operation the we want to perform on the file. To follow is an example.

```
FILE *infile;

infile = fopen("ibm_stock_prices", "r");
```

The first argument to `fopen` is the string `ibm_stock_prices`, which is the name of the file to open. The second argument is the operation we want to perform on this file. Several useful *modes* are `"r"` for reading, `"w"` for writing (a file opened with this mode will lose its previous contents), `"a"` for appending (here, previous contents are not lost; new data is added to the end of the file), `"r+"` for reading and writing. Note that both arguments must be character strings; therefore, they are surrounded by double quotes in this example. In this case, we are opening the file called `"ibm_stock_prices"` for reading.

If the `fopen` call is successful, the function returns a file pointer to the physical file. If the open for some reason fails (such as the file could not be found), then the function returns a null pointer. Recall that a null pointer is an invalid pointer that has the value NULL. It is *always* good practice to check if the `fopen` call was successful.

```
       FILE *infile;

       infile = fopen("ibm_stock_prices", "r");

       if (infile == NULL)
          printf("fopen unsuccessful!\n");
```

Now with the file pointer properly mapped to a physical file, we can use fscanf and fprintf to read and write it just as we used printf and scanf to read the standard devices. The functions fscanf and fprintf both require a file pointer as their first argument to indicate on which stream the operations are to be performed. The example in Figure 18.4 demonstrates.

Here, we are reading from an ASCII text file called ibm_stock_prices and writing to a file called buy_hold_or_sell. The input file contains a floating point

```
1    #include <stdio.h>
2    #define LIMIT 10000
3
4    int main()
5    {
6
7      FILE *infile;
8      FILE *outfile;
9      double prices[LIMIT];
10     char answer[10];
11     int i = 0;
12
13     infile  = fopen("ibm_stock_prices", "r");
14     outfile = fopen("buy_hold_or_sell", "w");
15
16     if (infile != NULL && outfile != NULL) {
17       /*  Read the input data */
18       while ((fscanf(infile, "%lf", &prices[i]) != EOF) && i < LIMIT)
19         i++;
20
21       printf("%d prices read from the data file", i);
22
23       /* Process the data... */
24          :
25          :
26
27
28       /* Write the output */
29       fprintf(outfile, "%s", answer);
30     }
31     else {
32       printf("fopen unsuccessful!\n");
33     }
34   }
```

Figure 18.4   An example of a program that performs file I/O

data item separated by white space. Even though the file can contain more, at most 10,000 items are read by this program using `fscanf`. The `fscanf` function returns a special value when no more data can be read from the input file, indicating the end of file has been reached. We can check the return value of `fscanf` against this special character, which is defined to the preprocessor macro `EOF`. The condition on the `while` loop causes it to terminate if `EOF` is encountered or if the limit of input values is exceeded. After reading the input file, the program processes the input data, and the output file is written with the value of the string `answer`.

The function `printf` is equivalent to calling `fprintf` using `stdout` as the file pointer. Likewise, `scanf` is equivalent to calling `fscanf` using `stdin`.

18.6 Summary

In this chapter, we examined the C facilities for performing input and output. Like many other current programming languages, C provides no direct support for input and output. Rather, standard library functions are provided for I/O. At their core, these functions perform I/O one character at a time using the `IN` and `OUT` routines supported by the underlying machine.

The key concepts that you should take away from this chapter are:

• **Input and output on streams.** Modern programming languages create a useful abstraction for thinking about I/O. Input and output occur on streams. The producer adds data to the stream, and the consumer reads data from the stream. With this relationship, both can operate at their own rate without waiting for the other to be ready to conduct the I/O. For example, a program generating output for the display writes data into the output stream without necessarily waiting for the display to keep pace.

• **The four basic I/O functions.** We discuss the operation, at a fairly detailed level, of four basic I/O functions: `putchar`, `getchar`, `printf`, and `scanf`. The latter two functions require the use of variable argument lists, which our LC-3 calling convention can easily handle because of the order in which we push arguments onto the run-time stack.

• **File I/O.** C treats all I/O streams as file I/O. Functions like `printf` and `scanf` are special cases where the I/O files are the standard output and input devices. The more general functions `fprintf` and `fscanf` enable us to specify a file pointer to which the corresponding operations are to be performed. We can bind a file pointer to a physical file on the file system using `fopen`.

Exercises

18.1 Write an I/O function call to handle the following tasks. All can be handled by a single call.

   a. Print out an integer followed by a string followed by a floating point number.

   b. Print out a phone number in (XXX)-XXX-XXXX format. Internally, the phone number is stored as three integers.

   c. Print out a student ID number in XXX-XX-XXXX format. Internally, the ID number is stored as three character strings.

   d. Read a student ID number in XXX-XX-XXXX format. The number is to be stored internally as three integers.

   e. Read in a line of input containing `Last name, First name, Middle initial age sex`. The name fields are separated by commas. The middle initial and sex should be stored as characters. Age is an integer.

18.2 What does the value returned by `scanf` represent?

18.3 Why is buffering of the keyboard input stream useful?

18.4 What must happen when a program tries to read from the input stream but the stream is empty?

18.5 Why does the following code print out a strange value (such as 1073741824)?

```
float x = 192.27163;
printf("The value of x is %d\n", x);
```

18.6 What is the value of `input` for the following function call:

```
scanf("%d", &input);
```

if the input stream contains

```
This is not the input you are looking for.
```

18.7   Consider the following program:

```
#include <stdio.h>

int main()
{
  int x = 0;
  int y = 0;
  char label[10];

  scanf("%d %d", &x, &y);
  scanf("%s", label);

  printf("%d %d %s\n", x, y, label);
}
```

    a. What gets printed out if the input stream is 46 29 BlueMoon?
    b. What gets printed out if the input stream is 46 BlueMoon?
    c. What gets printed out if the input stream is 111 999 888?

18.8   Write a program to read in a C source file and write it back to a file called "condensed_program" with all *white space* removed.

18.9   Write a program to read in a text file and provide a count of

    a. The number of strings in the file, where a string begins with a non–white space character and ends with a white space character.
    b. The number of words in the file, where a word begins with an alphabetic character (e.g., a–z or A–Z) and ends with a nonalphabetic character.
    c. The number of unique words in the file. Words are as defined in Part *b*. The set of unique words has no duplicates.
    d. The frequency of words in order of most frequent to least frequent. In other words, analyze the text file, count the number of times each word occurs, and display these counts from most frequent word to least frequent.

19

Data Structures

19.1 Introduction

C, at its core, provides support for three fundamental types of data: integers, characters, and floating point values.[1] That is, C natively supports the allocation of variables of these types and natively supports operators that manipulate these types, such as + for addition and * for multiplication. As we traversed the topics in the second half of this textbook, we saw the need for extending these basic types to include pointers and arrays. Both pointers and arrays are derived from the three fundamental types. Pointers point to one of the three types; we can declare arrays of int, char, or double.

Ultimately, though, the job of the programmer is to write programs that deal with real-world objects, such as an aircraft wing or a group of people or a pod of migrating whales. The problem lies in the reality that integers, characters, and floating point values are the only things that the underlying computing system can deal with. The programmer must map these real-world objects onto these primitive types, which can be burdensome. But the programming language can assist in making that bridge. Providing support for describing real-world objects and specifying operations upon them is the basis for *object orientation*.

Orienting a program around the objects that it manipulates rather than the primitive types that the hardware supports is the basic precept of object-oriented programming. We take a small step toward object orientation in this chapter by examining how a C programmer can build a type that is a combination of the

---

[1] Enumerations are another fundamental type that are closely tied to integer types.

more basic types. This aggregation is called a *structure* in C. Structures provide the programmer with a convenient way of representing objects that are best represented by multiple values. For example, an employee might be represented as a structure containing a name (character string), job title (character string), department (perhaps integer), and employee ID (integer) within a corporate database program. In devising such a database program we might use a C structure.

The main theme of this chapter is C's support for advanced data structures. First, we examine how to create structures in C and examine a simple program that manipulates an array of structures. Second, we examine dynamic memory allocation in C. Dynamic allocation is not directly related to the concept of structures, but it is a component we use for the third item of this chapter, linked lists. A linked list is a fundamental (and common) data organization that is similar to an array—both store collections of data items—but has a different organization for its data items. We will look at functions for adding, deleting, and searching for data items within linked lists.

19.2 Structures

Some things are best described by an aggregation of fundamental types. For such objects, C provides the concept of structures. Structures allow the programmer to define a new type that consists of a combination of fundamental data items such as int, char, and double, as well as pointers to them and arrays of them. Structure variables are declared in the same way variables of fundamental data types are declared. Before any structure variables are declared, however, the organization and naming of the data items within the structure must be defined.

For example, in representing an airborne aircraft, say for a flight simulator or for a program that manages air traffic over Chicago, we would want to describe several flight characteristics that are relevant for the application at hand. The aircraft's flight number is useful for identification, and since this would typically be a sequence of digits and characters, we could use a character string for representing it. The altitude, longitude, latitude, and heading of the flight are also useful, all of which we might store as integers. Airspeed is another characteristic that would be important, and it is best represented as a double-precision floating point number. Following are the variable declarations for describing a single aircraft in flight.

```
char flightNum[7];   /* Max 6 characters       */
int altitude;        /* in meters              */
int longitude;       /* in tenths of degrees   */
int latitude;        /* in tenths of degrees   */
int heading;         /* in tenths of degrees   */
double airSpeed;     /* in kilometers/hour     */
```

If the program modeled multiple flights, we would need to declare a copy of these variables for each one, which is tedious and could result in excessively long code. C provides a convenient way to aggregate these characteristics into a single type via the `struct` construct, as follows:

```
struct flightType {
    char flightNum[7];    /* Max 6 characters         */
    int altitude;         /* in meters                */
    int longitude;        /* in tenths of degrees     */
    int latitude;         /* in tenths of degrees     */
    int heading;          /* in tenths of degrees     */
    double airSpeed;      /* in kilometers/hour       */
};
```

In the preceding declaration, we have created a new type containing six *member* elements. We have not yet declared any storage; rather we have indicated to the compiler the composition of this new type. We have given the structure the *tag* `flightType`, which is necessary for referring to the structure in other parts of the code.

To declare a variable of this new type, we do the following:

```
struct flightType plane;
```

This declares a variable called `plane` that consists of the six fields defined in the structure declaration but otherwise gets treated like any other variable.

We can access the individual members of this structure variable using the following syntax:

```
struct flightType plane;

plane.airSpeed = 800.00;
plane.altitude = 10000;
```

Each member can be accessed using the variable's name as the base name followed by a dot . followed by the member name.

The variable declaration `plane` gets allocated onto the stack if it is a local variable and occupies a contiguous region of memory large enough to hold all member elements. In this case, if each of the fundamental types occupies one LC-3 memory location, the variable `plane` would occupy 12 locations.

The allocation of the structure is straightforward. A structure is allocated the same way a variable of a basic data type is allocated: locals (by default) are allocated on the run-time stack, and globals are allocated in the global data section. Figure 19.1 shows a portion of the run-time stack when a function that contains the following declarations is invoked.

```
int x;
struct airplaneType plane;
int y;
```

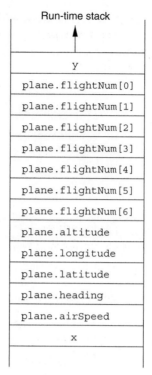

Figure 19.1   The run-time stack showing an allocation of a variable of structure type

Generically, the syntax for a structure declaration is as follows:

```
struct tag {
  type1 member1;
  type2 member2;
  ...
  typeN memberN
} identifiers;
```

The `tag` provides a handle for referring to the structure later in the code, as in the case of later declaring variables of the structure's format. The list of members defines the organization of a structure and is syntactically a list of declarations. A member can be of any type, including another structure type. Finally, we can optionally include identifiers in a structure's declaration to actually declare variables of that structure's type. These appear after the closing brace of the structure declaration, prior to the semicolon.

19.2.1 `typedef`

C structures enable programmers to define their own types. C `typedef` allows programmers to name their own types. It has the general form

```
typedef type name;
```

This statement causes the identifier `name` to be synonymous with the type `type`, which can be any basic type or aggregate type (e.g., a structure). So for instance,

```
typedef int Color;
```

allows us to define variables of type `Color`, which will now be synonymous with integer. Using this definition, we can declare (for a bitmapped image, for example):

```
Color pixels[500];
```

The `typedef` declaration is particularly useful when dealing with structures. For example, we can create a name for the structure we defined earlier:

```
struct flightType {
    char flightNum[7];   /* Max 6 characters       */
    int altitude;        /* in meters              */
    int longitude;       /* in tenths of degrees   */
    int latitude;        /* in tenths of degrees   */
    int heading;         /* in tenths of degrees   */
    double airSpeed;     /* in kilometers/hour      */
};

typedef struct flightType Flight;
```

Now we can declare variables of this type by using the type name `Flight`. For example,

```
Flight plane;
```

is now equivalent to the declaration `struct flightType plane;` that we used previously.

The `typedef` declaration provides no additional functionality. However, it gives clarity to code, particularly code heavy with programmer-defined types. Well-chosen type names connote properties of the variables they declare even beyond what can be expressed by the names of the variables themselves.

19.2.2 Implementing Structures in C

Now that we have seen the technique for declaring and allocating variables of structure type (and have given them new type names), we focus on accessing the member fields and performing operations on them. For example, in the following code, the member `altitude` of the structure variable of type `Flight` is accessed.

```
int x;
Flight plane;
int y;

plane.altitude = 0;
```

Here, the variable `plane` is of type `Flight`, meaning it contains the six member fields we defined previously. The member field labeled `altitude` is accessed using the variable's name followed by a period, followed by the member field label. The compiler, knowing the layout of the structure, generates code that accesses the structure's member field using the appropriate offset. Figure 19.1 shows the layout of the portion of the activation record for this function. The compiler keeps track, in its symbol table, of the position of each variable in relation to the base pointer R5, and if the variable is an aggregate data type, it also tracks the position of each field within the variable. Notice that for the particular reference `plane.altitude = 0;`, the compiler must generate code to access the second variable on the stack and the second member element of that variable.

Following is the code generated by the LC-3 C compiler for the assignment statement `plane.altitude = 0;`.

```
AND   R1, R1, #0    ; zero out R1

ADD   R0, R5, #-12  ; R0 contains base address of plane
STR   R1, R0, #7    ; plane.altitude = 0;
```

19.3 Arrays of Structures

Let's say we are writing a piece of software to determine if any flights over the skies of Chicago are in danger of colliding. For this program, we will use the `Flight` type that we previously defined. If the maximum number of flights that will ever simultaneously exist in this airspace is 100 planes, then the following declaration is appropriate:

```
Flight planes[100];
```

This declaration is similar to the simple declaration `int d[100]`, except instead of declaring 100 integer values, we have declared a contiguous region of memory containing 100 structures, each of which is composed of the six members indicated in the declaration `struct flightType`. The reference `planes[12]`, for example, would refer to the thirteenth object in the region of 100 such objects in memory. Each object contains enough storage for its six constituent member elements.

Each element of this array is of type `Flight` and can be accessed using standard array notation. For example, accessing the flight characteristics of the first flight can be done using the identifier `plane[0]`. Accessing a member field is done by accessing an element of the array and then specifying a field: `plane[0].heading`. The following code segment provides an example. It finds the average airspeed of all flights in the airspace monitored by the program.

```
int i;
double sum = 0;
double averageAirSpeed;

for (i = 0; i < 100; i++)
   sum = sum + plane[i].airSpeed;

averageAirSpeed = sum / 100;
```

We can also create pointers to structures. The following declaration creates a pointer variable that contains the address of a variable of type `Flight`.

```
Flight *planePtr;
```

We can assign this variable as we would any pointer variable.

```
planePtr = &plane[34];
```

If we want to access any of the member fields pointed to by this pointer variable, we could use an expression such as the following:

```
(*planePtr).longitude
```

With this cumbersome expression, we are dereferencing the variable `planePtr`. It points to something of type `Flight`. Therefore when `planePtr` is dereferenced, we are accessing an object of type `Flight`. We can access one of its member fields by using the dot operator (.). As we shall see, refering to a structure with a pointer is a common operation, and since this expression is not very straightforward to grasp, a special operator has been defined for it. The previous expression is equivalent to

```
planePtr->longitude
```

That is, the expression `->` is like the deference operator `*`, except it is used for deferencing member elements of a structure type.

Now we are ready to put our discussion of structures to use by presenting an example of a function that manipulates an array of structures. This example examines the 100 flights that are airborne to determine if any pair of them are potentially in danger of colliding. To do this, we need to examine the position, altitude, and heading of each flight to determine if there exists the potential of collision. In Figure 19.2, the function `PotentialCollisions` calls the function `Collide` on each pair of flights to determine if their flight paths dangerously intersect. (This function is only partially complete; it is left as an exercise for you to write the code to more precisely determine if two flight paths intersect.)

Notice that `PotentialCollisions` passes `Collide` two pointers rather than the structures themselves. While it is possible to pass structures, passing pointers is likely to be more efficient because it involves less pushing of data onto the run-time stack; that is, in this case two pointers are pushed rather than 24 locations' worth of data for two objects of type `Flight`.

```
1    #include <stdio.h>
2    #define TOTAL_FLIGHTS 100
3
4    /* Structure definition */
5    struct flightType {
6      char flightNum[7];    /* Max 6 characters        */
7      int altitude;         /* in meters               */
8      int longitude;        /* in tenths of degrees    */
9      int latitude;         /* in tenths of degrees    */
10     int heading;          /* in tenths of degrees    */
11     double airSpeed;      /* in kilometers/hour      */
12   };
13
14   typedef struct flightType Flight;
15
16   int Collide(Flight *planeA, Flight *planeB); void
17   PotentialCollisions(Flight planes[]);
18
19   int Collide(Flight *planeA, Flight *planeB)
20   {
21     if (planeA->altitude == planeB->altitude) {
22
23       /** More logic to detect collision goes here **/
24     }
25     else
26       return 0;
27   }
28
29   void PotentialCollisions(Flight planes[])
30   {
31     int i;
32     int j;
33
34     for (i = 0; i < TOTAL_FLIGHTS; i++) {
35       for (j = 0; j < TOTAL_FLIGHTS; j++) {
36         if (Collide(&planes[i], &planes[j]))
37           printf("Flights %s and %s are on collision course!\n",
38                   planes[i].flightNum, planes[j].flightNum);
39       }
40     }
41   }
```

Figure 19.2   An example function based on the structure `Flight`

19.4 Dynamic Memory Allocation

Memory objects (e.g., variables) in C programs are allocated to one of three spots in memory: the run-time stack, the global data section, or the *heap*. Variables declared local to functions are allocated during execution onto the run-time stack by default. Global variables are allocated to the global data section and are accessible by all parts of a program. Dynamically allocated data objects—objects that are created during run-time—are allocated onto the heap.

In the previous example, we declared an array that contained 100 objects, where each object was an aircraft in flight. But what if we wanted to create a flexible program that could handle as many flights as were airborne at any given moment, whether it be 2 or 20,000? One possible solution would be to declare the array assuming a large upper limit to the number of flights the program might encounter. This could result in a lot of potentially wasted memory space, or worse, we might underestimate the number of flights, which could have potentially devastating repercussions. A better solution is to dynamically adapt the size of the array based on the number of planes in the air. To accomplish this, we rely on the concept of dynamic memory allocation.

In a nutshell, dynamic memory allocation works as follows: A piece of code called the memory allocator manages an area of memory called the heap. Figure 19.3 is a copy of Figure 12.7; it shows the relationship of the various regions of memory, including the heap. During execution, a program can make requests to the memory allocator for contiguous pieces of memory of a particular

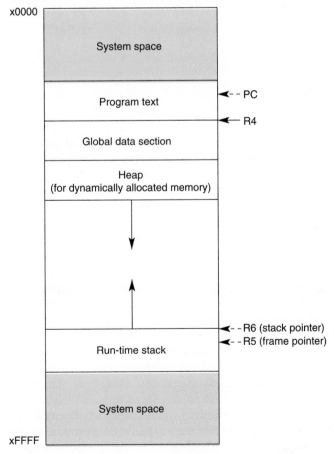

Figure 19.3   The LC-3 memory map showing the heap region of memory

size. The memory allocator then reserves this memory and returns a pointer to the newly reserved memory to the program. For example, if we wanted to store 1,000 flights' worth of data in our air traffic control program, we could request the allocator for this space. If enough space exists in the heap, the allocator will return a pointer to it. Notice that the heap and the stack both grow toward each other. The size of the stack is based on the depth of the current function call, whereas the size of the heap is based on how much memory the memory allocator has reserved for the requests it has received.

A block of memory that is allocated onto the heap stays allocated until the programmer explicitly deallocates it by calling the memory deallocator. The deallocator adds the block back onto the heap for subsequent reallocation.

19.4.1 Dynamically Sized Arrays

Dynamic allocation in C is handled by the C standard library functions. In particular, the memory allocator is invoked by the function `malloc`. Let's take a look at an example that uses the function `malloc`:

```
int airbornePlanes;
Flight *planes;

printf("How many planes are in the air?");
scanf("%d", &airbornePlanes);

planes = malloc(24 * airbornePlanes);
```

The function `malloc` allocates a contiguous region of memory on the heap of the size in bytes indicated by the single parameter. If the heap has enough unclaimed memory and the call is successful, `malloc` returns a pointer to the allocated region.

Here we allocate a chunk of memory consisting of `24 * airbornePlane` bytes, where `airbornePlanes` is the number of planes in the air as indicated by the user. What about the 24? Recall that the type `Flight` is composed of six members—an array of 7 characters, 4 integers, and a double, each occupy a single two-byte location on the LC-3. Each structure requires 24 bytes of memory. As a necessary convenience for programmers, the C language supports a compile-time operator called `sizeof`. This operator returns the size, in bytes, of the memory object or type passed to it as an argument. For example, `sizeof(Flight)` will return the number of bytes occupied by a variable of type `Flight`, or 24. The programmer does not need to calculate the sizes of various data objects; the compiler can be instructed to perform the calculation.

If all the memory on the heap has been allocated and the current allocation cannot be accomplished, `malloc` returns the value `NULL`. Recall that the symbol `NULL` is a preprocessor macro symbol, defined to a particular value depending on the computer system, that represents a null pointer. It is good programming practice to check that the return value from `malloc` indicates the memory allocation was successful.

The function `malloc` returns a pointer. But what is the type of the pointer? In the preceding example, we are treating the pointer that is returned by `malloc` as a pointer to some variable of type `Flight`. Later we might use `malloc` to allocate an array of integers, meaning the return value will be treated as an `int *`. To enable this, `malloc` returns a generic data pointer, or `void *`, that needs to be *type cast* to the appropriate form upon return. That is, whenever we call the memory allocator, we need to instruct the compiler to treat the return value as of a *different* type than was declared.

In the preceding example, we need to type cast the pointer returned by `malloc` to the type of the variable to which we are assigning it. Since we assigned the pointer to `planes`, which is of type `Flight *`, we therefore cast the pointer to type `Flight *`. To do otherwise makes the code less portable across different computer systems; most compilers generate a warning message because we are assigning a pointer value of one type to a pointer variable of another. Type casting causes the compiler to treat a value of one type as if it were of another type. To type cast a value from one type to a `newType`, we use the following syntax. The variable `var` should be of `newType`. For more information on type casting, refer to section D.5.11.

```
var = (newType) expression;
```

Given type casting and the `sizeof` operation and the error checking of the return value from `malloc`, the correct way to write the code from the previous example is:

```
int airbornePlanes;
Flight *planes;

printf("How many planes are in the air?");
scanf("%d", &airbornePlanes);

/* A more correctly written call malloc */
planes = (Flight *) malloc(sizeof(Flight) * airbornePlanes);
if (planes == NULL) {
    printf("Error in allocating the planes array\n");
    :
    :
}
plane[0].altitude = ...
```

Since the region that is allocated by `malloc` is contiguous in memory, we can switch between pointer notation and array notation. Now we can use the expression `planes[29]` to access the characteristics of the 30th aircraft (provided that `airbornePlanes` was larger than 30, of course). Notice that we smoothly switched from pointer notation to array notation; this flexibility has helped make C a very popular programming language. Other derivative languages, C++ in particular, keep this duality between pointers to contiguous memory and arrays.

The function `malloc` is only one of several memory allocation functions in the standard library. The function `calloc` allocates memory and initializes it to the value 0. The function `realloc` attempts to grow or shrink previously allocated regions of memory. To use the memory allocation functions of the C standard library, we need to include the `stdlib.h` header file. Can you use `realloc` to create an array that adapts to the size of the data size—for example, write a function `AddPlane()` that adds a plane if the current size of the `planes` is too small? Likewise, write the function `DeletePlane()` when the size of the array is larger than what is required.

A very important counterpart to the memory allocation functions is a function to *deallocate* memory and return it to the heap. This function is called `free`. It takes as its parameter a pointer to a region that was previously allocated by `malloc` (or `calloc` or `realloc`) and deallocates it. After a region has been `free`'d, it is once again eligible for allocation. Why is deallocation necessary? As we shall see, there is a class of data structures that dynamically grow and shrink as the program executes. For the shrinking operation, we put allocated memory back on the heap so that we can use it again in subsequent allocations.

19.5 Linked Lists

Having discussed the notion of structures and the concept of dynamic memory allocation, we are now ready to introduce a fundamental data structure that is pervasive in computing. A *linked list* is similar to an array in that both can be used to store data that is best represented as a list of elements. In an array, each element (except the last) has a next element that follows it sequentially in memory. Likewise in a linked list, each element has a next element, but the next element need not be sequentially adjacent in memory. Rather, each element contains a pointer to the next element.

A linked list is a collection of *nodes*, where each node is one "unit" of data, such as the characteristics of an airborne aircraft from the previous section. In a linked list we connect these nodes together using pointers. Each node contains a pointer element that points to the next node in the list. Given a starting node, we can go from one node to another by following the pointer in each node. To create these nodes, we rely on C structures. A critical element for the structure that defines the nodes of a linked list is that it contains a member element that points to nodes like itself. The following code demonstrates how this is accomplished. We use the `Flight` type we defined in the previous sections. Notice that we have added a new member element to the structure definition. It is a pointer to a node of the same type.

```
typedef struct flightType Flight;
struct flightType {
  char flightNum[7];   /* Max 6 characters        */
  int altitude;        /* in meters               */
  int longitude;       /* in tenths of degrees    */
  int latitude;        /* in tenths of degrees    */
  int heading;         /* in tenths of degrees    */
  double airSpeed;     /* in kilometers/hour       */
  Flight *next;
};
```

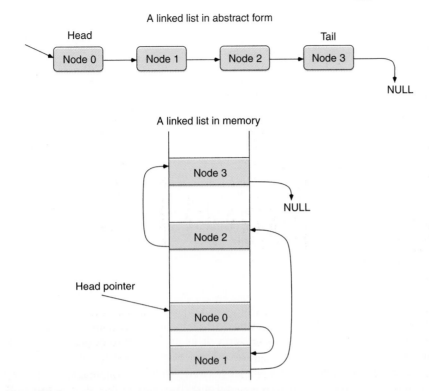

Figure 19.4 Two representations for a linked list

Like an array, a linked list has a beginning and an end. Its beginning, or *head*, is accessed using a pointer called the *head pointer*. The final node in the list, or tail, points to the NULL value. Figure 19.4 shows two representations of a linked list data structure: an abstract depiction where nodes are represented as blocks and pointers are represented by arrows, and a more physical representation that shows what the data structure might look like in memory.

Despite their similarities, arrays and linked lists have fundamental differences. An array can be accessed in random order. We can access element number 4, followed by element 911, followed by 45, for example. A simple linked list must be traversed sequentially starting at its head. If we wanted to access node 29, then we must start at node 0 (the head node) and then go to node 1, then to node 2, and so forth. But linked lists are dynamic in nature; additional nodes can be added or deleted without movement of the other nodes. While it is straightforward to dynamically size an array (see Section 19.4.1 on using malloc), it is much more costly to remove a single element in an array, particularly if it lies in the middle. Consider, for example, how you would remove the information for a plane that has just landed from the air traffic control program from Section 19.3. With a linked list we can dynamically add nodes to make room for more data, and we can delete nodes that are no longer required.

19.5.1 An Example

Say we want to write a program to manage the inventory at a used car lot. At the lot, cars keep coming and going, and the database needs to be updated continually—a new entry is created whenever a car is added to the lot and an entry deleted whenever a car is sold. Furthermore, the entries are stored in order by vehicle identification number so that queries from the used car sales-people can be handled quickly. The information we need to keep per car is as follows:

```
int  vehicleID;     /* Unique identifier for a car */
char make[20];      /* Manufacturer              */
char model[20];     /* Model name                */
int  year;          /* Year of manufacture       */
int mileage;        /* in miles                  */
double cost;        /* in dollars                */

Car *next;          /* Points to a car_node      */
```

In reality, a vehicle ID is a sequence of characters and numbers and cannot be stored as a single `int`, but we store it as an integer to make the example simpler.

The frequent operations we want to perform—adding, deleting, and searching for entries—can be performed simply and quickly using a linked list data structure. Each node in the linked list contains all the information associated with a car in the lot, as shown. We can now define the node structure, which is then given the name `CarNode` using `typedef`:

```
typedef struct carType Car;

struct carType {
  int  vehicleID;     /* Unique identifier for a car */
  char make[20];      /* Manufacturer              */
  char model[20];     /* Model name                */
  int  year;          /* Year of manufacture       */
  int mileage;        /* in miles                  */
  double cost;        /* in dollars                */

  Car *next;          /* Points to a car_node      */
};
```

Notice that this structure contains a pointer element that points to something of the same type as itself, or type `Car`. We will use this member element to point to the next node in the linked list. If the `next` field is equal to `NULL`, then the node is the last in the list.

```
1   int main()
2   {
3     int op = 0;   /* Current operation to be performed.     */
4     Car carBase; /* carBase an empty head node              */
5
6     carBase.next = NULL;   /* Initialize the list to empty   */
7
8     printf("==========================\n");
9     printf("=== Used car database ===\n");
10    printf("==========================\n\n");
11
12    while (op != 4) {
13      printf("Enter an operation:\n");
14      printf("1 - Car aquired. Add a new entry for it.\n");
15      printf("2 - Car sold. Remove its entry.\n");
16      printf("3 - Query. Look up a car's information.\n");
17      printf("4 - Quit.\n");
18      scanf("%d", &op);
19
20      if (op == 1)
21            AddEntry(&carBase);
22      else if (op == 2)
23            DeleteEntry(&carBase);
24      else if (op == 3)
25            Search(&carBase);
26      else if (op == 4)
27            printf("Goodbye.\n\n");
28      else
29            printf("Invalid option. Try again.\n\n");
30    }
31  }
```

Figure 19.5   The function `main` for our used car database program

Now that we have defined the elementary data type and the organization of data in memory, we want to focus on the flow of the program, which we can do by writing the function `main`. The code is listed in Figure 19.5.

With this code, we create a menu-driven interface for the used car database. The main data structure is accessed using the variable `carBase`, which is of type `CarNode`. We will use it as a *dummy* head node, meaning that we will not be storing any information about any particular car within the fields of `carBase`; instead, we will use `carBase` simply as a placeholder for the rest of the linked list. Using this dummy head node makes the algorithms for inserting and deleting slightly simpler because we do not have to deal with the special case of an empty list. Initially, `carBase.next` is set equal to `NULL`, indicating that no data items are stored in the database. Notice that we pass the address of `carBase` whenever we call the functions to insert a new car in the list (`AddEntry`), to delete a car (`DeleteEntry`), and to search the list for a particular car (`Search`).

```
1    Car *ScanList(Car *headPointer, int searchID)
2    {
3      Car *previous;
4      Car *current;
5
6      /* Point to start of list */
7      previous = headPointer;
8      current = headPointer->next;
9
10     /* Traverse list -- scan until we find a node with a    */
11     /* vehicleID greater than or equal to searchID          */
12     while ((current != NULL) &&
13            (current->vehicleID < searchID)) {
14       previous = current;
15       current  = current->next;
16     }
17
18     /* The variable previous points to node prior to the    */
19     /* node being searched for. Either current->vehicleID   */
20     /* equals searchID or the node does not exist.          */
21     return previous;
22   }
```

Figure 19.6   A function to scan through the linked list for a particular vehicle ID

As we shall see, the functions AddEntry, DeleteEntry, and Search all rely upon a basic operation to be performed on the linked list: scanning the list to find a particular node. For example, when adding the entry for a new car, we need to know where in the list the entry should be added. Since the list is kept in sorted order of increasing vehicle ID numbers, any new car node added to the list must be placed *prior* to the first existing node with a larger vehicle ID. To accomplish this, we have created a support function called ScanList that traverses the list (which is passed as the first argument) searching for a particular vehicle ID (passed as the second argument). ScanList always returns a pointer to the node **just before** the node for which we are scanning. If the node we are scanning for is not in the list, then ScanList returns a pointer to the node **just prior** to the place in the list where the node would have resided. Why does ScanList return a pointer to the previous node? As we shall see, passing back the previous node makes inserting new nodes easier. The code for ScanList is listed in Figure 19.6.

Next we will examine the function to add a newly acquired car to the database. The function AddEntry gets information from the user about the newly acquired car and inserts a node containing this information into the proper spot in the linked list. The code is listed in Figure 19.7. The first part of the function allocates a CarNode-sized chunk of memory on the heap using malloc. If the allocation fails, an error message is displayed and the program exits using the exit library call, which terminates the program. The second part of the function reads in input from the standard keyboard and assigns it the proper fields within the new node. The third part performs the insertion by calling ScanList to find the place in the list to insert the new node. If the node already exists in the list then an error message is displayed and the new node is deallocated by a call to the free library call.

```
1    void AddEntry(Car *headPointer)
2    {
3      Car *newNode;        /* Points to the new car info       */
4      Car *nextNode;       /* Points to car to follow new one  */
5      Car *prevNode;       /* Points to car before this one    */
6
7      /* Dynamically allocate memory for this new entry.        */
8      newNode = (Car *) malloc(sizeof(Car));
9
10     if (newNode == NULL) {
11       printf("Error: could not allocate a new node\n");
12       exit(1);
13     }
14
15     printf("Enter the following info about the car.\n");
16     printf("Separate each field by white space:\n");
17     printf("vehicle_id make model year mileage cost\n");
18
19     scanf("%d %s %s %d %d %lf",
20           &newNode->vehicleID, newNode->make, newNode->model,
21           &newNode->year, &newNode->mileage, &newNode->cost);
22
23     prevNode = ScanList(headPointer, newNode->vehicleID);
24     nextNode = prevNode->next;
25
26     if ((nextNode == NULL) ||
27         (nextNode->vehicleID != newNode->vehicleID)) {
28       prevNode->next = newNode;
29       newNode->next = nextNode;
30       printf("Entry added.\n\n");
31     }
32     else {
33       printf("That car already exists in the database!\n");
34       printf("Entry not added.\n\n");
35       free(newNode);
36     }
37   }
```

Figure 19.7 A function to add an entry to the database

Let's take a closer look at how a node is inserted into the linked list. Figure 19.8 shows a pictorial representation of this process. Once the proper spot to insert is found using ScanList, first, the prevNode's next pointer is updated to point to the new node and, second, the new node's next pointer is updated to point to nextNode. Also shown in the figure is the degenerate case of adding a node to an empty list. Here, prevNode points to the empty head node. The head node's next pointer is updated to point to the new node.

The routine to delete a node from the linked list is very similar to AddEntry. Functionally, we want to first query the user about which vehicle ID to delete and then use ScanList to locate a node with that ID. Once the node is found, the list is manipulated to remove the node. The code is listed in Figure 19.9. Notice that once

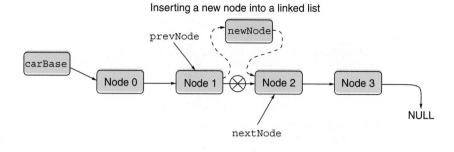

Inserting a new node into a linked list

Inserting into an empty list

Figure 19.8   Inserting a node into a linked list. The dashed lines indicate newly formed links

```
1   void DeleteEntry(Car *headPointer)
2   {
3     int vehicleID;
4     Car *delNode;        /* Points to node to delete         */
5     Car *prevNode;       /* Points to node prior to delNode  */
6
7     printf("Enter the vehicle ID of the car to delete:\n");
8     scanf("%d", &vehicleID);
9
10    prevNode = ScanList(headPointer, vehicleID);
11    delNode  = prevNode->next;
12
13    /* Either the car does not exist or              */
14    /* delNode points to the car to be deleted.      */
15    if (delNode != NULL && delNode->vehicleID == vehicleID) {
16      prevNode->next = delNode->next;
17      printf("Vehicle with ID %d deleted.\n\n", vehicleID);
18      free(delNode);
19    }
20    else
21      printf("The vehicle was not found in the database\n");
22  }
```

Figure 19.9   A function to delete an entry from the database

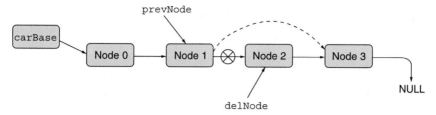

Figure 19.10 Deleting a node from a linked list. The dashed line indicates a newly formed link

```
1   void Search(Car *headPointer)
2   {
3     int vehicleID;
4     Car *searchNode;     /* Points to node to delete to follow */
5     Car *prevNode;       /* Points to car before one to delete */
6
7     printf("Enter the vehicle ID number of the car to search for:\n");
8     scanf("%d", &vehicleID);
9
10    prevNode = ScanList(headPointer, vehicleID);
11    searchNode  = prevNode->next;
12
13    /* Either the car does not exist in the list or          */
14    /* searchNode points to the car we are looking for.      */
15    if (searchNode != NULL && searchNode->vehicleID == vehicleID) {
16      printf("vehicle ID : %d\n", searchNode->vehicleID);
17      printf("make       : %s\n", searchNode->make);
18      printf("model      : %s\n", searchNode->model);
19      printf("year       : %d\n", searchNode->year);
20      printf("mileage    : %d\n", searchNode->mileage);
21
22      /* The following printf has a field width specification on */
23      /* %f specification.  The 10.2 indicates that the floating */
24      /* point number should be printed in a 10 character field  */
25      /* with two units after the decimal displayed.             */
26      printf("cost       : $%10.2f\n\n", searchNode->cost);
27    }
28    else {
29      printf("The vehicle ID %d was not found in the database.\n\n",
30              vehicleID);
31    }
32  }
```

Figure 19.11 A function to query the database

a node is deleted, its memory is added back to the heap using the `free` function call. Figure 19.10 shows a pictorial representation of the deletion of a node.

At this point, we can draw an interesting parallel between the way elements are inserted and deleted from linked lists versus arrays. In a linked list, once we have identified the item to delete, the deletion is accomplished by manipulating a few pointers. If we wanted to delete an element in an array, we would need to move all elements that follow it in the array upwards. If the array is large, this can result in a significant amount of data movement. The bottom line is that the operations of insertion and deletion can be cheaper to perform on a linked list than on an array.

Finally, we write the code for performing a search. The `Search` operation is very similar to the `AddEntry` and `DelEntry` functions, except that the list is not modified. The code is listed in Figure 19.11. The support function `ScanList` is used to locate the requested node.

19.6 Summary

We conclude this chapter by a summarizing the three key concepts we covered.

- **Structures in C.** The primary objective of this chapter was to introduce the concept of user-defined aggregate types in C, or structures. C structures allow us to create new data types by grouping together data of more primitive types. C structures provide a small step toward object orientation, that is, of structuring a program around the real-world objects that it manipulates rather than the primitive types supported by the underlying computing system.

- **Dynamic memory allocation.** The concept of dynamic memory allocation is an important prerequisite for advanced programming concepts. In particular, dynamic data structures that grow and shrink during program execution require some form of memory allocation. C provides some standard memory allocation functions such as `malloc`, `calloc`, `realloc`, and `free`.

- **Linked lists.** We combine the concepts of structures and dynamic memory allocation to introduce a fundamental new data structure called a linked list. It is similar to an array in that it contains data that is best organized in a list fashion. Why is the linked list such an important data structure? For one thing, it is a dynamic structure that can be expanded or shrunk during execution. This dynamic quality makes it appealing to use in certain situations where the static nature of arrays would be wasteful. The concept of connecting data elements together using pointers is fundamental, and you will encounter it often when dealing with advanced structures such as hash tables, trees, and graphs.

19.1 Is there a bug in the following program? Explain.

```
struct node {
  int count;
  struct node *next;
};

int main()
{
  int data = 0;
  struct node *getdata;

  getdata->count = data + 1;
  printf("%d", getdata->count);
}
```

19.2 The following are a few lines of a C program:

```
struct node {
  int count;
  struct node *next;
};

main()
{
  int data = 0;
  struct node *getdata;

        :
        :

  getdata = getdata->next;

        :
        :
}
```

Write, in LC-3 assembly language, the instructions that are generated by the compiler for the line getdata = getdata->next;.

19.3   The code for `PotentialCollisions` in Figure 19.2 performs a pairwise check of all aircraft currently in the airspace. It checks each plane with every other plane for a potential collision scenario. This code, however, can be made more efficient with a very simple change. What is the change?

19.4   The following program is compiled on a machine in which each basic data type (pointer, character, integer, floating point) occupies one location of memory.

```
struct element {
  char  name[25];
  int   atomic_number;
  float atomic_mass;
};

is_it_noble(struct element t[], int i)
{
  if ((t[i].atomic_number==2)   ||
      (t[i].atomic_number==10)  ||
      (t[i].atomic_number==18)  ||
      (t[i].atomic_number==36)  ||
      (t[i].atomic_number==54)  ||
      (t[i].atomic_number==86))
    return 1;
  else
    return 0;
}

int main()
{
  int x, y;
  struct element periodic_table[110];

     :
     :
  x = is_it_noble(periodic_table, y);
     :
     :
}
```

   a. How many locations will the activation record of the function `is_it_noble` contain?

   b. Assuming that `periodic_table`, x, and y are the only local variables, how many locations in the activation record for `main` will be devoted to local variables?

The LC-3 ISA

A.1 Overview

The Instruction Set Architecture (ISA) of the LC-3 is defined as follows:

Memory address space 16 bits, corresponding to 2^{16} locations, each containing one word (16 bits). Addresses are numbered from 0 (i.e, x0000) to 65,535 (i.e., xFFFF). Addresses are used to identify memory locations and memory-mapped I/O device registers. Certain regions of memory are reserved for special uses, as described in Figure A.1.

Bit numbering Bits of all quantities are numbered, from right to left, starting with bit 0. The leftmost bit of the contents of a memory location is bit 15.

Instructions Instructions are 16 bits wide. Bits [15:12] specify the opcode (operation to be performed), bits [11:0] provide further information that is

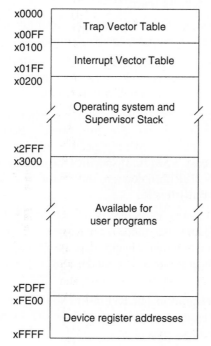

x0000	Trap Vector Table
x00FF	
x0100	Interrupt Vector Table
x01FF	
x0200	Operating system and Supervisor Stack
x2FFF	
x3000	Available for user programs
xFDFF	
xFE00	Device register addresses
xFFFF	

Figure A.1 Memory map of the LC-3

needed to execute the instruction. The specific operation of each LC-3 instruction is described in Section A.3.

Illegal opcode exception Bits [15:12] = 1101 has not been specified. If an instruction contains 1101 in bits [15:12], an illegal opcode exception occurs. Section A.4 explains what happens.

Program counter A 16-bit register containing the address of the next instruction to be processed.

General purpose registers Eight 16-bit registers, numbered from 000 to 111.

Condition codes Three 1-bit registers: N (negative), Z (zero), and P (positive). Load instructions (LD, LDI, LDR, and LEA) and operate instructions (ADD, AND, and NOT) each load a result into one of the eight general purpose registers. The condition codes are set, based on whether that result, taken as a 16-bit 2's complement integer, is negative (N = 1; Z, P = 0), zero (Z = 1; N, P = 0), or positive (P = 1; N, Z = 0). All other LC-3 instructions leave the condition codes unchanged.

Memory-mapped I/O Input and output are handled by load/store (LDI/STI, LDR/STR) instructions using memory addresses to designate each I/O device register. Addresses xFE00 through xFFFF have been allocated to represent the addresses of I/O devices. See Figure A.1. Also, Table A.3 lists each of the relevant device registers that have been identified for the LC-3 thus far, along with their corresponding assigned addresses from the memory address space.

Interrupt processing I/O devices have the capability of interrupting the processor. Section A.4 describes the mechanism.

Priority level The LC-3 supports eight levels of priority. Priority level 7 (PL7) is the highest; PL0 is the lowest. The priority level of the currently executing process is specified in bits PSR[10:8].

Processor status register (PSR) A 16-bit register, containing status information about the currently executing process. Seven bits of the PSR have been defined thus far. PSR[15] specifies the privilege mode of the executing process. PSR[10:8] specifies the priority level of the currently executing process. PSR[2:0] contains the condition codes. PSR[2] is N, PSR[1] is Z, and PSR[0] is P.

Privilege mode The LC-3 specifies two levels of privilege, Supervisor mode (privileged) and User mode (unprivileged). Interrupt service routines execute in Supervisor mode. The privilege mode is specified by PSR[15]. PSR[15] = 0 indicates Supervisor mode; PSR[15] = 1 indicates User mode.

Privilege mode exception The RTI instruction executes in Supervisor mode. If the processor attempts to execute an RTI instruction while in User mode, a privilege mode exception occurs. Section A.4 explains what happens.

Supervisor Stack A region of memory in supervisor space accessible via the Supervisor Stack Pointer (SSP). When PSR[15] = 0, the stack pointer (R6) is SSP.

User Stack A region of memory in user space accessible via the User Stack Pointer (USP). When PSR[15] = 1, the stack pointer (R6) is USP.

A.2 Notation

The notation in Table A.1 will be helpful in understanding the descriptions of the LC-3 instructions (Section A.3).

A.3 The Instruction Set

The LC-3 supports a rich, but lean, instruction set. Each 16-bit instruction consists of an opcode (bits[15:12]) plus 12 additional bits to specify the other information that is needed to carry out the work of that instruction. Figure A.2 summarizes the 15 different opcodes in the LC-3 and the specification of the remaining bits of each instruction. The 16th 4-bit opcode is not specified, but is reserved for future use. In the following pages, the instructions will be described in greater detail. For each instruction, we show the assembly language representation, the format of the 16-bit instruction, the operation of the instruction, an English-language description of its operation, and one or more examples of the instruction. Where relevant, additional notes about the instruction are also provided.

Table A.1   Notational Conventions

Notation	Meaning
xNumber	The number in hexadecimal notation.
#Number	The number in decimal notation.
A[l:r]	The **field** delimited by bit [l] on the left and bit [r] on the right, of the datum A. For example, if PC contains 0011001100111111, then PC[15:9] is 0011001. PC[2:2] is 1. If l and r are the same bit number, the notation is usually abbreviated PC[2].
BaseR	Base Register; one of R0..R7, used in conjunction with a six-bit offset to compute Base+offset addresses.
DR	Destination Register; one of R0..R7, which specifies which register the result of an instruction should be written to.
imm5	A 5-bit immediate value; bits [4:0] of an instruction when used as a literal (immediate) value. Taken as a 5-bit, 2's complement integer, it is sign-extended to 16 bits before it is used. Range: $-16..15$.
LABEL	An assembly language construct that identifies a location symbolically (i.e., by means of a name, rather than its 16-bit address).
mem[address]	Denotes the contents of memory at the given address.
offset6	A 6-bit value; bits [5:0] of an instruction; used with the Base+offset addressing mode. Bits [5:0] are taken as a 6-bit signed 2's complement integer, sign-extended to 16 bits and then added to the Base Register to form an address. Range: $-32..31$.
PC	Program Counter; 16-bit register that contains the memory address of the next instruction to be fetched. For example, during execution of the instruction at address A, the PC contains address $A + 1$, indicating the next instruction is contained in $A + 1$.
PCoffset9	A 9-bit value; bits [8:0] of an instruction; used with the PC+offset addressing mode. Bits [8:0] are taken as a 9-bit signed 2's complement integer, sign-extended to 16 bits and then added to the incremented PC to form an address. Range $-256..255$.
PCoffset11	An 11-bit value; bits [10:0] of an instruction; used with the JSR opcode to compute the target address of a subroutine call. Bits [10:0] are taken as an 11-bit 2's complement integer, sign-extended to 16 bits and then added to the incremented PC to form the target address. Range $-1024..1023$.
PSR	Processor Status Register; 16-bit register that contains status information of the process that is running. PSR[15] = privilege mode. PSR[2:0] contains the condition codes. PSR[2] = N, PSR[1] = Z, PSR[0] = P.
setcc()	Indicates that condition codes N, Z, and P are set based on the value of the result written to DR. If the value is negative, N = 1, Z = 0, P = 0. If the value is zero, N = 0, Z = 1, P = 0. If the value is positive, N = 0, Z = 0, P = 1.
SEXT(A)	Sign-extend A. The most significant bit of A is replicated as many times as necessary to extend A to 16 bits. For example, if A = 110000, then SEXT(A) = 1111 1111 1111 0000.
SP	The current stack pointer. R6 is the current stack pointer. There are two stacks, one for each privilege mode. SP is SSP if PSR[15] = 0; SP is USP if PSR[15] = 1.
SR, SR1, SR2	Source Register; one of R0..R7 which specifies the register from which a source operand is obtained.
SSP	The Supervisor Stack Pointer.
trapvect8	An 8-bit value; bits [7:0] of an instruction; used with the TRAP opcode to determine the starting address of a trap service routine. Bits [7:0] are taken as an unsigned integer and zero-extended to 16 bits. This is the address of the memory location containing the starting address of the corresponding service routine. Range 0..255.
USP	The User Stack Pointer.
ZEXT(A)	Zero-extend A. Zeros are appended to the leftmost bit of A to extend it to 16 bits. For example, if A = 110000, then ZEXT(A) = 0000 0000 0011 0000.

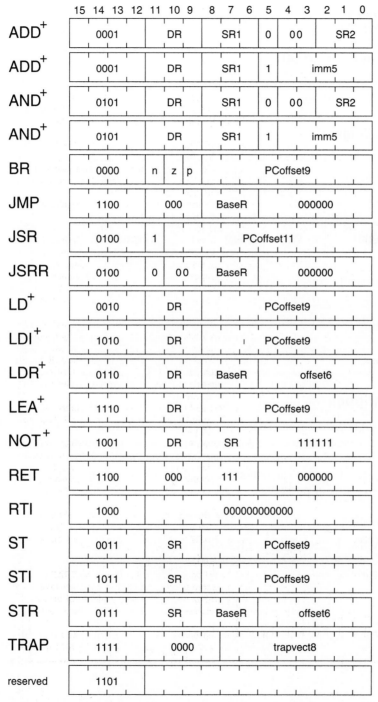

Figure A.2 Format of the entire LC-3 instruction set. **Note:** + indicates instructions that modify condition codes

ADD   **Addition**

Assembler Formats

    ADD   DR, SR1, SR2
    ADD   DR, SR1, imm5

Encodings

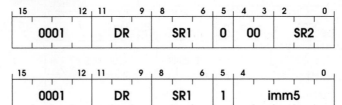

Operation

```
if (bit[5] == 0)
     DR = SR1 + SR2;
else
     DR = SR1 + SEXT(imm5);
setcc();
```

Description

If bit [5] is 0, the second source operand is obtained from SR2. If bit [5] is 1, the second source operand is obtained by sign-extending the imm5 field to 16 bits. In both cases, the second source operand is added to the contents of SR1 and the result stored in DR. The condition codes are set, based on whether the result is negative, zero, or positive.

Examples

    ADD   R2, R3, R4   ; R2 ← R3 + R4
    ADD   R2, R3, #7   ; R2 ← R3 + 7

AND   **Bit-wise Logical AND**

Assembler Formats

    AND DR, SR1, SR2
    AND DR, SR1, imm5

Encodings

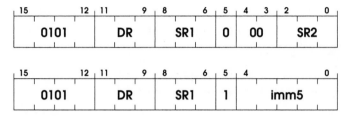

Operation

```
if (bit[5] == 0)
      DR = SR1 AND SR2;
else
      DR = SR1 AND SEXT(imm5);
setcc();
```

Description

If bit [5] is 0, the second source operand is obtained from SR2. If bit [5] is 1, the second source operand is obtained by sign-extending the imm5 field to 16 bits. In either case, the second source operand and the contents of SR1 are bit-wise ANDed, and the result stored in DR. The condition codes are set, based on whether the binary value produced, taken as a 2's complement integer, is negative, zero, or positive.

Examples

    AND R2, R3, R4   ;R2 ← R3 AND R4
    AND R2, R3, #7   ;R2 ← R3 AND 7

BR

Conditional Branch

Assembler Formats

BRn   LABEL   BRzp   LABEL
BRz   LABEL   BRnp   LABEL
BRp   LABEL   BRnz   LABEL
BR†   LABEL   BRnzp LABEL

Encoding

15 12	11	10	9	8 0
0000	n	z	p	PCoffset9

Operation

```
if ((n AND N) OR (z AND Z) OR (p AND P))
  PC = PC‡ + SEXT(PCoffset9);
```

Description

The condition codes specified by the state of bits [11:9] are tested. If bit [11] is set, N is tested; if bit [11] is clear, N is not tested. If bit [10] is set, Z is tested, etc. If any of the condition codes tested is set, the program branches to the location specified by adding the sign-extended PCoffset9 field to the incremented PC.

Examples

BRzp   LOOP   ; Branch to LOOP if the last result was zero or positive.
BR†   NEXT   ; Unconditionally branch to NEXT.

---

†The assembly language opcode BR is interpreted the same as BRnzp; that is, always branch to the target address.

‡This is the incremented PC.

JMP
RET

Jump

Return from Subroutine

Assembler Formats

```
JMP   BaseR
RET
```

Encoding

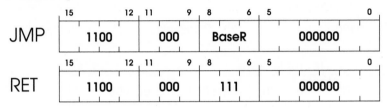

Operation

```
PC = BaseR;
```

Description

The program unconditionally jumps to the location specified by the contents of the base register. Bits [8:6] identify the base register.

Examples

```
JMP   R2     ; PC ← R2
RET          ; PC ← R7
```

Note

The RET instruction is a special case of the JMP instruction. The PC is loaded with the contents of R7, which contains the linkage back to the instruction following the subroutine call instruction.

JSR
JSRR

Jump to Subroutine

Assembler Formats

```
JSR    LABEL
JSRR   BaseR
```

Encoding

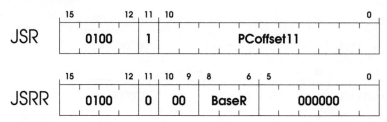

Operation

```
TEMP = PC;†
if (bit[11] == 0)
    PC = BaseR;
else
    PC = PC† + SEXT(PCoffset11);
R7 = TEMP;
```

Description

First, the incremented PC is saved in a temporary location. Then the PC is loaded with the address of the first instruction of the subroutine, causing an unconditional jump to that address. The address of the subroutine is obtained from the base register (if bit [11] is 0), or the address is computed by sign-extending bits [10:0] and adding this value to the incremented PC (if bit [11] is 1). Finally, R7 is loaded with the value stored in the temporary location. This is the linkage back to the calling routine.

Examples

```
JSR    QUEUE  ; Put the address of the instruction following JSR into R7;
              ; Jump to QUEUE.
JSRR   R3     ; Put the address following JSRR into R7; Jump to the
              ; address contained in R3.
```

---

†This is the incremented PC.

LD   **Load**

Assembler Format

LD   DR, LABEL

Encoding

Operation

```
DR = mem[PC† + SEXT(PCoffset9)];
setcc();
```

Description

An address is computed by sign-extending bits [8:0] to 16 bits and adding this value to the incremented PC. The contents of memory at this address are loaded into DR. The condition codes are set, based on whether the value loaded is negative, zero, or positive.

Example

LD   R4, VALUE   ; R4 ← mem[VALUE]

---

†This is the incremented PC.

LDI   **Load Indirect**

Assembler Format

LDI DR, LABEL

Encoding

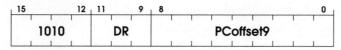

15 12	11 9	8 0
1010	DR	PCoffset9

Operation

DR = mem [mem [PC† + SEXT (PCoffset9)]];
setcc ();

Description

An address is computed by sign-extending bits [8:0] to 16 bits and adding this value to the incremented PC. What is stored in memory at this address is the address of the data to be loaded into DR. The condition codes are set, based on whether the value loaded is negative, zero, or positive.

Example

LDI   R4, ONEMORE   ; R4 ← mem[mem[ONEMORE]]

---

†This is the incremented PC.

LDR

Load Base+offset

Assembler Format

LDR   DR, BaseR, offset6

Encoding

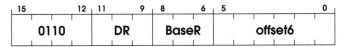

Operation

```
DR = mem[BaseR + SEXT(offset6)];
setcc();
```

Description

An address is computed by sign-extending bits [5:0] to 16 bits and adding this value to the contents of the register specified by bits [8:6]. The contents of memory at this address are loaded into DR. The condition codes are set, based on whether the value loaded is negative, zero, or positive.

Example

LDR   R4, R2, #−5   ; R4 ← mem[R2 − 5]

LEA
Load Effective Address

Assembler Format

    LEA   DR, LABEL

Encoding

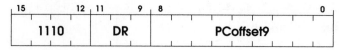

Operation

```
DR = PC† + SEXT(PCoffset9);
setcc();
```

Description

An address is computed by sign-extending bits [8:0] to 16 bits and adding this value to the incremented PC. This address is loaded into DR.‡ The condition codes are set, based on whether the value loaded is negative, zero, or positive.

Example

    LEA   R4, TARGET   ; R4 ← address of TARGET.

---

†This is the incremented PC.

‡The LEA instruction does not read memory to obtain the information to load into DR. The address itself is loaded into DR.

NOT

Bit-Wise Complement

Assembler Format

NOT   DR, SR

Encoding

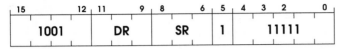

15	12	11	9	8	6	5	4	3	2	0
1001		DR		SR		1		11111		

Operation

```
DR = NOT(SR);
setcc();
```

Description

The bit-wise complement of the contents of SR is stored in DR. The condition codes are set, based on whether the binary value produced, taken as a 2's complement integer, is negative, zero, or positive.

Example

NOT   R4, R2   ; R4 ← NOT(R2)

RET[†]   **Return from Subroutine**

Assembler Format

    RET

Encoding

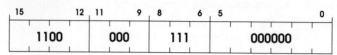

15	12	11	9	8	6	5	0
1100		000		111		000000	

Operation

PC = R7;

Description

The PC is loaded with the value in R7. This causes a return from a previous JSR instruction.

Example

    RET   ; PC ← R7

[†]The RET instruction is a specific encoding of the JMP instruction. See also JMP.

RTI

Assembler Format

RTI

Encoding

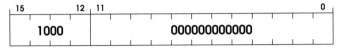

15	12	11	0
1000		000000000000	

Operation

```
if (PSR[15] == 0)
   PC = mem[R6]; R6 is the SSP
   R6 = R6+1;
   TEMP = mem[R6];
   R6 = R6+1;
   PSR = TEMP; the privilege mode and condition codes of
   the interrupted process are restored
else
   Initiate a privilege mode exception;
```

Description

If the processor is running in Supervisor mode, the top two elements on the Supervisor Stack are popped and loaded into PC, PSR. If the processor is running in User mode, a privilege mode violation exception occurs.

Example

RTI   ; PC, PSR ← top two values popped off stack.

Note

On an external interrupt or an internal exception, the initiating sequence first changes the privilege mode to Supervisor mode (PSR[15] = 0). Then the PSR and PC of the interrupted program are pushed onto the Supervisor Stack before loading the PC with the starting address of the interrupt or exception service routine. Interrupt and exception service routines run with Supervisor privilege. The last instruction in the service routine is RTI, which returns control to the interrupted program by popping two values off the Supervisor Stack to restore the PC and PSR. In the case of an interrupt, the PC is restored to the address of the instruction that was about to be processed when the interrupt was initiated. In the case of an exception, the PC is restored to either the address of the instruction that caused the exception or the address of the following instruction, depending on whether the instruction that caused the exception is to be re-executed. In the case of an interrupt, the PSR is restored to the value it had when the interrupt was initiated. In the case of an exception, the PSR is restored to the value it had when the exception occurred or to some modified value, depending on the exception. See also Section A.4.

   If the processor is running in User mode, a privilege mode violation exception occurs. Section A.4 describes what happens in this case.

ST

Store

Assembler Format

ST   SR, LABEL

Encoding

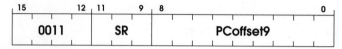

15 12	11 9	8 0
0011	SR	PCoffset9

Operation

mem[PC† + SEXT(PCoffset9)] = SR;

Description

The contents of the register specified by SR are stored in the memory location whose address is computed by sign-extending bits [8:0] to 16 bits and adding this value to the incremented PC.

Example

ST   R4, HERE   ; mem[HERE] ← R4

---

†This is the incremented PC.

STI

Store Indirect

Assembler Format

STI   SR, LABEL

Encoding

Operation

mem[mem[PC† + SEXT(PCoffset9)]] = SR;

Description

The contents of the register specified by SR are stored in the memory location whose address is obtained as follows: Bits [8:0] are sign-extended to 16 bits and added to the incremented PC. What is in memory at this address is the address of the location to which the data in SR is stored.

Example

STI   R4, NOT_HERE   ; mem[mem[NOT_HERE]] ← R4

---

† This is the incremented PC.

STR

Store Base+offset

Assembler Format

    STR   SR, BaseR, offset6

Encoding

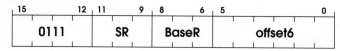

15 12	11 9	8 6	5 0
0111	SR	BaseR	offset6

Operation

```
mem[BaseR + SEXT(offset6)] = SR;
```

Description

The contents of the register specified by SR are stored in the memory location whose address is computed by sign-extending bits [5:0] to 16 bits and adding this value to the contents of the register specified by bits [8:6].

Example

    STR   R4, R2, #5   ; mem[R2 + 5] ← R4

TRAP   System Call

Assembler Format

TRAP   trapvector8

Encoding

Operation

R7 = PC;[†]
PC = mem[ZEXT(trapvect8)];

Description

First R7 is loaded with the incremented PC. (This enables a return to the instruction physically following the TRAP instruction in the original program after the service routine has completed execution.) Then the PC is loaded with the starting address of the system call specified by trapvector8. The starting address is contained in the memory location whose address is obtained by zero-extending trapvector8 to 16 bits.

Example

TRAP   x23   ; Directs the operating system to execute the **IN** system call.
             ; The starting address of this system call is contained in
             ; memory location x0023.

Note

Memory locations x0000 through x00FF, 256 in all, are available to contain starting addresses for system calls specified by their corresponding trap vectors. This region of memory is called the Trap Vector Table. Table A.2 describes the functions performed by the service routines corresponding to trap vectors x20 to x25.

[†] This is the incremented PC.

Unused Opcode

Assembler Format

Encoding

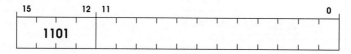

Operation

Initiate an illegal opcode exception.

Description

If an illegal opcode is encountered, an illegal opcode exception occurs.

Note

The opcode 1101 has been reserved for future use. It is currently not defined. If the instruction currently executing has bits [15:12] = 1101, an illegal opcode exception occurs. Section A.4 describes what happens.

Table A.2	Trap Service Routines	
Trap Vector	Assembler Name	Description
x20	GETC	Read a single character from the keyboard. The character is not echoed onto the console. Its ASCII code is copied into R0. The high eight bits of R0 are cleared.
x21	OUT	Write a character in R0[7:0] to the console display.
x22	PUTS	Write a string of ASCII characters to the console display. The characters are contained in consecutive memory locations, one character per memory location, starting with the address specified in R0. Writing terminates with the occurrence of x0000 in a memory location.
x23	IN	Print a prompt on the screen and read a single character from the keyboard. The character is echoed onto the console monitor, and its ASCII code is copied into R0. The high eight bits of R0 are cleared.
x24	PUTSP	Write a string of ASCII characters to the console. The characters are contained in consecutive memory locations, two characters per memory location, starting with the address specified in R0. The ASCII code contained in bits [7:0] of a memory location is written to the console first. Then the ASCII code contained in bits [15:8] of that memory location is written to the console. (A character string consisting of an odd number of characters to be written will have x00 in bits [15:8] of the memory location containing the last character to be written.) Writing terminates with the occurrence of x0000 in a memory location.
x25	HALT	Halt execution and print a message on the console.

Table A.3	Device Register Assignments	
Address	I/O Register Name	I/O Register Function
xFE00	Keyboard status register	Also known as KBSR. The ready bit (bit [15]) indicates if the keyboard has received a new character.
xFE02	Keyboard data register	Also known as KBDR. Bits [7:0] contain the last character typed on the keyboard.
xFE04	Display status register	Also known as DSR. The ready bit (bit [15]) indicates if the display device is ready to receive another character to print on the screen.
xFE06	Display data register	Also known as DDR. A character written in the low byte of this register will be displayed on the screen.
xFFFE	Machine control register	Also known as MCR. Bit [15] is the clock enable bit. When cleared, instruction processing stops.

A.4 Interrupt and Exception Processing

Events external to the program that is running can interrupt the processor. A common example of an external event is interrupt-driven I/O. It is also the case that the processor can be interrupted by exceptional events that occur while the program is running that are caused by the program itself. An example of such an "internal" event is the presence of an unused opcode in the computer program that is running.

Associated with each event that can interrupt the processor is an 8-bit vector that provides an entry point into a 256-entry *interrupt vector table*. The starting address of the interrupt vector table is x0100. That is, the interrupt vector table occupies memory locations x0100 to x01FF. Each entry in the interrupt vector table contains the starting address of the service routine that handles the needs of the corresponding event. These service routines execute in Supervisor mode.

Half (128) of these entries, locations x0100 to x017F, provide the starting addresses of routines that service events caused by the running program itself. These routines are called *exception service routines* because they handle exceptional events, that is, events that prevent the program from executing normally. The other half of the entries, locations x0180 to x01FF, provide the starting addresses of routines that service events that are external to the program that is running, such as requests from I/O devices. These routines are called *interrupt service routines*.

A.4.1 Interrupts

At this time, an LC-3 computer system provides only one I/O device that can interrupt the processor. That device is the keyboard. It interrupts at priority level PL4 and supplies the interrupt vector x80.

An I/O device can interrupt the processor if it wants service, if its Interrupt Enable (IE) bit is set, and if the priority of its request is greater than the priority of the program that is running.

Assume a program is running at a priority level less than 4, and someone strikes a key on the keyboard. If the IE bit of the KBSR is 1, the currently executing program is interrupted at the end of the current instruction cycle. The interrupt service routine is **initiated** as follows:

1. The processor sets the privilege mode to Supervisor mode (PSR[15] = 0).
2. The processor sets the priority level to PL4, the priority level of the interrupting device (PSR[10:8] = 100).
3. R6 is loaded with the Supervisor Stack Pointer (SSP) if it does not already contain the SSP.
4. The PSR and PC of the interrupted process are pushed onto the Supervisor Stack.
5. The keyboard supplies its 8-bit interrupt vector, in this case x80.
6. The processor expands that vector to x0180, the corresponding 16-bit address in the interrupt vector table.
7. The PC is loaded with the contents of memory location x0180, the address of the first instruction in the keyboard interrupt service routine.

The processor then begins execution of the interrupt service routine.

The last instruction executed in an interrupt service routine is RTI. The top two elements of the Supervisor Stack are popped and loaded into the PC and PSR registers. R6 is loaded with the appropriate stack pointer, depending on the new value of PSR[15]. Processing then continues where the interrupted program left off.

A.4.2 Exceptions

At this time, the LC-3 ISA specifies two exception conditions: privilege mode violation and illegal opcode. The privilege mode violation occurs if the processor encounters the RTI instruction while running in User mode. The illegal opcode exception occurs if the processor encounters the unused opcode (Bits [15:12] = 1101) in the instruction it is is processing.

Exceptions are handled as soon as they are detected. They are *initiated* very much like interrupts are initiated, that is:

1. The processor sets the privilege mode to Supervisor mode (PSR[15] = 0).
2. R6 is loaded with the Supervisor Stack Pointer (SSP) if it does not already contain the SSP.
3. The PSR and PC of the interrupted process are pushed onto the Supervisor Stack.
4. The exception supplies its 8-bit vector. In the case of the Privilege mode violation, that vector is x00. In the case of the illegal opcode, that vector is x01.
5. The processor expands that vector to x0100 or x0101, the corresponding 16-bit address in the interrupt vector table.
6. The PC is loaded with the contents of memory location x0100 or x0101, the address of the first instruction in the corresponding exception service routine.

The processor then begins execution of the exception service routine.

The details of the exception service routine depend on the exception and the way in which the operating system wishes to handle that exception.

In many cases, the exception service routine can correct any problem caused by the exceptional event and then continue processing the original program. In those cases the last instruction in the exception service routine is RTI, which pops the top two elements from the Supervisor Stack and loads them into the PC and PSR registers. The program then resumes execution with the problem corrected.

In some cases, the cause of the exceptional event is so catastrophic that the exception service routine removes the program from further processing.

Another difference between the handling of interrupts and the handling of exceptions is the priority level of the processor during the execution of the service routine. In the case of exceptions, we normally do not change the priority level when we service the exception. The priority level of a program is the urgency with which it needs to be executed. In the case of the two exceptions specified by the LC-3 ISA, the urgency of a program is not changed by the fact that a privilege mode violation occurred or there was an illegal opcode in the program.

From LC-3 to x86

As you know, the ISA of the LC-3 explicitly specifies the interface between what the LC-3 machine language programmer or LC-3 compilers produce and what a microarchitecture of the LC-3 can accept and process. Among those things specified are the address space and addressability of memory, the number and size of the registers, the format of the instructions, the opcodes, the data types that are the encodings used to represent information, and the addressing modes that are available for determining the location of an operand.

The ISA of the microprocessor in your PC also specifies an interface between the compilers and the microarchitecture. However, in the case of the PC, the ISA is not the LC-3. Rather it is the x86. Intel introduced the first member of this ISA in 1979. It was called the 8086, and the "normal" size of the addresses and data elements it processed was 16 bits. The typical size of addresses and data today is 32 bits. From the 8086 to the present time, Intel has continued implementations of this ISA, the 80286 (in 1982), 386 (in 1985), 486 (in 1989), Pentium (in 1992), Pentium Pro (in 1995), Pentium II (in 1997), Pentium III (in 1999), and Pentium IV (in 2001).

The ISA of the x86 is much more complicated than that of the LC-3. There are more opcodes, more data types, more addressing modes, a more complicated memory structure, and a more complicated encoding of instructions into 0s and 1s. However, fundamentally, they have the same basic ingredients.

You have spent a good deal of time understanding computing within the context of the LC-3. Some may feel that it would be good to learn about a *real* ISA. One way to do that would be to have some company such as Intel mass-produce LC-3s, some other company like Dell use them in their PCs, and a third company such as Microsoft compile Windows NT into the ISA of the LC-3. An easier way to introduce you to a *real* ISA is by way of this appendix.

We present here elements of the x86, a very complicated ISA. We do so in spite of its complexity, because it is the most pervasive of all ISAs available in the marketplace.

We make no attempt to provide a complete specification of the x86 ISA. That would require a whole book by itself, and to appreciate it, a deeper under-standing of operating systems, compilers, and computer systems than we think is reasonable at this point in your education. If one wants a complete treatment, we recommend *Intel Architecture Software Developer's Manual*, volumes 1, 2, and 3, published by Intel Corporation, 1997. In this appendix, we restrict our-selves to some of the characteristics that are relevant to application programs. Our intent is to give you a sense of the richness of the x86 ISA. We introduce these characteristics within the context of the LC-3 ISA, an ISA with which you are familiar.

B.1 LC-3 Features and Corresponding x86 Features

B.1.1 Instruction Set

An instruction set is made up of instructions, each of which has an opcode and zero or more operands. The number of operands depends on how many are needed by the corresponding opcode. Each operand is a data element and is encoded according to its data type. The location of an operand is determined by evaluating its addressing mode.

The LC-3 instruction set contains one data type, 15 opcodes, and three addressing modes: PC-relative (LD, ST), indirect (LDI, STI), and register-plus-offset (LDR, STR). The x86 instruction set has more than a dozen data types, over a hundred opcodes, and more than two dozen addressing modes (depending on how you count).

Data Types

Recall that a data type is a representation of information such that the ISA provides opcodes that operate on information that is encoded in that representation.

The LC-3 supports only one data type, 16-bit 2's-complement integers. This is not enough for efficient processing in the real world. Scientific applications need numbers that are represented by the floating point data type. Multimedia applications require information that is represented by a different data type. Commercial applications written years ago, but still active today, require an additional data type, referred to as *packed decimal*. Some applications require a greater range of values and a greater precision of each value than other applications.

As a result of all these requirements, the x86 is designed with instructions that operate on (for example) 8-bit integers, 16-bit integers, and 32-bit integers, 32-bit floating point numbers and 64-bit floating point numbers, 64-bit multimedia values and 128-bit multimedia values. Figure B.1 shows some of the data types present in the x86 ISA.

Opcodes

The LC-3 comprises 15 opcodes; the x86 instruction set comprises more than 200 opcodes. Recall that the three basic instruction types are operates, data movement, and control. Operates process information, data movement opcodes move information from one place to another (including input and output), and control opcodes change the flow of the instruction stream.

In addition, we should add a fourth category to handle functions that must be performed in the real world because a user program runs in the context of an operating system that is controlling a computer system, rather than in isolation. These instructions deal with computer security, system management, hardware performance monitoring, and various other issues that are beyond what the typical application program pays attention to. We will ignore those instructions in this

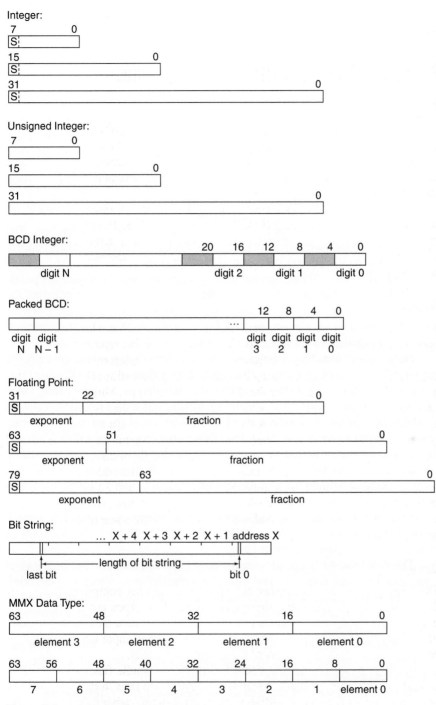

Figure B.1   A sample of x86 data types

appendix, but please note that they do exist, and you will see them as your studies progress.

Here we will concentrate on the three basic instruction types: operates, data movement, and control.

Operates   The LC-3 has three operate instructions: ADD, AND, and NOT. The ADD opcode is the only LC-3 opcode that performs arithmetic. If one wants to subtract, one obtains the negative of an operand and then adds. If one wants to multiply, one can write a program with a loop to ADD a number some specified number of times. However, this is too time-consuming for a real microprocessor. So the x86 has separate SUB and MUL, as well as DIV, INC (increment), DEC (decrement), and ADC (add with carry), to name a few.

A useful feature of an ISA is to extend the size of the integers on which it can operate. To do this one writes a program to operate on such *long* integers. The ADC opcode, which adds two operands plus the carry from the previous add, is a very useful opcode for extending the size of integers.

In addition, the x86 has, for each data type, its own set of opcodes to operate on that data type. For example, multimedia instructions (collectively called the MMX instructions) often require *saturating arithmetic*, which is very different from the arithmetic we are used to. PADDS is an opcode that adds two operands with saturating arithmetic.

Saturating arithmetic can be explained as follows: Suppose we represent the degree of grayness of an element in a figure with a digit from 0 to 9, where 0 is white and 9 is black. Suppose we want to add some darkness to an existing value of grayness of that figure. An element could start out with a grayness value of 7, and we might wish to add a 5 worth of darkness to it. In normal arithmetic, $7 + 5$ is 2 (with a carry), which is lighter than either 7 or 5. Something is wrong! With saturating arithmetic, when we reach 9, we stay there—we do not generate a carry. So, for example, $7 + 5 = 9$ and $9 + n = 9$. Saturating arithmetic is a different kind of arithmetic, and the x86 has opcodes (MMX instructions) that perform this type of arithmetic.

Scientific applications require opcodes that operate on values represented in the floating point data type. FADD, FMUL, FSIN, FSQRT are examples of floating point opcodes in the x86 ISA.

The AND and NOT opcodes are the only LC-3 opcodes that perform logical functions. One can construct any logical expression using these two opcodes. However, as is the case with arithmetic, this also is too time-consuming. The x86 has in addition separate OR, XOR, AND-NOT, and separate logical operators for different data types.

Furthermore, the x86 has a number of other operate instructions that set and clear registers, convert a value from one data type to another, shift or rotate the bits of a data element, and so on.

Table B.1 lists some of the operate opcodes in the x86 instruction set.

Data Movement   The LC-3 has seven data movement opcodes: LD, LDI, ST, STI, LDR, STR, and LEA. Except for LEA, which loads an address into a register,

Table B.1	Operate Instructions, x86 ISA
Instruction	Explanation
ADC x, y	x, y, and the carry retained from the last relevant operation (in CF) are added and the result stored in x.
MUL x	The value in EAX is multiplied by x, and the result is stored in the 64-bit register formed by EDX, EAX.
SAR x	x is arithmetic right is shifted n bits, and the result is stored in x. The value of n can be 1, an immediate operand, or the count in the CL register.
XOR x, y	A bit-wise exclusive-OR is performed on x, y and the result is stored in x.
DAA	After adding two packed decimal numbers, AL contains two BCD values, which may be incorrect due to propagation of the carry bit after 15, rather than after 9. DAA corrects the two BCD digits in AL.
FSIN	The top of the stack (call it x) is popped. The sin(x) is computed and pushed onto the stack.
FADD	The top two elements on the stack are popped, added, and their result pushed onto the stack.
PANDN x, y	A bit-wise AND-NOT operation is performed on MMX values x, y, and the result is stored in x.
PADDS x, y	Saturating addition is performed on packed MMX values x, y, and the result is stored in x.

they copy information between memory (and memory-mapped device registers) and the eight general purpose registers, R0 to R7.

The x86 has, in addition to these, many other data movement opcodes. XCHG can swap the contents of two locations. PUSHA pushes all eight general purpose registers onto the stack. IN and OUT move data between input and output ports and the processor. CMOVcc copies a value from one location to another only if a previously computed condition is true.

Table B.2 lists some of the data movement opcodes in the x86 instruction set.

Table B.2	Data Movement Instructions, x86 ISA
Instruction	Explanation
MOV x, y	The value stored in y is copied into x.
XCHG x, y	The values stored in x and y are swapped.
PUSHA	All the registers are pushed onto the top of the stack.
MOVS	The element in the DS segment pointed to by ESI is copied into the location in the ES segment pointed to by EDI. After the copy has been performed, ESI and EDI are both incremented.
REP MOVS	Perform the MOVS. Then decrement ECX. Repeat this instruction until ECX = 0. (This allows a string to be copied in a single instruction, after initializing ECX.)
LODS	The element in the DS segment pointed to by ESI is loaded into EAX, and ESI is incremented or decremented, according to the value of the DF flag.
INS	Data from the I/O port specified by the DX register is loaded into the EAX register (or AX or AL, if the size of the data is 16 bits or 8 bits, respectively).
CMOVZ x, y	If ZF = 1, the value stored in y is copied into x. If ZF = 0, the instruction acts like a no-op.
LEA x, y	The address y is stored in x. This is very much like the LC-3 instruction of the same name.

Table B.3   Control Instructions, x86 ISA

Instruction	Explanation
JMP x	IP is loaded with the address x. This is very much like the LC-3 instruction of the same name.
CALL x	The IP is pushed onto the stack, and a new IP is loaded with x.
RET	The stack is popped, and the value popped is loaded into IP.
LOOP x	ECX is decremented. If ECX is not 0 and ZF = 1, the IP is loaded with x.
INT n	The value n is an index into a table of descriptors that specify operating system service routines. The end result of this instruction is that IP is loaded with the starting result of the corresponding service routine. This is very much like the TRAP instruction in the LC-3.

Control   The LC-3 has five control opcodes: BR, JSR/JSRR, JMP, RTI, and TRAP. x86 has all these and more. Table B.3 lists some of the control opcodes in the x86 instruction set.

Two Address versus Three Address

The LC-3 is a three-address ISA. This description reflects the number of operands explicitly specified by the ADD instruction. An add operation requires two source operands (the numbers to be added) and one destination operand, to store the result. In the LC-3, all three must be specified explicitly, hence the name three-address ISA.

Even if the same location is to be used both for one of the sources and for the destination, the three addresses are all specified. For example, the LC-3 ADD R1,R1,R2 identifies R1 as both a source and the destination.

The x86 is a two-address ISA. Since the add operation needs three operands, the location of one of the sources must also be used to store the result. For example, the corresponding ADD instruction in the x86 ISA would be ADD EAX, EBX. (EAX and EBX are names of two of the eight general purpose registers.) EAX and EBX are the sources, and EAX is the destination.

Since the result of the operate is stored in the location that originally contained one of the sources, that source operand is no longer available after that instruction is executed. If that source operand is needed later, it must be saved before the operate instruction is executed.

Memory Operands

A major difference between the LC-3 instruction set and the x86 instruction set is the restriction on where operate instructions can get their operands. An LC-3 operate instruction must obtain its source operands from registers and write the result to a destination register. An x86 instruction, on the other hand, can obtain one of its sources from memory and/or write its result to memory. In other words, the x86 can read a value from memory, operate on that value, and store the result in memory all in a single instruction. The LC-3 cannot.

The LC-3 program requires a separate load instruction to read the value from memory before operating on it, and a separate store instruction to write the result in memory after the operate instruction. An ISA, like the LC-3, that has this restriction is called a *load-store* ISA. The x86 is not a load-store ISA.

B.1.2 Memory

The LC-3 memory consists of 2^{16} locations, each containing 16 bits of information. We say the LC-3 has a 16-bit address space, since one can uniquely address its 2^{16} locations with 16 bits of address. We say the LC-3 has an addressability of 16 bits, since each memory location contains 16 bits of information.

The x86 memory has a 32-bit address space and an addressability of eight bits. Since one byte contains eight bits, we say the x86 memory is byte addressable. Since each location contains only eight bits, four contiguous locations in memory are needed to store a 32-bit data element, say locations X, X+1, X+2, and X+3. We designate X as the address of the 32-bit data element. In actuality, X only contains bits [7:0], X+1 contains bits [15:8], X+2 contains bits [23:16], and X+3 contains bits [31:24] of the 32-bit value.

One can determine an LC-3 memory location by simply obtaining its address from the instruction, using one of the three addressing modes available in the instruction set. An x86 instruction has available to it more than two dozen addressing modes that it can use to specify the memory address of an operand. We examine the addressing modes in Section B.2 in the context of the x86 instruction format.

In addition to the larger number of addressing modes, the x86 contains a mechanism called *segmentation* that provides a measure of protection against unwanted accesses to particular memory addresses. The address produced by an instruction's addressing mode, rather than being an address in its own right, is used as an address within a segment of memory. Access to that memory location must take into account the segment register that controls access to that segment. The details of how the protection mechanism works will have to wait for later in your studies.

However, Figure B.2 does show how an address is calculated for the register+offset addressing mode, both for the LC-3, and for the x86, with segmentation. In both cases, the opcode is to move data from memory to a general purpose register. The LC-3 uses the LDR instruction. The x86 uses the MOV instruction. In the case of the x86, the address calculated is in the DS segment, which is accessed via the DS register. That access is done through a 16-bit *selector*, which indexes into a segment descriptor table, yielding the *segment descriptor* for that segment. The segment descriptor contains a *segment base register* and a *segment limit register*, and the protection information. The memory address obtained from the addressing mode of the instruction is added to the segment base register to provide the actual memory address, as shown in Figure B.2.

B.1.3 Internal State

The internal state of the LC-3 consists of eight 16-bit general purpose registers, R0 to R7, a 16-bit PC, and a 16-bit PSR that specifies the privilege mode, priority, and three 1-bit condition codes (N, Z, and P). The user-visible internal state of

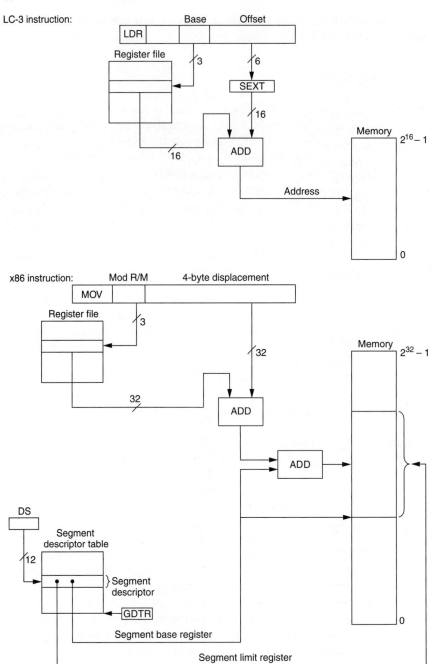

Figure B.2   Register+offset addressing mode in LC-3 and x86 ISAs

the x86 consists of application-visible registers, an Instruction pointer, a FLAGS register, and the segment registers.

Application-Visible Registers

Figure B.3 shows some of the application-visible registers in the x86 ISA.

Corresponding to R0 through R7, the x86 also has eight general purpose registers, EAX, EBX, ECX, EDX, ESP, EBP, ECI, and EDI. Each contains 32 bits, reflecting the normal size of its operands. However, since the x86 provides opcodes that process 16-bit operands and 8-bit operands, it should also provide 16-bit and 8-bit registers. The ISA identifies the low 16 bits of each 32-bit register as a 16-bit register and the low 8 bits and the high 8 bits of four of the registers as 8-bit registers for the use of instructions that require those smaller operands. So, for example, AX, BX, to DI are 16-bit registers, and AL, BL, CL, DL, AH, BH, CH, and DH are 8-bit registers.

The x86 also provides 64-bit registers for storing values needed for floating point and MMX computations. They are, respectively, FP0 through FP7 and MM0 through MM7.

General Purpose Registers:

31		0		
	AX	EAX	AL = EAX [7:0]
	DX	EDX	DL = EDX [7:0]
	CX	ECX	CL = ECX [7:0]
	BX	EBX	BL = EBX [7:0]
	BP	EBP	AH = EAX [15:8]
	CI	ECI	DH = EDX [15:8]
	DI	EDI	CH = ECX [15:8]
	SP	ESP	BH = EBX [15:8]

Floating Point Registers:

63	0
	FP0
	FP1
	FP2
	FP3
	FP4
	FP5
	FP6
	FP7

Multimedia Registers:

63	0
	MM0
	MM1
	MM2
	MM3
	MM4
	MM5
	MM6
	MM7

Figure B.3   Some x86 application-visible registers

System Registers

The LC-3 has two system-level registers—the PC and the PSR. The user-visible x86 has these and more.

Figure B.4 shows some of the user-visible system registers in the x86 ISA.

Instruction Pointer

The x86 has the equivalent of the LC-3's 16-bit program counter. The x86 calls it an *instruction pointer* (IP). Since the address space of the x86 is 32 bits, IP is a 32-bit register.

FLAGS Register

Corresponding to the LC-3's N, Z, and P condition codes, the x86 has a 1-bit SF (sign flag) register and a 1-bit ZF (zero flag) register. SF and ZF provide exactly the same functions as the N and Z condition codes of the LC-3. The x86 does not have the equivalent of the LC-3's P condition code. In fact, the P condition code is redundant, since if one knows the values of N and Z, one knows the value of P. We included it in the LC-3 ISA anyway, for the convenience of assembly language programmers and compiler writers.

The x86 collects other 1-bit values in addition to N and Z. These 1-bit values (called *flags*) are contained in a 16-bit register called FLAGS. Several of these flags are discussed in the following paragraphs.

The CF flag stores the *carry* produced by the last relevant operation that generated a carry. As we said earlier, together with the ADC instruction, CF facilitates the generation of procedures, which allows the software to deal with larger integers than the ISA supports.

The OF flag stores an *overflow* condition if the last relevant operate generated a value too large to store in the available number of bits. Recall the discussion of overflow in Section 2.5.3.

Figure B.4   x86 system registers

The DF flag indicates the *direction* in which string operations are to process strings. If DF = 0, the string is processed from the high-address byte down (i.e., the pointer keeping track of the element in the string to be processed next is decremented). If DF = 1, the string is processed from the low-address byte up (i.e., the string pointer is incremented).

Two flags not usually considered as part of the application state are the IF (*interrupt*) flag and the TF (*trap*) flag. Both correspond to functions with which you are familiar.

IF is very similar to the IE (interrupt enable) bit in the KBSR and DSR, discussed in Section 8.5. If IF = 1, the processor can recognize external interrupts (like keyboard input, for example). If IF = 0, these external interrupts have no effect on the process that is executing. We say the interrupts are *disabled*.

TF is very similar to *single-step mode* in the LC-3 simulator, only in this case it is part of the ISA. If TF = 1, the processor halts after every instruction so the state of the system can be examined. If TF = 0, the processor ignores the trap and processes the next instruction.

Segment Registers

When operating in its preferred operating mode (called *protected mode*), the address calculated by the instruction is really an offset from the starting address of a segment, which is specified by some *segment base register*. These segment base registers are part of their corresponding *data segment descriptors*, which are contained in the *segment descriptor table*. At each instant of time, six of these segments are active. They are called, respectively, the *code segment* (CS), *stack segment* (SS), and four data segments (DS, ES, FS, and GS). The six active segments are accessed via their corresponding segment registers shown in Figure B.4, which contain pointers to their respective segment descriptors.

B.2 The Format and Specification of x86 Instructions

The LC-3 instruction is a 16-bit instruction. Bits [15:12] always contain the opcode; the remaining 12 bits of each instruction are used to support the needs of that opcode.

The length of an x86 instruction is not fixed. It consists of a variable number of bytes, depending on the needs of that instruction. A lot of information can be packed into one x86 instruction. Figure B.5 shows the format of an

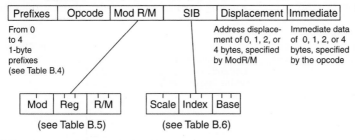

Figure B.5   Format of the x86 instruction

x86 instruction. The instruction consists of anywhere from 1 to 15 bytes, as shown in the figure.

The two key parts of an x86 instruction are the opcode and, where necessary, the ModR/M byte. The opcode specifies the operation the instruction is to perform. The ModR/M byte specifies how to obtain the operands it needs. The ModR/M byte specifies one of several addressing modes, some of which require the use of registers and a one-, two-, or four-byte displacement. The register information is encoded in a SIB byte. Both the SIB byte and the displacement (if one is necessary) follow the ModR/M byte in the instruction.

Some opcodes specify an immediate operand and also specify the number of bytes of the instruction that is used to store that immediate information. The immediate value (when one is specified) is the last element of the instruction.

Finally, the instruction assumes certain default information with respect to the semantics of an instruction, such as address size, operand size, segment to be used, and so forth. The instruction can change this default information by means of one or more prefixes, which are located at the beginning of the instruction.

Each part of an x86 instruction is discussed in more detail in Sections B.2.1 through B.2.6.

B.2.1 Prefix

Prefixes provide additional information that is used to process the instruction. There are four classes of prefix information, and each instruction can have from zero to four prefixes, depending on its needs. Fundamentally, a prefix overrides the usual interpretation of the instruction.

The four classes of prefixes are lock and repeat, segment override, operand override, and address override. Table B.4 describes the four types of prefixes.

Table B.4	Prefixes, x86 ISA
Repeat/Lock	
xF0 (LOCK)	This prefix guarantees that the instruction will have exclusive use of all shared memory until the instruction completes execution.
xF2, xF3 (REP/REPE/REPNE)	This prefix allows the instruction (a string instruction) to be repeated some specified number of times. The iteration count is specified by ECX. The instruction is also terminated on the occurrence of a specified value of ZF.
Segment override	
x2E(CS), x36(SS), x3E(DS), x26(ES), x64(FS), x65(GS)	This prefix causes the memory access to use the specified segment, instead of the default segment expected for that instruction.
Operand size override	
x66	This prefix changes the size of data expected for this instruction. That is, instructions expecting 32-bit data elements use 16-bit data elements. And instructions expecting 16-bit data elements use 32-bit data elements.
Address size override	
x67	This prefix changes the size of operand addresses expected for this instruction. That is, instructions expecting a 32-bit address use 16-bit addresses. And instructions expecting 16-bit addresses use 32-bit addresses.

B.2.2 Opcode

The opcode byte (or bytes—some opcodes are represented by two bytes) specifies a large amount of information about the needs of that instruction. The opcode byte (or bytes) specifies, among other things, the operation to be performed, whether the operands are to be obtained from memory or from registers, the size of the operands, whether or not one of the source operands is an immediate value in the instruction, and if so, the size of that immediate operand.

Some opcodes are formed by combining the opcode byte with bits [5:3] of the ModR/M byte, if those bits are not needed to provide addressing mode information. The ModR/M byte is described in Section B.2.3.

B.2.3 ModR/M Byte

The ModR/M byte, shown in Figure B.5, provides addressing mode information for two operands, when necessary, or for one operand, if that is all that is needed. If two operands are needed, one may be in memory, the other in a register, or both may be in registers. If one operand is needed, it can be either in a register or in memory. The ModR/M byte supports all cases.

The ModR/M byte is essentially partitioned into two parts. The first part consists of bits [7:6] and bits [2:0]. The second part consists of bits [5:3].

If bits [7:6] = 00, 01, or 10, the first part specifies the addressing mode of a memory operand, and the combined five bits ([7:6],[2:0]) identify which addressing mode. If bits [7:6] = 11, there is no memory operand, and bits [2:0] specify a register operand.

Bits [5:3] specify the register number of the other operand, if the opcode requires two operands. If the opcode only requires one operand, bits [5:3] are available as a subopcode to differentiate among eight opcodes that have the same opcode byte, as described in Section B.2.2.

Table B.5 lists some of the interpretations of the ModR/M byte.

Table B.5			ModR/M Byte, Examples		
Mod	Reg	R/M	Eff. Addr.	Reg	Explanation
00	011	000	[EAX]	EBX	EAX contains the address of the memory operand. EBX contains the register operand.
01	010	000	disp8[EAX]	EDX	Memory operand's address is obtained by adding the displacement byte of the instruction to the contents of EAX. EDX contains the register operand.
10	000	100	disp32[-][-]	EAX	Memory operand's address is obtained by adding the four-byte (32 bits) displacement of the instruction to an address that will need an SIB byte to compute. (See Section B.2.4 for the discussion of the SIB byte.) EAX contains the register operand.
11	001	110	ESI	ECX	If the opcode requires two operands, both are in registers (ESI and ECX). If the opcode requires one operand, it is in ESI. In that case, 001 (bits [5:3]) are part of the opcode.

Table B.6			SIB Byte, Examples	
Scale	Index	Base	Computation	Explanation
00	011	000	EBX+EAX	The contents of EBX are added to the contents of EAX. The result is added to whatever is specified by the ModR/M byte.
01	000	001	2 · EAX + ECX	The contents of EAX are multiplied by 2, and the result is added to the contents of ECX. This is then added to whatever is specified by the ModR/M byte.
01	100	001	ECX	The contents of ECX are added to whatever is specified by the ModR/M byte.
10	110	010	4 · ESI + EDX	The contents of ESI are multiplied by 4, and the result is added to the contents of EDX. This is then added to whatever is specified by the ModR/M byte.

B.2.4 SIB Byte

If the opcode specifies that an operand is to be obtained from memory, the ModR/M byte specifies the addressing mode, that is, the information that is needed to calculate the address of that operand. Some addressing modes require more information than can be specified by the ModR/M byte alone. Those operand specifiers (see example 3 in Table B.5) specify the inclusion of an SIB byte in the instruction. The SIB byte (for scaled-index-base), shown in Figure B.5, provides scaling information and identifies which register is to be used as an index register and/or which register is to be used as a base register. Taken together, the SIB byte computes scale · index + base, where base and/or index can be zero, and scale can be 1. Table B.6 lists some of the interpretations of the SIB byte.

B.2.5 Displacement

If the ModR/M byte specifies that the address calculation requires a displacement, the displacement (one, two, or four bytes) is contained in the instruction. The opcode and/or ModR/M byte specifies the size of the displacement.

Figure B.6 shows the addressing mode calculation for the source operand if the instruction is as shown. The prefix x26 overrides the segment register and specifies using the ES segment. The ModR/M and SIB bytes specify that a four-byte displacement is to be added to the base register ECX + the index register EBX after its contents are multiplied by 4.

B.2.6 Immediate

Recall that the LC-3 allowed small immediate values to be present in the instruction, by setting inst[5:5] to 1. The x86 also permits immediate values in the instruction. As stated previously, if the opcode specifies that a source operand is an immediate value in the instruction, it also specifies the number of bytes of the instruction used to represent the operand. That is, an immediate can be represented in the instruction with one, two, or four bytes. Since the opcode also specifies the size of the operand, immediate values that can be stored in fewer bytes than the

Prefix	Opcode	ModR/M	SIB	Displacement
00100110	00000011	10000100	10011001	32 bits
ES override	ADD r32, m32	disp32 [][] EAX	EBX * 4 + ECX	

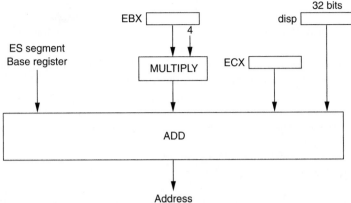

Figure B.6   Addressing mode calculation for Base+ScaledIndes+disp32

operand size are first sign-extended to their full size before being operated on. Figure B.7 shows the use of the immediate operand with the ADD instruction. The example is ADD EAX, $5. We are very familiar with the corresponding LC-3 instruction: ADD R0,R0,#5.

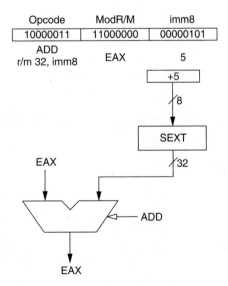

Figure B.7   Example x86 instruction: ADD EAX, $5

B.3 An Example

We conclude this appendix with an example. The problem is one we have dealt with extensively in Chapter 14. Given an input character string consisting of text, numbers, and punctuation, write a C program to convert all the lowercase letters to uppercase. Figure B.8 shows a C program that solves this problem. Figure B.9 shows the annotated LC-3 assembly language code that a C compiler would generate. Figure B.10 shows the corresponding annotated x86 assembly language code. For readability, we show assembly language representations of the LC-3 and x86 programs rather than the machine code.

```
#include <stdio.h>

void UpcaseString(char inputString[]);

main ()
{
    char string[8];

    scanf("%s", string);
    UpcaseString(string);
}

void UpcaseString(char inputString[])
{
  int i = 0;

  while(inputString[i]) {
    if (('a' <= inputString[i]) && (inputString[i] <= 'z'))
      inputString[i] = inputString[i] - ('a' - 'A');
    i++;
  }
}
```

Figure B.8   C source code for the upper-/lowercase program

```
; uppercase:  converts lower- to uppercase
              .ORIG  x3000
              LEA    R6, STACK
MAIN          ADD    R1, R6, #3
READCHAR      IN                       ; read in input string: scanf
              OUT
              STR    R0, R1, #0
              ADD    R1, R1, #1
              ADD    R2, R0, x-A
              BRnp   READCHAR
              ADD    R1, R1, #-1
              STR    R2, R1, #0         ; put in NULL char to mark the "end"
              ADD    R1, R6, #3         ; get the starting address of the string
              STR    R1, R6, #14        ; pass the parameter
              STR    R6, R6, #13
              ADD    R6, R6, #11
              JSR    UPPERCASE
              HALT
UPPERCASE     STR    R7, R6, #1
              AND    R1, R1, #0
              STR    R1, R6, #4
              LDR    R2, R6, #3
CONVERT       ADD    R3, R1, R2         ; add index to starting addr of string
              LDR    R4, R3, #0
              BRz    DONE               ; Done if NULL char reached
              LD     R5, a
              ADD    R5, R5, R4         ; 'a' <= input string
              BRn    NEXT
              LD     R5, z
              ADD    R5, R4, R5         ; input string <= 'z'
              BRp    NEXT
              LD     R5, asubA          ; convert to uppercase
              ADD    R4, R4, R5
              STR    R4, R3, #0
NEXT          ADD    R1, R1, #1         ; increment the array index, i
              STR    R1, R6, #4
              BRnzp  CONVERT
DONE          LDR    R7, R6, #1
              LDR    R6, R6, #2
              RET
a             .FILL  #-97
z             .FILL  #-122
asubA         .FILL  #-32
STACK         .BLKW  100
              .END
```

Figure B.9   LC-3 assembly language code for the upper-/lowercase program

```
.386P
.model FLAT

_DATA    SEGMENT                    ; The NULL-terminated scanf format
$SG397   DB        '%s', 00H        ; string is stored in global data space.
_DATA    ENDS


_TEXT    SEGMENT

_string$ = -8                       ; Location of "string" in local stack
_main    PROC NEAR
         sub    esp, 8              ; Allocate stack space to store "string"
         lea    eax, DWORD PTR _string$[esp+8]
         push   eax                 ; Push arguments to scanf
         push   OFFSET FLAT:$SG397
         call   _scanf

         lea    ecx, DWORD PTR _string$[esp+16]
         push   ecx                 ; Push argument to UpcaseString
         call   _UpcaseString

         add    esp, 20             ; Release local stack space
         ret    0
_main    ENDP

_inputString$ = 8                   ; "inputString" location in local stack
_UpcaseString PROC NEAR
         mov    ecx, DWORD PTR _inputString$[esp-4]
         cmp    BYTE PTR [ecx], 0
         je     SHORT $L404         ; If inputString[0]==0, skip the loop
$L403:   mov    al, BYTE PTR [ecx]  ; Load inputString[i] into AL
         cmp    al, 97             ; 97 == 'a'
         jl     SHORT $L405
         cmp    al, 122            ; 122 == 'z'
         jg     SHORT $L405
         sub    al, 32             ; 32 == 'a' - 'A'
         mov    BYTE PTR [ecx], al
$L405:   inc    ecx                ; i++ %$
         mov    al, BYTE PTR [ecx]
         test   al, al
         jne    SHORT $L403         ; Loop if inputString[i] != 0
$L404:   ret    0
_UpcaseString ENDP
_TEXT    ENDS
END
```

Figure B.10   x86 assembly language code for the upper-/lowercase program

The Microarchitecture of the LC-3

We have seen in Chapters 4 and 5 the several stages of the instruction cycle that must occur in order for the computer to process each instruction. If a microarchitecture is to implement an ISA, it must be able to carry out this instruction cycle for every instruction in the ISA. This appendix illustrates one example of a microarchitecture that can do that for the LC-3 ISA. Many of the details of the microarchitecture and the reasons for each design decision are well beyond the scope of an introductory course. However, for those who want to understand **how** a microarchitecture can carry out the requirements of each instruction of the LC-3 ISA, this appendix is provided.

C.1 Overview

Figure C.1 shows the two main components of an ISA: the *data path*, which contains all the components that actually process the instructions, and the *control*, which contains all the components that generate the set of control signals that are needed to control the processing at each instant of time.

We say, "at each instant of time," but we really mean **during each clock cycle**. That is, time is divided into *clock cycles*. The cycle time of a microprocessor is the duration of a clock cycle. A common cycle time for a microprocessor today is 0.5 nanoseconds, which corresponds to 2 billion clock cycles each second. We say that such a microprocessor is operating at a frequency of 2 gigahertz.

At each instant of time—or, rather, during each clock cycle—the 49 control signals (as shown in Figure C.1) control both the processing in the data path and the generation of the control signals for the next clock cycle. Processing in the data path is controlled by 39 bits, and the generation of the control signals for the next clock cycle is controlled by 10 bits.

Note that the hardware that determines which control signals are needed each clock cycle does not operate in a vacuum. On the contrary, the control signals needed in the "next" clock cycle depend on all of the following:

1. What is going on in the current clock cycle.
2. The LC-3 instruction that is being executed.
3. The privilege mode of the program that is executing.
4. If that LC-3 instruction is a BR, whether the conditions for the branch have been met (i.e., the state of the relevant condition codes).

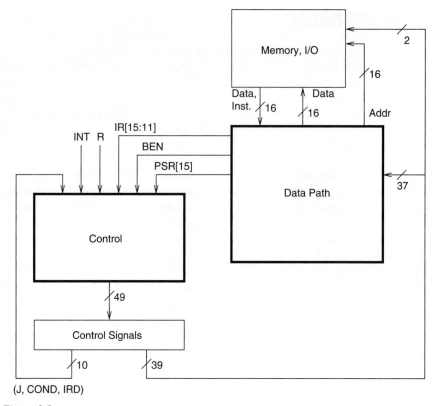

Figure C.1   Microarchitecture of the LC-3, major components

5. Whether or not an external device is requesting that the processor be interrupted.

6. If a memory operation is in progress, whether it is completing during this cycle.

Figure C.1 identifies the specific information in our implementation of the LC-3 that corresponds to these five items. They are, respectively:

1. J[5:0], COND[2:0], and IRD—10 bits of control signals provided by the current clock cycle.

2. inst[15:12], which identifies the opcode, and inst[11:11], which differentiates JSR from JSRR (i.e., the addressing mode for the target of the subroutine call).

3. PSR[15], bit [15] of the Processor Status Register, which indicates whether the current program is executing with supervisor or user privileges.

4. BEN to indicate whether or not a BR should be taken.

5. INT to indicate that some external device of higher priority than the executing process requests service.

6. R to indicate the end of a memory operation.

C.2 The State Machine

The behavior of the LC-3 microarchitecture during a given clock cycle is completely determined by the 49 control signals, combined with nine bits of additional information (inst[15:11], PSR[15], BEN, INT, and R), as shown in Figure C.1. We have said that during each clock cycle, 39 of these control signals determine the processing of information in the data path and the other 10 control signals combine with the nine bits of additional information to determine which set of control signals will be required in the next clock cycle.

We say that these 49 control signals specify the *state* of the control structure of the LC-3 microarchitecture. We can completely describe the behavior of the LC-3 microarchitecture by means of a directed graph that consists of nodes (one corresponding to each state) and arcs (showing the flow from each state to the one[s] it goes to next). We call such a graph a *state machine*.

Figure C.2 is the state machine for our implementation of the LC-3. The state machine describes what happens during each clock cycle in which the computer is running. Each state is active for exactly one clock cycle before control passes to the next state. The state machine shows the step-by-step (clock cycle–by–clock cycle) process that each instruction goes through from the start of its FETCH phase to the end of that instruction, as described in Section 4.2.2. Each node in the state machine corresponds to the activity that the processor carries out during a single clock cycle. The actual processing that is performed in the data path is contained inside the node. The step-by-step flow is conveyed by the arcs that take the processor from one state to the next.

For example, recall from Chapter 4 that the FETCH phase of every instruction cycle starts with a memory access to read the instruction at the address specified by the PC. Note that in the state numbered 18, the MAR is loaded with the address contained in PC, the PC is incremented in preparation for the FETCH of the next LC-3 instruction, and, if there is no interrupt request present (INT = 0), the flow passes to the state numbered 33. We will describe in Section C.6 the flow of control if INT = 1, that is, if an external device is requesting an interrupt.

Before we get into what happens during the clock cycle when the processor is in the state numbered 33, we should explain the numbering system—that is, why 18 and 33. Recall, from our discussion of finite state machines in Chapter 3, that each state must be uniquely specified and that this unique specification is accomplished by means of the state variables. Our state machine that implements the LC-3 ISA requires 52 distinct states to describe the entire behavior of the LC-3. Figure C.2 shows 31 of them plus pointers to three others (states 8, 13, and 49). Figure C.7 shows the other 18 states (plus 8, 13, and 49) that are pointed to in Figure C.2. We will come into contact with all of them as we go through this appendix. Since k logical variables can uniquely identify 2^k items, six state variables are needed to uniquely specify 52 states. The number next to each node in Figure C.2 is the decimal equivalent of the values (0 or 1) of the six state variables for the corresponding state. Thus, the state numbered 18 has state variable values 010010.

Now, then, back to what happens after the clock cycle in which the activity of state 18 has finished. Again, if no external device is requesting an interrupt,

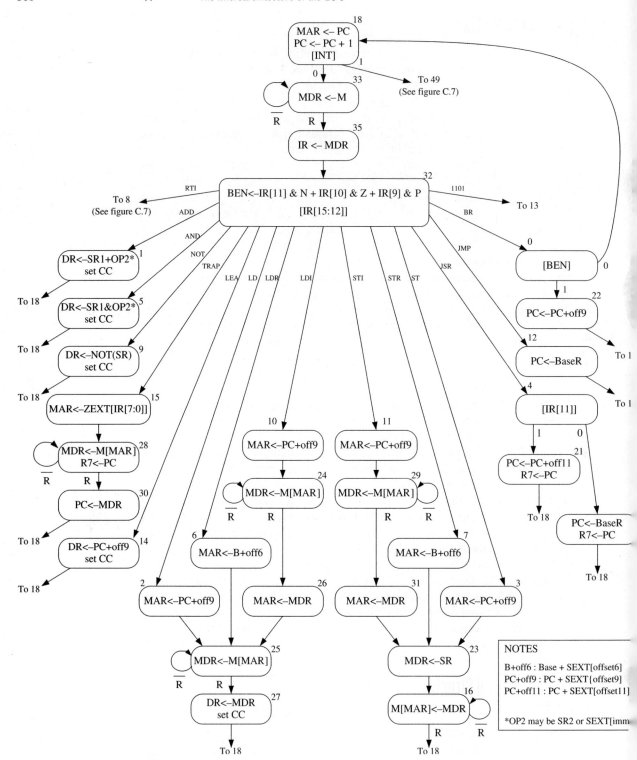

Figure C.2   A state machine for the LC-3

the flow passes to state 33. In state 33, since the MAR contains the address of the instruction to be processed, this instruction is read from memory and loaded into the MDR. Since this memory access can take multiple cycles, this state continues to execute until a ready signal from the memory (R) is asserted, indicating that the memory access has completed. Thus the MDR contains the valid contents of the memory location specified by MAR. The state machine then moves on to state 35, where the instruction is loaded into the instruction register (IR), completing the fetch phase of the instruction cycle.

Note that the arrow from the last state of each instruction cycle (i.e., the state that completes the processing of that LC-3 instruction) takes us to state 18 (to begin the instruction cycle of the next LC-3 instruction).

C.3 The Data Path

The data path consists of all components that actually process the information during a cycle—the functional units that operate on the information, the registers that store information at the end of one cycle so it will be available for further use in subsequent cycles, and the buses and wires that carry information from one point to another in the data path. Figure C.3, an expanded version of what you have already encountered in Figure 5.9, illustrates the data path of our microarchitecture of the LC-3.

Note the control signals that are associated with each component in the data path. For example, ALUK, consisting of two control signals, is associated with the ALU. These control signals determine how the component will be used each cycle. Table C.1 lists the set of control signals that control the elements of the data path and the set of values that each control signal can have. (Actually, for readability, we list a symbolic name for each value, rather than the binary value.) For example, since ALUK consists of two bits, it can have one of four values. Which value it has during any particular clock cycle depends on whether the ALU is required to ADD, AND, NOT, or simply pass one of its inputs to the output during that clock cycle. PCMUX also consists of two control signals and specifies which input to the MUX is required during a given clock cycle. LD.PC is a single-bit control signal, and is a 0 (NO) or a 1 (YES), depending on whether or not the PC is to be loaded during the given clock cycle.

During each clock cycle, corresponding to the "current state" in the state machine, the 39 bits of control direct the processing of all components in the data path that are required during that clock cycle. The processing that takes place in the data path during that clock cycle, as we have said, is specified inside the node representing the state.

C.4 The Control Structure

The control structure of a microarchitecture is specified by its state machine. As described earlier, the state machine (Figure C.2) determines which control signals are needed each clock cycle to process information in the data path and which

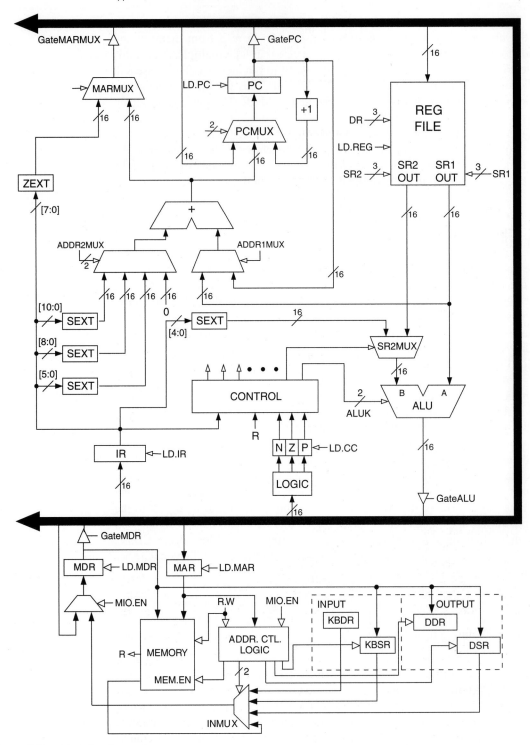

Figure C.3   The LC-3 data path

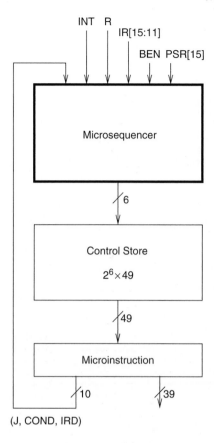

Figure C.4 The control structure of a microprogrammed implementation, overall block diagram

control signals are needed each clock cycle to direct the flow of control from the currently active state to its successor state.

Figure C.4 shows a block diagram of the control structure of our implementation of the LC-3. Many implementations are possible, and the design considerations that must be studied to determine which of many possible implementations should be used is the subject of a full course in computer architecture.

We have chosen here a straightforward microprogrammed implementation. Each state of the control structure requires 39 bits to control the processing in the data path and 10 bits to help determine which state comes next. These 49 bits are collectively known as a *microinstruction*. Each microinstruction (i.e., each state of the state machine) is stored in one 49-bit location of a special memory called the control store. There are 52 distinct states. Since each state corresponds to one microinstruction in the control store, the control store for our microprogrammed implementation requires six bits to specify the address of each microinstruction.

Table C.1   Data Path Control Signals

Signal Name	Signal Values	
LD.MAR/1:	NO, LOAD	
LD.MDR/1:	NO, LOAD	
LD.IR/1:	NO, LOAD	
LD.BEN/1:	NO, LOAD	
LD.REG/1:	NO, LOAD	
LD.CC/1:	NO, LOAD	
LD.PC/1:	NO, LOAD	
LD.Priv/1:	NO, LOAD	
LD.SavedSSP/1:	NO, LOAD	
LD.SavedUSP/1:	NO, LOAD	
LD.Vector/1:	NO, LOAD	
GatePC/1:	NO, YES	
GateMDR/1:	NO, YES	
GateALU/1:	NO, YES	
GateMARMUX/1:	NO, YES	
GateVector/1:	NO, YES	
GatePC-1/1:	NO, YES	
GatePSR/1:	NO, YES	
GateSP/1:	NO, YES	
PCMUX/2:	PC+1	;select pc+1
	BUS	;select value from bus
	ADDER	;select output of address adder
DRMUX/2:	11.9	;destination IR[11:9]
	R7	;destination R7
	SP	;destination R6
SR1MUX/2:	11.9	;source IR[11:9]
	8.6	;source IR[8:6]
	SP	;source R6
ADDR1MUX/1:	PC, BaseR	
ADDR2MUX/2:	ZERO	;select the value zero
	offset6	;select SEXT[IR[5:0]]
	PCoffset9	;select SEXT[IR[8:0]]
	PCoffset11	;select SEXT[IR[10:0]]
SPMUX/2:	SP+1	;select stack pointer+1
	SP−1	;select stack pointer−1
	Saved SSP	;select saved Supervisor Stack Pointer
	Saved USP	;select saved User Stack Pointer
MARMUX/1:	7.0	;select ZEXT[IR[7:0]]
	ADDER	;select output of address adder
VectorMUX/2:	INTV	
	Priv.exception	
	Opc.exception	
PSRMUX/1:	individual settings, BUS	
ALUK/2:	ADD, AND, NOT, PASSA	
MIO.EN/1:	NO, YES	
R.W/1:	RD, WR	
Set.Priv/1:	0	;Supervisor mode
	1	;User mode

Table C.2	Microsequencer Control Signals	
Signal Name	**Signal Values**	
J/6: COND/3:	COND0	;Unconditional
	COND1	;Memory Ready
	COND2	;Branch
	COND3	;Addressing Mode
	COND4	;Privilege Mode
	COND5	;Interrupt test
IRD/1:	NO, YES	

Table C.2 lists the function of the 10 bits of control information that help determine which state comes next. Figure C.5 shows the logic of the microsequencer. The purpose of the microsequencer is to determine the address in the control store that corresponds to the next state, that is, the location where the 49 bits of control information for the next state are stored.

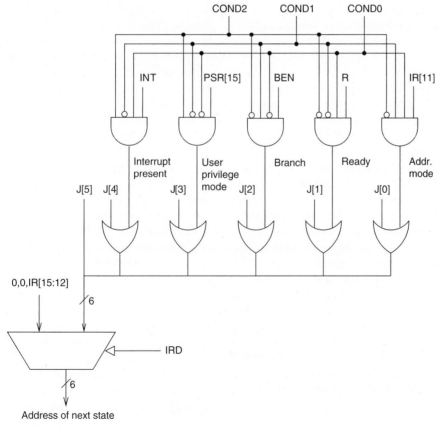

Figure C.5   The microsequencer of the LC-3

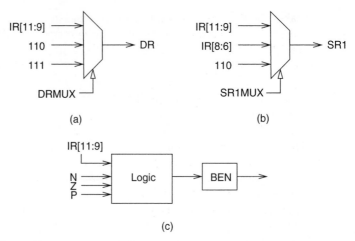

Figure C.6   Additional logic required to provide control signals

Note that state 32 of the state machine (Figure C.2) has 16 "next" states, depending on the LC-3 instruction being executed during the current instruction cycle. This state carries out the DECODE phase of the instruction cycle described in Chapter 4. If the IRD control signal in the microinstruction corresponding to state 32 is 1, the output MUX of the microsequencer (Figure C.5) will take its source from the six bits formed by 00 concatenated with the four opcode bits IR[15:12]. Since IR[15:12] specifies the opcode of the current LC-3 instruction being processed, the next address of the control store will be one of 16 addresses, corresponding to the 15 opcodes plus the one unused opcode, IR[15:12] = 1101. That is, each of the 16 next states is the first state to be carried out after the instruction has been decoded in state 32. For example, if the instruction being processed is ADD, the address of the next state is state 1, whose microinstruction is stored at location 000001. Recall that IR[15:12] for ADD is 0001.

If, somehow, the instruction inadvertently contained IR[15:12] = 1101, the unused opcode, the microarchitecture would execute a sequence of microinstructions, starting at state 13. These microinstructions would respond to the fact that an instruction with an illegal opcode had been fetched. Section C.6.3 describes what happens.

Several signals necessary to control the data path and the microsequencer are not among those listed in Tables C.1 and C.2. They are DR, SR1, BEN, INT, and R. Figure C.6 shows the additional logic needed to generate DR, SR1, and BEN.

The INT signal is supplied by some event external to the normal instruction processing, indicating that normal instruction processing should be interrupted and this external event dealt with. The interrupt mechanism was described in Chapter 8. The corresponding flow of control within the microarchitecture is described in Section C.6.

The remaining signal, R, is a signal generated by the memory in order to allow the LC-3 to operate correctly with a memory that takes multiple clock cycles to read or store a value.

Suppose it takes memory five cycles to read a value. That is, once MAR contains the address to be read and the microinstruction asserts READ, it will take five cycles before the contents of the specified location in memory are available to be loaded into MDR. (Note that the microinstruction asserts READ by means of two control signals: MIO.EN/YES and R.W/RD; see Figure C.3.)

Recall our discussion in Section C.2 of the function of state 33, which accesses an instruction from memory during the FETCH phase of each instruction cycle. For the LC-3 to operate correctly, state 33 must execute five times before moving on to state 35. That is, until MDR contains valid data from the memory location specified by the contents of MAR, we want state 33 to continue to re-execute. After five clock cycles, the memory has completed the "read," resulting in valid data in MDR, so the processor can move on to state 35. What if the microarchitecture did not wait for the memory to complete the read operation before moving on to state 35? Since the contents of MDR would still be garbage, the microarchitecture would put garbage into IR in state 35.

The ready signal (R) enables the memory read to execute correctly. Since the memory knows it needs five clock cycles to complete the read, it asserts a ready signal (R) throughout the fifth clock cycle. Figure C.2 shows that the next state is 33 (i.e., 100001) if the memory read will not complete in the current clock cycle and state 35 (i.e., 100011) if it will. As we have seen, it is the job of the microsequencer (Figure C.5) to produce the next state address.

The 10 microsequencer control bits for state 33 are as follows:

```
IRD/0        ; NO
COND/001     ; Memory Ready
J/100001
```

With these control signals, what next state address is generated by the microsequencer? For each of the first four executions of state 33, since $R = 0$, the next state address is 100001. This causes state 33 to be executed again in the next clock cycle. In the fifth clock cycle, since $R = 1$, the next state address is 100011, and the LC-3 moves on to state 35. Note that in order for the ready signal (R) from memory to be part of the next state address, COND had to be set to 001, which allowed R to pass through its four-input AND gate.

C.5 Memory-Mapped I/O

As you know from Chapter 8, the LC-3 ISA performs input and output via memory-mapped I/O, that is, with the same data movement instructions that it uses to read from and write to memory. The LC-3 does this by assigning an address to each device register. Input is accomplished by a load instruction whose effective address is the address of an input device register. Output is accomplished by a store instruction whose effective address is the address of an output device register. For example, in state 25 of Figure C.2, if the address in MAR is xFE02,

Table C.3   **Truth Table for Address Control Logic**

MAR	MIO.EN	R.W	MEM.EN	IN.MUX	LD.KBSR	LD.DSR	LD.DDR
xFE00	0	R	0	x	0	0	0
xFE00	0	W	0	x	0	0	0
xFE00	1	R	0	KBSR	0	0	0
xFE00	1	W	0	x	1	0	0
xFE02	0	R	0	x	0	0	0
xFE02	0	W	0	x	0	0	0
xFE02	1	R	0	KBDR	0	0	0
xFE02	1	W	0	x	0	0	0
xFE04	0	R	0	x	0	0	0
xFE04	0	W	0	x	0	0	0
xFE04	1	R	0	DSR	0	0	0
xFE04	1	W	0	x	0	1	0
xFE06	0	R	0	x	0	0	0
xFE06	0	W	0	x	0	0	0
xFE06	1	R	0	x	0	0	0
xFE06	1	W	0	x	0	0	1
other	0	R	0	x	0	0	0
other	0	W	0	x	0	0	0
other	1	R	1	mem	0	0	0
other	1	W	1	x	0	0	0

MDR is supplied by the KBDR, and the data input will be the last keyboard character typed. On the other hand, if the address in MAR is a legitimate memory address, MDR is supplied by the memory.

The state machine of Figure C.2 does not have to be altered to accommodate memory-mapped I/O. However, something has to determine when memory should be accessed and when I/O device registers should be accessed. This is the job of the address control logic shown in Figure C.3.

Table C.3 is a truth table for the address control logic, showing what control signals are generated, based on (1) the contents of MAR, (2) whether or not memory or I/O is accessed this cycle (MIO.EN/NO, YES), and (3) whether a load or store is requested (R.W/Read, Write). Note that, for a memory-mapped load, data can be supplied to MDR from one of four sources: memory, KBDR, KBSR, or DSR. The address control logic provides the appropriate select signals to the INMUX. For a memory-mapped store, the data supplied by MDR can be written to memory, KBSR, DDR, or DSR. The address control logic supplies the appropriate enable signal to the corresponding structure.

C.6 Interrupt and Exception Control

The final piece of the state machine needed to complete the LC-3 story are those states that control the initiation of an interrupt, those states that control the return from an interrupt (the RTI instruction), and those states that control the initiation

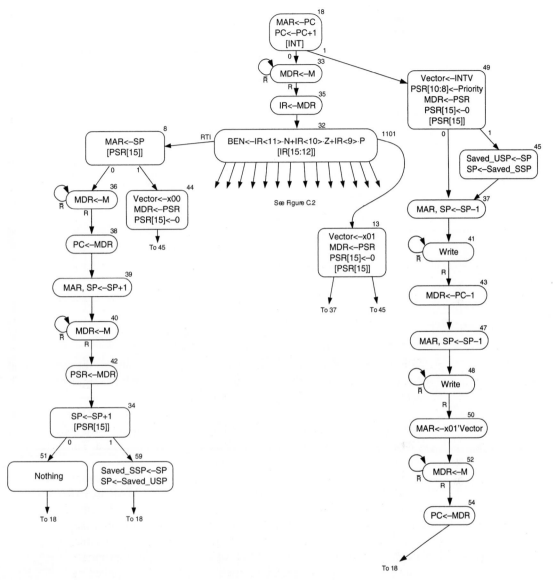

Figure C.7   LC-3 state machine showing interrupt control

of one of the two exceptions specified by the ISA. The two exceptions are a privilege mode violation and an illegal opcode. Figure C.7 shows the state machine that carries these out. Figure C.8 shows the data path, after adding the additional structures to Figure C.3 that are needed to make interrupt and exception processing work.

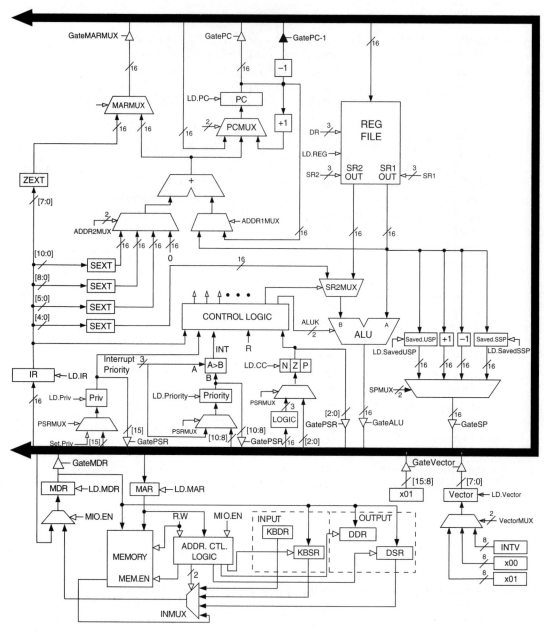

Figure C.8   LC-3 data path, including additional structures for interrupt control

C.6.1 Initiating an Interrupt

While a program is executing, an interrupt can be requested by some external event so that the normal processing of instructions can be preempted and the control can turn its attention to processing the interrupt. The external event requests an interrupt by asserting its interrupt request signal. Recall from Chapter 8 that if the priority level of the device asserting its interrupt request signal is higher than the priority level of the currently executing program, INT is asserted and INTV is loaded with the appropriate interrupt vector. The microprocessor responds to INT by initiating the interrupt. That is, the processor puts itself into supervisor mode, pushes the PSR and PC of the interrupted process onto the supervisor stack, and loads the PC with the starting address of the interrupt service routine. The PSR contains the privilege mode PSR[15], priority level PSR[10:8], and condition codes PSR[2:0] of a program. It is important that when the processor resumes execution of the interrupted program, the privilege mode, priority level, and condition codes are restored to what they were when the interrupt occurred.

The microarchitecture of the LC-3 initiates an interrupt as follows: Recall from Figure C.2 that in state 18, while MAR is loaded with the contents of PC and PC is incremented, INT is tested.

State 18 is the only state in which the processor checks for interrupts. The reason for only testing in state 18 is straightforward: Once an LC-3 instruction starts processing, it is easier to let it finish its complete instruction cycle (FETCH, DECODE, etc.) than to interrupt it in the middle and have to keep track of how far along it was when the external device requested an interrupt (i.e., asserted INT). If INT is only tested in state 18, the current instruction cycle can be aborted early (even before the instruction has been fetched), and control directed to initiating the interrupt.

The test is enabled by the control signals that make up COND5, which are 101 only in state 18, allowing the value of INT to pass through its four-input AND gate to contribute to the address of the next state. Since the COND signals are not 101 in any other state, INT has no effect in any other state.

In state 18, the 10 microsequencer control bits are as follows:

```
IRD/0        ; NO
COND/101     ; Test for interrupts
J/100001
```

If INT = 1, a 1 is produced at the output of the AND gate, which in turn makes the next state address not 100001, corresponding to state 33, but rather 110001, corresponding to state 49. This starts the initiation of the interrupt (see Figure C.7).

Several functions are performed in state 49. The PSR, which contains the privilege mode, priority level, and condition codes of the interrupted program, are loaded into MDR, in preparation for pushing it onto the Supervisor Stack. PSR[15] is cleared, reflecting the change to Supervisor mode, since all interrupt service routines execute in Supervisor mode. The 3-bit priority level and 8-bit interrupt vector (INTV) provided by the interrupting device are recorded. PSR[10:8] is loaded with the priority level. The internal register Vector is loaded with INTV.

Finally, the processor must test the old PSR[15] to see which stack R6 points to before pushing PSR and PC.

If the old PSR[15] = 0, the processor is already operating in Supervisor mode. R6 is the Supervisor Stack Pointer (SSP), so the processor proceeds immediately to states 37 and 44 to push the PSR of the interrupted program onto the Supervisor Stack. If PSR[15] = 1, the interrupted process was in User mode. In that case, the USP (the current contents of R6) must be saved in Saved_USP and R6 must be loaded with the contents of Saved_SSP before moving to state 37. This is done in state 45.

The control flow from state 49 to either 37 or 45 is enabled by the 10 microsequencer control bits, as follows:

```
IRD/0        ; NO
COND/100     ; Test PSR[15], privilege mode
J/100101
```

If PSR[15] = 0, control goes to state 37 (100101); if PSR[15] = 1, control goes to state 45 (101101).

In state 37, R6 (SSP) is decremented (preparing for the push), and MAR is loaded with the address of the new top of the stack.

In state 41, the memory is enabled to WRITE (MIO.EN/YES, R.W/WR). When the write completes, signaled by R = 1, PSR has been pushed onto the Supervisor Stack, and the flow moves on to state 43.

In state 43, the PC is loaded into MDR. Note that state 43 says MDR is loaded with PC-1. Recall that in state 18, at the beginning of the instruction cycle for the interrupted instruction, PC was incremented. Loading MDR with PC-1 adjusts PC to the correct address of the interrupted instruction.

In states 47 and 48, the same sequence as in states 37 and 56 occurs, only this time, the PC of the interrupted process is pushed onto the Supervisor Stack.

The final task to complete the initiation of the interrupt is to load the PC with the starting address of the interrupt service routine. This is carried out by states 50, 52, and 54. It is accomplished in a manner similar to the loading of the PC with the starting address of a TRAP service routine. The event causing the INT request supplies the 8-bit interrupt vector INTV associated with the interrupt, similar to the 8-bit trap vector contained in the TRAP instruction. This interrupt vector is stored in the 8-bit register INTV, shown on the data path in Figure C.8.

The interrupt vector table occupies memory locations x0100 to x01FF. In state 50, the interrupt vector that was loaded into Vector in state 49 is added to the base address of the interrupt vector table (x0100) and loaded into MAR. In state 52, memory is enabled to READ. When R = 1, the read has completed and MDR contains the starting address of the interrupt service routine. In state 54, the PC is loaded with that starting address, completing the initiation of the interrupt.

It is important to emphasize that the LC-3 supports two stacks, one for each privilege mode, and two stack pointers (USP and SSP), one for each stack. R6 is the stack pointer and is loaded from the Saved_SSP when privilege changes from User mode to Supervisor mode, and from Saved_USP when privilege changes from Supervisor mode to User mode. Needless to say, when the Privilege mode changes, the current value in R6 must be stored in the appropriate "Saved" stack pointer in order to be available the next time the privilege mode changes back.

C.6.2 Returning from an Interrupt, RTI

The interrupt service routine ends with the execution of the RTI instruction. The job of the RTI instruction is to restore the computer to the state it was in when the interrupt was initiated. This means restoring the PSR (i.e., the privilege mode, priority level, and the values of the condition codes N, Z, P) and restoring the PC. Recall that these values were pushed onto the stack during the initiation of the interrupt. They must, therefore, be popped off the stack in the reverse order.

The first state after DECODE is state 8. Here we load the MAR with the address of the top of the Supervisor Stack, which contains the last thing pushed (that has not been subsequently popped)—the state of the PC when the interrupt was initiated. At the same time, we test PSR[15] since RTI is a privileged instruction and can only execute in Supervisor mode. If PSR[15] = 0, we can continue to carry out the requirements of RTI.

PSR[15] = 0 ; RTI Completes Execution

States 36 and 38 complete the operation of restoring PC to the value it had when the interrupt was initiated. In state 36, the memory is read. When the read is completed, MDR contains the address of the instruction that was to be processed next when the interrupt occurred. State 38 loads that address into the PC.

States 39, 40, 42, and 34 restore the privilege mode, priority level, and condition codes (N, Z, P) to their original values. In state 39, the Supervisor Stack Pointer is incremented so that it points to the top of the stack after the PC was popped. The MAR is loaded with the address of the new top of the stack. State 40 initiates the memory READ; when the READ is completed, MDR contains the interrupted PSR. State 42 loads the PSR from MDR, and state 34 increments the stack pointer.

The only thing left is to check the privilege mode of the interrupted program to see whether the stack pointers have to be switched. In state 34, the microsequencer control bits are as follows:

```
IRD/0        ; NO
COND/100     ; Test PSR[15], privilege mode
J/110011
```

If PSR[15] = 0, control flows to state 51 (110011) to do nothing for one cycle. If PSR[15] = 1, control flows to state 59 where R6 is saved in Saved_SSP and R6 is loaded from Saved_USP. In both cases control returns to state 18 to begin processing the next instruction.

PSR[15] = 1 ; Privilege Mode Exception

If PSR[15] = 1, the processor has a privilege mode violation. It is attempting to execute RTI while the processor is in User mode, which is not allowed.

The processor responds to this situation by pushing the PSR and the address of the RTI instruction onto the Supervisor Stack and loading the PC with the starting address of the service routine that handles privilege mode violations. The processor does this in a way very similar to the mechanism for initiating interrupts.

First, in state 44, three functions are performed. The Vector register is loaded with the 8-bit vector that points to the entry in the interrupt vector table that contains the starting address of the Privilege mode violation exception service routine. This 8-bit vector is x00. The MDR is loaded with the PSR of the program that caused the violation. Third, PSR[15] is set to 0, since the service routine will execute with Supervisor privileges. Then the processor moves to state 45, where it follows the same flow as the initiation of interrupts.

The main difference between this flow and that for the initiation of interrupts flow comes in state 50, where MAR is loaded with x01'Vector. In the case of interrupts, Vector had previously been loaded in state 49 with INTV, which is supplied by the interrupting device. In the case of the privilege mode violation, Vector was loaded in state 44 with x00.

Two other minor differences reflect the additional functions performed in state 49 if an interrupt is initiated. First, the priority level is changed, based on the priority of the interrupting device. We do not change the priority in handling the privilege mode violation. The service routine executes at the same priority as the program that caused the violation. Second, a test to determine the privilege mode is performed for an interrupt. This is unnecessary for a privilege mode violation since the processor already knows it is executing in User mode.

C.6.3 The Illegal Opcode Exception

At the outset of Section C.6, we said the LC-3 ISA specifies two exceptions, a privilege mode violation and an illegal opcode. The privilege mode violation, as you have just seen, occurs when the processor tries to execute the RTI instruction while in User mode. The illegal opcode exception occurs if the instruction being processed specifies the undefined opcode (i.e., 1101) in bits [15:12] of the instruction. The action the processor takes is very similar to what happens when a privilege mode exception is detected. That is, the PSR and PC of the program are pushed onto the Supervisor Stack and the PC is loaded with the starting address of the Illegal Opcode Exception service routine. That initiates the service routine. From there, the service routine does whatever has been specified as the corrective action when an illegal opcode is detected.

The fact that the processor is in state 13 is enough to know that an illegal opcode is being processed. The reason: the only way it could get there is via the IR decode state 32. State 13 starts the initiation of the exception. State 13 is very similar to state 49, which starts the initiation of an interrupt, and state 44, which starts the initiation of a privilege mode violation. As with states 49 and 44, the Vector register is loaded in preparation for vectoring to the Interrupt Vector Table to find the starting address of the service routine. The exception vector in this case is x01. As with states 49 and 44, state 13 sets the Privilege mode to Supervisor (PSR[15] ← 0), since the service routine executes in Supervisor mode. Also like those states, it loads the PSR into the MDR to start the process of pushing the PSR onto the Supervisor Stack.

Like state 44, it does not change the priority of the running program, since the urgency of handling the exception is the same as the urgency of executing the program that contains it. Like state 49, it tests the Privilege mode of the program that contains the illegal opcode, since if the currently executing program is in User mode, the stack pointers need to be switched as was described in Section C.6.1. Like state 49, the processor then microbranches either to state 37 if the stack pointer is already pointing to the Supervisor Stack, or to state 45 if the stack pointers have to be switched. From there, the initiating sequence continues in states 37, 41, 43, etc., identical to what happens when an interrupt is initiated (Section C.6.1) or a privilege mode exception is initiated (Section C.6.2). The PSR and PC are pushed onto the Supervisor Stack and the starting address of the service routine is loaded into the PC, completing the initiation of the exception.

C.7 Control Store

Figure C.9 completes our microprogrammed implementation of the LC-3. It shows the contents of each location of the control store, corresponding to the 49 control signals required by each state of the state machine. We have left the exact entries blank to allow you, the reader, the joy of filling in the required signals yourself. The solution is available from your instructor.

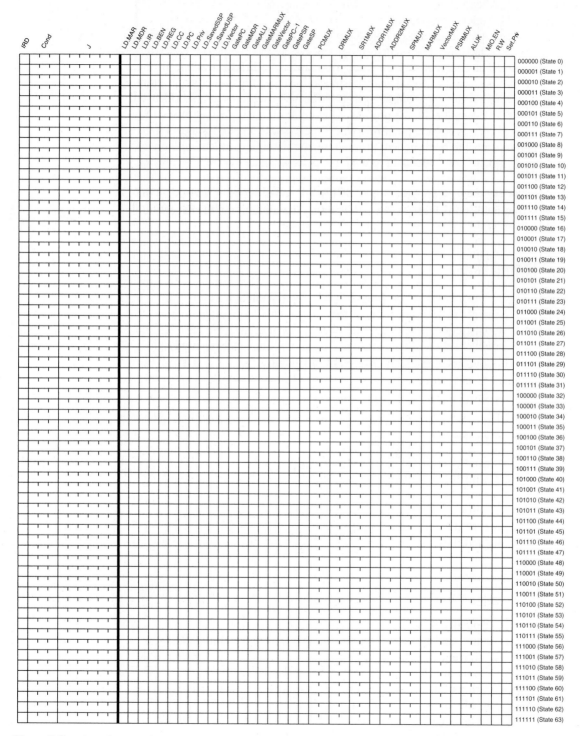

Figure C.9   Specification of the control store

The C Programming Language

D.1 Overview

This appendix is a C reference manual oriented toward the novice C programmer. It covers a significant portion of the language, including material not covered in the main text of this book. The intent of this appendix is to provide a quick reference to various features of the language for use during programming. Each item covered within the following sections contains a brief summary of a particular C feature and an illustrative example, when appropriate.

D.2 C Conventions

We start our coverage of the C programming language by describing the lexical elements of a C program and some of the conventions used by C programmers for writing C programs.

D.2.1 Source Files

The C programming convention is to separate programs into files of two types: source files (with the extension `.c`) and header files (with the extension `.h`). Source files, sometimes called `.c` or dot-c files, contain the C code for a group of related functions. For example, functions related to managing a stack data structure might be placed in a file named `stack.c`. Each `.c` file is compiled into an object file, and these objects are linked together into an executable image by the linker.

D.2.2 Header Files

Header files typically do not contain C statements but rather contain function, variable, structure, and type declarations, as well as preprocessor macros. The programming convention is to couple a header file with the source file in which the declared items are *defined*. For example, if the source file `stdio.c` contains the definitions for the functions `printf`, `scanf`, `getchar`, and `putchar`, then the header file `stdio.h` contains the declarations for these functions. If one of these functions is called from another `.c` file, then the `stdio.h` header file should be `#included` to get the proper function declarations.

D.2.3 Comments

In C, comments begin with the two-character delimiter /* and end with */. Comments can span multiple lines. Comments within comments are not legal and will generate a syntax error on most compilers. Comments within strings or character literals are not recognized as comments and will be treated as part of the character string. While some C compilers accept the C++ notation for comments (//), the ANSI C standard only allows for /* and */.

D.2.4 Literals

C programs can contain literal constant values that are integers, floating point values, characters, character strings, or enumeration constants. These literals can be used as initializers for variables, or within expressions. Some examples are provided in the following subsections.

Integer

Integer literals can be expressed either in decimal, octal, or hexadecimal notation. If the literal is prefixed by a 0 (zero), it will be interpreted as an octal number. If the literal begins with a 0x, it will be interpreted as hexadecimal (thus it can consist of the digits 0 through 9 and the characters *a* through *f*. Uppercase *A* through *F* can be used as well. An unprefixed literal (i.e., it doesn't begin with a 0 or 0x) indicates it is in decimal notation and consists of a sequence of digits. Regardless of its base, an integer literal can be preceded by a minus sign, –, to indicate a negative value.

An integer literal can be suffixed with the letter *l* or *L* to indicate that it is of type long int. An integer literal suffixed with the letter *u* or *U* indicates an unsigned value. Refer to Section D.3.2 for a discussion of long and unsigned types.

The first three examples that follow express the same number, 87. The two last versions express it as an unsigned int value and as a long int value.

```
87      /*  87 in decimal     */
0x57    /*  87 in hexadecimal */
0127    /*  87 in octal       */
-24     /* -24 in decimal     */
-024    /* -20 in octal       */
-0x24   /* -36 in hexadecimal */
87U
87L
```

Floating Point

Floating point constants consist of three parts: an integer part, a decimal point, and a fractional part. The fractional part and integer part are optional, but one of the two must be present. The number preceded by a minus sign indicates a negative value. Several examples follow:

```
1.613123
.613123
1.         /* expresses the number 1.0 */
-.613123
```

Floating point literals can also be expressed in exponential notation. With this form, a floating point constant (such as 1.613123) is followed by an *e* or *E*. The *e* or *E* signals the beginning of the integer exponent, which is the power of 10 by which the part preceding the exponent is multiplied. The exponent can be a negative value. The exponent is obviously optional, and if used, then the decimal point is optional. Examples follow:

```
6.023e23        /* 6.023 * 10^23      */
454.323e-22     /* 454.323 * 10^(-22) */
5E13            /* 5.0 * 10^13         */
```

By default, a floating point type is a `double` or double-precision floating point number. This can be modified with the optional suffix *f* or *F*, which indicates a `float` or single-precision floating point number. The suffix *l* or *L* indicates a `long double` (see Section D.3.2).

Character

A character literal can be expressed by surrounding a particular character by single quotes, e.g., `'c'`. This converts the character into the internal character code used by the computer, which for most computers today, including the LC-3, is ASCII.

Table D.1 lists some special characters that typically cannot be expressed with a single keystroke. The C programming language provides a means to state them via a special sequence of characters. The last two forms, octal and hexadecimal, specify ways of stating an arbitrary character by using its code value, stated as either octal or hex. For example, the character 'S', which has the ASCII value of 83 (decimal), can be stated as '\0123' or '\x53'.

String Literals

A string literal within a C program must be enclosed within double quote characters, ". String literals have the type `char *` and space for them is allocated in

Table D.1	Special Characters in C
Character	**Sequence**
newline	\n
horizontal tab	\t
vertical tab	\v
backspace	\b
carriage return	\r
formfeed	\f
audible alert	\a
backslash \	\\
question mark ?	\?
single quote '	\'
double quote "	\"
octal number	\0nnn
hexadecimal number	\xnnn

a special section of the memory address space reserved for literal constants. The termination character `'\0'` is automatically added to the character string. The following are two examples of string literals:

```
char greeting[10] = "bon jour!";
printf("This is a string literal");
```

String literals can be used to initialize character strings, or they can be used wherever an object of type `char *` is expected, for example as an argument to a function expecting a parameter of type `char *`. String literals, however, cannot be used for the assignment of arrays. For example, the following code is **not** legal in C.

```
char greeting [10];

greeting = "bon jour!";
```

Enumeration Constants

Associated with an enumerated type (see Section D.3.1) are enumerators, or enumeration constants. These constants are of type `int`, and their precise value is defined by the enumerator list of an enumeration declaration. In essence, an enumeration constant is a symbolic, integral value.

D.2.5 Formatting

C is a freely formatted language. The programmer is free to add spaces, tabs, carriage returns, new lines between and within statements and declarations. C programmers often adopt a style helpful for making the code more readable, which includes adequate indenting of control constructs, consistent alignment of open and close braces, and adequate commenting that does not obstruct someone trying to read the code. See the numerous examples in the C programming chapters of the book for a typical style of formatting C code.

D.2.6 Keywords

The following list is a set of reserved words, or keywords, that have special meaning within the C language. They are the names of the primitive types, type modifiers, control constructs, and other features natively supported by the language. These names cannot be used by the programmer as names of variables, functions, or any other object that the programmer might provide a name for.

auto	double	int	struct
break	else	long	switch
case	enum	register	typedef
char	extern	return	union
const	float	short	unsigned
continue	for	signed	void
default	goto	sizeof	volatile
do	if	static	while

D.3 Types

In C, expressions, functions, and objects have types associated with them. The type of a variable, for example, indicates something about the actual value the variable represents. For instance, if the variable kappa is of type int, then the value (which is essentially just a bit pattern) referred to by kappa will be interpreted as a signed integer. In C, there are the *basic data types*, which are types natively supported by the programming language, and *derived types*, which are types based on basic types and which include programmer-defined types.

D.3.1 Basic Data Types

There are several predefined basic types within the C language: int, float, double, and char. They exist automatically within all implementations of C, though their sizes and range of values depends upon the computer system being used.

int

The binary value of something of int type will be interpreted as a signed whole number. Typical computers use 32 bits to represent signed integers, expressed in 2's complement form. Such integers can take on values between (and including) $-2,147,483,648$ and $+2,147,483,647$.

float

Objects declared of type float represent single-precision floating point numbers. These numbers typically, but not always, follow the representations defined by the IEEE standard for single-precision floating point numbers, which means that the type is a 32-bit type, where 1 bit is used for sign, 8 bits for exponent (expressed in bias-127 code), and 23 bits for fraction. See Section 2.7.1.

double

Objects declared of type double deal with double-precision floating point numbers. Like objects of type float, objects of type double are also typically represented using the IEEE standard. The precise difference between objects of type float and of type double depends on the system being used; however, the ANSI C standard specifies that the precision of a double should never be less than that of a float. On most machines a double is 64 bits.

char

Objects of character type contain a single character, expressed in the character code used by the computer system. Typical computer systems use the ASCII character code (see Appendix E). The size of a char is large enough to store a character from the character set. C also imposes that the size of a short int must be at least the size of a char.

Collectively, the int and char types (and enumerated types) are referred to as *integral* types, whereas float and double are floating types.

Enumerated Types

C provides a way for the programmer to specify objects that take on symbolic values. For example, we may want to create a type that takes on one of four values: Penguin, Riddler, CatWoman, Joker. We can do so by using an *enumerated* type, as follows:

```
/* Specifier */
enum villains { Penguin, Riddler, CatWoman, Joker };

/* Declaration */
enum villains badGuy;
```

The variable badGuy is of the enumerated type villains. It can take on one of the four symbolic values defined by enumerator list in the specifier. The four symbolic values are called *enumeration constants* (see Section D.2.4) and are actually integer values.

In an enumerator list, the value of the first enumeration constant will be 0, the next will be 1, and so forth. In the type villains, the value of Penguin will be 0, Riddler will be 1, CatWoman will be 2, Joker will be 3. The value of an enumerator can be explicitly set by the programmer by using the assignment operator, =. For example,

```
/* Specifier */
enum villains { Penguin = 3, Riddler, CatWoman, Joker };
```

causes Penguin to be 3, Riddler to be 4, and so forth.

D.3.2 Type Qualifiers

The basic types can be modified with the use of a type qualifier. These modifiers alter the basic type in some small fashion or change its default size.

signed, unsigned

The types int and char can be modified with the use of the signed and unsigned qualifiers. By default, integers are signed; the default on characters depends on the computer system.

For example, if a computer uses 32-bit 2's complement signed integers, then a signed int can have any value in the range $-2,147,483,648$ to $+2,147,483,647$. On the same machine, an unsigned int can have a value in the range 0 to $+4,294,967,295$.

```
signed int c;     /* the signed modifier is redundant */
unsigned int d;

signed char j;    /* forces the char to be interpreted
                     as a signed value */

unsigned char k;  /* the char will be interpreted as an
                     unsigned value */
```

long, short

The qualifiers `long` and `short` allow the programmer to manipulate the physical size of a basic type. For example, the qualifiers can be used with an integer to create `short int` and `long int`.

It is important to note that there is no strict definition of how much larger one type of integer is than another. The C language states only that the size of a `short int` is less than or equal to the size of an `int`, which is less than or equal to the size of a `long int`. Stated more completely and precisely:

```
sizeof(char) <= sizeof(short int) <= sizeof(int) <= sizeof(long int)
```

New computers that support 64-bit data types make a distinction on the `long` qualifier. On these machines, a `long int` might be a 64-bit integer, whereas an `int` might be a 32-bit integer. The range of values of types on a particular computer can be found in the standard header file `<limits.h>`. On most UNIX systems, it will be in the `/usr/include` directory.

The following are several examples of type modifiers on the integral data types.

```
short int q;
long int p;
unsigned long int r;
```

The `long` and `short` qualifiers can also be used with the floating type `double` to create a floating point number with higher precision or larger range (if such a type is available on the computer) than a `double`. As stated by the ANSI C specification: the size of a `float` is less than or equal to the size of a `double`, which is less than or equal to the size of a `long double`.

```
double x;
long double y;
```

const

A value that does not change through the course of execution can be qualified with the `const` qualifier. For example,

```
const double pi = 3.14159;
```

By using this qualifier, the programmer is providing information that might enable an optimizing compiler to perform more powerful optimizations on the resulting code. All variables with a `const` qualifier must be explicitly initialized.

D.3.3 Storage Class

Memory objects in C can be of the *static* or *automatic* storage class. Objects of the automatic class are local to a block (such as a function) and lose their value once their block is completed. By default, local variables within a function are of the automatic class and are allocated on the run-time stack (see Section 14.3.1).

Objects of the *static* class retain their values throughout program execution. Global variables and other objects declared outside of all blocks are of the static class. Objects declared within a function can be qualified with the `static` qualifier to indicate that they are to be allocated with other static objects, allowing their value to persist across invocations of the function in which they are declared. For example,

```
int Count(int x)
{
  static int y;

  y++;
  printf("This function has been called %d times.", y);
}
```

The value of y will not be lost when the activation record of Count is popped off the stack. To enable this, the compiler will allocate a static local variable in the global data section. Every call of the function count updates the value of y.

Unlike typical local variables of the automatic class, variables of the static class are initialized to zero. Variables of the automatic class must be initialized by the programmer.

There is a special qualifier called register that can be applied to objects in the automatic class. This qualifier provides a hint to the compiler that the value is frequently accessed within the code and should be allocated in a register to potentially enhance performance. The compiler, however, treats this only as a suggestion and can override or ignore this specifier based on its own analysis.

Functions, as well as variables, can be qualified with the qualifier extern. This qualifier indicates that the function's or variable's storage is defined in another object module that will be linked together with the current module when the executable is constructed.

D.3.4 Derived Types

The derived types are extensions of the basic types provided by C. The derived types include pointers, arrays, structures, and unions. Structures and unions enable the programmer to create new types that are aggregations of other types.

Arrays

An array is a sequence of objects of a particular type that is allocated sequentially in memory. That is, if the first element of the array of type T is at memory location X, the next element will be at memory location $X + $ sizeof(T), and so forth. Each element of the array is accessible using an integer index, starting with the index 0. That is, the first element of array list is list[0], numbered starting at 0. The size of the array must be stated as a constant integral expression (it is not required to be a literal) when the array is declared.

```
char string[100]; /* Declares array of 100 characters */
int  data[20];    /* Declares array of 20 integers */
```

To access a particular element within an array, an index is formed using an integral expression within square brackets, [ ].

```
data[0]         /* Accesses first element of array data */
data[i + 3]     /* The variable i must be an integer */
string[x + y]   /* x and y must be integers */
```

The compiler is not required to check (nor is it required to generate code to check) whether the value of the index falls within the bounds of the array. The responsibility of ensuring proper access to the array is upon the programmer. For example, based on the previous declarations and array expressions, the reference `string[x + y]`, the value of `x + y` should be 100 or less; otherwise the reference exceeds the bounds of the array `string`.

Pointers

Pointers are objects that are addresses of other objects. Pointer types are declared by prefixing an identifier with an asterisk, `*`. The type of a pointer indicates the type of the object that the pointer points to. For example,

```
int *v;    /* v points to an integer */
```

C allows a restricted set of operations to be used on pointer variables. Pointers can be manipulated in expressions, thus allowing "pointer arithmetic" to be performed. C allows assigment between pointers of the same type, or assignment, of a pointer to 0. Assignment of a pointer to the constant value 0 causes the generation of a null pointer. Integer values can be added to or subtracted from a pointer value. Also, pointers of the same type can be compared (using the relational operators) or subtracted from one another, but this is meaningful only if the pointers involved point to elements of the same array. All other pointer manipulations are not explicitly allowed in C but can be done with the appropriate casting.

Structures

Structures enable the programmer to specify an aggregate type. That is, a structure consists of member elements, each of which has its own type. The programmer can specify a structure using the following syntax. Notice that each member element has its own type.

```
struct tag_id {
   type1 member1;
   type2 member2;
   :
   :
   typeN memberN;
};
```

This structure has member elements named `member1` of type `type1`, `member2` of `type2`, up to `memberN` of `typeN`. Member elements can take on any basic or derived type, including other programmer-defined types.

The programmer can specify an optional tag, which in this case is `tag_id`. Using the tag, the programmer can declare structure variables, such as the variable `x` in the following declaration:

```
struct tag_id x;
```

A structure is defined by its tag. Multiple structures can be declared in a program with the same member elements and member element identifiers; they are different if they have different tags.

Alternatively, variables can be declared along with the structure declaration, as shown in the following example. In this example, the variable firstPoint is declared along with the structure. The array image is declared using the structure tag point.

```
struct point {
  int x;
  int y;
} firstPoint;


/* declares an array of structure type variables */
struct point image[100];
```

See Section 19.2 for more information on structures.

Unions

Structures are containers that hold multiple objects of various types. Unions, on the other hand, are containers that hold a single object that can take on different predetermined types at various points in a program. For example, the following is the declaration of a union variable joined:

```
union u_tag {
  int    ival;
  double fval;
  char   cval;
} joined;
```

The variable joined ultimately contains bits. These bits can be an integer, double, or character data type, depending on what the programmer decides to put there. For example, the variable will be treated as an integer with the expression joined.ival, or as a double-precision floating point value with joined.fval, or as a character with joined.cval. The compiler will allocate enough space for union variables as required for the largest data type.

D.3.5 typedef

In C, a programmer can use typedef to create a synonym for an existing type. This is particularly useful for providing names for programmer-defined types. The general form for a typedef follows:

```
typedef type name;
```

Here, type can be any basic type, enumerated type, or derived type. The identifier name can be any legal identifier. The result of this typedef is that name is a synonym for type. The typedef declaration is an important feature for enhancing code readability; a well-chosen type name conveys additional information about the object declared of that type. Following are some examples.

```
typedef enum {coffee, tea, water, soda} Beverage;
Beverage drink;     /* Declaration uses previous typedef */
typedef struct {
    int xCoord;
    int yCoord;
    int color;
} Pixel;

Pixel bitmap[1024*820]; /*Declares an array of pixels*/
```

D.4 Declarations

An *object* is a named section of memory, such as a variable. In C, an object must be declared with a declaration before it can be used. Declarations inform the compiler of characteristics, such as its type, name, and storage class, so that correct machine code can be generated whenever the object is manipulated within the body of the program.

In C, functions are also declared before they are used. A function declaration informs the compiler about the return value, function name, and types and order of input parameters.

D.4.1 Variable Declarations

The format for a variable declaration is as follows:

```
[storage-class] [type-qualifier] {type} {identifier} [ = initializer] ;
```

The curly braces, { }, indicate items that are required and the square brackets, [ ], indicate optional items.

The optional *storage-class* can be any storage class modifier listed in Section D.3.3, such as static.

The optional *type-qualifier* can be any legal type qualifiers, such as the qualifiers provided in Section D.3.2.

The *type* of a variable can be any of the basic types (int, char, float, double), enumerated types, or derived type (array, pointer, structure, or union).

An *identifier* can be any sequence of letters, digits, and the underscore character, _. The first character must be a letter or the underscore character. Identifiers can have any length, but for most variables you will use, at least 31 characters will be significant. That is, variables that differ only after the 31st character might be treated as the same variable by an ANSI C compiler. Uppercase letters are different from lowercase, so the identifier sum is different from Sum. Identifiers must be different from any of the C keywords (see Section D.2.6). Several examples of legal identifiers follow. Each is a distinct identifier.

```
blue
Blue1
Blue2
_blue_
bluE
primary_colors
primaryColors
```

The *initializer* for variables of automatic storage (see Section D.3.3) can be any expression that uses previously defined values. For variables of the static class (such as global values) or external variables, the initializer must be a constant expression.

Also, multiple identifiers (and initializers) can be placed on the same line, creating multiple variables of the same type, having the same storage class and type characteristics.

```
static long unsigned int k = 10UL;
register char l = 'Q';
int list[100];
struct node_type n;   /* Declares a structure variable */
```

Declarations can be placed at the beginning of any *block* (see Section D.6.2), before any statements. Such declarations are visible only within the block in which they appear. Declarations can also appear at the outermost level of the program, outside of all functions. Such declarations are *global variables*. They are visible from all parts of the program. See Section 12.2.3 for more information on variable declarations.

D.4.2 Function Declarations

A function's declaration informs the compiler about the type of value returned by the function and the type, number, and order of parameters the function expects to receive from its caller. The format for a function declaration is as follows:

```
{type} {function-id}([type1] [, type2], ... [, typeN]);
```

The curly braces, { }, indicate items that are required and the square brackets, [ ], indicate items that are optional.

The *type* indicates the type of the value returned by the function and can be of any basic type, enumerated type, a structure, a union, a pointer, or void (note: it cannot be an array). If a function does not return a value, then its type must be declared as void.

The *function-id* can be any legal identifier that has not already been defined.

Enclosed within parentheses following the *function-id* are the types of each of the input parameters expected by the function, indicated by *type1*, *type2*, *typeN*, each separated by a comma. Optionally, an identifier can be supplied for each argument, indicating what the particular argument will be called within the function's definition. For example, the following might be a declaration for a function that returns the average of an array of integers:

```
int Average(int numbers[], int howMany);
```

D.5 Operators

In this section, we describe the C operators. The operators are grouped by the operations they perform.

D.5.1 Assignment Operators

C supports multiple assignment operators, the most basic of which is the simple assigment operator `=`. All assignment operators associate from right to left.

A standard form for a simple assignment expression is as follows:

```
{left-expression} = {right-expression}
```

The *left-expression* must be a modifiable object. It cannot, for example, be a function, an object with a type qualifier `const`, or an array (it can, however, be an element of an array). The *left-expression* is often referred to as an *lvalue*. The *left-expression* can be an object of a structure or union type.

After the assignment expression is evaluated, the value of the object referred to by the *left-expression* will take on the value of the *right-expression*. In most usages of the assignment operator, the types of the two expressions will be the same. If they are different, and both are basic types, then the right operand is converted to the type of the left operand.

The other assignment operators include:

```
+=   -=   *=   /=   %=   &=   |=   ^=   <<=   >>=
```

All of these assignment operators combine an operation with an assignment. In general, `A op= B` is equivalent to `A = A op (B)`. For example, `x += y` is equivalent to `x = x + y`.

Examples of the various assignment operators can be found in Sections 12.3.2 and 12.6.4.

D.5.2 Arithmetic Operators

C supports basic arithmetic operations via the following binary operators:

```
+   -   *   /   %
```

These operators perform addition, subtraction, multiplication, division, and modulus. These operators are most commonly used with operands of the basic types (`int`, `double`, `float`, and `char`). If the operands have different types (such as a floating point value plus an integer), then the resulting expression is converted according to the conversion rules (see Section D.5.11). There is one restriction, however: the operands of the modulus operator `%` must be of the integral type (e.g., `int`, `char`, or enumerated).

The addition and subtraction operators can also be used with pointers that point to values within arrays. The use of these operators in this context is referred to as pointer arithmetic. For example, the expression `ptr + 1` where `ptr` is of type `type *`, is equivalent to `ptr + sizeof(type)`. The expression `ptr + 1` generates the address of the next element in the array.

C also supports the two unary operators `+` and `-`. The negation operator, `-`, generates the negative of its operand. The unary plus operator, `+`, generates its operand. This operator is included in the C language primarily for symmetry with the negation operator.

For more examples involving the arithmetic operators, see Section 12.3.3.

D.5.3 Bit-Wise Operators

The following operators:

```
&     |     ^     ~     <<     >>
```

are C's bit-wise operators. They perform bit-wise operation only on integral values. That is, they cannot be used with floating point values.

The left shift operator, <<, and right shift operator, >>, evaluate to the value of the left operand shifted by the number of bit positions indicated by the right operand. In ANSI C, if the right operand is greater than the number of bits in the representation (say, for example, 33 for a 32-bit integer) or negative, then the result is undefined.

Table D.2 provides some additional details on these operators. It provides an example usage and evaluation of each with an integer operand x equal to 186 and the integer operand y equal to 6.

D.5.4 Logical Operators

The logical operators in C are particularly useful for constructing logical expressions with multiple clauses. For example, if we want to test whether both condition A and condition B are true, then we might want to use the logical AND operator.

The logical AND operator takes two operands (which do not need to be of the same type). The operator evaluates to a 1 if both operands are nonzero. It evaluates to 0 otherwise.

The logical OR operator takes two operands and evaluates to 1 if either is nonzero. If both are zero, the operator evaluates to 0.

The logical NOT operator is a unary operate that evaluates to the logical inverse of its operand: it evaluates to 1 if the operand is zero, 0 otherwise.

The logical AND and logical OR operators are *short-circuit* operators. That is, if in evaluating the left operand, the value of the operation becomes known, then the right operand is not evaluated. For example, in evaluating (x || y++), if x is nonzero, then y++ will not be evaluated, meaning that the side effect of the increment will not occur.

Table D.3 provides some additional details on the logical operators and provides an example usage and evaluation of each with an integer operand x equal to 186 and the integer operand y equal to 6.

Table D.2	Bit-Wise Operators in C		
Operator Symbol	Operation	Example Usage	x=186 y=6
&	bit-wise AND	x & y	2
|	bit-wise OR	x | y	190
~	bit-wise NOT	~ x	−187
^	bit-wise XOR	x ^ y	188
<<	left shift	x << y	11904
>>	right shift	x >> y	2

Table D.3	Logical Operators in C		
Operator Symbol	Operation	Example Usage	x=186 y=6
&&	logical AND	x && y	1
||	logical OR	x || y	1
!	logical NOT	!x	0

D.5.5 Relational Operators

The following operators:

```
==   !=   >   >=   <   <=
```

are the relational operators in C. They perform a relational comparison between the left and right operands, such as equal to, not equal to, and greater than. The typical use of these operators is to compare expressions of the basic types. If the relationship is true, then the result is the integer value 1; otherwise it is 0. Expressions of mixed type undergo the standard type conversions described in Section D.5.11. C also allows the relational operators to be used on pointers. However, such pointer expressions only have meaning if both pointers point to the same object, such as the same array.

D.5.6 Increment/Decrement Operators

The increment/decrement operators in C are ++ and --. They increment or decrement the operand by 1. Both operators can be used in *prefix* and *postfix* forms.

In the prefix form, for example ++x, the value of the object is incremented (or decremented). The value of the expression is then the value of the result. For example, after the following executes:

```
int x = 4;
int y;

y = ++x;
```

both x and y equal 5.

In the postfix form, for example x++, the value of the expression is the value of the operand prior to the increment (or decrement). Once the value is recorded, the operand is incremented (or decremented) by 1. For example, the result of the following code:

```
int x = 4;
int y;

y = x++;
```

is that x equals 5 and y equals 4.

Like the addition and subtraction operators, the increment and decrement operators can be used with pointer types. See Section D.5.2.

D.5.7 Conditional Expression Operators

The conditional expression operator in C has the following form:

```
{expressionA} ? {expressionB} : {expressionC}
```

Here, if *expressionA* is logically true, that is, it evaluates to a nonzero value, then the value of the entire expression is the value of *expressionB*. If *expressionA* is logically false, that is, it evaluates to zero, then the value of the entire expression is the value of *expressionC*. For example, in the following code segment:

```
w = x ? y : z;
```

the value of the conditional expression x ? y : z will depend on the value of x. If x is nonzero, then w will be assigned the value of y. Otherwise w will be assigned the value of z.

   Like the logical AND and logical OR operators, the conditional expression short-circuits the evaluation of *expressionB* or *expressionC*, depending on the state of *expressionA*. See Section D.5.4.

D.5.8 Pointer, Array, and Structure Operators

This final batch of operators performs address-related operations for use with the derived data types.

Address Operator

The address operator is the &. It takes the address of its operand. The operand must be a memory object, such as a variable, array element, or structure member.

Dereference Operator

The complement of the address operator is the dereference operator. It returns the object to which the operand is pointing. For example, given the following code:

```
int *p;
int x = 5;

p = &x;
*p = *p + 1;
```

the expression *p returns x. When *p appears on the left-hand side of an assignment operator, it is treated as an lvalue (see Section D.5.1). Otherwise *p evaluates to the value of x.

Array Reference

In C, an integral expression within square brackets, [ ], designates a subscripted array reference. The typical use of this operator is with an object declared as an array. The following code contains an example of an array reference on the array list.

```
int x;
int list [100];

x = list [x + 10];
```

Structure and Union References

C contains two operators for referring to member elements within a structure or union. The first is the dot, or period, which directly accesses the member element of a structure or union variable. The following is an example:

```
struct pointType {
    int x;
    int y;
};
typedef pointType Point;

Point pixel;

pixel.x = 3;
pixel.y = pixel.x + 10;
```

The variable `pixel` is a structure variable, and its member elements are accessed using the dot operator.

The second means of accessing member elements of a structure is the arrow, or `->` operator. Here, a pointer to a structure or union can be dereferenced and a member element selected with a single operator. The following code demonstrates:

```
Point pixel;
Point *ptr;

ptr = &pixel;
ptr->x = ptr->x + 1;
```

Here, the pointer variable `ptr` points to the structure variable `pixel`.

D.5.9 `sizeof`

The `sizeof` operator returns the number of bytes required to store an object of the type specified. For example, `sizeof(int)` will return the number of bytes occupied by an integer. If the operand is an array, then `sizeof` will return the size of the array. The following is an example:

```
int list[45];

struct example_type {
    int     valueA;
    int     valueB;
    double valueC;
};
typedef struct example_type Example;

...

sizeA = sizeof(list);      /* 45 * sizeof(int)  */
sizeB = sizeof(Example);   /* Size of structure */
```

Table D.4   Operator Precedence, from Highest to Lowest. Descriptions of Some Operators are Provided in Parentheses

Precedence Group	Associativity	Operators
1 (highest)	l to r	`()` (function call) `[ ]` (array index) `.` `->`
2	r to l	`++` `--` (postfix versions)
3	r to l	`++` `--` (prefix versions)
4	r to l	`*` (indirection) `&` (address of) `+` (unary) `-` (unary) `~` `!` `sizeof`
5	r to l	`(type)` (type cast)
6	l to r	`*` (multiplication) `/` `%`
7	l to r	`+` (addition) `-` (subtraction)
8	l to r	`«` `»`
9	l to r	`<` `>` `<=` `>=`
10	l to r	`==` `!=`
11	l to r	`&`
12	l to r	`^`
13	l to r	`|`
14	l to r	`&&`
15	l to r	`||`
16	l to r	`?:`
17 (lowest)	r to l	`=` `+=` `-=` `*=` etc.

D.5.10 Order of Evaluation

The order of evaluation of an expression starts at the subexpression in the innermost parentheses, with the operator with the highest *precedence*, moving to the operator with the lowest precedence within the same subexpression. If two operators have the same precedence (for example, two of the same operators, as in the expression 2 + 3 + 4), then the *associativity* of the operators determines the order of evaluation, either from left to right or from right to left. The evaluation of the expression continues recursively from there.

Table D.4 provides the *precedence* and *associativity* of the C operators. The operators of highest precedence are listed at the top of the table, in lower numbered precedence groups.

D.5.11 Type Conversions

Consider the following expression involving the operator *op*.

```
A op B
```

The resulting value of this expression will have a particular type associated with it. This resulting type depends on (1) the types of the operands *A* and *B*, and (2) the nature of the operator *op*.

If the types of *A* and *B* are the same and the operator can operate on that type, the result is the type defined by the operator.

When an expression contains variables that are a mixture of the basic types, C performs a set of standard arithmetic conversions of the operand values. In general, smaller types are converted into larger types, and integral types are converted into floating types. For example, if *A* is of type `double` and *B* is of type `int`, the result is of type `double`. Integral values, such as `char`, `int`, or an enumerated type, are converted to `int` (or `unsigned int`, depending on the implementation). The following are examples.

```
char   i;
int    j;
float  x;
double y;

i * j     /* This expression is an integer */
j + 1     /* This expression is an integer */
j + 1.0   /* This expression is a float    */
i + 1.0   /* This expression is a float    */
x + y     /* This expression is a double   */
i + j + x + y        /* This is a double */
```

As in case (2) above, some operators require operands of a particular type or generate results of a particular type. For example, the modulus operator `%` only operates on integral values. Here integral type conversions are performed on the operands (e.g., `char` is converted to `int`). Floating point values are not allowed and will generate compilation errors.

If a floating point type is converted to an integral type (which does not happen with the usual type conversion, but can happen with casting as described in the next subsection), the fractional portion is discarded. If the resulting integer cannot be represented by the integral type, the result is undefined.

Casting

The programmer can explicitly control the type conversion process by *type casting*. A cast has the general form:

```
(new-type) expression
```

Here the expression is converted into the *new-type* using the usual conversion rules described in the preceding paragraphs. Continuing with the previous example code:

```
j = (int) x + y; /* This results in conversion of
                    double into an integer */
```

D.6 Expressions and Statements

In C, the work performed by a program is described by the expressions and statements within the bodies of functions.

D.6.1 Expressions

An expression is any legal combination of constants, variables, operators, and function calls that evaluates to a value of a particular type. The order of evaluation is based on the precedence and associativity rules described in Section D.5.10.

The type of an expression is based on the individual elements of the expression, according to the C type promotion rules (see Section D.5.11). If all the elements of an expression are `int` types, then the expression is of `int` type. Following are several examples of expressions:

```
a * a + b * b
a++ - c / 3
a <= 4
q || integrate(x)
```

D.6.2 Statements

In C, simple statements are expressions terminated by a semicolon, `;`. Typically, statements modify a variable or have some other side effect when the expression is evaluated. Once a statement has completed execution, the next statement in sequential order is executed. If the statement is the last statement in its function, then the function terminates.

```
c = a * a + b * b;   /* Two simple statements */
b = a++ - c / 3;
```

Related statements can be grouped togethered into a compound statement, or *block*, by surrounding them with curly braces, { }. Syntactically, the compound statement is the same as a simple statement, and they can be used interchangeably.

```
{                      /* One compound statement */
 c = a * a + b * b;
 b = a++ - c / 3;
}
```

D.7 Control

The control constructs in C enable the programmer to alter the sequential execution of statements with statements that execute conditionally or iteratively.

D.7.1 If

An `if` statement has the format

```
if  (expression)
    statement
```

If the *expression*, which can be of any basic, enumerated, or pointer types, evaluates to a nonzero value, then the *statement*, which can be a simple or compound statement, is executed.

```
if (x < 0)
    a = b + c; /* Executes if x is less than zero */
```

See Section 13.2.1 for more examples of `if` statements.

D.7.2 `If-else`

An `if-else` statement has the format

```
if (expression)
    statement1
else
    statement2
```

If the *expression*, which can be of any basic, enumerated, or pointer type, evaluates to a nonzero value, then *statement1* is executed. Otherwise, *statement2* is executed. Both *statement1* and *statement2* can be simple or compound statements.

```
if   (x < 0)
      a = b + c; /* Executes if x is less than zero */
else
      a = b - c; /* Otherwise, this is executed.  */
```

See Section 13.2.2 for more examples of `if-else` statements.

D.7.3 `Switch`

A `switch` statement has the following format:

```
switch(expression)   {
case const-expr1:
      statement1A
      statement1B
      :

case const-expr2:
      statement2A
      statement2B
      :

      :
      :

case const-exprN:
      statementNA
      statementNB
      :

}
```

A `switch` statement is composed of an *expression*, which must be of integral type (see Section D.3.1), followed by a compound statement (though it is not required to be compound, it almost always is). Within the compound statement exist one or more `case` labels, each with an associated constant integral expression, called *const-expr1*, *const-expr2*, *const-exprN* in the preceding example. Within a `switch`, each `case` label must be different.

When a `switch` is encountered, the controlling *expression* is evaluated. If one of the case labels matches the value of *expression*, then control jumps to the statement that follows and proceeds from there.

The special case label `default` can be used to catch the situation where none of the other case labels match. If the `default` case is not present and none of the labels match the value of the controlling expression, then no statements within the `switch` are executed.

The following is an example of a code segment that uses a `switch` statement. The use of the `break` statement causes control to leave the `switch`. See Section D.7.7 for more information on `break`.

```
char k;

k = getchar();
switch (k)   {
case '+':
  a = b + c;
  break;        /* break causes control to leave switch */

case '-':
  a = b - c;
  break;

case '*':
  a = b * c;
  break;

case '/':
  a = b / c;
  break;
}
```

See Section 13.5.1 for more examples of `switch` statements.

D.7.4 While

A `while` statement has the following format:

```
while (expression)
  statement
```

The `while` statement is an iteration construct. If the value of *expression* evaluates to nonzero, then the *statement* is executed. Control does not pass to the subsequent statement, but rather the *expression* is evaluated again and the process is repeated. This continues until *expression* evaluates to 0, in which case control passes to the next statement. The *statement* can be a simple or compound statement.

In the following example, the `while` loop will iterate 100 times.

```
x = 0;
while   (x < 100)   {
  printf("x = %d\n", x);
  x = x + 1;
}
```

See Section 13.3.1 for more examples of `while` statements.

D.7.5 `For`

A `for` statement has the following format:

```
for (initializer;  term-expr; reinitializer)
   statement
```

The `for` statement is an iteration construct. The *initializer*, which is an expression, is evaluated only once, before the loop begins. The *term-expr* is an expression that is evaluated before each iteration of the loop. If the *term-expr* evaluates to nonzero, the loop progresses; otherwise the loop terminates and control passes to the statement following the loop. Each iteration of the loop consists of the execution of the *statement*, which makes up the body of the loop, and the evaluation of the *reinitializer* expression.

The following example is a `for` loop that iterates 100 times.

```
for (x = 0; x < 100; X++)   {
    printf("x = %d\n", x);
}
```

See Section 13.3.2 for more examples of `for` statements.

D.7.6 `Do-while`

A `do-while` statement has the format

```
do
   statement
while (expression);
```

The `do-while` statement is an iteration construct similar to the `while` statement. When a `do-while` is first encountered, the *statement* that makes up the loop body is executed first, then the *expression* is evaluated to determine whether to execute another iteration. If it is nonzero, then another iteration is executed (in other words, *statement* is executed again). In this manner, a `do-while` always executes its loop body at least once.

The following `do-while` loop iterates 100 times.

```
x = 0;
do {
    printf("x = %d\n", x);
    x = x + 1;
}
while (x < 100);
```

See Section 13.3.3 for more examples of `do-while` statements.

D.7.7 Break

A break statement has the format:

```
break;
```

The break statement can only be used in an iteration statement or in a switch statement. It passes control out of the smallest statement containing it to the statement immediately following. Typically, break is used to exit a loop before the terminating condition is encountered.

In the following example, the execution of the break statement causes control to pass out of the for loop.

```
for (x = 0; x < 100; x++)  {
    :
    :
  if (error)
      break;
    :
    :
}
```

See Section 13.5.2 for more examples of break statements.

D.7.8 continue

A continue statement has the following format:

```
continue;
```

The continue statement can be used only in an iteration statement. It prematurely terminates the execution of the loop body. That is, it terminates the current iteration of the loop. The looping expression is evaluated to determine whether another iteration should be performed. In a for loop the *reinitializer* is also evaluated.

If the continue statement is executed, then x is incremented, and the *reinitializer* executed, and the loop expression evaluated to determine if another iteration should be executed.

```
for (x = 0; x < 100; x++)  {
    :
    :
  if (skip)
      continue;
    :
    :
}
```

See Section 13.5.2 for more examples of continue statements.

D.7.9 `return`

A `return` statement has the format

```
return expression;
```

The `return` statement causes control to return to the current caller function, that is, the function that called the function that contains the `return` statement. Also, after the last statement of a function is executed, an implicit return is made to the caller.

The `expression` that follows the `return` is the return value generated by the function. It is converted to the return type of the function. If a function returns a value, and yet no `return` statement within the function explicitly generates a return value, then the return value is undefined.

```
return x + y;
```

D.8   The C Preprocessor

The C programming language includes a preprocessing step that modifies, in a programmer-controlled manner, the source code presented to the compiler. The most frequently used features of the C preprocessor are its macro substitution facility (`#define`), which replaces a sequence of source text with another sequence, and the file inclusion facility (`#include`), which includes the contents of a file into the source text. Both of these are described in the following subsections.

None of the preprocessor directives are required to end with a semicolon. Since `#define` and `#include` are preprocessor directives and not C statements, they are not required to be terminated by semicolons.

D.8.1 Macro Substitution

The `#define` preprocessor directive instructs the C preprocessor to replace occurrences of one character sequence with another. Consider the following example:

```
#define A B
```

Here, any token that matches A will be replaced by B. That is, the *macro* A gets *substituted* with B. The character A must appear as an individual sequence, i.e., the A in APPLE will not be substituted, and not appear in quoted strings, i.e., neither will "A".

The replacement text spans until the end of the line. If a longer sequence is required, the backslash character, \, can be used to continue to the next line.

Macros can also take arguments. They are specified in parentheses immediately after the text to be replaced. For example:

```
#define REMAINDER(X, Y)    ((X) % (Y))
```

Here, every occurrence of the macro COPY in the source code will be accompanied by two values, as in the following example.

```
valueC = REMAINDER(valueA, valueB + 15);
```

The macro REMAINDER will be replaced by the preprocessor with the replacement text provided in the #define, and the two arguments A and B will be substituted with the two arguments that appear in the source code. The previous code will be modified to the following after preprocessing:

```
valueC = ((valueA) % (valueB + 15));
```

Notice that the parentheses surrounding X and Y in the macro definition were required. Without them, the macro REMAINDER would have calculated the wrong value.

While the REMAINDER macro appears to be similar to a function call, notice that it incurs none of the function call overhead associated with regular functions.

D.8.2 File Inclusion

The #include directive instructs the preprocessor to insert the contents of a file into the source file. Typically, the #include directive is used to attach header files to C source files. *C header files* typically contain #defines and declarations that are useful among multiple source files.

There are two variations of the #include directive:

```
#include <stdio.h>
#include "program.h"
```

The first variation uses angle brackets, < >, around the filename. This tells the preprocessor that the header file can be found in a predefined directory, usually determined by the configuration of the system and which contains many system-related and library-related header files, such as stdio.h. The second variation, using double quotes, " ", around the filename, instructs the preprocessor that the header file can be found in the same directory as the C source file.

D.9 Some Standard Library Functions

The ANSI C standard library contains over 150 functions that perform a variety of useful tasks (for example, I/O and dynamic memory allocation) on behalf of your program. Every installation of ANSI C will have these functions available, so even if you make use of these functions, your program will still be portable from one ANSI C platform to another. In this section, we will describe some useful standard library functions.

D.9.1 I/O Functions

The `<stdio.h>` header file must be included in any source file that contains calls to the standard I/O functions. Following is a small sample of these functions.

getchar

This function has the following declaration:

```
int getchar(void);
```

The function `getchar` reads the next character from the standard input device, or `stdin`. The value of this character is returned (as an integer) as the return value.

The behavior of `getchar` is very similar to the LC-3 input TRAP (except no input banner is displayed on the screen).

Most computer systems will implement `getchar` using buffered I/O. This means that keystrokes (assuming standard input is coming from the keyboard) will be buffered by the operating system until the Enter key is pressed. Once Enter is pressed, the entire line of characters is added to the standard input stream.

putchar

This function has the following declaration:

```
void putchar(int c);
```

The function `putchar` takes an integer value representing an ASCII character and puts the character to the standard output stream. This is similar to the LC-3 TRAP OUT.

If the standard output stream is the monitor, the character will appear on the screen. However, since many systems buffer the output stream, the character may not appear until the system's output buffer is *flushed*, which is usually done once a newline appears in the output stream.

scanf

This function has the following declaration:

```
int scanf(const char *formatstring, *ptr1, ...);
```

The function `scanf` is passed a format string (which is passed as pointer to the initial character) and a list of pointers. The format string contains format specifications that control how `scanf` will interpret fields in the input stream. For example, the specification `%d` causes `scanf` to interpret the next sequence of non–white space characters as a decimal number. This decimal is converted from ASCII into an integer value and assigned to the variable pointed to by the next pointer in the parameter list. Table D.5 contains a listing of the possible specifications for use with `scanf`. The number of pointers that follow the format string in the parameter list should correspond to the number of format specifications in the format string. The value returned by `scanf` corresponds to the number of variables that were successfully assigned.

Table D.5	scanf **Conversion Specifications**
scanf Conversions	Parameter Type
%d	signed decimal
%i	decimal, octal (leading 0), hex (leading 0x or 0X)
%o	octal
%x	hexadecimal
%u	unsigned decimal
%c	char
%s	string of non–white space characters, \0 added
%f, %e	floating point number
%lf	double precision floating point number

Table D.6	printf **Conversion Specifications**
printf Conversions	Printed as
%d, %i	signed decimal
%o	octal
%x, %X	hexadecimal (a–f or A–F)
%u	unsigned decimal
%c	single char
%s	string, terminated by \0
%f	floating point in decimal notation
%e, %E	floating point in exponential notation
%p	pointer

printf

This function has the following declaration:

```
int printf(const char *formatString, ...);
```

The function printf writes the format string (passed as a pointer to the initial character) to the standard output stream. If the format string contains a format specification, then printf will interpret the next parameter in the parameter list as indicated by the specification, and embed the interpreted value into the output stream. For example, the format specification %d will cause printf to interpret the next parameter as a decimal value. printf will write the resulting digits into the output stream. Table D.6 contains a listing of the format specifications for use with printf. In general, the number of values following the format string on the parameter list should correspond to the number of format specifications in the format string. printf returns the number of characters written to the output stream. However, if an error occurs, a negative value is returned.

D.9.2 String Functions

The C standard library contains around 15 functions that perform operations on strings (that is, null-terminated arrays of characters). To use the string functions from within a program, include the <string.h> header file in each source file that contains a call to a library string function. In this section, we describe two examples of C string functions.

strcmp

This function has the following declaration:

```
int strcmp(char *stringA, char *stringB);
```

This function compares `stringA` with `stringB`. It returns a 0 if they are equal. It returns a value greater than 0 if `stringA` is lexicographically greater than `stringB` (lexicographically greater means that `stringA` occurs later in a dictionary than `stringB`). It returns a value less than 0 if `stringA` is lexicographically less than `stringB`.

strcpy

This function has the following declaration:

```
char *strcpy(char *stringA, char *stringB);
```

This function copies `stringB` to `stringA`. It copies every character in `stringB` up to and including the null character. The function returns a pointer to `stringA` if no errors occurred.

D.9.3 Math Functions

The C standard math functions perform commonly used mathematical operations. Using them requires including the `<math.h>` header file. In this section, we list a small sample of C math functions. Each of the listed functions takes as parameters values of type `double`, and each returns a value of type `double`.

```
double sin(double x);    /* sine of x, expressed in radians   */
double cos(double x);    /* cosine of x, expressed in radians */
double tan(double x);    /* tan of x, expressed in radians    */
double exp(double x);    /* exponential function,  e^x        */
double log(double x);    /* natural log of x                  */
double sqrt(double x);   /* square root of x                  */
double pow(double x, double y)   /* x^y -- x to the y power   */
```

D.9.4 Utility Functions

The C library contains a set of functions that perform useful tasks such as memory allocation, data conversion, sorting, and other miscellaneous things. The common header file for these functions is `<stdlib.h>`.

malloc

As described in Section 19.3, the function `malloc` allocates a fixed-sized chunk from memory.

This function has the following declaration:

```
void *malloc(size_t size);
```

The input parameter is the number of bytes to be allocated. The parameter is of type `size_t`, which is the same type returned by the `sizeof` operator (very often, this type is `typedef`ed as an unsigned integer). If the memory allocation goes successfully, a pointer to the allocated region of memory is returned. If the request cannot be satisfied, the value NULL is returned.

free

This function has the following declaration:

```
void free(void *ptr);
```

This function returns to the heap a previously allocated chunk of memory pointed to by the parameter. In other words, free deallocates memory pointed to by ptr. The value passed to free must be a pointer to a previously allocated region of memory, otherwise errors could occur.

rand **and** srand

The C standard utility functions contain a function to generate a sequence of random numbers. The function is called rand. It does not generate a truly random sequence, however. Instead, it generates the same sequence of varying values based on an initial *seed* value. When the seed is changed, a different sequence is generated. For example, when seeded with the value 10, the generator will always generate the same sequence of numbers. However, this sequence will be different than the sequence generated by another seed value.

The function rand has the following declaration:

```
int rand(void)
```

It returns a pseudo-random integer in the range 0 to RAND_MAX, which is at least 32,767.

To seed the pseudo-random number generator, use the function srand. This function has the following declaration:

```
void srand(unsigned int seed);
```

Useful Tables

E.1 Commonly Used Numerical Prefixes

Table E.1	Numerical Prefixes			
Amount	Commonly Used Base-2 Approx.	Prefix	Abbreviation	Derived From
10^{24}	2^{80}	yotta	Y	Greek for eight: okto
10^{21}	2^{70}	zetta	Z	Greek for seven: hepta
10^{18}	2^{60}	exa	E	Greek for six: hexa
10^{15}	2^{50}	peta	P	Greek for five: pente
10^{12}	2^{40}	tera	T	Greek for monster: teras
10^{9}	2^{30}	giga	G	Greek for giant: gigas
10^{6}	2^{20}	mega	M	Greek for large: megas
10^{3}	2^{10}	kilo	k	Greek for thousand: chilioi
10^{-3}		milli	m	Latin for thousand: milli
10^{-6}		micro	μ	Greek for small: mikros
10^{-9}		nano	n	Greek for dwarf: nanos
10^{-12}		pico	p	Spanish for a little: pico
10^{-15}		femto	f	Danish and Norwegian for 15: femten
10^{-18}		atto	a	Danish and Norwegian for 18: atten
10^{-21}		zepto	z	Greek for seven: hepta
10^{-24}		yocto	y	Greek for eight: okto

E.2 Standard ASCII codes

Table E.2   The Standard ASCII Table

ASCII Character	Dec	Hex	ASCII Character	Dec	Hex	ASCII Character	Dec	Hex	ASCII Character	Dec	Hex
nul	0	00	sp	32	20	@	64	40	`	96	60
soh	1	01	!	33	21	A	65	41	a	97	61
stx	2	02	"	34	22	B	66	42	b	98	62
etx	3	03	#	35	23	C	67	43	c	99	63
eot	4	04	$	36	24	D	68	44	d	100	64
enq	5	05	%	37	25	E	69	45	e	101	65
ack	6	06	&	38	26	F	70	46	f	102	66
bel	7	07	'	39	27	G	71	47	g	103	67
bs	8	08	(	40	28	H	72	48	h	104	68
ht	9	09	)	41	29	I	73	49	i	105	69
lf	10	0A	*	42	2A	J	74	4A	j	106	6A
vt	11	0B	+	43	2B	K	75	4B	k	107	6B
ff	12	0C	'	44	2C	L	76	4C	l	108	6C
cr	13	0D	-	45	2D	M	77	4D	m	109	6D
so	14	0E	.	46	2E	N	78	4E	n	110	6E
si	15	0F	/	47	2F	O	79	4F	o	111	6F
dle	16	10	0	48	30	P	80	50	p	112	70
dc1	17	11	1	49	31	Q	81	51	q	113	71
dc2	18	12	2	50	32	R	82	52	r	114	72
dc3	19	13	3	51	33	S	83	53	s	115	73
dc4	20	14	4	52	34	T	84	54	t	116	74
nak	21	15	5	53	35	U	85	55	u	117	75
syn	22	16	6	54	36	V	86	56	v	118	76
etb	23	17	7	55	37	W	87	57	w	119	77
can	24	18	8	56	38	X	88	58	x	120	78
em	25	19	9	57	39	Y	89	59	y	121	79
sub	26	1A	:	58	3A	Z	90	5A	z	122	7A
esc	27	1B	;	59	3B	[	91	5B	{	123	7B
fs	28	1C	<	60	3C	\	92	5C			124	7C
gs	29	1D	=	61	3D	]	93	5D	}	125	7D
rs	30	1E	>	62	3E	^	94	5E	~	126	7E
us	31	1F	?	63	3F	_	95	5F	del	127	7F

E.3 Powers of 2

Table E.3	Powers of 2	
Amount	Decimal Conversion	Common Abbreviation
2^1	2	—
2^2	4	—
2^3	8	—
2^4	16	—
2^5	32	—
2^6	64	—
2^7	128	—
2^8	256	—
2^9	512	—
2^{10}	1,024	1K
2^{11}	2,048	2K
2^{12}	4,096	4K
2^{13}	8,192	8K
2^{14}	16,384	16K
2^{15}	32,768	32K
2^{16}	65,536	64K
2^{17}	131,072	128K
2^{18}	262,144	256K
2^{19}	544,288	512K
2^{20}	1,048,576	1M
2^{30}	1,073,741,824	1G
2^{32}	4,294,967,296	4G

Solutions to Selected Exercises

Solutions to selected exercises can be found on our website:
http://www.mhhe.com/patt2

j

The Standard ASCII Table

Character	Dec	Hex	Character	Dec	Hex	Character	Dec	Hex	Character	Dec	Hex
nul	0	00	sp	32	20	@	64	40	`	96	60
soh	1	01	!	33	21	A	65	41	a	97	61
stx	2	02	"	34	22	B	66	42	b	98	62
etx	3	03	#	35	23	C	67	43	c	99	63
eot	4	04	$	36	24	D	68	44	d	100	64
enq	5	05	%	37	25	E	69	45	e	101	65
ack	6	06	&	38	26	F	70	46	f	102	66
bel	7	07	'	39	27	G	71	47	g	103	67
bs	8	08	(	40	28	H	72	48	h	104	68
ht	9	09	)	41	29	I	73	49	i	105	69
lf	10	0A	*	42	2A	J	74	4A	j	106	6A
vt	11	0B	+	43	2B	K	75	4B	k	107	6B
ff	12	0C	'	44	2C	L	76	4C	l	108	6C
cr	13	0D	–	45	2D	M	77	4D	m	109	6D
so	14	0E	.	46	2E	N	78	4E	n	110	6E
si	15	0F	/	47	2F	O	79	4F	o	111	6F
dle	16	10	0	48	30	P	80	50	p	112	70
dc1	17	11	1	49	31	Q	81	51	q	113	71
dc2	18	12	2	50	32	R	82	52	r	114	72
dc3	19	13	3	51	33	S	83	53	s	115	73
dc4	20	14	4	52	34	T	84	54	t	116	74
nak	21	15	5	53	35	U	85	55	u	117	75
syn	22	16	6	54	36	V	86	56	v	118	76
etb	23	17	7	55	37	W	87	57	w	119	77
can	24	18	8	56	38	X	88	58	x	120	78
em	25	19	9	57	39	Y	89	59	y	121	79
sub	26	1A	:	58	3A	Z	90	5A	z	122	7A
esc	27	1B	;	59	3B	[	91	5B	{	123	7B
fs	28	1C	<	60	3C	\	92	5C			124	7C
gs	29	1D	=	61	3D	]	93	5D	}	125	7D
rs	30	1E	>	62	3E	^	94	5E	~	126	7E
us	31	1F	?	63	3F	_	95	5F	del	127	7F